# A PIECE OF THE ACTION

## HOW THE MIDDLE CLASS
## JOINED THE MONEY CLASS

# Joseph Nocera

Rock Valley College
Educational Resources
Center

SIMON & SCHUSTER
*New York   London   Toronto   Sydney   Tokyo   Singapore*

SIMON & SCHUSTER
Rockefeller Center
1230 Avenue of the Americas
New York, New York 10020

Designed by Irving Perkins Associates, Inc.
Manufactured in the United States of America

2   4   6   8   10   9   7   5   3   1

Library of Congress Cataloging-in-Publication Data
Nocera, Joseph.
A piece of the action : how the middle class joined
the money class / Joseph Nocera.
p.   cm.
Includes bibliographical references and index.
1. Middle class—United States—Economic conditions. 2. Financial services industry—United States—History. 3. United States—Economic
conditions—1945– I. Title.
HT690.U6N6   1994
305.5'5'0973—dc20                     94-27618   CIP
ISBN: 0-671-66756-4

# Contents

Introduction: The Money Revolution     9

## Part I
## THE SHAPE OF THE WAVE

1   The Drop, *September 1958*     15
2   The Man with the Golden Touch, *February 1966*     34
3   Delusions and the Madness of Bankers, *November 1966*     53
4   The Great Wall of Q, *February 1970*     70
5   "Here Come the Revolutionaries," *July 1970*     89
6   The Luckiest Entrepreneur, *May 1975*     106
7   The World's Most Hated Bank, *August 1977*     126
8   The Discreet Charms of the CMA, *September 1977*     149

## Part II
## GROUND ZERO

9   The Great Inflation, *July 1979*     167
10   "Please Don't Take It Away!" *March 1981*     187
11   Mr. Regan Goes to Washington, *September 1981*     207

## Part III
## BULLS AND BEARS

12   The Maestro of Magellan, *August 1982*     231
13   Socks 'n' Stocks, *November 1982*     250
14   The People's Nest Egg, *April 1984*     275
15   The Pleasure Palace in the Sky, *May 1984*     297
16   The Bull's Last Stampede, *January 1987*     325
17   "This Is a War over Here," *October 1987*     346
18   Peter Lynch's Long Good-bye, *March 1990*     366
19   The Triumph of Main Street, *August 1993*     390

# CONTENTS

Acknowledgments                 407
Notes                           411
Selected Bibliography           449
Index                           452

# Introduction:
# The Money Revolution

Spring is the busiest time.

That's what they'll tell you in the "financial services industry"—the clumsy, all-purpose term that encompasses all the mutual fund companies and investment firms now spanning the nation, all the insurance companies and brokerage houses, all the S&Ls and banks and credit unions of every shape and size: the thousands upon thousands of entities that compete for the chance to handle our money. They know the routine by now; they've seen it enough times that they can predict what's going to happen. Each spring, as the April 15 tax deadline approaches, the number of incoming phone calls begins to increase, a little more each week, until they are double their usual volume. The branch offices become crowded with customers and potential customers, as people jostle each other to pore over the merchandise or angle for a quiet word with an overworked salesperson.

For those in the business, spring has become a version of Christmastime—one of the most important selling seasons of the year.[1] Except, of course, the merchandise they are offering isn't toys or clothes. It's equity mutual funds. It's certificates of deposit. It's annuities. It's municipal bond funds and individual stocks and overseas funds and hundreds of other tempting "financial products"—to use another of those unfortunate but useful phrases that have entered the language. In the spring, the industry has come to understand, millions of Americans go shopping for an investment, searching for a place to invest $2,000 or so in an Individual Retirement Account. That's something we do now in America, pretty much as a matter of course: we shop for investments. Shopping for investments has become our habit and our responsibility, our burden and our thrill. It is an activity that has insinuated itself into the rhythms of middle-class life.

Whenever a large behavioral change enters the realm of habit—whenever it becomes akin to watching television or using a personal computer, something that was once new and strange but is now second nature—we tend to

forget where it came from, and what life was like before its arrival on the
scene. This is so even when the change in question is relatively recent, as is
the case here. This book is a history of one such enormous change in
American life: the astonishing transformation of the financial habits of the
middle class. By this I'm referring not only to the process that led us to
become investors, though that's certainly a large part of it. Rather, I'm
speaking about a broader set of habits that have resulted from Americans
having to take charge of their own financial lives, habits that include changes
in the way we borrow, the way we save, even the way we think about our
money. Over the past two decades, we've been participating in nothing less
than a money revolution. This is not a term I use lightly. When one recalls
what the financial life of the middle class was like twenty years ago—when
thrift was the highest virtue, when the daily movement of the Dow Jones
average had almost no relevance to our lives, when few of us knew what a
mutual fund was, much less the distinction between, say, a growth fund and
a balanced fund—it's hard not to conclude that this transformation has,
indeed, been revolutionary.

It's always difficult to pinpoint precisely where social revolutions spring
from, and the money revolution is no exception. If you ask the marketers at
the big mutual fund companies, they'll tell you that it is we who have
instigated the changes, by grabbing control of our financial destiny and
forcing the nation's financial institutions to cater to our yearnings. "People
want control," a marketer at Fidelity Investments told me several years ago.
"They want to make their own decisions." No doubt there is some truth in
what the man says.

But it's equally true, I think, that most of us perceive the money revolution as being fueled by "them"—the nation's financial companies—rather
than by us. We feel pulled into it by forces larger than ourselves. We didn't
*demand,* for example, the right to be able to make an instant personal loan
by pulling a piece of plastic out of our pocket, to cite another financial
innovation that helped instigate a huge behavioral change. Somebody, somewhere, had to create those things we now know as Visa and MasterCard, and
then they had to persuade us to use them. And, in addition, the social and
economic conditions had to be exactly right to cause this practice of paying
by credit card to catch on—to cause it, that is, to become one of our new
financial habits. The history of the money revolution is a history of all those
somebodies, somewhere—the inventors of credit cards, the creators of discount brokerages, the marketers of mutual funds—*and* a history of those
larger forces, such as inflation and financial deregulation, that made such
innovations all but inevitable, *and* a history of our own evolving attitudes,
which caused us to embrace these innovations. It's pointless, it seems to me,

to try to place one factor over all the others, and in the pages that follow, I've tried not to do that. Had any one ingredient been missing, this stew would never have been made. Of that I'm convinced.

I'm equally convinced, by the way, that the money revolution has been, in general, a force for good. Without question, it's created a layer of complication to our already complicated lives, adding responsibilities that didn't exist before, making it necessary for us to learn about things that never used to be among our concerns. We can make mistakes with our money now, and those mistakes can be costly. Markets, as we've learned again and again in recent years, can go down as well as up. Taking control of our finances can be quite nerve-racking at times. But we also have tools and resources at our disposal that were formerly unavailable to us, and we have been handed possibilities for making money that had always been out of our reach. The financial markets were once the province of the wealthy, and they're not anymore; they belong to all of us. We've finally gotten a piece of the action. If we have to pay attention now, if we have to come to grips with our own tolerance for risk, if we're forced to spend a little time learning about which financial instruments make sense for us and which ones don't, that seems to me an acceptable price to pay. Democracy always comes at some price. Even financial democracy.

Sometimes change comes about in an obvious and dramatic way, but more often it takes place gradually and even imperceptibly. It's only afterward, when the dust has settled, that we suddenly have the presence of mind to look up and see that everything is different. The money revolution has been a work in progress for some thirty years now, but it's only been quite recently that we've finally been able to look up and see how much has changed. When did we start putting our savings in money market funds instead of bank passbook accounts? When did we start using credit cards for items that used to require a trip to see the loan officer at the bank? When did mutual funds capture our fancy? When did we become so aware of yield that we began moving our money around to capture an extra half a percentage point? When did we start keeping track of the Japanese stock market? When did this all happen? *How* did this all happen?

Here is how it happened.

# Part I

# THE
# SHAPE
## OF THE
# WAVE

# CHAPTER 1

# The Drop

## *September 1958*

AMERICA BEGAN TO CHANGE on a mid-September day in 1958, when the Bank of America dropped its first 60,000 credit cards on the unassuming city of Fresno, California. That's a word they liked to use in the credit card business to characterize a mass mailing of cards: a "drop," and it is an unwittingly apt description. There had been no outward yearning among the residents of Fresno for such a device, nor even the dimmest awareness that such a thing was in the works. It simply arrived one day, with no advance warning, as if it had dropped from the sky. Over the course of the next twelve years, before the practice of mass card mailings was outlawed, banks would blanket the country with 100 million credit cards of one sort or another, and it would always have that same feeling. It would always seem as though those first hundred million credit cards had simply fallen from the sky.

Not that anybody made much of the drop back in 1958. Because this was the first test of its BankAmericard program (as it was called), the Bank of America purposely kept things low-key. The *Fresno Bee* managed to sandwich six paragraphs on the bank's new credit card program on an inside page between the business briefs and the livestock report. The headlines that day centered on the outbreak of fighting between Communist and Nationalist Chinese forces near the island of Quemoy; in Fresno, the lead local story was about a proposed reorganization of the police and fire departments. The Dow Jones Industrial Average began the day at 524, in the midst of a decade-long bull market. But since we were still a good twenty-five years away from the time when the stock market would be among the daily concerns of the middle class, nobody paid much attention to it.

Like so many subsequent moments in the evolution of personal finance in America, it was years before the significance of that date became clear—

years before the Bank of America would celebrate its original BankAmeri-card as the first all-purpose credit card to take root; when it would note with pride its history as the precursor to Visa, one of the two giant credit card systems; when it would draw attention to its role in helping to make credit cards the most ubiquitous financial instrument since the check, an unam-biguous commercial success story. Thirty years later, when most of us had developed feelings about credit cards that were nothing if not ambiguous, the bank even used the anniversary as the centerpiece of a marketing cam-paign.

As it turns out, the Fresno drop also marked the beginning of something larger: the first stirring of what would become a full-scale financial revolu-tion in America. A money revolution, you might call it. Here began the trickle of what we now call financial products, aimed largely at the middle class, that would become, by the 1980s, an avalanche. Here marked the first inkling of the gradual but enormous changes in the financial habits and assumptions of the middle class. Here is when a simple, ordered, highly regulated world began to evolve, for better or worse, into an immensely complicated universe. Though this transformation wouldn't become appar-ent for several decades, and though it continues to this day, this is when the American middle class began to change the way it thought about, and dealt with, its money.

It's oddly appropriate that the Bank of America wound up being the insti-gator of the credit card—and, by implication, everything that followed—for the bank was a unique institution in the 1950s, in many ways a harbinger of what was to come. Until it was finally overtaken in 1982 by Citibank, it was the largest bank in America, and indeed, for much of its existence, it was the largest bank in the world. What made it unusual was the route it had chosen to get there. Although every bank took in deposits from consumers and offered checking accounts, most of them were not especially interested in serving their middle-class depositors. There was no particular need to be interested. By law, all banks paid the same interest on passbook accounts, the primary vehicle for middle-class savings. In the 1950s, that rate never climbed above 3 percent. Checking accounts offered no interest at all, again by law. Other alternatives for middle-class savings were largely nonexistent. Since there was nothing to differentiate one bank from another, most people chose the bank that was most convenient. To the extent that banks bothered to do anything that might be considered marketing, such efforts usually consisted of offering, say, a free toaster to customers who opened up a

Christmas Club account. At most banks, such accounts also lacked interest payments.

It wasn't just the law that held bankers back; snobbery was at work too. Up until the late 1970s, when alternatives to passbook accounts finally forced banks to pay attention to their middle-class customers, most bankers looked down their noses at such business. Within the culture of banking, it was corporations that mattered, not consumers. Making loans to large companies was the most prestigious activity in all of banking; making consumer loans, on the other hand, was considered slightly disreputable, and such loans were ceded to finance companies, which were also considered slightly disreputable. This was so even though, as Bank of America executives were fond of pointing out, bankers were quite happy to lend large sums to finance companies, which would relend that money at far higher interest rates to people in need of short-term loans. This distinction between a bank's loan customers and a finance company's loan customers, which had less to do with the law than with institutional prejudice, was nonetheless one of those unwritten but inviolable lines of demarcation that then characterized American finance.

Bank of America was different. It was a bank with the mentality of a finance company and proud of it. It eagerly embraced the customers other banks disdained, and in that embrace it found enormous success. The bank had been founded in 1904 by the legendary A. P. Giannini, the son of an Italian immigrant who had settled in San Jose, California, forty-five miles south of San Francisco. Giannini was a particular American archetype: the populist entrepreneur. A big, blustery, blunt-spoken man, he had both predatory instincts and a common touch, along with an instinctive knack for commerce. At the age of fifteen, he joined his stepfather's produce wholesale company, and helped build it into the dominant company of its kind on the West Coast. At the age of thirty-four, he began his second, more enduring career as a banker. His explicit goal in starting his bank was to make money available for "his" people in and around the San Francisco area, many of whom were the Italian immigrant farmers in the Santa Clara Valley who sold their fruits and vegetables to Giannini's produce company. He named his new institution the Bank of Italy.

To a remarkable degree, Giannini held to that original goal, although his definition of "his" people expanded as his ambitions did. Long after the bank had delved into other businesses, like corporate lending, Giannini never forgot that it had been built by attracting deposits from, and lending money to, "the little fellow," as he called his customers. He never let anyone else forget it either. He was full of aphorisms promoting the essential goodness of the common man and the wisdom of lending to him. "The little fellow is the best customer that a bank can have, because he is with you," Giannini once told a congressional committee. "Whereas the big fellow is only with you so long as he can get something out of you; and when he cannot, he is not for you anymore." He saw clearly that by making thousands of small loans, rather than fewer but larger commercial loans, the bank's own risks were reduced. He understood that loyalty bred loyalty. After the San Francisco earthquake of 1906, when other banks in the area wanted to enforce a six-month moratorium on loans, Giannini went down to the pier, used a plank and two barrels to set up a desk, and began to lend money to virtually anyone who asked for it. By 1918, fourteen years after it was founded, the Bank of Italy was the fourth largest bank in California, with $93 million in assets. Three years later, after an acquisition binge, it was the state's biggest bank. By 1945, it had a new name, Bank of America, and assets of $5 billion. It had become the largest bank in the world.

In focusing on "the little fellow," Giannini was a good sixty years ahead of his time; when Citibank finally grew large enough to overtake Bank of America, its surge was largely the result of its own willingness to chase after the middle class. But Giannini had another, larger vision of banking in America, which he pursued during the second half of his life with a relentless single-mindedness. He saw a nation where a handful of large banks would have branches all across the country, and a banking system that would allow customers to use branches not only to make deposits or obtain loans, but to buy insurance and conduct all their financial business. In this, too, Giannini was ahead of his time; not until the late 1970s, after the regulatory barriers separating financial institutions had begun to crumble, did Giannini's idea of a financial "supermarket" come into vogue.

The trouble with being ahead of your time is that very few people are out there with you. So it was with Giannini. No matter how hard he pushed for his grand vision, he met fierce, unyielding resistance. At every turn, he ran headlong into a different, more powerful strain of populism: the country's deep and abiding suspicion of the power of bankers. It is that fear of bankers—a fear that goes back to America's agrarian roots, when the annual preharvest bank loan was as vital to a farmer's well-being as the weather itself—that has largely shaped federal bank policy for most of this century. Bank laws have been driven by the idea, often unspoken, that small banks are more benign than big banks, and that local bankers, living and working in a community, will react more favorably to local borrowers than will larger, more remote institutions. This is why, to this day, there is still no bank in America that can truly be said to operate nationwide and why the country has closer to 11,000 banks than the 1,000 or so Giannini envisioned.

This fear of bankers infuriated Giannini. He saw it as fundamentally irrational, a product, as he once described it, "of horse and buggy minds." It was incomprehensible to him that the government would allow nationwide department stores but not nationwide banks. More than that, it offended him that people would fear his ambitions, for it so deeply violated his sense of himself as a paternalistic force for good. He lashed out at state and federal regulators intent on curbing his expansionist appetites. Usually, he lost. In 1927, Congress passed the McFadden Act, the first of the modern bank laws, which outlawed interstate banking. According to a number of accounts, the law was aimed squarely at Giannini, who by then owned a bank in New York. After President Franklin Roosevelt ordered his famous bank holiday in 1932, regulators came very close to refusing to allow Bank of America to reopen with other banks, an action that would have destroyed it. The Depression only made Washington even more wary of banks, and the result was the Glass–Steagall Act, which created strict barriers separating banks from the likes of insurance companies and investment firms. By the time Giannini died in 1949, at the age of seventy-nine, his bank, like every other bank in the country, had seen its options drastically pared back and its turf much more narrowly defined.

Ah, but what turf it was! Here was Bank of America's singular advantage: Its home base was California—sunny, glorious California, the second-largest state (in terms of land mass),[1] the fastest-growing, and after World War II especially, the most dynamic. Perhaps most important of all, sunny, fast-growing, dynamic California was one of the few places in the country that allowed statewide branch banking. This was also something that had embroiled Giannini in bitter feuds with regulators; a California banking commissioner once called the idea of statewide branch banking un-American. But this time Giannini won. In New York, by contrast, branches were only permitted citywide, and in many states, such as Texas and Illinois, even that much was forbidden. In Texas, banks were allowed one physical location, and nothing else. Years later, after technology and urbanization began to make such rules archaic, disputes actually broke out over whether the installation of automatic teller machines violated the prohibition against branch banking.

Is it any wonder that Bank of America became the biggest bank in the country? With branch banking as its engine, operating in a state as big and as fast-growing as California, how could it *not* have become the biggest bank? Between 1940 and 1960, California more than doubled in population, growing from 6.9 million to 15.7 million people, becoming the nation's most populous state. During those same years, Bank of America's sprawling branch system rose from fewer than 500 branches to more than 700. Newcomers streaming into the state could usually find a Bank of America branch just around the corner.[2] And because the shadow of Giannini still hung so heavily over the bank, it had never lost that obsessive focus on its constituency, which it now defined as the broad middle class that had begun to spring up after World War II. At the Bank of America, the branch manager was king; everything headquarters did was aimed at making it easier for him to attract customers and to give them what they wanted. And what did those customers want? They wanted credit.

Consumer credit—that is, the taking on of personal debt—has always occupied a peculiar place in the American psyche. On the one hand, there is no aspect of personal finance more likely to inspire anxiety and even fear. At any given moment in our history, one can find ringing denunciations of consumer credit and "usurious" interest rates, calls for reform, worries that things have finally gotten out of hand. "Rather go to Bed supperless than rise in Debt," wrote Ben Franklin, and Americans have been echoing that sentiment ever since. Credit historian Lewis Mandell points out that in the early 1800s, many states, upon being granted statehood, passed a usury ceiling, rolling back interest rates, as their very first law. Among the reasons banks originally refused to make consumer loans widely available was out of a belief that too much consumer credit was dangerous and that people needed to be protected from themselves.

On the other hand, among the reasons finance companies prospered was because they saw this refusal by banks to make personal loans as a yawning void, which they rushed to fill. Despite the denunciations, despite the free-floating anxiety, Americans have always borrowed money to buy things—if not from a bank, then from *somebody*: from a finance company or a credit union or a department store or a loan shark, for that matter. There isn't another Western country that has relied so heavily on consumer credit; between 1958 and 1990, there was never a year when the amount of outstanding consumer debt wasn't higher than it had been the year before.

Years later, a retired Bank of America executive could look back on his lifetime in the credit card industry and say proudly, "Consumer credit built this country." Whatever one's feelings about personal debt, it is difficult to disagree with this assertion. The rise of the consumer society, in particular, would not have been possible without a widespread willingness to take on personal debt. How could General Motors have sold its first mass-market automobiles without that other mass-market innovation, the auto loan? How could Singer have sold sewing machines without extending credit? How could Sears have sold refrigerators?[3] Even during the Depression, credit was important; in many ways, it was the grease that oiled the economy. People asked for credit because they didn't have any choice; merchants granted it because *they* didn't have any choice. These were painful, discouraging transactions for everyone involved—a constant reminder of how tough times were and how close people were to the brink.[4]

Well into the 1950s and beyond, the Depression remained the nation's dominant economic memory. It had been such a searing experience that people who lived through it adopted a set of financial habits and attitudes that would last long after the event itself had receded into the country's subconscious. The ethos of thrift was one natural result of the Depression experience. So was an aversion to financial risk. That's why so few people even thought about the stock market and why the vast majority of Americans were content to keep their money in bank passbook accounts. Such accounts were federally insured, which meant they were secure. In the wake of the Depression, security was what mattered.

The desire of the middle class to take on debt in the 1950s was the first crack in the relentless financial logic of the Depression. For the burgeoning middle class, seeking a loan was no longer an act of desperation but one of cautious optimism, no longer primarily about need but about want. Loren Baritz, an historian of the middle class, reports that between 1947 and 1959, the percentage of families earning under $3,000 dropped from 46 to 20, "while the percentage of families earning between $7,000 and $10,000, a high middle class income, rose from 5 to 20 during the same period." "The onslaught of consumer goods," as Mandell calls it, had begun in earnest: televisions, refrigerators, new models of automobiles, and a dozen other modern conveniences. People wanted these things. The logic of the Depression said they should go without until they had saved the money to buy them. But Americans were tired of going without. So rather than wait and save, they took out personal loans or bought on the installment plan. And when they saw that nothing bad happened as a result, they did it again, adding the television loan to the refrigerator loan to the auto loan. "Of all families within the income range from $3,000 to $4,000, 48 percent had installment payments to meet," noted economist John Kenneth Galbraith in *The Affluent Society*, his best-selling attack on the consumer society Americans were greeting with such enthusiasm. "For nearly a third of those," Galbraith added ominously, "the payments commanded more than a fifth of the family income before taxes."

Thus did Americans begin to spend money they didn't yet have; thus did the unaffordable become affordable. And thus, it must be said, did the economy grow. Between 1945 and 1960, consumer credit simply exploded, going from $2.6 billion to $45 billion. A decade later, it stood at $105 billion. It was as if the entire middle class was betting that tomorrow would be better than today.

Almost alone among banks, Bank of America understood this growing optimism and fed off it. Like other forms of credit in other times, installment credit was controversial in the 1950s. In the first eight years after World War II, as installment loans grew by an astounding 700 percent, there was increasing concern in Washington and among many economists that personal debt was rising too fast. "Can the bill collector be the central figure in the good society?" wrote Galbraith, who, like many intellectuals, objected not only to the rise in debt but to the consumer mentality that spawned it. *The New York Times* editorialized on several occasions that installment loans needed to be brought under control. The Federal Reserve was ordered to produce studies on the subject. (They were inconclusive.) President Eisenhower even asked Congress for authority to rein in consumer credit. (It was never granted.)

Yet the Bank of America never flinched: People were asking for installment loans, so it would provide them. Other banks might cede this business to finance companies, but it would not. It had one plan for television buyers and another for refrigerator buyers—at one point in the 1950s, the bank had a $60 million portfolio made up mostly of $200 refrigerator loans. It became such a huge generator of auto loans that, at its peak, it did 85 percent of the state's auto loan business. "People would come into the bank four and five times a year, whenever they needed extra funds," recalls Kenneth Larkin, a lifelong Bank of America executive who retired in 1984. "There was vacation. There were back-to-school clothes. There were the holidays. There was tax time. There were medical emergencies."

Larkin was the assistant manager of the bank's Bakersfield branch at the time, rising steadily through the ranks. This meant that like every other officer in the bank's sprawling branch system, a big part of his job was devoted to making small loans to consumers. Among the things he most remembers is how cumbersome it used to be to make a small personal loan. Every time a man came into the branch to get a loan—a loan customer was invariably a man in those days—he had to sit down with the loan officer and fill out his family history, even if he'd just been there a few months before. The loan officer had to reevaluate the man's fitness to get a loan. The man had to return to the branch with his wife to sign a note. Only then would the loan officer transfer the funds to the man's account. With that much effort needed to generate a $300 loan, it was difficult to turn much of a profit, despite the volume of such business.

This was duly noted at the bank's San Francisco headquarters, and it led to several innovations—evolutionary steps, they would seem now, in making personal loans available to the middle class. One wrinkle was called Timeplan, which created for the middle class something it had never had before: a line of credit. Under the plan, approved customers could draw up to $1,000—and it was up to them to choose how much they wanted to borrow, and for what purpose. It was one of the bank's most popular loan programs.

And the other innovation? That was the credit card.

It emerged from a think tank, a fact that suggests that some things had changed at the bank since the death of its founder. Bank of America still saw itself as "an institution run in the interest . . . of the people it serves" (as Giannini used to phrase it), and still clung proudly to its role as the financial institution most closely aligned with "the little fellow." But in the fashion of many institutions that came of age in the 1950s, it began to operate in ways that were less instinctive and more rigorously managerial. Its ranks began to be filled with middle managers, who wrote position papers and conducted studies. And for a time at least, it had an in-house think tank— "not an egg-head group," its former leader insists, but a practical group, interested in divining which new products a bank customer might use and a bank might want to offer. It was called the Customer Services Research Department.

The leader of the group was a man named Joseph Williams, forty-one years old, a Philadelphia banker so disenchanted with the way banking was done in the East, and so enamored of Giannini's philosophy, that practically the first thing he did upon returning from Germany after World War II was drive across the country to San Francisco and ask for a job at the Bank of America. By 1956, when he convinced management that a small research group was the sort of thing a forward-thinking bank ought to have, he was among its growing corps of middle managers.

In theory, Williams and the six people in his department were supposed to be able to pursue any idea that struck their fancy. In practice, there was never any doubt that the bank's management expected to see a proposal for an all-purpose credit card. Three times before, the bank had explored the possibility of issuing credit cards, most recently the previous year. A credit card clearly dovetailed with the direction the bank—and the country—was headed. Consumer credit was spilling out in every direction. Most Americans by then had a dozen or more different forms of credit: a gasoline card from an oil company, five or six department store charge plates, a Sears card, some airline charge accounts if they traveled, installment loans for autos and refrigerators, and maybe a loan or two from a finance company.

In a holdover from the Depression, they also usually had "an account" at
the neighborhood pharmacy, the neighborhood grocery store, and a half-
dozen other local stores. The value of a single card that could replace all
those other forms of credit would be so instantly obvious, the bank believed,
that not only would it be embraced by its current customers, but it would
serve as a powerful tool in the bank's continuing quest to clasp ever more
members of the middle class to its bosom.

Nor was Bank of America alone in thinking about an all-purpose credit
card. This was an idea very much in the air by the late 1950s. On the East
Coast, Chase Manhattan Bank was quietly preparing to issue credit cards,
something it would do (with disastrous results) five months after Bank of
America's Fresno drop. American Express, after much hesitation, was getting ready to launch its first charge card,[5] after having given its upstart rival,
Diners Club, an eight-year head start. Diners Club, in fact, had been the first
charge card in America that could be used at more than one establishment.
Its founder, a New York businessman named Frank X. McNamara, liked to
say that he was visited with the crucial burst of inspiration one afternoon at
a midtown restaurant when he finished lunch only to realize that he hadn't
brought enough money to pay for it.[6] As the name implies, Diners Club
began life as a restaurant charge card, but even after it outgrew its origins,
it was still aimed primarily at businessmen, men who traveled to different
cities, stayed in different hotels, and ate in different restaurants. Its appeal
was convenience rather than credit, which it did not offer. (Customers were
expected to pay their bills in full at the end of each month.) American
Express, which would soon dominate the "travel and entertainment" sector
Diners Club pioneered, would stick to that same formula. But even without
offering credit, Diners Club provided the conceptual breakthrough: it showed
that one card could be used to buy different things at different places.

By the mid-1950s, there had been at least a dozen attempts to create an
all-purpose credit card. A number of small banks, eager to find a niche that
would distinguish them from their larger rivals, had been the first to experiment with credit cards—much to the annoyance of bigger banks; one early
credit card experimenter was described as "lowering banking's image by
engaging in an activity more properly associated with pawn shops. . . ."
These early efforts invariably failed.

Being the good middle manager that he was, Williams studied those
failures and came away encouraged. The other programs had been small-
scale; Bank of America had a much larger canvas to work with. The other
programs hadn't been structured properly; Bank of America would do it
right. Williams had friends at Sears and Mobil Oil, and those friends secretly allowed his team to observe their credit operations. Out of this latter

research, incidentally, came a number of the standard features of credit cards, features that have remained remarkably unchanged to this day. The idea of a one-month grace period, a time during which customers could pay off their balances without facing interest charges, emerged from that research, as did the idea of charging 18 percent a year on credit card loans—a figure that would be seemingly set in stone for the next thirty years, even as every other manner of interest rate fluctuated wildly. There was no black magic involved: The bank just assumed that if a one-month grace period and a monthly interest charge of 1½ percent (which amounts to 18 percent a year) was good enough for Sears, with its fifty years of credit experience, then it was good enough for the Bank of America.

By the middle of 1957, Williams was making presentations to the bank's top management and gearing up for a launch of BankAmericard the following year. Every step was taken cautiously. Fresno was chosen as the first test site partly because of its size—with a population around 250,000, it offered the critical mass the bank thought necessary to make a credit card work—and partly because a staggering 45 percent of Fresno's families did at least some business with the Bank of America. But at least as important was Fresno's relative isolation; if the card bombed, the bank reasoned, the damage to its reputation would be minimal.

To talk now to people who were there at the creation is to be impressed with something else—something that takes you by surprise after all this time, even though it shouldn't. Today, credit cards are so commonplace that everything about them seems second nature: the physical feel of them, the way a transaction is conducted, the look of the statement that comes at the end of the month—everything. But nothing was second nature then. Nothing about how credit cards should work was obvious. The credit card trailblazers like Joe Williams were making it up as they went along, groping for answers that didn't yet exist, learning a business as they were inventing it.

So invent it they did. They concluded, on the basis of nothing but their own intuition, that credit limits for the cards should range between $300 and $500. In that age before instant electronics, they came up with the concept of "floor limits" ranging from $25 to $100, which allowed the cardholder to charge that much without the merchant having to call the bank to get approval. They decided that the merchant who accepted a BankAmericard would have to pay Bank of America 6 percent of the purchase price—the "merchant discount," it was called, which was expected to be a crucial source of profit—plus $25 a month for the "imprinters" the bank gave it. The bank had started using computers, so engineers were brought in to program them to perform such novel tasks as alerting the bank when credit card customers were spending more than their limit allowed. The bank's marketing staff assumed that advertising would have to be unsubtle and nonstop. ("The plan represented a new buying habit and therefore required heavy educational promotion," as the bank's in-house historian euphemistically put it.)

Most important of all, Williams and his group saw that a credit card could be used in two ways. It could be used either as a device offering convenience—as a Diners Club card did—or as a device generating an instant personal loan. A BankAmericard would be able to do both, depending on the cardholder's preference. In hindsight, that is what made BankAmericard so different from any financial product that had come before it. It put the onus entirely on the customer. It was he or she alone who got to make the key decisions about how and when to spend large sums of money—and how and when to pay it back. It could be used impulsively or carefully, frequently or sparingly, for emergencies or for shopping sprees. And then, when the bill arrived, it was he or she alone who decided whether to pay back the money all at once (with no interest), or in installments (with interest). The crucial point is that the customer was in control of financial decisions that had always before required the explicit approval of a banker or loan officer. One major reason previous credit card programs had flopped was that most banks feared giving their customers that much control. Bank of America had no such qualms.

Williams also had to solve a peculiar paradox, one that would crop up again and again in those early years. It's another one of those things we have tended to forget as credit cards have become commonplace: A successful credit card program requires the participation of not just customers but store owners as well. In fact, it requires thousands of store owners, who have to be recruited with the promise that there will be enough cardholders to make accepting the card—and handing over 6 percent of the purchase price to a bank—worth their while. At the same time the bank is recruiting merchants, though, it must also recruit cardholders—promising them that there will be enough merchants signed up to make carrying the card worth *their* while. It was a chicken-and-egg dilemma. Which came first, the customers or the merchants?

The "drop" was Williams's solution to this problem. Rather than recruit cardholders, he decided to create them. He would mail cards to anyone who did business with Bank of America, free of charge.[7] He fully expected them to view the arrival of the card as a wonderful new service the bank was providing. If they didn't see it that way, Williams assumed that they would just toss it away.

Whatever the drawbacks of the drop—as it turns out, there were many—it had one overriding virtue. Fresno's shop owners knew for a fact that, on the day the program began, some 60,000 people would be holding BankAmeri-cards. That was a powerful number, and it had its intended effect. Merchants began to sign on. Not the big merchants, like Sears, which had its own proprietary credit card and saw the bank's entry into the credit card business as a form of poaching. Rather, it was the smaller merchants who first came around. Larkin remembers visiting a drug store in Bakersfield, hoping to persuade its owner to accept BankAmericard. "When I explained the concept of our credit card," he says, "the man almost knelt down and kissed my feet. 'You'll be the savior of my business,' he said. We went into his back office," Larkin continues. "He had three girls working on Burroughs bookkeeping machines, each handling 1,000 to 1,500 accounts. I looked at the size of the accounts: $4.58. $12.82. And he was sending out monthly bills on these accounts. Then the customers paid him maybe three or four months later. Think of what this man was spending on postage, labor, envelopes, stationery! His accounts receivables were dragging him under."

A store owner who accepted the credit card was, in effect, handing his back office headaches over to the Bank of America. The bank would guarantee him payment—within days instead of months—and would take over the role of collecting from the customers. As for the bank, in addition to taking its 6 percent cut, the card was a way to get its hooks into businessmen who were not yet Bank of America customers.

Whenever you're trying to do something new in business, you have to make some assumptions that can't be tested beforehand. In the case of BankAmericard, some of the assumptions Williams made were clearly naive. One, certainly, was his belief that people would react to the arrival of that first card with equanimity; he never understood the emotional power of this new device, the way it would bring people's conflicting feelings about credit bubbling to the surface.

He missed something else, too. Williams was a Bank of America man through and through, but he'd never been a *loan* man at the BofA, which meant that his passionate belief in the goodness of the common man had never been tempered by the experience of lending him money. He'd never had the experience of looking a man who was behind in his payments straight in the eye, and asking him when he'd be able to start paying back the loan. He'd never had to order the repossession of a new car. One of the reasons an all-purpose credit card was such a revolutionary device was that it made the act of borrowing money so much more impersonal than it had ever been before; with cards coming in the mail, nobody was going to be looking anybody straight in the eye. Yet at the same time, it was much more dependent on the sheer good faith of the borrower, since no collateral was involved. A subtle but important shift was taking place in the dynamic between lender and borrower, and Williams, so busy struggling over the complicated details—and so convinced that the BankAmericard was destined for instant success—was oblivious.

Thus he wound up assuming that only around 4 percent of credit card users would get behind on their payments. That, after all, was the percentage of the bank's installment loan customers who were delinquent, and he saw no reason why credit card delinquencies would be any different. He also assumed, as the author of an in-house BankAmericard history would later report, that "collections would never be a problem" and that "everyone would love Bank of America." The writer added dryly: "All of the mistakes and problems that resulted, and extended themselves for a year and a half, were inextricably bound up in these . . . determinations."

The Fresno drop went smoothly. More to the point, perhaps, it went quietly. "There wasn't a big parade or anything," recalls Williams, but there wasn't a great outcry either—no ringing condemnations of the evils of credit, nor any of the loud protestations about unwanted credit cards that would come later, and would be such a hallmark of the early phase of the credit card business. More than 300 small shop owners were signed up by the time of the launch, with more promising to do so once they were sure that people were using the card. Williams remembers that Florsheim Shoes—another of those institutions tied to the rise of the middle class— was the first chain of stores to accept BankAmericard. The card was a novelty at first; just as Americans spent hours staring at the test pattern of their new TV, so did the citizens of Fresno gather around the checkout counter to watch someone pay with a BankAmericard. This was the 1950s, after all, a time of wonder at the miraculous march of progress. BankAmericard was part of that march.

The advertising campaign unveiled in Fresno was also a classic product of the 1950s, managing to evoke that guileless mix of ambition and innocence we've come to associate with that era. "Carry Your Credit in Your Pocket!" those first ads exuberantly announced. "Just One Payment to Make at the End of the Month!" they added. "It's easy to know where your money goes when you see it there in black and white in one concise statement!" the copy read. "You can budget payments, too, if you wish and still add more purchases on your BankAmericard—thanks to the *flexible payment* feature. . . ." It's as if no one at the bank could conceive that there might ever be a problem with letting any member of the middle class carry its credit in his pocket; as if a "flexible payment feature" posed no potential dangers;

as if everything associated with having a credit card was good and wholesome and quintessentially American.

In fact, that is exactly what the bank believed. Throughout its long history of extending consumer credit, Bank of America had always made an implicit distinction between "good" credit and "bad" credit. The kind of credit it extended, of course, was the good kind: the kind that made it possible for good, upstanding citizens to achieve the American dream. The kind that made the consumer society tick. The kind that was based on "the inherent honesty of the great majority of people," as Ken Larkin later put it. This sentiment did not change just because the bank was now issuing credit cards.

Williams himself had an almost prudish view of his new device. "The biggest thing a credit card can do is enable families to take advantage of sales—to buy your skis in the summer and your barbecue grill in the winter," he says. "I wanted people to understand that their goal should be to make credit pay them, instead of having them pay for credit. If they overspent," he adds with a paternalistic smile, "then you might have to rap their knuckles once in a while."

Larkin recalls the bank's nervousness when it decided to expand the program to Los Angeles. Los Angeles was home to (in his words) "the fast Hollywood crowd, the blue suede shoe boys." Partly, that nervousness stemmed from the bank's fears—not unjustified—that there might be problems in Los Angeles with credit card fraud and with collections. But it was also due to the fact that, although the blue suede shoe boys would undoubtedly enjoy having a credit card, they were probably not going to use it to buy skis in the summer.

In the end, though, the main thing old Bank of America hands remember about the Fresno test is how short it was. It had only been running for a few months when the bank began hearing rumors that another California bank was going to inaugurate a competing credit card—and would make its first drop in San Francisco, Bank of America's backyard. A friendly merchant slipped a copy of the other bank's plans to someone at Bank of America, which not only confirmed the rumor but galvanized everyone associated with BankAmericard. Suddenly, all the caution that had characterized the Fresno experience was abandoned.

Within three months, the bank was rushing credit cards to customers in Modesto, north of Fresno, and in Bakersfield to the south. By March 1959, tens of thousands of BankAmericards were being given to customers in San Francisco and Sacramento; by June, tens of thousands more were arriving in the mail in dreaded Los Angeles. In each of these cities, every employee in every Bank of America branch was assigned to sign up merchants, which they did with abandon. By October 1959, thirteen months after the Fresno test had begun, BankAmericards had been dropped in every nook and cranny in California. In that time, some 2 million cards were put into circulation; more than 20,000 merchants had agreed to accept it. The other California bank never bothered to unveil its competing card. And two months after that, Joe Williams resigned.[8]

What had gone wrong? It's hard, in hindsight, to think of anything that didn't go wrong. The bank's frantic effort to push credit cards out the door had degenerated into a small catastrophe. Delinquent accounts? They weren't 4 percent as Williams had predicted; they were 22 percent. Collections? Williams, convinced the BankAmericard program would never have to worry about collecting on its loans, hadn't even bothered to set up a collections department. Fraud? It was rampant. Resistance to the bank? It was everywhere, especially among the larger merchants, who hated the idea of paying 6 percent to the Bank of America, and resented its attempt to get into the credit card business. Bank of America salesmen got nowhere with them. As a result, those early merchants were dominated by "the league of pawn shops, taverns, and bail bond houses," as one writer would later describe it.

The biggest disaster was in Los Angeles, just as the bank had feared. Here is where Bank of America got its first lesson in credit card fraud. Crooks were quick to decipher the symbols on a stolen credit card, so they knew what the floor limit was. That way, they could make hundreds of small purchases under the limit without having to worry about a merchant calling the bank and finding out the card was stolen. Prostitutes lifted cards from johns. Merchants by the hundreds cheated the BofA. Thieves broke into the bank's warehouse and stole unembossed BankAmericards, which they then offered to sell back to the BofA. Because credit card crime was so new, the bank had a hard time getting the police interested in pursuing these thefts; because it feared the thieves would emboss the cards and use them, it often did buy them back.

It was in Los Angeles that Bank of America also first learned something about the risks that came with handing out credit cards indiscriminately. You couldn't drop thousands of credit cards on a large American city and not expect to have problems; it was crazy to think otherwise. In Los Angeles, there were problems with people getting duplicate cards; problems with once-good customers seeing the card as free money and running up charges they had no intention of repaying; problems with people who were simply not good credit risks getting the card. In one case, the branches were asked to come up with a list of people who should not get a BankAmericard;

because of a mixup, everyone on the list got a card. Later, Williams would blame the Los Angeles branches, claiming that they had been too lax in compiling their lists of customers who should be mailed BankAmericards. Most other bank executives, though, blamed Williams for not realizing that not all Bank of America customers were equally credit-worthy. According to this view, his lack of loan experience was his crucial flaw, as was his unwillingness to confront head-on the mounting problems. Whenever other executives asked him what he was doing to stanch the red ink, he would airily dismiss their concerns. "All is well," he would say. But it wasn't. By the time Williams left, fifteen months after the launch, the bank had officially lost $8.8 million on its new credit card program. For a bank in the 1950s, that was a huge sum of money. And that wasn't the half of it. The real figure—when hidden costs like advertising and overhead were included—was closer to $20 million.

As painful as this financial loss was for the bank, the loss of face hurt almost as much. Williams's decision to mail out the bank's new credit card created a furor across the state. "Regularly there appeared an item," according to the bank's own account, "usually a report or a statement from a congressman that [said]: 'a rapidly expanding credit-oriented economy is morally and financially ruinous to the public welfare.' " Larkin went to church one Sunday morning and heard his minister denounce credit cards from the pulpit. Editorial writers all over California took up the cry, pointing out that people were being handed a device they had never asked for and didn't want—one that could only get them into trouble. Others objected to the fine print they found buried in the cardholder agreement. It said that the person to whom the card was issued could be held responsible for any purchase made, even if the card had been lost or stolen. After this became widely known, there was another round of condemnation.


Eventually, it all came to a head. A moment arrived when the bank's top management, stung by the growing criticism and unable to ignore the mounting losses, had to decide whether to stay in the credit card business or abandon it, as so many smaller banks had done before it. In the bank's own retelling, this moment came during a series of meetings of its Managing Committee, a small group chaired by the bank's chief executive, a soft-spoken, gentlemanly man named Clark Beise. Naturally, the BankAmericard program had acquired the stench of failure; no one in the bank wanted to be associated with it. The facts, as they were presented to the committee, were awful. No one could say with any certainty whether the program was salvageable. The head of the bank's installment loan division was asked to sit in on these sessions, which he did "with misgivings."[9] And naturally, the members of the committee, these rational, 1950s legatees of their boisterous founder, looked out into the future of their bank and their country and saw credit cards as a part of both. (Besides, adds the bank's credit card historian, they realized that "every conceivable mistake had already been made.")

Did it really happen that way? It's impossible to know for sure, since virtually everyone involved in that decision is now deceased. But that's the legend as it has been handed down, and subsequent events would suggest that it is reasonably close to the mark. After Williams left the bank, a massive effort was begun to clean up after him. First, all of the men who had been part of Williams's team were given new assignments as far away from credit cards as possible. Then, the business was turned over to the loan men. "That's when the bank began to bring installment credit thinking to the management of credit cards," says Larkin. A collections department was set up. An antifraud unit was established. Losses were written off. People who were clearly not planning on paying their bills had their cards taken away; merchants suspected of cheating the bank were dropped from the program. At the same time, realizing the need to lower the resistance of larger, more reputable merchants, the new credit card department began cutting the merchant discount, in some cases to as low as 3 percent.

And for the first time, the bank faced up to the realization that not everyone in California was as convinced of the virtues of credit as it was. This is what Williams had most lost sight of as he had prepared to unleash his new device upon an unsuspecting world. It is what the bank most needed to come to terms with now. In an attempt to repair its tattered image—to explain itself, really—the bank's advertising department wrote an open letter to its customers across the state, 3 million families in all. Part apologia, part sales-pitch, the letter was both an admission that it had offended people with its mass mailings of cards, and an attempt to recapture the moral high ground from its critics. It read in part:

> As for its encouraging extravagance, it seems to us that this is a problem which every individual must resolve for himself. Only you can determine to what extent your income and circumstances permit you to buy on credit. It is not our intention to encourage "easy money" or a "free spending program." In fact, we believe our job is to assist you in any way possible to maintain sound and sensible control of your finances.

It took well over a year for the BankAmericard program to right itself, but gradually it did. In his 1960 report to shareholders, Beise predicted that the

BankAmericard would soon become "a significant source of earnings." By the following April, the card had turned a profit.

Between 1958 and 1966, Bank of America had the California credit card business all to itself. Other banks, knowing about the huge early losses but not about the later profits, stayed away. For much of that time, the number of BankAmericards grew only slightly: The bank was largely content to manage the million or so cards that remained in circulation after the program had been cleaned up. It would be another five years before the bank dropped cards again in any significant number.

Yet a funny thing was happening. Each year, the cards in circulation were gaining a little wider acceptance. Each year, more customers were taking them out of their desk drawers and using them. In 1960, 233,585 were in use; by 1964, that number was up to 430,442; by 1968, it was over a million. Each year Bank of America customers used the card to buy more things ($59 million worth of sales in 1960; $400 million by 1968), and to take on more debt ($28 million in 1960 versus $252 million in 1968). And each year, the card made more money for the bank, from $179,000 in 1961 to $12.7 million in 1968.

Today, credit card executives like to say that the card has become so entwined in the fabric of American life that most people have no choice but to carry one. Their feelings about debt, and about the card itself, are largely irrelevant. "Have you ever tried to rent a car without one?" asks Alex "Pete" Hart, the former head of MasterCard. But that wasn't true in the 1960s. People did have a choice. There was no imperative to use a credit card. In the spring of 1965, the bank conducted a widely publicized stunt, in which a man lived for a month without cash, using only a BankAmericard to make purchases. But the stunt was hardly necessary, for by then it was obvious that the card was gaining acceptance. For whatever reason, more and more Californians were choosing to use it—choosing to make their own decisions about the level of personal debt they could carry comfortably, implicitly accepting the bank's shifting of responsibility from itself to them.

The first shot in the money revolution had been fired.

## CHAPTER 2

# The Man with the Golden Touch

## *February 1966*

T HE GREATEST POPULARIZER of the stock market—the man who spent his career trying to convince the middle class that stocks and bonds should be a part of their lives—died in his bed, at his Long Island retreat, on October 6, 1956. He was seventy years old, and though the moment of death had arrived suddenly, the real surprise is that he lived as long as he did.

He had been an invalid for more than a decade, having suffered a series of heart attacks when he was fifty-eight, followed by an intense and unrelenting angina that would stay with him the rest of his life. On bad days, the angina might strike as often as 127 times: He knew the precise number because he kept close track of his attacks, and then grimly related the latest count to friends and relatives in the long, windy, self-absorbed letters for which he was renowned among his circle. A lifelong carouser and incorrigible womanizer—"getting my batteries recharged" was his euphemism for philandering—he bridled at the regimen prescribed by his doctor, who, adhering to the conventional medical wisdom of the day, told him he would have to remain bedridden and housebound if he expected to stay alive. Told to stop drinking, he cut back to two martinis a day. Ordered to stop traveling, he merely cut out business travel, continuing to rotate among his three residences, in Barbados, Palm Beach, and Southampton, Long Island. In his late sixties, he found temporary relief from his angina when a doctor prescribed a new and radical treatment, dosages of radioactive iodine, which he called "atom bomb cocktails." The pains temporarily gone, he then went to his reunion at Amherst College, where he caroused so gaily and drank so freely that he suffered a major relapse.

And of course it was unthinkable that he would stop working, no matter what his doctor said. It would be nearly ten years after his first heart attack before he stepped into his office again—this appearance also made possible by the atom bomb cocktails—yet there was no question that he was still the man in charge. His days on Long Island revolved around two events: a bridge game with a handful of wealthy women who made up his entourage, and a two-hour phone call to his firm's managing partner, in which he would pepper the man with questions, requests, demands of every kind. "*Why* . . . had the monthly report not reached him? *Why* hadn't he been informed of a partner's wife's mother's illness?" his younger son later wrote, gently mocking his daily demands. Two weeks before his death, a former partner would later recount (as if to prove the son's point), he asked to see the text for the upcoming annual report. "It could not be released until he approved every word and illustration."

By then, the angina pains had returned, and he had come back from a stay in Barbados with a mysterious skin ailment, though neither condition seemed to suggest a serious turn for the worse. In early October, however, he developed uremia. On October 5, he lapsed into a coma, and the next day, Charles Edward Merrill was dead. Of the hundreds who attended his funeral—the industrialists whose stock he had underwritten, the partners he had made wealthy, the family he had tried, however imperfectly, to love, even some of the women he had seduced—most had known him as Charlie. Good Time Charlie Merrill. He was a piece of work.

His firm, of course, was Merrill Lynch, Pierce, Fenner & Beane, which he founded as Charles E. Merrill & Co. in the first few days of 1914, and which became in his lifetime the largest and most successful brokerage house Wall Street had ever seen. In effect, Merrill worked the opposite side of the street from A. P. Giannini: The latter operated on the banking side of personal finance, while the former worked the investment side— the riskier, stock market side. But in many ways they were kindred spirits. They both had outsized egos, personalities that overwhelmed, and a sense of zealotry that bordered on the messianic. In business at least, they shared a rigid sense of morality: Merrill always had contempt for those in the brokerage business—and in his mind, that included just about everybody who didn't work for him—who held to a different, looser set of standards. Most importantly, they both bet correctly that success in their particular spheres of personal finance lay with attracting the middle class, instead of catering to the rich. "Bringing Wall Street to Main Street" was the way Merrill liked to describe his life's work, and although his life ended well before his work was done, those words would echo through the decades, as events gradually conspired to push Americans in the direction Merrill had always tried to lead them. In time, his central idea, that the middle class should be investors as well as savers, would be at the heart of the money revolution.

                              *     *     *

All his life, Merrill was his own best mythmaker, and the myth he spun
about his early days in New York ranks among his finest creations. The year
was 1907; Merrill was twenty-two years old, an ambitious, inexperienced
young man whose job history up to that point amounted to playing semipro
ball and editing a small newspaper. The son of a struggling doctor, he had
grown up in a series of small towns in Florida, and had been forced to drop
out of Amherst College during one of his father's periodic financial droughts.
The chief circumstance behind his move to New York was his engagement
to a Smith College student: Her father was a New York textile executive,
and at his daughter's request, the man agreed to take on Merrill, whom he
had never met. Merrill was hired as an office boy, earning $15 a week.

   His arrival in the city coincided with a market crash; credit was tight. His
new employer (as he later told the story) had been unable to persuade any
bank in the city to lend it $300,000, money it had to have to stay afloat. In
desperation, the company sent its office boy to one of New York's newest
banks, to make one last stab at getting the loan. Somehow, the office boy
maneuvered his way into the bank president's office. The dialogue supposedly went like this:

   "Young man, I understand you want to borrow $300,000."
   "Yes, sir, that's what I'm here for."
   "How old are you?"
   "Twenty-two."
   "Don't you know there's a panic on?"
   "Yes, sir, I certainly do," replied the office boy. "But don't you know
that it takes just one good panic to get a new bank going?" At which point,
the bank president roared with laughter and gave Charlie Merrill the money.

   It is an utterly improbable story, the kind that only a man of astounding
bluster and ego could tell on himself with a straight face. But Charlie Merrill
was always such a man—perfectly willing to hear others describe him as
larger than life since that's what he believed himself. The mundane facts are
not quite so legendary, but impressive enough: He showed talent in that first
job, rose quickly through the ranks, earned a salary of $100 a week within
two years, spent much of the money in the clubs of New York accompanied
by women who were not his fiancée, broke off his engagement, and quit his
job. It wasn't long before he landed at his first Wall Street firm, where the
pattern repeated itself. This time he revived the firm's moribund bond department, got in return 10 percent of his department's profits, perfected
the art of crashing society parties with his pal and coworker Eddie Lynch
(the Lynch of Merrill Lynch), had a huge blowup with his boss, and quit

the firm after feeling he'd been cheated in several of the firm's financial dealings. In his next Wall Street job, he lasted less than eight months, quitting this time when his boss tricked him into tearing up his employment contract and forced him to take a $50-a-week pay cut. By then, Merrill was beginning to realize that he was not cut out to work for someone else. He also realized that Wall Street was the arena where he wanted to spend his life. In 1914, with $6,000 in capital, he hung out his own shingle. He was twenty-nine years old. He struggled for eighteen months to put together his first underwriting, but after that, he quickly put together seven more. By the time he was thirty-one, Merrill was a millionaire.

Merrill had a small handful of great business insights in his life, two of which were in evidence even before he struck out on his own. The first was his belief that Wall Street could not prosper in the long run unless it broadened its horizons. The stock and bond markets were completely and unapologetically an insider's game in the early part of this century; the ultimate insider was J. P. Morgan. The markets were run by Morgan and other wealthy insiders for their own benefit, and woe to anyone who tried to interfere. Small investors were not just scorned; their business was often turned away even when it arrived over the transom. Yet within two years of his arrival on Wall Street, Merrill was writing articles in popular magazines soliciting small accounts, promising readers that "a new guild has sprung up in the [investment] banking profession which does not despise the modest sums of the thrifty." This was an exaggeration. There was no new guild. There was only him.

Merrill's second insight had to do with the changing nature of American industry. The most powerful investment banks of the day tended to finance only the most powerful industries, the railroads and the utilities, and to promote their stock. Merrill quickly came to the view that those stocks were overvalued, and turned his attention instead to what we would now call "emerging growth stocks"—the nascent auto industry, for instance, and most especially, chain stores. Chain stores were sprouting up across America, but despite their spectacular growth, Wall Street viewed them as fads. Merrill viewed them as the future of retailing, and he became their champion. He financed S. S. Kresge & Co., Safeway Stores, McCrory Corp., and many others. When one became weakened, he would arrange the merger that would save it; when a key executive departed, Merrill would maneuver to install his own man; when things became stickiest, Merrill would step in and take control. Whenever his firm handled a chain store financing, he always bought a large number of warrants, convertible into stock, for himself. This both ensured him a say in the operation of the stores, and showed his customers that he was willing to put his money where his mouth was.

("If a stock is good enough to sell, it's good enough to buy," he liked to say.) It also made him extremely rich; he was the largest single stockholder of Safeway Stores. Even after other firms began clamoring for a slice of this obviously lucrative business, it remained predominately his, so closely was he identified with chain store financing. Until quite recently, Safeway was run by his grandson, Peter Magowan.[1]

For most of the Roaring Twenties, Merrill combined his two insights with happy results. He continued to finance chain stores—which brought in underwriting revenues for the firm—and to promote their stock to his growing network of customers—which brought in commission revenue for the firm. In effect, his small customers were investing in the same stores they were shopping in. He set up branch offices in cities like Detroit, Chicago, and Los Angeles, all connected to the main office by Teletype wire. (Hence the Wall Street term "wirehouse.") He was a believer in the virtue of long-term investments, and was outraged whenever he overheard one of his salesmen encouraging someone to buy a stock to make a fast profit. During World War I, he pushed his staff to sell Liberty Bonds, not only because it would help finance the war effort but because he could see the connection to his larger beliefs. "People who start buying bonds from motives of patriotism will continue to do so because they are the most convenient form of safe investment," he wrote.

And on March 31, 1928, he was the first to tell his clients to get out of the stock market. This was another of those stories Merrill would recount for the rest of his life, but this was no exaggeration: He saw the great crash coming, and he said so. He saw it, in fact, nineteen months before it happened, at a time when stock prices were still rocketing upward and when the small investors Merrill wanted in the market were finally racing in. But they were doing so in the wrong way and for the wrong reasons—piling up margin debt in a speculative orgy, clamoring to get aboard as the train was leaving the station. It was one of those moments that are always obvious in hindsight: The moment when speculative excess replaces sober-minded judgment, and greed replaces fear as the market's reigning emotion. At this moment in 1928, like all such moments, the telltale signs were there for all to see, but no one saw them because they were caught up in the market's euphoria. All except Charlie Merrill.

Over the protests of his partner Lynch, Merrill wrote an impassioned letter to his customers, urging them to "take advantage of present high prices and put your own financial house in order." Three months later, the market took its first big tumble, but came roaring back. Merrill wangled an appointment to see Calvin Coolidge, whose presidency was nearing an end, pleaded with the President to help dampen the wild speculation, even offered him a partnership in the firm after he left the White House—with his only task being to speak out publicly against speculation and margin debt. Coolidge was unmoved. By February 1929, as the market was making its last wild climb, Merrill was liquidating much of his firm's stock portfolio. "Many fine reputations have been built up in this era of extraordinary prosperity, which will not stand the acid test when troublesome times are here," he predicted to Lynch. And when the crash finally arrived that fall—and Merrill's firm came through it largely unscathed because of his actions—he abandoned the brokerage side of his business, handing over the firm's retail network to another wirehouse, while retaining its underwriting side. He would later claim that he was disgusted by what he had seen during the last days of the bull market—the way brokers had pushed small investors toward disaster for a commission. And no doubt he was sincere. But it's also true that the 1930s would have been an impossible time to sell stocks to the common man. Small investors were slaughtered in the crash; they weren't about to come near the market. Whatever the case, Merrill did not return to the brokerage business for a decade.

He was a celebrity by then, his business pronouncements listened to respectfully, his divorces grist for the gossip columnists. When he decided to divorce his second wife Hellen, whom he had married a week after his first divorce, the twists and turns in the proceedings were recounted with the kind of joyous abandon the tabloids reserve for such events. (She sought an injunction to prevent him from getting a Reno divorce; he retaliated by claiming that she was unfit to have custody of their son James: "Pawn in Parents' Fight" ran a tabloid caption when James was barely a teenager.)

Periodically, Charlie Merrill would vow to change his ways, and no doubt he was sincere about this, too. When he had first married Hellen, a stunning twenty-five-year-old magazine editor, in 1925, he had stayed home at nights, and even attended church for a while. But ultimately, he was incapable of changing, so even though he was no longer in the brokerage business, and even though he was married to a beautiful woman whose company he enjoyed, he spent the 1930s the way he spent most of his life—in constant pursuit of deals and women. Always, he carried around a palpable pride, and a need to place himself at the center of any orbit he was in. "Whatever he decided to serve," his son James Merrill once wrote, "the victim was meant to choke it down and be grateful."

James Merrill, of course, would go on to become one of America's finest poets; he was also one of the rare homosexual men in the 1950s who lived his life, in large measure, in general disregard of the closet. At first, Charlie

Merrill had a difficult time comprehending both these aspects of his son's life. Once, after Merrill learned his son was having an affair with a professor at Amherst College, he was filled with such instant rage that he fleetingly contemplated having the professor killed. And though Merrill realized early on that his son was unlikely ever to join the firm, he was still not disposed to look kindly on a vocation so profitless (in the literal sense) as poetry—at least not until the president of Amherst assured Merrill that his son had "professional" talent.

Indeed, to read James Merrill's memoirs is to get the strong sense that the younger man spent much of his youth struggling to break free from the older man's dominance.[2] Fleeing New York in his twenties, James Merrill spent several years in Europe, a continent where the Merrill name held no sway, as he notes with palpable relief. Several years earlier, James Merrill had briefly contemplated a far more drastic step than moving to Europe: He let it be known that he was thinking about renouncing his inheritance. Having known poverty, Charlie Merrill found such a notion incomprehensible. More than that, though, it was a blow to his ego—and it was ego, finally, that drove his incessant deal making and womanizing, his never-ending search for conquests.

Just as it was ego that propelled him toward one last conquest of the brokerage industry at the age of fifty-four.

In the fall of 1939, a broker named Winthrop Smith invited Charlie Merrill to visit him in Chicago on his way to the West Coast. Smith had worked for Merrill in the 1920s and now ran the Chicago office of E. A. Pierce & Co., the wirehouse that had taken over Merrill's branch offices. The agreement between the two firms was due to expire at the end of the year, and Smith feared that if Merrill reclaimed his branch offices, Pierce & Co. would not survive. Because of the Depression and the looming prospect of war, the market had been terrible, and wirehouses like Pierce & Co., with its forty branches and 20,000 miles of wire, had been especially hard hit. Smith had talked to his managing partner, Edward Pierce, and had convinced him that there was only one man who could save the firm: Charlie Merrill. If he were willing to merge his underwriting firm with Pierce's wirehouse, Smith told Merrill, Pierce would step aside and allow Merrill to become managing partner. As for what Merrill would get out of it, Smith was shrewdly downbeat. "A man in your tax bracket would be a fool to come in," he later claimed to have told his old boss. But maybe, he added, Merrill might be able to reclaim his old slogan about bringing Wall Street to Main Street.

Maybe he could show Wall Street a few new tricks. In the face of such an appeal, Merrill was defenseless.

The merger was announced in January and completed in April. Merrill put up $2.5 million in return for a majority stake in the new firm, which was christened Merrill Lynch, E. A. Pierce, and Cassatt & Co.[3] Three days after assuming control, Merrill called a conference of his new partners, where he laid out his plans. In effect, Merrill was planning to apply to the brokerage industry the same principles that had made chain stores so successful: the mass marketing techniques, the emphasis on high volume and low cost, the saturation advertising, the nationwide distribution network. To the snickers of his competitors and the skepticism of many of his new partners, he would run his new firm as if it were a supermarket. It was his last great business insight.

On the face of it, there was scarcely an industry in America less amenable to mass marketing techniques than the brokerage business. It had always been a high-cost, low-volume industry that made its money by catering to the wealthy. Indeed, Merrill's own cost structure was instructive: At the end of the 1930s, his firm was spending $14.29 on each transaction but taking in only $10.17. "When you figure that one of our clients, the Carnation Milk Company, can content the cow, milk it, pasteurize the milk, put the milk in the can, put a label on it, put it in a box, advertise it, ship it all over the world, and sell the can of milk for five cents, then you realize how perfectly frantic these figures make me feel," Merrill said. His first order of business was to slash costs, which he did ruthlessly, employing Smith as his designated hatchet man. He and Smith even closed the large, plushly appointed room where customers had always been able to watch the ticker. He put 100 brokers in that space instead.

He then took steps to make it less expensive for customers to do business with the new firm. Services that brokers had always charged for—collecting dividends, for instance—Merrill Lynch would now do for free. Merrill announced that his new firm would charge only the minimum fixed commission rate for stock trades, as set by the New York Stock Exchange, eliminating the commission surcharge many brokers added. He was "downscaling," we'd say now. The tonier investment banks on Wall Street hated what he was doing and would look down their noses at Merrill Lynch forever after. Their attitude would always rankle Merrill Lynch employees, but Merrill himself could not have cared less.

Merrill's strategy hinged on drawing small investors into the market. This was a daunting mission. In 1939, the Roper organization conducted a poll for the New York Stock Exchange to gauge the public's attitude toward the market. The findings were damning. Those members of the public who weren't ignorant of the workings of the market were suspicious of them, Roper found. People didn't trust the hot tips they got from brokers. They were convinced that brokers foisted bad stocks on clients. Fifty percent of those polled said that rich customers got better treatment than the less affluent. Merrill Lynch did its own study, asking people to rank all the possible places they might put their money. Most of those polled put stocks at the bottom.

To change that perception, Merrill launched a public relations campaign that would continue long after his own life. Partly, the campaign was an explicit effort to prove to the small investor that a Merrill Lynch broker operated on a higher moral plane than his less scrupulous competitors. A Merrill Lynch man would always disclose his firm's interest in any stock he was promoting, Merrill announced. Merrill insisted that the firm publish its financial results each year, even though it was not required to. Since customers didn't want hot tips, Merrill Lynch would provide them with impartial research. A Merrill Lynch man would be trained at a school Merrill set up in 1945 for new brokers, many of whom were drawn from the ranks of the new veterans returning from World War II.

And finally, a Merrill Lynch man would be paid a salary. To Merrill, this was the most important change of all—and the one his brokers most resented. Historically, brokers made their money on commissions that were added to the price of a stock or a bond that a broker bought or sold for a client. This system had a glaring built-in conflict (as it does to this day), pitting the need of the broker for commission revenue against the desire of the customer for sound and stable investments. From time immemorial, unscrupulous brokers "churned" accounts to reap commissions, but even honest brokers faced temptation. A broker with a clientele full of contented customers was—and still is—a broker who will soon be looking for a new job. Brokers needed *trades* to make money.

Putting his brokers on salary was Merrill's way of eliminating the temptation. A salaried broker, he believed, would be better able to guide clients to long-term investments without having to worry about the need to generate periodic trades. And the customer, listening to his broker's advice, would know that it wasn't motivated by the prospect of commissions. For the rest of his life, Merrill never changed his view about this, and despite periodic grumbling from the brokers, he refused to reintroduce a system of pay based on commissions.

There was another aspect to the Merrill Lynch public relations campaign, one that had less to do with heralding the firm and more to do with reacquainting Americans with stocks and bonds. Merrill believed that people wouldn't come to the stock market until they understood it. He also believed that once people did understand it—once they saw how much they could make with a steady, long-term investment program—they would flock to the market. He thus gave himself the task of *making* them understand it. "It was probably the biggest job in mass education that's ever confronted any business at any time in the history of this country," he would say years later. This was hyperbole, of course, though for Merrill it was less hyperbolic than usual.

This mass education campaign took shape after the end of the Second World War (and after the onset of Merrill's various ailments), when he watched the rise of the middle class and quickly saw the implications for his business. Here, at last, were the potential customers he had yearned for all his life—Americans who were not rich, but still had disposable income that could be sensibly invested. It was up to him to persuade them.

There was almost nothing Merrill Lynch wouldn't do to spread the good word. It was said that $1 out of every $4 spent on advertising by Wall Street was spent by Merrill Lynch, a figure Merrill liked to toss off with both pride (he was doing *his* part) and disdain (nobody else was doing theirs). The firm published an endless stream of reports, investment magazines, pamphlets—11 million pieces in 1955 alone—with titles like *How to Invest* and *How to Read a Financial Report.* In 1948, it ran perhaps the most famous financial ad in history in *The New York Times,* a densely written, 6,000-word tract entitled "What Everybody Ought to Know About This Stock and Bond Business." Merrill Lynch gave big lectures and small seminars, with day-care provided so that both husband and wife could attend. It held a popular series of investment courses for women only. It set up tents at country fairs and erected an investment booth in New York's Grand Central Station. It ran a brokerage on wheels. Once, it even gave away stock in a contest sponsored by Wheaties.

Did it work? Within the narrow confines of Wall Street, it worked spectacularly. By the time he died in 1956, Merrill had put together the distribution network he'd always dreamed of: With its 122 offices, its 119 partners, and its 5,800 employees, Merrill Lynch was the country's first truly nationwide brokerage house, its reach immense, its name by far the best-known in the business. It did nearly 20 percent of the odd lot volume on the New York Stock Exchange (an odd lot is a trade of less than 100 shares) and 12 percent of the larger, round lot volume. With $83.5 million in revenues, it was the largest firm on Wall Street, and with $18 million in profits, it was among the most profitable. It had proudly spent $20 million in advertising over the course of the previous decade, and advertising would remain one of

Merrill's legacies; Merrill Lynch was running television ads years before anyone else in the business. And it had garnered 440,000 customers, which was three times more than its nearest competitor. Of those, 79 percent earned less than $10,000 a year.

And yet one ends up wondering whether Merrill felt disappointed by what he achieved in his lifetime. As grand as his accomplishments were, they simply did not lead to the kind of sweeping change in America's financial habits that he had hoped for. Those 440,000 customers may have been a large number by Wall Street's standards, but they were a pittance in the grand scheme of things, especially considering the growing prosperity of the middle class. And despite the firm's success, Wall Street remained unmoved by his example. When Merrill died, his voice was nearly as lonely as when he'd first landed on Wall Street, enthusiastically soliciting "the modest sums of the thrifty."

Late in his life, during that short period in 1953 when he found temporary relief from his angina, Merrill made a speech to the firm's partners that hinted at his frustration that his ideas had not been embraced. He was a frail man by then, stooped and small, and he shuffled slowly to the podium after he was introduced. Although the speech was meant to be a celebration of Merrill's short-lived return to the office, it had an edginess, a bitterness even, that he could not disguise. "Thirteen years ago, I said—and I meant it then and I mean it now—I do not want to be a partner in the only firm that makes money when everybody else in the same industry is dying of starvation. Actually, it isn't a case of starvation. It's just plain dry rot."

For the next ten minutes, as he gripped the podium to steady himself, he bemoaned Wall Street's various failings—its failure to change its pay system, as he had done. It had failed to advertise and promote its business—the way Merrill Lynch had. American business had failed to persuade the middle class to come into the market—as he had urged. Brokers had failed to understand the greatness of their products—despite his many attempts to explain it to them. "If the average man had invested a set sum of money every year since 1937 . . . and reinvested his dividends every year, he would have done considerably better than if he put the same amount of money out at ordinary . . . compound interest. [But] you could tell that story to nine out of ten men in our line of business, and they wouldn't even listen to you, much less believe it," he growled.

No wonder so few people had come to the stock market! Everyone had failed him. Including, perhaps, the American public itself. Despite everything he had done, there were only 6.5 million individual investors at the time Merrill made his speech. That amounted to 4 percent of the country. Had the other 96 percent listened to Merrill, they would have participated as

the Dow Jones average made its steady climb during the 1950s. They would
have made a great deal of money. But they were not yet ready, and nothing
Merrill could say or do could make them ready.

∽

THE STOCK MARKET WASN'T COMPLETELY DORMANT in the 1950s, of course.
It wasn't like the 1930s. Each year, as the Dow Jones average rose, from
192 in 1950 to 679 by the end of the decade, so did the volume of shares
traded—an obvious indication that more people were buying stocks. Figures
compiled by the New York Stock Exchange showed that in the mid-1950s,
about 500,000 people a year were becoming new stockholders. By the end
of the decade that number had jumped to a million a year; in all, reported the
exchange in 1959, 12.5 million people were investing in the market—nearly
double the number Charlie Merrill had cited in his valedictory speech a half-
dozen years before.

Although the exchange would trumpet these figures as proof that America
was flocking to the market, it seems more likely that they represented a
narrower phenomenon. The Americans who were becoming interested in the
stock market were, for the most part, members of the new, and newly
prosperous, white collar class: doctors and lawyers and, most especially,
men (and the occasional woman) who staffed the growing middle-
management ranks of America's corporations.[4] These same corporations—
IBM, Eastman Kodak, Pan American, and dozens of others—were also the
growth stocks of the day, which may explain why those who worked for
them would begin to get interested in the market. Buried in the stock
exchange's figures is an intriguing list of cities with the highest proportion
of stockholders: at the top of the list, Hartford, Connecticut, a city dominated by five of the nation's largest insurance companies; Wilmington,
Delaware, where DuPont had become one of America's giant corporations;
and Rochester, New York, headquarters to Eastman Kodak and Xerox.

In the early 1960s, the market got much rockier, the classic example
being its wild swing in the wake of the Kennedy assassination: In twenty-
seven minutes of trading, the market lost $13 billion in value, only to gain
it all back when the stock exchange reopened a few days later. In general,
though, the upward momentum continued. In 1960, the Dow Jones average
reached 685; by the end of 1962, it was over 900. And *still* the market
remained not much more than a curiosity to most people.[5]

But by 1965 that had changed; the market had become interesting to many
Americans again. It was not, however, the result of anything Merrill Lynch
did, even though the firm continued to promote the virtues of the market as

if it half-expected its founder to phone in his daily critiques from the grave. Instead, what caught the public's attention was the spectacular performance of a young immigrant from Shanghai named Gerald Tsai, Jr. Tsai was a money manager at an investment company based in Boston, called Fidelity Management and Research, and what he managed was a mutual fund. A mutual fund was an investment vehicle that allowed people to purchase shares not in a single stock, but in a group of stocks, which were bought and sold by a professional fund manager like Tsai. The money manager served as a proxy for the fund's shareholders, making the investment decisions that most individual investors had neither the time nor the knowledge to make themselves. In effect, a fund manager was a buffer between market and investor.

For most of their history, mutual funds had had an insignificant role in the market; at the end of World War II, all the funds put together held only $1 billion. But in the mid-1960s, they suddenly became hot: In 1965, $2.4 billion streamed into the market via mutual funds. Among the reasons for their popularity was that they held out the prospect, as *The New Yorker*'s John Brooks would later put it, "[of] making 'people's capitalism' a reality instead of a catch phrase." In other words, they appealed to the middle class. And thus the irony: Charlie Merrill, the champion of the middle-class investor, hated mutual funds.

The reason for Merrill's dislike of mutual funds is lost to history,[6] but his view on the subject was well-known among the Merrill Lynch hierarchy. Former Treasury Secretary Donald Regan, who joined Merrill Lynch in 1946, and ran the firm in the 1970s, remembers writing a memo as a young staff assistant, suggesting that the firm start its own mutual fund. "I'm not going to touch this one," his boss said. "Merrill will have a fit." In his brash innocence, Regan insisted on having the memo shown to Merrill—and the great man did, indeed, have a fit. Merrill's prejudice made such a deep impression that even after he had died, the firm still refused to have anything to do with mutual funds.

Here, plainly, was Charlie Merrill's blind spot. How could someone who believed so fervently in the importance of bringing the middle class to the market miss the deep appeal of mutual funds? How could he fail to see that people would embrace the idea of having a fund manager serve as their market proxy? For all his foresight about the middle class and the market, Charlie Merrill never grasped the power of the mutual fund as an investment idea. It was the one great insight into his business that he missed.

\* \* \*

Not that the inherent power of the idea was what first got people interested in the mid-1960s. No, it was another kind of power to which Americans have always been susceptible: the power of a star. That's what Gerald Tsai was. Brooks would later compare Tsai to Greta Garbo: someone who "courted publicity while quite sincerely shunning it." The Garbo analogy is fitting in another way: Though he was in the business of investing people's money, Tsai got the kind of adulatory press normally reserved for movie stars—and not just in the business publications, but in popular magazines like *Newsweek,* which ran a long story on him in the late 1960s. ("Gerald Tsai Jr.," swooned *Newsweek,* "radiates total cool.") The celebrity fund manager is not such an oddity anymore, of course, but Tsai was the first.

Tsai was in his midthirties when he caught the country's attention, managing Fidelity's Capital Fund, which he had started from scratch in 1957, at the age of twenty-eight, and turned into a $340 million mutual fund. He was a short, handsome man, his eyes impassive, his hair slicked back neatly, his elegant French cuffs prominent in most photographs he posed for. Reporters who managed to get in to see him inevitably noticed his precise manner, his manicured hands, and the temperature of his office, which was noticeably cold. Because of his Oriental background—and because sensitivities about such matters were rather duller than they are today—reporters found it easy to imbue him with an air of mystery. From our latter-day perspective, though, it appears that most of the mystery was merely the result of Tsai's refusal to describe his upbringing in Shanghai when reporters asked him about it. He was inevitably described as crafty and even, on occasion, "inscrutable."

Most of all, though, reporters noticed his investing style. Everyone noticed his investing style. It was one of the reasons he was famous. He operated during an era we now know as the Go-Go Years, and he became the personification of the go-go style of investing. The Go-Go Years, which ran from the mid- to late 1960s, were a time when the market, like so many other aspects of American life, seemed to turn its back on the quiet 1950s. Throughout the 1950s, the stock market had made a slow but steady climb; during the Go-Go Years, it got zippy and overheated. Glamorous growth stocks like Polaroid and LTV rocketed upward. Speculation was rampant, as it always is as a bull market nears its end—not that anyone thought the end was near. And riding the bull most spectacularly were the new breed of mutual fund portfolio managers, who seemed to be able to dip in and out of the growth stocks and the gyrations of the market itself with the greatest of ease. This being the 1960s, they were invariably young, and it was usually noted that they sported sideburns, as if this signified their rebellion against their elders. The best of them were far outpacing the market averages, chalking up annual gains of 30 and 40 percent. The press began calling them gunslingers.

Tsai was the fastest gun of all. Few were as nimble: at a time when many mutual funds held stocks for decades, he had no qualms about turning over his entire stock portfolio in a year's time. Or as audacious: at a time when mutual fund managers bought and sold stocks in small increments, Tsai traded big blocks of a company's stock in one fell swoop. Or as unpredictable: Tsai had a fondness for technical stock market data, and he loved to try to time big market moves. "It was a beautiful thing to watch," his employer once said of him. "What grace, what timing—glorious!"

And few could match his results. That's the other reason he was famous. The growth funds run by Tsai and the other gunslingers were often called performance funds, for their explicit aim was to outperform the market. (Their implicit aim was to outperform each other.) Every year Tsai ran Fidelity Capital, it was near the top in terms of its annual gain. Once, in 1962, Tsai got caught in a market downdraft, but he recovered with such astonishing speed that his fund gained 68 percent in the next three months. In 1965, his last year at Fidelity, his fund gained close to 50 percent while the Dow itself rose only 15 percent. Thanks largely to Tsai's growing legend, Fidelity's small handful of funds grew from $239 million in 1955 to $1.5 billion a decade later.

On the other hand, thanks largely to Fidelity, Gerry Tsai was able to become a legend. He may have been the right man for his time, but he also worked for the right company—the fund company that, more than any other, exalted performance, and championed the radical idea that a fund should be managed not by a committee of stodgy, anonymous men, but by one person, who would be free to follow his own market instincts. It is not too much to say, in fact, that Fidelity invented both concepts and that without these two radical notions—of measurable performance and solo fund managers—mutual funds would never have caught the public's fancy the way they did. Portfolio managers, with their brash manners and controversial ways, competing against each other and the market: *that* was compelling in a way that a hundred of Charlie Merrill's pamphlets were not. That was irresistible.

Fidelity was owned by Edward Crosby Johnson 2d; it would be difficult to conjure up a more unlikely radical. In person, he seemed almost a caricature of the proper Bostonian: a discreet, reserved, formal man who favored bow ties and was known to everyone, at all times, as "Mr. Johnson." A corporate lawyer, Johnson had a lifelong love affair with the market: He once famously told the writer Adam Smith that "the market is like a beautiful woman—endlessly fascinating, endlessly complex, always changing, always mystifying.'' When offered the chance, in 1943, to take over an inconsequential fund called Fidelity Fund, which held around $3 million, he jumped at it. In 1952, he hired Tsai as a stock analyst, and began to change the very nature of the business he now found himself in.

Until Johnson arrived on the scene, mutual funds were run conservatively, in large part because so many of them were located in Boston, which was an extremely conservative town, at least when it came to money. The Boston financial district was dominated by trustees, who had a fiduciary duty to preserve the capital that had been entrusted to them. Not surprisingly, they tended to view their mission as avoiding losses rather than achieving gains. Although mutual funds had no such legal restrictions, they were run with the same mind-set; investment decisions were usually made by committees only after much deliberation.

Although Johnson was every bit the Boston conservative in bearing and manner, he was not at all conservative about money management. To him, the point of the exercise was not to preserve capital, but to add to it—the more the better. His benchmarks were the broad market averages, such as the Standard & Poors 500 and the Dow Jones Industrial Average; beating those averages was the goal he set for his funds. And his fundamental belief was that in order for a fund to beat the averages with any regularity, it had to be managed not by a committee, but by one person, who used his own instincts and knowledge to trade stocks. ''Two men can't play a violin,'' he liked to say. Thus did he create a new species, the portfolio manager, and a new kind of mutual fund investing. Very quickly, firms cropped up to monitor the performance of these newly aggressive funds, and published the results. By 1958, when Tsai began managing Fidelity Capital, the essential framework was in place.

Did Johnson understand the way his radical changes would excite both the press and the public? It seems unlikely. For one thing, he was never the missionary that Charlie Merrill was; he wasn't really thinking about trying to bring the middle class into the market, though that turned out to be one of the primary consequences of his innovations. He also didn't understand that he had created a system that lent itself naturally to press coverage. The press loves anything that smells of a horse race, and that is what the mutual fund industry was now poised to become: an exciting annual race between portfolio managers and the market averages. It also has an institutional weakness for stars, and Johnson's system practically guaranteed that star portfolio managers would emerge—people who not only beat the market, but did it with some flair. Yet even as the press coverage highlighted Tsai's performance and brought hundreds of millions of dollars into Fidelity, Johnson always felt uncomfortable around the press. Even good publicity struck him as unseemly. Also, he harbored a suspicion that Tsai's glowing press clippings went to his head, allowing him to become, as John Brooks would tactfully phrase it, "self-confident with fame and success." Tsai's sense of omnipotence, Johnson always felt, played at least some role in Tsai's decision to leave Fidelity in 1965. After his famous protégé had left, Johnson made it known within the firm that press inquiries were not to be answered.


What happened to Tsai after he left Fidelity is the most famous story of the Go-Go Years. Johnson was sixty-seven years old in 1965, and when Tsai turned in his magnificent 50 percent gain that year—the second best of all the performance funds—he approached Johnson to ask about succession. He wanted to know whether he would be chosen to run Fidelity when the older man retired. Johnson said no: he expected his son to take over the company when that day finally came. Edward Crosby Johnson 3d—known to everyone as Ned—occupied an office near Tsai's, where he managed Fidelity's Trend Fund and had proved to be a pretty terrific stock picker himself. He and Tsai had had a strained, competitive relationship for years. Tsai must surely have known that this would be the answer, for father and son were close, but it was not an answer he was willing to accept.

Tsai moved to New York, rented fancy quarters on Fifth Avenue, and announced that he would start up a new growth fund, which he named the Manhattan Fund. There was a mad rush to get into the fund, as people clamored to grab a piece of the Tsai magic. Hoping to raise $25 million, he raised ten times that much. The Manhattan Fund's fees were egregiously high—an 8.5 percent upfront commission (called a "load" in the fund business), plus a stiff annual management fee. No one cared. There were a number of other funds with track records every bit as good as Tsai's. It didn't matter. Gerald Tsai was the mutual fund manager everybody wanted—the man with the golden touch. In February 1966, when the fund opened for business, it had 125,000 shareholders. Within two years, it had around 220,000 shareholders, and held some $525 million.

And, of course, that's when Tsai lost his golden touch. In retrospect, he could not have picked a worse moment to start a new fund; the very month the Manhattan Fund began operation, the market hit its all-time high, not quite grazing 1,000. Then it started to drop. By October it had lost 250 points. It quickly reversed course again, gaining back a third of the loss by the end of the year. The Manhattan Fund spiked up and down, and up and down again, before ending its first year pretty much where it had begun. But because of the high fees, investors had lost around 10 percent of their money. The next year, 1967, was a better one, both for the market and the Manhattan Fund. But in 1968 the roof fell in on Tsai.

It turns out that 1968 was the last gasp for the Go-Go Years, too, though no one could see it at the time. The market was still zigging and zagging, and money was pouring into mutual funds at an unprecedented rate: $1.6 billion for the first three months of 1968 alone. Because Tsai was still the most famous fund manager in the country, a fair amount of that money wound up with the Manhattan Fund. Tsai invested it as he always had. He still made market moves full of daring and bravado, still bought and sold blocks of stock with the same swagger and confidence, still gobbled up huge stakes in all his favorite glamour stocks. ("If he ever sells Polaroid," a broker said at the time, "it will be like President Johnson shorting [Savings] Bonds.") But it didn't work anymore. The same stocks that had once risen practically on his say-so now tumbled when he bought them. His fabled instincts abandoned him. That spring, as the market made a strong rally, Tsai missed it completely.

By July of 1968, the Manhattan Fund had lost 6.6 percent of its value; among the 300 largest funds, only six had done worse. Investors, many of them novices who had put money into the fund after reading about the great Tsai, bailed out frantically. Still, Tsai had one more ace to play. In August, he sold his firm to a giant insurance company in return for $30 million in stock, and soon afterward hung up his spurs, a gunslinger no more. Gerry Tsai had bailed out too.

Later, Tsai would complain[7] that "[I] had one bad year, in 1968, and I've been killed in the press ever since. . . . I don't think it's fair." And perhaps it wasn't. Within a few years, most mutual funds were down as sharply as the Manhattan Fund had once been. One after another, the gunslingers of the era were hanging up their spurs, having been whipped by the market. But Tsai was more famous than all of them put together, and the first to crash to boot; it's hard to see how he could have expected to be treated any differently. He who lives by the press dies by the press. Any movie star could have told him that.

Later, too, writers like John Brooks and Adam Smith, both of whom chronicled the Go-Go Years, would treat Tsai's rise and fall as a parable for the era. Brooks, in particular, was openly scornful of Tsai's investment methods, viewing them as little more than rank speculation. He saw Tsai's fall from grace as a kind of deserved comeuppance for his free-wheeling investment style, a metaphor for the excesses of the age.

But their disapproving eyes caused Brooks and Smith to miss as much as they saw. Yes, the Go-Go Years had their share of excess—probably more than their share, inasmuch as they represented the end of a bull market, when things tend to get out of hand. And yes, novice investors got burned, as they usually did when they rushed in at the end. But as much as Tsai may have represented the end of that era, he also represented the beginning of something. He was a glimpse into the future. The system that Johnson established, and that Tsai epitomized—"the cult of performance," in Smith's words—that was here to stay. And in focusing so gleefully on Tsai's post-Fidelity performance, the writers missed something else. Eventually, Johnson did retire, handing over the reins of power to his son Ned, just as he had said he would. Barely noticed at the time, this would turn out to be an event of far more significance than the rise and fall of Gerry Tsai.

CHAPTER 3

# Delusions and the Madness of Bankers

*November 1966*

THERE ARE FEW THINGS more impossible to sustain in American business than a profitable monopoly, as Bank of America was about to discover. For eight sweet years, it had had the California bank credit card market entirely to itself. Its BankAmericard had become an increasingly accepted part of the vaunted California lifestyle. Its long-running television advertising campaign, centering around a cartoon symphony conductor drawn to resemble Toscanini (the tag read: "Best way to conduct your shopping!"), was among the most recognizable in the state. For five of those eight years, starting in 1961, the card had been an ever-increasing source of profit. But it couldn't last, and it didn't.

Sometime in early 1966, Bank of America's credit card executives began hearing a rumor that four of its biggest California bank rivals were plotting to break jointly into the business; they were going to call their common program Master Charge. Even earlier than that, word had filtered back that First National City Bank of New York (now known as Citibank) was negotiating to buy Carte Blanche, one of the travel and entertainment cards. Such a move would give First National City a web of customers and merchants that would extend nationwide—something no bank in the country could then say—and would pose a different kind of threat to Bank of America. Meanwhile, other banks began hearing rumors that Bank of America was going to push its own program beyond California. After years of relative quiet, the banking industry was awhirl in rumors about credit cards—about possible thrusts and potential parries. For practically the first time since the Depression, banks were contemplating the possibility of openly competing with each other.

The rumors, in turn, helped bring about the next great wave of credit card mailings, a wave that swept the nation in the late 1960s. It was not banking's finest moment. Fueled by panic and jealousy, bankers jumped into a business about which they knew practically nothing and for which they were utterly unprepared. Large banks and small banks, bank consortiums and single banks, banks that made consumer loans and banks that didn't—in one fell swoop, they all became issuers of credit cards, mailing out such now-forgotten labels as Everything Cards, Town & Country Cards, Midwest Bank Cards, Interbank Cards, and dozens more. During a four-year span that ended in 1970, bankers blanketed the nation in credit cards. The country had never seen anything quite like it.

Most credit card veterans now view the late 1960s as a time of madness, culminating in staggering losses to the banks, public embarrassment, and federal legislation. But they also now believe that the madness was necessary. From that chaos emerged the electronic credit card system that now exists. Without it, bank credit cards might never have become what they are today: the plastic symbol of the money revolution.

It wasn't entirely panic and jealousy that stoked the madness of the late 1960s. It never is at first. When asked, bankers could trot out a handful of reasonably persuasive rationales. One was the conviction that credit cards might be the product that finally gave banking the means to escape the yoke of state and federal regulations. As it happens, quite a few financial innovations over the last twenty-five years have been driven by this goal; one way to view the astounding changes in personal finance is to see them as efforts to evade the straitjacket of regulation—capitalism's instinctive response when circumstances change but regulations don't. For instance, bankers began to realize that a credit card was a device that might enable them to expand their turf legally. Rather than wait for customers to walk in the door, they could troll for new loan customers through the mail, using cards as the lure.

Secondly, there was a feeling among bankers that as consumer credit became increasingly accepted in American life, people would be more willing to "revolve" their credit card balances—that is, stretch their balances out beyond the grace period, and thus pay interest on the money they owed. Finally, even the most above-the-fray banker had to see that to stay out of the business was to risk being left behind. One banker remembers standing in line to check out of a hotel; as he watched everyone else in the line pull out either an American Express card or a BankAmericard to pay the bill, he suddenly realized that this was a business he needed to be in.

Hovering over all these rationales, though, was a more basic motive: the palpable fear of the biggest bank in the country. Publicly, the Bank of America had always downplayed the success of its BankAmericard, but that could only work for so long. Eventually, the other California banks figured out that the BankAmericard was turning a handsome profit, and they watched with increasing anxiety as their biggest rival's most revolutionary product continued to gain acceptance. Bankers outside California were no less anxious, especially once they realized that Bank of America would not be content with California. It wanted the rest of America, too. There was a genuine sense among other large banks that Bank of America had to be stopped, or at least slowed down; and if one can point to a single spark that led to the credit card explosion of the late 1960s, this was it.

The spark was lit on March 25, 1966. On that day, Kenneth Larkin submitted a memo to his superiors suggesting that the bank begin franchising BankAmericards in other states. Larkin had risen to the rank of vice president in the consumer credit department, and was already beginning to assume his role as the bank's most visible credit card spokesman, a position he would not relinquish until he retired. He was—and is—a big, sweet, gentle man, steeped in the ethos of the bank where he spent his career. As passionate a believer in the virtue of consumer credit as Giannini himself, Larkin has never had so much as a moment's doubt about the value of credit cards to consumers. His obvious decency made him a formidable spokesman for his cause; when he declared, as he did early in 1967, that "the credit card is an entirely decent and honorable means of extending . . . installment credit," there could be no doubting his sincerity.

Larkin's memo was not a bolt from the blue. In typical Bank of America fashion, a consensus had formed among the top executives that the time had come for BankAmericard to extend its reach beyond California. It was the logical next step. A credit card that could only be used in California had severe limitations. Commerce crossed state boundaries. People crossed state boundaries. If a credit card was going to be truly useful, it would have to cross state boundaries too. They could see that at Bank of America: they could see the way the American penchant for travel had rendered state boundaries meaningless. They wanted a card that would do the same. "The ultimate objective of this program is to make the name BankAmericard a household word throughout the nation," Larkin wrote.

Reflecting the essential gentility of the banking world, Larkin recoiled at the prospect of having Bank of America march into other states and sign up merchants and customers itself, even though such a move would have been completely legal. Instead, he came up with the idea of enlisting out-of-state banks as partners instead of enemies. As Larkin envisioned the system, a "licensee" would pay a $25,000 entry fee to Bank of America. In return, the larger bank would turn over the credit card software it had developed, and would show the smaller bank how to run a credit card operation. The smaller bank would then run its own program, mailing its own BankAmeri-cards to people in its own territory, signing up its own merchants, and enlisting its own smaller "licensee" banks to the cause. And, of course, it would reap its own profits or absorb its own losses. Although Bank of America took a small additional royalty, most of that money went to support a national advertising campaign; the licensing program was not intended to be a big money maker for the BofA. Yet every time a new bank was added to the system, Bank of America did wind up making more money, because its own card activity lurched upward. The reason was that there was sud-denly a new group of out-of-state merchants ready to accept BankAmeri-cards from anyone, including visiting Californians—and a new group of out-of-state cardholders, ready to use their BankAmericards when they trav-eled to California. Bank of America's own balance sheet offered all the proof you needed that the more places a credit card could be used, the more people would use it. To be indispensable, a card had to be universal.

Even before Larkin had put pen to paper, First National City made it official: it purchased a 50 percent stake in Carte Blanche. That was in late 1965. The following March, Larkin submitted his memo. In May, Bank of America began approaching selected banks about joining its new system. June: five Chicago banks announced that they would form a regional credit card pro-gram. August: a group of big banks, led by Marine Midland in Buffalo and Pittsburgh National, began meeting secretly in Buffalo to form what would become the Interbank Card Association. October: the BofA's California rivals announced their new Master Charge group. November: the Chicago banks began dropping credit cards. That same month, Bank of America signed up banks in Portland, Philadelphia, Seattle, and Boston.

With every succeeding month, the pace quickened. In April 1967, the Federal Reserve reported that 627 banks were in the credit card business, up from seventy just a few years before. Two months later, the Master Charge group, which had merged with the Interbank group, began dropping cards.[1] Then, in August, First National City, forced to sell its stake in Carte Blanche by the Justice Department (which raised antitrust objections), began drop-ping its own proprietary card, called the Everything Card. In October, the Federal Reserve did another survey: in the space of six months, the number of banks issuing credit cards had risen by more than 200. There was no doubt by then that Americans were feeling inundated with credit cards;

according to one estimate, 32 million cards were issued in 1967 alone. The madness had begun.

It's Chicago the credit card old-timers always cite whenever they talk about the bad old days. There were plenty of other disasters, but Chicago was the paradigmatic disaster, the purest case study of what could go wrong. The old-timers chuckle now as they recall Chicago—now that the credit card business has become as sleek and refined as a fighter jet. But it wasn't funny at the time. It was scary.

The original idea in Chicago was to apply the principle of universality—the same principle behind Bank of America's franchising push—on a smaller, regional scale. The banks, none of which had ever issued a credit card before, formed a group, called the Midwest Bank Card Association, whose purpose was to connect each bank's credit card to all the other cards in the association. (Master Charge and Interbank were started for the same reason.) Thus, a customer carrying Continental Bank's Town and Country card would be able to use it in a store that had been signed up by Harris Trust. In other words, the banks were creating a situation in which they would have to cooperate and compete at the same time. The problem was that they mainly just competed.

The banks had tentatively agreed that they would hold off mailing credit cards until early in 1967. But one bank, hoping to get a jump on the others, decided to start mailing cards early. It would make its drop in November, in time (it hoped) to take advantage of the Christmas season. The others, already skittish about the bruising competition they knew was coming, were spooked into following suit. So they all began mailing cards in November, well before they were ready, whipped into a lather by their fear of each other. When the great Chicago credit card blitz finally ended a few months later, some 5 million cards had been mailed.

Five million credit cards! And it wasn't just the number of cards that was so alarming, it was the obvious haste with which those 5 million names had been compiled. In their desire to get cards into the mail, banks had issued them indiscriminately: people with bad credit histories got them along with people with good credit histories. Fixed-income pensioners got them along with middle-class families. Convicted criminals got credit cards. If you lived in the suburbs, where the Chicago banks were desperate to gain a toehold, but couldn't because of Illinois' restrictive banking laws, you were likely to wind up with eight or ten or fifteen cards before it was over. Suburban teenagers were mailed cards, as were suburban preschoolers, suburban infants, and in several notorious cases surburban dogs. Wright Patman, the old-style Texas populist who was then the chairman of the House Banking and Currency Committee, held a hearing triggered by the Chicago experience during which he held up two cards issued to a woman in Peoria, Illinois. The woman, he thundered, had died five months before the cards were mailed. For a time, everyone in Chicago had a story like that.

The mass mailing of unsolicited credit cards provoked enormous anxiety among those who received them—just as it had in California eight years before. Chicagoans complained that they had not asked for this new device, and they resented what they saw as the banks' efforts to tempt them into spending beyond their means. People worried about their own will power. They worried about this intrusion into their financial life. They worried about their potential liability: what happened if the cards were stolen? Who was responsible? Thousands of Chicagoans cut up their cards and sent them back to the bank. Others complained about the many errors: cards with misspelled names, bills for items that had never been purchased—and the near-impossibility of getting the bank to fix the computer's mistake.

But the anxiety went beyond the incompetence of the mass mailings themselves. It reflected a deeper fear many people harbored about the rise of consumer credit and the growing view that debt was an acceptable financial tool. Although consumer credit had been growing rapidly well before the full-scale introduction of credit cards, the cards' visibility made them the obvious symbol of this trend. Patman, who hated credit cards and wanted them outlawed, summed up the feelings of many people when he opened his congressional hearing by saying, ''I am probably old-fashioned . . . but the thought that debt will replace thrift is repulsive to me.''

The mass mailings may have caused most of the public outcry, but for the banks, it was only one headache among many. The signing of merchants was done every bit as shoddily as the mass mailings and with the same dismal results. Credit card fraud reached a scale that would never be rivaled. Chicago postal clerks were discovered carting off bags of unmailed credit cards to sell on the black market. (The price for a stolen card was said to be $50.) Petty thieves broke into mailboxes to grab cards. The Mafia got involved—as it would in other cities—trafficking in stolen cards, counterfeiting them, conspiring with crooked merchants to submit phony sales slips. The massive thefts only heightened the anxiety among legitimate customers, who now had to worry not only about all the unwanted cards that had arrived, but about all the unwanted cards that *hadn't* arrived. It also heightened their anger, made them feel that if they threw their cards away and someone wound up stealing them, it was the bank's problem, not theirs. And it *was* the bank's problem; with all the bad publicity the card drops generated, no bank had the nerve to press someone to pay a credit card charge they claimed not to have made, no matter how shaky the claim.

There didn't seem to be anything the Chicago banks could do right. About a month after the initial drop, a Continental Illinois employee was taking several cartons of credit card sales slips to the bank's computer center, four blocks away. There was a blizzard that day, causing him to slip and fall. When he did, most of the paperwork blew away. The incident made the six o'clock news. Another time, a van filled with new credit cards overturned, spilling cards in every direction. That made the news too: the newspapers had pictures the next day of people grabbing credit cards by the handful, presumably for later use. Even the most innocuous moves backfired: Chicago's First National was widely ridiculed for staging a parade to introduce its credit card and having young women pass out applications to passersby. This sort of garish promotion didn't fit with people's idea of how a bank should behave.

By the summer of 1967, three of the banks had concluded that their only hope was to withdraw their cards and issue new ones. They would wipe the slate clean, accept their losses, and start all over. But in some ways, the slate could not be wiped clean. Chicago had captured the attention of the entire country, and the act of withdrawing cards wouldn't change that. And a tone had been established among the growing legions of credit card critics that would take years to erase—a tone that combined fear, outrage, and withering contempt. This tone reached its apotheosis in March 1970, when *Life* magazine published a cover story on credit cards, an article so scornful that two decades later bankers could still recite its more inflammatory passages from memory. "American banks have mailed more than 100 million credit cards to unsuspecting citizens of the Republic during the last four years," the article began, "and have offered each recipient not only a handful of 'instant cash' but a dreamy method of buying by signature after the lettuce runs out." The first paragraph continued:

One should not conclude that bankers no longer consider money a sacred commodity. They do. They do. But the soberest of trust institutions now suggest that we forget those strictures on thrift with which they belabored us so vigorously in the past and "live better" by refusing to "settle for second best." This means that our friendly banker hopes we will run up credit-card bills we cannot pay off in 25 days and will allow him to charge us EIGHTEEN percent a year on the resultant debt. It does not mean that he trusts us. He will put us on the "hot list" in a flash if we go broke in the process or try to support mistresses at his expense.

The same tone could be heard in Congress, where the mass mailings quickly became a popular issue. Bankers had only themselves to blame for that: they had buried the country in credit cards without being remotely prepared to solve the hundreds of problems, both large and small, that were bound to arise—everything from questions about privacy rights to whether divorced couples were responsible to pay for each other's charges, to the various liability questions that generated so much fear and anger. With no clear answers coming from the banks, Congress jumped into the breach. The irascible Patman, whose deep mistrust of bankers was perhaps his most notable feature as House Banking chairman, held his first hearings on the subject in November 1967. He spent the hearings in high dudgeon, fulminating not just about the mailings but about the very existence of credit cards, which he saw as an insidious plot by banks "to totally dominate consumer credit." The 18 percent interest was "usurious," he declared. The merchant discount he described as "skimming." The mailing of unsolicited cards, he said flatly, "is . . . upon its face an unsound and unsafe banking practice." "I think the banks, ever since the moneychangers were driven out of the temple of God, have been trying to perfect some plan whereby they can collect from both sides," he railed; credit cards, he concluded, had finally made that possible. Then Patman turned the floor over to his lead witness, Betty Furness, who was President Lyndon Johnson's consumer affairs adviser. She declared that credit cards were "modern traps" that would lead Americans to become "hopeless addicts." Over in the Senate, another longtime critic of the banks, Sen. William Proxmire of Wisconsin led the charge against mass mailings: "Unless we bring unsolicited credit cards under control," he said at one hearing, "we are likely to produce a nation of credit drunks."

Although congressional critics blamed credit cards for everything from increased bankruptcies to rising inflation, the central objection always came back to the idea of temptation, of sin. It was a moral objection at bottom, a feeling that by giving people credit cards, banks were doing the devil's work. And what seemed most objectionable of all was that the Americans being led astray by their banks were the members of the middle class. Unlike the American Express card, which—in addition to being payable in full each month—was aimed at wealthier Americans, bank cards were aimed at the suburbanite as well as the penthouse dweller, the secretary as well as the executive. There was an undeniable paternalism embedded in the criticism, a sense that people needed to be protected from themselves. "I am by no means trying to make a point that knowledgeable, reliable citizens should be denied credit," Furness said. "But . . . a great many Americans don't know how to use credit." She added, "A man isn't allowed to use a car until he can prove he knows how. Why should he be given credit until he can prove he knows how to use it?'' So pervasive was this sentiment that when Proxmire's bill banning the mailing of unsolicited cards made it to the Senate floor, it passed 79–1. By May 1970, the mass mailings had been banned.[2]

In the face of this fusillade of criticism, the banking industry kept a stiff upper lip. Not once did bank lobbyists concede that maybe the mass mailings had been bungled or acknowledge that the ensuing problems might have created some justified anxiety among its customers. Always, they dismissed reports of losses due to credit cards as unfounded rumor.

But this was a smoke screen. Within the tight little world of consumer banking, the reigning emotion was terror. The losses were far higher than anyone would ever know. In Chicago, a consensus formed among bank analysts that the combined card losses amounted to around $6 million; in fact, they were at least $25 million and possibly much higher. Indeed, the Chicago banks came very close to selling their card business to American Express; they changed their minds when they realized that such a sale would force them to disclose, for the first time, the true extent of their credit card losses. In New York, where some of the biggest banks in the country were dropping cards, losses were estimated in the $250 million range. The Federal Reserve did a study in 1970, and concluded that losses resulting from fraud alone would top $115 million, up from $20 million four years before. In September 1970, a new credit card newsletter, the *Nilson Report,* glumly predicted in its third issue that the ''heyday of bank card growth may be over as officials begin to wonder if there will ever be such a thing as 'profits.' '' (''Biggest disappointment,'' the newsletter added: ''too many customers pay promptly.'')

And the numbers alone didn't begin to convey the sinking sensation many bankers felt that they had unleashed a monster they could not control. ''There was hysteria in the bank,'' one New York banker would later write, after describing the losses, the mismanagement, the fraud, the credit card sales drafts piling up in boxes—and the complete inability of the bank to get its arms around any of it.[3] He concluded morosely, ''The best that we can hope for—now that we're hooked as deeply as we are—is that eventually we'll get the system running as best it can and perhaps it will turn a profit. I doubt it will ever earn back what went into it.''

As to why it had all gone so badly, this same banker had a theory. ''Banking is thoroughly regulated,'' he wrote, ''our [interest] rates are the same as anyone else's in town. The credit card business is not formally regulated by government, and we were innocents in the grown-up world of business.''

*    *    *

What the banks couldn't see in their despair were the glimmers of hope. But they were there if you looked for them. One, oddly enough, was the legislation banning mass mailings. Credit card veterans have always contended that despite the obvious problems, the mass mailings were crucial because they got so many cards in circulation all at once—a prerequisite for mass acceptance. There came a point, however, when banks needed to stop sending out cards and start grappling with problems. The ban allowed that process to begin. Another healthy sign was that, for all the protestations, Americans were using their bank credit cards; by 1970, some 29 million people had used a bank card at least once, and many of them were using it regularly.

Most of all, you could start to make out the beginnings of a nationwide system—or, more precisely, two systems—as a shakeout began. One group of banks, including most of those in Chicago, were coalescing around the Master Charge card. And other banks, including Chase Manhattan and Chicago's First National City,[4] became BankAmericard licensees. One after another, the independent cards that had popped up in the late 1960s succumbed to the inevitable and joined either Master Charge or BankAmericard. By 1970, Master Charge operated in forty-nine states, and BankAmericard in forty-four. Within these two systems, chaos still reigned, but the emergence of the systems themselves suggested at least some semblance of order.

What was most needed at this critical juncture was for someone to emerge who could lead the way—someone who was not paralyzed by the chaos, but galvanized by it. And lo and behold, there he was.

HIS NAME WAS DEE WARD HOCK, and if you found his surname almost comically apt for someone in the credit card business, you were best advised to keep it to yourself. Dee Hock took himself much too seriously to see the humor. He took his mission much too seriously too, which he came to define as making BankAmericard, which he ran from 1970 to 1984 (and whose name he changed to Visa along the way), the premier payment system in the world. This was the sort of grandiose phrase that came naturally to Dee Hock and a fair indication of the depths of his ambition. What he meant was that he expected Visa someday to replace the current "premier payment system," which was, well, cash. To anyone expressing skepticism about this goal, Hock would refer the skeptic to the dictionary, where money was defined as "something generally accepted as a medium of exchange." That's what a credit card was, in his view: a device that was accepted as a medium of exchange between a buyer and a seller. Just like cash. "He used to say that money had evolved from shells to green paper to the artful arrangement of binary digits," a former employee recalls. That's the other thing a credit card did: in an electronic banking system, it set into motion a computer, which triggered the rearrangement of a person's binary digits. Thus completing the exchange of value. Dee Hock wanted Visa to control the binary digits.

It was strange, in a way. Hock had spent most of his early career as a loan officer, yet the installment loan aspect of the credit card, which is all most bankers cared about, never captured his imagination. It scarcely seemed to interest him. He could talk for hours about credit cards without ever mentioning the word "debt." He firmly believed that the worst marketing mistake in history was calling it a "credit card"; such a name, he felt, belittled its larger possibilities. In fact, the card itself seemed almost incidental to his purposes. It was his firm view that once you understood that a credit card was a "value-exchange device," it didn't matter whether it was a piece of plastic or a grain of sand.

Or maybe it wasn't so strange: Dee Hock was driven by the need to think the big thoughts, and they didn't get much bigger than devising the next evolution in the nation's payment system. It gave him purpose in a way that merely establishing the infrastructure for a smoothly functioning credit card industry never could. Once, he persuaded Visa's international board to pass a resolution that began: "Resolved: That the Visa system should become the premier worldwide system for the exchange of value. . . ." The bankers, who were never especially comfortable with Hock's big ideas, passed it, one suspects, because that was easier than not passing it. Not passing it meant that Hock's face would get red, and the veins in his neck would become visible, and he would become almost physically ill, as he did whenever the board contested him on something he cared about deeply. Not passing it meant that he would begin an unrelenting campaign to get them to change their minds before the next board meeting, and it might even mean that he would threaten to quit. The bankers passed it, but they never really believed it, not the way Hock did. Eventually, this would create a chasm between Hock and his board that would be unbridgeable. But that would come later.

He was forty-one years old when he first grabbed hold of the throttle at BankAmericard and began to land the thing; for the next fourteen years, until he abruptly walked away from the business, he was the central figure in the world of credit cards. He was the one everyone else was forced to react to. He ruffled the most feathers. His ideas were the most hotly debated. His speeches provoked the fiercest responses—speeches he insisted on writing himself, holing up in his office for as long as two weeks at a time, and then emerging with his latest eloquent, passionate cri de coeur, which he invariably copyrighted. He transformed the credit card business, and he polarized it. Dee Hock was one of those people who are completely anonymous outside their area of influence, and completely dominant within it.

His tendency to dominate came naturally, a by-product of the fierce and, at times, quixotic pride that burned within him. All his life, he carried around a large chip on his shoulder; it was one of the most obvious things about him. Born in 1930, Hock was a classic child of the Depression, the youngest son of a utility lineman who scratched out a living in the then-rural town of North Ogden, Utah. He was a loner from the time he was old enough to read, something he did insatiably. He began working part-time when he was twelve years old, almost always at jobs that required hard, manual labor. In high school and junior college, he excelled at debating, a skill that would prove valuable in his subsequent career. Although his formal education ended after two years of junior college, his breadth of knowledge was staggering. On the things that mattered to him, Hock was self-taught. He read Plato and Aristotle, Yeats and Emerson, Voltaire and Bacon—and then he read them again. He would quote from the classic works of Western thought whenever he found an appropriate occasion, which in his case was all the time. His speeches were dotted with quotations from Marcus Aurelius and Machiavelli; when critics complained about high interest rates, Hock liked to refer them to Sir Francis Bacon's essay, "Of Usury": "[I]t is a vanity to conceive that there would be ordinary borrowing without profit, and it is impossible to conceive the number of inconveniences that will ensue, if borrowing be cramped."

There was, undoubtedly, a fair amount of vanity behind these allusions, but they also suggested something else about Hock: a lingering resentment toward people who had the kind of education he could never afford, and who therefore could pick and choose from life's possibilities in a way that he had never been able to do. When a magazine writer once asked him why he hadn't become a lawyer, he replied that he hadn't even known what lawyers did until he read Clarence Darrow when he was twenty-five years old. Job seekers who possessed MBAs from Harvard arrived at Visa with two strikes against them; Hock took a certain smug glee in not hiring them. In 1981, a professor from Harvard Business School showed up at Visa, hoping to analyze the organization for one of the school's famous case studies. Although Hock seemed almost to toy with him, the professor was dazzled by what he found at Visa, and most especially by its leader, whom he quoted at length mocking (among other things) "the ponderous tomes . . . written by professors of business administration."

People like Hock often do well in American life. Their upbringing, their lack of higher education, their gnawing belief that they began life behind the eight ball—this is a combustible mixture that can fuel an unquenchable desire to prove themselves among their better-credentialed peers. Unlike their better-credentialed peers, however, they often back into the field they conquer rather than choose it consciously. This is hardly surprising, since they usually begin their adult life needing mainly to make some money. In Hock's case, financial necessity caused him to back into the small loan business. Newly married, not yet twenty-one years old, Hock took a job as a loan officer in the Utah office of a West Coast finance company. It was the first job he could find after being laid off as a bricklayer's helper.

Finance companies were at the bottom of the food chain of American finance: they lent money to the people who had no place else to turn. They made loans to working-class Americans, to the poor, to people who had had previous problems with debt, and also to millions of Americans whose own banks considered the small loan business beneath their notice, as so many did in the 1950s. But because finance companies supplied credit to a riskier group of people than banks, their default rate was necessarily higher—as was the interest they charged.[5] The worst of the finance companies deserved their seedy reputation, but even for the best of them, it was a gritty, merciless business, in which the essential act consisted of judging whether someone pleading for a loan—someone with minimal financial resources to back up the request—was likely to pay it back. The other essential act was getting the money back when you judged wrong.

As unpleasant as the work was, and as distasteful as Hock found it, he had a knack for it. In collecting an overdue payment, Hock never threatened, he persuaded, by convincing the delinquent borrower that paying back the finance company was the most honorable thing he could do. One thing led to another: success in Utah brought promotions, until finally he found himself in Los Angeles, a middle manager. Everyone could see he was a comer. And not long afterward he quit in a huff.

On three separate occasions, Hock was employed by finance companies; all three times he earned a reputation as a star; every time he walked away in disgust. It wasn't the finance business that bothered him so much as it was corporate life in general. Practices that other people accepted as the way of the world caused Hock to boil with rage. One reason he always wrote his own speeches at Visa was because he remembered how much it rankled him whenever he had had to ghost-write a speech for one of his finance company bosses. The rituals of corporate bureaucracy drove him to distraction. His prickly uprightness made him difficult to deal with and quick to anger, and what angered him most was his belief that he wasn't being treated fairly. Whether justified or not, it was something he felt often.

Hock left his last finance company position early in 1966, and decided to look for a lending job with a bank; he soon wound up at the National Bank of Commerce in Seattle (later known as Rainier Bank). You might think that such a bank, a haughty institution long accustomed to sniffing at the kind of small consumer loans Hock had made all his life, would cause the chip on Hock's shoulder to grow even larger. But just the opposite took place. In spite of its arrogance—or perhaps because of it—National Bank of Commerce had an aura of propriety, of noblesse oblige, even, that matched Hock's own sense of those things. It was ramrod straight, and so was he. The president was known to toss off a Latin phrase or two, which must have appealed to Hock. And his job had appeal, too. For here is where Hock came face to face with his future. A short time after he joined the bank, he was made the assistant to the head of the bank's new credit card division.

National Bank of Commerce was an early, if somewhat reluctant, Bank-Americard licensee; it was one of those banks that got into the business only because it saw every other bank getting in, and felt it had no choice. Hock helped launch its program. His big ideas about credit cards were years away from gestation, but still, it was new and exciting. It also offered him a chance to do things his way for a change. Prior to the launch, he and several colleagues visited Bank of America to be instructed in the ways of the credit card business. Hock, typically, lost patience with the bank bureaucrats assigned to teach the crew from Seattle, and spent his days prowling the back office, asking pointed questions of the people doing the real work. Over dinner each night, he and the other visitors from Seattle would then compare what they had learned that day, taking particular note of the discrepancy between what the bureaucrats were teaching versus the tricks of the trade Hock was picking up in the back office. As a result, National Bank of Commerce's entry into the credit card business went relatively smoothly. Although the bank suffered its share of losses, there was never that panicky feeling that everything was spiraling out of control. It was never like Chicago.

Even as Hock's bank was getting the kinks out of its BankAmericard program, one final disaster was beginning to unfold. Unlike the mass mailings, however, this one was shaping up out of public view, where it would remain: even Wright Patman never found out about it. The problem was, even though the various BankAmericard licensees were learning how to manage credit cards, and even though more and more banks were becoming BankAmericard members, the BankAmericard system, upon which all the member banks depended, was falling apart. The behind-the-scenes apparatus—the "interchange" system, as it was later called—that Bank of America had cobbled together to facilitate its dream of a nationwide credit card program was no longer functioning properly. In fact, it was no longer functioning at all.

It is impossible to overstate the importance of a workable interchange system; without it, nationwide bank credit cards simply cannot exist. Because the vast majority of credit card transactions involve two separate banks—one that handles the merchant's business, and another that issues the credit card to the customer—banks have to have a mechanism that allows them to "settle" their accounts with each other. Simply stated, Bank of America set up a system whereby the merchant bank would reimburse the store for every credit card sale it made—minus the merchant discount, which it kept for itself. Then the merchant bank would send out the sales drafts to the member banks around the country whose customers had made those purchases. The customers' banks, in turn, would reimburse the merchant bank, taking a fractional amount of the transaction for itself: the interchange fee, this latter amount was called. Finally, the customer's bank would bill the customer for the item. When the customer paid, the transaction was complete.

This description makes interchange sound relatively straightforward, and today it is. Every night at Visa and MasterCard, an array of powerful computers sorts through millions of transactions, divvying them up among thousands of banks, adding and subtracting the various fees involved. Banks and merchants alike now take the process completely for granted. Yet interchange has a lot to do with giving a credit card its power as a financial device. A merchant will accept a credit card because he knows, absolutely, that his bank will reimburse him, no matter what. A bank will pay the merchant, knowing absolutely that it will get its money from other banks. A customer will take his credit card out of his wallet knowing absolutely that it is as acceptable to the merchant as cash. Interchange is the structure that supports our faith that a credit card will do what we expect it to do.

But for interchange to work, the bankers themselves have to have faith in the system's rules and regulations. They have to be willing to agree to some procedure for settling the inevitable disputes that arise (which bank should have to swallow fraudulent sales drafts, for instance). They have to have a mechanism for solving the numerous complex problems that any nationwide system of interchange poses. Mostly, though, they have to believe the system is fair, and that everybody is playing by the same rules.

Is it surprising to learn that member banks were flouting the rules, cheating each other, entangling themselves in yet another layer of chaos? Perhaps not. The same mind-set that drove bankers to mail credit cards to dogs and infants also drove them to bend the interchange system to their own advantage. Card-issuing banks would receive sales drafts from a merchant bank and then sit on them for weeks at a time, earning interest on money that didn't really belong to them. Or they would unilaterally refuse to accept certain sales drafts from a merchant bank, claiming they were invalid for some preposterous reason. Or the merchant bank would lie about the size of the merchant discount, in order to lower the fee it had to pay to the credit card banks. These measures would then bring retaliation. "I thought a bank was shafting us on the merchant fee they sent us," recalls one banker, "so I decided we would just start sending them zero. Two weeks later, the head of their card program called the head of ours and started screaming, 'You're sending us zero, you bastard! I *know* your merchant discount isn't zero.' "[6]

Even without the mistrust, the interchange system was bound to break down as more banks signed on. It was one thing to settle accounts with five banks or even twenty-five. It was another thing to settle accounts with 150 banks, with millions of cardholders, with $2 billion in sales, and to do it without computer help, with sales drafts flying back and forth across the country every day, with balances that didn't add up correctly half the time— with, as one banker would later put it, "millions of dollars floating all over hell's half-acre in back rooms."

Then there was the business of "authorization," which went hand in hand with interchange. Authorization is what makes it possible for a merchant to know that the card being presented to him is valid, and that the cardholder is not exceeding his credit limit. This is another one of those things we scarcely think about, now that it's done electronically. The merchant runs the card through an electronic device, punches in a few numbers, and within seconds he knows whether the purchase is approved. But the electronics didn't exist then, so the merchant had to call his bank, and while he was put on hold, his bank would make a long distance call to the bank that had issued the credit card, and while *it* was put on hold, the clerk on the other end of the line would pull out a fat printout of names and numbers and look up the customer's balance to see if the purchase could be approved—all while the customer and the merchant stood in the store, waiting for the reply. And that was when the system was operating *smoothly*. Sometimes the merchant got a busy signal. Other times his call went unanswered, something that happened most often when a customer with a card from an East Coast bank tried to buy something late in the day in California. And if he couldn't get through, the merchant then had to decide whether to accept the card or lose the sale. And if he took the card, and it turned out to be stolen, all hell would break loose as the banks fought over who should absorb the loss. There were a hundred problems like that.

What was worse, Bank of America was plainly incapable of fixing the problems. None of the member banks trusted it: its enormous size bred a natural suspicion among the smaller banks, as did the incessant rumors that certain banks had been able to cut licensing deals not available to everyone else. Also, Bank of America officials had never established a means for solving disputes or working out problems; as conflicts arose, they seemed bewildered. They didn't even have a way to enforce their own rules, except to toss a bank out of the system. But such drastic action was unthinkable, and the member banks knew it.

Larkin and other Bank of America officials would always describe subsequent events as a logical progression, a graceful transfer of power from the bank to the licensees. "The children had become adults," he says. That Bank of America acted with grace is beyond dispute; on the other hand, it didn't have much choice. By 1968, Larkin's "children" were in open revolt.

That October, Bank of America's credit card executives called a meeting, held in Columbus, Ohio, to clear the air. Well over 100 bankers crowded into a hotel conference room, and though the details of the meeting have faded with the passage of time, the tenor of the affair remains vivid in the minds of those who attended. The Bank of America executives saw the meeting as a chance to sort out the technical problems with interchange and authorization, and to assure the member banks they were getting the problems under control. But of course it's impossible to get anything substantive done when there are 100 angry people in a room, each of whom has his own priorities and complaints and ideas. The meeting quickly degenerated into a shouting match. "By noon the first day," recalls one participant, "everyone could see that it was a shambles." The bankers broke for lunch. When they returned to the meeting room, they found Dee Hock standing in front of them, ready to take control of their destiny.

## CHAPTER 4

# The Great Wall of Q

## *February 1970*

SEVEN YEARS AFTER Gerry Tsai left Fidelity Investments, the elder Mr. Johnson finally turned over his beloved firm to his only son. The transfer of power officially took place in the fall of 1972, when Edward C. Johnson 2d named Edward C. Johnson 3d president of the parent company, Fidelity Management and Research. By then, the elder man was seventy-four; his son Ned forty-two.

The Go-Go Years had come and gone, and to an alarming degree, so had the money that had flowed into Fidelity during those happy days. Although the Dow Jones average was on the upswing in 1972, the rise was a tease; this was the heyday of the illusory "nifty-fifty" market.[1] All the broader averages were down, and in time the Dow would join them, dropping from 1052 in 1973 to 578 less than two years later—"the culmination," notes financial journalist Peter L. Bernstein, "of the worst bear market in common stocks since the Great Crash of 1929."

Inevitably, the money held in mutual funds dropped along with the market. The money in Fidelity's funds had ballooned to $4.3 billion by 1969; barely a year later, close to $1 billion of that was gone, and assets continued to dwindle in the years that followed. Trend Fund alone dropped from $1.4 billion in 1967 to $450 million in 1974. Part of the loss was due to the decline in the funds' value: whenever a fund has a losing day, it necessarily contains less money than it did the day before. But far more was the result of investors pulling their money out of the company in the 1970s. "The public," recalls Leo Dworsky, a longtime Fidelity hand, "was voting with its money."

"Net redemptions" is the term they use in the mutual fund business when more money flows out of a fund than flows in; by the early 1970s, it was the condition of the industry. The novice investors who had been lured by the hot performance funds were now the most anxious to get their money back in the bank. As is so often the case, these were the people who least understood the ramifications of their investment: it hadn't really dawned on them that in the stock market, rewards always come with risks attached, or that the market had to go down sooner or later. Nor had their brokers apprised them of these eternal truths. Everyone now agrees that brokers wildly oversold the virtues of mutual funds during the Go-Go Years, which only exacerbated the later disenchantment.

Mr. Johnson himself was a dispirited man by the early 1970s. He had had his one great idea, and it had changed his industry, but he needed a new idea, and he didn't have it. His was the mind of a professional investor, which had served him well in his day; needing now to capture the hearts and minds of the novice investors who were fleeing his company, he was lost. One Fidelity executive, sensing his confusion, made a brief, failed stab at pushing him aside.

In June 1971, he received a final, discouraging blow. That month, Fidelity lost an important lawsuit.[2] Brought by a lawyer who specialized in suits against securities firms, it charged that Fidelity had engaged in the practice of "splitting commissions" among various brokerage houses. In fact, Fidelity *had* split commissions. Everyone split commissions in those days. Commissions, which were fixed by the New York Stock Exchange, were absurdly high, especially for institutions like mutual fund companies that traded stocks in large volume but lacked a seat on the exchange. Because the stock exchange forbade volume discounts, it became standard procedure for such an institution to ask the brokerage house making its trades to redirect a portion of the oversized commission to other investment houses as a reward for providing, say, research information. The procedure was finally halted by the Securities and Exchange Commission in 1968; the suit against Fidelity covered the years before 1968, when the legality of splitting commissions was still murky.

In ruling against Fidelity, a federal appeals court described commission-splitting as an act of "gross misconduct."[3] The words cut Mr. Johnson to the quick. All his life, he had been the very model of WASP integrity and moral probity. The phrase "gross misconduct"—shouted from the business pages of *The New York Times* and the *Wall Street Journal* in the wake of the ruling—rang in his ears. It didn't matter that the ruling was aimed not at him personally but at an industrywide practice. He took it personally anyway, so personally that there are those at Fidelity who believe that he never really recovered. Once his son was officially in charge, Mr. Johnson largely withdrew as a presence from Fidelity, though he remained its chairman for another four and a half years.[4] He still kept an eye on the market he so loved, but his watchfulness had an almost wistful quality, as if he knew his day had passed. "Homer," he wrote to a friend shortly before he retired for good, "let's start a little mutual fund, you and me." By then it was obvious that if someone at Fidelity was going to find the next great idea, it was going to have to be Ned Johnson, not his father.

The big question back then—back before people at Fidelity became accustomed to his quirky brilliance and eccentric methods, before they began to appreciate his almost Japanese style of indirect management, before they understood that he had an extraordinary intuitive feel for the way the money revolution would play out—the big question back then was whether Ned Johnson could find the next big idea if he tripped over it. The general consensus, in those darkest of days, was that he could not. It wasn't that his Fidelity colleagues didn't like Ned Johnson, it was that they scarcely knew him. Although he had been employed at his father's company since 1957, he was, to an amazing degree, a cipher to the people he worked with.

Partly, this was a natural consequence of the Yankee reserve he inherited from his father. Like his father, Ned Johnson had a fierce sense of both privacy and propriety. His discretion was absolute. In his first decade and a half at Fidelity, Ned Johnson rarely let his hair down, and certainly never revealed his dreams and ambitions. At rare[5] company gatherings, he was a wallflower. He was a nice enough fellow, but always in the bland, uncommitted way that often characterizes office friendships—"jovial" is how one former colleague remembers him. With the exception of his father, the people he was closest to did not work at Fidelity. In the office, he still called his father "Mr. Johnson," just like everyone else.

He also had a patrician's aversion to the spotlight, so much so that even after he was managing Trend Fund—and turning it into one of the most successful growth funds in America—he managed to remain anonymous. Brokers would plead with Johnson to make a speech or attend a forum—to make the kind of public appearance that could only bring money into Trend Fund—and he would invariably turn them down. On the rare occasion when he accepted such an offer, he usually did poorly. Gunslingers like Tsai excited audiences with their charisma; Ned Johnson put audiences to sleep. And this was another reason he seemed such a cipher: Up to the moment he became Fidelity's president, there was nothing about him that seemed special or out of the ordinary. He did not exude the kind of natural authority one expects from a leader. Quite the contrary: his former Harvard roommate, a venture capitalist named Arthur DuBow, told one writer that Johnson "was not that strong a personality'' as a college student. Twenty years later, that was still the majority opinion.

Johnson did have one noticeable personality quirk. He had about him an air of distractedness that could rival the most absent-minded professor. His train of thought seemed to wander from the subject at hand, even during the most pointed conversations. His speech had a vaporous quality; he liked to waft sentences into the air, and let them float there until they evaporated. He had a disconcerting way of tossing out ideas that seemed, on their face, complete non sequiturs (though they usually weren't), and an annoying tendency to answer a question by asking another question. He seemed constitutionally incapable of giving a straightforward ''yes'' or ''no'' answer about anything.

Later, after he had transformed Fidelity into the most successful company to emerge from the money revolution, this style of his would be rather offhandedly described as part of his brilliance, an example of the free-ranging quality of his mind. But that was hindsight. When the new head of Fidelity Investments began staring off into space during meetings, it did not inspire confidence among the troops. ''Ned was just an apparition floating around the building,'' recalls Caleb Loring, who was the Fidelity executive closest to his father.[6] ''Nobody suspected that Ned had the kind of mind he turned out to have.''

Mr. Johnson had been grooming his son to take over practically from the moment he was born, something the men around him realized only gradually—and which they had a hard time taking seriously when they did realize it. Given the way events played out, however, the grooming could hardly have been more misguided. Fidelity's success under Ned Johnson would be very much tied to the needs and aspirations of the middle class, yet there was nothing about his upbringing or training that would suggest that he had any particular feel for middle-class life. He grew up in a proper, upper-class household in the Boston suburbs, the kind of household where the children ate with their nannies and maids, rather than their parents, so as not to interrupt the adult conversation. Like his father, Johnson attended Milton Academy and Harvard University, where, his former roommate told a reporter, he was a mediocre student who kept to himself—though he did have a passion for the market that was unique among his peers. Every Sunday, he returned home to have lunch with his father. Johnson spent the next two years in the Army, where he did not exactly embrace the lifestyle of his fellow soldiers. ''I spent a relaxing two years in Baumholder, Germany, acquiring a taste for the fine wines of the Mosel and Nahe Rivers,'' he would later write. He tooled around Germany in a newly purchased Porsche. After his stint in the Army, he worked at a bank before joining Fidelity.

Once there, the son began jumping through a series of hoops the father placed in his path. There was a long apprenticeship, with Ned starting as a stock analyst, learning how to "cover" companies and to gauge their stock potential. Then came the tour of duty as a portfolio manager; Mr. Johnson put his son in charge of a fund called Trend Fund, where the new manager quickly displayed a style completely different from Tsai's—"I was uncomfortable with all that *activity*," he once said of Tsai's trading habits—and yet just as successful. Johnson also managed the new Magellan Fund, which gained 106 percent during one of the years he ran it.

These early jobs were intended to uncover whether Ned had the necessary skills to manage large sums of money. In Mr. Johnson's view—in everyone's view—successful portfolio management was the key to everything at a mutual fund company; it was the engine that drove the firm. But there were also other, vaguer tests—"general tests of human probity," as Loring would describe them, "which Ned may have realized were tests, or may not have." In the older man's view, moral uprightness was the other crucial attribute for someone in line to run a mutual fund company. "I've got to be satisfied," Mr. Johnson would say constantly, as he evaluated his son. Eventually he was.

But surely for the wrong reasons. For though Ned Johnson could manage money with the best of them, he did not strictly think like a professional investor. That would turn out to be his greatest strength. He had other qualities, too, that his father had neither instilled nor tested, having no idea they would serve any purpose: ambition that went far beyond the boundaries of investment management; a gift for marketing; an uncanny instinct for what people wanted; and more. One childhood trait that served Johnson well during the money revolution was his love of tinkering with things mechanical: it would lead him directly to computers. In this he could not have been more different from his father, who hadn't the slightest interest in gadgets. Heredity may have put Ned Johnson in line to succeed his father, but it was more luck than anything else that he turned out to be the right man for the job. "It was as though," reflected Loring, "a greater hand had decreed it."

And then another bit of luck: at the same time Ned Johnson was taking control of Fidelity, the next big innovation in personal finance was lurking just around the corner. Needless to say, when he saw it, he did not trip.

❧

"THE CORNER," IN THIS CASE, was the Securities and Exchange Commission. Under the Investment Company Act of 1940, the SEC had regulatory authority over the mutual fund industry—power that very much included the right to approve or disapprove new funds. In February 1970, the prospectus for a new fund, called the Reserve Fund, was sent to the agency, where it sat unapproved (though not disapproved) for the next two and a half years—"quite possibly the longest gestation period on record," one of the coinventors would later grouse, still irked by the memory. It wasn't until September 1972 that the fund was freed from its regulatory limbo; the other coinventor, with equally dark memories, firmly believes that the regulators gave them the go-ahead to offer it to the public only because "they were sure it was going to die." More likely, they sat on the prospectus because they had trouble understanding what it was supposed to do. No one at the SEC had ever seen anything like the Reserve Fund before. It certainly wasn't an equity mutual fund. Its creators would eventually call it a money market mutual fund; in the prospectus, they described it simply as "a cash management vehicle."

Here we stand, a little more than two decades later, and money market funds seem to us the most commonplace of "cash management vehicles." They do simple, ordinary things. They offer us a place to store our savings or park our cash, and return to us, in addition to the principal, a sum that strongly resembles interest. If we want to withdraw our money, we can do so easily, by writing out something that strongly resembles a check. By all appearances, in other words, a money market fund strongly resembles that most mundane of cash management vehicles: the bank account. So casual have we become about these funds that by 1991, we had put well over $400 billion in the more than 300 money funds in existence.

Yet as ordinary as the money market fund may seem to us now, its effect on American finance has been profound. It stands as the seminal invention in the money revolution, at least on the investment side. It was the first truly different wrinkle in personal finance since the credit card. It was the first product to cross previously iron-clad boundaries between banks and other financial institutions, not to mention the psychological (but no less iron-clad) boundaries separating "savings" money and "investment" money in the minds of most Americans. When the financial habits of the middle class began to change, of necessity, toward the end of the decade, the money market fund was the product that made such changes feasible, and even thinkable. Its creation signaled the beginning of the end for the old world of personal finance.

*       *       *

The two men generally credited with inventing the money market fund are Henry B. R. Brown and Bruce R. Bent. The way the story goes—which is to say, the way Brown and Bent have told and retold it over the years—they were a pair of insurance company renegades (Brown the short one with the rigid bearing of an ex-Marine, Bent the tall, gangly one with the casual manner of a practiced nonconformist), who in the spring of 1968 walked away from their safe, well-paying, bureaucratic jobs at the Teachers' Insurance and Annuity Association to strike out on their own. They set up offices in midtown Manhattan, naming their new investment firm Brown & Bent (eventually renamed Reserve Management Corporation). Two years later—a terrible two years, during which they did no business, and exhausted most of their own money—they devised their masterstroke.

All this is true enough. What their story misses, though, is any larger sense that a money fund—or something quite like it—was inevitable right about then. If Brown and Bent hadn't come up with the idea, somebody else would have; indeed, a handful of people were already moving in that direction. William Donoghue, who would later become the money funds' chief proselytizer, recalls having the idea himself in 1973, only to discover that others had gotten there first. In San Jose, a Merrill Lynch broker named James Benham came up with the concept not long after Brown and Bent. Benham's fund, called the Capital Preservation Fund, wound up being America's second money market fund.

No, the instigator of the money fund was not so much a particular human being as the times themselves. By the early 1970s, Americans were feeling the first lashes of inflation. Inflation made money market funds inevitable.

Inflation began, almost everyone agrees now, with President Johnson's infamous 1960s guns-and-butter strategy: his decision to finance the Vietnam War and the Great Society by creating a budget deficit—"printing money," his critics would call it—instead of raising taxes. For more than two decades, inflation had been nonexistent. But in 1967, the cost of living, as measured by the Consumer Price Index, rose 3 percent. The following year the CPI rose another 4.7 percent. And on it went: 6.2 percent in 1969; 5.6 percent in 1970. President Richard Nixon, desperate to regain control over the economy, succeeded in turning back inflation temporarily, but only by imposing draconian mandatory wage and price controls in the summer of 1971. As soon as the controls came off, inflation roared back. In 1974, as a result of the Arab oil embargo, the Consumer Price Index rose an almost unthinkable 12 percent, as America got its first modern taste of double digit inflation. The country did not react with equanimity. One labor leader openly predicted that unless inflation were stopped, there would soon be "riots in supermarkets."

As inflation ebbed and flowed, so did interest rates. This is also a phenomenon we've become used to, but it was new then—new and unsettling. In the fall of 1969, when interest rates on short-term Treasury bills[7] reached 8 percent, it marked a level that hadn't been approached since before the Civil War. There was, however, one interest rate that was *not* ebbing and flowing in lock step with the T-bill. The interest paid to small savers, on the money they kept in bank passbook accounts, was stuck at 4½ percent, seemingly oblivious to the chaotic events engulfing the rest of the American economy. In 1973, the rate rose, grudgingly, to 5 percent. There it stayed for the next six years—when it rose another quarter of a percent, to 5¼.

The interest banks paid to consumers was stuck for a very good reason: that's where the Federal Reserve Bank wanted it to be. Under another one of those Depression-era bank regulations, the Federal Reserve had control over how much interest banks could pay their customers. Its power over bank interest rates was embodied in a rule called Regulation Q, which owed its existence to the Depression-era belief that banks had gotten into trouble in the 1930s because they paid too much interest in competing for deposits. This was quite true in 1933, when Regulation Q took effect; more than 4,000 banks closed that year, and the practice of overpaying for deposits had a lot to do with those closings. Forty years later, however, Reg Q had the perverse effect of forcing banks to pay too little interest on their customers' deposits. It had gone from being a rule that protected banks from themselves to being a rule that protected banks from the vagaries of the real world. Banks were actually able to take advantage of inflation and high interest rates—for while Reg Q allowed banks to collect deposits at artificially low rates, they could then turn around and lend out that money at the prevailing rate of 10 or 11 percent. Not surprisingly, Q was one regulation bankers did not complain about.

So long as inflation was negligible, nobody else complained either; Regulation Q had no meaning in American life. But once inflation began to bubble up, Reg Q had a great deal of meaning. It meant that the middle class was losing money in its own bank accounts—and the government was not only allowing this to happen, it was *causing* it to happen. This was obvious to anyone who took the time to think it through. If you had money in the bank earning 4½ percent annual interest, in a year when inflation rose by 6 percent, you lost, in effect, 1½ percent of that money's earning power. If you had money in the bank earning 4½ percent in a year when T-bill rates hit, say, 8½ percent, you were losing the chance to make an additional 4 percent of real world interest. This was not only obvious, it was untenable. Something had to give; somebody was bound to figure out a way around Regulation Q. The people who did so were Bruce Bent and Henry Brown on

the East Coast and James Benham on the West Coast. For that's what their
money market fund was, ultimately: it was the way around Q. It was the
most logical response to the disparity between market interest rates and the
lower rates forced on the country's savers by the Fed.

Though they did not instantly grasp the ultimate significance of the money
market fund, Brown and Bent understood completely that they were making
the first real assault on Regulation Q. Here is Henry Brown describing the
moment of epiphany: "It was a frustrating time," he wrote in an unpublished chronicle, of their disastrous first two years in business. ("Bent
calculated that the proprietor of the hot dog stand at the corner of Sixth
Avenue and 53rd Street was making twice as much money as either of
them.") In a moment of desperation, Bent one day asked Brown:

" 'How do you get money?'

" 'By paying more [interest] than anyone else,' Brown replied."

Thus did the light bulb go on. "So now we had to figure out some way
we could pay higher interest," continued Bent. "Where could we find an
aberration in the marketplace?" Regulation Q created the aberration. The
two men first planned to exploit their discovery by starting a state-chartered
bank someplace where Reg Q was not part of the state banking laws, but that
idea turned out to be unworkable. Brown picks up the tale:

> But then the search was widened to [include] other ways of packaging similar
> products, and all of a sudden, a hole in the Great Wall of Q miraculously
> opened up. "One day we were sitting around trying to sort out this situation,"
> Bruce Bent recalls, "[and] I said, 'What about a mutual fund?' " . . . They sat
> down and boned up on the Investment Company Act of 1940, and found, to
> their surprise, that nothing in the law seemed to stand in their way.

Although making it a reality would turn out to be full of complications,
the idea itself was fairly straightforward. They would create a mutual fund
that would invest, as Brown puts it, "in short-term instruments of indebtedness." In their first prospectus, Brown and Bent laid out plans for a fund
that would rely primarily on two such instruments, T-bills and jumbo certificates of deposit (that is, CDs containing $100,000 or more), which had
been deregulated in the mid-1960s, and therefore offered market interest
rates. Just as investors in an equity fund reap the returns gained by the fund
manager, investors in a money market fund would be able to reap the
interest rates these instruments yielded.[8] By sticking only to short-term
debt—and mostly government debt, at that—Brown and Bent were ensuring
that their fund's yield would always reflect the current market interest rate

while dramatically reducing the potential risk to the investor's principal. As for the two inventors, they would make their money by imposing a number of small management and administrative fees.[9] Here, indeed, was the hole in the Great Wall of Q. It was big enough to drive a truck through.

Out on the West Coast, James Benham was coming up with the same brainstorm, independent of Brown and Bent. He, however, *did* see the larger significance. Even after creating the money fund, Brown and Bent assumed its usefulness would be primarily as a cash management device for companies, rather than as a product that freed the middle-class saver from the shackles of regulated rates. From the first, however, Benham saw banks and the government as the enemy, and the middle-class depositor as the person he was out to rescue. "I came at it," he says now, "from the perspective of the little guy." Benham was an angry man in the early 1970s, angry and scared and, to be frank about it, a little paranoid. He was in his mid-thirties then, a tall, talkative trumpet-playing Virginian, who had been a federal bank examiner before becoming a stockbroker. From his perspective as a semi-insider, he had become convinced that the American financial system was on the verge of total collapse. He had the kind of dark vision of America very much in keeping with that tumultuous age of Watergate, except that his was viewed through the prism of finance. The financial system, in his view, was as corrupt as the Nixon administration. The nation's bankers, the bureaucrats at the Treasury Department, even his own bosses at Merrill Lynch: they all lied about the health of the financial system, which Benham saw as being held together by baling wire. When this perspective led him to advise his customers to sell off their stock holdings as quickly as possible, his Merrill Lynch superiors demanded that he become more bullish. Benham refused.[10] "I used to corner people at parties," he told a reporter years later, "and go at them like a preacher: 'Don't you *know* how stressed this financial system is? How *thin* this ice is?'"

He has a vivid memory from those days. In January 1970, with Treasury bills still yielding that historic 8 percent, he saw hundreds of people lined up outside the Federal Reserve Bank of San Francisco. They were standing in line to buy T-bills, which could be purchased for a minimum of $1,000, a sum within the reach of most middle-class savers. There were similar lines in front of all the Federal Reserve Banks that January during the weekly Treasury auctions; small savers purchased somewhere between $250 million and $500 million worth of government bonds in a flurry of panicky buying. For years, as a broker, Benham had been promoting Treasury bills as a good place for his customers to park their cash. But even he was struck by the sight of small savers standing in line for the chance to get 8 percent interest on their money. He was also struck by what happened next. The next month, Paul Volcker, who was then Undersecretary of the Treasury for Monetary Affairs, announced that the department was raising the minimum T-bill purchase from $1,000 to $10,000. In doing so, the Treasury Department was explicitly placing government notes out of the reach of the middle class. The reason Volcker gave for this action was that processing these small purchases was costing the government too much money. But did Benham believe that? Not for a second. The real reason, he was sure, was to force small savers to keep their money in the bank, where Regulation Q was eating away at it. It was all part of the grand conspiracy.[11]

Benham became the avenging angel of the middle class. His idea was even simpler than Brown and Bent's. The fund he had in mind would invest in only one thing—short-term Treasuries. The minimum investment in his fund was set at the old Treasury minimum, $1,000; additional investments could be made for as little as $100. In August 1971, Benham quit his job at Merrill Lynch and formed the company that would manage his new fund. He remembers that date vividly too. The same month, President Nixon took the dollar off the gold standard, and announced his wage and price controls—two actions that, in his mind, further signaled the coming collapse.

Benham's fund prospectus arrived at the SEC a year after Brown and Bent's. Its course was no smoother. Benham had planned to call his fund the First Safe Fund, which he considered an accurate description since there wasn't a security in the country safer than a Treasury bill, backed by "the full faith and credit of the United States." The SEC, however, was not about to approve any mutual fund with the word "safe" in the title. The agency told Benham it wouldn't even consider his fund until he changed the name. Reluctantly, he did.

Then, late in the registration process, came a far more damaging shot across the bow. Someone from the Federal Home Loan Bank Board—the agency regulating the S&L industry—sent a letter to the SEC requesting that the minimum investment in Benham's Capital Preservation Fund (as he had renamed it) be raised to $10,000. The SEC called Benham and suggested that he do that. It was a devastating request—unthinkable, really, for it would destroy the purpose of the fund. If he agreed, his fund would be no more accessible to the middle class than T-bills themselves. Benham was distraught. "I had put every cent I had into this idea. I had remortgaged my house. I had a family to support. And all I could think was that somebody was trying to squash us."

What he did instead was rewrite the prospectus to disguise the fund's true nature. The new prospectus still allowed it to buy T-bills, but it also stated that the fund would be able to buy longer-term debt securities, corporate debt, bonds of every kind. "We threw the kitchen sink in there," Benham recalls. The strategy worked. The SEC, thinking that Benham's fund was a variant of a bond fund, stopped asking him to raise the minimum.

Over the next two decades, Benham would go on to build his firm, Benham Capital Management, into a highly successful fund company, and he would also calm down considerably about the financial system's prospects for meltdown. But the memory of that letter can still stir in him those old paranoid feelings. "I remember we asked the SEC who at the Home Loan Bank Board had written the letter," he recalls, his voice rising. " 'We can't tell you that!' they said. Then, after we were up and running, we requested a copy of the letter. This time they said they'd 'lost' it. And of course nobody at the SEC could remember who wrote it." He snorts his disbelief, and then his voice suddenly drops. "It was right around the time of Watergate," he concludes darkly. "Makes you wonder."

Brown and Bent's Reserve Fund and Benham's Capital Preservation Fund were finally approved by the SEC in the fall of 1972, within two weeks of each other. The world did not beat a path to their respective doors. Brown and Bent had always assumed that once they got past the SEC, the rest would be easy; corporate finance officers would flock to money market funds, since corporations in those days had millions of dollars sloshing around in interest-free bank accounts. To their horror, they now discovered that their assumption was wrong. Most of the time, they couldn't even get in to see the finance officer, much less persuade him to put the company's spare cash in money funds.

They next turned to the brokerage industry. For decades, brokerage firms had labeled their customers' spare cash "free credit balances," and paid out no interest on that money. A fund that allowed such cash to accrue interest would be of enormous benefit to customers; indeed, today there isn't a brokerage house in the country that doesn't stick its customers' cash in money market funds, quite a few of which are managed by Brown and Bent. In those days, however, brokerage firms invested their customers' free credit balances for their own accounts. It was the dirty little secret of the business. Not surprisingly, brokers showed no more interest in money funds than corporate finance officers.

By January 1973, Brown and Bent were in trouble. More than a year had passed since the SEC had approved their fund, yet they were as broke as ever—so broke, in fact, that they were about to sell a controlling interest in their company for $300,000, just to gain a little more time. And that's when the gods intervened. A *New York Times* business reporter chose that moment to write a little article about this new cash management vehicle of theirs. It ran on the front page of the Sunday business section, under the headline: "Overnight Mutual Fund for Surplus Assets." That's all it took. "On the Monday morning following . . . the *Times* article," Brown later wrote, "our phone began ringing off the hook." To their surprise, the callers were not corporate finance officers or conscious-stricken brokers but individuals—people who saw the fund for what it was: an alternative to a bank account. "I knew a lot of guys on Wall Street," recalls Bent, "and they would send their mothers to me. The mothers would say, 'My son says you have a good thing.' " By the end of February, the fund had $2 million in assets. By the end of the year, it was up to $100 million. The proposed sale of the company was canceled.

As for Benham, he also wound up selling his new fund largely through word of mouth, though typically he took the more offbeat path. He hitched his fortunes to the well-known financial rabble-rouser, Howard Ruff. A Mormon, a gold bug, and a rabid conservative, Ruff believed that inflation was God's punishment on a society run amok. Inflation, he was convinced, would lead to anarchy, and he spent much of his time imploring people to begin preparing for that eventuality by hoarding precious metals like gold and silver, as well as food and toilet paper and ammunition. "RELOCATE if you live in an endangered city," he wrote. "Have an alternate SOURCE OF HEAT," he wrote. His vision of the coming apocalypse represented the extremes of panic that inflation could induce; his 1970s-era book, *How to Prosper During the Coming Bad Years,* was a runaway best-seller.

After reading a small item about Benham's fund, Ruff brought Benham into his fold, touting his money fund in his newsletter and books, and making Benham part of his traveling road show. "The five-cent tour," Benham used the call it, because for $25, you not only got a fiery, head-for-the-hills speech from Ruff, but also a free copy of his book, which retailed for $24.95. Of course, Ruff believed that money market funds only made *short-term* sense, since in the long term, the world was more or less coming to an end, an eventuality that would render even Treasury bills worthless. On this point (and many others) Benham disagreed, but he was in no position to dissent too strongly. Every little bit helped, even when the help came from Howard Ruff.

The other thing that helped, of course, was continued high interest rates. That was always the heart of the matter. With money market funds, people were getting higher yields than they could get at the bank. For Benham, this point was made in spades in 1977, when short-term Treasury rates momentarily dipped below the bank rate of 5 percent. There was a tremendous outflow of cash, as Benham's customers rushed to get their money back into passbook accounts, which were suddenly the better deal. By the time the redemptions had ended, Benham's Capital Preservation Fund had shrunk by a staggering 90 percent. Then interest rates started rising again, and so did the assets in the fund.

As painful as that outflow was at the time, it was also an event filled with encouraging omens for the money fund pioneers. It meant that people were shedding the inertia that had been the hallmark of personal finance since the Depression. They were beginning to understand that inflation was a different phenomenon requiring a different response—a willingness (for instance) to keep an eye on interest rates. Not everybody had gotten to this point, of course; not even more than a tiny minority: in any chart of financial assets in the early and mid-1970s, the assets in money market funds barely register. But it was a start. In the words of banking consultant Edward Furash, the early money fund investors had begun the process of abandoning the "Depression mentality" and acquiring the "inflation mentality."

The outflow also suggested something else that would benefit money funds. If people were willing to move money back and forth between money market funds and banks, it meant that in their own minds, at least, the only difference between the two vehicles was the interest they paid. A blurring had begun between saving and investing, which could only help money funds. A money market fund, no matter how much it looked like a bank account, was still a form of mutual fund—by definition, an investment vehicle. It did not come with federal deposit insurance, the way a bank account did. The possibility—remote though it might be—always existed that some principal might be lost. Yet people were willing to use money market funds the same way they used bank accounts. And the more they used them that way, the more comfortable they became with the idea, and the more blurring took place.

This blurring, it should be noted, was decidedly not another of those lucky accidents of the money revolution. It was quite calculated. Although they were mistaken about the Reserve Fund's potential audience, Brown and Bent always understood that they were competing with banks for money, and from the start, they worked hard to overlay a kind of bank-account sheen on their money fund. Customers didn't have to pay an upfront load to buy shares in their fund, for instance, the way they did with a typical mutual fund.[12] More importantly, Brown wrote a series of computer programs designed to make the Reserve Fund mirror the workings of a bank account. (Everyone who got into the money fund business replicated Brown's work.) The most important was a program that allowed for something called "dollar pricing." If you bought shares in a traditional mutual fund, your return was reflected in the fluctuations of the share price. If you bought shares in the Reserve Fund, however, the share price would always be fixed at $1.00. What fluctuated instead was the yield, which (thanks to another of Brown's programs) was updated every day to reflect the changes in the fund. By separating principal from yield, dollar pricing made it appear that a money fund investment was simply accruing daily interest as time went on—just the way a bank account did. It was a critical step.

There was one other crucial innovation that helped blur the distinction between a money fund and a bank account, but it wasn't something Brown or Bent could take credit for. Rather, the innovator was the newly installed president of Fidelity Investments, who had been watching the development of the money fund with keen interest. A year and a half after the Reserve Fund gained SEC approval, Ned Johnson introduced Fidelity's first money market fund. It came with a novel twist. You could write checks against it. When Johnson figured out how to add check writing to a money market fund, the blurring was complete.

YEARS LATER, JOHNSON WAS ASKED ABOUT THE CIRCUMSTANCES under which the idea first came to him—this seemingly wild notion that checks could be attached to money market funds. It was an idea so unusual that it violated just about every piece of conventional wisdom the mutual fund industry held dear, and yet one whose importance was so instantly obvious that everyone in the business rushed to duplicate it.

Johnson was slouched down in a large, comfortable easy chair in his large, comfortable office in Fidelity's Boston headquarters. This was the summer of 1987, by which time Fidelity was plainly the dominant mutual fund company in America. Among the cognoscenti, it was universally acknowledged that his Fidelity Daily Income Trust (FDIT, or Fidit, as it was called)—the first money market fund to include check writing—marked the moment when the company's turnabout began. Johnson stared at the ceiling, looking slightly pained at the self-aggrandizement the question seemed to call for. The walls were filled with elegant paintings, the room dotted with beautiful artifacts. A Quotron machine blinked in the background. Reporters who visited Johnson in the past always took note of the little frog icons scattered about the room—a kind of eccentric homage to that first money fund, which, within the company, had been symbolized by a frog. (Fidit, ribit—get it?) But now most of the porcelain frogs had been placed in a display case that stood in the hallway leading to his office, a somewhat more formal acknowledgment of the importance of the fund in Fidelity's history.

For a long time, Johnson seemed lost in his own thoughts. He stared off into space. "Oh, I don't know," he said finally, with a small, tight sigh. "Ideas bubble up and down, and the ones that keep coming back usually have the most merit." Then he let the sentence float above the room until it was gone.


The idea had bubbled up early. Everyone realizes that now. While keeping his own counsel, Ned Johnson had clearly been thinking about what he would do differently when he took over. Even as assets continued to pour out of the company, his father was unable to budge from the narrow view that Fidelity existed to sell equity mutual funds. Ned Johnson never had the same emotional attachment to the stock market; what he saw when he looked at Fidelity was a company that sold products no one was buying. To him, the solution was to create new products that people would want. But until his father stepped aside, Johnson held back; no one else in the firm even knew he harbored such heretical thoughts. He was a little like Gorbachev must have been as he rose through the ranks of the Soviet hierarchy—full of strange ideas and big ambitions and radical plans, but biding his time, biting his tongue, never openly contradicting his superior, which in Johnson's case was a father he adored.

By the time his moment did come, Fidelity was suffering not only from a loss of assets, but from a crisis of confidence. Fund sales had dried up, as the company's traditional sales force—the nation's brokers—had turned against them. And the market itself had also turned against Fidelity. Its fund managers had a miserable time coping with the gyrating, frustrating market of the early 1970s, and several of them lost their nerve. One portfolio manager became so paralyzed by the continuing losses that one day he went down to the trading room and told the traders, "If any other portfolio manager buys anything, buy it for me. If they sell something and I own it, sell it for me."

The ascension of Ned Johnson did nothing to calm the firm's jitters. Some of the firm's best analysts and portfolio managers, worried about the company's future, began jumping ship. "Ned's being heir apparent is precisely why a lot of talented people left," says one of those who departed. Nor did it help morale that one of Johnson's first tasks, necessitated by the dwindling assets, was to inaugurate a belt-tightening program, which included layoffs. What he expressly didn't do—though it wasn't noticed until years later— was cut back in the equity department. The fund managers, the large complement of stock analysts who traveled the country looking at companies, even the handful of technical "chartists" who attempted to discern the direction of the market—not one lost his job. None even took a pay cut. Johnson would say later that he kept the equity staff intact because he believed, just as his father did, that one day the market would rebound, and he wanted the firm to be ready. Unlike his father, however, he was unwilling to wait for that to happen. By then, he realized, it might be too late.

So he turned to money market funds. In this he was not alone; arch-rival Dreyfus, which was then a larger and better-known mutual fund company, had already created a money market fund after seeing the success of the Reserve Fund. Other fund companies followed suit. They all viewed money funds as a stopgap measure that could keep them afloat until the stock market turned around. A money market fund would never be a major source of profit for a mutual fund company—because of the pressure to keep yields as high as possible, the management fee would necessarily be small—but it was a finger in the dike.

What was unique to Johnson was his insistence that Fidelity's money market fund come with check-writing privileges. He never considered doing it any other way, even though it proved to be a daunting technical challenge, requiring a complicated arrangement with a bank, and complex computer capabilities. It was expensive. It cost Fidelity time—time during which Dreyfus and the others came out with their money funds. And all the while the market continued to swoon, and money continued to leave Fidelity.

As word of his fund's prospectus spread, the mutual fund industry was stunned at what Ned Johnson was trying to do. It wasn't so much the technical hurdles that stunned them, but the philosophy that underlay his willingness to allow customers to write checks against their money market fund. In doing so, Johnson was turning his back on one of the industry's most firmly held beliefs. "Make it easy to put money into a fund," went the old mutual fund saw, "but hard to take money out." It often took weeks to redeem mutual fund shares—weeks of paperwork going back and forth in the mail, with silly requirements for notaries and signature guarantees and the like. Though no one ever said it in so many words, the idea was that if you made it hard for people to withdraw from a fund, they wouldn't bother.

Check writing turned this idea on its head. With Johnson's fund, it would actually be easier to take money out of a money market fund than to put it in. "Our philosophy was that if you made it easy to withdraw your money, you'd wind up getting more of it," says Johnson now. It sounds like a very basic observation, but it was a powerful new notion at the time. It meant that Johnson had begun to think of Fidelity not as a company that managed funds but as one that sold *products*, the same as any other consumer goods company. Consumer companies succeeded not by resisting the wishes of customers but by embracing those wishes. Customers returned to McDonald's because it made their life easier, not harder. Ned Johnson was going to do that now too. He was going to treat investors like consumers, people whose money he had to fight for, since they had other places to put it—and would soon have many more such places. That's what check writing implied.

Johnson's instincts proved to be completely right, of course. After a year and a half of pushing his employees to bring the fund to life, the Fidelity Daily Income Trust was an instant, unqualified hit when it opened in May 1974. Customers loved the check-writing feature (even if there was an initial requirement that no check could be written for less than $1,000: "We didn't want people using it to pay for their dry cleaning," one ex-employee remembers). With check writing, FDIT didn't just resemble a bank account; it was better than a bank account. Federal Reserve rules required banks to offer passbook accounts that paid interest or checking accounts that didn't. Fidelity was offering check writing and interest in the same account. By the end of 1974, the fund had pulled in $500 million, much of it from people who had never put a penny in a Fidelity fund before. Soon, people at Fidelity were revising their opinion of their new boss.

Unlike Bent and Brown, or Benham, Ned Johnson did not rely on word of mouth to promote his new fund. Here came the next new wrinkle: he relied on advertising, just like any other consumer-product company. This was another one of those decisions that made everyone at Fidelity nervous. But what choice did he have? The broker network was dead. Even if that hadn't been the case, what broker would be willing to sell a money market fund, which had no commission attached? So Fidelity had to learn how to sell the fund itself. Johnson hired an ad man named Alan Holliday, who happened to be a long-time Fidelity investor. Holliday began writing a series of ads for the fund. "Fidelity's Money Market Fund," read the headline of one early ad, "the one with the check redemption feature." If this effort seems less than inspired, the fault lay not with Holliday but with the SEC, which considered his work so racy that the agency regularly called Johnson to force him to tone it down. One touch Holliday always put in the ads was a little picture of a phone at the bottom corner. This was at Johnson's insistence; he was sure the picture would offer a subliminal reinforcement to the basic message, which was that people should call Fidelity's new 800 number and obtain a money market fund prospectus.

And so it went: the need to advertise led to the need to deal with customers directly. Johnson hired people whose sole duty was to answer the phones. There were five of them in the beginning, stuck in a little windowless room, frantically writing down orders and requests. As FDIT got more popular, the five were overwhelmed, and pretty soon there wasn't an executive in the place who wasn't answering the phones during peak times, Johnson included. This, in turn, led to a new computerized phone system, like the ones the airlines used for their reservation systems. And that led to new and more sophisticated computers, and new personnel to handle customer requests and market the fund and man the computers. Before FDIT, Fidelity had been, in effect, a wholesale company, providing a product to retailers. Now it was turning into a retail company, selling directly to customers. With at least this one product, the money market fund, Johnson had control of his destiny in a way he'd never had before.

And gradually, it all led to the next big idea: if you could sell money market funds directly to the public, why couldn't you sell equity mutual funds that way too? Why did you have to continue relying on brokers who were so openly hostile? And why did you even have to impose a load on mutual funds? That money was supposed to be a commission for the brokers, but they had lost interest in selling the product.

The answer was that you didn't have to do any of those things. You could sell mutual funds the same way you sold money market funds: directly to the public, without having to charge a commission that went to a middleman. You could advertise mutual funds and promote their performance yourself. You could have your phone staff handle requests for mutual funds as well as money market funds. You could program your computers to spit out statements, and chart the daily changes in the funds. You could turn your entire operation into a retail operation, instead of just the money market fund division. You could control *all* of your own destiny, not just a piece of it.

To Johnson, this was the inescapable logic of the success of his money market fund. As he would prove over the next decade, it was a logic he willingly and eagerly embraced.

## CHAPTER 5

# "Here Come the Revolutionaries"

## *July 1970*

W HEN BUSINESSMEN ARE at loggerheads, bickering over how to solve some sticky crisis, their first instinct is to form a committee. Committees offer at least the illusion of progress. Thus it was that on that October afternoon in 1968, Dee Hock stood up after lunch before the assembled group of angry BankAmericard members and suggested that they form a committee. More specifically, he proposed that the licensees set up a permanent, seven-member "executive" committee that could advise the Bank of America on how to right its troubled credit card program. This was hardly an innovative solution, but the bankers were so happy to hear somebody suggest *something* that they stood up and applauded. After electing Hock chairman, they all went home, feeling slightly cheerier than they had when the day began.

Except Hock. For despite being the person to broach the idea to the others, he himself was not at all convinced it would work, and he'd offered it up to the idea-starved bankers only after much pleading from the Bank of America, which didn't dare make the suggestion itself. Yet the committee that emerged from that hornet's nest of a meeting wound up working remarkably to Hock's advantage. Once Hock placed himself at the center of the process, he could begin maneuvering everybody in the direction he wanted them to go. This he did over the next seven months, in a feat of politicking so deft that most bankers never realized they were being maneuvered.

He employed his chairmanship as a bully pulpit, which he used to convince both the member banks and the Bank of America that licensing had reached a dead end. He did this by showing them that their problems were actually worse than they thought. He preached to them about how credit card crime had become a national, rather than a local, problem, with the Mafia muscling into the stolen card business. He showed them how interchange was a mess not at one bank or even a hundred, but at all of them. ("The present system of drawing individual drafts daily on every bank in the system, and of *mailing the actual items to each bank* simply will not hold up under future growth," Hock later wrote.)[1] He talked about how the haphazard authorization system was not just inefficient but deeply damaging, and about how the current rules allowing each bank to conduct its own BankAmericard advertising campaign was making for duplication, not to mention some truly bad advertising. (One bank was promoting its Bank-Americard as "the card you can't go berserk with.")

Armed with this broader information, Hock was able to impress on everyone just how intractable their difficulties had become. And *still* they made no headway. "It became quite clear," Hock later wrote, "that the voluntary group, working with [the Bank of America] under the powers of the existing licensing agreements, could not begin to cope with the problems that required immediate attention."

Surely, this was the outcome Hock expected. More than likely, it was the outcome he had hoped for. The lack of progress would make the assembled bankers more desperate than ever, and their growing desperation would lead them to the second part of Hock's unspoken agenda. If BankAmericard were to remain viable, some completely new organization would have to rise from the ashes to save it. Hock had not yet figured out what shape this organization would take. But he knew one thing: the new group would have to strip Bank of America of its proudest creation. That is to say, it would have to gain control of the BankAmericard trademark, while breaking free of the bank.

What made Hock think he could pull off such a feat? The simple answer was that nobody had a bigger stake in saving the system than Bank of America. It was by far the largest issuer of BankAmericards and the only issuer in the country making any money; those profits would vanish if the system collapsed. And to its credit, even the Bank of America seemed to realize that the creation had outgrown the creator.

Seeing how events were moving, the Bank of America could have made things difficult. But it never did. It let Hock play out his hand. There were rough patches along the way, of course, and inevitable resentments. "Here come the revolutionaries," Larkin used to crack when Hock and his staff walked into a negotiating session with bank officials. Yet it was Larkin's job to negotiate this separation with Hock, and he did so graciously, because that was the way a Bank of America man was supposed to act at such times. Larkin was a gentleman, at a bank run by gentlemen.

By the spring of 1969, Hock had convinced all involved that the old licensing system was untenable. That May, with the Bank of America's blessing, he formed one more committee, consisting of himself and three hand-picked allies. On a Monday morning, the four men checked into the Alta Mira Hotel in Sausalito, California, where they stayed for the rest of the week. Their mission was to devise the shape of the new organization that everyone now agreed needed to be created. As Hock later put it, in a speech, "We, like the founding fathers, have the need for a more sophisticated vehicle to insure to all the benefits to be derived from combined effort."

Can you picture the joy with which Hock greeted the task that faced him that week? At the midpoint of his life, resigned to being a minor banking executive in Seattle, he was suddenly being handed the chance to leave his mark upon the world. (*Just like the founding fathers!*) If it worked as he hoped, his new organization would not only save a troubled industry, but would touch the life of every American who carried a credit card. One of Hock's least attractive qualities is his false modesty, but he was never modest about what he created that week. He fell in love with what he did in Sausalito.

What was there to love? Quite a bit, if you were Dee Hock. The organization that emerged from that week's retreat was full of the kind of paradoxes that engaged his mind. For instance, although it was being set up to solve a specific set of credit card problems, Hock refused to discuss any such problems in Sausalito. The four men could only discuss principles, he said; if the principles[2] of the new organization were sound, then the solutions would fall into place. The most basic principle: who should own the group? The member banks should own it jointly, they decided. This principle embodied not one but two paradoxes. The first was that through the creation of this cooperative venture, the member banks would be better able to compete with each other in the credit card business. The second was that such an organization, where bankers met regularly, abided by joint operating regulations, and shared data, managed nonetheless to stay on the right side of the nation's antitrust laws.

Another principle decided that week: the new organization would be run by a group of directors—"small enough to work effectively, yet large enough to represent all interests and areas adequately"—which would consist of officials of the member banks. Hock shrewdly worked out a cumulative voting system that prevented any one kind of bank from dominating the twenty-four-member[3] board: eastern banks couldn't blackball western banks, big banks couldn't steamroller small ones.[4] He replaced the loosely worded BankAmericard interchange payment system with a new system, based on a sliding scale of fees, that would be paid to the new organization. He established a series of stiff fines to prevent member banks from cheating the system. To assuage the Bank of America's pride, he devised a plan to give it a larger say for the first few years, granting it five board seats, a number that would be gradually reduced to one. By the time he was done, he had created a for-profit, member-owned, Delaware-incorporated company, which he named National BankAmericard Inc.: NBI for short. This is the organization we now know as Visa.

In his more prosaic moments, Hock would describe NBI as an enabling organization, which it certainly was. Its purpose—in addition to keeping the BankAmericard system from collapsing—was to build the behind-the-scenes apparatus that would enable banks to run their credit card operations smoothly and profitably. The banks always saw its role as this and nothing more. Hock, however, viewed his brainchild as a great deal more, and at times, he could lapse into a description that bordered on the rhapsodic. "This was the first time in a 200- or 300-year-old industry—and perhaps the first time in any commercial enterprise—that an enormous number of immensely powerful, tradition-bound enterprises voluntarily surrendered autonomy to a central organization for a common purpose," he declared on more than one occasion. "Visa transcended language, politics, economic theory, culture, currency, geography, and law."

Power at NBI would reside with the board of directors. As the president of NBI, Hock would have a seat on the board; theoretically, his voice would be one among many. But it was implausible that Hock would be content merely carrying out whatever directives emerged from the quarterly board meetings. It was a point of pride with him that because he didn't trust power, didn't like what it did to people, he had seen to it that the only power that resided with his own position as president of NBI was the power to persuade. But this was Hock at his most coy. It was precisely his ability to persuade that made him powerful.

He proved it right away, by inducing the BankAmericard members to join the newly created NBI. There was no subtlety now. In late June 1970, he put out the word that if the licensees were going to join the new association, they would have to do so by September 28—thereby setting one of those completely arbitrary deadlines that takes on a life of its own. He insisted that every NBI board member be a top official at the bank, not some powerless middle manager. The members agreed. He wrote bylaws that gave NBI the power to establish operating regulations, set ground rules, impose penalties.

They agreed. Bank of America wanted $5 million for its trademark; Hock, knowing the new organization would never be able to afford that much all at once, offered the bank twice as much, so long as the payments could be spread out. Larkin and his superiors agreed. He held a meeting with the chairmen of the largest banks in the system, laid out the plan, and asked them to approve the new corporation. They did. When he sent the plan to all the other banks that June, he told them he would not negotiate changes or make exceptions. By the time the deadline arrived, only twenty-two banks had not signed up. Soon afterward, everyone was on board.

And on July 9, 1970, even before the members had all joined, the new corporation held its first formal board meeting. Samuel Stewart, a courtly Southerner who was one of Bank of America's three top executives, was elected chairman of the board.[5] Then, according to the minutes of that meeting, "Mr. Stewart reviewed and the Board approved . . . the provisions of an employment contract under which Dee W. Hock would be employed as president." They gave him a three-year contract, a salary of $40,000, the authority to begin hiring a staff, and a mandate to save them from themselves. By the time that first contract expired, he had done that and quite a bit more. For better or worse, what Hock did in those early years at NBI is what made bank credit cards an integral part of American life.

*FOR BETTER OR WORSE.* Which was it? Which *is* it? In some deep way, this has always been the central question about credit cards. Did the easy access to credit made possible by bank cards enhance our lives, giving us access to middle-class accoutrements that had been previously out of reach? Or did it make it more difficult, since that money eventually had to be repaid? Were Americans capable of using credit wisely? Or was it inevitable that credit cards would eventually cause financial distress? Americans were inclined to think the worst. When the credit card fiasco of the late 1960s aroused critics like Ralph Nader and Wright Patman, the only people who rose in defense of bank cards were the bankers themselves. The phrase "credit card society" was coined right around this same time; the country quickly embraced its wholly negative connotation.

Indeed the central contradiction embedded in America's historic attitude toward credit—that we viewed it as dangerous and even sinful while using it more freely than any society ever has—was only exacerbated by the popularity of credit cards. It brought credit out of the closet, made us grapple with our subconscious feelings about debt and temptation. It symbolized all our mixed and muddled feelings on the subject.

There *was* temptation in credit cards, after all—how could anyone deny it? Almost from the moment bank cards were created, bankers insisted that the American middle class handled credit responsibly. "Ninety-eight percent of the people with cards just do very well," Ken Larkin liked to say, voicing the unanimous opinion of the banking community. Yet it was also true that every year increasing numbers of people filed for bankruptcy. Surely, credit card debt had *something* to do with that fact.

Similarly, if people harbored a suspicion that they bought more impulsively because their credit cards made such buying easy, they were right. People spent more in a store when they used a credit card than when they used cash—that was a verifiable fact. Indeed, it was a key selling point in the early days, when the banking industry was trying to persuade merchants to accept cards. Why would people spend more with cards than cash? Who could say? "Plastic cards have an anesthetizing effect," speculates Stephen M. Pollan, the writer and financial adviser. "They allow people to temporarily ignore the question of whether they can really afford something or not."

Credit cards, in sum, were a psychological minefield, though not a minefield any banker wanted to muck around in. Consequently, the first serious inquiry into American attitudes toward credit cards was conducted not by a banker but by a curious academic. His name was Lewis Mandell, who was then an economist at the University of Michigan.[6] Each year, the university's Survey Research Center, where Mandell worked, conducted a massive Survey of Consumer Finances. In the early 1970s, when he noticed that more than half of the people surveyed had a credit card, Mandell began including questions about credit card attitudes and habits. At around the same time Dee Hock was gearing up NBI, Mandell was arriving at a simple, startling conclusion: "Americans," he wrote in a short book entitled *Credit Card Use in the United States,* "are far more likely to use credit cards than to approve of them."

"Few Americans tend to think of credit cards as a good thing whether they use them or not," Mandell noted. "Some 75 percent of all respondents said that credit cards made it too easy to buy things that they may not really want or can't really afford. On the other hand," he added, noting the incongruity that still exists, "when asked about the advantages of credit cards, the most frequent response related to the credit feature—the fact that a family could buy without having the money and pay the bank back over time."

Mandell found that 81 percent of families with an income of at least $25,000 used credit cards while fewer than 20 percent of families making less than $3,000 relied on credit cards. This made obvious sense, of course—as Mandell put it, "[I]t is reasonable to assume that persons with higher incomes, who purchase more goods, will be more apt to use a mechanism such as the credit card which facilitates these transactions." (They were also more apt to be able to get their hands on credit cards than low-income families.) Another of Mandell's findings was that the younger the family, the better the chance that it relied on credit cards. This, too, made sense, partly because of the stiff resistance to credit cards among older people, but also because credit cards have always felt less threatening to younger people, whose careers are just beginning, and who can feel optimistic about their prospects for promotions and raises. It was logical that young married couples, with small children, were the most likely to carry large revolving balances, and that people in the western half of the country were more likely to carry credit cards than people in the East (since bank credit cards had begun as a West Coast phenomenon).

Logic explained only so much, however. Because the subject of money is so fraught with emotion, there would always be patterns of behavior that were inexplicable except to the person exhibiting the behavior. How to explain, for instance, that people who used credit cards tended to write more checks per month than those who didn't? This finding directly contradicted the theory, widely held in banking circles, that credit cards would help eliminate checks. When asked to name the advantages of credit cards, almost no one mentioned one of their biggest advantages—the initial "float" that gave users a month-long, interest-free loan before the bill came due. When asked to name the disadvantages of credit cards, barely 10 percent of those surveyed mentioned the biggest disadvantage: the 18 percent-a-year interest rate, which was much higher than the interest on other kinds of loans. In fact, Mandell noted, "There is some recent evidence that a large proportion of credit card users don't know the interest that they must pay on their account."[7] The economist was particularly perplexed by the percentage of wealthier families who carried a credit card balance. It was only 15 percent, but that seemed awfully high to Mandell, since they clearly had the means to avoid those lofty interest rates. Their behavior, Mandell concluded, was "irrational."

Most of all, though, Mandell discovered that people were afraid of their own consumer impulses. What they most dreaded was not the card itself but their ability to handle their new freedom to go into debt whenever they wanted: "[F]ully three-quarters of all American families said that such a card tempts one to buy more than is necessary. This reason," Mandell added, "was given more frequently in every conceivable type of grouping." And then he quoted some of those surveyed. A "well-educated thirty-eight-year-old westerner, who uses several cards himself" said, "I think, as a whole, Americans are poor managers of money, and credit cards just add to this." A fifty-nine-year-old man said, "[The banks] force these things onto people. Young people get into trouble with them because they haven't had the experience." A fifty-three-year-old widow said that cards were "bad, if used for pleasure." A "fifty-five-year-old westerner with a grade school education who didn't use any cards" said, "I'd put a match to them. They are a detriment, the biggest one the United States ever had."

Did Dee Hock ever give any thought to this most elemental of credit card paradoxes? His fondness for paradoxes notwithstanding, the answer seems to be: not if he could help it. Surely, he had to understand the mixed feelings many Americans had when they pulled out their credit cards; his finance company career had forced him to see firsthand the dangers of debt. He had even known what it was to fear his own consumer desires; once, after quitting one of his finance company jobs, he had cut up his own store charge plate.

Yet the subject of debt was just not something he ever talked about very much. Yes, when the occasion called for it, he could trot out the statistics that proved that the middle class could handle debt.[8] He could defend the 18 percent interest rate with the best of them. But on the question of whether debt was good or bad, healthy or unhealthy, an engine of American prosperity or the surest route to hell—that was a debate that never engaged him. When it came to the one thing cards were most often used for—the creation of an instant, unsecured personal loan—he would say only what was expected of him, and nothing more.

Did he prefer not to talk about debt because it diminished, in his mind at least, the true potential of the bank card? Probably. Was he averting his gaze from something he preferred not to dwell on? Quite possibly. Did he think that his central idea—namely that a plastic card should be seen as a "medium of exchange" interchangeable with cash—was so compelling that the issue of debt scarcely deserved to be uttered in the same breath? Without a doubt.

But in the beginning especially, there was another reason he didn't spend much time dwelling on how Americans felt about the product he was trying to get them to use. He had too much else to do. He was trying to dig BankAmericard out of its hole while there was still time.

ALMOST FROM THE START, there were whispers, closed-door meetings, furtive huddles in the halls of Dee Hock's new association. No one can remember anymore when the whispers started, only that they began early, and that you could hear them if you put your ear to the ground. Of the handful of men whom Hock hired in the fall of 1970, at least four were plotting his overthrow.

On the one hand, theirs was a hopeless exercise. Did they really believe they could go to the NBI board of directors, as they planned to do, and persuade it to fire the very man who had dreamed up the organization most bankers viewed as their last, best hope for credit card survival? The answer should have been obvious. Not that the coup instigators ever got the chance to find out. Well before they were ready to carry out their plans, Hock uncovered the plot and fired the ringleader. Then he fired two of the other three plotters, but spaced out the dismissals over the course of a year, so that the departures would seem unconnected. The board never even knew a plot had been afoot.

On the other hand, you could see the plotters' point. Most of these early hires were older men, in the twilight of their careers, brought in because of their credit card experience. Their station in life caused them to expect a certain corporate style: nice offices, long lunches, easy-to-meet deadlines. At NBI, however, the pace was frenetic, the deadlines unceasing. The quarters, leftover Bank of America office space, were so cramped that you had to go through Hock's office to get to the bathroom. And as for lunch, it was gulped on the run—assuming there was time to eat at all.

Most of all, none of these men—or any of the hundreds of employees who followed them—had ever come up against a boss like Dee Hock before. It was not so much that he was a benevolent tyrant; it was that he seemed to have a small handful of personalities residing within him, one of which was the benevolent Hock, another the tyrannical Hock. In one moment, he was asking you about your health and insisting you take some time off, sending flowers to your wife because you'd been away from home for so long, fighting with the board to get you a bonus he felt you deserved. In the next moment, he could turn on you, transforming himself into a different creature, dark and unlikable.

He would "devastate" people, recalls one former NBI hand; "he could be fairly savage to people," says another. He employed a style of management that would later be called "creative tension," pitting one executive against another. Occasionally, he held "blue sky sessions" with his staff, meaning that any idea was open to discussion. But as soon as someone brought up an idea Hock disagreed with, he would cut him down mercilessly. "It seemed that the only way he could build himself up was by tearing the people around him down," recalls an ex-employee.

Those were two of Hock's personalities. Here was a third: It would be late
in the afternoon, and Hock would wave you into his office. He was in a
mood to talk. He would talk about his frustrations with the board and about
his dreams for his beloved payment system, about his childhood in hard-
scrabble Utah and his love of the Great Books. Two or three hours later, you
went home feeling that you knew this boss better than you'd ever known a
boss in your life, and feeling closer to this boss as well. Yet that warm
feeling passed quickly, because you also knew the lengths to which Hock
went to keep you at a distance. It was extraordinarily rare for an NBI
employee to so much as step inside Hock's house, for instance. The distance
between his personal life and his work life was both absolute and unbridgeable.

A fourth personality: Hock was the micromanager from hell—so obsessive about details that for the first year he insisted that no letter could leave
NBI headquarters without his personal approval. He was known to make his
staff redo the cover of the annual report nine times before he would approve
it. He tinkered endlessly with the copy of BankAmericard ads. He had an
obsession with neatness; employees who left papers on their desks were sure
to find a cranky note from Hock the next morning. Even after he had stopped
reading the outgoing correspondence and was delegating responsibility, "he
continued"—in the flowery words of the Harvard professor who wrote the
Visa case study—"to probe the thoughts of his key managers with a me-
ticulous precision that bordered on inquisition."

He had other idiosyncrasies as a manager, not the least of which was that
he didn't view himself as a manager, but rather as a leader—an important
distinction in his mind. "Most great leaders," he declared to the man from
Harvard, "don't follow strict rules. . . . Management," he continued, "is
an art. . . ." Hock, of course, saw himself as an artist of the first rank, but
from his staff's point of view, he used some awfully strange brush strokes.
He wouldn't allow employees to put nameplates on their office doors. He
insisted that the corporate directory be alphabetized by first names, even
after the staff had grown to several hundred. And every six months or so, he
would reorganize the executive ranks. At NBI, he liked to say, they were in
the business of managing change; changing the innards of the organization
helped remind people of that.

His relations with the board of directors was a trickier bit of business. He
couldn't get away with bullying the board, nor could he reorganize it at will.
He had to employ other techniques to get what he wanted. He had to lobby
and line up allies. He had to make speeches and employ personal appeals.
His most dramatic technique, which he resorted to more often than he should

have, was to threaten to resign; such threats often came during negotiations over Hock's salary. Mostly, though, he simply wore the board down in his relentless pursuit of his goals. For weeks prior to a board meeting, Hock and his staff would practice their presentation, until he was satisfied that there was nothing the board members could ask him that he couldn't answer. And then, during the meeting, Hock would make his case—"lecturing us as if we were children," recalls a former board member—with a kind of lead-with-the-chin belligerence that seemed to defy disagreement.

Hock had one last personality in his repertoire, and in those early days especially, it was the most important of all. For all his flaws, Dee Hock could be a genuinely inspiring man. He was a figure of true charisma, the central focus at NBI, the person whose approval every employee yearned for. Even at his bullying worst, he had a remarkable ability to create a feeling of esprit. He made it possible for people to believe what he himself believed: that in creating this new payment system, they were doing something that mattered a great deal. "He saw himself as a revolutionary," recalls one longtime Visa employee, "and he made you think of yourself that way too." A job interview with Hock consisted of listening to him talk, as he spun out his vision of a plastic future, in which a small card would unlock the financial universe. He could be mesmerizing at such moments, especially to someone who had never thought about payment systems or the nature of money as an "exchange device." It was hard not to be hooked. "In the early years," says a longtime Visa hand named Robert Miller, "I would have done anything for him."

NBI offered no benefits in the beginning. The pay was miserable. The hours were long. It didn't matter. What mattered was that Dee Hock—*with your help!*—was changing the world. In the cool light of day, this seems like a terribly inflated claim to make for what is, after all, only a credit card. But at the root of Hock's charisma was his ability to inspire others to embrace his grand vision—and inspire them to reach heights they had never before approached.

"How could you hate a guy who pulled the best out of you when you didn't think you had anything left?" reflects Thomas Honey, a former Visa executive who fell out of Hock's good graces toward the end of the eleven years he spent there. Honey continues:

> A lot of it was oppressive—the hours spent sitting around endless board meetings, or getting beaten up by Hock, or doing things that seemed crazy. I think a lot of people have the impression that there were only those hateful parts. But that's not true. It was a time of great highs and lows—a time in our

lives we all cherish. If there is one reason we still talk about it, it is because we want it back.

As much as anything, computer technology made the money revolution possible. Computers are the hidden spine of every modern financial device; they are what separate the old world of Charlie Merrill and A. P. Giannini from the new one that Ned Johnson and Dee Hock were building. True, some clever soul could have created a money market fund without computers, but it could never have been made to look and feel like a bank account, which was the key to its success. And plainly, bankers could make loans without computers, as they had done for centuries. But they couldn't make unsecured personal loans triggered whenever a borrower handed a piece of encoded plastic to a merchant.

Think for a minute about what happens today when you pay for something with a credit card. The storekeeper runs your card through a little machine that is part telephone and part computer, an action that triggers a phone call. When the call goes through, he then keys in the purchase price. While he fills out the credit receipt, you and he wait for the machine to "authorize" the purchase. If the process takes more than a minute, you begin to get impatient. This is not because a minute is a long time, but because you expect the process to go faster than that. It's the same impatience that you feel at a long red light.

What you don't see in this process is . . . well, you don't see much of anything. You don't see the impressive network that connects credit card computer centers all over the world. You don't see the electron speeding from your credit card, finding the right computer, searching through a database to make sure that credit limit is large enough to afford to purchase, and finally sending the answer back to the merchant. You're also not seeing the way other computers are processing the transaction for other reasons: setting up the interchange fees among the banks that are party to the transaction, storing the information so that it will appear on your next bill, and so on. It's a complicated array of things that you don't see, but it all happens so quickly and smoothly that you don't even think about it.

Here, then, was another paradox: computers weren't important only because they managed highly complex tasks; they were important because they *disguised* highly complex tasks. By making a complicated process invisible, computers allowed people to forget about the complexity, and focus instead on what was visible: namely, how easy the thing was to use. "For a great financial device to catch on," says banking consultant Edward Furash, "it must appear simple." That was true of money market funds; it was true of mutual funds; it was true of automatic teller machines; and it was especially true of credit cards. Hock is the one who stitched together the disguise. Even the bankers who dislike him give him his due for erecting the system—"the switch," as they call it in the trade—that exists today.

He did it by building a huge computer network, anchored by two monster mainframes that took up the better part of a new low-rise office building in nearby San Mateo, California. Once they were up and running, the mainframes would act as the pulsing heart of Hock's payment system. Just as the heart circulates blood through the body, so did NBI's computers keep the flow of information moving, sucking in authorization requests from merchants and pushing out answers, absorbing the day's transactions from around the world—more than 200 million transactions in 1974, nearly 6 billion by 1992—and automatically settling up with every bank in the system, so that each banker that issued a BankAmericard knew when he got to work in the morning how much his bank had paid out the day before and how much it had taken in.

The idea of setting up a national computer network was not original to Hock. Even before NBI was formed, many bankers had concluded that such a system was necessary. Most immediately, computers were needed to handle the authorization process. Computers, as everyone in the business realized, would cut down drastically on the time it took for a merchant to obtain an authorization; they would make authorizations more accurate; they would eliminate the time-zone problem, in which a person from Boston couldn't charge something late in the day in Los Angeles because his bank back at home was closed. And on and on.

In fact, the first organization to propose a central authorization system wasn't a bank at all; it was American Express. The company had in mind a giant system that would handle not only BankAmericard but Master Charge cards and American Express cards. Although many bankers were amenable to this idea, Hock was not among them. Because American Express issued its own plastic card—its own "medium of exchange" as he tended to think of it—Hock believed that the company was the implacable enemy of the nation's banks, and he was determined to treat it as such. At one of his first board meetings, Hock stopped the American Express effort cold. We have to control our own destiny, he argued to the board; we can't be at the mercy of a potential competitor like American Express. Therefore, he said, NBI would build its own system, for the exclusive use of its members. A few days later, a small notice appeared in *The American Banker,* the daily newspaper of the banking industry, announcing that NBI was abandoning the talks with American Express and would build its own authorization system. To the general disbelief of the industry, Hock set out to build his system. He called it BankAmericard Service Exchange: BASE I.

The only thing their disbelief really showed was how paralyzed the banking industry had become. As it turns out, the hardware Hock employed to create his system was strictly off the shelf. Special software had to be written, but IBM and Digital Equipment Corporation were already building machines with more than enough power to handle the needs of a nationwide credit card system. And businesses like the airlines had already shown that you could create a network linking computers across the country via telephone lines.

By May of 1972, Hock had hired a computer staff to his liking—he'd fired his first computer staff after it drew up plans for a $10 million state-of-the-art system—and he had a design he could live with: by using existing technology, the new team had cut the price to $3 million. Hock took that figure to the board, which approved the expense. He also promised the board that their long-awaited authorization system would be up and running by April 1, 1973—an impossible deadline, of course.

It was also a dangerous deadline, for Hock had never tried to build something for the system before. As an outsider in the tight little world of consumer banking, he didn't have a lifetime of friendships he could fall back on. He could not afford to fail to deliver on this promise—it was still too early in the game, and there was too much at stake.

Perhaps that explains why, for most of the next year, Hock was an even more demanding boss than he had been before. He seemed to be everywhere, doing everything—riding herd over the computer group, overseeing the construction of the new building in San Mateo, hiring staff, traveling the country, preparing the banks for the big change that was coming. Rumors began filtering across the country that Interbank, the competing association managing Master Charge, was putting together its own authorization system, which only prodded everyone at NBI to stay longer and work harder. "We were running on fear," recalls Aram Tootelian, a computer specialist who set up BASE I.

Did they meet the deadline? Of course they did. In July, Tootelian was hired to oversee the project. Four months later, NBI took delivery of several Digital mainframe computers, though they could not be installed because the San Mateo building had not been completed. It was a mess that fall; heavy rain turned the San Mateo construction site into a pool of mud. A feeling of gloom descended upon the NBI computer staff. But then, in January, they held a big meeting with the seventy-six largest member banks,[9] and it was there that they could see that they were closing in on their goal. The members were no longer squabbling with each other; progress was visible. By February, small-scale testing had begun. Over the next few months, there was the usual bout of last-minute catastrophes, but finally, on March 30,

NBI and the banks were all connected, and ready for their first full-scale, two-hour test. It failed. The next day, they did it again. This time—O lucky day!—everything worked. By April 4, the members began using the new system for a few hours a day, and by May 1, 1973, the system was running twenty-four hours a day.

The project had taken nine months, start to finish. It had cost $3 million, just as Hock had promised. Within a year, it had saved its members at least $30 million. And it finally smoked out Interbank. After Hock introduced BASE I at a press conference in San Francisco, Interbank hastily announced that it was also working on a proprietary authorization system for Master Charge. That system would be up and running, Interbank promised, by May . . . *1974*. You could almost hear the chortles at NBI.

That first system was not completely computerized—not the way authorization is today, when a credit card purchase can be approved without the intervention of a single human being. Still, it was a huge step forward. When a merchant called to get a purchase approved, the call was automatically "switched" by the NBI system to the right bank: no more fumbling for the correct phone number. The customer's outstanding balance was on computer, as was any information about whether the card was stolen: no more fumbling with unwieldy printouts either. If the bank was closed, the call would be automatically "switched" to NBI, which acted as a backup for all the member banks. During peak hours, it could process 5,000 requests an hour. There were duplicate computers in case the main ones broke down.

The point is this: it worked exactly the way it was supposed to work. On the day BASE I went into effect, the average time it took to approve an authorization request dropped from over five minutes to around fifty-six seconds. By today's standards—with the average approval time now down to around seven seconds—this still seems like a long time. But for someone standing at a checkout counter in 1973, the difference between five minutes and fifty-six seconds was enormous. Quite often, it was the difference between deciding to use a credit card and deciding that it was easier to use cash. This was the moment when credit cards passed over the threshold from mildly useful device to near-necessity.

A year later, just as Interbank was getting the bugs out of its authorization computers, Hock once again held a press conference, this time to announce that BankAmericard interchange had also been computerized. Now the "clearing" and "setting" process would be done electronically as well. Again, Hock had brought the project in on time and on budget—BASE II, as the system was called, cost around $7 million—and again, the members saw benefits right away. BASE II cut out $12 million in mailing costs alone in its first year of operation. And again, Interbank was forced to make the embarrassing announcement that it was also creating a computerized interchange system, except that it wasn't . . . quite . . . ready . . . yet. That's the way it usually went for Interbank in those mid-1970s days. It was the larger of the two systems, with more cards in circulation and higher sales volume. But that was because Interbank had three and four times the member banks that NBI did, not because it ran a better system. In the offices of NBI, the contempt for their credit card rival was palpable, the sense of superiority not even thinly disguised. "There was a certain arrogance in the way we did things," recalls a veteran Visa hand. When, in 1974, Hock proposed that NBI take over the international side of BankAmericard, which was still run by Bank of America and beginning to face the same problems that had once tormented the American members, who was going to tell him he couldn't?

Certainly not the board. However much his manner grated, they were deeply gratified by what he had accomplished. He had used the new organization as the means to solve their once-intractable problems. With his system of rules and fees, he had eliminated their attempts to take advantage of each other, and finally put them in a position to make a profit on credit cards. He had coordinated such important matters as promotion and advertising—BankAmericard's first nationwide slogan was "Think of It as Money." By 1974, BankAmericard had overtaken American Express in sales volume, and was closing in on the much larger Interbank. Hock's computerized "switch" had made credit cards such an integral part of American life that even critics like William Proxmire began carrying them.[10]

Once, late in his tenure at Visa, Hock told a reporter that he had never expected to last more than three years; he assumed that to do the job right, he'd have to so alienate the member banks that they would get rid of him. It's hard to know whether he really believed that or not, but it's certainly not how things turned out. After his first three-year contract was up, the board granted Hock a new four-year pact, with a healthy raise. They also offered to set up a deferred income program that would assure him income for the rest of his life. (Hock turned the offer down.) Far from being alienated, they were thrilled.

And they would have stayed thrilled if only Hock had been content to manage what he had put in place. "Visa was a *switch*," grumbled Ken Larkin many years later, still rankled by Hock's refusal to accept that assessment. "That's all it was." But Hock could never accept that; he had bigger ideas, grander plans. By then, Dee Hock himself had begun to "think of it as money." That is, he had begun to believe that the very nature of money was about to be transformed by electronic networks like the one he had just built—and that whoever controlled those networks would also control the nation's "medium of exchange." It was this belief, and Hock's insistent attempts to act on it, that brought him during the next decade into increasingly bitter conflict with the bankers whose hides he had just saved.

## CHAPTER SIX

# The Luckiest Entrepreneur

## *May 1975*

A SUCCESSFUL COMPANY in America almost always creates, over the course of its life, a kind of internal mythology—a stock set of images and stories that are passed along over the years, refined and embroidered until they form a seamless corporate narrative. At Apple Computer, the corporate mythology begins in Steve Jobs's garage, where he and his friend Steve Wozniak created the personal computer. At Electronic Data Systems, it begins when founder H. Ross Perot picked up a copy of *Reader's Digest* in a barbershop, read Thoreau's famous words—"The mass of men lead lives of quiet desperation"—and had his epiphany.

And at Charles Schwab & Co., the corporate mythology begins on May 1, 1975—"Mayday," as they still call it on Wall Street, the momentous day when the New York Stock Exchange, after 183 years of enforcing a system of fixed brokerage commissions, was forced by the government to loosen its grip on commission prices so that they could be set by the forces of competition. Schwab desperately wanted to be one of those forces. It was a speck of a firm then, located not on Wall Street but in the outback of San Francisco, and founded expressly in anticipation of Mayday. Its founder and namesake, a short, shy, thirty-eight-year-old man whose previous financial venture had ended in ignominious failure, believed that an event as seismic as Mayday might create for him, at long last, a place in the financial firmament. His idea—and as usual in the money revolution, he was not the only one who had it—was that the deregulation of commissions would give rise to a new kind of brokerage firm: a firm that competed solely on the basis of price. His firm would not offer advice the way a traditional brokerage house did; it would not compile reams of research reports; it would not be staffed with energetic brokers who made handsome livings persuading customers to trade stocks. It would simply execute stock trades efficiently, for rock-bottom commissions. Even before Mayday arrived, a dozen different firms had popped up hoping to do the same thing Schwab wanted to do.[1] They were called discount brokerages.

The coming of Mayday made discount brokerages theoretically possible, but they were far from a sure thing. As the Schwab people tell the story now, the new firms were nervous about how the big wirehouses would react to their existence. Their greatest fear was that the big firms would engage in a price war, driving commissions so low that their new competitors would be run out of business. Most worrisome of all was the potential reaction of Merrill Lynch. Not only was Merrill Lynch the biggest wirehouse, but Donald Regan, who by then was running the place, was the only head of a major firm to come out in favor of commission deregulation. Everyone at Schwab assumed that Merrill Lynch would lower rates. But then Mayday arrived, and the small Schwab staff awoke to find on the front page of the *Wall Street Journal* the amazing news that Merrill Lynch was not lowering its retail commissions after all. It was *raising* them, by 10 percent.

Or so the story goes. Actually, the article in question was on page 5 of the *Journal,* not page 1; the average price increase was closer to 3 percent than the 10 percent the Schwab people remember; and the news was not a shock in any case, since it was widely known that the wirehouses did not intend to lower the commissions they charged to small investors. But it's hardly surprising that in the retelling, this bit of news would become larger and more dramatic than it really was. For Schwab, it was a moment of surpassing importance. "It created the umbrella for discount stock-brokerage," says Hugo Quackenbush, Schwab's longtime head of public relations (and keeper of the mythology). "It was one of those accidents that allowed the birth of this industry."

Regan's decision to raise the commissions Merrill Lynch charged to small customers seems fraught with significance not only because of what it has meant for Schwab—namely, everything—but because of what it has meant to the money revolution. Here was the next new financial option, which was able to blossom because larger competitors remained unaware of the threat it posed. Here was the next kind of financial firm that was proving that there were other routes besides the traditional ones. Here was the next new idea that hinged on the assumption that there were at least some Americans willing to make their own financial decisions, and assume their own level of risk.

And when Regan raised commissions on Mayday, he also signaled a changing of the guard. At that moment, it was Charles Schwab, not Regan, who was poised to champion the causes Charlie Merrill had championed all his life. It was Schwab who picked up Merrill's old slogan about "bringing

Wall Street to Main Street" and carried it into the modern age. Don Regan had known Charlie Merrill personally, had sipped brandy with the old man in Southampton, and had risen to run his old firm, something he did with tremendous vigor and no small amount of success. But he was not, in the end, the great man's natural heir. Chuck Schwab was.

Long before the word became chic, Chuck Schwab saw himself as an entrepreneur—a maverick by inclination, an outsider by choice. After he had gotten rich and famous and was expected to tell some stories about himself, he unswervingly turned to the ones that showed off his early entrepreneurial instincts. He could tell you the walnut story ("I remember, as a boy, picking up walnuts, sacking them, and then selling them for $5 a 100-pound sack"), the caddie story, or—his personal favorite—the chicken story. The latter begins with Schwab, as a twelve-year-old, making a little pocket money by selling eggs door-to-door, and reaches its climax a year later, by which time he is working every chicken-related profit angle known to man: raising the chickens, selling the eggs, killing the fryers and preparing them for market, even peddling "chicken fertilizer." It ends with Schwab "liquidating" the business, after realizing that there is more profit and less work in caddying. By then, he's fourteen.

People are usually more complicated than their personal store of uplifting anecdotes make them seem, and Schwab is no exception. Although he ran a maverick company in a nascent industry—much scorned by the Wall Street big boys—there would always be a part of him that wanted to play with the big boys. He yearned for acceptance. He had the bland good looks of a frat boy, which he had once been. He was both extremely unassuming—the result of a painful shyness—and intensely competitive.

This is an odd combination of traits for someone who professes to be an entrepreneur. But then, Schwab did not always act the part of the classic entrepreneur. There was something oddly languid about him, a blitheness about the way he ran his firm that bordered on the careless. Most entrepreneurs are fanatically hands-on personalities; Ned Johnson used to so involve himself in the minutiae of his company's computers that he sometimes knew the actual programming code. Schwab wasn't like that at all. He kept tight control only over the one aspect of the business where he was the acknowledged in-house expert—advertising and marketing. Otherwise, he allowed his lieutenants to go their own way, often to his detriment. There were never any formal staff meetings; most times, company strategy got decided over lunch at a nearby Chinese restaurant, where the handful of people running the company would yell and argue until some kind of rough consensus emerged, at least until the next day's lunch. In these sessions, Schwab acted more like a peacemaker than a founder. His employees all loved him, which he cared about more than he probably should have. Anyone who worked for Schwab in the old days can recall times when their boss called some obviously incompetent employee into his office, intending to fire the man, and wound up giving him a raise instead.

On the other hand, his competitive nature was never far from the surface. "Work hard, play hard" was the company ethos, and nobody worked harder than Schwab. There were days when he took customer orders in the morning, worked on the next day's ads in the afternoon, and then stuffed envelopes at night. He was not above sweeping the floors if that's what was needed. If he was going to fail, it was not going to be from lack of effort. And if he was going to succeed, he wasn't going to be satisfied with some middling success; he wanted the world to stand up and take notice. One former Schwab lieutenant remembers talking to his new boss shortly after Mayday, when the firm had only a dozen or so employees, and asking him how big he wanted the firm to get. "*Big*," replied Schwab. The aide persisted: was there any size at which he would begin to feel that it was more than he could manage? "No," shrugged Schwab. The aide tried one more time: "Would you rather have $100 million in revenues and 10 percent profit, or $50 million in revenues and 25 percent profit?" Without hesitating, Schwab chose the former. "You give me the growth," he said, "and I'll worry about the profit later." Peter Moss, another of Schwab's early lieutenants, remembers that sometimes, after a particularly exhilarating day, he and Schwab would talk dreamily about the firm's "manifest destiny." They actually used those words. It was as if Schwab felt that, after his early missteps, he had finally stumbled upon his fate. Given the amount of sheer good luck he entertained along the way, who can doubt it?

He was a California boy, brought up in comfortable suburban circumstances, "on the upper end of the middle class," as he describes his upbringing. Charles Schwab was born in Sacramento in 1937, grew up in nearby Woodland, and spent his teenage years in Santa Barbara, where the family moved when his father, a lawyer, joined a small firm there. The chicken story notwithstanding, he did not evince much in the way of maverick behavior: he was a nice, pleasant boy growing up in nice, pleasant surroundings. He did have an early interest in the stock market, but there was nothing terribly passionate about it, and when he went to college at Stanford, although he played the market a bit, he never let it interfere with his true passion, which was golf.

Schwab's first job in the investment industry was with a small Bay Area firm that published an investment newsletter and managed some portfolios. Within a few years, however, he had quit the firm, and with two confederates, set up his own shop, intending to publish their own investment newsletter. At the age of twenty-five, Schwab was, indeed, an entrepreneur.

Though Schwab would later say that he never had the slightest interest in following in his father's footsteps and becoming a lawyer, he did have a role model of sorts. His father's brother, William Schwab—Uncle Bill, as he is known in the Schwab mythology—was an entrepreneur. By all accounts, Uncle Bill was one of those curmudgeonly yet lovable characters who made and lost small fortunes with regularity. He lived in Sacramento, where he flew his own airplane and dabbled in whatever business caught his fancy, oil and boxes and timber and even, for a short time, money market funds. Schwab greatly admired his uncle, and the feeling appears to have been mutual. Early on, Uncle Bill invited his nephew to serve on the board of directors of a company he owned, and several times he hired his nephew as an adviser on deals he was putting together. Always, Uncle Bill was drawn to Schwab's ventures, where he would hover in the background, popping up to lend a hand at the most propitious moments.

As it turns out, young Schwab needed all the help he could get. He was not the "instinctive" entrepreneur he thought he was; some of the most essential acts of entrepreneurship were anathema to him. In particular, he hated the act of selling, something that became apparent as Schwab's company foundered. "Within the first two years we ran out of money," he later recalled. "I was on the brink of losing it all." Then, in what would become the pattern of his business life, he caught a break. On "the edge of the abyss," he met a man named Jack Shelton, an expert in a new selling technique called direct mail marketing. Marketing by mail was not only an effective way to gain newsletter subscribers, it was also enormously appealing to someone like Schwab, who much preferred its impersonal sell to the kind of one-on-one selling that characterizes, for instance, the brokerage business. Under Shelton's guidance, Schwab began learning the art of writing an effective direct sales pitch. The newsletter began to gain subscribers.

Buoyed by the newsletter's success, Schwab decided to expand. He became a gunslinger, like Gerry Tsai. Schwab's firm started a fund, called Investment Indicators, that was among the first no-load mutual funds in the country. This being the height of the Go-Go Years, the money flowed in: Investment Indicators was soon the largest mutual fund in California, with some $20 million in assets. Alas, as quickly as it grew, it fell apart just as fast. And the reason it did—in another recurring theme of his career—was that Schwab became careless.

Most states have their own securities laws, and out-of-state financial entities wishing to do business in that state must register with the local authorities and agree to abide by its laws. As his business boomed, Schwab increasingly ignored this requirement, accepting money from people in several states where the fund was not registered. Forever afterward, he would blame the ensuing disaster on the state bureaucrats and their petty ways. But really, he should have known better.

It was the Texas regulators who blew the whistle on Schwab. Upon realizing that he was operating an unregistered mutual fund, the bureaucrats demanded that he not only refund to Texas investors their original investment, but that he tack on 6 percent interest for good measure. When Schwab responded by suing the state of Texas, the federal regulators swooped in to finish him off. The SEC quickly moved to block sales of the fund, not just in Texas, but everywhere, an action that was effectively a death sentence. As Schwab's suit inched its way through the Texas courts, his small company slowly went broke. By the time it was over, in 1972, Schwab's reputation had been muddied, his firm had gone bust, and he was more than $100,000 in debt. He was also single; his marriage collapsed as his business problems mounted up.

And that's when Uncle Bill swooped in. Even as Schwab was struggling to save his original firm, Uncle Bill put up $100,000, allowing his nephew and four partners to start a second investment company, which they named First Commander Corporation. But it, too, had the whiff of failure; with Schwab's attention still directed toward Texas, the new firm did almost no business. Uncle Bill soon bailed out, though he did so without taking any of his money out of the company, accepting notes instead. A year later, the other four partners were gone. By 1973, Schwab had the place to himself. His first real piece of business arrived soon thereafter, again through the auspices of his uncle, who got him retained to manage the sale of a small timber company in which Uncle Bill held a minority interest.

Still, Schwab floundered. What was First Commander in business to *do*? He really couldn't say. What was his strategy? He didn't have one. How was he going to make money? He didn't know. Yet he seemed strangely confident he would come up with *something*. And so he did. Schwab had a friend at the firm of Scudder, Stevens & Clark, Hugo Quackenbush, who began telling Schwab that commissions were going to be deregulated, and that this might be something he could take advantage of. Why not turn First Commander into one of the new discount brokers that were sure to spring up? Quackenbush suggested.

Schwab loved the idea. For starters, it appealed to that side of him that disliked personal selling. For a variety of reasons, discounting has to be a reactive business; the customer has to be the one to pick up the phone and initiate a trade. Also, Schwab had built up a healthy suspicion of brokers over the years. He had been a stock trader much of his life; he understood the conflict of interest brokers faced every day. Surely, he thought, there was a place for firms that avoided the old broker's conflicts—firms that appealed to customers who knew exactly what stocks they wanted to buy and sell, and simply needed their trades carried out efficiently and cheaply.

In April 1974, he got a chance to try out this new idea. That month, the New York Stock Exchange, under government pressure, began to allow unfixed commissions, on a trial basis, for any trade of $2,000 or less. Schwab was ready. He ran a series of small ads in the *Wall Street Journal,* announcing commission prices at the newly renamed Charles Schwab & Co., ranging between 30 and 80 percent below the fixed commission rates, depending on the size of the trade. (The bigger the trade, the larger the discount.) Sure enough, people began calling, and transacting business through this new firm. Not a lot of people, but enough to make Schwab think that, finally, he was onto something that might work.

Still, he proceeded cautiously. He did so in part because his past failures were still so fresh, and in part because this was, after all, just a test. The real event, Mayday, was still a year away. When it came—and when he saw how Merrill Lynch reacted—that's when he knew he had a business.

Or so the story goes.

❧

TWO MONTHS BEFORE MAYDAY, the Vietnam War ended. As the North Vietnamese army moved triumphantly into Saigon, the last remaining Americans scrambled onto helicopters and military planes, fleeing the country. The images of those scenes—of desperate South Vietnamese being pushed away from Army helicopters as they lifted off the American embassy roof— were haunting and unforgettable. And one wonders whether Wall Street even noticed.

Wall Street was itself under siege in those days, and had been for seven long years. Its dominant institution, the New York Stock Exchange, was being attacked relentlessly, and was slowly crumbling under the barrage. In retrospect, it is hard to see how it could *not* have crumbled. For the stock exchange was, quite simply, a cartel—a monopoly entrenched not by law but merely by tradition, by force of unexamined habit. As the assault escalated, and the full extent of the exchange's monopolistic practices gained public exposure, people became offended. "Nowhere in the United States," one angry mutual fund executive declared in the early 1970s, "is a group of businessmen given the right to organize themselves into an association with the power to maintain a marketplace for their joint use and then to fix prices to be charged in that market, to restrict entry to that market, and to boycott competing markets. . . ."[2]

In fact, fixing prices and restricting entry is *exactly* what the stock exchange had been founded to do. Its origins go back to 1792, when a group of brokers, fearful of losing business to new competitors, met secretly in a New York hotel, emerging with a pact that read in part: "[W]e will not buy or sell from this date . . . any kind of Public Stock at a less rate than one-quarter of one percent Commission on the Specie value, and . . . we will give preference to each other in our Negotiations." For nearly two centuries, these essential terms remained unchanged. Commissions went up, of course—they averaged around 40 cents a share by 1970—but they were always fixed. Membership in the exchange was expanded—there were about 1,400 exchange seats by the early 1970s—but it was still highly restricted, and brought uncalculable benefits to its members. Members still gave each other preferential treatment. But the greatest benefit of all was the iron-clad rule—Rule 390, it was called—that all stocks listed on the exchange could only be bought and sold through a member firm. Perhaps these were acceptable business practices in the 1790s, but by the 1970s, they appeared to be in rather blatant violation of the nation's antitrust laws.

It is tempting, and not inaccurate, to fit the stock exchange's woes into the context of the times. Here was an important American institution like other important American institutions—like the government, or organized religion—that had been held in high esteem in the America of the 1950s, and was viewed much more skeptically by the America of the early 1970s.[3] Also, like those other institutions in which people were losing faith, the stock exchange was not accustomed to having its practices questioned; as a result, it reacted both defensively and arrogantly. Donald I. Baker, the antitrust lawyer at the Justice Department most responsible for making Mayday a reality, remembers the first extensive government hearing, held by the Securities and Exchange Commission, and aimed at exploring the ramifications of the NYSE monopoly. It was July of 1968, and the exchange's opponents included not just the institutions that were paying absurdly high commissions because of the stock exchange cartel, but a handful of the country's most eminent economists—Paul Samuelson of MIT, Henry Wallich of Yale, William Baumol of Princeton. All of them "lambasted the stock exchange scheme," as Baker puts it now. When its turn came, the exchange offered up only its own house economist, who prattled on about how the stock market was a "delicate mechanism" that would be endangered if commissions were unfixed. It was an impossibly lame performance, the product of the exchange's arrogant conceit that this whole business of having to justify itself was beneath its notice. In time, the phrase "delicate mechanism" would have the same effect on 1970s-era critics of the New York Stock Exchange as the phrase "executive privilege" had on 1970s-era critics of the Nixon White House. People would roll their eyes when they heard those words.

The exchange's practices were under assault for a more urgent reason: they were hopelessly outdated. The investment world was in the midst of massive and profound changes; the stock exchange, and its member firms, were still operating as though it were the 1920s. Financial journalist Chris Welles wrote a fine book about the events leading up to Mayday, which he entitled, quite appropriately, *The Last Days of the Club*. Anything that made the NYSE seem less like a club and more like a business was stoutly resisted. When some of the larger firms wanted to offer stock to the public, a move that would provide increased capital and stability, the exchange's board of directors, which included many of its most influential members, wouldn't countenance it. The small specialist firms who worked on the exchange floor (and had one of the sweetest monopolies ever devised: *all* trading in the stocks under their purview had to go through them) had always used paper to transact business; computers made that paperwork unnecessary, yet the firms refused to install new technology. Even the way commissions were set was rooted in the clubby nature of the stock exchange. Any time there was a slump in business, the NYSE would simply race to the SEC to get a rate increase to make up the shortfall. And the rates themselves were based on methods of conducting business that were no longer applicable, now that big institutions like mutual funds were buying and selling huge blocks of stock. This new trading encompassed not only obvious economies of scale, but even a different mind-set, one that put execution and price over hand-holding and advice.

As these two powerful forces—the modern needs of institutional investors, and the entrenched practices of the stock exchange—began colliding, something had to give. Usually, it was the NYSE. In 1969, Donaldson, Lufkin & Jenrette, a young, aggressive firm, announced that it was going public, even if it meant resigning from the NYSE. The exchange backed down. Alternative markets like NASDAQ began cropping up that used technology the stock exchange resisted; the exchange reacted by trying to emasculate its new competition, as it always had before. This time, the government wouldn't let it. The pressure on member firms to align their commission prices with the new realities of the marketplace brought about the convoluted system of "give ups" and "split commissions" and "soft dollar'' compensation that became so prevalent; thus did the exchange bend without breaking.

The culmination of these smaller collisions was the back office crisis of the late 1960s and early 1970s. As the big institutions issued ever more frequent buy-and-sell orders, the member firms that executed the trades (by hand, using paper) couldn't keep up. Errors began piling up, as did the paperwork itself; back offices all over Wall Street became ensnarled in their own paper. In time, the crisis grew so severe that Wall Street and Washington began to fear for the health of the financial system. Though the financial system survived in the end, the back office crisis was a disaster for the New York Stock Exchange just the same. It gave the lie to the NYSE's most basic arguments in favor of fixed commissions. For instance, the exchange's lobbyists used to claim that if commissions were unfixed, small firms would fall by the wayside. But they were falling by the wayside anyway.[4] How much worse could it be if they were forced to compete on price? Wasn't it far more likely that such competition would breed—in the words of the Justice Department—"efficiency, innovation and healthy, progressive change,'' qualities conspicuously lacking on Wall Street?

Right up to the end, the stock exchange and its member firms refused to concede the obviousness of this point, except on the rarest of occasions. The first and most notable such occasion took place on a November night in 1970 at the Waldorf Astoria, when then-NYSE president Robert Haack made a speech in which he boldly called for "negotiated rates'' on commissions.[5] The speech came some two and a half years after the Justice Department had begun beating the drums in favor of reform; among the growing circle of experts who thought about the issue, Haack had done not much more than recite the emerging conventional wisdom. Yet within the exchange, reaction to Haack's speech was so unremittingly hostile that within a year, he announced that he would soon be stepping down as NYSE president. This was a preemptive move, since there was no possibility that he would be reappointed to the post.

Three years later, the exchange actually went to the SEC to ask for a commission rate increase of 10 to 15 percent, an amount worth some $300 million a year to the member firms. It was an act of stunning chutzpah, for by then it was plain that fixed commissions were doomed. Pressure from the government had already forced the NYSE to deregulate commissions for trades over $300,000, and two congressional committees were pushing legislation to unfix all commissions. The stock exchange wound up getting its increase from the SEC, but the victory was Pyrrhic. In return, it was forced to agree to phase in deregulated commissions, a process to be completed no later than April 30, 1975. And *still*, there were pockets of resistance. James Needham, who followed Haack as the president of the NYSE, brazenly told reporters as late as the fall of 1974 that "if we don't get what we want"— that is, if the SEC didn't back down from its Mayday edict—"[I'll] see them on the steps of the courthouse at Foley Square."[6] Through it all, in fact, there was only one head of one member firm that consistently and openly sided with the forces of change.

That was Donald Regan.


The key to understanding Regan's posture was this: although Merrill Lynch was an important member of the New York Stock Exchange, it was not a member of the club—and hadn't been since Charlie Merrill had "down-scaled" back in the 1940s. Although it was a partnership, it was run in a far more businesslike fashion than any other Wall Street firm. It also did grubby things like advertise (on television, no less!),[7] which the rest of Wall Street considered undignified. But the crux of the matter was that, within the clubby world of the stock exchange, Merrill Lynch, for all its heft, lacked prestige; it was a firm (so it was whispered) run by a bunch of dumb Irish ex-Marines whose only skill was peddling stocks to the unwashed middle class.

Wall Street's dismissive attitude was infuriating to everyone at Merrill Lynch, but it did give Regan certain advantages. The firm's sheer size guaranteed that Regan was a player on Wall Street, yet since he was not a part of the club, he could criticize it with impunity. He had a gruff, direct, overpowering personality—the kind that both embraced controversy and enjoyed seeing his name in the paper, something most club members avoided at all cost. (Once, when he was interviewing a job applicant who had a fairly high profile, he pointedly told the man: "You've been in the papers a lot. I'm not too sure you'd be very happy here because at Merrill Lynch there is only one spokesman. . . .") Even before he was officially Merrill Lynch's chairman, Regan spoke out in favor of commission deregulation—in remarks beautifully timed to reap maximum press exposure, coming two weeks after Haack had made his heretical speech.[8] Then, when Haack resigned as NYSE president, Regan made a point of adding him to Merrill Lynch's board of directors.

Regan was an Irish ex-Marine, all right, but he wasn't dumb. He absolutely understood that Merrill Lynch could only benefit from the changes taking place on Wall Street. Donaldson, Lufkin & Jenrette may have been the first member firm to go public, but Merrill Lynch was right behind it; in June 1971, it issued stock that brought in $56 million in working capital, and created over 200 instant millionaires, as Merrill Lynch partners became shareholders in a public company. The back office crisis, so disastrous for everyone else on Wall Street, was a windfall for Merrill Lynch: not only did it have the money and manpower to solve its own problems, but the exchange came to Regan and begged him to swallow up one of his competitors, which was about to go under. "They did everything but get down on their knees," Regan recalls now, which of course he enjoyed immensely. After they'd begged long enough, he agreed.

Most importantly, the breakup of the club was crucial to Regan's larger ambitions for his firm, and the most likely way to break up the club was to unfix commissions. That one act had the potential to transform Wall Street completely, to render useless the clubby relationships that had always bonded an investment banker to his clients, and to create in their place—to borrow a Wall Street phrase that gained currency in the 1980s—"a transaction oriented environment." Once commissions were deregulated, firms would be forced to compete for business; the spoils would go to the best competitors. As in any other business, that meant giving the best service at the lowest price, which Regan was sure Merrill Lynch could offer. If Regan wanted to shed Merrill Lynch's reputation as a mere wirehouse—and he did, desperately—and if he wanted to force his way into the growing institutional side of the investment business—which he did even more desperately—he needed Mayday. It was his best hope for replacing the snobbish ethos of the club with the more cutthroat mores of competition.[9]

Regan himself would always deny that he was motivated by self-interest. He insists that he was acting purely out of his belief in the tenets of free enterprise. "I couldn't believe then—and I *still* can't believe—how capitalists could be practicing cartelism," he says.[10] He also claims, with the same blustery vehemence, that he was consciously acting in his role as the champion of the small investor. "They were our clients," he says now. "Why shouldn't I try to get a lower price for them?" This contention, however, stretches the limits of credulity. Although his speeches were dotted with assertions that unfixed commission would be a boon to investors, his firm's actions sent out a different signal. In March 1974, at the beginning of that trial period when small commissions were deregulated, Merrill Lynch grandly unveiled a "sharebuilding" plan for small investors; though it supposedly offered lower commissions, it was so full of caveats that rare was the investor who saved money using the plan. Four months later, Merrill Lynch raised commissions on small trades by 5 percent, while announcing that it would begin to negotiate commission rates with its big institutional clients.[11] And on Mayday, of course, the firm again raised the rates it charged small investors.

Why? The simple answer is that Mayday was never about middle-class investors; it was always about the growing power of institutional traders. It was the trading habits of the mutual funds and pension funds that made fixed commissions untenable, their pressure that brought about the reforms, their business that the member firms scrambled to keep. Small investors were never going to get the kind of commission breaks that institutions could command, and that was especially true if they did business with a newly public company that needed a steady revenue source to make up for the millions it was spending to break into the lucrative institutional business. In effect, Merrill Lynch's retail customers were paying the price, in the form of higher commissions, for Regan's ambitious strategy.

The more complicated answer is that Regan really didn't have much choice. Merrill Lynch's dominance as a wirehouse was profound: in 1974, it generated $800 million in revenues, which was four times as much as the second-ranking wirehouse, E. F. Hutton. But this dominance had a price. The firm had over 200 branch offices by the mid-1970s, and a sales force of almost 6,000 brokers. It had fancy new headquarters. It had layers of middle managers. Although Charlie Merrill would have found it heretical, this entire structure was supported by commissions. That's because, within a few years of assuming the chairmanship of Merrill Lynch, Regan had abandoned Merrill's old salary system and converted to the same commission-based system that everyone else on Wall Street used. As a result, a Merrill Lynch broker's income was directly pegged to how much commission revenue he shook out of his customers. If Merrill Lynch cut retail commissions, the brokers lost income and the firm's enormous overhead became that much more burdensome; the mere rumor of a commission cut was enough to set the broker network buzzing angrily. Merrill Lynch could not afford to have its brokers angry. To cut retail commissions by 50 percent the way Schwab was doing—well, that was out of the question. You couldn't have a system that both paid brokers a percentage of the commissions they generated *and* offered cut-rate commissions to customers; it just wasn't possible. You had to choose one or the other. Merrill Lynch executives would later claim that they secretly drew up plans for a discount operation, which they could have pulled off the shelf if they had wanted to. But they never did pull it off the shelf. They never dared.

❧

THERE'S A FINAL REASON WHY THE SCHWAB STAFF WOKE UP on Mayday to discover that Merrill Lynch was not going to put them out of business. Like all the big wirehouses, Merrill Lynch had a hard time taking discounting seriously. The way the discounters went about their business violated too many of the ancient truisms of the brokerage business. "Stocks are sold, not bought" went one such axiom—meaning that most Americans still did not come easily to a decision to buy or sell a stock or bond. They had to be cajoled, prodded, convinced. Brokers activated this process by picking up the phone, planting an idea, slowly reeling in the customer. Ross Kenzie, the longtime manager of Merrill Lynch's Cleveland office, was legendary within the firm for the way he supposedly trained new brokers: in order to impress upon them the importance of making phone calls, he used to tape one of their hands to the phone during their first week on the job.[12]

At Schwab, however, it was the customer who had to pick up the phone. Employees were supposed to sit at their desks and wait for people to call; then, when people did call, they were under explicit instruction not to offer advice or suggestions. Their job was to write down the caller's order, and pass it along the Schwab pipeline, where other employees made the trade and billed the caller. At that point, of course, the caller became a customer, with an "account" at Schwab. Yet even then, no one at Schwab solicited additional business, something a wirehouse would have done as a matter of course. Discounters were operating on a different theory, which grew out of another truism of the brokerage business: "Ten percent of the customers provide 90 percent of the revenues." It was this 10 percent, the most active investors, that discounters hoped to attract—investors who knew their own minds, and were tired of the incessant phone calls from their brokers. In one of his first ads, Schwab's slogan was: "Call us because no sales person will ever call you."

Although Schwab would always trumpet this difference between his firm and the wirehouses, he was to some degree making a virtue out of necessity. The path he chose was every bit as preordained as Regan's post-Mayday path. The same arithmetic that applied to Regan applied to him: it was simply impossible to employ full-service brokers earning commissions while offering cut-rate commissions to customers. Thus he hired glorified telephone operators and paid them around $10,000 a year, because that's what he could afford.[13]

An even more onerous straitjacket was an SEC regulation called the know-your-customer rule. It said that a broker couldn't give a customer advice until he understood something of the customer's circumstances. Once a broker knew (for example) that his client was an elderly man dependent on dividend income, he was expected—nay, he was bound—to suggest an appropriately conservative portfolio. Paradoxically, the only legal way the discounters could get around the know-your-customer rule was by knowing nothing about their customers' financial circumstances. You couldn't be accused of giving out inappropriate advice if you gave out no advice at all. Schwab's no-advice policy, besides being cost-effective, kept him on the right side of the law.

The creation of the discount business was, in hindsight, another of those moments that one could find from time to time in this early phase of the money revolution—a moment when you could see a subtle shift taking place between buyer and seller. Unlike the big firms, the discounters were placing the onus on the buyer to make his own decisions, and to take greater responsibility for his financial actions. And on some deep level, Schwab understood this. But no one can ever remember him talking about it in the beginning. He was too busy trying to survive.

Charles Schwab & Co. was swamped from the start. That's how the old-timers would always remember it. Once Mayday arrived, there was always more business than the tiny firm could handle; and one gets the distinct impression, listening to former employees recall the constant chaos, that for the first half-dozen years of the firm's life, there was scarcely a moment when everyone there didn't have that slightly queasy feeling that they'd never be able to dig out. There was always a paperwork backlog, always a batch of errors that needed untangling, always a need for capital, always some problem with one of the regional exchanges. The top executives, Schwab included, were always being pulled away from their other tasks to man the phones temporarily or help reduce the back office backlog. This helped create the feelings of camaraderie so important to a new company, but it didn't do much to alleviate the chaos.

You might think, listening to these old stories, that the entire middle class had flocked to the new discounters. But that was hardly the case. The middle class had turned against the stock market as it sank during the 1970s; a *Census of Shareowners* put out by the New York Stock Exchange in 1978 concluded that there had been "a net decline of some 5½ million individual owners of corporate stocks or mutual funds between 1970 and 1975." (Added the horrified exchange, "There is no indication that this trend has been reversed.") Rather, Schwab's early customers were a much narrower segment of the population—inveterate investors who traded no matter which way the market was going. And even *they* didn't flock to the discounter; it was more drizzle than deluge.

No, Schwab's chronic inability to keep pace was due less to the influx of customers than to his own haphazard business practices. Although he was constantly hiring, the volume of phone calls and stock trades—from four trades a day in April 1974, to seventy-five a day by the summer of 1975, to

400 a day by 1977—always seemed to leapfrog right after a Schwab hiring binge. In 1978, Schwab executives decided that their only hope lay in computerizing the entire operation, even though the move entailed tremendous risk. This was still years before the big Wall Street firms embraced computers, and the kind of system Schwab needed didn't exist. Nevertheless, the firm's executives devised and installed a sophisticated system that allowed Schwab's phone operators to "input" a customer's order directly into the computer. By then, Schwab was handling 800 trades a day; no sooner had the computer been installed than orders jumped to 2,000 a day. The computers were as overwhelmed as the employees had always been.

There were other problems too. Resistance to the new firm among traditional brokerage houses was fierce. When Schwab attempted to negotiate a lease for a branch office in a Seattle building that also housed a regional, full-service firm, the larger firm threatened to move out of the building if Schwab were given a lease. On several occasions, the Pacific Stock Exchange slapped the hand of the new firm for petty rules violations—actions that seemed primarily aimed at intimidating Schwab. Once, company officials were asked to present themselves to the SEC, though as the meeting went on, it plainly had no identifiable agenda. "I think they just wanted to measure our character," a former employee now surmises.

The resistance made it difficult to find qualified employees, especially anyone with experience in the brokerage industry. As a result, Schwab's early executive team was put together as haphazardly as everything else. The number two man had just quit his job at a regional firm and was driving to Mexico in his Volkswagen bug when he stopped, on a lark, at the Schwab office in San Francisco, took a peek around, and wound up going to work there. Peter Moss, the company's strategic planner, began his Schwab relationship as an angry customer, who became so annoyed at the firm's inability to reconcile his account that one day he jumped over the counter and did it himself. Schwab's chief deal maker, Rich Arnold, was a pet-shop owner-turned-financial adviser.

Even when the company tried to do things in an organized fashion, they could wind up feeling slapdash. In the late 1970s, Moss persuaded Schwab to set up an elaborate telephone answering operation in Reno, Nevada, arguing that having one central location for phone operators would save the company money. When Moss's assumptions turned out to be wrong, he then convinced Schwab that he could recoup the mounting losses by contracting out the Reno facility to other companies that used 800-numbers, most of which were the kind of fly-by-night record companies that advertised Elvis Presley collections on television at 3:00 A.M. No sooner had the deals been signed, however, than Elvis died; the phone lines were so jammed with callers wanting to buy his records that for several days, Schwab customers couldn't get through. Such was life at Charles Schwab & Co.

To listen to this litany of woe is to wonder how the firm stayed in business for two weeks, much less two decades. A good part of the reason is that the classic Schwab customer was willing to put up with a lot to get the kind of commission breaks the firm was offering. Die-hard investors were often stunned by Schwab's prices; part of the lore of the firm is the story of a man so bowled over by the commission Schwab planned to charge him for an options trade—$34 instead of the $175 his usual broker would have charged—that he brought his lawyers to the Schwab office to make sure it was all on the up and up. Word of mouth was a great Schwab ally. So was its puppy-dog eagerness to please, which made it hard for customers to stay mad at Schwab. Schwab himself has a theory that the firm succeeded in part because it was on the West Coast, where people were more open to new ideas. No doubt his location was important, though perhaps for a different reason. Schwab's San Francisco office was a half-hour's drive from Silicon Valley, where a new kind of American industry was emerging. This new computer industry had different ways of doing things, including different ways of rewarding employees. Instead of paying straight salaries, these companies often granted stock options; as a result thousands of computer jocks began to own—and to trade—stocks. As often as not, they were predisposed to trade with Schwab. This was a small trend, not yet discernible to the census takers at the New York Stock Exchange. But if you worked for Schwab, it was something you could see clearly. It was a small, encouraging glimpse into the future.

And finally, Schwab grew because not all that was haphazard was bad. Sometimes when Chuck Schwab lurched and stumbled, he wound up falling into a pot of gold. From his luckiest accidents emerged real insight, and out of these insights came a sense of direction so clear, so well lit, that there was no way he could miss it.

The first of these lucky accidents was precipitated by the arrival, one last time, of Uncle Bill. He showed up two months after Mayday, which is how long it took him to realize that his nephew was really onto something this time, and that he wanted in. As always, he arrived with money in hand, $300,000 this time, proposing to invest it in the company in return for a small ownership slice. As always, Schwab badly needed the money. He needed money to grow, but he also needed it because brokerage firms have capital requirements the same as banks do; they must hold a small percentage of assets aside to cover margin calls or unforeseen losses. Though it's not the kind of fact that got enshrined in the firm's mythology, Schwab was always bumping up against its capital requirements and, on occasion, violating them. This was one of those times. The firm's trades were being restricted by the Philadelphia Stock Exchange until it found more capital.

Uncle Bill's money came with a condition attached. He wouldn't invest unless his nephew agreed to open a branch office in his home town of Sacramento. Such an office would employ Uncle Bill's son-in-law as its manager. (Perhaps no less important, it would also give Uncle Bill a place to hang around.)

As much as Schwab needed the money, he resisted at first. In theory, discounters didn't need branch offices, since there was nothing an employee in a branch office could do that an employee on the telephone couldn't. All the East Coast discounters avoided branch offices, relying on telephones and advertising as their basic tools. Fancy branch offices, it was thought, had more to do with ego than business; they were precisely the kind of extravagance that made traditional brokerage firms like Merrill Lynch so expensive to operate.

Besides, Schwab argued, the California state capital hardly seemed like the kind of place where a discount broker could thrive—it was too small, too staid, too full of midlevel bureaucrats with their midlevel salaries. But Uncle Bill would not budge: it was Sacramento or nothing. So Sacramento it was. Uncle Bill rented space in an inexpensive storefront across from a state office building, and in September 1975, Charles Schwab & Co.'s first branch office opened for business.

What happened next was a revelation. Schwab's volume—both the number of trades transacted each day, and the number of customers who called each day—immediately lurched upward. How much it jumped is lost to history, but everyone at Schwab noticed it. Plainly, the increased business was related to the opening of Uncle Bill's branch office, since most of the new customers lived in the Sacramento area. Yet Schwab had done only minimal local advertising to announce the new office. Stranger still, the new office, while busy, did not seem anywhere near as hectic as the added business would imply.

The only answer that made sense was that branches did matter after all—they mattered psychologically. It wasn't so much that people would insist on visiting the branch office every time they wanted to make a stock trade, they just needed to know it was there. There was something reassuring about seeing a real office—something that made a financial enterprise seem more solid than when it was represented merely by an ad in the *Wall Street Journal*. Most of Schwab's new Sacramento customers came into the branch office when they first opened their accounts, but not all of them did.

Some of them simply walked by the office. That was enough. Once they had seen it, they were able to pick up the phone and make a stock trade through Schwab.

Over and over, this pattern would be repeated. After Sacramento was up and running, a Seattle man came to Schwab and made the same pitch Uncle Bill had made. He wanted to put money in the firm, but only if he could open a branch in his home town. This time, Schwab was more receptive to the notion. The Seattle branch wasn't even in a storefront—it was in a high-rise office building—but the results were the same. Schwab then hired his old friend Hugo Quackenbush, who had already invested in the firm, to open a branch in Los Angeles, and cut a deal with a Phoenix investor to open a branch in that city. In both cases, the effect was a major upsurge in volume. In 1977, when Schwab opened the next branch office, in Denver, the firm decided to monitor the results. Before the branch opened, Schwab had about 300 Colorado customers. Within a year, that number jumped to nearly 2,000. That clinched it. From that moment on, Schwab spent every spare dollar opening new branches. It was clear that a branch's value as an engine of growth far outweighed the added cost.

On the East Coast, competing discounters scoffed at Schwab's branch office strategy. "It seemed completely logical to concentrate all my operations in one place," says one of Schwab's former competitors, long since out of business. "What I didn't appreciate until it was too late was that branches made people feel better." That's the insight Schwab had accidentally stumbled upon. *Branches made people feel better.* "They wanted to kick the tires," is how one old Schwab hand describes it.

Schwab's second insight, not unrelated to the first, had to do with another of the discounter's basic tools: advertising. To pick up a copy of the *Wall Street Journal* in the mid-1970s was to realize that advertising was becoming increasingly important as new financial institutions and products emerged. All the money market funds advertised, of course, as did most full-service brokerage firms. The discounters quickly joined their ranks—they had to, since they had no other means of selling their services. The classic discounter ad would offer a comparison between the discounter's commissions and a full-service broker's commissions. Though Schwab's ads were a cut above those, with flashier headlines and sharper language, they stuck to that basic formula.

In late 1976, the *San Francisco Examiner* did a story about the new firm. Included with the story was a photograph of Schwab, wearing a crisp white shirt and aviator glasses, and smiling that smile that would soon become famous, a smile that was friendly and earnest and ambitious and a little sheepish all at once—a smile that was impossible to resist. When Quackenbush saw the smile in that picture—when he saw how perfectly it represented his image of the firm—he bought the picture from the *Examiner,* and persuaded Schwab to use it in an ad. In the ad, Schwab's picture ran alongside a headline that read: ''The other brokers laughed when I cut commissions.''

Actually, the other discounters laughed when they saw this ad; to them, it was the final proof that Schwab's ego had gotten the better of him. But they were wrong again. Schwab's essential shyness made him reluctant to put his own face in an ad, and it was something he would never have done without prodding. But once the results came in, his reservations evaporated. Ads that used Schwab's face did better than ads that didn't. In direct marketing, you went with what worked. Schwab's face worked.

And it would always work. It would work for the same reason the branch offices worked: when people saw Schwab's friendly face and his eager smile, they felt better. They felt they could entrust this man with their money. Discounting had taken an extremely personal business, revolving around a broker's relationship with his customers, and made it impersonal. By using his face in his company's ads, Schwab was making it personal again. It wasn't especially logical, of course: when you called the Schwab 800-number, you were likely to get some twenty-five-year-old kid making $10,000 a year. But somehow, it didn't *feel* impersonal. Somehow you felt as though you knew your broker. You knew him because you saw him every day when you opened your *Wall Street Journal.* Sure, you were talking to some kid on the other end of a phone line, but he wasn't your broker. Not really.

Your broker was Chuck Schwab.

CHAPTER 7

# The World's Most Hated Bank

*August 1977*

B Y NOW YOU could see it if you looked closely enough: you could see the broad outlines of the money revolution. It was like a wave that had formed but hadn't yet crested, its shape discernible but its impact still to be felt.

Most of the elements that would make up the money revolution were in place. The ordered, straightforward universe of personal finance had started to get complicated, as new products were created, and new financial companies formed. The continued spasms of inflation were beginning to take a psychic toll, as Americans worried about the erosion of their savings and standard of living. The Depression-era ethos continued to fade, the best evidence being the unstoppable rise of personal debt in America, as credit card use grew at rates that sometimes topped 30 percent a year.

And all across the financial spectrum, in a dozen different ways, a blurring was beginning to occur. One example was the psychological blurring between what constituted "saving" and what constituted "investing," caused by the invention of money market funds. Another was the blurring of the functions that had always separated the various kinds of financial institutions. Banks were making consumer loans that had once been the province of finance companies; mutual fund companies were offering "checks," just like banks; discounters were luring customers who "belonged" to wirehouses. The regulations that historically kept financial institutions from invading each other's turf were starting to be viewed as irritating impediments: you might not be able to crash through them with a full frontal assault, but that didn't mean you couldn't sneak around them with a little cleverness.

A good example of these changes was the emergence of a product called the NOW account. First devised in 1970, the NOW account was brought to market two years later, after a long court battle. Its inventor was an obscure savings and loan executive named Ronald Haselton, who ran an S&L in Worcester, Massachusetts. And its explicit purpose was to evade the regulations that kept Haselton from offering a service he wanted to offer, namely checking accounts.

S&Ls had long been prevented from offering checking accounts, and it is quite possible that once upon a time, this ban made sense. By the 1970s, however, its practical effect was to force an S&L customer needing to pay some bills to withdraw money from his interest-bearing savings account, walk across the street to his local bank, and redeposit the money in a noninterest bearing checking account. "Mr. Haselton considered this ridiculous," two bank historians later wrote, "and vowed to do something about it." What he did was invent something he called a Negotiable Order of Withdrawal—or NOW account. It was a checking account, issued by an S&L, that paid interest.

But how could this be possible in the face of banking regulations? The answer was that, technically, the NOW account did not violate the regulations, it *evaded* them. Haselton had created his new account by taking advantage of some loopholes he had found in the regulations, and his strict interpretation was upheld in court. By 1976, the NOW account had been given explicit congressional approval—but only in New England, and only on a temporary basis.[1] This tentativeness on the part of Congress—its unwillingness to shut down a popular new product, while trying to keep it from spreading any further—was also a hallmark of this early phase of the money revolution.

As with any historical trend, this all seems much clearer now than it did at the time. We know now that every time someone chipped away at the regulatory wall, the pressure on the rest of the wall became that much greater, until finally it began to collapse of its own weight. We also know that when Ned Johnson attached a check to a money market fund, when Chuck Schwab began offering the alternative of cut-rate commissions, when Ron Haselton found a way to get around some Depression-era regulations, these were not anomalous acts. Although each man was acting independently, they were part of something larger. Even as their innovations were shaping the future of personal finance, they themselves were in the grip of forces they did not yet fully understand or appreciate.

There was, however, a small group of people who by the mid-1970s had begun to think about the money revolution in broad terms—to look across the divide separating financial institutions and openly wonder what the effect would be once the wave reached the shore. Of most significance, this group was the first to wonder what it would be like not just for the institutions involved but for their customers. That this was something worth thinking about should also have been clear by then. Americans had seen their financial assets quadruple in the twenty years since 1950, going from $295 billion to $1.3 trillion, and there was no reason to doubt that those assets would continue to grow sharply over the next twenty years. Moreover, middle-class Americans didn't think of themselves as only "bank customers" or only "brokerage customers"—which is how the institutions tended to think of them. They crossed financial borders every day. The money revolution would put their burgeoning assets up for grabs, but to be able to attract that money, financial institutions would have to learn to view a customer as someone with a wide range of financial needs and desires, rather than as, say, an occasional buyer of shares in IBM. They had to learn to think the way the small group at SRI International had begun to think.

SRI was—and is—a large nonprofit contract researcher located in a suburban neighborhood in Menlo Park, California. Formerly an arm of Stanford University[2]—and originally named Stanford Research Institute—SRI is known today for its work in the area of computer security and its research for the Defense Department. But over the years, it has been involved in an eclectic variety of projects. It is famous in banking circles, for instance, for developing the standards, still in use today, for bank checks—that bewildering array of numbers, in their odd, bulky typescript, at the bottom of any check, is the handiwork of SRI. And so are those take-your-own-blood-pressure machines you find in pharmacies, which an SRI team developed in the 1970s.

In 1974, SRI's president, Charles Anderson, asked an employee named Carl Spetzler to form a small SRI consulting group that would focus on financial institutions. The impetus for this request was an offhanded question asked by one of SRI's outside board members: Why, he wondered, wasn't SRI doing anything in the area of financial services, which seemed to be so ripe for the kind of consultative work SRI specialized in? The answer was simple: no one had thought of it. As to why Anderson chose Spetzler to set up the SRI Financial Group (later renamed the Financial Industries Center—or "the center"), one can only guess. "My understanding of financial services was that I had a checking account," says Spetzler.

Spetzler's expertise was in an esoteric discipline known as decision analysis. A specialty emerging from the Harvard Business School in the early 1960s, its essential premise was that by applying rigorous, mathematical modeling to the business decision-making process, one could impose rationality on managerial decision-making. For the untutored, it was arcane beyond belief (and in seeming defiance of common sense); decision analysis

textbooks were filled with indecipherable equations and intimidating matrixes. (Within SRI, Spetzler was known as a man who could never resist a
good matrix.) Even to the tutored, it was heavy sledding. At SRI, Spetzler
had been a key member of the decision analysis consulting group, helping
to turn it into a nice little profit center for the nonprofit research facility.

The first consulting contracts Spetzler landed for his new group came
about because of his willingness to admit his own ignorance about financial
services. He could persuasively claim that he brought a fresh perspective to
the subject, having never been steeped in decades of hoary lore and regulatory tradition; thus he could see things other experts couldn't. One thing
he saw, as he once wrote in a memo, was that "[Americans] talk about and
legislate against financial concentration, but the financial industries are probably the least concentrated and most fragmented of any in this country."[3]
He was struck by the inefficiency built into the structure of American finance: not only were there tens of thousands of financial institutions, but
each industry segment had its own set of overlapping sales agents—180,000
brokers! 250,000 life insurance salesmen!—all offering their own (skewed)
advice. Even the regulatory apparatus was inefficient, with banking alone
regulated by the comptroller of the currency, the Federal Reserve, the Federal Deposit Insurance Corporation, and state authorities. One of Spetzler's
earliest matrixes attempted to show which financial institutions offered what
services. He came up with twenty-two different kinds of institutions and
forty-two different kinds of services—"a bewildering array of incomprehensible alternatives to the individual," is how he described it. One of SRI's
early findings was that the typical middle-class American patronized at least
six different financial institutions.

Spetzler's other early insight, which alternately amused and appalled him,
was how little financial executives understood about their own industry. The
problem, as he saw it, was that each fragment of the industry had become
so comfortable with its own niche "that they would only write about their
own little fragment," as he once put it. When he visited banks, executives
trotted out reams of statistics about how much a typical checking account
held, and how many checking accounts supported each branch, but when
Spetzler asked about the net worth of customers and how that related to the
size of a checking account, he got blank stares. He quickly realized that the
center could generate clients if it did nothing else but try to understand
financial services, in the broadest sense, and then explain it back to the
people who worked in the industry.

And so that's what he set out to do. He would draw little cartoons to
illustrate how the world was changing: the first panel showed six financial
institutions, with names like U Betcha Life Insurance Co. and Overnight

Success Brokerage Firm, standing next to each other, separated by a series of walls. The second panel showed the same six institutions, in what looked like the aftermath of an earthquake: the buildings were in the same locations, but the walls had crumbled badly. And the man at U Betcha Life Insurance was casually climbing into Overnight Success Brokerage Firm's space. He would draw diagrams showing the extent to which formerly discreet financial products had begun to overlap. He had charts that ranked products according to their degree of complication (cash was simplest; commodities and stock options the most complicated), and other charts that rated products according to how much personal selling was required. In both cases, he simply ignored the old divisions; implicitly he was encouraging his clients to do likewise. Early on, Spetzler hired a man named James Fuller, who had worked in the securities industry, and Fuller persuaded him to do a full-scale study of the investment business. Among the study's bolder forecasts was its prediction that banks would eventually own discount brokers. This was startling news to brokers and bankers alike, most of whom assumed that the Glass–Steagall Act would prevent such a combination. But it didn't. The SRI consultants reached their conclusion by doing something few bankers had done in forty years. They read the Glass–Steagall Act.

And early in 1977, Spetzler authorized an attempt to find out, in a precise and detailed fashion, the myriad ways Americans used the financial products at their disposal—*all* the financial products, from credit cards to certificates of deposit, from life insurance to mutual funds.[4] The study was called Consumer Financial Decisions, and it would be one of the group's most enduringly important projects, its publication standing as a kind of formal recognition that the money revolution had arrived. Even the most insular banker couldn't ignore it anymore. For those involved, working on Consumer Financial Decisions was an exhilarating experience, a time when they felt like advance scouts, clearing the path an entire industry would soon follow. For most of those who worked on the study, it ranks among the highlights of their lives.


One wonders now whether a consultant named Andrew Kahr was among those who felt exhilarated by their work at SRI. An intense, wiry man in his early thirties, Kahr had to be the most unlikely looking financial consultant in America; with long, stringy hair that flowed to his shoulders, he bore a resemblance to Tiny Tim, the novelty act from the 1960s. His range of eccentricities were equally unusual for someone in his line of work, and a source of much amusement to his SRI colleagues. Years later, they could still recall how he so hated changing paper in the typewriter that he would write every-thing single-spaced, leaving no discernible margins in any direction, so that each page was little more than a sea of black lettering. These eccentricities were always recounted fondly, though; his former colleagues realize now—and most of them realized at the time—that part of what made their time at SRI so special was that it gave them the chance to work alongside Andrew Kahr. Despite the fact that he was a part-timer—a consultant to the consult-ant—he quickly became the most memorable figure to work at the center.

But to ask Kahr how *he* felt during his time at SRI was to invite from him a dismissive frown and a helpless shrug. It was such a vague and subjective question; it was like asking him about politics or history, both of which he also found unappealingly subjective, since they required one to make judg-ments based on instincts and leanings rather than on cold and irrefutable data. He said once that what he most admired about Franklin Roosevelt was that he was the only President to have been reelected three times. That was an unassailable fact. As to whether Roosevelt should be admired for any larger accomplishment—for ending the Depression, say—Kahr was loath to express himself, since after all there was a school of thought that said that Hitler ended the Depression by starting World War II. There was no open-and-shut case, in other words; to admire Roosevelt for ending the Depres-sion meant having an opinion, and Andrew Kahr's main opinion about opinions was that they were worthless.

Lay before him a printout of seemingly random data, however, and Kahr was in his element. He could see patterns invisible to everyone else, and could squeeze meaning from numbers that no one else could discern. From data, Kahr could identify behavior, trends, and much else. He understood people better through the interpolation of numbers than through the more typical forms of human discourse—probably liked them better that way, too. In addition, the traditions and regulations of American finance were largely irrelevant to Kahr, since his mind instinctively rearranged things in patterns he found more meaningful. In the whole of the money revolution, no one was as good at getting around even the most stubborn regulation barriers as he was. "The Swiss cheese of regulation," he called it; had there been no government regulations to elude, "most of what I've done couldn't have been conceived." Kahr liked to say that he had no desire to enter a business in which he did not have an unfair advantage, but his chief unfair advantage was his own powerful mind.

In his book *The Big Store,* the writer Donald Katz refers to Kahr as "the noted financial inventor."[5] This description is accurate so far as it goes: Kahr was an unknown in the culture at large but among the financial cognoscenti, he was, indeed, "noted." He took pride in never having business stationery or even an office. Yet because of his ideas and his spreading reputation, business people knew where to find him, refused to be put off by his appearance, and threw him work.

He was also, unquestionably, a financial inventor. But the phrase doesn't quite do him justice; it misses the way his inventions simply shredded the legal distinctions that had existed for so long, rendering them as moot as a law could be while remaining on the books. And it misses the awe in which Kahr was held among many of the people who worked with him. "I know very few people I would put in a class with Andrew," says his friend John "Mac" McQuown, no slouch himself as a financial innovator.[6] "He has this phenomenal capacity to look at a very complex problem, analyze all the elements, sort them out in his mind, and then come up with a system," adds a former business partner named Adolph Mueller. "That is his genius." To them, that's what Kahr was, finally—an odd, narrow, data-obsessed genius. The money revolution provided the hothouse where Kahr's genius could bloom.

He had always been considered a genius; it was one of the conditions of his life. Andrew Kahr was born in 1941 and grew up on Manhattan's Upper East Side, his father a psychiatrist, his mother (once the children were grown) a published art historian. So prodigious were his abilities that by the time he was fourteen, he had begun his freshman year at Harvard. His major—indeed, his gift—was mathematics.

Like many a talented young man, Kahr was not humble about his talents. On the contrary, his ego was the most noticeable thing about him. Howard Raiffa, a professor at the Harvard Business School, taught a graduate-level applied mathematics course, which Kahr took in his junior year, and thought the young student was "trying to pass himself off as a math genius. . . . I didn't take him too seriously." But then he found out just how young Kahr was and began to take him quite seriously. He became Kahr's mentor, and as he got to know his young protégé, he learned several surprising things. The first was that Kahr found mathematics uninteresting. And the second was that Kahr was as captivated by business as he was bored by mathematics. Georges Doriot, the great venture capitalist, lectured at the business school; Kahr religiously audited Doriot's classes. As he approached graduation, Kahr told Raiffa that he wanted to attend the business school. Raiffa begged him to get a Ph.D. in math instead. So Kahr entered MIT, emerging two years later with a Ph.D. after solving two previously unsolved problems in logic. "Once Andrew wrote his thesis," Raiffa adds, "he was offered a *lot* of positions in math.'' He spurned them all to return to Harvard. But not in the MBA program. Barely old enough to drink, Kahr was an assistant professor of the Harvard Business School.

He went to work as the junior man in the same department as Raiffa, who, as it happens, was among a small group of mathematically inclined professors trying to develop the new "science" of decision analysis; the longtime head of the group, Robert Schlaiffer, is known as the father of the discipline. It should have been the perfect spot for Kahr, for here was a subject that combined his gift for mathematics with his love for business. But it didn't work out that way. He lacked a teacher's temperament; he could not bring himself to simplify for the sake of clarity, for example. As a result, the case studies he wrote for the decision analysis course were bewilderingly complex, so much so that decades later, people could still remember how impossible they were to get through. Nor was Kahr much easier to follow in the classroom. (Not that Kahr was the only offender: at one point, the students became so frustrated with decision analysis that some of them held a public burning of Schlaiffer's textbook.) And Kahr's relations with Schlaiffer never got much beyond testy. As the guiding light of decision analysis, Schlaiffer expected a certain amount of deference. This was something Kahr was incapable of giving, and the two men would have shouting matches that reverberated down the hall; another decision analysis professor recalls Kahr telling Schlaiffer once, "You should engage your mind before you open your mouth."

"Our friendly Martian" they began to call him behind his back at Harvard, and the stories his colleagues told about him started to take on a mythic quality. One kind of Kahr story tended to stress (perhaps to the point of exaggeration) his gifts, which even at the business school were considered extraordinary. How he taught himself Japanese in six months, for instance, or how he once wrote a finance text, said to be brilliant, which he refused to publish because he didn't feel it was good enough. A second kind of Kahr story stressed his lack of social skills. How he had to be reminded of the necessity of saying "please" and "thank you," or how he alienated colleagues with his biting sarcasm. One suspects that these stories are also a little exaggerated, for Kahr certainly had his share of friends at the business school. But it's true enough that he had no tolerance for the requirements of academic life, social or otherwise. His attitude seemed to be that his intellect exempted him from the petty demands of polite society.

Also, he thought the pay stank. In some ways this may have been what most set Kahr apart from his academic peers: In a milieu where money was not supposed to matter, Kahr was completely open about his desire to get rich. At Harvard, he was constantly setting up little companies on the side, looking for opportunities that might take off. (They never amounted to much.) He used to tell people that he wanted to make $10 million by the time he was thirty, so he could retire; years later, when asked why it was so important to him not to have to work, he replied: "Having to work means you're not free." He wasn't one of those people who believed that money was a way of keeping score. Rather, he wanted to be wealthy so that he wouldn't have to go to work solely to earn money. This thing that most of us accept as a part of life's essential shape—the need to earn a living—Kahr saw as an annoying constraint. And he hated constraints even more than he hated opinions.

In 1968, realizing that he was never going to get rich as an academic, Kahr abandoned Harvard for an executive position with a small conglomerate in Massachusetts. For Kahr, this turned out to be a far more miserable experience than Harvard had been, and when he quit that job two years later, he promised himself that he'd never work for anyone else again. That pretty much ruled out everything except consulting. Consulting got him to San Francisco, when a Harvard friend recommended him to someone at Wells Fargo. When that contract ended, someone at Wells Fargo recommended him to someone else who needed consulting help. That's always the way it was with Kahr; he cringed at the thought of having to sell himself, but he never had to. He got work because word of his prodigious analytic talent was passed along the corporate grapevine. By the mid-1970s, AT&T was a client, and Bechtel and several ambitious California S&Ls. And SRI.

Spetzler knew about Kahr because they had been in the same field; the one book Kahr had coauthored at Harvard was a decision analysis textbook. Although Kahr had since abandoned decision analysis, Spetzler jumped at the chance to bring him on as a consultant at SRI. Kahr was no more likely to get rich at SRI than at Harvard, for the think tank was notorious for its tightfisted ways. But it was at SRI that Andrew Kahr found the money revolution, and saw in it the opportunities he had been seeking.


When you ask them now what they remember about the Consumer Financial Decisions, it turns out that they recall less about the big things—the major findings, the sweeping pronouncements—than about the odd little facts they stumbled across along the way. That, and the shared anecdotes that are part of any memorable group experience. Barbara Casey, a young woman fresh out of Harvard Business School who would become the project manager, remembers her initial bewilderment at one such odd fact, which has remained lodged in her brain ever since: 65 percent of those surveyed claimed not to own a car. This was impossible, of course; upon further examination, it turned out that most people who were paying off a car loan answered "no" when asked whether they owned their own car. On the other hand, she also remembers her growing horror as it gradually dawned on her that this project that was originally slated to cost $40,000 was going to cost closer to $1.5 million—a sum Spetzler approved before he had lined up the clients to pay for it. And *everybody* remembers the time that Kahr, McQuown, and Fuller went to Citibank to ask for money to help underwrite the survey.

Sitting across the table from the SRI group was a team of young Citibank executives led by a woman named Mary Falvey, who was well known to the visitors. She had worked at one of SRI's competitors, McKinsey & Co., prior to joining Citibank; before that, she had been a student at the Harvard Business School, where she had studied under, and been duly intimidated by, Andrew Kahr. She was not intimidated now, however. After the presentation, Falvey began peppering the SRI representatives with skeptical questions. "I started asking Andrew, 'How are you going to handle this, how are you going to handle that?' " she recalls. He didn't have the answers, and what was worse, he had to admit that he didn't have the answers. This was almost more than he could bear, and with each new question, Kahr's face got redder, and his temper got shorter, until he could no longer restrain himself. "If you think this is going to be one of those fill-in-the-blanks studies, *like the kind you used to do at McKinsey*," he fairly spat at his former student, "you are sadly mistaken!" As the Citibank executives looked at him in stunned amazement, you could almost see Fuller and McQuown trying to crawl under the boardroom table.

But in the end, it *wasn't* one of those fill-in-the-blanks studies. That's why it was so expensive. Even with fifty corporate sponsors, the survey wound up costing SRI money. SRI contracted with one opinion firm to find an appropriate cross section of middle-class Americans, 4,000 in all, who were paid $10 to fill out a voluminous questionnaire. And it hired the Gallup Organization to find another 2,000 affluent Americans—defined as people who made more than $30,000 a year—and to interview them about their finances, a process that took hours. For this, they received $20. The "affluents," especially, found the idea of talking about their money off-putting; SRI persuaded them to open up by promising to send them a report detailing what other affluent people did with *their* money. Still, with over 5,000 questions, most of which Kahr wrote, the survey ran to more than 200 pages. Those who took the time to answer them were grossly underpaid.

Here's one other thing everyone remembers: they remember Kahr's insistence that the only questions worth asking were those that examined past behavior. "People can never tell you what they'll do [in the future]," he says. "I myself believe only in asking what they've done." It was pointless to ask people how they would react to a new financial product or a new set of financial circumstances; no matter what they told you, they couldn't know the answer until the circumstance was upon them. They could only legitimately describe what they had done in the past, and why: why they had four life insurance policies instead of one; what had caused them to open a new bank account; how frequently they paid down their credit card debt. What could you learn about the future by asking questions about the past? Quite a bit, if you had Andrew Kahr interpreting the data. "Many fundamental patterns came up on my personal screen," he says now.

One big surprise to emerge from the study was how much money people had in the bank. The savings balance in the typical "affluent" passbook account was an astonishing $40,000, but even for the least affluent people included in the survey (those who made $15,000 a year) a typical savings account might hold as much as $10,000. Savings and checking accounts amounted to 16 percent of total household assets; only real estate consumed a higher percentage. People didn't save with an eye toward passing money on to their heirs or for any particular purpose, SRI discovered. They just saved. In many cases, they put money in the bank with one hand while revolving their credit card debt with the other hand—behavior that made no sense at all.

Putting money in a passbook account was still the ingrained habit of the middle class. The more sophisticated savers knew enough to prefer S&L passbook acounts to bank accounts; since 1966, S&Ls had been allowed to pay slightly higher interest rates than banks. (By the late 1970s, S&Ls were paying 5.5 percent; banks, 5.25 percent.) But the number of people who realized that inflation was eroding their savings appeared to be minimal. The firms offering money market funds may have felt deluged with new business, but in this larger context, the money flowing out of banks and into money funds was not much more than a trickle. "Savings accounts," concluded SRI, "are a preferred vehicle for meeting all major household financial goals, even 'keeping up with inflation.' " This last belief was crazy, of course, but there it was.

Kahr, who was analyzing the savings data as it came in, quickly saw the situation for what it was: a gravy train for the banks. In an internal memo, he noted that because of the effect of Regulation Q, "these large accounts are obviously highly profitable when prevailing rates of interest are reasonably high. For instance, if funds can be invested to yield even 8% . . . the institution will earn *$250 per year* on a $10,000 account paying 5¼% to the depositor. By the same token," he added, "the depositor will stand to gain this $250, or a major portion of it, if he accepts an opportunity to . . . invest directly.''

A second big finding was that America was a risk-averse nation, at least when it came to money. ''In spite of their tremendous diversity in financial resources and demographic traits, households exhibit a remarkably consistent pattern of financial conservatism,'' wrote the authors of Consumer Financial Decisions. ''[O]nly 2% of the nonaffluent males and 5% of affluent males indicate that they are willing to assume 'substantial risk' . . . [and] in both income groups, females are more risk averse than are males with similar incomes.''

The implications of this finding could be seen in a dozen different ways. How else to explain why relatively few people had moved their savings to money market funds? Such funds may have been a much better deal than a bank account, but they lacked deposit insurance, which meant they were necessarily riskier. How else to explain that only around 10 percent of the households surveyed had ever used an automatic teller machine? Because ATMs were still so new they too were seen as risky. Since the entire brokerage business was predicated on the willingness of customers to assume risk, SRI made a special effort to pin down the accuracy of the old wirehouse adage about 10 percent of the customers supplying 90 percent of the revenue. What it discovered had to be discouraging news to anyone in the brokerage industry: that mythical 10 percent was, if anything, an overstatement. In reality, a mere ½ of 1 percent of households could be considered active traders. Worse, the wirehouses didn't even have these customers to themselves. Many of them had relationships with up to twenty other financial institutions, including other brokerage firms.

The SRI study was filled with illuminating nuggets like that. Its authors saw the coming popularity of home equity loans. They showed that most people did not view their credit card balance as a loan. They documented the fact that even with the growth of bank cards, the most widely dispersed credit card in America was the Sears charge card, which was held by half the families in the country. (Sears executives, of course, had long known this fact, and were not at all happy about having to share it with the rest of the world.)

Finally, the SRI team concluded that the most important factor driving consumer financial decisions was nothing more than inertia. This may have been the most crucial finding of all. ''Limited consumer knowledge about financial matters and social psychology can help explain the [inertia],'' the authors wrote. ''The individual feels financial matters are both important and complex. He must resolve the situation, yet he knows his knowledge is insufficient. . . . Comparison shopping only prolongs and accentuates the discomfort. He can best deal with this uncomfortable, dissonant position by ignoring financial issues altogether. Inertia and reliance on friends are psychologically efficient solutions.''

So: people tended to buy life insurance not because they felt an urgent need, but because they happened to bump into their friend the life insurance salesman who talked them into it. They tended to be so wedded to old habits and patterns that they would avoid learning about a new financial product if it meant having to do something differently. They put their money in the bank, opened a non-interest-bearing checking account, took advice from a stockbroker who never picked winners—all for one reason. That's what they had always done. Consumer Financial Decisions did not miss the irony: "The customers, who are not forcing the revolutionary changes now under way, will select the winners."

From these collected insights came some predictions about the future, many of which would turn out to be prescient. Because such a large percentage of America's financial assets resided in passbook accounts, those accounts would serve as the primary battleground in the years to come, SRI concluded. The money revolution would be, at its core, a tug-of-war for "savings," with nonbanks trying to pull savings out of banks and S&Ls, while banks and S&Ls pulled just as hard to keep that money right where it was. Because nonbank institutions—brokerage houses especially—held sway over such a small percentage of the nation's financial consumers, they would be the ones pulling hardest. "Cross-selling"—the ability of a firm that traditionally sold one kind of financial product to begin marketing new and different products—would be among the key skills in the coming battles. To succeed, firms would have to develop broad relationships with customers and offer a variety of products.

And yet, because of America's ingrained financial inertia, all of this would be much harder to accomplish than anyone quite realized. Kahr first understood this when he examined the responses to a series of questions he had written aimed at divining why people chose one bank over another. No matter how he phrased the questions, the answer was always the same: people banked wherever it was most convenient. Nothing else mattered— not lower loan rates, not exceptional customer service, not even *bad* service. "You could look at that," says Kahr now, "and say, 'Every fool knows that the key to retail banking is location. So what?' But the 'so what' was that if you were going to create new products and pay lip service to better customer service or better accuracy or timeliness, you had better understand how difficult it's going to be [to show] that those things really have any value in the customer's mind." Breaking the hold of inertia, the tug of old habits, would require something extraordinary. To Kahr, at least, it was clear that in order to compete in the coming battle for savings, you needed a financial product at least as powerful as the inertia it was confronting. You also needed an extremely powerful event—something with the approximate psychological force of the Depression, an event so jarring that Americans would be forced to abandon old habits. Kahr had already devised a powerful product, which Merrill Lynch was in the process of developing. And America itself would provide the second requirement soon enough.

EVEN AS CARL SPETZLER AND HIS SRI TEAM were crisscrossing the country in search of sponsors to underwrite Consumer Financial Decisions, another, much more public event was taking place that helped make the shape of the wave that much clearer. In August 1977, Citibank launched the credit card drop to end all credit card drops. In terms of its size and scope—not to mention the pure, uncoiled ambition it revealed—no drop in the short history of the credit card business had ever come close to it or ever would again. By the time Citibank was finished, it had mailed an overwhelming 26 million credit card solicitations. In the process, it sent a signal about the future that you could scarcely miss if you were a banker. The coming battles weren't going to be fought only between brokerage houses and banks, or between mutual fund companies and banks. They were also going to be fought between banks and other banks, or rather, between most banks and one huge, unruly, gleefully cutthroat bank, which, though legally confined to the state of New York, seemed to have set its sights on taking over the world. It wasn't just consumers who were going to have to break free of old habits. Once Citibank publicly took off the gloves—and there was never any doubt that that's what it did in August 1977—everyone else in banking would have to do the same.

*Citibank.* To even mention the word in a room full of bankers was to tempt fate: as likely as not, someone would erupt in outrage, spewing unbankerly venom at an institution they had all come to despise. Bank of America, it was true, was still the largest in the country, but its days as a banking predator were largely over. Now it was Citibank, which by 1971 had surpassed Chase Manhattan in deposits to become the nation's second-largest bank, that was widely perceived as the predator, the bank that refused to play by the unspoken rules of the game. ''The world's most hated bank,'' the newsletter writer Spencer Nilson once called it, speaking for most of the banking fraternity. But it was a title in which most Citibank executives took a certain smug pride. It was Citibank that had set up Citicorp in the late 1960s as the nation's first bank holding company, an act that both telegraphed its expansionist dreams and gave notice that it would not be bound by the old edicts.[7] It was Citibank that had created the first negotiated CD in the early 1960s, and the first floating prime rate a decade later.

And every year, it was Citibank that cut a little further into Bank of America's once imposing lead, as its aggressive, acerbic chairman, Walter Wriston, spoke openly of his zealous goal of 15 percent annual growth, and goaded his staff to meet that objective. (Or else!) Oh, how other bankers hated Wriston for that! Actually, there were quite a few things about Wriston they hated; he had, the writer John Brooks once pointed out, "a widespread reputation for such not necessarily bankerly qualities . . . as a strong streak of intellectuality, a tendency to call a spade a spade in public, and a fondness for wisecracking to the press." What they mostly hated, though, was his overweening ambition for the institution he ran—his overt desire to have Citibank become the biggest, the strongest, the best-known, the most innovative bank in the country—the kind of ambition not seen in banking since A. P. Giannini. Do you *know* what Wriston was doing by the mid-1970s? Wriston was filling the ranks of Citibank middle management with people who had never been in banking—people from General Foods, who had marketing backgrounds and understood that bank accounts could be thought of as "product lines" and peddled like breakfast cereal. Wriston was rejecting the gentlemanly culture that had long existed in banking and replacing it with the corporate version of a Darwinian death struggle. Wriston was telling his head of personnel to hire "troublemakers" and was rewarding risk takers, sometimes even when they fell on their faces. Wriston was opening offices in ninety-two countries. Wriston was so crazy for growth that he was diving into the murky business of Third World loans, waving off objections to the idea of lending billions to small, shaky governments with perhaps his most famous (and certainly his most wrong-headed) utterance: "A country does not go bankrupt."

Here was another thing about Wriston that drove them all crazy: Wriston was virtually the only banker in America who wanted to see the regulatory barriers torn down. He took this stance for the same reason Don Regan had wanted to see brokerage commissions unfixed. The regulations made the culture of the gentlemanly banker possible. The famous maxim about how the three most important numbers in banking were 3-6-3—take in money at 3 percent, lend it out at 6 percent, and be on the golf course by 3:00 P.M.—that was a direct outgrowth of banking regulation. If you took away the regulations, bankers would suddenly have to compete as never before, just as Wall Street had had to learn to compete once fixed commissions had been abolished.

Wriston had a second argument for wanting to tear down the barriers. He realized, well before most other bankers, that there was precious little banks could do that other financial institutions couldn't. He used to say that he had seen the future of banking in America: "Don Regan runs it, and it's called Merrill Lynch, Pierce, Fenner and Smith." "Banks take deposits . . . and pay interest on them," he said in a famous speech he delivered in the spring of 1980. "So do brokers, money market mutual funds, and all the S&Ls owned by companies like Sears Roebuck, National Steel, Beatrice Foods, and the Baldwin Piano Company." Of all these institutions taking deposits and paying interest, only banks and S&Ls had to pay, by law, below-market interest rates, thanks to Regulation Q. And it wasn't just Regulation Q that galled Wriston; it was Glass–Steagall, it was the McFadden Act, which outlawed interstate banking, it was all of them. Bankers had always assumed that the regulatory structure acted as a shield, protecting them from the vagaries of the marketplace. Wriston realized that just the opposite was true. "Surely it must be obvious by now that the wall built by Glass and Steagall and their friend McFadden to keep people out of the fort [of banking] is today serving an entirely different purpose," he said in that same speech. "All it does now is keep the bankers locked inside while everyone else with imagination and drive harvests the cash crops growing beyond the stockade." For most of Wriston's fourteen years as the head of Citicorp, his chief in-house lawyer played a role very similar to Andrew Kahr's role at SRI. He looked for tiny cracks in the wall and then tried to turn them into gaping holes. "We were changing banking!" exults a former Citibank executive; but other bankers, who still viewed the wall as protection, watched this process with something akin to terror.


Among the survivors of Citibank's Darwinian struggle was John S. Reed, a young man still in his thirties who was fast becoming something of a legend within the bank. He was Wriston's golden boy and had been since he was in his midtwenties: promoted every ten months his first five years at the bank; named senior vice-president by the age of thirty (the youngest in the bank's 172-year history); regularly handed the most important assignments, or at least the ones closest to Wriston's heart, which was pretty much the same thing. Reed was thirty-eight years old in 1977, and with his boyish good looks appeared to be younger still. Yet, within Citicorp, he was already being talked about as a leading contender to replace Wriston when the chairman retired, as he was expected to do in 1984.

From the moment he set foot in the place, in the spring of 1965, John
Reed was at home in Citibank's ruthless corporate culture. He didn't just
thrive in it, but became in time, as at least one writer[8] has suggested, its very
embodiment. However much he may have looked like a boy scout, he was,
in banker's terms, a corporate killer: a brusque, demanding, driven executive who gave no quarter and expected none in return. In a place that prized
risk taking, no one could roll the dice quite like Reed. In a place that didn't
coddle its employees, no one could be as brutal. He regularly put the people
who worked for him under enormous stress, and then almost casually tossed
them aside when they burned out. "He had no fear of firing anyone," recalls
a former associate, "even people he considered friends. He had no loyalty."
He never seemed less comfortable than when he was in an elevator with a
handful of his own employees. Even the executives who reported directly to
him found him a difficult man to know, much less like. Yes, he was brilliant—that practically went without saying—but he was also "icy" and
"harsh," lacking the diplomatic skills and qualities of empathy required of
good executives. The only time he ever engaged in small talk, recalls one of
his former aides, was when he was "sitting around evaluating the people
who worked for him—usually in fairly catty terms—in the presence of other
people who worked for him."

He was tremendously ambitious, too, though that also probably goes
without saying. He used to tell associates that there were only two jobs that
could cause him to leave Citicorp: chairman of the Federal Reserve system,
or president of MIT, his alma mater. He had a particular genius for subtle—
and sometimes not-so-subtle—self-promotion. Once, he created a small
furor at the bank by posing with his wife and children for a two-page ad for
*Scientific American* that ran in *The New York Times*. Among his equally
ambitious colleagues, this was considered an unseemly way to raise one's
public profile. His drive, in fact, took its toll on his family, particularly his
wife; *The New York Times,* in an otherwise glowing profile, once alluded to
"the emotional stress his long hours and work-related travel placed on
[her]." After her problems became evident, he was a changed man—everyone noticed it right away—rigorously leaving the office at 5:30 P.M.
(though he made up for it by starting work at 4:30 A.M.), cutting back on his
travel, and softening the rough edges of his management style, becoming,
in the words of one former associate, less of a "robot." Yet even that helped
fuel his rise, since he was now seen as a more "rounded" executive.

Although Reed had already caught Wriston's eye by the late 1960s, his
reputation at Citibank wasn't cemented until 1969, when he agreed to take
on the monumental task of cleaning up the bank's back office, which had
fallen into such disarray that it had begun to pose a threat not just to

Wriston's 15 percent growth target, but to any growth at all. Reed was twenty-nine years old when he was installed to ride herd over the Operating Group (as the back office was called);[9] by the time he left six years later, he had turned chaos into order: automating everything in sight; setting up systems that more closely resembled an assembly line at General Motors than anything bankers were used to; grabbing control of costs by slashing jobs by the thousands.

Wriston, meanwhile, was coming to the stark conclusion that his growth targets would still remain unattainable unless the bank embarked on some dramatic new course. Third World loans alone just weren't going to get him where he wanted to go, nor would commercial lending, Citibank's longtime strength. Only the consumer could take him where he wanted to go; only by making a major push into retail banking, where the bank was traditionally weak, could Citi grow as big and as fast as he dreamed. In 1975, Wriston tapped his golden boy to make his dream come true.

If Reed's tenure as the head of operations clinched his reputation, his time as the head of Citibank's consumer group created his legend. They can tell you, his old bank colleagues can, about his "Letter from the Beach," which he wrote early in 1976 during a vacation in the Virgin Islands, outlining his grand plan to conquer consumer banking, and about his famous "banana books," thick volumes of statistics and information his division generated each quarter, which were bound in yellow covers (hence the term "banana book"), which Reed pored over, extracting illuminating bits of data that served as his signposts. They can tell you about how he became such a champion of consumer banking that when the national Consumer Bankers Association was thinking of changing its name to something a bit more highbrow, Reed threatened to pull Citi out of the organization if the word "consumer" was dropped. They can tell you about his fanatical focus on the consumer possibilities in technology—the way a computer and a piece of plastic together could open up new vistas for banks—and how he made that focus the linchpin of his strategy. Chemical Bank had been the first New York bank to introduce one such use of computers and a plastic card—the automatic teller machine—but it was John Reed who made it an accepted part of banking, practically shoving ATMs down the throats of reluctant customers. Reed spent untold millions at an R&D facility he set up in California that did nothing but test new consumer uses for technology. Reed's old colleagues, most of whom have scattered to the winds, can tell you, finally, about all the dazzling risks their former boss took, and the dazzling amount of money he lost—somewhere around $500 million before he was done, an incomprehensible sum to just about every other banker in America. Over at Bank of America, Kenneth Larkin watched in slack-jawed astonishment. "Reed did things that would have gotten me fired in a year," he once remarked.

And, of course, they can tell you about the drop. The drop was something.

Several events coincided to made the Citibank drop possible, converging so neatly that they must have seemed to Reed like a gift from the gods. The first, which took place in June 1976, was Dee Hock's reluctant decision to abandon his long-held position on an issue called duality. "Duality" refers to the now-common practice of allowing a bank to issue both Visa and MasterCard. In the mid-1970s, however, this practice was very much against the rules, thanks mainly to Hock, who violently opposed duality. Banks could be part of one system or the other, but they couldn't be part of both. Hock's rationale was that it was as important for Interbank and NBI to compete with each other as it was for the banks to compete among themselves, and that duality would destroy the competition between the two organizations. The minute banks could join both organizations, he believed (correctly, as events would prove), the two systems would be seen as interchangeable.

Since 1971, NBI had been fighting a lawsuit brought by the Worthen Bank in Arkansas, a BankAmericard member that wanted to issue Master Charge cards as well. For five years, the case had inched its way through the courts. But in the winter of 1975, just when it finally seemed as though the case might come to trial, the Justice Department sent a letter to NBI, in which it refused to side with Hock, and implied that it might well take Worthen's position. The letter convinced Hock that he was engaged in a struggle he could not win, so he caved in—wrongly, he now believes. "It is my biggest regret," he would later say, "that I didn't continue the fight."[10] But there were certainly no regrets at Citibank, which up until then had been a Master Charge issuer. Just as Reed and his team were trying to devise ways to expand their consumer business, they were suddenly presented with an option they hadn't considered before: the option of issuing a second credit card. By February 1977, Citibank had joined NBI, though it had not yet issued cards.

The second event was Hock's announcement a few months later that he was renaming both the organization he ran and the card it supported "Visa." Hock could toss off a raft of good reasons for doing this but the main reason was that the word "BankAmericard" just didn't roll trippingly off the tongue, especially the tongues of people in Japan and Argentina and Germany, and all the other countries where Hock was trying to establish beachheads for his payment system. He loved the fact that the word "visa" was pronounced the same way in every language. He saw the name change as another small step in his never-ending drive to create a new international currency—a currency that he hoped would now be called Visa.

Hock unveiled the name change at a banking convention in Orlando in the fall of 1976. The name change would take place the following year, he said, and added that Visa would spend around $50 million on "brand" advertising to acclimate people to the change. Most of the bankers in the room that day viewed the announcement as typical Hock—much ado about very little[11]—but the two Citibank representatives attending the conference felt otherwise. Their names were David Phillips, a direct marketing expert who was one of Reed's top aides, and Richard Kane, who ran the consumer group's credit card division. "A sum like that wasn't quite what they spend on a Colgate campaign, but in the banking business in 1977 it was an incredible number," Kane recalls. "We sat around afterward reflecting on how the American consumer was going to be talked to on national television about a credit card name in a way that has never happened before." Adds Phillips, "We kept thinking, 'What an opportunity!' "

It was an opportunity to insert the chisel once more into the regulatory wall. This time, the wall was the one erected by the McFadden Act, which prevented interstate banking, and which Reed had been trying to break down practically from the moment he took over the consumer group. In Reed's mind—and Wriston's, too—there was never any question that developing the consumer business at Citibank meant developing it *nationally*, banking regulations be damned. There was simply no way the two men were going to be content slapping up new branches and automatic teller machines in New York City, or even New York State. (Statewide branch banking was finally allowed in New York in 1976.) Though Reed's group was convinced that the old banking regulations were doomed, they weren't going to be content to wait for the laws to disappear, either—not when Merrill Lynch had a full-fledged national distribution system, and would soon be trying to lure people away from banks. To compete, Citibank would have to have a national distribution system, too. So what if the banking laws expressly forbade such a thing? At Citibank in the mid-1970s, the stench of hubris was very much in the air.

But how could a bank "go national" and still remain within the letter of the law? That answer was credit cards. Just as the Chicago banks had once dropped credit cards in the Illinois suburbs to attract suburban customers, so could Citibank now use credit cards to try to attract customers all across the nation. It was all theoretically feasible by the mid-1970s; the emergence of credit bureaus, for instance, made it possible to evaluate the creditworthiness of potential customers in faraway locales. The only thing holding bankers back was tradition. And Lord knows, Citibank was never going to let tradition stand in its way.

There was one other piece of information, culled from Reed's extensive research, that made the opportunity irresistible. "We understood that the consumer didn't have the slightest idea which bank he had his card with," recalls Phillips. "We had tested that." This was also in no small part Dee Hock's doing; because of his unyielding insistence that the word "Bank-Americard" be the prominent name on the card, the individual banks were forced to put their own names on the back of the card, practically in fine print.[12] Over time, people tended to forget that they got the card not from some central BankAmericard behemoth, but from a local bank. Now Citibank planned to take advantage of that forgetfulness. It would use the name change from BankAmericard to Visa as its cover.

A bank couldn't just drop credit cards in America anymore; that was against the law. It had to send direct mail solicitations, asking people if they wanted its card, and wait for a positive response. The Citibank solicitations, which were mailed in the late summer and early fall of 1977, read in part:

> A person with your excellent credit standing deserves the best there is. So, we have set aside a new Visa card especially for you. To get your Visa card, all you have to do is return the Reserved Invitation below. . . . Visa is replacing BankAmericard and is now the most widely accepted personal credit card in the world. . . . Best of all . . . THERE'S NO CHARGE TO OBTAIN YOUR VISA CARD.

You will notice that the word "Citibank" never appears in the above paragraph. Later, as news stories began to be written about Citibank's massive credit card blitzkrieg, its executives would strongly deny that there was anything deceptive about what they had done. But that was public relations double-talk. Citibank was counting on the fact that people wouldn't realize they already stood to receive a Visa card—it would come automatically from whichever bank had issued their BankAmericard. Clearly, the mailing was supposed to make people think that only by sending in their application to Citibank could they get this wonderful new card they were hearing so much about on television. And it worked. By the time the mailing had ended, Citibank had issued 3 million Visa cards, making it the nation's second-largest Visa issuer, after only Bank of America. When you added its Master Charge portfolio to its new Visa portfolio, Citibank had become, in one stroke, the largest issuer of bank cards in the world. This is a position it has never relinquished.

It was in many ways a classic Reed foray—lightning quick, extremely bold, infuriating to other bankers (who felt Citibank was trying to trick their customers), and staggeringly expensive. Having never done anything in credit cards on this scale before, Citibank made gigantic mistakes, granting cards to tens of thousands of people who quickly defaulted. As the losses rose to $100 million, to $200 million, to $300 million, Reed never flinched. Neither did Wriston. No matter how high the losses got, the executives in Reed's group were never told that they couldn't spend what they needed to spend. Of course, that just added to the reasons other bankers hated Citibank: Not only did it have money to burn, it was quite willing to burn it.

The Citibank mailings drew three kinds of responses from other bankers. From the bankers in the states hit with Citibank mailings came the expected howls of outrage—the accusations of trickery, and the mounting anger over Citibank's attempt to pick off customers in "their" territory. A second reaction came from bankers in states where Citibank didn't mail, especially New York and California, home to such large credit card banks as Bank of America and Chase Manhattan. Bankers at those institutions assumed an attitude of bemused contempt, as they watched Citibank's losses mount, and sniffed at the many mistakes it had made in its rush to issue Visa cards. And the third reaction came from bankers inside Citicorp itself. Their reaction was one of deep resentment toward this young upstart, who seemed to have such a Svengalilike hold on Wriston. They couldn't understand it: why didn't Wriston just pull the plug on Reed, admit that it was all a big mistake, and try something else? This reaction reached its apotheosis in 1980, a year in which none of the bank's top 250 executives received bonuses, in no small part because John Reed had to take another $100 million loss. "As you can imagine," says Kane now, "visiting the executive dining room at the end of that year was not a pleasant experience."

We know now that all three reactions were misguided. The first category of bankers—those whose BankAmericard customers were lured to Citibank—were wrong to assume that anybody could be considered "their" customer anymore. The second category of bankers—those who scoffed from the sidelines—were wrong to assume that the sidelines were the place to be. Yes, Citibank made mistakes; its credit standards were sloppy; it had a lot to learn. But because it had been willing to absorb the mistakes, even at such immense cost, it was able to stake a lead as an issuer of credit cards that would never be challenged. By the mid-1980s, Citibank's credit card operation was a money machine; one out of every five American families had some kind of banking relationship with Citi, and the great majority of those relationships revolved around credit cards. And as for the third category of bankers—those who worked at Citibank—there were plenty of years when their bonuses were directly traceable to the profits flowing from Reed's creation.

You didn't have to wait until the mid-1980s to realize how it was going to turn out, either. In 1980, the year the Citicorp bonuses were wiped out, a credit card consultant named Helene Duffy predicted that Reed's strategy would ultimately succeed. She pointed out, among other things, that Citibank had established credit card relationships with 4 million families, 5 percent of all American households. "One must admire the aplomb with which Citibank identifies 'our market,' " she added wryly. " 'Our market,' in this instance, means the United States of America."

BARBARA CASEY, THE YOUNG SRI RESEARCHER who had been named project manager for Consumer Financial Decisions, will always remember the day the Citibank solicitations arrived in the mail. She was in Pittsburgh, trying to drum up sponsors for the survey, but wasn't finding many takers among the city's bankers. They were gentlemanly about it, of course: "You don't understand," one kindly banker told her one day. "This is *Pittsburgh*. We're an isolated market here. What's going on in New York doesn't mean that much to us."

The next morning the city of Pittsburgh was swamped with Visa solicitations from Citibank. Since most bankers lived in affluent neighborhoods, they all received mailings; when they arrived in the office, it was all anyone could talk about. There was some gallows humor, especially when some junior officers discovered they had been offered higher lines of credit than their bosses. But in the main, the atmosphere was somber. "People looked shell-shocked," recalls Casey, who was still making her rounds. It was at that moment that bankers in Pittsburgh realized that they weren't as isolated as they had assumed. No one was isolated anymore.

"That day," says Casey, "we got clients in Pittsburgh."

# CHAPTER 8

# The Discreet Charms of the CMA

## *September 1977*

Donald Regan once said in a speech that his favorite Merrill Lynch branch was one located near Tampa, Florida. What he liked about it, he went on to explain, was that it was shaped like a box—more specifically, a box with four entrances, one in each direction. And it was the four doors that captured his imagination, because they seemed a kind of physical embodiment for his scheme to transform Merrill Lynch as the money revolution approached.

As he envisioned it, one door would be the entrance to Merrill Lynch, Pierce, Fenner & Smith, member of the New York Stock Exchange, brokerage to the middle class, wirehouse extraordinaire. A second door would lead to Merrill Lynch Realty, a business Regan thought would go hand in hand with the brokerage industry.[1] The third door would open into Merrill Lynch's Insurance—another business that Regan was sure would mesh well with selling stocks and bonds.

And as for the fourth door, Regan's most fervent hope was that it would someday be the entrance to the Merrill Lynch Bank & Trust. Walter Wriston had it right: Don Regan wanted to be in banking. More precisely, he wanted to be in the business of attracting the consumer deposits that had always flowed to banks as a matter of course. Later they would come up with a phrase for what Regan wanted to do; it was called "gathering assets," and it would soon be the key to everything.

What Regan did not want, however, was to be in banking the way Wriston was in banking, with a hundred bureaucrats looking at his balance sheet, and stiff capital requirements to abide by, and all kinds of regulations about what he could and could not do. Regan wanted to be the kind of post-Glass–Steagall, post-McFadden Act banker that everyone assumed was on the horizon, the kind of banker who could gather deposits (nationwide!) with one hand, while underwriting stocks and offering mutual funds with the other. Then again, Wriston wanted to be that kind of banker too; he could hardly wait for Glass–Steagall to fall, and was doing his best to bring it about as quickly as possible. The difference between the two men was that Wriston was inside the wall trying to break out while Regan was outside the wall trying to break in. As events would prove, Regan's was the easier task.

In the almost eighty years of its existence, Merrill Lynch has twice been in the grip of a completely dominating personality. The first, obviously, was Charlie Merrill, whose hold on his firm remained unshakable long after his death, as his various beliefs and prejudices took on the aura of a sacred text. Merrill's grip wasn't broken until 1968, fully twelve years after he died, when the next dominant figure attained a position of power within the firm. That was Don Regan. Regan was every bit the force of nature Merrill had been, every bit the irascible executive, every bit the egocentric boss.

He was also every bit the b.s. artist. "Reporters liked him at first," writes former White House speechwriter Peggy Noonan, describing Regan when he served in Ronald Reagan's White House, "not only because he was good copy but because every now and then you could look up from your pad and catch that wry twinkle in those eyes, a look that said, Of course I'm full of it, so are you. . . . It's all a glorious con, welcome to life." Noonan goes on: "[Y]ou can see it all the minute you meet him, he loves his power and his fame. But . . . he has the Irish disease: He cannot resist a good line . . . and he cannot resist appearing to be tough and mean when in fact . . . you could tell, he wasn't so tough and he wasn't so mean."

Well, maybe you could tell that from the vantage point of the White House in the 1980s, but if you worked at Merrill Lynch in the 1970s, what you mainly saw was that he was tough and mean. His toughness, to be sure, had a hopelessly exaggerated quality: he would bang his fist on the desk when he wanted something done *right now!*; he would bark out orders and expect them to be done *yesterday!*; when he opposed something, he would tell the poor schmo who had proposed it that it would only get done *over my dead body!* "Someone was always knifing, sandbagging, bashing, or snookering some jackass, Joe Schmo, or betrayer," recalls Noonan. Regan himself liked to boast: "I don't get ulcers. I give 'em!"

That Regan's aggressively autocratic style got results is undeniable. In 1971, his first full year as chief executive, Merrill Lynch earned $70 million on revenues of $676 million. A decade later, profits were up threefold, on revenues that exceeded $3 billion. Perhaps because of his Marine background, he had a military man's love of the bold stroke: when he decided that Merrill Lynch needed to beef up its research department, he simply got a copy of *Institutional Investor*'s annual listing of the best Wall Street analysts and hired as many as he could, often doubling or tripling their salaries. "It was a display of financial muscle perhaps not seen on lower Manhattan since the 1920s," Chris Welles later wrote. Indeed, by the time Regan left in early 1981, the most striking fact about the firm wasn't that it was so much bigger but that it was so plainly different. You couldn't call it a wirehouse anymore, not if you wanted to be fair; it had outgrown the label. Regan's goal of breaking into the institutional side of the business had been accomplished. Merrill Lynch paid commissions instead of salaries, and offered mutual funds, money market funds, and real estate services as well as stocks and bonds. It was a public company instead of a private partnership. Its slogan—"Merrill Lynch is bullish on America"—which was created early in Regan's tenure, was among the best-known lines in America. It was headquartered in a large and handsome new building, which Regan had named—with a typical Reganesque flourish—One Liberty Place. And if Merrill Lynch wasn't quite a bank by the time he walked out the door, it was certainly headed in that direction.

The downside of Regan's blustery, brook-no-dissent style was that he wound up being surrounded by yes-men. His working premise, never stated directly but never far from the surface, was that he was smarter than the people around him. Those who accepted that premise prospered during his regime. Those who didn't were "idiots" or "dopes," and he rode them mercilessly, until he had ridden them right out of the firm. Several of the "idiots" had been his only intellectual equals at Merrill Lynch, but Regan's deep-seated need to be the Big Cheese made it impossible for him to tolerate their presence.

And when he left the firm himself to go to Washington as Ronald Reagan's first Treasury Secretary in 1981,[2] the shadow he cast was every bit as long as Merrill's had been. His handpicked successor, an unassuming man named Roger Birks, seemed to view his mission as carrying forward the Regan strategy[3]—a view that Regan did nothing to discourage whenever he attended some Merrill Lynch social function, where he was the center of attention, just as he had been when he was running the place. Four years after Regan had left, a young executive named Robert Rittereiser[4] was given the task of reviewing the firm's entire strategy. Among Rittereiser's conclusions was that it made no sense for Merrill Lynch to be in the real estate business. Yet when he stood before the company's board of directors and delivered his verdict, the directors looked at him as if he had lost his mind. "But Don Regan said it was great business!" they replied as one.

It wasn't until the market crash of 1987 that Regan's hold on Merrill Lynch began to loosen, and it was another few years still before the firm shook it off entirely. In 1989, with Merrill Lynch struggling to rebound from the crash, Regan gave an interview to *Fortune* magazine that was cuttingly critical of his old firm. The week that issue of *Fortune* came out, a visitor to the Merrill Lynch offices was likely to notice a very odd thing. In one office after another, there was a small, square spot on one wall where the paint seemed brighter and fresher than the rest of the wall. That's the spot where the photograph of Don Regan had once hung.

He was an impossible man to know. That's one thing they all still remember about Regan: for someone who took such evident relish in being a public figure, he was a very private person. For much of his career, he commuted from Princeton, New Jersey; the distance alone kept his colleagues at arm's length. Perhaps the biggest difference between Charlie Merrill and Regan was that Regan was a devoted family man, with no discernible interest in the indiscriminate womanizing that was Merrill's lifelong weakness. But his devotion to his family also meant that Regan was usually out the door at 5:30, heading for the commuter train. Rare were the times that he stayed after work to have a martini with the boys, though such after-hours cama- raderie could have helped his career.

So what did they know about him? They knew only what he let them know, which wasn't much. They knew he was Boston Irish or, more pre- cisely, Cambridge Irish, the rare townie accepted at Harvard, where he won a scholarship set aside for the locals. They didn't know, however, that he'd had an older brother who'd died, a fact they first learned, to their great surprise, when they read the autobiography he wrote in 1988. They knew about all the jobs he'd held as he worked his way through school, and how the experience of working those jobs—and paying taxes on his wages—had turned him into a conservative Republican when everyone around him was a Roosevelt Democrat, his parents included. "I was an usher when Social Security went into effect," he used to explain, "so I knew what it was like to have money deducted from a paycheck—money that I had *earned*!" His colleagues knew he had been in the Marine Corps during World War II, but they knew next to nothing of his combat experience. Even in his autobiog- raphy, Regan barely glances over the five different theaters he fought in, including Okinawa, where he commanded over 1,200 men, a fact left out of the book. He dwells longer on his time in Quantico, Virginia, because that's where he met Ann Buchanan, who would soon become his wife. Here, however, he omits something from his book that everyone at Merrill Lynch was acutely aware of. Ann Buchanan was the niece of Merrill's right-hand man, Win Smith. And as the young Regan began to climb the greasy pole—and as it became obvious that he was a personal favorite of not just Smith but Merrill himself—there was no small amount of gossip that his family connections lay behind his swift and regular promotions. For there was one other thing everybody knew about Don Regan: he planned on running the firm someday. This was not something he ever admitted, of course, but he didn't have to. He wore it on his sleeve.

Regan would always bridle at the gossip. In his mind, he succeeded because he worked hard—because he had *earned* it, by God. And if the old man took a shine to him, it was probably because he reminded Merrill of someone the founder greatly admired: himself. Regan was brash from the minute he walked in the door, completely unafraid to contradict a senior man if he thought he was right. He first came to Merrill's attention as a result of one such incident, in which he interrupted a senior partner's lecture about Merrill Lynch sales techniques to tell the man point-blank that he didn't have the faintest idea how the men in the field were selling stocks and bonds. Merrill happened to be sitting in the room. "That Regan is a fresh SOB," he is supposed to have said; it was not meant as a criticism. In 1953, when Regan made partner at the age of thirty-five—at the time, the youngest general partner in the firm's history—it was Merrill who lent Regan the $10,000 he needed to buy into the partnership. When a promotion caused "a certain amount of discontent" (in Regan's discreet phrase), it was Merrill who soothed his worries. "Hell, there isn't a job in this firm that a man your age can't handle if he applies himself," the founder said, as he and his protégé sipped brandy at Merrill's Long Island estate. Then he bestowed the ultimate Merrill compliment: "I know—I did it myself when I was younger than you."

Whatever the reason, nothing seemed to slow Regan down, no matter how many feathers he ruffled. After an early tour of duty in the Washington branch office, Regan became the special assistant to Robert Magowan, who ran the firm's sales department—and was Merrill's son-in-law. In 1960, after running the Philadelphia office for a few years, he became the head of administration. Then he was put in charge of Magowan's old division, which had been renamed Marketing and Sales, and where by all accounts he shone. He was a member of the firm's operating committee, set up its first planning department, became one of three officials designated as "executive assistant to the president." By 1968, not yet fifty years old, he was president himself.

This, in fact, was the one time his enemies within the firm did manage to slow him down. Soon after Regan became president of Merrill Lynch, a handful of partners arrayed against him managed to install a new chief executive officer, a man named James E. Thomson, who was only a few years from retirement. Thomson's promotion was meant as a stalling tactic, to give the anti-Regan faction a few more years to coalesce around an alternate candidate. Some stalling tactic it turned out to be: Regan responded by acting as if Thomson had already retired. Thomson was almost never quoted in the press; it was always Regan. Regan was the mastermind behind the acquisition of a firm called Lionel D. Edie, which had a strong mutual fund division, and which brought Merrill Lynch—at last!—into the mutual fund business. In January 1969, it was Regan, not Thomson, who chaired a two-day conference of the firm's partners, in which he outlined the goals for the next five years. That same year, *Forbes* magazine proclaimed that Regan was leading "a quiet revolution" at Merrill Lynch; Thomson wasn't even mentioned. By the time Thomson retired at the end of 1970, there was not the slightest doubt who the next CEO would be.

Thomas Chrystie, who spent the 1970s as one of Regan's lieutenants, likes to say that the Regan era comprised four phases. In the earliest phase, Regan grappled with Merrill Lynch's back-office problems, while recasting the firm in his image. The second phase consisted of his successful attempt to bull his way into the institutional business. And the final phase, which took place toward the end of the 1970s, saw Regan's growing involvement in national economic affairs. People who watched him then were convinced that he was angling for a top Washington post—which, of course, he was.

It is the third phase, though, that seems most significant in retrospect. For it was during this stretch—which began, roughly, when Mayday arrived—that Regan's already big plans for the firm became geometrically bigger. Suddenly he was no longer content to play on Wall Street's stage—even if he was the strongest player, running the best-known firm. The third phase was when he yearned to be a real estate broker, a life insurer, a banker—when he wanted Merrill Lynch to be everywhere, doing everything. At one point, he became embroiled in serious merger discussions with James Robinson, the new CEO of American Express; the combination, had it come to pass, would have created the country's first financial supermarket.[5] Even without the merger, though, Regan's goal remained constant. "What we're trying to do," he liked to say, "is see how many financial services we can perform for people—legally and profitably." After Mayday, he understood that there was nothing to stop him from pursuing that goal. Nothing but the "sandbagging jackasses" on his own staff, who were worried about where

Regan's new ambitions would lead, and tried to resist him. Not that they ever had a chance.

There were two people who were instrumental in setting Regan on this new path. The first was a man named Ted Braun, an outside management consultant whose career had largely revolved around Merrill Lynch. Braun was as much a fixture at the firm as any senior partner; he and Charlie Merrill had first worked together in the 1930s. Because he was such a strong link to the past, his opinions carried weight. And his opinion—which he began voicing in the 1960s—was that Merrill Lynch needed to diversify.

Regan was never especially generous in parceling out credit for things that happened on his watch; with Braun, he was positively niggardly. "*I* played the catalyst!" he later boasted. Well, maybe. At the least, Braun and Regan were thinking along the same lines. The stock market, Braun (and Regan?) believed, was a fickle mistress—when it was up, business boomed; when it was down, business vanished. Merrill Lynch did more than 10 percent of the stock trades conducted on the New York Stock Exchange, but the volume of those trades could careen wildly from year to year, and even from month to month. This was an impossible situation for a soon-to-be-public company with enormous fixed costs: it needed earnings that didn't rise and fall with each blip of the Dow Jones average. "If we didn't diversify," Regan would later say (echoing Braun?), "we would never control our own destiny."

As for the second instrumental person, that was Andrew Kahr.

They met maybe twice, Regan and Kahr, in circumstances so unremarkable that years later, Regan would draw a blank when asked about Kahr. Yet their effect on each other was profound. Regan gave Kahr the thing he most needed as he began to make his way as a consultant: credibility. Once Kahr left his mark on Merrill Lynch, there could be no doubting the power of his ideas. And Kahr gave Regan something he needed just as badly. He handed Regan a product that ripped away the old financial barriers like nothing that had come before. Kahr's product was called a cash management account, and it was the one that woke everyone up—especially bankers, who understood at last the threat they faced.

What was it about a cash management account that made it such a threat to the existing order? The short answer was that it took disparate elements— each of which had previously been connected to one particular segment of the financial world—and gathered them together in one account. So: a CMA was anchored by a stock and bond portfolio, which firms like Merrill Lynch traditionally offered. But it also had a money market fund attached to it—a product that had been the province primarily of mutual fund companies like Fidelity and Dreyfus. In addition to paying "market" interest on any cash a customer put into his CMA, the money fund also regularly swept in dividends and other payouts, allowing that money to begin earning interest for the customer. The money fund, of course, had check-writing privileges—formerly the sole province of banks. And to top it off, a CMA came with a Merrill Lynch plastic card, thus cutting into the banking business in yet another way. The card alone was a remarkable creature. It could serve as a debit card or a credit card depending on the circumstances: If the customer had enough cash in his money market account, funds would be immediately "debited" to cover the charge. If he didn't, the charge would trigger a margin account—in effect, allowing the customer to borrow the money retroactively against the value of his stock portfolio. This was not a small point: just as home equity loans would later "liquefy" the rising value of a home—allowing the home owner access to some of that gain without having to sell his house—so did the CMA make it possible for a customer to liquefy his portfolio without having to sell his stocks and bonds.

The CMA was a device that crossed once-uncrossable barriers. It gave customers a way to cut out some of the myriad overlap that was so prevalent in the financial universe. And it was an enormously complex device that created a great deal of financial simplification. In all these ways and more, it was the quintessential money revolution product. Though it was not meant for everybody—not with Merrill Lynch requiring every new CMA customer to have a beginning balance of $20,000, either in stocks, bonds, or cash—it was a window into the future.

Typically, Merrill Lynch history has since been rewritten to expunge the name of a mere free-lance consultant from its official version of the invention of the cash management account. In this version, it is Tom Chrystie who has the masterstroke one December day in 1975—a day he spent at Menlo Park, brainstorming with the SRI financial group. "Andrew Kahr was not the key guy," Chrystie insists. Everyone else at that meeting insists just as firmly that Kahr *was* the key guy. Given Kahr's subsequent track record, one would have to conclude that the weight of the evidence is in his favor.

What everyone involved does agree on is that the cash management account grew out of that daylong meeting at SRI. Having just been put in charge of Merrill Lynch's new holding company—a job that meant he was supposed to lead the diversification effort—Chrystie found on his new desk a stack of proposals from SRI. "They wanted to write books about financial services that we would underwrite," he says derisively. He called Carl Spetzler intending to turn the proposals down, but Spetzler persuaded him to spend a day at SRI first, where he could sit in an office and listen as the SRI consultants pitched him their best diversification ideas. Grudgingly, he agreed.

It was a long day. The SRI staff was full of ideas. Spetzler had become fixated on the idea of financial planning for the middle class,[6] and pushed Chrystie to let SRI explore the idea of a financial planning unit for Merrill Lynch.[7] Other members of the team had their own pet projects, most of which Chrystie summarily rejected. Only toward the end of the day did the CMA begin to take shape.

Kahr had conceived of something along the lines of a cash management account even before he signed on with SRI; he had tried to get Wells Fargo interested in it in an earlier consulting stint. During Chrystie's visit, caught up in the spirit of the moment, he basically handed the idea over to Merrill Lynch. SRI wound up with a $100,000 contract to develop the CMA in concert with Merrill Lynch, over the next six months. With the SRI financial group not even a year old, it seemed a healthy sum to Spetzler. In retrospect—with Merrill Lynch's CMA now holding more than $250 billion in assets, and all the competing CMAs holding tens of billions more—he gave the thing away.

From the point of view of a wirehouse, circa 1975, the CMA had a serious drawback: by making it possible for customers to earn interest on their cash, through the money market feature, a brokerage firm would be depriving itself of the easy profits that resulted from investing its customers' free credit balances for its own account. Chrystie, of course, immediately understood this, and according to one published account,[8] he and Kahr began arguing about the importance of the free credit balance:

> By paying customers interest on their money [in a CMA], Chrystie contended, the firm would be throwing away its "ace in the hole." Kahr had a different view of things. "It's not your ace in the hole," he declared coolly. "It's your Achilles' heel." At a time of ravaging inflation and high interest rates, he argued, people were less likely to sit back while a financial intermediary earned interest on their money.

Before he left that day, Chrystie recognized that Kahr was right. For someone steeped in the traditions of a wirehouse, it was a significant breakthrough.

Chrystie also deserves credit for much of what happened next. He was the one who sold the idea to Regan. He lined up the arguments for why something this radical made sense for Merrill Lynch. He figured out how much the new account might cost the firm in lost free credit balances, and how the earnings from the new product might offset those easy profits. He investigated the technical feasibility of the CMA. One large potential stumbling block was that under the rules of the credit card associations, only a bank could issue a credit card. To get around this stricture, Kahr proposed that Merrill Lynch ask a bank to issue a credit card on its behalf. But that still meant that a willing bank had to be found, and that one of the credit card associations had to agree to this rather blatant stretching of the rules. Another problem was creating computer programs sophisticated enough to sweep cash into money funds each night or trigger margin accounts. This was all new territory.

Chrystie spent four months laying the groundwork. By the time he was ready to show the cash management account to Regan, he had enlisted some fifty people at Merrill Lynch to work part-time on the project. He swore them all to secrecy.

He finally unveiled the project in April 1976. The forum he chose was a meeting of Merrill Lynch's operating committee, which comprised all the top executives. Kahr and Spetzler gave a presentation, as did Chrystie, spelling out this bold new product idea they were calling, somewhat apologetically, a cash management account. (They vowed to come up with a snappier name.) James Fuller, from SRI, was also present that day, and what sticks in his mind is the cacophony of protests that arose when the presentations had ended. "It's obviously too complicated," the marketing vice president began. "The brokers will see right through it," added the vice president in charge of the branch system. "I couldn't possibly interface with a bank every night," complained the operations vice president. "And besides all that," added the general counsel, "it's illegal." As each man had his say, Regan remained silent. Then, after an appropriately dramatic pause, he spoke. "I've heard all the nay-sayers," he said. "I'd like to tie a can to someone's tail and see if we can get it done."

Afterward, Regan called Chrystie into his office. "I don't want anyone in the firm to know about this yet." Chrystie informed Regan that at least fifty people knew already. "How are you going to keep this confidential?" Regan demanded. Chrystie suggested that he draft a memo for Regan to sign, but by the time he had finished, Regan had written his own memo. "Not since the Manhattan Project has there been such a need for secrecy," it began forbiddingly. "If there is any leak, and we can trace it, that person will no longer be working for Merrill Lynch." Well, that was Don Regan. He couldn't help himself.

*       *       *

The next year was spent ironing out the bugs. The easy part, it turns out, was lining up the bank that would issue the card for Merrill Lynch,[9] making sure the federal government wouldn't object, and getting NBI to go along with the subterfuge that would allow Merrill Lynch to issue a plastic card. Indeed, Dee Hock could not have been more enthused about an idea if he had thought of it himself. Such a product played right into his vision of plastic cards as a powerful, flexible "payment device," as opposed to a "mere" credit card. That Merrill Lynch hoped to crash an association intended only for banks was irrelevant to him. The more the merrier, in his view.[10]

No, the big problems with the cash management account were never with the people outside Merrill Lynch; they were with the people inside the firm. It was extraordinarily difficult, technically. "Interfacing" with a bank each night, "sweeping" cash each day into interest-bearing accounts, automatically "liquefying" a stock portfolio when the occasion demanded—these were all immensely complex tasks, requiring applications far beyond anything Merrill Lynch had attempted before. And once the programmers had finished, the marketers had to start worrying about how to sell it: how to make something new and complicated seem simple and understandable and desirable.

But the biggest roadblock was that almost everybody at Merrill Lynch wanted their revolutionary new product to flop. To them, it was an expensive sideshow, irrelevant to the needs of a wirehouse, which was in the business (to be perfectly blunt about it) of generating commissions. The cash management account, which was costing millions of dollars, was consuming enormous energies, and was even requiring the installation of an entirely new computer system, *would never generate a penny in new commissions*. Not only that, it would rob the firm of its free credit balances. What good was *that*? The brokers were apoplectic; the way they saw it, they were being asked to sell something that brought them nothing in return. And if the brokers were upset, then management was upset, since keeping the brokers happy was what management existed to do. Paul Stein, the young executive given the unenviable task of marketing the CMA, recalls that when he began his new assignment in July 1977, a higher-ranking executive pulled him aside. "Your job," the man said, "is to sink it in the Atlantic by next April."

There was only one reason the CMA didn't die an early death. Don Regan wanted it to live. That's all that mattered. Even he had his doubts on occasion, which Chrystie repelled by reminding Regan that brokerage firms weren't the only ones who could create a product like this: a bank could do it, and so could Sears Roebuck. From time to time, Regan needed to hear that.

The rest of the firm never saw those doubts, however. What it saw was Regan's seemingly pigheaded insistence that the firm forge ahead, no matter what the cost in money and morale. The other executives finally came to the grudging realization that Regan would never back away from the CMA during a meeting of the operating committee early in 1978. By then, the CMA had been unveiled in a handful of states, and it was floundering badly. At last, its opponents thought, they had some ammunition: in the market-place, where it mattered, the product was failing.

Regan was not noticeably ill-tempered that day; he heard them all out, didn't call anyone an idiot or bang his fist on the table. "I appreciate your recommendation," he began when they had finished. Then he paused to create the sense of drama he so loved. "But there's been a vote taken here today, and it's one to nothing. I'm the one, and you guys are the nothing. We go forward." And with that, he walked out of the conference room.

Years later, after the CMA had become an acknowledged success, they would all concede that that meeting was the key moment. Regan himself would happily recount the story over the years—as it became Exhibit A in the case he would build for himself as the "godfather" of the CMA. That was when the sandbagging jackasses had to stop their sniveling and get on board. And it was a lucky thing they did. The loss of the free credit balance turned out to be a nonevent,[11] more than made up for by the annual fee attached to the CMA. Chrystie had estimated that the CMA might attract 100,000 customers; by the time the bull market was in full swing in the mid-1980s, it had well over a million customers, making up 20 percent of the Merrill Lynch customer base. Many of those customers were new ones, who moved their brokerage business to Merrill Lynch specifically to open a CMA.

The cash management account also turned out to be an illumination for Merrill Lynch, for as a gatherer of assets, it was an astonishing thing. The total assets in a CMA—the combined value of the stocks, bonds, and cash—were much larger than Merrill Lynch had expected—as much as ten times larger. Chrystie had based his early predictions about the size of individual accounts on the size of traditional Merrill Lynch accounts. But the CMA was a far stronger magnet than a traditional brokerage account. People really liked the idea of being able to use one account to do a half-dozen different things; it *did* make life simpler. As a result, the CMA attracted billions of dollars of assets that Merrill Lynch had never seen before—stock certificates residing at other firms, cash from bank CDs, money salted away in money market funds. "For the first time," says one executive, "we got a true picture of our customers' assets." It was an eye-opener. It reinforced the firm's realization that its piece of the financial pie was a mere sliver in the large scheme of things. Even the densest executives had to see that the CMA offered the best chance of grabbing a larger piece.[12]

Yet one also winds up feeling that those years of internal resistance took a toll.[13] Although the CMA became, in time, a significant weapon in Merrill Lynch's arsenal, it was never as powerful as it might have been. With the money revolution gaining momentum, asset-gathering was poised to become the single most valuable skill for any financial company. Those who emphasized that skill would wind up the winners. But Merrill Lynch, despite creating in the CMA an extremely powerful asset gatherer, could never take the full plunge. For all its power as a financial device, the CMA was never powerful enough to change the culture of the firm. At Merrill Lynch, they could never break free of the idea that persuading people to trade stocks was the preeminent goal, and the brokers could never get past the fact that the CMA was a product that brought no commissions. The reward system at Merrill Lynch never adapted to the CMA; the traditional method of paying brokers was simply too entrenched.

Regan's successor, Roger Birks, says that one of his biggest regrets during his early-1980s tenure was his inability to change the way the firm made money. "I wish we had been able to move to an annual fee arrangement with our customers, with no commissions involved," he says. Regan would always argue that he had no choice when he abolished Charlie Merrill's old salary system in the late 1960s; Merrill Lynch was losing too many brokers to other firms. In the short term, his logic made sense. But given the way the world was changing, one can't help thinking that it was Merrill who had it right all along.


In July 1977, the cash management account, as it was officially known—they never did come up with a snappier name—was unveiled at a press conference. Two months later, Merrill Lynch began to roll it out, rather tepidly it would seem now. It was just a test, the firm assured its brokers, hoping to quell any possible rebellion. That was the first mistake. "If you were a salesman," Stein says now, "why would you put a valued customer into a product that was only being tested?" The firm chose to roll it out in three cities: Denver, Atlanta, and Columbus. These cities were picked because there was nothing in the banking laws of Colorado, Georgia, and Ohio that would seem to prohibit a CMA. Another mistake: the wording of the law could not have been less relevant. What mattered was whether the city's leading bankers would object to the CMA, and whether the chief regulator was a golfing buddy of the most powerful bank president. Finally, once the CMA was introduced, there was very little advertising or promotion. It was as if Merrill Lynch was trying to sneak its revolutionary new product past everybody.

Which, in fact, it *was* trying to do. Money market funds had been born in relative obscurity, and had built their customer base quietly, without arousing the ire of the nation's bankers. Paul Stein, who was in charge of the rollout, hoped to do the same with the CMA. But it was an impossible hope. Merrill Lynch's brokers may not have appreciated their new weapon, but most bankers understood it right away. With a CMA, people could write checks! They could earn interest on their savings! They could even use a credit card! *That's what banks did!* It *had* to be illegal! And if it wasn't illegal, they would make it illegal. Stein spent the better part of the next three years fighting legislative and court battles in some two dozen states; his battles began almost from the moment of the rollout. In Denver, Merrill Lynch ran a small ad in the local papers. Almost immediately, Merrill Lynch was sued by the Colorado Bank Board.

And when Stein tried to hire local lawyers and lobbyists, he discovered how enmeshed local power brokers are in each other's business. The big law firms all had banks on retainer, as did the local lobbyists. Stein laid out his case at several law firms he wanted to hire, arguing that the CMA was plainly legal in Colorado. His argument carried no weight. "Boy, are you in trouble," several lawyers told him.

And so it went. Early in 1978, as Merrill Lynch prepared to introduce the CMA in Oregon, Stein flew to Eugene to meet the state banking commissioner, a man named John Olin. "This is to let you know," Olin began, "that if you offer it here, we'll have to take you to court." Olin was a colorful character, and when reporters asked him about Merrill Lynch's new financial product, he summed up the views of many bankers. As far as he was concerned, he said, the CMA looked like a duck, walked like a duck, and quacked like a duck. Therefore, he concluded, "it should be regulated by whoever is charged with regulating the ducks."

And yet, despite everything, the CMA began to catch on. To entice the brokers to promote the product, Stein began offering trips to Hawaii to the salesmen who opened the most accounts. To appease the state regulators, he learned to approach banking officials—and line up lawyers and lobbyists—before rolling out the CMA. And despite the lack of publicity, the CMA began getting great word of mouth. There were stories about people getting $25,000 cash advances with the Visa card, or buying a car with the card. People heard about the money market fund feature, offering market interest rates, and the monthly statement feature, which gave an accounting of their entire financial life that month. They liked these features. A notorious bank robber opened a CMA, and used its debit card to charge his getaway rent-a-car—and then deposited the money he'd just stolen in its money fund. In Oregon, the cash management account was finally allowed not because the bank regulators had a sudden change of heart but because Oregonians were outraged that everyone in the country had access to it except them.

Most of all, it caught on because of a stroke of timing. At the same time the CMA was being launched, the economic climate in America was changing dramatically. Interest rates were going up, not just a little at a time, but in great leaps. The Consumer Price Index was also rising rapidly. There had been price rises before, of course, but never like this: they had never been so frightening or so seemingly unstoppable. Americans across the economic spectrum had the feeling, as the writer Nicholas Lemann later put it, that "at the level of ordinary life, as opposed to public affairs, things seemed to be out of control."

And yet, even as interest rates and inflation were setting postwar records, bank savings accounts were still paying only 5¼ percent interest, thanks to Regulation Q. The disparity had become intolerable. If you had money in the bank, as most middle-class Americans did, you could no longer afford to ignore the growing differential. It was costing you too much. For the first time, you had to begin exploring alternatives that had always been a little beyond your frame of reference, like money market funds and cash management accounts. Suddenly, you had to start thinking about where best to put your money, and what to do with it, and how to keep pace with this new threat to your savings.

You had to start thinking this way because you were suddenly living in the Age of Inflation.

# Part II

# GROUND ZERO

# GROUND
# ZERO

# CHAPTER 9

# The Great Inflation

## *July 1979*

INFLATION IN THE late 1970s and early 1980s—The Great Inflation, as Theodore H. White once aptly labeled it—trickled in with one President, Jimmy Carter, and limped out with another, Ronald Reagan. But in between it raged out of control, a brushfire that seemingly could not be contained, no matter how many firefighters were parachuted in or how many assaults were made.

It scared us, this inflation; it scared us terribly, and it changed us. Inflation splintered the status quo every bit as much as the Vietnam War did. Among other things, it helped fuel the rise of special interest politics, causing Americans to become selfish in a way they really hadn't been before. People had responded to the Depression by helping each other out as best they could, but inflation had the opposite effect on us. It created an ethos in which people felt justified in cutting special deals for themselves, even when the net effect of those deals was to ratchet up the inflation rate. Whenever a union chief won a demand that his members receive wage increases exceeding the cost of living, his action made inflation worse for all of us, who had to bear the cost of those higher wages for the lucky few. Whenever the elderly lobby won an automatic cost of living adjustment to their Social Security payments, they fueled inflation. But when government officials argued that the "spiral of inflation" could only be stopped if Americans were willing to sacrifice for the common good, they got nowhere. Americans weren't willing to sacrifice for the common good, not when it came to inflation. Inflation didn't just have a corrosive effect on our money; it had a corrosive effect on us.

Inflation changed our politics, too. Just as the Depression paved the way for Franklin Roosevelt and twenty years of Democratic control of the White House, so did inflation pave the way for Ronald Reagan and twelve years of

Republican control of the White House. It wasn't the only reason for this change, of course, but it was a bigger one than it is usually given credit for. The term "tax-and-spend Democrat," which Reagan and George Bush both hurled so effectively in their successful presidential campaigns, was intended as much as anything to conjure up the specter of those days when inflation raged, and we all felt helpless to do anything about it. Politicians who taxed and spent were politicians who inflated the economy—and then robbed the people of the means to keep pace with the menace they had created. And they were also politicians who had proved as helpless in the face of inflation as the rest of us.

Finally, inflation altered forever the relationship of the middle class to its money. Here is when old behaviors were abandoned and new financial habits acquired—habits that would remain with us long after inflation had subsided, just as the habits acquired during the Depression lasted long after that traumatic time had receded into memory. Looking back, it almost seems as though, in some strange, preordained way, everything that had previously taken place in the money revolution had been leading up to this point. Most certainly, everything that happened afterward flowed from it. The Age of Inflation was the money revolution's ground zero. It marked the moment when everything changed—when the financial life of the middle class would never again be simple or ordered or easy.


The politician whose career was most damaged by inflation—the one we think of instinctively when we are reminded of those bad times—is Jimmy Carter. The portrait of a politician flailing futilely at inflation is the portrait of Carter in his cardigan sweater, staring sincerely into the television monitor as he delivers yet another of his many exhortations, urging us to shoulder our part of the burden for the good of all. Carter was big on shared sacrifice; it was something he believed in passionately. But as a result, every one of his many inflation-fighting plans was rooted in the notion that inflation could only be beaten if people were willing to give up something they wanted (a price hike, a wage increase, a cost of living adjustment) to help the country. When we proved unwilling to do that—and when Carter proved unable to back up his exhortations with either a carrot or a stick—we booted him out of office. However much his reputation has been rehabilitated since, he has never shed the stigma of the President Who Couldn't Stop Inflation. There was something truly frightening about watching this obviously good-hearted man fail so miserably in dealing with the issue that mattered most to the middle class. That's also part of what made inflation itself so frightening, and why it sticks with us still.

Inflation was not a new phenomenon when Jimmy Carter came to office, of course; since Lyndon Johnson, Presidents had been struggling to get it under control, with varying degrees of success. Nixon had imposed his wage and price controls in the early 1970s, and after an initial outbreak of double-digit inflation in 1974,[1] Gerald Ford had instituted his widely ridiculed WIN program. (The initials stood for Whip Inflation Now; when Ford announced the program in a televised address, he wore a WIN button in his lapel.) Still, within two years, the rate of inflation, as measured by the Consumer Price Index, was under 5 percent a year. Ford's problem was that in focusing so exclusively on inflation, he had allowed unemployment to rise to a politically unacceptable 8 percent. Nothing hurt him more than that when he ran against Carter in 1976.

Carter's problem, on the other hand, was that he came to office with a belief, born of a deadly combination of hubris and an utter lack of knowledge about macroeconomics, that he could handle everything at once. He could control inflation while bringing down unemployment, and he could balance the federal budget (widely thought to be a leading cause of inflation) while adding dozens of new programs. But of course the world doesn't work that way: you can't balance the budget if you're planning only to *add* federal programs, as Carter seemed to be suggesting. And according to classic Keynesian macroeconomic theory, which was still the reigning dogma when Carter became President, you couldn't manage both inflation and employment at the same time, either. Keynesians[2] believed that capitalism's two most intractable problems stood opposite each other like the ends of a seesaw: one couldn't go down without the other going up. Indeed, it was widely believed among mainstream economists that the one sure way to rid the country of inflation was simply to plunge it into a recession. Several of Carter's top economic advisers[3] urged him to do exactly that—to get "his" recession out of the way early, as they used to phrase it. The new President wouldn't countenance the suggestion, however. "High unemployment is a morally unacceptable way of combating inflation," he said in his first official pronouncement on the subject, "and I totally reject that approach."

So what did that leave him with? Not much, as it turns out, something Carter began to realize after he had been in office for a while. There's only so much the government can do to influence the direction of an economy in any case, which is why it is ultimately unfair to expect any President to be able to solve the nation's economic problems more or less single-handedly. This is especially true when the problem is inflation. "When price inflation becomes a normal state of affairs," points out the writer Charles Morris, "inflationary assumptions weave themselves into every day's transactions, and the inflationary process becomes so deeply embedded in the economy

that it is beyond the reach of policy tinkering by presidential advisers.''
That's what economists meant when they talked about the inflationary spiral:
workers, anticipating inflation, clamored for higher wages to keep up with
the cost of living. Businesses, anticipating wage hikes, raised prices to
protect their profit margins. Social Security recipients, their monthly checks
indexed to the cost of living, began getting larger checks. Which triggered
more inflation. Which triggered a new round of wage demands. Which
triggered a new round of price increases. The *expectation* of inflation was
creating inflation; it was a psychological phenomenon as much as anything
else.

A President couldn't stop inflation by unilaterally rolling back world oil
prices, even though they were probably the single leading cause of inflation
in the late 1970s. (This was the era, you'll recall, when OPEC seemed as
powerful as any entity on earth.) He couldn't outlaw food shortages, either,
which drove up supermarket prices. He could soften or eliminate inflationary regulations—costly antipollution rules, for instance—but for Carter, that
was almost as unthinkable as creating unemployment by bringing on a
recession. In the end, the most a President could do was jawbone,[4] the way
John F. Kennedy had once famously jawboned the steel industry, shaming
steel executives into rolling back price increases. By vocally critiquing
on-going wage negotiations or by publicly criticizing companies that raised
prices, a President just might begin to change the inflationary psychology
that was gripping the nation. Carter's early anti-inflation plans—indeed, all
his anti-inflation plans—revolved around a complicated series of "voluntary" wage and price guidelines, which both business and labor were supposed to abide by. But precisely because the guidelines were voluntary, they
could only work if they were backed by the moral suasion of the President.
Carter had to be willing to use his weight as the leader of the country to point
an accusatory finger at those who failed to abide by the guidelines.

Here, however, Carter was sabotaged by another hubristic assumption. In
part, he accepted the various guideline schemes placed before him because
his economic team could come up with nothing better. But he also accepted
them because he thought of himself as the kind of President who would have
no difficulty pointing the accusatory finger when necessary. One of his
campaign mantras had been his line about always telling the American
people the truth—even when the truth might not be what we wanted to hear.
After he was installed in the Oval Office, reading the steady profusion of
memos that poured in from aides, Carter's favorite response was to write
back: "Be Bold!"

But Jimmy Carter *wasn't* bold. In economic matters, he was terribly,
infuriatingly, timid. Within the confines of the White House, Carter used to

egg his staff on to stand up to the greatest Democratic special interest of them all, organized labor.[5] Yet whenever he faced a moment of truth with labor, the President always wilted. At Carter's urging, for instance, the administration inserted itself into more than a half-dozen big labor negotiations, attempting to keep the wage settlements low. But the White House always lost its nerve in the end; not only did it never openly criticize an agreement struck by labor and management, in several cases it actually applauded settlements that were clearly inflationary. This happened most vividly in late 1977, when the administration's sudden change of heart allowed the United Mine Workers to extract a 37 percent wage increase from the nation's coal companies, after a bitter strike.[6] After that, no union ever took Jimmy Carter seriously again.[7]

Carter also liked to think of himself as a President who could make the "hard choices" that needed to be made—and damn the political consequences. But this self-image was also largely delusional. Inflation was an issue that absolutely demanded hard choices; every decision facing Carter that held out the potential to slow down the inflation rate always came with some political cost. For instance: was it worth holding down federal pay raises even if the cost might be losing civil service reform, which Carter badly wanted? Should the President veto a bill laden with pork barrel spending, which would add to the federal deficit, when such a move would alienate crucial congressional allies, whom Carter needed to pass legislation he cared about? Should he oppose a request by the powerful California congressional delegation to place (inflationary) tariffs on Mexican tomatoes? Or should he give in to such a demand because it was important to placate California? When faced with this kind of hard choice, Carter opted for the politically palatable choice far more than he would care to admit. This was also apparent early on. Just four months after taking office, Carter held a press conference during which he unveiled his first anti-inflation effort. Toward the end of it, a reporter asked him how he could square his anti-inflation program with "your recent approval of higher milk subsidies that will raise the price of milk by an estimated six cents a gallon." "Milk," replied the President, "is a special case." But they were all special cases. That was the trouble.

Inevitably, inflation began creeping up soon after Carter took office. Having come down to 4.9 percent in 1976, Ford's last year in office, the Consumer Price Index (CPI) rose 6.7 percent in 1977, Carter's first year as President. Carter's response to this worrisome—but still manageable—rise was to announce his first set of voluntary guidelines, and to exhort America, a number of times, to share in the sacrifice. And . . . *nothing*. Carter's guidelines and his speeches had about the same effect on the American economy as a pebble dropped into the ocean. Within the first three months of 1978, food prices rose more than 15 percent, gasoline more than 11 percent, medical costs more than 9 percent. In April, the CPI rose 0.9 percent—which translated to an annual rate of 11 percent. Hourly wages were higher, in part because Carter had not been willing to face the political consequences of vetoing a hike in the minimum wage, and in part because unions were openly thumbing their noses at the guidelines. Businesses, in deciding how high to raise prices, were also ignoring the guidelines, though less brazenly. Worker productivity had been flat since Carter took office— part of a long-term trend, though no one could know that at the time—which added to the inflation rate. Then again, what wasn't inflationary? Charles Schultze, who, as head of the Council of Economic Advisers, was Carter's chief economic adviser, had come to the conclusion that the core inflation rate—that is, the amount of inflation that resulted "naturally," without any external events like an OPEC price hike or sudden food shortages—was 6 percent.

Before the year was out, Carter had unveiled two more anti-inflation programs—both variations on the same "guideline" theme; he had added literally hundreds of people to the administration rolls as inflation fighters, most of them at the Council on Wage and Price Stability (COWPS), a once-tiny group that mushroomed into a large bureaucracy in the Carter years; he had begun appearing before the country in that famous cardigan sweater, pleading with the country to get behind his program, feeble though it obviously was. And *still* nothing. When 1978 had ended, the Consumer Price Index had gone up 9 percent, dangerously close to the double-digit level. In two years' time, in other words, the rate of inflation had almost doubled. More importantly, it had gone from being something that the country found troubling to something it found frightening. "It is impossible to overestimate the importance of the inflation issue. . . ." began a late-1978 memo to the President from his longtime media consultant, Gerald Rafshoon. "It affects every American in a very palpable way. It causes insecurity and anxiety. It threatens the American Dream." Every word Rafshoon wrote was true. The Age of Inflation was in full swing.

Among the many ineffectual moves Carter made as he desperately tried to grab control of inflation was his decision, in the fall of 1978, to bring into the White House a genial, uninhibited, outspoken professor of political economy, on leave from Cornell University, and to make him the administration's "inflation czar." The professor's name was Alfred Kahn. He was sixty-one years old when he went to the White House, where he was handed a post where his duties were utterly undefined—and which he was temperamentally ill-equipped to handle in any case. And yet by the time Carter left office two years later, Kahn had become by far the most memorable figure of all of the President's economic advisers. Inflation may have been the scourge of the nation, but it was certainly fun to watch Kahn try to fight it—if, in fact, one can describe what he was doing as "inflation fighting." With Fred Kahn it was sometimes hard to tell.

If you lived through the Age of Inflation, you no doubt remember Alfred Kahn, the rumpled professor with the thick stack of briefing papers seemingly sewn to his arm, the man whose combination of self-deprecating wit and breathtaking, almost pathological, candor caused him to say (it sometimes seemed) whatever unedited phrase happened to pop into his head.[8] Kahn was the Carter administration official who once called the Arab oil producers "schnooks," and the one who described Carter's wage and price guidelines—which he himself was supposed to be administering—as "those stinking guidelines." He was the one who didn't even bother to mouth the administration party line. "I don't want to think it is hopeless," he would tell reporters. "But if the prospect were that we would run 13 percent for the rest of the year, obviously one would have to give up." Once, when he was testifying before Congress, a subcommittee chairwoman angrily demanded to know how he, as inflation czar, could support the administration's decision to continue the government's sugar-price-support program—a policy, she pointedly noted, that aided 13,000 sugar producers to the detriment of the tens of millions of Americans who merely *bought* sugar. This of course was another of those "hard choices" Carter had ducked, and Kahn, knowing that, was quiet for a moment. Then he replied, "Let the record reflect an embarrassed silence."[9] The room burst into laughter. Another time, after he had said once too often that he thought the country was headed for a "real depression" if inflation wasn't stopped, he got a call from Stuart Eizenstat, Carter's chief domestic adviser. "Fred," said Eizenstat gently, "please try not to use that word. It scares people." A few days later, Kahn was delivering his stock speech, and when he got to the part where he usually predicted a depression, he said, "We're going to have a . . . I don't care what you call it. Let's call it a banana." And for the rest of the speech, he used the word "banana" whenever he meant "depression." That was the classic Fred Kahn incident. He was always going off half-cocked like that, and everyone loved him for it. "He is the sort of guy," *New York Times* columnist James Reston wrote, "who can make failure seem attractive."

Among those who loved Kahn for his reckless candor was Carter himself; in some small way, he envied his inflation adviser's freedom to say what he really thought and to hell with the consequences. "You're my college professor," Carter used to tell him fondly, by which he meant that he relished having someone around who could play the role of loose cannon, saying the hard truths that Carter himself didn't dare. Of all his economic advisers, Fred Kahn was the only one who was ever willing to "Be Bold!" a stance from which Carter drew vicarious enjoyment.

Sometimes it even did some good. In late 1979, just as Congress was completing work on the Chrysler bailout bill—putting the finishing touches on a package of loan guarantees intended to ensure the auto giant's survival—the United Auto Workers announced the terms of a new labor contract with Chrysler. The union had negotiated wage and benefit increases totaling $1.5 billion—the same amount, Kahn angrily pointed out to the President, as the loans the government was about to guarantee. Carter wrote back (typically), "Don't be intimidated by Fraser," referring to UAW Pres. Douglas Fraser, thereby giving Kahn tacit permission to attack the settlement, which he did. Within days, Sen. William Proxmire, who was handling the Chrysler bill, rewrote the legislation, doubling the amount of required union concessions.

Such victories, however, were rare. Far more often, when Kahn said something politically awkward, other, higher-ranking officials would publicly disassociate the administration from its inflation czar, thus rendering him even more ineffective than he already was. "I was the front man," says Kahn, "and I hated it." But he never did anything about it. Kahn had one aide, a savvy Democratic operative named Alvin From, who was constantly trying to shape his boss into more of a player—pushing him to think more before he spoke, to grab hold of the inflation program and make it his own, to develop some political guile. But it just wasn't in him. He may be the only White House aide in history who voluntarily gave up scheduled time with the President because he had nothing specific to tell Carter that day.

As a result, despite his incorrigible outspokenness, Kahn was the wrong man for the job, a fact that did not escape him. Indeed, his brutal honesty, which was what most people admired about him, was actually a detriment to the work at hand: if the inflation czar was on record saying that his task was "hopeless," why should anyone else have hope? How could the populace not sag, collectively, upon hearing such a remark? Kahn also had no instinct at all for the kind of White House hand-to-hand combat that would have been required to turn himself into something more than a figurehead. "I always felt like somebody outside the huddle trying to get in," he complains now.

Most of all, though, he was wrong for the job because he had little to add to the administration's store of anti-inflation ideas. He had been handed the job not because he knew anything about curbing inflation, but because he had pulled off the administration's one genuine economic accomplishment.

As head of the Civil Aeronautics Board, he had led the successful drive to deregulate the airline industry. But Kahn hadn't the faintest idea what to tell the President to do about inflation. "I could never think up enough magic bullets," he says now, with a small sigh. Eventually, he came to the conclusion that no one could—no economist, at least. Inflation, he once wrote in a memo to Carter, wasn't just a matter of economics. "It is a deeply sociological, psychological, political phenomenon. It is . . . a reflection of a society in dissolution [resulting from] a weakening of the social fabric. . . . To turn responsibility for devising policies and programs for dealing with that kind of deeply social phenomenon to a group of professional economists is in very large measure to turn it over to the wrong kinds of people." Undoubtedly, such sentiments contained a dollop of truth. But even here Kahn's candor did no good. Such sentiments were not going to help Jimmy Carter grapple with inflation. And they weren't going to help us, either.

If there is one reason why the country chose to find comic relief in the antics of Fred Kahn—why it preferred laughing at his jokes to raging at his ineffectiveness—it may have been because his appointment coincided with the absolutely worst of the inflation years: by then people needed some comic relief. October 1978, when Kahn was named inflation czar, turned out to be the moment when inflation moved firmly into the double digits. And there wasn't a thing Fred Kahn, or anyone else in the administration, could do about it. Kahn would grant interviews, make speeches, set up White House anti-inflation groups, travel to meet union and business leaders, and do a million other things—and OPEC would break his heart by raising oil prices 14 percent in a single stroke, something it did in December 1978. The Producer Price Index, another important government inflation indicator, would rise 1.3 percent in a single month, which translated to a 15 percent annual rate. That happened in January 1979. The Teamsters would announce that it had agreed to a new three-year basic contract, calling for a 30 percent wage hike; it did so in April 1979. Meat prices would rise 85 percent in a single three-month period. This happened in the spring of 1979.

Oh, it was bad in 1979, and everybody felt it. By February, it was no secret that double-digit inflation had arrived; the only question was how high would it get. Pretty damn high, was the answer; by the end of 1979, the Consumer Price Index would climb 13.3 percent, the worst since 1946. Interest rates that year climbed toward 12 percent. Ralph Nader called for a one day "buying strike" to protest inflation. The UAW's Fraser said publicly what many business and union leaders believed privately: that Carter's program had "self-destructed." And then summer arrived, and a bad situation got worse. In June, after an OPEC oil meeting, the ministers announced that they had decided to nearly double the price of oil, from $12.50 a barrel to around $22 a barrel. Carter, returning home from a summit meeting in Tokyo, skipped a planned trip to Hawaii to take command of the looming crisis. And how did he take command? He made a speech.

Perhaps you remember that speech. Aside from the Camp David accords and the Iranian hostage crisis, it ranks among the most unforgettable events of Carter's presidency—and the strangest, too. This was the infamous "malaise" speech, the one in which he never actually used the word "malaise," yet managed to convey a sense of gloom and American helplessness in the face of OPEC that was positively depressing. It was also the culmination of the strangest week of his presidency—a week in which he essentially went on retreat at Camp David, making no comments or public appearances the entire time, while jetting in all kinds of people to visit him and critique his performance as President. That same week, Carter demanded letters of resignation from every member of his Cabinet, accepted five of them, persuaded G. William Miller, whom he had recently appointed to be Federal Reserve Board chairman, to become his Treasury Secretary instead, and—in an effort to prevent panic in the financial markets, which were becoming unglued by his behavior—named Paul Volcker, the head of the New York Fed, to the vacated Federal Reserve chairmanship. And *then*, having done all that, Carter went on television and made the malaise speech.

To read that speech now is to realize that although its raison d'être was the energy crisis, its subtext was inflation. As much as the energy crisis was about oil shortages and our own gnawing sense of national impotence, it was just as much about higher prices. "When we import oil," Carter said at one point, "we are also importing inflation. . . ." More than that, many economists believed that OPEC price decisions acted as a kind of trigger mechanism that set off the next inflationary explosion. Of the Carter aides who believed the malaise speech was a terrible mistake, the most vehement was Vice President Walter Mondale; his argument was directly connected to his sense of how people were reacting to inflation. "He rejected the diagnosis that the country was suffering from some sort of . . . emotional collapse," wrote Elizabeth Drew of *The New Yorker* in her postmortem. "He argued that the anxiety . . . was based on inflation . . . ; people were finding that their savings were turning to water, that they couldn't afford housing, that they couldn't help their children get an education. He argued that in these circumstances it is harder to appeal to people, that their sense of survival comes first. He argued that the need was not to scold people for being 'selfish,' but to respond to what was bothering them.''

Indeed, there was no easier task for a newspaper reporter in 1979 than to find middle-class Americans who could describe, with great passion, the way inflation was changing their lives for the worse. Here were the Ronczys of Chicago, Edward and Josephine, both in their midfifties, looking forward to "early retirement, a few more luxuries . . . to the time when financial pressures would ease a bit," according to *The New York Times*. "But then came the years of surging inflation and at best those dreams have been pushed further into the future.'' There were the Sheppards of Los Angeles, Tyrone and Ada, in their thirties, earning a combined $45,000, living with their young son in a handsome $100,000 home. "It's a battle just to stay where you are," groaned Tyrone. In one inspired bit, a *Times* reporter described the plight of a couple he called Robert and Nancy T., who had two children in college and a third about to enter. They were toying with the once heretical notion of taking on debt to pay the tuition bills. "They do not like the idea [of remortgaging their house]," the reporter added, "but it is no longer unthinkable.'' A few sentences later, Nancy T. was revealed to be Nancy Teeters—a governor of the Federal Reserve Board.

"By the summer of 1979," wrote Theodore White, the great chronicler of presidential campaigns, "no other issue could rival the inflation as a pressure on the American mind. . . .'' White composed the most vivid contemporary account of the Age of Inflation in his 1982 book, *America in Search of Itself: The Making of the President 1956–1980*. He was sixty-seven years old when he wrote this final book of his storied career (he died four years later), and the combination of his age and the fifteen years he had spent as a foreign correspondent gave him something most Americans lacked: perspective. "The inflation in the United States had, by 1979, not yet reached panic proportions," he pointed out:

Panics, like those of Germany in the 1920s, or China in the 1940s, are bursts of insanity. I remember not only my own madness in the late years of the war in China, but the madness of others. I recall scouring through Chungking, China's wartime capital, in 1944 in a ricksha, with a sack of worthless paper money. I was looking for cheese: only three stores still had stocks of imported Swiss cheese in cans. I bought out their entire stock. . . .

Yet he also understood how inflation scared the middle class—how it warped their perception of their own financial situation, and caused, as White put it, "a contagion of fear.'' One of White's talents was his ability to intuit the mood of the nation, and then to convey that mood on the printed page. "It required no public opinion surveys to recognize that Americans had begun to shiver at the way prices were rising," he intuited in his last book—and then he showed America shivering:

> Conversation in the nation . . . was stained and drenched in money talk, by what it cost to live or what it cost to enjoy life.
>
> In the upper classes, one heard cocktail chatter about the cost of a new suit or dress: "I just paid four hundred dollars for a two hundred dollar suit." . . . Then the "sticker shock," as the well-to-do as well as the commoner went to shop for new cars. . . . The meal at the restaurant, with the host sneaking a glance at the tab and stunned, surreptitiously adding up the figures to verify the total. . . . [I]n California, the epicenter of real estate inflation, the incessant, obsessive chatter, among gentry and cottage dwellers alike, about housing prices, [because] the house you bought was your main stake in the great gamble, the house financed the children's college, the house was the only safe investment, to have and to hold, as [inflation] made money a deceit. . . .
>
> But the conversation among poor people, among ordinary people, was far more significant. They winced and ached. Some mysterious power was hollowing their hopes and dreams, their plans for a house or their children's college education. They felt the government must do something. It must either protect them from inflation, or it must stop inflation. . . .
>
> What the great inflation had done, by 1979, was to separate America into layers of different but resentful (or greedy) people. Promises had been made to all of them over the two decades; but now the promises were being redeemed in money which might become as worthless as Confederate dollars. . . . [T]hose who had believed those promises, those who still held war bonds . . . or put their dollars in savings banks—all those had been cheated. What they saved today would at the 1980 inflation rate be worth half as much five years later. . . .
>
> Faith in one's own planning was dissolving—all across the nation. The bedrock was heaving.

"Inflation," White concluded, "is the cancer of modern civilizations."

White was harsh in his judgment of the economic stewardship of Jimmy Carter—"who had promised so much, and meant so well" but "could apparently do nothing" about inflation—a judgment that would only be strengthened with the passage of time, as more was learned about what had gone on in the White House during those years. To read old memos written by Carter's advisers is to wonder sometimes what parallel universe they were living in. There was something about their efforts that strikes one now as oddly disconnected from the difficult reality of American life. The memos have the opaque texture of empty rhetoric, the programs a grasping-atstraws quality. "Our [anti-inflation] activities have to be visible, sustained and planned," a Carter aide named Anne Wexler wrote the President, echoing the words of a hundred similar missives. "They must build on each other and reinforce a constant theme, rather than appearing to be ad hoc reactions to current developments." But what activities was she talking about? And how would they be planned? And how would they reinforce a constant theme? And what was the theme, anyway?

Yet while America viewed the White House as doing nothing to stop inflation, inside the administration it felt completely different. Inside, it felt as though there weren't enough hours in the day to attend all the meetings, write all the memos, deliver all the testimony, conduct all the negotiations, and do all the other things that needed to be done *right this second*. What had happened, of course, was that the anti-inflation program had taken on a life of its own. Those administering the program gradually stopped thinking of their work as a means to an end and began seeing it as an end in itself. Actions were being dictated by an internal logic quite apart from any effect they might have on the rate of inflation.

This spectacle of White House aides frantically chasing each other's tails deserves at least a little sympathy. They genuinely didn't know what else to do. No one knew what to do. As Barry Bosworth, Carter's former head of COWPS, told the economics writer Robert Samuelson at the time, "Nobody in the economics profession can even agree on what [inflation] is. The last decade has left the theory of inflation behavior and how to deal with it in tatters."[10]

Another problem, though—to be less sympathetic—was that there just weren't enough people working for Jimmy Carter who were personally affected by inflation. So many of Carter's aides were in their twenties or early thirties—chief of staff Hamilton Jordan, for instance, was thirty-two; press spokesman Jody Powell just a few years older. Young and single, living in one-bedroom apartments and making more money than they'd ever seen in their lives, they were oblivious to the psychological and economic pressures inflation placed on middle-class families. "Inflation had no meaning in my life," admits Josh Gotbaum, Kahn's twenty-something executive assistant. "I was just a kid then," sighs Alice Rogoff, who worked for the administration as a special assistant to the director of the Office of Management and Budget. "Maybe that's why I never felt it was a scary time."

"The White House was filled with people like that," says Al From. "They didn't have kids. They didn't own homes. They spent all their time at work. They didn't have to see any normal people if they didn't want to." David Rubenstein, who was all of twenty-six when he worked as Eizenstat's deputy in Jimmy Carter's White House, grudgingly agrees: "Back then, a prime rate of 20 percent [a figure reached in 1980] didn't mean a thing to me. Now I think, 'My God! How did people buy houses? How did the economy function?' "

Al From, on the other hand, though far less powerful than the likes of Jordan or Powell or Rubenstein, was older than most White House aides. He owned a house and was raising a family, for whom he was the sole financial provider. He absolutely understood the pressures on middle-class families— the way, as he puts it, "inflation undermines the middle class"—because he felt those pressures himself. Perhaps that is why he was one of the few Carter aides who could clearly see how fundamentally pointless the administration's anti-inflation programs had become. He was certainly the only one willing to say it out loud, which he did with infuriating shrillness.

Once, he bluntly told Kahn in a memo, "Of course the President would like to do more public events with you—you're more popular than he is—but that doesn't change the fact that we have nothing to say." Again and again, he tried to make the White House see that all the anti-inflation programs in the world didn't mean a thing *if they didn't drive down the rate of inflation*; otherwise everything they did was mere wheel spinning. From's greatest frustration, though, was that he could never make his colleagues understand, until it was much too late, that inflation was the overriding concern of the middle class. It used to infuriate him the way the liberals in the administration tried to cast inflation as an issue affecting only the weak and the poor: "Such a portrayal of inflation's impact is likely to create a negative reaction among the much broader constituency of middle Americans who are reeling from high inflation," he fired back. "[I]ts greatest danger is to our economic security, the security that most Americans are seeking." Unemployment was the historic Democratic issue, but unemployment only affected the unemployed. Inflation affected everybody. That was the cruel political calculus.

"The Democrats always underestimated inflation," says From today. And the price they paid was high: for the next three presidential elections, Carter's inability to deal with inflation cost his party the middle class vote.[11]

SOMETIME IN THE EARLY FALL OF 1979, by which time it had become embarrassingly clear that the administration's various inflation plans were a bust, Alfred Kahn went over to the Federal Reserve to have lunch with the new chairman, Paul Volcker. It was there and then that Kahn learned that the White House was about to be pushed aside in the inflation battle. "The program's clearly not working, Fred," Kahn remembers Volcker telling him. "I have the only other weapon in town. I'm going to have to use it." What could Kahn say? He knew that the weapon Volcker had in mind—an ambitious plan to choke inflation by slowing the growth of the money supply—was not just strong medicine but radical medicine, with the real potential to send the country into a recession. He also knew that it could not happen at a worse time for Carter, since the presidential primary season was about to get under way, with Sen. Ted Kennedy poised to run against the incumbent from his own party. Kahn sighed. Then he looked at Volcker and said, "You're right."

In theory, there was nothing to keep Volcker from carrying out his plan except the other members of the Federal Reserve's board of governors, who would have to approve any shift in the way the Fed handled the money supply. The Federal Reserve was an independent body, and its independence was supposed to insulate it from political pressures. In practice, however, Federal Reserve chairmen operated in the real world of politics and policy, dealing on a regular basis with Presidents and Treasury officials, legislators and bankers, and other assorted mortals. The Fed's conduct of the nation's monetary policy (as the regulation of the money supply is called) always has political implications, and as a practical matter most Fed chairmen find it difficult to chart a monetary course openly opposed by the President.

Though he had been Fed chairman for only a few months, Volcker understood this better than anyone in Washington. He had been a Treasury Department official under four successive Presidents, always in the thick of things. (Ford had named him chairman of the New York Fed.) "[Volcker's] training was so extensive," writes William Greider in *Secrets of the Temple,* his detailed account of Volcker's tenure as Federal Reserve chairman, "that he resembled a senior civil servant in the British system, a career man who stays in government while the elected officials come and go, who accumulates great influence because he knows every issue more thoroughly than the politicians he advises." Preparing the groundwork for the changes he had in mind, Volcker began quietly telling the White House of his plans.

Kahn aside—and on a matter of this magnitude, his opinion carried zero weight—Carter's advisers were unanimously opposed to Volcker's scheme. They were appalled, actually. What appalled them was not so much Volcker's desire for tighter money, which everyone in the White House knew was coming; rather, it was the *way* Volcker was planning to regulate the money supply that horrified them. Traditionally, the Federal Reserve regulated money indirectly, by fiddling with interest rates, moving them up or down a quarter of a percent at a time. Volcker was convinced that this approach was too incremental to curb an inflation so powerful that it was causing people to feel, in his words, "that things were out of control." Feeling the need to do something more drastic, he decided that the Federal Reserve should control the growth of money directly, by regulating the amount of money the nation's banks had to hold in reserve. "In effect," he later wrote, "our emphasis would shift from controlling the price of money to its quantity." One strong possibility was that interest rates, no longer controlled by the Federal Reserve, would skyrocket. But no one could say for sure, since the radical solution Volcker was proposing was untested in postwar America. In a universe still dominated by Keynesian economics, Volcker was about to put into practice a theory that had been devised by—and was being actively promoted by—a group of conservative economists known as "monetarists." Led by Milton Friedman, the monetarists were challenging some of the most basic tenets of Keynesian theory. Although Volcker would later take pains to disassociate himself from "the extreme claims" of the monetarists—a veiled dig at Friedman—he had come around to their view that taking control of the money supply directly was the only way to slow down virulent inflation. He also thought it might help change the inflationary psychology. "People don't need an advanced degree in economics to understand that inflation has something to do with too much money," Volcker wrote. "[I]f we could get out the message that when we say we're going to control money, we mean we're going to deal with inflation, then we would have a chance of affecting ordinary people's behavior."

As the days passed, Volcker received a series of ever-more pressing phone calls from Schultze and other White House officials, urging him to reconsider. But there was never such a call from Carter himself, which Volcker took to mean that the President would not oppose him. His instincts were right. When, in early October 1979, he finally called the White House to tell Schultze that he and his board of governors had formally agreed to move in this new direction, Schultze quickly acquiesced. "I told Volcker the President wouldn't attack him," says Schultze, and except for a single lapse in the heat of the election campaign, Carter never did, not even as Volcker's tight money policy sank what slim political hopes he had left. "What the hell," shrugs Schultze now. "We didn't have a better mousetrap."

Although Volcker did turn out to have the better mousetrap in the end, this would not become apparent for quite some time—far too late, certainly, for Jimmy Carter. On the contrary, his radical shift in monetary policy appeared at first to have about as much effect on inflation as Carter's various programs, which is to say none at all. It did, however, have a huge effect on interest rates, just as Schultze and the others had feared. The prime rate, which had been hovering in the 12 percent range, rocketed to 15.75 percent that fall. Ted Kennedy, out on the stump, began calling for mandatory wage and price controls as the only way to bring inflation down. Kahn, in a speech to the National Press Club around this time, said bluntly (of course!) that if Carter lost the upcoming election, it would be "overwhelmingly" due to his failure to bring down inflation. Then, in January, the Labor Department confirmed that the Consumer Price Index rose 13.3 percent in 1979, and two days after that, Carter released his annual economic report to Congress, which has to rank as one of the most pessimistic documents ever released by an American President, gloomier even than Carter's malaise speech. In the report, the administration said that it anticipated that the Gross National Product would drop by 1 percent in 1980, while unemployment would rise to 7.5 percent. In other words, the President of the United States was *predicting* that the country would be thrown into a recession—and in an election year. This wasn't just an unusual admission; it was unheard of. In the same report, the administration also predicted a second straight year of double-digit inflation, something America hadn't seen since World War I. A new word had been added to the nation's political discourse: "stagflation." It meant an economy that was both stagnating and inflating at the same time—something the Keynesian textbooks said wasn't supposed to be possible. But apparently it was possible. In fact, it was happening.

And then, just when you thought things couldn't possibly get any worse, they did.

On Friday, February 22, 1980, the Labor Department announced the sharpest monthly rise yet in the Consumer Price Index—1.4 percent, a figure that projected to an annual inflation rate of around 17 percent. While this might seem like just one more numbing inflation report piled atop all the other numbing inflation reports, it was not. The rise in the CPI was the highest one-month gain since the Arab oil embargo of 1973. And it was accompanied by the news that the major banks were raising their prime rate by ¾ of a point, to 16.5 percent—the single largest one-day rise in a decade. The combination of the two announcements made banner headlines all across the country, for the news seemed to signal, in some deep way, that the economy was on the verge of disintegrating. Having had the weekend to absorb the bad news, the bond market crashed when it opened the following Monday.

The news had a galvanizing effect on the Carter administration. Perhaps this was because the New Hampshire primary was only days away, and Kennedy had been hammering away at the inflation issue. Or maybe it was because the White House economists understood that the new inflation numbers, bleak as they were, hid an even glummer reality. There was no aberrational event that could explain away this rise—no oil shock, no sudden food shortages, no new spike in interest rates to dampen the housing market. "The underlying rate of inflation has started to explode," admitted one administration official.

Whatever the reason, Carter and his aides reacted, for the first time in four years, with a real sense of urgency. There were the usual flurry of emergency meetings—but this time Carter himself attended. Publicly, a solemn President said that inflation had reached "a crisis stage." He asked his advisers to come up with yet another inflation plan—one that might actually work this time—and shortly afterward, he and his aides began a series of extraordinary private meetings with the congressional leadership in a dramatic attempt to rewrite the 1981 federal budget, which Carter had already submitted to Congress a few weeks earlier. That original budget, which assumed a deficit of $15 billion,[12] had been greeted with derision, especially on Wall Street, which saw an out-of-balance budget as sending "the wrong signal" about inflation. Now, Carter wanted to lead a bipartisan effort to achieve a balanced budget. To underscore how seriously he regarded this task, he took the highly unusual step of having Volcker attend most of the sessions.[13] Three weeks later, on the 14th of March, Carter came before the nation to announce that the budget was in balance—and to unveil a new, tougher inflation policy. Naturally, that resulted in the biggest disaster of all.

By this time, the nation's economic elites—the editorial writers and columnists, the economic seers at the big Wall Street firms, the CEOs and labor leaders, even the financial markets themselves—had become a kind of Greek chorus, passing collective judgment on each of Carter's attempts to grapple with inflation. Always before, those judgments had been negative. And so it was now. The Monday following Carter's announcement, the Dow Jones average dropped twenty-three points. On Tuesday, Proxmire, the Senate's most influential voice on inflation, called Carter's new program "much weaker than I had hoped or expected."[14] On Wednesday, the big banks raised the prime rate to 19 percent. The "new, tougher" inflation package, the chorus concluded, contained nothing that was either new or tough: it was (sigh) typical Jimmy Carter. This assessment, however, was not quite accurate. Along with new wage and price guidelines and a freeze on federal employment, Carter did have one new wrinkle. His plan called for federal controls on consumer credit. Essentially, what he was trying to do was rein in credit card debt. Not only was this a new idea, but it was the first new inflation-fighting idea that the inflation czar himself could claim credit for. In talking to a number of iconoclastic economists, Kahn had become persuaded by them that the growth in consumer debt, and especially credit card debt, helped propel the inflationary spiral. When Americans borrowed to sustain a lifestyle that inflation was pushing out of reach, went the theory, they were effectively pumping money into the economy. The act of trying to keep pace with inflation was fueling inflation.

"It was not considered a respectable position by an economist," admits Kahn, especially the economists working at the Council of Economic Advisers—which is why Kahn didn't make much headway the first few times he brought up the subject. But he kept plugging away at it, suggesting it in the frequent memos he wrote to the President, and even mentioning it in speeches as a "possibility." He remembered the credit controls that had existed during the Korean War, which required large down payments and short payback schedules, and he thought a similar program would help restrain borrowing now. When Carter finally decided to include credit controls in his last inflation package, against the advice of people like Schultze and Treasury Secretary Miller, one gets the strong sense that he was thinking that since nothing *they* had suggested was working, why not give this thing a shot? What harm could it do?

Under the law, only the Federal Reserve could impose credit controls, and Volcker was distinctly unenthused about the notion. The Fed chairman went along largely because he felt he owed it to the President, who a few months before had backed Volcker's monetary shift. Even after agreeing to controls, however, he and his staff had tried to water them down, exempting, writes Greider, "automobiles, furniture and appliances, home-improvement loans and mortgages." "When the President and the Federal Reserve chairman announced their initiatives," added Greider, "[Fed officials] joked among themselves about the many loopholes written into the controls. They were confident that lenders and borrowers would find them."

What happened next was amazing. People not only didn't find the loopholes, they refused to look for them. The entire country simply stopped borrowing. "No one had ever seen anything like it," recalls Volcker. Kahn made speeches suggesting that people cut up their credit cards, and thousands did so—sending their sliced-up cards to the White House in a show of support for the President's program. It was quickly apparent, however, that cutting up their credit cards was the worst thing they could have done, both for Carter and themselves. For months, consumer borrowing was the only thing that had kept the recession at bay; when the borrowing stopped, the economy collapsed—"within a matter of days," writes Volcker. Embroiled in a nasty fight for the nomination, grappling by then with the hostage crisis in Iran and the Soviet Union's invasion of Afghanistan, his popularity at an all-time low—this was the moment that Jimmy Carter finally got "his" recession.[15]

As quickly as he "decently" could, Volcker undid the credit controls. By

July, they were gone. He also loosened the money supply temporarily to revive the economy. Meanwhile, the balanced budget was quickly jettisoned, as Congress added billions in additional spending to revive the economy. Interest rates plummeted, the recession ended almost as quickly as it had begun, and even the CPI slowed down for a few months, though not enough to prevent a second consecutive year of double-digit inflation.

But it was too late for Jimmy Carter. Everything he had tried had failed, and he had nothing left. He was done trying to fight inflation. Inside the White House, the anti-inflation machinery was still in place, its gears whirring louder than ever, but that's all it was now: noise and motion. Right up until election day, nothing changed. Once, when the CPI dropped, Jody Powell pathetically suggested that Carter make a self-deprecating remark about it to reporters, just to draw attention to this rare bit of good news. And to the bitter end, Carter could never make the "hard choices" that were needed to put even the tiniest dent in inflation. Not long before the election, Kahn tried to get Carter to take a large Army contract away from Kerr–McGee, the Oklahoma oil company, which COWPS had found in violation of the price guidelines. But then the Army weighed in, claiming that the Kerr–McGee contract was important to the national security, and that was that.

And all the while, Carter's opponent in the general election, Ronald Reagan, was using inflation as a club with which to bludgeon the President. The first page of the first campaign memo Reagan received, back in 1979, had said, "By a wide margin, the most important issue in the minds of voters today is inflation." He never forgot it. "When [Carter] took office," Reagan used to say in his stump speech, "inflation was 4.8 percent and he said he was going to do something about it. And he did. It's now averaging 16.4 percent." A week before the election, the two men held their one and only debate. Reagan was well ahead in the polls, but toward the end of that debate, he administered the coup de grace when he looked into the camera and asked: "Are you better off than you were four years ago?"

Thanks to inflation, we were not better off, and we knew it. At that moment, Jimmy Carter's last, flickering hopes of winning reelection were gone for good.

## CHAPTER 10

# "Please Don't Take It Away!"

## *March 1981*

P EOPLE HAVE AN amazing ability to adapt to changing circumstances; it's an all-too-familiar part of the human condition. We can cope, when we have to, with war and deprivation and upheavals of every sort. We can survive anarchy and natural disasters. And when we have to, we can adjust to shifting economic circumstances. For seventy years, in the states that made up the Soviet Union, people adapted to an economy that simply did not function the way its leaders said it did; indeed, it barely functioned at all. In America in the 1930s, people likewise coped with the hand they had been dealt—scrimping and sharing and doing what they had to do to outlast the Depression.

That's what happened during the Age of Inflation, too. Americans found themselves facing a set of economic circumstances radically different from any that had existed in their memory—circumstances that included not just double-digit inflation, but wildly gyrating interest rates, a gradual lowering of their standard of living,[1] and a situation where many of the basic financial vehicles Americans had relied upon for decades, such as regulated bank savings accounts, were no longer viable. And how did people react to these cataclysmic changes? They adapted.

Economists used to marvel at the dramatic, quantifiable changes in the behavior of the middle class. "It turns out that people can scramble and keep up longer than you think they can," Barry Bosworth once remarked. That's part of the reason why stamping out inflation was so hard: people spent as much time adapting to it as they did complaining about it. Americans who lived on fixed incomes devised strategies to keep their income rising with the inflation rate. People who could feel their standard of living slipping away tried to figure out ways to pull it back up. The most common way was to insert both spouses into the workforce; this was the moment that saw one of the seismic shifts in American life, the emergence of two-income couples. Wives joined the workforce by the millions, motivated in part by the need to keep pace with inflation. Whereas two-income couples made up a third of the nation's families in the late 1960s, a decade later, that number had risen to around 45 percent.

Another example of this process of adaptation was the way the mortgage market changed once interest rates and inflation began to rise. In an earlier age, people bought a house with the expectation that they would live in it long enough to pay off a thirty-year fixed mortgage, after which they would own it free and clear. But as interest rates climbed into the stratosphere, the old thirty-year fixed mortgage became a relic, replaced by adjustable rate mortgages. The great appeal of ARMs was that they offered below-market rates the first year or two, and then only gradually approached market interest rates. There was some risk involved, to be sure—who could say where interest rates would be a few years hence?—but what choice did people have? Indeed, even if rates didn't go down, people adapted: an unspoken assumption of this new class of mortgage holders was that they wouldn't be paying off that mortgage all that long anyway. Nobody did that anymore.

"Paying off the mortgage on the family home," *The New York Times* lamented in the spring of 1979, "was once as ingrained in the national psyche as buying the home." The *Times* went on to describe these payments as a "sacred American value" that was being abandoned. But there was never anything sacred about paying off a mortgage; it was simply a sensible way to act given the economic conditions of the time. In an era of inflation and high interest rates, such behavior no longer made sense. What made sense instead was *not* paying off the mortgage, refinancing whenever rates dropped or selling one house for a new one, which kicked in a new adjustable rate mortgage.

No longer was a house "merely" a roof over one's head, either. Gradually, it grew into something quite a bit more: for most families, it was their largest and most important financial asset. It was also the one asset whose value only seemed to go in one direction: up. This is the phenomenon Theodore White had been referring to when he described a house as "your main stake in the great gamble . . . the only safe investment." As people latched onto this fact, a mad scramble ensued, and Americans used every penny they could spare to buy the most expensive house they could afford. Between 1975 and 1978, home mortgages in America rose from $479 billion to $737 billion.

That houses went up in price was a direct by-product of inflation; hard assets always rise in inflationary times. That people began thinking about their homes in this fundamentally new way was a direct by-product of the fact that they were rising in value. People no longer bought a house so much as they "invested" in one; the down payment was their "equity stake." And after four or five years, by which time their investment had doubled in value, they might well be moved to treat it like any other investment—by engaging in some profit taking and plunging the capital gains into a more expensive investment—i.e., another house. Of course, everyone else's house was also doubling in value, but never mind. It happened all the time. Sometimes, in fact, it could border on the ridiculous. There were middle-class Americans—not a lot, but enough so that you noticed—who became so caught up in making money on their homes that they would purchase a new one every six months or so. After living in it long enough to escape the short-term capital gains tax, they would then "flip" it to the next buyer and start all over again. So long as real estate prices went only upward, this was a no-lose strategy—unless, of course, you wanted to live someplace for longer than six months.

Marshall Loeb, who was the editor of *Money* magazine in the early 1980s, used to say that this was when money became "the most discussed topic among consenting adults." Surely he was right about this. As a subject to be talked about—out loud among friends, rather than privately with one's banker—money came out of the closet during the Age of Inflation. Partly, this new willingness to talk about money was the natural result of having to learn about money. Quite often, people made their first investment in a money market fund after seeing a friend do it first and talking to him about it.

But the money talk always had another, darker undercurrent. It became nearly impossible to go to a dinner party in a large American city and not wind up spending half the night discussing real estate prices; the topic became, as one writer put it, "the great conversation starter in the social life of the middle class." This talk had less to do with middle-class learning than with middle-class bragging, a not-so-private mental totting up of profits, as people compared how much prices had risen in the various neighborhoods they lived in. Among those who already owned a home, the talk had an awed, slightly obsessive, even giddy quality; among those who didn't, it had an awed, slightly embittered, and frankly envious quality. A house wasn't just part of the American dream anymore; it was part of the money revolution. And that was sad.

❧

OF THE MANY WAYS AMERICANS ADAPTED TO INFLATION, two changes stood above the rest. The first was a pronounced shift in the attitude of the middle class, particularly those young enough to have missed the Depression, toward credit and credit cards. The second was a shift away from regulated bank passbook accounts and toward "savings" vehicles that offered market rates of returns. In the first instance, Americans began borrowing as they'd never borrowed before—borrowing that was facilitated by the near universal acceptance of credit cards, a condition that had arrived by the late 1970s. In the second instance, Americans in large numbers finally realized, to their dismay, that they were being killed by Regulation Q, which held bank interest rates down even as "market" interest rates were rising rapidly. This was when the imperatives of inflation overtook the power of inertia, as the middle class began moving its savings out of bank passbook accounts and into money market funds. It was also the moment when it was clear beyond all doubt that the money revolution had arrived.

How well had Dee Hock done his job? Here's how well: in 1970, the year Hock established National BankAmericard Inc., Americans used the two competing bank cards, BankAmericard and Master Charge, to charge around $7 billion worth of goods. By 1973, when Hock installed NBI's computerized authorization system, credit card spending was growing at a rate of about $3.5 billion a year and had reached $13.8 billion. Then it *really* began taking off: $22 billion in accumulated bank card spending in 1976; $31.7 billion the following year; $44.5 billion the year after that. By the time the Age of Inflation was petering out, in 1982, the figure stood at over $66 billion. In a decade, credit card spending had quadrupled. Even after taking inflation into account, this was an impressive gain.

Around 60 million people held either a Master Charge or a Visa card by 1978; according to one estimate,[2] only 11.5 million people in the entire country who could qualify for a bank card chose not to have one. Most Americans had at least two credit cards,[3] while around 20 million people had three or more. And they were using them to buy more expensive things: the typical credit card purchase had risen from less than $20 to around $60 in the 1970s. "If this current rate of growth continues," wrote Spencer Nilson, the credit card newsletter publisher, "the major banking interests will be in a position to dominate the credit card industry—and through it, influence . . . the credit spending habits and lifestyle of all consumers."

Nilson was only half right. Banks were indeed poised to dominate the credit card business, finally overwhelming the long-standing resistance of most major retail chains, while rendering competing cards such as Carte Blanche and oil company cards practically obsolete. Ultimately, only American Express had the wherewithal to withstand the onslaught of bank credit cards.[4]

But Nilson was wrong to predict that credit cards would be responsible for changing the "credit spending habits" of Americans. He had it backward: it was the credit spending habits of Americans that was responsible for increased credit card use. Credit cards were undoubtedly making it easier for Americans to borrow with newfound abandon. But credit cards were not the only reason this was happening or even the main reason. *Inflation* is what drove people to take on more debt; credit cards simply provided an easy means to do so.

In 1975, for instance, a year when credit card debt totaled close to $15 billion, total consumer borrowing[5] stood at $167 billion. By 1979, with the inflation rate in double digits, credit card spending had more than tripled. But the rate of total consumer borrowing had also grown rapidly: it was closing in on $315 billion. This was the real eye-popping figure, and the one that held the most significance. A 90 percent jump in total consumer borrowing in only three years represented the kind of frenetic borrowing that hadn't been seen in America since the early 1950s. In the 1950s, however, interest rates had been low, consumer desires were ready to explode, and the burgeoning middle class had been full of optimism about the future. The conditions for borrowing were ideal. In the mid- and late 1970s, by contrast, interest rates were at historic highs, and Americans were decidedly pessimistic about the future. And yet the middle class in the 1970s seemed to be outborrowing its 1950s counterpart. Historically, whenever consumer debt reached 2.5 percent of total disposable income, it would be followed by an immediate slowdown in borrowing; collectively Americans seemed to know that they had reached a danger point. But in 1978, consumer debt regularly topped 3 percent of disposable income, yet there wasn't so much as a hint of a slowdown. "Attitudes toward incurring more debt have held up despite the tremendous buildup in debt," a bewildered economic pollster said at the time, "and that is at variance with previous experience."

*At variance with previous experience?* Previous experience was meaningless. It had been obliterated by inflation. That was the whole point: the old rules no longer applied. Thrift, for instance, had long been the great American virtue, something good people practiced as a matter of course. In a time of double-digit inflation, however, thrift was something foolish people practiced. Thrift in an inflationary age meant paying for tomorrow's more expensive goods with yesterday's diminished dollars. It was dumb. Borrowing, on the other hand, meant purchasing yesterday's less expensive goods with tomorrow's inflated dollars. That was smart. "The buy-in-advance syndrome," one economist called it. Why did people continue to take on more debt when previous experience suggested they should be slowing down? Because borrowing was the economic response that made the most sense.

Early in 1980, Kenneth Larkin gave a speech at a banking convention in which he outlined some of the new American attitudes toward credit. Larkin was by then the head of Bank of America's credit card division, among the nation's most accomplished credit card spokesmen. Yet even he seemed to find the new eagerness for debt a bit unsettling. In preparing his speech, he had stumbled across a paper written by two University of Southern California "futurists," entitled "Social Changes Affecting the Consumer Finance Industry, Period 1980–2000." Their findings were at the heart of his talk.

"The young adult (25–44-year-old) segment of the population will grow significantly over the next twenty years," Larkin said, quoting the USC scholars:

By 2000 it will include those who were born between 1956–1975 and who are today 4–23 years old. During the formative years of their attitudinal development they will have seen the traditional values espoused in *Poor Richard's Almanack* turned upside down. They are learning important new values, such as:
1. It doesn't pay to save for a rainy day.
2. Buy now, not later: prices will invariably go up and the purchasing power of your dollar will invariably go down.
3. Stretch your financial obligations over as long a period of time as possible.
4. Borrowing improves your credit rating.
5. Pay your bills as late as you can (without jeopardizing your credit rating).

These, truly, were the lessons of inflation. "If you're in debt," a Brookings Institution economist named Joseph Minarek said at the time, "you're better off because inflation is paying part of the debt." That's what people had figured out; that's why they were borrowing.

In many ways, financial attitudes had begun to break down along generational lines, with people under forty representing what the banking consultant Edward Furash would later call the Inflation Generation. Inflation was shaping them every bit as much as the Depression had shaped their parents. Here, for example, was a young Paine Webber economist named Christopher Rupkey making the case for borrowing by his generation— something he did with a glee that his elders could only have found unseemly. " 'Never buy what you can't afford' was the admonition of our parents," he began in a *New York Times* article he wrote in the spring of 1979. "Today, the statement has been changed to, 'You can't afford not to buy it.' "

> More young couples live in the same comfortable homes and sit in the same sumptuous sofas that are equal or better than those of their parents, many of whom worked for years to obtain what their children get with a simple flash of the credit card. . . .
> It took us only until puberty to learn the catch phrase "There is no tomorrow." With inflation depreciating [our] joint annual earnings . . . the response was to enjoy the fruits of our labors today. . . .

"Get your money out of the bank and spend it!" Rupkey exhorted his readers at the close of his article. "Inflation gives the most it has to give to those with the largest pile of debts."

Strangely, despite the run-up in debt and the new attitudes engendered by inflation, bank credit card divisions were again losing money. For a few years in the mid-1970s most bank card operations were profitable; in 1978, according to Nilson's figures, banks made an average of $22 for every $1,000 charged, a rate of return of just over 2 percent. In 1979, however, credit cards barely broke even, and by the first half of 1980, they were back in the red: Nilson figures that banks were losing $30 to $50 per $1,000 charged.[6] It wasn't quite the bad old days all over again, but if you were a banker, you couldn't be blamed for feeling a distinct, uneasy sense of déjà vu.

There were two reasons for this new wave of losses. The first was that banks were just as vulnerable to the effects of high interest rates as any other business. Rising interest rates increased the cost of money for a bank just as it did for General Motors or IBM. But thanks to state usury laws, banks (unlike General Motors and IBM) were prevented from passing on their higher costs to their middle-class customers.

Only three states lacked usury ceilings in the late 1970s: Hawaii, New Hampshire, and California. Although usury ceilings varied widely, from a high of 24 percent (South Dakota and Ohio) to a low of 10 percent (Arkansas), most of them ranged between 12 and 18 percent. Plainly, with the cost of money at or above the usury ceiling, profits were pretty much out of the question. Some savvy customers even learned how to take advantage of the disparity: by drawing down a large cash advance against a bank card in a state with a low usury ceiling, and then putting that advance in a high-interest-rate money market fund, they could make a profit on the spread. This action infuriated bankers, but they were helpless to do anything about it.

The credit card operation that was losing the most in the late 1970s was of course John Reed's at Citibank. This was partly due to the simple fact that it had the most cards in circulation, but it was also because, unlike its nationwide network of customers, the bank itself was stuck in New York, where usury laws limited consumer interest to 18 percent for the first $500 of debt, and 12 percent for everything above $500. Every time interest rates went up another notch, so did the bank's mounting losses. But when Citicorp's lobbyists went to the legislature to plead for temporary relief, they got nowhere. The second largest bank in America asking for the right to charge more interest? A more hopeless cause would be hard to imagine. So Reed did the next best thing. He left New York.

Or rather, his credit card division left. Ever attentive to the loopholes in the banking laws, Citicorp's lawyers had begun to realize that nothing prevented them from setting up a separate bank subsidiary in a different state, which would handle only credit card business. This path was further greased by an important Supreme Court ruling, which stated that when a bank and its credit card customers were located in different states, the usury law in effect was the bank's. "When we saw that," says Citibank's Richard Kane, "we realized that we could choose our headquarters state based on its usury laws."

But why stop there? Why not choose a headquarters state on the basis of its willingness to *eliminate* its usury law. Why not approach the governor of a sparsely populated state in the middle of the country, where white-collar jobs were in short supply? You could explain to this man that if his state was willing to abolish its usury ceiling, you could guarantee him a minimum of 2,000 new jobs—and desk jobs at that. You could make this approach, oh, a month before the end of the legislative session. And then you could stand back and watch as the governor and key legislators drafted a bill, held hearings, conducted committee mark-ups and floor debates, and had the thing signed into law thirty days later, just as the legislative term expired. Then, when the law passed, you could have the satisfaction of watching half the politicians of New York come crawling to you, begging you to keep those jobs in New York, even promising to loosen its own usury laws. Sorry, you could tell half the politicians of New York: too late.

And that is how it came to be that in January 1981, Citibank's credit card division moved to South Dakota, where it remains to this day, the largest employer in the city of Sioux Falls. That is also how it came to be that usury laws were eliminated as an important factor in the granting of consumer loans in America. Other states, especially Maryland and Delaware, followed South Dakota's example and eased or eliminated their usury laws in order to lure banks with big credit card operations. Many of them came. Once again, the money revolution had managed to void a handful of laws that had been around for a very long time—in this case, for as long as the Republic itself. Inflation, in fact, had even voided the ancient concept of usury itself.

The second problem banks were grappling with was what to do about all those people who were using credit cards *and not paying anything for them.*[7] There were millions of them—nay, tens of millions—and they weren't doing anything fraudulent or illegal or even unethical. All they had to do was pay off their balance each month. By doing so, they avoided interest payments, and ever since Bank of America had dropped its first cards in 1958, interest was the only sum customers had ever had to pay for the "privilege" of using a credit card.

At any given moment, half the nation's bank credit card customers were building up debt and paying interest, while the other half were avoiding interest. That's what credit card surveys always showed. As the number of credit card holders grew, and as inflation imposed its relentless logic, people began to gain a new awareness of the implications that came with certain credit card actions. In particular, they began to understand the meaning of the word "float." When a customer used a credit card to buy something at the beginning of the billing cycle, and then didn't pay the bill until the tail end of the "grace period," the bank had, in essence, "floated" the customer a month-long interest-free loan. Once again, savvier customers figured out how to maximize this advantage, learning the precise moment to make big purchases so that the bill would not come due for forty-five or even sixty days. Once again, bankers could only grit their teeth in response.

One of the great misconceptions people used to have about credit cards is that, by paying in full at the end of each month, they were acting as "good customers." But bankers never wanted them to pay in full; for a bank, that defeated the whole purpose of credit cards, which was to create debt. Bankers had a word for people who paid off their balances each month: freeloaders. The way they saw it, the banking industry was providing a service of indesputable value. They were providing Americans—and people the world over—not only the means to trigger an instant, no-questions-asked personal loan, but also the means to walk into any decent-sized establishment, practically anywhere on the planet, and walk out with something they wanted simply by proffering a little piece of encoded plastic. Surely, that was worth

*something*, even for those who eschewed the debt feature of the card. That
so many customers paid nothing at all for the service cards rendered in
linking buyer to seller caused the nation's bankers to feel, well, cheated.

You might think that this would have been an easy problem to solve: If
an industry wants to charge for a service that was once free, it just does so.
But this industry didn't dare make such a move. Its hurdles included both
fierce customer resistance and a host of state regulations that impinged on its
freedom to add charges at will.[8] Credit card marketing surveys consistently
showed customers responding negatively when asked their reaction to the
possibility of a monthly or annual fee. "[V]irtually no one liked the idea,"
concluded the authors of one such study. "Indeed, the initial reaction was
usually anger, ranging in intensity from irritation to outrage."

So once again the nation's credit card bankers, faced with a need to do
something, found themselves unable to act. Even as profits turned to losses
in the late 1970s, no credit card banker was willing to make the first move
to impose a fee. They all feared the wrath of legislators, of judges, of
customers—and they feared each other. If Bank A imposed a fee, wouldn't
Bank B respond by launching a marketing campaign to point out that its card
was still free? It was a legitimate worry.

There things stood—and there they would have continued to stand, except
that in the spring of 1980, Jimmy Carter imposed his disastrous credit
control program. Although bankers complained bitterly about the program,
it wound up giving them the cover they needed to impose annual fees.
"Jimmy Carter," Ken Larkin later admitted, "did us one of the biggest
favors any President ever did the banking industry." Because the controls
included a freeze on new accounts, Carter's action meant that for this one
moment, Bank B was prevented by regulatory fiat from soliciting Bank A's
customers. By the time Volcker lifted the controls four months later, just
about every bank in the credit card game had imposed a small annual
fee—$10 or $15 or $20. The fees created a valuable new income stream for
the banks, and ended the "freeloading" they so loathed.

Millions of credit card customers all over the country reacted by pulling
their business away from their bank; Bank of America lost several hundred
thousand accounts to such protests. But the protests were futile, because
when the protesters searched for a new "free" credit card, they discovered
that they all now came with fees attached. The only other option was to
refuse to take a credit card altogether, and though surveys suggested that as
many as half the country's credit card users were vowing to do precisely
that, they never did. By 1980, refusing to use a credit card wasn't much of
an option anymore.

With usury laws conquered and annual fees a reality, all the bankers needed to do was wait: Wait for inflation to subside; wait for interest rates to go down; wait for the profits to start rolling in. Soon enough, they did.

⟞

And then there were money market funds.

In any accounting of the winners and losers in the Age of Inflation, money market funds had to rank among the biggest winners of all. In 1974, as the nation suffered through its first postwar bout of double-digit inflation, money fund assets rose from $1.7 billion to $3.7 billion. Though this amounted to a gaudy 117 percent gain, the total was still a pittance; commercial banks and S&Ls still held more than $335 billion in passbook accounts alone. Money funds took their next big jump in 1978, when the CPI rose 9 percent. Assets climbed to $10.9 billion. Then, in 1979, as inflation was peaking, money fund assets began registering gains like that every few months: $15.6 billion by February; $32.5 billion by August; $45 billion by December. "If predictions for 1980 are accurate," complained Lawrence Connell, Jr., the chairman of the National Credit Union Administration, "the 90 or so money market mutual funds within eight years will have accumulated a pool of savings that took 23,000 credit unions some sixty years to accumulate." In fact, when 1980 ended, money market funds held $84 billion, which was $15 billion *more* than credit unions. Two years after that, they held, stunningly, over $200 billion.

There was no dispute about why this was happening. The middle class had discovered money market funds because the "real world" interest rates they offered, compared to the 5¼ percent interest Regulation Q allowed banks to pay, had become too large to ignore. In 1974, the widest difference between regulated passbook rates and unregulated money market rates had been about 4 percent. In 1980 and 1981, the spread between the regulated and unregulated rates could get as wide as 11 or 12 percent. Although they were technically investment vehicles, money market funds were now seen as basically turbo-charged savings accounts, a notion the fund industry did nothing to discourage. According to an SRI survey, by 1980, 42 percent of the nation's households "understood money market funds well enough to decide whether to buy one or not"—a tremendously high number for a product that had been virtually unknown until a few years before. Much of this understanding had been acquired by word of mouth; the funds, in the words of their chief proslytizer, William Donoghue, "were just riding the wave." By then, the question was no longer whether you dared risk your savings in a money market fund. The question had become: How could you *not* risk your money in such a fund?

Congress—or at least those members of Congress who sat on the Senate banking committee—seemed surprisingly sanguine about allowing money market funds to continue to pluck billions of dollars of middle-class money from the nation's banks.[9] "I think money market funds deserve to be commended," said Proxmire at a hearing he chaired in January 1980—the first of many hearings devoted to the subject of these funds. The powerful bank and S&L lobbyists turned out in force that day, fully prepared to launch an attack on their newfound enemy. But before they got their chance, the subcommittee heard from a panel of high-ranking federal regulators, each of whom went on record as favoring money market funds. Each of them took turns dismissing the idea that money funds were underregulated, or excessively risky, as banks were claiming. And they rejected the favorite argument of the bank lobby that since money funds offered check writing, just as banks did, they should be forced to abide by the same reserve requirements. (Such requirements would cause money market yields to drop dramatically, thus negating their advantage.)

For his part, Proxmire seemed smitten with this latest financial innovation. "[They] are a textbook example of a market response to the need for financial services that were not being offered by other financial intermediaries," he said at that January hearing. "I think that as long as interest rates remain relatively high and Regulation Q continues to preclude small savers from getting a market rate of interest in their savings, the money market mutual fund will continue to prosper." To the dismay of the bank lobby, Proxmire was utterly unperturbed by this prospect, for his own solution to their dilemma was quite the opposite of theirs. They wanted to suppress money funds; he wanted to give the banks the freedom to set their own interest rates. "The success of the money market funds serves to underscore the need for the Congress to take action this year to get rid of Regulation Q," he said bluntly.

Washington, however, moves at its own pace, which is usually glacial. And so it was here. By early 1980, in spite of Proxmire's prodding, Congress and the financial regulators had taken only a few tiny steps to make banks more competitive with money market funds. The first of these, which took effect on June 1, 1978, was a new banking product created by legislative mandate, called the money market certificate. Although this new bank vehicle offered interest that was moderately competitive with money funds, it required a minimum deposit of at least $10,000—money that could not be touched for six months. Savers who needed to withdraw cash earlier than that had to pay a steep penalty. It didn't take a marketing genius to see that this new product was going to have rather limited appeal.

As the outflow of savings accelerated, the banking industry became increasingly anxious. If it could get no satisfaction in Washington, there were other places where the battle could be joined. There were the states. At the state level, banks could try to do what they had failed to do in Washington: regulate the money market funds out of business. "I had a magic number in mind—$100 billion," recalls David Silver, who was then the head of the Investment Company Institute, which is the mutual fund lobby. "I used to say that when the assets in money funds hit $100 billion, that's when the attack from the banks would come." Silver was off by $20 billion; when the attacks began in earnest, money funds had reached $80 billion.

It is impossible to know for sure whether the attacks that ensued were orchestrated out of the American Bankers Association offices in Washington; the bank lobbyists deny it to this day. Maybe they didn't have to orchestrate it. Maybe local bankers, feeling beleaguered by the success of money funds, decided spontaneously to fight back. It's certainly conceivable. What is known for sure is that in quite rapid succession, skirmishes broke out between banks and money market funds in some two dozen states. In almost every case, the tactics and strategies were similar, as were the results. One of the first such skirmishes, and the one that set the tone for all the battles to come, was fought in Utah, in the first few months of 1981. The battle of Utah became a kind of proxy for the nation, as this small state, with its closely knit power structure and its 18,000 money fund investors, wound up deciding for the rest of the nation whether money funds would live or die. Those were the real stakes, and everyone involved knew it.

"IT STARTED," recalls the former chief counsel for the Utah Bankers Association, "when the bankers in Utah became concerned about the deal Merrill Lynch had with that bank in Columbus, Ohio. You know, the one where they had that cash management account with money market funds on which people could write checks."

Peter Billings, who is still a practicing attorney in Salt Lake City, sits back in his chair and begins reminiscing about the famous legislative fight, which took place a decade before, in which he played so prominent a role:

> The money funds were paying higher interest rates than banks. The banks figured that there was a statutory limitation on interest rates. I prepared a legal

opinion [to that effect]. Then I got in touch with the commissioner of financial institutions and asked him to get an order for Merrill Lynch to cease and desist.

The commissioner asked the attorney general for his opinion, and he gave him a copy of the opinion I had written. And in effect, the attorney general adopted my opinion.

The commissioner of financial institutions, it almost goes without saying, was a former bank president. His name was Mirvin Borthick. The lawyer who "adopted" Billings's opinion was not the attorney general himself, but a local lawyer, deputized to ride herd over this issue. (This was not unusual in Utah.) His law firm represented an S&L. That's the way it worked in a small state capital like Salt Lake City, where everyone knew everyone else, and their business interests were hopelessly intertwined. It came as no surprise that the banking commissioner would be inclined to see things from the perspective of his friend the lobbyist. Merrill Lynch responded to the attorney general's opinion by ignoring it.

Then, in early 1980, in anticipation of the 1981 legislative session, Borthick formed a committee, composed entirely of members of the Utah banking fraternity, to rewrite the state's antiquated state banking laws. By the time they had finished, they had written a huge new bill, running over 400 pages, that contained exactly one controversial paragraph. But what a paragraph! It required that any money market fund that offered check-writing privileges—a feature, of course, offered by every money fund in existence—be brought under the jurisdiction of the commissioner for financial institutions. For his part, Borthick knew exactly what he was going to do once he had money market funds in his grasp. "I would have approached it as illegal banking," he says now. "We felt very strongly that they were taking *our* deposits."

Meanwhile, at Merrill Lynch, Paul Stein, who was still heading up the firm's CMA efforts, started hearing rumors that the product was about to run into trouble in Utah. The cash management account was doing well in the state, as was the firm's principal money market fund, called the Merrill Lynch Ready Asset Trust, which at the time was the largest mutual fund in history, with over $11 billion in assets. As a precautionary move, Stein retained a local attorney named James B. Lee, who, despite his impeccable establishment credentials—his father had been governor of Utah—agreed to represent the firm. Lee quickly learned of the committee rewriting the banking laws, and found the offending paragraph. But when he tried to present Merrill Lynch's position on the matter, he got nowhere. On January 1, 1981, the Utah legislative session began. Within days, the proposed banking code had received the sponsorship of the senator who chaired the relevant committee. Senate Bill 134, it was named. Its anti–money market fund paragraph was very much intact.

Right away, hard and bitter feelings developed between the protagonists. From early January to early March—the length of the Utah legislative term— the air was thick with barely veiled insults and whispered suspicions. Lee was considered a turncoat for his willingness to represent Merrill Lynch; his firm lost business as a result of his stance. From the other side, it was darkly (and wrongly) rumored that Jake Garn, Utah's senior senator who had just become Senate Finance Committee chairman, had secretly agreed to use his clout to help stifle money market funds in his home state.[10] People who had been friends for years would stride past each other in the state capitol without a nod of acknowledgment. The sense of Us against Them was powerful—Utahans against outsiders, local banks against big East Coast securities firms, and even, it must be said, Mormons against Jews. Silver, who is Jewish, does not remember any overt anti-Semitism, but Stein and Lee do. They recall a meeting, when tempers were short, in which a probank legislator walked into a conference room, eyed the assembled Merrill Lynch team, and said, "I suppose these are your goddamn Jewish lawyers from New York."

When non-Jews start muttering about Jews and money, it can often mean that they feel threatened by forces they can't control and often don't even fully comprehend. Without question, the banks and the S&Ls in Utah—like banks and S&Ls all over the country—felt threatened by such forces. And if they lashed out at the "outsiders" and even "the Jews," it was because they did not know whom else to blame for their problems. In the end, it wasn't money market funds or CMAs that were draining the banks of their deposits. It was the times themselves. If money funds hadn't existed, something else would have come along to perform the same function. The banks and the S&Ls were the victims of broad historical forces—forces that had been gaining strength for years, and were culminating now in this transformation of the financial landscape.

In attempting to rid their state of money market funds, Utah's bankers were really trying to turn back the clock. "If 'they' will stay out of the banking business, we won't get in the securities business," one banker said angrily during a meeting with state senators. They wanted the old world again, the one where banks did one thing, wirehouses another, and mutual fund companies a third. They wanted the world the way it was before all the blurring began, before inflation started changing the behavior of the middle class, before everything got so confusing and complicated. What the bankers didn't see—what they refused to see, though the evidence was everywhere—was that that world was gone forever.

*   *   *

In late January 1981, David Silver of the ICI arrived in Utah to join forces with Stein and Lee. When he got to Salt Lake City, the *Salt Lake Tribune* put his picture on the front page of the business section. The photograph showed him striding purposefully into town; the image it inevitably conjured up was of a balding, bespectacled gunslinger in a three-piece suit, toting a briefcase instead of a six-shooter. " 'High Noon' in Utah for Banking Law,'' read the accompanying headline. The two sides were heading for a showdown, and everybody could smell it.

Because a legislative term in Utah only lasts sixty days, bills have to move quickly, and it wasn't long before Senate hearings were scheduled for SB 134. In preparing for the hearings, Borthick rewrote the disputed paragraph, and offered up the new version as a "compromise." The new paragraph stated that any money fund that offered two-party checks would be exempt from the new law. However, third-party checks would still fall under its purview.

Stein and Silver did not consider this new language a compromise so much as a choke hold. A two-party check is a check a person writes out to himself, which he either cashes at a bank or deposits into his bank account. If he deposits it, of course, a bank might put a hold on the check for a few days, earning interest on the float in the interim. A third-party check, by contrast, is one that is written out to *a third party*—a store, the gas company, a person owed money by the check writer. With a third-party check, the float works in favor of the check writer instead of against him. More importantly, third-party checks are what make money funds both liquid and easy to use. They also give people the sense that a money fund is a banklike product. By insisting on this two-party check restriction, the banks were trying to force money fund assets back into bank accounts, at least for a few days at a time, while trying to make the funds less attractive to customers.

Despite Lee's protests, the chairman of the committee attached Borthick's new paragraph to the bill. Stein and Silver declared that if the bill passed in its present form, money market funds would be withdrawn from the state of Utah. No response. The bill passed the committee, 4–2, and was sent to the Senate floor for a final vote. The legislative term had three weeks to go.

By then, you could not step into the state capitol without seeing the swarms of lobbyists for both sides. When a senator walked down the corridor, he would be set upon by three or four or five bank lobbyists at a time, who would surround the poor man until he had heard them out. The pressure on these part-time legislators was enormous; if they were businessmen (as many were), the lobbyist they heard from most often was their own banker, the person who had the power to grant them a business loan—or to deny them one.

More surprising was the pressure being applied by the other side. This pressure, which was orchestrated by Stein and Silver, was coming from the 18,000 Utah voters who had some of their savings in money market funds. After getting all the money fund companies to send out urgent letters to their Utah customers, Stein and Silver had the makings of a powerful grassroots lobby. This new lobby didn't gather in the halls of the capitol, or hold protest marches on Salt Lake City. But it had its ways. "I don't know if I'm getting more phone calls than the rest of you," one state senator said during the floor debate, "but I estimate I've had somewhere between 150 and 200 phone calls in the last few days."

> The citizens who are calling are extremely well informed, and extremely anxious to maintain what they consider their one chance to get something in an interest rate that people with a great deal of money have always been able to get. The people I'm hearing from are not wealthy either. I've had letters from widows . . . from young people, from old people, from middle-aged people. They all know what they are talking about.

Robert Sykes, a thirty-three-year-old legislator who championed the cause of the money market funds in the House, remembers the constituent pressure in somewhat less exalted terms. "I had people call me and say, 'I'll be watching how you vote very carefully.' They were very blunt about it."

On March 3, 1981, the full Senate took up SB 134. The legislative session had nine days left. Despite the size of the bill, there was still only one paragraph in dispute, and even the janitors in the capitol could recite the arguments of both sides. Still, there was protocol to be followed. In Utah, when a controversial measure came to the floor, advocates for both sides were usually asked to sum up their views one last time prior to the vote. This they did, making the same arguments they'd been reciting for months. Then it was time to vote.

More than a decade later, almost no one on the floor that day can remember the vote count, crucial though it was at the time. What they remember instead was the scene in the visitors gallery. High above the Senate floor, the gallery was packed with bankers from all over Utah. Every senator with a line of credit from any bank in Utah could see his bank's president in the gallery, peering over the railing, watching him intently—looking, recalls one participant, "like a vulture." As the roll was called, most of those opposing the bill glanced up at the gallery as they voted, as if to plead for mercy from their bankers. On the crucial vote—on an amendment to delete the third-party check paragraph—only ten senators had need for mercy. The other fifteen sided with the bankers. Two anticlimactic votes later, the banking bill had passed the Senate. The bankers were halfway home.

They were jubilant, of course; on the scratchy dictabelt that recorded the moment, you can hear a cheer erupt from the gallery when the voting ends. And they were confident. The money funds had poured everything they had into the fight, spending upward of $1 million on such tactics as inflammatory newspaper ads intended to rouse those who had assets in money funds. Yet the bankers had emerged victorious. As Lee trudged out of the gallery, he and Desmond Barker, a local public relations man who had worked with him, bumped into a banker they both knew. "Congratulations," said Lee. Barker couldn't resist adding, "But it ain't over yet." The banker retorted, "We'll knock you over in the House."

It's a week later. March 10, 1981. The legislative term has two days left. Although SB 134 only landed on the desks of the House members the previous Thursday, it has to be debated and voted on today. *Has* to be. Otherwise, there's not enough time. This is the last stand for the money funds.

Even at this late date, the vote is too close to call. Nobody knows where the Speaker of the House stands; he won't say. A number of legislators tell Sykes, who is leading the fight against the bill, that although they support him, they hope to be able to vote with the banks if it doesn't affect the outcome. Sykes is a second-term House member; this is his first big legislative battle. Opposing him is a man named Sherman Harmer, Jr., a veteran committee chairman.

The protocol in the House is the same as in the Senate: before the vote, speakers from both sides get to press their arguments. This time, the money fund lobbyists trot out an elderly woman named Afton Forsgren. A retired schoolteacher, she knows just about everyone in the House by name. She is so frail she has to be helped to the podium. "Please, don't take it away!" she pleads in her soft, shaky voice, echoing the newspaper and radio ads Stein and Silver have been running daily.

The speeches over, the Speaker opens the floor to motions from House members. Sykes jumps up and demands a vote "to strike the enacting motion." It is a rarely employed parliamentary maneuver. The rookie has just thrown the veteran a curveball.

"To attempt to strike an enacting clause!" one of the probank legislators would later say in disgust. "You just don't *do* that." Sykes's move is plainly preemptive—he is trying to cut down the bill before any real debate can take place.

Under the rules, the debate that follows a motion such as the one Sykes has just offered is brief: one minute per speaker. Sykes completely ignores the substance of the argument, stressing instead the lateness of the session, and the numbing length of the bill. "I sat down last night intending to get through the important parts, and about midnight I fell asleep with the bill in my lap," he laments. All he is suggesting is that the House should have the same time to study the bill as the Senate had, he says. Is that so unreasonable? Harmer spends his minute ridiculing Sykes's rationale.

The Speaker calls for the ayes and the nays. The ayes have it, he quickly declares—implausibly, since the ayes and the nays sound exactly the same. Perhaps he is signaling his own position. Harmer requests an electronic rollcall.

From the floor of the House, the members can watch the votes adding up on the large electronic scoreboard. As the numbers inch upward, they resemble hands climbing a rope: first one side is ahead, then the other. With less than a minute remaining, though, everyone has voted, and the banks hold a one-vote lead, 38–37. But suddenly—inexplicably—there is a flurry of vote switching, bringing the count to 39–36 in favor of the Sykes motion. The Speaker bangs his gavel down. "Voting is closed," he announces. "The motion passes."

Where there were cheers in the gallery the week before, one can now hear on the scratchy dictabelt an audible gasp. Harmer leaps out of his seat. "Mr. Speaker," he says, panic-stricken, "four people came up to me and said that they voted yes on the [Sykes motion] so that they can recall it." Under Utah parliamentary rules, this is quite common; it's a hedge legislators use to force a second vote on a controversial issue. Indeed, it is so common that Harmer himself is among those who voted *for* the Sykes motion. "When you add those votes to the 'no' votes," he insists, "the [Sykes] motion would have never carried. So I move to reconsider our action on SB 134."

Now it's Sykes's turn to speak. "I believe in the last, let's see, three days of the session it takes a two-thirds vote to reconsider."

The Speaker: "That's correct. It will take a two-thirds vote."

Suddenly, Harmer realizes the magnitude of his blunder. Caught unprepared by Sykes's gambit, he allowed legislators opposing the motion to vote for it, for parliamentary reasons, not realizing he would be unable to bring it up again because of the two-thirds rule. More humiliating still, he has voted that way himself! "Fellow representatives," he says, in a tone of absolute anguish, "that's one of the worst parliamentary blunders I have ever seen." He begs the legislators to give him a chance to undo the damage, but they won't. They can't. Unless he can muster a two-thirds vote to reconsider, the Speaker tells him, the banking bill is officially dead. And that he cannot do.

They did wind up with a banking bill in Utah in 1981. The next day, having no other choice, the bankers agreed to remove the offending paragraph. In return, Stein, Silver, and Lee agreed to support the rest of the bill. It flew through the legislature the next day; no one in the House seemed to care anymore that they hadn't had time to read it.

But the effects of the battle of Utah would linger. As other states introduced legislation to restrict money market funds, Silver used the same grassroots strategy he had honed in Utah to defeat the proposed legislation. "We got it refined to where, in Kentucky I think, we heard about a money market amendment one morning, and had ads on the air three hours later," Silver recalls. "The next day, the amendment was withdrawn."

The hard feelings lingered, too. When Sykes ran for reelection the following year, the bank lobby poured money into his opponent's campaign; Sykes lost by 51 votes. And for months afterward, bankers in Utah talked openly about mounting another assault on money funds. But it wasn't going to happen. Borthick, especially, had lost his stomach for the fight. At their convention that summer, he told them that if they still wanted to fight money market funds, they would have to do it alone.

"I almost stopped Merrill Lynch in their tracks," Borthick would say a decade later. And he was right. But almost wasn't good enough; and while Silver spent the next year putting out fires in other states, money funds were never so seriously threatened again. Too many voters had too much money in them to allow it to happen. Money funds were a fixture in the emerging world of personal finance, and there was nothing any bank could do about it. Even the most stubborn banker had to accept this reality, and had to realize what came next. Unable to beat the money funds, the banks had only one other option: they had to join 'em.

## CHAPTER 11

# Mr. Regan Goes to Washington

## *September 1981*

W E NEED TO return for a moment to Washington during that awful month of March 1980, when Jimmy Carter was making his last, dismal attempt to gain the upper hand over inflation, and the economy was falling off the cliff. On the last day of that month—a full year before the Utah money fund fight reached its climax—Carter signed into law a piece of legislation called the Depository Institutions Deregulation and Monetary Control Act. It was nothing less than the most ambitious effort to rewrite the nation's Depression-era financial regulations since, well, since the Depression.

As you might expect, the Depository Institutions Deregulation and Monetary Control Act was a law of immense complexity. Its many provisions included new rules freeing the S&L industry from some of the tighter restrictions placed on it. It legalized NOW accounts nationwide, instead of just in New England. It allowed the paying of interest on bank checking accounts. And most infamously (at least in retrospect), it raised the amount covered by Federal Deposit Insurance from $40,000 per account to $100,000.[1] Although the Carter administration was in wholehearted agreement with the thrust of the law—namely, to create a body of regulation that better reflected the new realities of the financial marketplace—and although numerous officials were involved in shaping it as it wended its way through Congress, it was, at its core, Proxmire's bill. It incorporated Proxmire's solution to the problem of regulated bank passbook accounts vying for deposits with unregulated money market funds. The Proxmire solution, of course, was to allow banks to pay market interest rates, and that's what the Depository Institutions Deregulation Act called for. To put it another way, a year before Utah, the federal government had officially ordered that Regulation Q be abandoned.

Still, passage of the new bill didn't mean that Reg Q would vanish overnight. The law called for Q to be phased out over a six-year period, and it left the details of the phaseout to a new committee, formed specifically to handle that task. The committee, called the Depository Institutions Deregulation Committee (DIDC for short), had other tasks as well: It was supposed to devise new financial products that would allow banks and S&Ls to compete with money funds, and to begin lifting the bewildering variety of interest rate ceilings imposed on so-called time deposits,[2] such as certificates of deposit.[3] At bottom, though, the DIDC's mission was a straightforward one: to deregulate bank interest rates.

On May 7, 1980, the DIDC met for the first time. It consisted of only six people, but they were the nation's six most powerful financial regulators. The chairmen of the Federal Deposit Insurance Corporation (FDIC), Federal Home Loan Bank Board (FHLBB), and National Credit Union Administration were members, as were the comptroller of the currency, the secretary of the Treasury, and the chairman of the Federal Reserve. They met on Paul Volcker's turf, in a large, ornate conference room at the Federal Reserve Bank. Volcker was elected chairman.

Because the DIDC came under the aegis of the Sunshine Act, the meeting began in open session, but Volcker soon moved to have it closed to the public. "[A]n open discussion of this topic would incur an unacceptable risk of fostering speculation in financial markets" was his official reason. With the safety of the nation's financial markets thus assured, the committee then took up the first item on its agenda: premiums.

*Premiums!* Do you know what premiums are? Or rather, do you know what they were? Premiums were the gifts bank customers used to get when they opened a new account—the place settings, the clock radios, the toasters, the hundreds of other favors banks and S&Ls had been giving away whenever they wanted to attract new money. That premiums existed because of Regulation Q was indisputable: since banks couldn't offer competitive interest rates, they needed some other way to lure new deposits; as banking evolved in postwar America, premiums became the way. As with every other aspect of banking, premiums were regulated: for deposits under $5,000 the gifts were not supposed to be worth more than $5; for deposits over $5,000, they were not supposed to exceed $10 in value.[4] But the old rules were being increasingly ignored, as banks and S&Ls, desperate for deposits, began offering ever-fancier premiums. "Abuse of premiums [is] spreading," one alarmed member of the DIDC told his colleagues at that first meeting. To say the irony was rich doesn't do irony justice. Here were the six men charged with freeing bank interest rates from the shackles of regulation, and their first debate revolved around reestablishing regulatory control over toasters and clock radios. The discussion had the unmistakable feel of Nero fiddling while Rome burned.

The committee met again in late May. This time, after going into closed session, the regulators at least talked about "strategies and possible regulatory initiatives relating to interest rate ceilings on various categories of accounts. . . ." Which is not to say they made any headway. In June, the committee entered into the record a letter from Fernand St. Germain, the Rhode Island congressman who then chaired a key banking subcommittee, pleading with it to create a bank account "that would have some of the characteristics of a money market fund." It demurred.

And so it went. By the end of 1980, the DIDC had met more than a half-dozen times and accomplished nothing. It had not devised a timetable for the elimination of Regulation Q. It had not created any new savings products to help the banks and S&Ls fend off the money funds. It hadn't even been able to reach a decision on the premium issue—not after some premium manufacturers complained to St. Germain, who quickly browbeat the committee into backing off a plan to eliminate them. "DIDC Still Rearranging Deck Chairs on the Titanic," read the headline in *Donoghue's Money Fund Report* after one of its meetings. Donoghue couldn't have been happier, since the continued existence of Regulation Q meant only good things for money market funds.

Did the members of the DIDC understand that as well? Of course they did. Did they want to do something to help banks and S&Ls compete with money market funds? Desperately. Yet they seemed to be paralyzed at the prospect of raising bank interest rates even a smidgen. And it soon became clear that the man most responsible for this paralysis was the one who was supposed to be leading the charge—the man who spoke in his famously inaudible mumbles, wore his famously inexpensive suits, and puffed away on his famously cheap cigars. The deregulation committee wasn't deregulating largely because of its chairman, Paul Volcker.

More than a decade later, it is impossible to read the transcripts and minutes of those old DIDC meetings without sensing Volcker's discomfort with what he was being asked to do. At the time, it was impossible to sit in on the DIDC sessions without seeing it firsthand. Volcker seemed to cringe whenever the subject turned to deregulation, to slink his 6 foot, 7 inch frame low in his seat, as he rubbed his furrowed brow and emitted, from time to time, the heaviest of sighs. His whole bearing seemed to suggest that he would rather be doing anything than *this*. Asking Paul Volcker to loosen the nation's banking regulations was like asking Picasso to paint a traditional portrait. It wasn't impossible . . . *exactly*. But it rubbed against his grain so fiercely as to be nearly unimaginable.

Not that Volcker didn't have his reasons for proceeding at the snaillike pace he had chosen. Yes, he realized that small savers were getting a lousy deal from their banks, but correcting that particular inequity just wasn't very high on his list of priorities. He had other things to worry about—bigger things, as he saw it. He was worried about the stability of the banking system; from where he was sitting the lifting of Regulation Q would not necessarily help the banks and S&Ls. His greatest fear, in fact, was that the elimination of interest rate ceilings would have the opposite of the intended effect. Instead of making the banks and thrifts healthier, by giving them the means to regain the deposits they had been losing, deregulation would cause the cracks already evident in the foundation of banking to grow so wide that the entire structure would collapse.

Nor could Volcker's fears be easily dismissed. Nobody could say for sure what the banking world would look like once interest rate ceilings were gone. It was not at all obvious, for instance, that bankers, after decades of handing out place settings to attract money, would know how to market their newly deregulated accounts. Wasn't it possible that banks would go crazy with their new freedoms, offering interest rates that were unrealistically high, in a mad scramble to buy back deposits lost to the money funds? Isn't that precisely what had happened in the 1930s, and had led to the imposition of Regulation Q in the first place?

As for the S&Ls' owners, they had come to view Regulation Q as the very foundation of their business. In the mid-1960s, when Reg Q was extended to encompass the thrift industry, the S&Ls had persuaded Congress to allow them to pay slightly higher interest than banks—¾ of a percent at first, gradually reduced to ¼ of a percent by the late 1970s. This was the so-called housing differential,[5] and over the years, it had become, for the S&L industry, the one indispensable tool in the struggle for deposits. The prospect of having to pay market interest rates on savings accounts terrified the S&L industry in no small part because it would mean the end of the differential.

Even with the differential, though, S&Ls were in a terrible bind during the Age of Inflation. As interest rates rose, more money was withdrawn from regulated passbook accounts than was deposited, which meant that S&Ls had to find some other means to attract new deposits.[6] The primary means in the late 1970s and early 1980s were a small handful of fixed-term instruments—such as those money market certificates, which had been legislated into existence in 1978—that offered interest that approached money fund yields. Yet these were imperfect instruments, lacking the liquidity and convenience of money funds, and thus they could not stop the bleeding altogether.[7] What's more, the new instruments inflicted their own kind of pain on the institutions they were supposed to help. Quite often, money that landed in a money market certificate came not from a money fund but from a savings account. That meant that an S&L was paying 10 or 11 percent to retain funds that were already on deposit, and that had previously cost it only 5½ percent.

And that only describes one side of the S&L balance sheet. On the other side—the lending side—things were even worse. S&Ls existed to do one thing: lend money for home mortgages. In the days before inflation, an S&L would write thirty-year mortgages by the bushelful, charging, say, 7 percent interest, which would be enough to turn a nice little profit. But when interest rates began reaching 10 percent and beyond, those mortgages resembled nothing so much as a noose, slowly strangling the institutions that had written them. S&Ls were "borrowing short and lending long," as they used to say—paying high short-term rates to attract money, while carrying a huge portfolio of low-interest, long-term loans. As a result, hundreds of S&Ls were technically insolvent, their doors kept open mainly because the government feared the cost of closing them down.[8] As rates kept rising, recalls Todd Conover, comptroller of the currency under Reagan, "people actually calculated the month a particular S&L was going to go out of business."

Under these circumstances, it was entirely legitimate to worry about the effect of eliminating Regulation Q. As late as the spring of 1981, despite everything that had happened, regulated bank accounts in America still held more than $350 billion, "earning" savers a miserly 5¼ percent (or a slightly less miserly 5½ percent in the case of S&Ls). This was down, to be sure, from a mid-1978 figure of almost $500 billion—which is pretty much the point at which people began to catch on to money market funds. Indeed, since money market funds held $115 billion by the spring of 1981, the correlation between the rise in their assets and the reduction of assets in passbook accounts was unmistakable. It was equally clear that this trend— the gradual transfer of savings from regulated passbook accounts to money market funds—was bound to continue so long as interest rates remained higher than the Reg Q ceilings. On the face of it, S&Ls would seem doomed if Regulation Q remained in effect—differential or no differential.

And yet $350 billion was still a lot of money, and even if the sum was primarily a testament to the power of inertia, the S&Ls were loath to let go of it: it was the only cheap money they had left. Given their mortgage portfolios, they desperately needed a cheap source of money just to survive. To eliminate Reg Q, or even to raise the ceiling a few percentage points, was to force banks and S&Ls to pay more for deposits that were just sitting there anyway. One could argue, as Volcker did, that increasing the cost of deposits would not only exacerbate the industry's losses, but threaten their survival. Or one could argue, as Proxmire did, that if Regulation Q wasn't lifted, middle-class money would continue to leave the banking system, bankers would never learn to adapt to the real world of competition, and unsophisticated small savers would continue to be treated unfairly. In effect, Volcker was saying they were damned if they did, while Proxmire was saying they were damned if they didn't.

Volcker's reluctance to tackle deregulation head-on went beyond his legitimate fears, however, and that was also obvious to anyone who attended those old DIDC meetings. Jimmy Carter's emphasis on deregulation was a new idea in Washington, based on the then-radical notion that the marketplace could do a better job of fostering competition and lowering prices than any federal bureaucrat wielding a regulatory club. Having spent a long and honorable career as a bank regulator, Volcker didn't just disagree with that central premise, he was offended by it. He seemed to feel that the country had been well served by its web of bank regulations and that it was counterproductive to abandon them—or even to loosen them a little. He also seemed to feel—and this is an attitude that came easily to any lifelong regulator, no matter how honorable—that he alone knew best. His attitude was paternal at bottom; but then, so is most government regulation. Volcker thought it best to have the DIDC meet in closed session, so it did, no matter how strenuously Proxmire objected. Volcker thought Congress was incapable of understanding the potential effect of lifting interest ceilings; thus he felt justified in dragging his feet, despite the new law's mandate. And as for the bankers and thrift operators, he certainly didn't believe *they* knew better than he how to solve their problems. "His concern was that if we gave bankers the right to pay whatever they wanted, they would do something stupid," says a former Treasury Department official. In the end, Volcker trusted neither bankers nor Congress nor the marketplace to keep the banking system healthy. He only trusted himself.

And yet notwithstanding the genuineness of worries, and the obvious sincerity of his desire to do right by the banking system, it's hard not to conclude that Volcker *was* Nero, and Rome *was* burning. His focus on banks and S&Ls at the expense of the larger, evolving world of American finance was so narrow as to be blinding. When people had the option of putting their savings in money funds paying double-digit yields, what was the sense of worrying about the S&L differential? When firms like Merrill Lynch, which stood outside the regulatory walls, could poach bank customers with ease, it was worth asking what purpose those walls still served. "The world was changing," complains Garn today. "Credit cards, computers, money market funds—these things were making the laws obsolete." Deregulation, he adds, had begun taking place long before the deregulation law was passed—thanks to the likes of Andrew Kahr and Ned Johnson. And thanks to inflation itself. The new economic condition had made many of the old rules outmoded and impractical, and that is what Volcker missed most of all. In the forest of the money revolution, he could only see the trees of bank regulation.

"Everybody," says Garn, "was frustrated with the DIDC." By early 1981, "everybody" included the incoming Reagan administration, which tended to view deregulation not so much as a new idea but as a new religion. This especially included Ronald Reagan's new Treasury Secretary, Donald Regan.

IN HIS MEMOIRS, Don Regan claims that he only met Ronald Reagan twice prior to the 1980 election, encounters that were so fleeting that at the second of them, Reagan could not recall his name. He goes on to say that although he happily voted for Reagan, the new President's decision to name him Treasury Secretary took him quite by surprise. In the strictest sense, perhaps, this account is accurate. But the impression it is meant to convey—that Regan never harbored the slightest thought about landing such a job, and took it only because (as he claims to have told Reagan), "How could any American say no when asked to serve by the President?"—that impression isn't even close.

Regan had been harboring such thoughts for years;[9] to the extent such a thing is possible, he had been campaigning to be Treasury Secretary for much of his tenure as the head of Merrill Lynch. He had tried to position himself, with some considerable success, as a Wall Street statesman, writing a book about Wall Street in 1972, testifying before Congress, sitting on any blue-ribbon panel that would have him. And while he may not have been close to Reagan himself, he had worked hard to build bridges to the Republican Party, efforts that included chairing several big fund-raisers. These were the occasions when Don Regan met the future President—a circumstance not likely to be forgotten. After the election, Regan's name quickly surfaced as a candidate for Treasury Secretary.[10] And why not? He was sixty-one years old. He had done everything he was going to do at Merrill

Lynch. He had the requisite heft for the position. And he plainly coveted the job, having done everything short of erecting a billboard in front of Merrill Lynch headquarters to signal his interest.

Still he was an odd choice, and not just because he and the new President barely knew each other. His understanding of politics and Congress lay somewhere between slim and nonexistent. He had no strong grasp of fiscal or monetary policy. His Merrill Lynch management style couldn't possibly work in Washington, a place where subordinates, instead of asking "How high?" when he said "Jump!" were more likely to leak his latest demand to the press. And most of all, he wasn't one of "them." Though a devoutly conservative man, he was not remotely in tune with the kind of conservatism being swept into power with Ronald Reagan. This was a new style of conservatism, radical in tone and intent, driven by ideology, and carrying both a chip on its shoulder and a take-no-prisoners attitude toward Washington. The young firebrands who served as Reagan's foot soldiers had nothing but scorn for the kind of complacent, corporate, old-fashioned conservatism represented by the likes of Don Regan.

Before becoming Treasury Secretary, Regan most likely would have agreed with George Bush's famous description of supply-side economics, which was at the heart of the Reagan revolution: "voodoo economics," Bush had called it back when he had opposed Reagan in the Republican primaries. Supply-side economics held that the way to shrink the federal deficit was not by raising taxes but by lowering them, because lower taxes would give Americans the kind of bald financial incentives they needed to increase productivity and "grow" the economy. This growth, in turn, would generate tax revenues far in excess of whatever money was lost through tax cutting. As for Regan's own economic beliefs, his friend William Rogers, the Wall Street lawyer and former Secretary of State, perhaps put it best: "Don," he said, "is not totally committed to any economic theory." Rather, he was an "inveterate pragmatist,"[11] committed mainly to whatever principles would generate the most profits for Merrill Lynch.

Say this for inveterate pragmatists: they can shed old personae as easily as a snake sheds skin. If Ronald Reagan believed in supply-side economics, then, by God, Don Regan would believe in it, too. Once he started to think about it, it occurred to him that the President's views and his own really weren't that far apart; he just hadn't realized it before! This happy thought came to him in a flash one afternoon early in his term, when one of his new assistant secretaries briefed him on the intricacies of supply-side theory. After the man had finished, Regan smiled and said, "I've always been a supply-sider."[12]

Meanwhile, Regan's management style was undergoing a remarkable metamorphosis. For instance: he didn't bang his fists on the table anymore. The Regan of yore—the Regan whose hold on Merrill Lynch was roughly equivalent to Louis XIV's hold on seventeenth-century France—that Regan vanished the moment he arrived in Washington, along with that aura he'd always had at Merrill Lynch, the one that telegraphed his belief that he was the smartest man in the room. One of the few times his inner circle saw him blow up was when he discovered his archrival, Office of Management and Budget head David Stockman, outflanking him during one of their internecine battles. Unfortunately for Regan, this occurred with some regularity, for Stockman, a thirty-four-year-old ex-congressman, was a Washington pro, a deft leaker who knew how to promote himself at the expense of his rivals. Regan was an amateur in this world, unaccustomed to working the back channels that are so necessary in Washington, at sea in this atmosphere of guile and intrigue. And it showed. "He was like an actor trying to learn Richard III for the first time, when the play is opening the next day," recalls a former aide. This same man adds that, in the beginning especially, Regan's views were so unformed that he tended to echo the opinions of whoever had last visited his office.

There was one area of his new job, however, where he was never insecure, and where he had an unquestioned grasp of the issues and their implications. The issue was the one most deeply entwined with the money revolution: the deregulation of the financial services industry.

It should come as no surprise that Don Regan had strong feelings about deregulation. However lacking in supply-side fervor, he had always had been passionate about competition and free enterprise; in his mind, those feelings were the reason he had become a Republican. Moreover, deregulation was the one public policy issue he had grappled with prior to joining the administration. Nobody had to brief Don Regan about how the regulatory barriers were crumbling; at Merrill Lynch, he'd been among those trying to break them down. Nobody had to explain to him about why Regulation Q had outlived its usefulness; Q was the reason the Merrill Lynch Ready Asset Trust was the biggest money market fund in the country, having swelled to more than $22 billion by the end of 1982. And certainly no one had to tell him how to think about Volcker's implicit argument that banks needed to be protected, via regulation, from themselves. He knew exactly what he thought about that line of reasoning. "On the day Regan became Treasury Secretary," recalls Chrystie, his former Merrill Lynch aide, "I was sure Regulation Q was dead." Chrystie adds: "If you told him that a lot of financial institutions weren't ready, that wasn't going to impress

Don Regan at all. His position was, If you can't do it, step aside for those who can.''

One former aide would later point out how convenient it was for Regan to be in favor of more competition, coming as he did from the Wall Street firm most accustomed to steamrolling anyone in its way. And while this is true enough, it does not give Regan his due. His belief in the virtues of free market competition was as much his bedrock creed as the importance of regulation was Volcker's. Deregulation was the one subject where he would revert to his old full-of-beans self: "Why the hell should the little guy have money in the bank and not get paid what the big guy gets?" he would bellow. And there was an exquisite paradox, which did not escape him. Here he was, the man (in his own mind, at least) most responsible for making life miserable for America's bankers, now suddenly charged with nursing the banking system back to health. How he loved that twist! "I'm the one who caused this problem," he was fond of saying, "so I might as well be the one to solve it." This sentiment was always followed by a self-satisfied chortle.

His first impulse upon taking office was to conduct an overhaul of the nation's financial laws, erasing those old war horses, the Glass–Steagall and McFadden acts, from the books and starting all over again. Here, however, he got one of his first bracing lessons in the realities of Washington. At Merrill Lynch, he could demand that something happen, and it would happen, no matter how strong the opposition. In Washington, he couldn't demand anything of anybody, especially Congress; the process didn't work that way. Among those most eager to explain this to Regan was Jake Garn, the grim, humorless Utah Republican who had just replaced Proxmire as chairman of the Senate banking committee.[13] Having been in the minority his entire Senate career, Garn was not about to cede power to anyone— certainly not to Regan, to whom he took an instant dislike. The first time Regan visited Garn, the new chairman brushed him away like a piece of lint. "The administration proposes and Congress disposes," Garn sniffed, upon learning of Regan's plans. All of which left Regan, an instinctive deregu- lator in an administration that fairly worshipped at the altar of deregulation, with only one narrow outlet for his free market impulses. The DIDC.

Of Regan's first DIDC meeting, held on March 26, 1981, little remains on the record: both the transcript and the summary are missing from the old DIDC files now residing at the National Archives. The few smatterings of paper left behind, however, herald a changing of the guard. Sometime before the meeting, Volcker quietly offered to turn over the chairmanship of the committee to Regan, who gladly accepted. (Volcker became vice-chairman.) The meeting was moved from its previous location at the Federal Reserve to the Treasury Building. It was conducted in open session. It began with the new Treasury Secretary reading a prepared text in which he came out foursquare in favor of lifting interest rate ceilings. And its tone was markedly different: there was a confidence about the appropriateness of deregulation that had been missing before, and a kind of bullheaded optimism in the face of the deep problems facing the S&Ls. "I should like to take this opportunity to reiterate that the problems of the thrift institutions are temporary and manageable, and should not be of concern to the general public," Regan pronounced as he opened his second meeting. Don Regan was in charge; everything was under control.

With each successive meeting Regan gained new allies as others with his point of view were named to succeed Carter-era bank regulators. Richard Pratt, the new head of the Federal Home Loan Bank Board (and thus the chief S&L regulator), made his initial DIDC appearance in June; William Isaac, the new FDIC chairman, joined the administration in time for the September session; Todd Conover, the incoming comptroller of the currency, made his first appearance at the December meeting. Though Regan's alliance with Pratt was always shaky—in the classic fashion of FHLBB chairmen, his only cause seemed to be the S&L differential—the new chairman seemingly had the votes to do what he wanted. Volcker, suddenly in the minority, did what he could to apply the brakes, using his intimidating presence and worried mien to keep Regan's enthusiasm for deregulation in some small check. But there was no way he could stop the thing entirely.

Even with Regan surrounded by his new allies, though, the same questions remained that had haunted Volcker throughout 1980. Would S&Ls, especially, be able to handle the deregulation of interest rates? What kind of timetable should be drawn up for eliminating interest rate ceilings? What new savings vehicles could be created so that banks and S&Ls would be competitive with money market funds? What made these questions especially vexing was that there was so little consensus among the institutions themselves. There were ideas and proposals all over the spectrum—though as a general rule of thumb, the larger the institution the better the chance that it would favor the abolition of interest rate ceilings. Citicorp, for instance, was aggressively pushing for change, while most small-town S&L operators were pushing just as aggressively to retain the status quo. The one thing everyone agreed on was that they wanted the DIDC to decide *something* so they at least knew where they stood. If they were going to be deregulated, they wanted some details. They wanted a schedule.

This Regan was determined to give them. At his first meeting in March, he had the committee come up with a four-year deregulation plan, which it put out for public comment. By the time the committee reconvened in late June, 500 letters had been received in reaction to the plan, evenly divided between those who supported it and those opposed. At the June meeting, the committee members went at it again. "Let me try this one on you," Regan said at one point, and then almost offhandedly[14] tossed off a deregulation schedule that closely resembled a schedule Citicorp had been pushing. Under this plan, each August, beginning in 1981, successive levels of time deposits would be deregulated, starting with four-year certificates of deposit and moving gradually toward shorter term instruments. Also, after shrinking the differential in half during the first two years of this plan, Regan wanted to eliminate it entirely by 1983.

"My only comment would be that I think four years is certainly as short as we can go on deregulation at the moment," responded Volcker, trying, as always, to slow things down. "I think the fact that we're letting people know there is something that they can depend on is quite important," added Irvine Sprague, the FDIC chairman, occupying the middle ground. (Isaac had not yet joined the administration.) "[We] would have been prepared to be much more liberal much sooner," chimed in Charles Lord, the acting comptroller of the currency, staking out the let's-get-on-with-it position. Nonetheless, when it came time to vote, everyone sided with Regan, including Volcker. In approving the schedule, the committee had at last begun the process of interest rate deregulation that Congress had mandated a year and a half before. August 1, the starting date, was only six weeks away.

Toward the end of that same meeting, the committee took up Q itself. Sprague was the instigator this time. A year before, he pointed out, the committee had voted to make some kind of decision about passbook rates by September 1981. Why not propose a new passbook ceiling now, at this June meeting, put it out for public comment, and gauge the reaction? Sprague suggested a new ceiling of 10¼ percent, almost double the current Regulation Q limit—high enough to get the attention of all interested parties. In defending this proposed ceiling, Sprague made what should have been the most obvious of points: "This basic [5¼] rate remained virtually unchanged for eight years while the rest of the world passed it by." The motion passed with only one dissent—not Volcker, as it happens, who was perfectly happy to put out anything for comment (since it meant delaying a final decision). The "nay" vote was cast by Pratt, worried that a doubling of the passbook rate would finish off even those S&Ls that had managed so far to remain solvent. With that done, the committee adjourned until September.

*     *     *

It turned out to be a terrible summer, the summer of 1981. The election of a new President had not caused Volcker to change his strategy of attacking inflation by controlling the money supply; if anything, Volcker went about his business with renewed resolve, steeling himself against criticism, impervious to doubt, convinced that the administration was filled—to put it more harshly than Volcker himself ever would—with supply-side lunatics. Volcker's determination was only heightened when the Reagan administration pushed through the meat of the supply-side program, a huge tax cut. Convinced that such a tax cut was about the most irresponsible thing the government could do at such a moment, Volcker again felt the onus on himself to bring inflation under control.

That summer was when it all came to a boil—when the consequences of Volcker's anti-inflation crusade were so painful that Americans were entitled to wonder whether the cure was worse than the disease. In attempting to squeeze inflation out of the economy, Volcker threw the country into the deepest recession since the Depression.[15] Interest rates were off the charts. They had already risen to new heights during the last year of the Carter administration, but it was the summer of 1981 when interest rates peaked. The prime lending rate seemed to be stuck at around 20 percent. Government debt of every kind—three- and six-month T-bills, as well as the "long bonds" of fifteen- and thirty-year durations—were paying out stratospheric yields, around 16 percent in the case of Treasury bills, with the long bond hovering close to 14 percent. Most of the summer, the average money market fund yield was between 16 and 17 percent; in August, at least three funds broke the 18 percent barrier. In their whole history, they would never yield more than they did that summer.

And the middle class was paying attention. The relationship between interest rates and the movement of middle-class money was never so clear as it was that summer. Money didn't stay in one place anymore; it went wherever interest rates were highest. During its June meeting, for instance, the DIDC voted to raise the interest rate ceiling on something called a small saver's certificate—essentially a thirty-month CD that had been created by Congress to help the small saver. With the ceiling lifted, the rates paid on the certificates jumped from around 12 percent to 16 percent. Instantly, the small saver's certificates swelled with new money; in August alone, S&Ls pulled in $6.5 billion. That was just one of a dozen examples of how middle-class savings had begun to follow interest rates.

Of course the preeminent example of this practice remained money market funds. When 1981 began, money market funds held a record $80 billion in assets. By the end of the year, that $80 billion figure had been washed away in a tidal wave of new money. During the course of the year, assets poured in at the rate of $2 billion a week, bringing the 1981 total to $183 billion in assets. And that 125 percent gain, impressive though it was, represented a mere fraction of the total 1981 money market *sales*. The latter amount—the amount of money that flowed *through* money market funds during the course of the year—was a staggering $452 billion. That is to say, only one out of every four dollars that went into a money fund during 1981 was still there at year's end.

Where had the rest of that money gone? A good deal of it, surely, had left money funds to pay bills.[16] But it also seems clear that people were moving their savings in and out of money funds for another reason: They were shopping around for the best yields they could find. Once people began to pay attention to interest rates, they realized that the financial universe was full of competing interest rates. Small saver's certificates offered one rate, T-bills another, money funds a third. They also discovered that money market funds were not generic, the way passbook accounts were. Different funds offered different yields, and though the gap between the highest yielding fund and the lowest yielding fund was small, it was still a gap. That gap mattered, in a way it never had before. *Money* magazine was publishing a monthly list of the highest yielding money funds by then, and it was startling, the effect that list had. Every month, the money funds at the top of the list were flooded with new money. Around this same time, a term came into vogue to describe this new phenomenon of Americans moving their money around from place to place, in search of an extra percentage point in interest. It was called "chasing yield," and it represented one of the great behavioral shifts in American finance.

There are, in retrospect, any number of reasons why the humble money market fund turned out to be the critical financial innovation of the money revolution. One of them, surely, was that it was largely responsible for instilling in millions of Americans the idea that chasing yield was something worth doing. More compelling still, it instilled the idea that those who failed to chase yield would lose. Just as the aversion to risk would be ingrained in anyone who had lived through the Depression, so would this new lesson embed itself in the subconscious of those who lived through the Age of Inflation. Long after inflation had been tamed, Americans would continue their sometimes frantic, sometimes giddy, sometimes sensible, sometimes insane, search for yield. Chasing yield would be the defining financial act of the middle class in the decade to come. It was how we had changed.

They were not a happy group, the members of the DIDC, when they reassembled at the Treasury Department in September. Their confidence in their mission, so much in evidence in previous DIDC sessions, had largely evaporated. Having taken the first step toward loosening Regulation Q—a step that had been very much predicated on interest rates dropping during the summer—DIDC members were now faced with a terrible dilemma. On the one hand, skyrocketing interest rates greatly increased the pressure on them to take some action that would give the American saver a reason to keep his money in the bank instead of handing it over to a money fund. On the other hand, skyrocketing interest rates greatly increased the pressure to do nothing of the kind—because any loosening of the ceilings would result in a further weakening of the banks and S&Ls, costing them many billions of dollars they couldn't afford in higher interest payments. Even Regan, the one DIDC member whose confidence had not flagged, seemed less blustery than usual.

The DIDC strategy had taken a beating in any case. The schedule the committee had approved in June was on hold after a district court judge ruled that it had been passed improperly.[17] And the proposal to double the Regulation Q ceiling, which was out for public comment, had received a huge and volatile reaction—4,571 comments in all. The reaction made clear just how divisive an issue it had become. The people who ran the smallest S&Ls, the ones that anchored every small-town Main Street in America, were livid. "The proposed increase on passbook savings rates to 10¼ percent is absurd," wrote the president of an S&L in McMinnville, Tennessee. The head of a thrift in Newton, Kansas, complained: "I know we can't stop the world in order to get off, but you people just don't realize what a nightmare [you've created]." From Little Falls, New Jersey: "To suggest any large increase is unthinkable unless it is the DIDC's intention to put the S&Ls into bankruptcy." For their part, the thousands of retirees who wrote in to support raising the Reg Q ceiling were every bit as vociferous.

And here was the DIDC put in the position of trying to turn water into wine. It was somehow supposed to loosen Regulation Q without destroying the thrift industry, while inventing financial products that could compete with products that had emerged from the marketplace.[18] It wasn't just a thankless task, it was a hopeless one, and if the members of the committee couldn't quite bring themselves to admit as much, they came as close as they ever would at that September session, as they prepared to vote on what to do about Regulation Q.

"[Treasury] thinks the passbook rate should be increased from its current 5¼ percent to 6¾ percent," Regan began:

You say to yourself, well, what happens if they pay market rates? Obviously, that's too expensive. But I think something has to be done here . . . to indicate to the small saver that all of these high interest rates are not going to be passed on to the big guy. Are we going to be able to keep [money in passbook accounts] by hiding it under the rug . . . and hoping that lethargy or sheer inertia will mean that the little guy will be kept there at his disadvantage?

VOLCKER: I come to a different conclusion because I do think our injunction—to have due regard for the safety and soundness of the depositary institutions—is relevant and important.

ISAAC: I'm very troubled by the potential earnings impact of the passbook increase. On the other hand, we do have to move these accounts into the realm of the marketplace as soon as possible.

LORD: [O]ne of the great mysteries of the moment is why people keep money in passbook accounts at any balance level. . . .[19]

They went around in circles like this for more than an hour, coming no closer to a consensus. Finally, it was time to vote. They didn't even bother with the original proposal to double the passbook rate; the summer's record interest rates had killed that idea off already, and everyone on the DIDC knew it. Instead, their first vote was on Regan's more modest plan to raise the Regulation Q ceiling from 5¼ percent to 6¾ percent. To his surprise, he lost, 3–2;[20] Pratt, Isaac, and Volcker all voted against him. Regan then offered another proposal, to raise the passbook rate by a mere half-percentage point, from 5¼ to 5¾ percent. Again, the vote was 3–2, but this time Regan won. Coming as it did at a time when double-digit interest rates had lost their ability to shock, it was the tiniest of changes, so insignificant that one might have expected it to be greeted with the collective yawn it deserved. Yet within a month, the committee had been forced to back away from even this minuscule change in the Regulation Q ceiling. Stranger still, it had been forced to do so by many of the same congressmen who had criticized it for moving too slowly.

•

What had happened? What had caused Congress, which had created the DIDC to do exactly what it was finally doing, to change its mind so suddenly—and over such small potatoes? Part of the answer was that the summer of 1981 had shaken Congress as badly as it had shaken everyone else. You didn't have to own a thrift, or regulate one, to understand the effect that record interest rates were having on the balance sheets of the nation's S&Ls: the thing had escalated into a bona fide crisis. But there is also a less generous answer, which is that the S&L industry was milking the crisis for all it was worth. The thrift industry had led a charmed life for a long time, its image burnished by the Frank Capra movie, *It's a Wonderful Life,* its role as the nation's primary mortgage lender one of the great sacred cows in American life, its Washington clout the stuff of legend. For years, its slow but steady profits had been as close to a sure thing as one could find in a capitalist economy. But the coming of inflation and high interest rates had eliminated the profits and ended the charmed life—and there wasn't even any way to fight back! How could you fight an economic condition? It was like punching at shadows. When the DIDC voted to increase the passbook rate by a half a percentage point that September, it gave the thrift industry a tangible target, an outlet for its accumulated frustration.

Congress bore the brunt of this frustration. That's the way it always worked with the S&L industry back then; Congress was where it went to get what it wanted. The thousands of thrift owners across the country began swarming over their legislative representatives, demanding that something be done to rein in the "out-of-control" DIDC. And congressmen and senators, most of whom had been oblivious to the workings of the DIDC, swarmed, in turn, over the regulators. Few legislators had more than the faintest idea what the dispute was about, and fewer cared to find out; all they knew was that back home, some important constituents were angry, and they wanted something done about it.

Even those members of Congress who did understand the dispute reacted in like fashion. In October, Fernand St. Germain—the same St. Germain who a year before had pleaded with the DIDC to create a banking vehicle that could compete with money funds—wrote a short, insistent letter to Regan, cosigned by three members of the banking committee, practically directing that the DIDC's September decision be reversed. One committee member went so far as to submit a bill to prevent the DIDC from raising regulated interest rates, which of course was the only thing the DIDC existed to do.

But the crucial event was a phone call from Jake Garn to Don Regan, which began with the Utah senator snarling, "You've really done it now!" A few days later, Regan went up to Capitol Hill to repair the damage, but it only got worse: Garn seemed positively gleeful to have this opportunity to dress down the Treasury Secretary. "My phone has been ringing off the hook," a former Treasury aide remembers Garn telling Regan. "People are telling me that this is the worst decision you have ever made! You really messed this up." It was a bizarre encounter, and what made it so was not just that Garn, who had supported the creation of the DIDC and generally favored deregulation, now seemed to be taking the opposite position. It wasn't even that Garn's ire was directed at such a ridiculously small increase in the passbook rate. No, what made the encounter so baffling was what happened next. When Garn had finished berating Regan, the Treasury Secretary calmly replied, "Ok, we'll change it." He seemed quite cavalier about his willingness to roll back the passbook rate—as if it were no big deal either way. The aide, who was Regan's point man on the DIDC, was stunned, but when he tried to say something, Regan quickly cut him off. They never discussed it again.

"Garn you could understand," the aide says now. "His attitude was: Do whatever makes everybody happy." Plainly, there were a lot of unhappy people in the thrift industry after that September meeting. But Regan's blithe reaction was something he never quite got over. "There was nothing Don would die for," he says now.

Now it was the elderly's turn to howl in outrage. "I was utterly disgusted this morning when I read that the one half of one percent boost in rates would not go into operation. . . ." "It is sad that the little guy doesn't count. . . ." "I resent your action; you do not represent the low-income taxpayer. . . ." "I am a widow . . . if I could get more interest on my small savings, it would help some. . . ." "It was you [Regan] who promised to 'strike a blow for the little guy.' I think your [decision] to defer was a blow at him, not for him. . . ." "WHY DID YOU DO THIS?"

But the deed was done. At its December meeting, the DIDC revoked the half-a-percentage-point increase in the passbook rate, deferred consideration of the long-term deregulation schedule, and temporarily abandoned efforts to come up with a short-term instrument that might compete with money market funds. It was a very short meeting. Regan didn't attend; he was at the doctor's. Isaac was the only committee member to urge the DIDC to hold firm, arguing that the committee's about-face would only strengthen the growing nonbank competition. "Virtually every week we've seen billions of dollars added to the money market funds," he said. "In February, two of the nation's largest financial organizations, Sears and Prudential, will unleash their marketing forces to sell money market funds nationwide. The loss of customers and market share could well become permanent and even more substantial." But when it came time to vote, the accumulated pressure brought to bear by Garn, St. Germain, and the S&L lobby outweighed Isaac's warning. Thus did Nero continue to fiddle, and Rome continue to burn.

⌒

THE DAY DID COME, OF COURSE, when banks and S&Ls began to offer market interest rates—a day that ultimately showed how prescient Isaac had been. It came more than a year after the DIDC's fateful September meeting, by which time interest rates were nearing single digits, making the move politically palatable, and the accumulated assets in money market funds had topped $230 billion, making it a good deal more pressing. More to the point, it came about not because of any action on the part of the DIDC, but because Congress finally grabbed hold of the thing, as it should have all along. On October 15, 1982, Ronald Reagan signed into law the second massive banking deregulation bill Congress had passed in two years. If the first one was Proxmire's baby, this one belonged to Garn and St. Germain, who patched it together in a series of uneasy compromises. It became known forever after as the Garn–St. Germain bill.

Why did Garn–St. Germain succeed is lifting interest rate ceilings when Don Regan and the DIDC had failed? Partly it was because Congress ignored Regulation Q, which was still too contentious, and concentrated instead on devising a new bank savings vehicle that would offer market interest rates.[21] More importantly, though, while the DIDC had only been charged with deregulating one side of the balance sheet—the deposit side—Congress deregulated the lending side as well, freeing the thrift industry to make loans far afield from its traditional base of home mortgages. Many of the other long-standing restrictions on the thrift industry were also loosened or abandoned. As part of the deal it cut to get these new freedoms, the industry grudgingly agreed to pay market interest rates for deposits. (It also agreed, even more grudgingly, to the elimination of the differential.) The operative theory was that thrifts would be able to afford to pay higher interest rates to depositors because the new lending freedoms would allow thrift owners to make more profitable loans. Well, it sounded good anyway.

That it didn't work out that way—that, on the contrary, the loosening of restrictions on S&Ls led to one of the greatest financial disasters of all time—is well known by now. Every credible account of the ensuing S&L crisis begins with the new lending freedom granted by Garn–St. Germain, and the abuses of those freedoms by the industry. Garn, while always denying that his bill sowed the seeds of the disaster, would later come to regret having his name so closely associated with the 1982 bill, feeling unfairly tarred by something he had once thought of as a great achievement. Or at least a necessary achievement. "People forget what it was like back then," he would complain bitterly. "They forget about the tens of billions of dollars going into money market funds. They forget about how all the depository institutions would be up here on Capitol Hill fighting over some little piece of turf." Then, after an anguished pause, he would ask plaintively, "What choice did we have?"

What choice *did* they have? The only other choice would have been to go in completely the other direction, and begin regulating money market funds, forcing down yields by government fiat. But that wasn't really much of a choice so long as Reagan was President, and interest rates were high. And not so long as the middle class remained wedded to money market funds, and to the idea that they had a God-given right to keep pace with inflation. Garn–St. Germain was driven by the need to allow banks and S&Ls to pay the same interest rates as money market funds, and everything else about it flowed from that need. Including its flaws.

Wouldn't you know it, though? In the end, Garn–St. Germain wound up tossing the ball right back to the DIDC. To be sure, the law's mandate to the committee this time was extremely specific: It gave the DIDC exactly two months to come up with a new, federally insured account that would be "directly equivalent to and competitive with" money market funds. The minimum balance could not exceed $5,000, and there could be no interest rate ceiling whatsoever. But *still*. . . After everything that had happened, Congress still had the same misplaced faith that a committee full of regulators could devise financial products to compete with those that arose from the marketplace.

When the DIDC convened a month later, not much had changed. Here was Don Regan, so happy to be finally deregulating that he could barely restrain himself. Here was Paul Volcker, sitting across from Regan, looking as glum as Regan looked gleeful. (Here was Pratt, still worried about losing the differential!) And here they all were arguing over the very same things they'd been arguing over for two-plus years. When the subject of the required minimum deposit was raised, for instance, Regan quickly suggested that they impose no minimum at all, and let the marketplace work it out, while Volcker wanted a minimum deposit of $5,000, which was the classic regulator's approach. The only reason they settled the argument this time was that Garn–St. Germain told them they had to. "I could go to $2,500," Volcker said finally. "I don't think it's a good idea, but it's just to get off the stalemate and get on with it." So $2,500 it was.

Then came the issue of attaching checks to this new account, the way money funds did. Regan wanted unlimited checking; Volcker wanted severe restrictions on the number of checks a customer could write against the account—none preferably.[22] Again, what would have been, pre-Garn–St. Germain, a stalemate, ended in compromise, with Volcker grudgingly agreeing to a three-check-per-month limit. Down the list of variables they went, arguing and compromising every step of the way, until finally they had created their new account. Whatever else you could say about this process of give-and-take, it did not much resemble the way money funds had come about.

Perhaps you remember this account—the one with the $2,500 minimum, and the three-check-per-month limit. Even with its regulatory restrictions, it was a very big deal when banks and thrifts were finally allowed to market it in mid-December 1982. It was called the money market deposit account, and part of the reason it was such a big deal was that it appeared at first as though Volcker's greatest fears were going to be realized. Given the freedom for the first time in some fifty years to offer any interest rate they pleased, bankers ran amok. At a time when money market fund rates had dipped to a little over 8 percent, most of the big banks in Atlanta, for instance, introduced their money market deposit accounts with interest rates of 20 percent or more. The most egregious of them, First DeKalb Bank, offered 25 percent interest, and threw in an E.T. doll. A bank that had been founded in 1879 offered an introductory interest rate of 18.79 percent. Bank of America set its first money market account interest rate at 11¼ percent, and handed $100 in cash to anyone who deposited more than $20,000. A bank in Boston gave out sixteen-piece dinnerware sets as premiums to anyone who opened one of the new accounts—thus proving that old habits died hard. Within two weeks, the Boston bank had handed out 4,700 sets. Indeed, in just its first week of existence, money market deposit accounts drew in $19 billion.

But the initial madness did not last long, and when those early inflated rates returned to earth, it was plain that money market funds, while bloodied, were still standing. They only lost $1.3 billion to the new accounts that first week, and once things settled down, it was obvious that money market funds were *still* able to offer higher interest rates than most banks and thrifts, primarily because their overhead was so much lower. The key advantage banks now had was federal deposit insurance. With the spread between bank yields and money fund yields having narrowed to one or two percentage points, instead of ten or twelve percentage points, there were plenty of people who were willing to forgo a little interest to get deposit insurance. But not nearly so many that money funds were destroyed: yield had become too important a goal for too many Americans. By the end of 1983, money market funds had dropped to $160 billion in assets. But then they began to rise again. By the end of 1984, money funds were above the $200 billion benchmark again, on their way to $400 billion and beyond.

Edward Furash, the banking consultant, believes that money funds thrived after interest rate deregulation because they were "quicker, faster, smarter—better able to get to the consumer's heart and mind through marketing." He also believes that they were able to hold on to middle-class money even without deposit insurance because, as he puts it, "the money funds lowered the consumer's perception of what constituted risk." William Donoghue has a different theory. He believes that in deciding to label the new bank account a money market deposit account, the DIDC did a great service to the money funds. "Money market deposit accounts were nothing like money market funds," he says. "They didn't operate in the same way at all. But by labeling the new account a 'money market' account, they legitimized money funds. It was as if the government was admitting there was no real difference between a money fund and a bank account." The point is: for many people there wasn't any difference.

And all the while, the Age of Inflation was winding down, as Volcker stuck to his tight money policy, and the country suffered through the wrenching recession of the early 1980s. Reagan did his part, too: when the nation's air traffic controllers went out on strike six months into his presidency, he took the kind of bold action Jimmy Carter never could. He fired them all. As cruel as this action was, it sent an unmistakable signal to both business and labor that the days of large, inflationary wage settlements were over. Companies could force tougher terms on the unions, and the federal government would not interfere. Whatever one thinks about this stance as social policy, as economic policy, it worked. The spiral of inflation was broken.

By the fall of 1982, the Age of Inflation had effectively come to an end. That year, the Consumer Price Index rose a meager 3 percent, and except for one year, it would stay in that general range for the rest of the decade. Which is not to say that people didn't think about inflation all the time, or worry about it, or talk about it—just as people had continued to worry about the Depression after it had ended. Nor is it to say that people didn't continue to treat their homes as an investment, to rely increasingly on credit and credit cards, or to chase yield, wherever they might find it. They continued doing all of those things. For by then, the Age of Inflation had done its work.

# Part III
# Bulls
# and
# Bears

## CHAPTER 12

# The Maestro of Magellan

## *August 1982*

THE GREAT BULL market of the 1980s—the second greatest bull market of this century, and the event that most dramatically shaped personal finance as Americans emerged from the Age of Inflation—began in the middle of August 1982. Or so it was always said later, once the extent and importance of the bull market had become clear, and it had entered the pantheon of watershed moments that comprised the money revolution. August 1982 would eventually be seen as the time when the stock market finally began to matter to the middle class, just as Charlie Merrill had hoped some sixty years before.

And it was true enough. On an otherwise inauspicious Friday in August—Friday the 13th, as it happens—the Dow Jones Industrial Average opened at 776.92. Up until then, all but one trading session that month had been a losing one; indeed, most trading sessions for the previous year and a half had resulted in losses. Volume was light. The market seemed moribund. But when trading ended that day, the Dow had risen twelve points. The following Monday it rose another four points, and the day after that, the 17th of August, it closed at 831.24, for a gain—highly unusual in the early 1980s—of close to forty points. Volume wasn't just heavy, it was history-making: More shares were traded the third week of August 1982 than had ever been traded in any five-day stretch before.[1] By the end of the month, the Dow stood at 901.31. It had gained 125 points in thirteen sessions.

The thing about big market shifts, though, is that their beginnings are always easy to pinpoint after the fact. You look at a graph of the market, find the lowest (or highest) point before the trend reverses and, *voilà,* that's when the bull (or bear) began. The moment of change is rarely so obvious when you're in the middle of it, surrounded by the chaos and white noise of the market, with no way of knowing whether today's good fortune is a harbinger or an aberration. Most certainly, that was true in August 1982. The signals being sent by the larger economy—signals that might propel the stock market in a particular direction—were ambiguous. The recession had not yet ended, unemployment was still very high, and corporate profits were mediocre—not exactly encouraging signs for the stock market. On the other hand, inflation and interest rates were coming down quickly; in fact, the August surge was triggered by the pronouncement by Salomon Brothers' highly influential interest rate forecaster, Henry Kaufman, the legendary Dr. Doom,[2] that interest rates would continue to fall for the next twelve months.

Still, Wall Street was hesitant to label the surge in stock prices the beginning of a bull market. One participant described the rise in stock prices as an "institutional buying panic"; another said flatly that he didn't trust the August rally. The community of traders and portfolio managers and analysts who make up Wall Street were acting a little like a freshly jilted suitor out on a first date with someone new: no matter how well the evening goes, he spends most of his time trying not to get his hopes too high, for fear of having his heart broken again. In August 1982, Wall Street didn't want to have its heart broken.

The market stalled the next month, ending September about five points lower than its August close. But in early October, it roared back, piling up another 100-plus points in five powerful trading sessions, with yet more record-setting volume. By October 22, the Dow had reached 1036.98, its highest point in a decade, and Wall Street seemed ready to fall in love again. Although this upswing could also be attributed to a precipitating event—the news that the Federal Reserve had begun to ease up on the money supply—there was none of the previous hesitation. "Prices of Stocks, Bonds Soar in Massive Buying Binge," the *Wall Street Journal* proclaimed exuberantly, adding that the buying was characterized by "investor euphoria." *Money* magazine, *Barron's,* Louis Rukeyser—all were quick to declare that a new bull market had begun. By December, a musical group in San Francisco had recorded a song called "Bull Market High."

What an eternity it had been between bull markets! What a long time it had been, in fact, between markets that could reasonably be described as decent. More than a decade had passed since the Go-Go era had ended, but one could make a strong case that the drought in stock prices had begun well before then and that much of the seeming bullishness of the late 1960s had been a cruel mirage. The charts clearly showed that the powerful postwar bull market had ended in February 1966, with the Dow peaking at 995.15.[3] Between then and the late summer of 1982—a sixteen-year period—the market had been characterized by a series of peaks and valleys so pronounced that a picture of the Dow Jones average resembled nothing so much as a mountain range. At the top of each peak, the Dow would graze the 1,000 point mark, sometimes barely topping it, sometimes just missing it. At the bottom of each subsequent valley, the market would drop anywhere from 250 to 400 points. In August 1982, the Dow stood 219 points below its February 1966 peak. No doubt there were people who could maneuver their way through these peaks and valleys, but there weren't many, and virtually none were small investors. For a small investor, negotiating such a market really was about as treacherous as climbing a mountain range.

Not that there were many small investors left. What was the point? Americans were far too concerned with figuring out ways to keep up with inflation to give much thought to a market that was going nowhere. Besides, the stock market didn't have much to offer people who were trying to ward off the corrosive effects of inflation. The stereotypical elderly investor, for instance, who traditionally held conservative stocks that paid out steady dividends, was far better off in a money fund, because the yield was much higher. A real speculator, of course, might be able to find a stock or two that could outsprint inflation, but for most people that course seemed awfully risky. By contrast, an investment in inflation-sensitive real estate seemed a sure thing.

In 1978, the New York Stock Exchange confirmed the widespread sense that the market had become an unwatched sideshow. In conducting one of its occasional surveys of "investor attitudes," it discovered "pervasive public preoccupation with 'preserving' capital and purchasing power to keep abreast of inflation." The exchange added, "Investments that are perceived as involving the least amount of risk rank highest today in the estimation of people who have funds to invest"—investments such as money market funds, real estate, and Treasury bonds.

Of course, if you worked for a brokerage firm, you didn't need the New York Stock Exchange to tell you how bad things were. What people at Merrill Lynch remember most vividly about the 1970s, besides the broad swath Don Regan cut through the firm, was how hard it was to make money the old-fashioned way: by persuading people to trade stocks. No wonder Regan had been so anxious to find other, sturdier pillars upon which to build the firm! The easiest product for the brokers to sell was the firm's money market fund, Ready Asset Trust—a product that brought in no commissions, which made Merrill Lynch brokers reluctant to peddle it.[4] Not that they had to. Once inflation set it, it was the customers who called the brokers, check in hand, ready to move their savings to a money market fund.

At Fidelity, too, they knew how dead the market was. They also saw it every day, as the firm's stock equity funds continued to shrivel. The 1970s and first few years of the 1980s were when Trend Fund, which Ned Johnson had once run with such success, lost more than two thirds of its assets; when Capital Fund, which Gerry Tsai had ridden to such prominence, did likewise; when every equity fund in the shop lost assets. "In 1968," recalls Leo Dworsky, the former Fidelity fund manager, "we were managing $4.6 billion, and 90 percent of it was in equity funds. In 1981, we were managing $12 billion in assets, and 20 percent was in equities. By 1982, we were up to $17 billion in assets, but only 12 percent of it was in equities." That is, of the $17 billion the firm had under management, only $2 billion were in the stock funds that had always been the heart and soul of the company.

Yet America's disenchantment with the stock market did not create the same atmosphere of gloom within Fidelity that one found at a brokerage firm. Quite the contrary: what old Fidelity hands remember about that era is not how grim it was, but how exciting—how exhilarating it was to be working at Fidelity. There was an enormous sense of ferment within the firm, which flowed from Ned Johnson's wispy, suggestive, elliptic sentences and spread to every corner of the company. Money was pouring into the firm's money market funds, but that was only part of it. People at Fidelity felt they were in the middle of a grand experiment, in which anything was possible, and nothing was too crazy to be tried once. Out of this experimentation, a new kind of mutual fund company—indeed, a new kind of financial services company—was gradually taking shape, one that was aimed not at the financial cognoscenti, but at everyone. This was the kind of firm that would prosper in the 1980s.

Of course, just as it is easier to pinpoint the beginning of a bull market long after the fact, so it is also easier to look back now at what Fidelity was doing during the late 1970s and see a recognizable pattern. Now that Fidelity has become one of the dominant financial institutions in America, it is clear that this was when the foundation for that dominance was built. One would like to believe that it was all part of some grand plan of Ned Johnson's—that he had some deep understanding of how the 1980s would unfold, and how the middle class would flock to the products he was creating—for that is what makes the most sense. Companies like Fidelity do not come to rule their particular universe by accident. But if Johnson did have such a plan, he kept it to himself. To talk about such a thing would mean revealing the depths of his ambition, and that he could never do. Even years later, when asked why he had taken this prescient step or that one, the explanations he would proffer would sound hopelessly mundane. "It just seemed like the obvious thing to do," he was likely to say—though that didn't answer the question of why, if it was so obvious, he was the only one who saw it. To that question, Johnson had no answer at all.

He himself had become only slightly less eccentric over the years. He was still notorious for tossing off those little flickers of insight that one practically had to grab out of the air before they vanished. There were those who thrived under his direction-by-indirection management style and those who found it so unnerving that they would quit in frustration two weeks after joining the company. His chief passion seemed to be computers: the installation, maintenance, and use of the giant mainframes that would be the backbone of the company in the 1980s was what most engaged him, and he was constantly in the computer room, watching, asking questions, tinkering with the machines. Naturally, his staff thought he was pouring too much money into computer capacity, and viewed his obsession as folly. Naturally, they would be proved wrong as soon as the bull market began.

More famously, there was Boston Coach, the car fleet Fidelity bought after Johnson became frustrated by his eccentric inability to hail a cab during the Boston rush hour. There wasn't an employee in the shop who didn't know the story behind Boston Coach, and very few who didn't offer it up to anyone wanting to know what Johnson was really like. To them, this was the quintessential Ned Johnson: though his genius may have been hidden from public view, he was quite demonstrably the kind of man who would buy his own private fleet company because he could never seem to catch a cab when he needed one. There were more than a few people at Fidelity, though, who found the story more annoying than amusing, for they felt that starting up so peripheral a business was both a waste of Johnson's time and the company's money. This time, they were probably right.

Yet the Fidelity Johnson was creating, while certainly different, was anything but eccentric. It was driven by the essential motives that drive most ambitious companies in America: a desire for growth, a thirst for market share, a hunger for dominance. In that respect, it was a far more conventional place than it had been under Johnson's father. And the things that made it different from other financial institutions stemmed primarily from the experience of operating a money market fund, which had been such a transforming event for Johnson. It wasn't just the American middle class that was learning the lessons of inflation; as it turns out, so was Ned Johnson.

For instance: during the Age of Inflation, Fidelity became a company that eschewed commissions. Money funds, of course, couldn't be sold on a commission basis, because the commission would cut too deeply into the funds' yields and negate their appeal. But once Fidelity learned how to market its money fund directly to the public, without relying on a commissioned sales force, Johnson took a far more dramatic step: he abandoned the commissions on Fidelity's other funds as well, and began selling them all directly to the public, cutting out the traditional broker-dealer network. This happened in 1979.

Though Johnson was not the first to take this step—that distinction belongs to his archrival Jack Bogle at the Vanguard Group, who made the move two years before—it was still a risky thing to do for someone in the fund business, which had always used brokers to distribute funds. Yet to hear Johnson tell it now, the decision to bring the business in-house was just so . . . *obvious*. "Brokers weren't selling our funds anyway," he says with a shrug. But the move had a host of repercussions, the most important of which was that it changed the focus of the company. Commission revenue is inexorably tied to the performance of the stock market; therefore, eliminating commissions helped bring employees around to the idea that Fidelity no longer lived and died by the vagaries of the Dow Jones average. Instead, Fidelity executives began to see that their real function was not trading stocks, or researching companies, or even selling mutual funds. It was gathering assets.

Secondly, Fidelity began relying heavily on technology, some of it immensely complicated, some of it laughably simple. "Do you know how mutual fund companies broke the stranglehold of the banks?" chuckles banking consultant Edward Furash. "They did it by using the telephone and the mail." Once it began selling mutual funds directly to the public, Fidelity had to set up those 800-numbers that became its lifeline. Once the public started buying those funds, they had to use those numbers: they had to dial a phone number they saw in an advertisement, and talk to an anonymous clerk on the other end of the line, who was an order taker rather than a salesman. (Schwab, of course, was operating on the same principles.) Then, after making the call, people would send a check in the mail to open an account, instead of handing it to a person on the other side of a desk. This act, simple though it was, ought not to be underestimated. It took a certain amount of faith on the part of the sender that he could mail money to a post office box in Boston and have it wind up in the right fund. It was also a fundamentally impersonal way of doing business, but then, personal finance was becoming more impersonal by the day. The concept of "customer service" had less to do with talking to someone face to face than it did with having phone calls answered promptly, statements delivered accurately, business conducted efficiently. This is why Johnson began investing in those massive mainframe computers, and setting up huge and sophisticated phone centers. He understood that people would judge the company on the basis of technology they never saw and were only dimly aware of. It was another revelation.

Finally, Fidelity was a place that was starting to resemble a giant con-

sumer goods company like Procter & Gamble more than a traditional provider of stock mutual funds. It was learning to think the way a classic
consumer products company thinks—trying to find out, first of all, what the
customer wants and then attempting to craft something that would scratch
that particular itch. And it was beginning to use the same business strategies
that had long characterized the giant packaged goods companies in America:
finding niche products that satisfied different customer segments; developing
"brand" awareness; emphasizing marketing and advertising. The only difference was that Fidelity was selling funds instead of soap.

For instance: when Fidelity began to realize that its money market fund
customers could be divided into different segments, the company brought
out a second money market fund, in May 1979, called Fidelity Cash Reserves, which was geared to the particular needs of small savers. The old
standby, FDIT, was then repositioned to appeal to wealthier money fund
investors. A few years earlier than that, Johnson had pushed the company to
create a municipal bond fund—a product that did not exist when he first
started thinking about it, but which he was convinced would have great
appeal among the middle class. He was right; Fidelity's municipal bond
fund garnered over $500 million in its first six months.[5] And that led to
another idea: since municipal bond funds were tax free, why not set up a
tax-free money market fund, which would invest only in tax-free government securities? So that came next. And then came the nation's first junk
bond fund,[6] and a handful of other bond funds, some conservative, others
riskier, each intended to appeal to some small segment of the market. Some
people wanted the safety of an income fund without losing the chance for the
potential big gains of a growth fund, so the company brought out some
equity-income funds. Gold prices were rising faster than anything during the
Age of Inflation, and demand for gold was strong; Fidelity began a gold
fund, which, like the gold funds of other mutual fund companies, instantly
became a stellar performer. And on and on. The goal was to have a flavor
for every taste; and if there was any single thing that tipped off the enormity
of Johnson's ambition, it was this willingness to slice the salami ever thin-
ner, in a furious effort to satisfy any conceivable investment desire. Such
product proliferation has since become one of the hallmarks of the mutual
fund industry, but nowhere has it been carried to such extremes as at Fidelity. By the mid-1980s the company offered more than 100 different
mutual funds; by the early 1990s, it had close to 200 funds. "We were in
the manufacturing business," recalls a former Fidelity executive. "We were
manufacturing funds."

There was another lesson Fidelity was learning during the Age of Inflation. "What we learned in the late 1970s was that yield sells," recalls Roger

Servison, a longtime Fidelity executive who is now the head of retail marketing. He remembers in particular a day in 1979 when the *Wall Street Journal* published for the first time a comparison between the yields on money market funds and certificates of deposit. The money funds, of course, were offering significantly higher rates of return. The phones rang incessantly that day, as people clamored to put money in Fidelity's money market funds, and from that point forward, the company pushed to advertise the yields of its money market funds, something the SEC resisted for a short time before giving way to the inevitable. From that point until the market crash of 1987, yield was the basic message of all Fidelity advertising. Most of the time, it was the only message.

Yet, even as he was changing the essential nature of Fidelity, transforming it from the stock fund boutique his father had run into something much bigger and broader, Ned Johnson had not forgotten about the market. In retrospect, that may have been his most prescient move of all.

Why, he was once asked, had he kept the equity department intact even as the company's stock funds lost around three quarters of their assets? Why had he remained so committed to equity funds—not just Trend and Capital funds, but Essex Fund, Salem Fund, Puritan Fund, Contrafund, Mercury Fund, Magellan Fund, and a half-dozen others? Why had he continued to employ nearly twenty stock analysts, to maintain a fabulously appointed "chart room" for the company's handful of technical analysts, and to continue to invest in a side of the company that was becoming (so it seemed) less and less relevant to Fidelity's fortunes? Upon hearing the question, Johnson sighed a little, and scratched his head, and screwed up his mouth in a way that conveyed his discomfort at having to reply. When he finally did reply, his answer was hopelessly mundane. "I just assumed that the equity market would eventually come back," he said with a small, sheepish shrug. "It always has before."

*It always has before.* So it has. Except that this time, when it came back, millions of middle-class Americans who had never given a thought to the stock market would have money "invested" in a money market fund. Which was operated by a mutual fund company. Which also had stock funds. These customers would have been trained by inflation to search for the highest yields they could find, wherever they might be. They would have learned the importance of paying attention to the broader financial world, which, they now knew, directly affected them. In other words, thanks to the changes wrought by inflation, the next bull market was bound to be noticed by the very people Charlie Merrill had always tried to lure into the market.

The evidence would suggest that this is what Ned Johnson really understood, in that opaque way of his—that it wasn't merely the eventual, inevitable return of a bull market that caused him to keep the stock funds at full throttle. It was that the potential investors in this bull market would be geometrically larger than ever before. That was the crucial fact: once inflation ended and interest rates dropped, Americans weren't going to return their money to the banks. They were going to continue to search for those double-digit yields they'd come to love. Sooner or later, Americans would come to the market because sooner or later, the market would be the only place they could get the kind of returns they now believed was their due. *It always had before.*

Plus, by then, Ned Johnson had another reason for betting on the return of the bull market. He had Peter Lynch running the Magellan Fund.

∽

WHEN PETER LYNCH WAS TEN YEARS OLD, his father died. The year was 1954, and the 1950s bull market was well under way—not that Lynch had even an inkling of it. He was a Boston Irish kid who lived in the suburbs, went to Mass every Sunday, rooted for the Red Sox, and grew up in a home where money was not scarce, but certainly tight. And in a roundabout way, it was the death of his father that caused Lynch first to become aware of and then fascinated by the stock market.

To support the family, his mother had to go to work (as a secretary); to have any spending money at all, her preteen son had to do likewise. So every summer for the next decade, Lynch worked as a caddie at one of Boston's exclusive country clubs—"a caddie," he recalls fondly, "during one of the greatest bull markets of all time." It was there that he first started to tune in to the stock market. How could he not? Any young man caddying at an exclusive country club in the 1950s was bound to hear stock tips being traded, stocks being discussed, the state of the market being talked about endlessly. The men who played golf in such places were precisely the men who bought stocks in that era. On occasion, Lynch would caddy for a stockbroker, and it was just like those old E. F. Hutton ads: "People really stopped in the middle of their back swing to hear what stock the broker was recommending on the next tee."

Unlike most caddies, however, Peter Lynch would remember the stock tips the broker had recommended, and when he got home he'd look up the stocks, noticing, as he puts it now, "that they always went up." And when he decided to learn something about the companies whose stocks he was following—to "hear their stories"—he discovered that it was like history class, which was one of his favorite subjects: "It was like trying to figure out how Hannibal managed to roam around for ten years in Italy, never losing a battle, and still wound up losing the war.'' He remembers all this with the clarity of someone who had had a revelation. Upon entering Boston College, he took $1,000 he had saved from those summers caddying and used it to buy his first stock. The company was called Flying Tiger Airlines, and he can recount every last detail, if you ask him to. He can tell you how he bought the stock because his research had led him to believe that air freight was poised to be the next great growth industry. How he paid around $10 a share. How the stock quickly took off, but for a completely unexpected reason: Flying Tiger turned out to be the airline that flew troops to Vietnam. How he began selling a few shares at $20, and was still selling off the last few shares as the stock rose to the mid-80s. How his investment in Flying Tiger put him through Wharton. It was always like that with Peter Lynch. Long after he had become the most famous mutual fund manager in America—known for (among other things) owning as many as 1,700 stocks at a time in his beloved Magellan Fund—he seemed to be able to recall every stock he'd ever bought or sold, in fact, every stock he'd ever *thought* about buying or selling. And if you asked him, he'd be only too happy to give you the details. One thing about Lynch: you never had to ask twice.

He became famous, of course, not because he owned a lot of different stocks in Magellan, or because he was willing to talk about them, but because the stocks he bought always seemed to go up. As they did, Magellan became practically a household name—an answer on ''Jeopardy,'' even—and so did he. Peter Lynch became famous, that is, for the same reason Gerry Tsai became famous: because he was astonishingly good, and because his performance grabbed hold of the imagination of the press and the public just as they were getting caught up in the bull market. Lynch came to symbolize the opportunities inherent in this, the first post–money revolution bull market—the first bull market in which anyone could participate, not just the wealthy. Twenty years after Tsai, he became the second portfolio manager in America to get the press of a movie star—better press, actually, for no reporter ever accused him of being ''inscrutable.'' On the contrary, his public persona was characterized by a kind of guilelessness that reporters—and the public—found irresistible.

In many ways, Peter Lynch played the same function for Ned Johnson that Tsai had played for his father. Like Tsai, he was the star portfolio manager of his era. Like Tsai, he became a magnet for assets, a flesh-and-blood advertisement for the delicious possibilities of making money in mutual funds. Like Tsai, he set a certain tone, both within Fidelity, as the other equity managers strove to emulate his style, and outside it, as people came to perceive Lynch as the prototypical Fidelity mutual fund manager. All of these things worked to Fidelity's advantage as the bull market took hold, and by the mid-1980s one had the strong sense that despite everything he'd done to change the nature of Fidelity, Ned Johnson's fortunes had become as linked to his superstar fund manager as his father's had been twenty years before. And that he felt every bit as ambivalent about it.

Here, though, Johnson turned out to be a good deal luckier than his father, or perhaps a shrewder judge of character. For there were also substantial differences between Lynch and his spiritual predecessor, which all worked to Johnson's advantage. Lynch, unlike Tsai, never had the slightest desire to take over the firm, or even to branch out on his own; he was perfectly content to manage the best-known mutual fund in America, while remaining fiercely loyal to Fidelity. There was nothing flamboyant about Lynch the way there had been about Tsai, nor anything that made it instantly obvious that he had a special gift for picking stocks—something he spent an absurd amount of energy denying in any case. This is not to imply that he lacked ego, or that he didn't have a star's unconscious belief that the world should revolve around him, only that he tended to ascribe his accomplishments to his work ethic rather than to his innate talent.

To put it another way, he was not a smoothie. He wore crumpled seer-sucker suits, and spoke in simple aphorisms that anyone could understand. And he could seem weirdly naive at times. Once, when he was in Detroit with another Fidelity fund manager, Lynch spent an hour one afternoon with Lee Iacocca, the chairman of the Chrysler Corporation. Lynch's decision to invest heavily in Chrysler in the early 1980s, when the company was tee-tering on the edge of bankruptcy, was probably the single greatest stock bet he made in his storied career at Magellan; perhaps not surprisingly, Lynch tended to think highly of Iacocca. Afterward, though, as the two Fidelity men were leaving the building, Lynch said, with absolute sincerity, "You know, *Iacocca* is one of the five greatest books of all time."

Even his stock picking lacked the kind of trendiness that one associates with Tsai. He himself had deeply middle-class instincts and tastes—which is perhaps why the middle class felt so comfortable with him as its desig-nated stock picker—and that was often reflected in the stocks he bought. He loved malls, for instance, and in searching for stocks, he would often go to the mall to see what people were buying, or to observe which stores were filled with customers. In the early years especially, he would fill his port-folio with companies like Dunkin' Donuts or Pep Boys, the auto supply company—the kind of places he himself might frequent. On the other hand, not long after Microsoft went public in 1983, in a frenzied public offering, Lynch made one of his occasional appearances on Louis Rukeyser's "Wall Street Week." When Rukeyser asked him how many shares of Microsoft he had bought for Magellan, Lynch replied that he hadn't bought any; it wasn't his kind of stock. In the end, though, the biggest difference between Lynch and Tsai was that the former was not a gunslinger playing out a hot hand, as Tsai turned out to be. He was something else entirely: a man whose performance as a stock picker was so sustained and so transcendent that he could arguably be called the greatest mutual fund manager who ever lived.

How transcendent? If you had put $1,000 in Magellan when he became its fund manager in 1977, that money would have grown to $27,000 thirteen years later, when he called it quits.[7] That twenty-six-fold gain is one of the singular statistics of the age. And it wasn't just the gain itself that was so impressive, it was the way he did it: in the thirteen years Lynch ran Magellan, there was not a single year when the fund lost money, and only two when it failed to beat the S&P 500 index. In his inaugural year, 1977, he rang up a 14 percent gain in a year when the S&P 500 index lost 7 percent. In 1980, a year in which the S&P 500 gained a healthy 32 percent, Peter Lynch came in with a staggering 70 percent gain; in 1985, the S&P 500 was up 31 percent, and Magellan 43 percent; in 1988, it was Magellan 22 percent; S&P 500, 16 percent. Six years into Lynch's term, Magellan already had the best ten-year record of any stock mutual fund in the country. When Lynch finally quit in 1990, Magellan was so popular that one out of every 100 American families had invested in it. By then it was the largest mutual fund in the country, with close to $13 billion in assets, a fact that should have mitigated against further big gains. And yet it still had the best ten-year record of any stock mutual fund in the country, still outperformed 99 percent of the nation's equity funds, and still beat the S&P 500 by an average of 6 percent a year. This, of course, was another reason why the middle class was so happy to have Peter Lynch manage its money. Actually, it was the main reason.

One wonders now about the root of his astonishing talent: Where *did* this gift for stock picking come from? Lynch's own explanation—that he simply worked hard, visited lots of companies, asked lots of questions, read lots of reports, et cetera—failed to satisfy on a number of levels. To buy into it, one had to ignore his obvious talent for sniffing out important trends, and then riding them as far as they could take him. In the early 1980s, for instance, he saw the coming boom in the financial services sector, and loaded up on every kind of financial stock he could think of. He was one of the first portfolio managers in America to realize that big gains could be made in foreign stocks. He had an uncanny knack for loading up on cyclical industries, like autos, just before the cycle moved in their direction: by the time Ford Motor Co. was making its huge gains in the mid-1980s, it was Magellan's largest holding. There were others who tended to ascribe his success to some inexplicable genius, but it is hard to spend any time with Lynch and come away thinking of him as a genius; he's just too relentlessly normal. The most likely answer was some combination of the two theories: that what he most resembled was a great athlete, who is born with an innate talent, but must be willing to hit a million baseballs or shoot a million jump shots in order for that talent to blossom. When Ned Johnson handed Lynch the reins of Magellan, in May of 1977, it was like handing the ball to Michael Jordan. All we could do—Ned Johnson and the middle class alike—was stand back and watch in admiration.

All things considered, the moment took a surprisingly long time in coming. When Peter Lynch was finally given Magellan to run, enough time had passed to make one wonder whether, just as Fidelity employees had once missed Ned Johnson's considerable gifts, Johnson, in turn, had missed Lynch's. Lynch had been associated with Fidelity since 1965, and had been a full-time research analyst since 1969. At a place like Fidelity, where mutual fund managers are at the top of the pecking order, most research analysts see their jobs as a testing ground, leading (they hope) to the more exalted position of fund manager. Lynch was no exception. And after two or three years as a stock researcher, an analyst is likely to get impatient if he isn't handed a fund. Again, Lynch was no exception. "I was starting to wonder if I was ever going to get a chance to play for the varsity," he would later say. Yet even though he spent eight years as a stock analyst, he never threatened to quit. It wasn't his style. "I just assumed things would work out," he says now.

The Go-Go Years were at their giddy height when Lynch first joined Fidelity, a wet-behind-the-ears summer intern, fresh out of Boston College. Gerry Tsai was the master of all he surveyed. Money was pouring into the stock funds. And as Lynch soaked it all in, he found it . . . *frustrating*. That's how he remembers it. Here he was, in the middle of more excitement than he'd ever seen in his life, and he still had business school ahead of him, and two years in the Army after that, to fulfill an ROTC commitment. He was going to miss all the fun, he feared.

As it turns out, he was right to have been worried. When Lynch returned to Fidelity in 1969, the fun *was* over; the worm had turned on the Go-Go Years. For Lynch, though, it was more than just the general malaise of the times that was troubling. With Tsai long departed, and Johnson no longer managing portfolios full-time—indeed, with most of the other Fidelity fund managers having retired or moved on—the funds were being run by a new generation of portfolio managers, all of whom were former Fidelity analysts. "All the funds had been taken," he recalls.

So he settled in for the long haul. The job of a Fidelity analyst—as it is for any stock analyst—is to cover a particular industry, and to make stock recommendations to Fidelity's fund managers. His first year as a full-time Fidelity analyst, Lynch was given the metal and chemical industries to follow. He was paid $16,000. The next year, he was bumped up to $17,000. In between, he turned down a job offer that would have paid him at least $55,000—"maybe $75,000 if I earned the bonus." Why would he turn down a chance to quadruple his salary? Because the job would have meant moving to Wall Street, and Lynch was too much the Boston boy to do that. Because it would have meant covering the metals industry, which he viewed as a sideways move, and one that would have kept him from his ultimate goal, managing a mutual fund. And because it would have meant walking out on Fidelity, which would have made him feel like an ingrate. It is certainly not accurate to portray Lynch as completely oblivious to money; by the late 1980s, he was earning some $3 million a year managing Magellan, and held company stock[8] said to be worth somewhere between $25 million and $50 million. It is accurate to say that he had a surprising amount of perspective for a young man in a hurry. He realized that the appeal of working for Fidelity—and the long-term prospects it offered him—out-weighed his short-term wish for a higher salary. It was one of his better bets.

What was the appeal of Fidelity to Lynch? It was everything about the place: he was one of those lucky people who finds in his very first job the perfect place for both his temperament and his talent. He liked the way the equity shop created an ethos of teamwork without sacrificing individuality. He liked the way the greenest rookies were encouraged to bring ideas to meetings or pop into the office of a portfolio manager to suggest a stock. He liked the fact that Fidelity lacked most of the trappings of bureaucracy. But he also liked the way the ultimate decision to buy or sell a stock resided with the individual portfolio manager. Ned Johnson believed that each portfolio manager should be able to follow his own instincts in picking stocks, just as his father had. At Fidelity, the proof of a manager's talents lay not with his style but with his results. Which was another thing Peter Lynch liked about Fidelity and, indeed, about the stock market in general: he liked the cult of performance. "At Fidelity," he says now, "if you write a report saying 'Buy International Paper' and the sucker goes up, no one will ever say you're doing a bad job. It's a very measurable business."

By 1974, Lynch had plainly paid his dues. But still his wait continued, for no funds were available for him to manage. So he spent the next three years as the head of the research department. Yet even after all that time, he was still surprised when, at the age of thirty-three, "they finally tapped me on the shoulder" in May 1977. The surprise was not so much that they were handing him the ball; rather, it was that the ball they were handing him was Magellan. It was a small fund, true enough, barely known to the outside world. But within Fidelity, it loomed large. Magellan was Ned Johnson's baby.

It had been started in 1963, with Johnson himself as its original fund manager. Two years later, it was closed to the public, and became primarily an investment vehicle for what might be called in-house money. Its assets included some employee profit-sharing funds and corporate funds, but mostly it contained Johnson family money. By the time Lynch took it over, Johnson no longer ran the fund, but it was still closed to the public, and its assets were still mostly his and his family's. It held, at that point, $6 million.

To beef it up a bit, Fidelity merged it with another fund, Essex, which had virtually collapsed in the 1970s, its assets dwindling from $100 million to $14 million. That gave Lynch $20 million to work with. (The merger also resulted in some tax advantages for Magellan.) But the fund remained closed to the public, which gave Lynch an important advantage: he didn't have to worry about coping with an influx of money from enthusiastic investors. Then again, in those days one would have been hard-pressed to find an enthusiastic investor anywhere in America.

There was, however, one obvious disadvantage to having your first portfolio be the one that contained the boss's money. The boss was going to watch what you were doing very closely. And for the next year, that's pretty much what happened. Lynch bought and sold stocks, and Ned Johnson looked over his shoulder. It was, Lynch would say later, "the greatest interplay I had with Ned Johnson in all my years at Fidelity." Johnson had a tendency to pop into his office around 6:00 P.M., and then just linger, asking Lynch why he was buying this or that, or reminiscing about the old days when he was running funds. By the time he got up to leave, two hours would have passed. Lynch used to commute home with his wife, and after this had happened a few times, he came up with a code phrase—he can't remember what it was—so that he could discreetly call her and tell her that the boss had just popped in, and they wouldn't be getting home any time soon.

You might expect the young novice to be intimidated by so much scrutiny from the man who signed his paychecks. But he wasn't. Lynch's distinctive, unorthodox style seemed to be fully formed from the moment he became a portfolio manager, and he was fearless about following his instincts—instincts that could not have been more different from Ned Johnson's. Lynch was a contrarian by temperament, a huge believer that you bought when everyone around you was selling. The more mundane the company, the better he liked it—he wanted to buy stock in companies he understood. ("I like to buy a business that any fool can run because eventually one will" was one of his aphorisms.) An anecdote he would recount endlessly after he became famous was the one about how he purchased stock in Hanes, the company that produced L'Eggs pantyhose, after his wife began buying the new pantyhose at the supermarket. But he was eclectic too: although Magellan was an aggressive growth fund, Lynch was willing to buy conservative stocks like textiles and utilities if he liked their "stories." His only rule, he once said, was that he had no rules. He wanted to be open to every idea, flexible enough to adapt to any circumstance, ready to pounce on anything that had the whiff of a "ten-bagger"—his favorite term for a big winner. In that sense, his guileless quality was among his biggest advantages: he was open to things more world-weary people were not.

Johnson had always been fascinated by the technical side of the market; Lynch could not have cared less about the technical indices. He didn't even much care which direction the market was heading, for he didn't believe that the direction of the market could tell him anything about the direction of a particular stock. And it was particular stocks he was interested in. If you bought the right stocks, he believed, it didn't matter what the broader market was doing: over the long haul, your stocks would go up. After he became well known, and people asked him where he thought the market was headed, he would reply that he had no idea. The "market," he felt, was a big distraction, and his ability to shut it out was another of his advantages.

Finally, he liked to have a lot of stocks in his portfolio. There was nothing so distinctive about his style as his willingness to stuff hundreds upon hundreds of stocks into Magellan—and nothing that so clearly set him apart from Johnson. Johnson's strategy had always been to hold a small handful of stocks, concentrated in an even smaller handful of industries. When he wanted to make a change, he did so cautiously, one stock at a time. Lynch, on the other hand, would buy entire industries—grab a piece of every company in a particular group, or every company in a variety of industry groups. He did this partly because he felt that in order to truly get a feel for a stock, he had to have a little money invested in it. But he also did it, as he used to explain, because "if you buy stock in ten different companies, maybe three will turn out to be total dogs, and another four will be okay, and the last three will be big winners. And while the money you lose on the bad stocks is limited to what you invested, the money you can make on the winners is unlimited. So your winners more than offset your losers. You don't even need to be right half the time!" There, in a nutshell, was the Peter Lynch theory of investing—simple, brilliant, and a tad disingenuous all at once.

There were times, in the beginning, when the boss felt moved to utter a few words of caution to the new portfolio manager, as he saw Lynch playing the game in a way that was so foreign to his own experience. But the words were never especially loud or forceful, and Lynch ignored them. Soon, Johnson was simply asking him why he had bought, say, Taco Bell; Lynch would explain his reasoning, and that would be that. And not long afterward, the older man stopped looking over the younger man's shoulder. And why not? Fidelity prized results, and Lord knows, Peter Lynch was supplying them. Besides, the core idea at Fidelity held that a fund manager's methods, no matter how unorthodox, weren't supposed to matter so long as he produced. That was as true for the rookie fund manager as it was for everyone else. Even if he was handling the boss's money.

Fidelity opened Magellan to the public in the summer of 1981, four years into the Lynch era, and to hear the executives tell it now, they did so because they could see the bull market coming, and they needed some way to get in front of it. All these years later, it is hard to know for sure whether they were really that farsighted at Fidelity—the bull market, after all, was still a year away—or whether they were lucky too. What can be said with some certainty is that the decision to open Magellan to the public spoke volumes about the kind of company Fidelity had become. It was a company that tried to respond to the wishes of the public, and there was a growing segment of the public that quite explicitly wanted Magellan. Fidelity knew this because, by the late 1970s, it had begun to receive letters and phone calls from customers who wanted to know why they couldn't get into this terrific fund they had noticed. It was also a company that understood the importance of being able to sell yield, and that's what Magellan could offer over every other stock fund in the shop—indeed, over most other stock funds in America. The top-ranking funds during the Age of Inflation had been the gold funds, but as inflation waned, they were bound to crash as the price of gold dropped. Stock funds with eye-popping records, but which had been obscured by the gold funds, were likely to come to the fore once that happened, and Magellan, under Lynch, was the fund with the most eye-popping record around. Of course, the ads for Magellan (and for every stock fund) always cautioned in the fine print that past performance could not guarantee future results: the SEC demanded such caveats. But implicitly, Fidelity was selling—and people were buying—the idea that the manager running this wonderful fund would be able to keep churning out these fabulous returns. And not just Fidelity. The entire mutual fund industry was doing the same thing: they had all learned that yield sold funds. For better or worse, the phenomenal success of mutual funds in the 1980s was built almost entirely on the promise of future yield, which in turn was based on past performance.

The deification of the best fund managers, of which Lynch was the preeminent example, would be fundamentally a by-product of their ability to deliver on that promise. There weren't that many, it turns out, who could do it consistently. But this was a lesson the middle class would learn later.

Johnson did one other thing that would affect both Magellan's fortunes and those of the mutual fund industry. In opening Magellan to the public, Johnson decided to slap a small, 2 percent commission on it, making it the nation's first "low-load" fund. The difference between this commission and the commission the company used to charge in the old, Go-Go days—besides being much smaller—is that Fidelity got to keep the money itself instead of handing it over to a broker.

The move itself was pure instinct. Johnson felt that if a fund truly performed, people wouldn't mind paying a small fee to get into it. Fidelity could then use that money to buy more advertising, and do more marketing, and have more people to answer the phones. The loads that Johnson imposed on his funds became, in time, a cash machine, helping make him one of the wealthiest men in America, and helping create the behemoth that Fidelity became. Gradually, other mutual fund companies that sold directly to the public did likewise, and soon the direct-market mutual fund universe was divided into two groups: the no-loads—which, as the name implies, consists of companies that do not put any loads on the funds they offer—and the low-loads, of which Fidelity is the preeminent example.[9]

Putting loads on his funds brought criticism that Johnson and Fidelity were acting piggishly—that the loads imposed far outstripped the company's need for the money. But Johnson's instincts were right. People were willing to pay extra for a fund that generated the kind of yield Peter Lynch was producing—the kind that allowed people to brag about their mutual fund. And if you wanted proof, all you had to do was look at what happened to Magellan. More money flowed into Magellan when it had a 2 percent load than when it had been free. In 1982, just as stock funds started to become popular again, Johnson upped the load to 3 percent. Now the money *really* streamed in. For nearly four years, Lynch had been able to become a hot fund manager without having to face the hot fund manager's problem: finding enough good stocks to invest the new money that comes streaming in from investors, all of whom want a piece of the hot fund. Suddenly Lynch faced that problem in spades. It got to the point where he went to Johnson and complained, for the one and only time in his career, that the fund was getting too big, and maybe they should close it to the public. Johnson said he'd think about it. The subject never came up again.

Magellan held around $200 million when that conversation took place. By the end of 1982, it was up to $458 million. It had been, of course, another glorious year for Magellan, which gained 48 percent while the S&P 500 rose a "mere" 21 percent. It was poised to become the fund with the best ten-year record, something it would achieve the following year. It was right around then that reporters began taking note not just of the fund but of its manager. Rukeyser was calling to ask if Lynch would appear on his show. *Barron's* added him to its regular panel of investment gurus. By the time 1983 had ended, Magellan's assets had grown to $1.6 billion, and interview requests for Lynch had grown in like fashion. At that point, one could safely say that his incredible ride was well under way.

And so, in its own way, was ours.

## CHAPTER 13

# Socks 'n' Stocks

## *November 1982*

ANDREW KAHR HAD been a busy man during the money revolution. Among a small but important circle of people, the fact that he had devised the Merrill Lynch cash management account had put him on the map, and he spent the next half-dozen years in a furious blizzard of creation. He had plans for brilliant new financial products he wanted to try, for new ways to evade the regulatory barriers that still existed, for new ventures he thought could be formed to some profitable end. Always, these ideas revolved around a certain set of themes, as he would later describe them: "Why did certain patterns [of financial behavior] exist? What was the impact of financial deregulation? Where was there an opportunity?" He himself was involved in a series of alliances, forming partnerships with acquaintances he thought could help him, hiring on to consult for this big company or that one, enmeshed in a web of constantly mutating associations. Throughout, he was trying to take advantage of the notoriety the CMA had gained for him while there was advantage to be taken. What he hoped to reap from this flurry of work and ideas and alliances was the one thing he had failed to reap from the CMA: money.

It's not quite right to say that Kahr had gotten nothing for his CMA efforts. In addition to a modest measure of renown, he'd gotten his agreed-upon consulting fee from SRI, which amounted to around $35,000. And Merrill Lynch, as a sop, had named Kahr a trustee of its CMA Money Trust. (The Money Trust was the money market fund attached to the cash management account.)[1] Like most such arrangements, the job was supposed to be a paid sinecure. But Kahr's tongue was too acerbic to allow him to be the sort of trustee Merrill Lynch wanted, and his stint did not last long. In September 1980—at a time when money market funds were being showered with middle-class savings, and the CMA Money Trust had swelled to $2.5

billion—the other four trustees voted to increase the management fees on the fund. Kahr voted against the increase, an action that caused the other board members to vote him off the board after his term expired. Kahr responded by quitting the board without waiting for his term to end. With that flourish, Andrew Kahr's relationship with Merrill Lynch came to its somewhat inevitable conclusion.

Even had he remained on the board, though, acting as a trustee for a money market fund was scarcely his idea of the big score. It wasn't going to make him rich, or transform his life, or allow him the freedom to make decisions about work irrespective of financial considerations. That is what he had been striving toward since he'd been a teenager; now in his midthirties, his goal was as elusive as ever. And even though the work he was getting was tremendously interesting—conducting studies for Sears as the retailing giant prepared its entry into financial services, working for a brief time with First Nationwide Savings (the big California S&L) on new ways to attract deposits, helping a friend sell an elite winery in Napa Valley, and so on—none of these projects were getting Kahr any closer to where he wanted to go.

Gradually, he realized that consulting was never going to get him to his destination. Consultants are hired guns, who rent out their brains for a fee. But Kahr didn't want to rent his brain out anymore; he wanted to have a piece of the action, to be able to partake of whatever profits his ideas might generate. If an idea of his made money for a company, then it should make money for him, too. And if an idea flopped, that was a risk he was willing to take. That was the kind of risk his old hero, Georges Doriot, used to take back when he was operating the first venture capital firm in America, gaining an equity stake in some fledgling company in return for start-up capital. Essentially, Andrew Kahr wanted an equity stake in his own mind.

So the proposals he started taking around to companies began to have a distinctly entrepreneurial flavor. Instead of offering to conduct studies, Kahr started to concentrate on devising new financial products, or on adding a twist to an existing product to give it a new, post–money revolution utility. Then he'd approach a company that was trying to adapt to the new financial realities, lay out his idea, and offer to get it up and running in return for, say, 20 percent of the profits it produced.

There were two rather obvious problems with Kahr's scheme. The first was that he was a terrible salesman. Picture him, in the late 1970s, sitting in a conference room in some corporate skyscraper somewhere, surrounded by a handful of perplexed executives, as he spewed out his complex, intimidating thoughts, occasionally pushing his shoulder-length hair out of the way as he talked. By corporate standards, it was an odd sight; the chances of such a meeting leading to an open-ended, multimillion-dollar contract for Kahr were slim, to put it mildly. But never mind that. Picture what it took even to get that far—the introductions that needed to be wangled, the phone calls made, the letters written. Even this was beyond Kahr's capacity. "When I first met him," recalls Adolph Mueller, one of his friends from that period, "he was an incredibly shy, antisocial person who couldn't sell anything. Once you got past that, he could sell an idea better than anyone because sooner or later, he would completely overwhelm someone with his intellect. But he couldn't get out of the box. He didn't know how to do it."

Hence, his need for alliances with people who believed in the potency of his ideas, but who had the contacts and social skills he lacked. Mueller, a well-to-do former banker, was one such acquaintance. McQuown was another. James Fuller, the gregarious former Wall Street executive who had worked with Kahr, at SRI was a third. All three became friends of Kahr's, and then business partners, but none of their partnerships overlapped; Kahr liked to keep his business dealings compartmentalized. And the division of labor was equally compartmentalized: his partners played Abbott to Kahr's Costello. They were the straight men, the pullers of strings to get Kahr in the door of some financial company or another.

Even after the contact had been made and the doors opened, however, there was a second hurdle to overcome. Large corporations are not entrepreneurial. They are bureaucratic. Big bureaucratic organizations hate taking chances. They have an extremely limited tolerance for an acid-tongued outsider like Kahr. And for most of them, the notion of sharing profits with such a person—indeed, with anyone at all—is anathema, no matter how brilliant his idea. Large companies usually don't mind paying handsomely for something they want, but they want the sum to be finite, and agreed in advance. What Kahr was asking for—an agreement with the potential to make him far wealthier than anyone working at the company—was something most companies wouldn't even countenance.

Mueller can remember approaching General Electric Credit Corporation about an innovative credit card Kahr had conceived; by the end of several meetings, GE had become extremely interested, but insisted that Kahr and Mueller's profit-sharing be capped at $1 million a year. The two men walked away from the deal. They went around and around with Household Finance, but got nowhere. Kahr and Mueller dickered with Beneficial Finance, even signed a contract, but it gradually became clear that Beneficial had no intention of pursuing Kahr's project, so that deal petered out. With McQuown, Kahr approached American Express about setting up a money market fund, which would have been a brilliant stroke, putting the company in the crucial business of gathering assets. Those negotiations also went nowhere.

And those were the *good* deals: the ones where Kahr and his partner actually sat down with the top executives of a company and tried to negotiate an agreement. Most of the time, it never even got that far. "For those two or three things where we had some sort of contract or were on the verge of one, there were probably about fifty where we couldn't get over this profit-sharing hurdle," recalls Mueller. "They would say, 'Come in and show us how to do it, and we'll pay you a quarter of a million dollars.' That was big money to us. But Andrew insisted, and I agreed, that it had to be profit sharing." And there the discussions would end.

Except in two cases. In 1981, Fuller, who had recently left SRI for Charles Schwab & Co., introduced Kahr to Schwab, who commissioned him to come up with a financial product that would do for Schwab what the CMA had done for Merrill Lynch. This Kahr accomplished with his usual flair—the ensuing product, called the Schwab One Account, improved on the CMA in several respects, and remains one of Schwab's most popular offerings to this day. Since Chuck Schwab saw himself as an entrepreneur, like Kahr, he had no problems turning over 20 percent of the profits to Kahr and his partner, who in this case was Fuller. After all, that's how entrepreneurs operated.

The other company to do business with Kahr in this era was a bit more surprising. It was a big, lumbering, Dallas-based finance company called the Associates, which at the time was owned by a well-known, New York–based conglomerate, Gulf + Western.[2] Then again, maybe it shouldn't have been such a surprise, since finance companies were no less immune to the effects of the money revolution than their more exalted brethren, the banks and brokerage houses and insurance companies. They, too, had to cope with a formerly well-defined world that had turned upside down. For finance companies, it was the widespread acceptance of bank credit cards that had changed their world—that, and the concomitant discovery by the banks that the middle class, as a group, were extremely desirable customers, which of course finance companies had long known. Once credit cards became commonplace, finance companies found themselves scrambling to maintain their loan portfolios, as banks began making the everyday loans to middle-class Americans that had always been the bread and butter of most finance companies.

Far better than many bankers, finance company executives understood the implications of the credit card business. But understanding the power of the credit card as a small loan device, and doing something to combat it, were two different tasks, and thus far, most finance companies had been unable to counteract the incursions of the bank credit card onto their once-profitable turf. This was especially true of the Associates, a once healthy company that had fallen on hard times. In 1976, Gulf + Western had fired the company president and brought in a new man, the wonderfully named Reece Overcash. Overcash, a hardened veteran of the business, was an acquaintance of Mueller's. A year later, through Mueller's intercession, Andrew Kahr showed up with an idea about how the Associates could reclaim some of the revenues it had lost to bank credit cards. Since banks were crossing into territory that had once "belonged" to finance companies, it was Kahr's thought that finance companies should begin crossing into territory controlled by banks. His audacious plan was to put a finance company into the credit card business.[3]

Kahr's first meeting with his potential client took place in the summer of 1977. The Merrill Lynch CMA wasn't even a product at that point; the first tests wouldn't come for another year. It didn't matter. When Overcash and his new company president, George Evans, listened to Kahr, they immediately knew he was onto something. "If you had any common sense, you had to realize that he had tremendous brain power," recalls Evans. "So I said, 'Let's meet again,' and the next time we met we spent nearly all day together, and we had other executives and our legal counsel and our controller in and out [of the meeting]." Within a very short time—a few weeks at most—the Associates was so convinced that Kahr's idea would work that they agreed to his stiff terms. Ten months later, they had a product.

Not that it was easy. Dealing with Andrew Kahr was never going to be easy for a big company. There were always going to be moments when he said things that were so impolitic that the people assigned to work with him wanted mainly to strangle him. Early on, Kahr reportedly threatened to sue his own client for breach of contract because it was taking the Associates so long to get started. And then, once the work began, Evans and Overcash had to listen to a constant stream of complaints about Kahr. "Basically," says Evans, "he drove everybody nuts." Staffers would storm out of meetings with him in a fury, only to be ordered back in by Evans. Evans, who oversaw Kahr's efforts, always got along with him, but Overcash kept his distance, preferring to avoid being drawn into some technical credit card discussions for which he had little understanding and less patience. Nonetheless, he fully understood the potential importance of Kahr's product for the Associates, so he, as much as Evans, turned his back on the chorus of complaints from those who had to work most closely with Kahr.

Does it need to be said that there were supposed to be impenetrable walls preventing finance companies from issuing bank credit cards? Perhaps it doesn't; finding ways around impenetrable walls was how Andrew Kahr made his living. In this case, the walls were the by laws of Visa and MasterCard, which explicitly forbade nonbank entities from joining the two credit card associations. But Kahr had already figured out a way around that one: just as Merrill Lynch was doing with the CMA, with Kahr's help, the Associates would search for a bank willing to act, essentially, as a "front," processing the credit card transactions for a fee. Kahr found his bank in Baton Rouge; perhaps not coincidentally, it was run by the brother of the banker who had agreed to process credit card transactions for Merrill Lynch. And to gain the approval of this arrangement from one of the credit card organizations, Kahr once again turned to Visa, knowing he could count on Hock's enthusiastic endorsement. With Hock arguing in the affirmative, the Visa board approved the arrangement at a meeting that took place on January 5, 1978. At the same meeting, the CMA deal was also approved.

Two months later, the Associates mailed solicitations to potential customers, and got a response so high that it virtually assured that the company's new Execu-Charge card—as it was called—would be a smash. Despite the glut of bank credit cards, Kahr had designed the Associates' card in such a way as to make it particularly attractive to a certain segment of the middle class—a segment, as it happened, that had no qualms about generating debt to maintain its standard of living.[4] Thus, while most bank credit cards had 50 percent of its customers "revolving" its debt, the Associates had upward of 90 percent of its customers taking on debt. Within six months, the Execu-Charge card had generated some $50 million worth of debt. By 1980, a mere two years after it had been inaugurated, the Associates had some 250,000 credit card customers across the nation, and was among the twenty-five largest credit card operations in America.

And still Kahr had one more trick up his sleeve—one more startling example of how good he was at exploiting the "Swiss cheese of regulation." He had never liked having to do business with a bank in order to issue credit cards; it put too many variables outside his control. What happened if the bank started making mistakes? Or if it decided one day that it no longer wanted to help out a finance company? Or if it started demanding changes in the contract? Kahr could envision a dozen scenarios like that, every one of which could only mean trouble for his client, the nonbank financial institution dependent on the goodwill of a bank, which in every other respect was a competitor. As its card program grew, the Associates also began to get nervous about the arrangement, fearing that the government might object. So once the Execu-Charge card was running smoothly, Kahr began contemplating an idea as outrageous as any he'd ever had. He started thinking about the possibility of having the Associates process its own credit card transactions, through its own bank.

Here he was truly entering a Houdini-like realm. Despite all the changes that had taken place in American finance, the laws preventing a nonbank entity from buying a bank seemed as airtight as ever. It was one of the true untouchables; the long-held belief, in Washington and elsewhere, that permitting nonbanks to own banks could only lead to abuse still held sway. Merrill Lynch and all the other nonbank financial institutions could try to perform banklike functions, and could create products that mirrored the workings of bank products, but nobody even thought about simply buying a bank outright. That was unambiguously against the law.

But what was a bank, exactly? It's not the sort of question most people would ever ask, and if they did, their answer would probably resemble Justice Potter Stewart's famous line about pornography: he might not be able to define it, but he knew it when he saw it. Yet, in the law, there were specific criteria separating banks from nonbanks. According to the Bank Holding Company Act of 1960, a bank was defined as an institution that did two things: accept deposits and make commercial loans. Kahr knew this because, as was his habit, he had gone back and read the Bank Holding Company Act, searching for loopholes that others had missed. He found his loophole in this very definition of a bank. What if you owned an institution that met only one of the conditions? What if your "bank" accepted deposits, but only made *consumer* loans instead of commercial loans? If you did that, you would have an institution that looked like a bank, smelled like a bank, and acted like a bank. But technically, it wouldn't be a bank, and therefore could be owned by a finance company. A bank that wasn't a bank. A nonbank bank.

Thus did the money revolution take one more lurch forward. On August 12, 1980, the Associates received the go-ahead from the comptroller of the currency, and transferred its credit card operation to newly named Associates National Bank, in Concord, California. Formerly, this institution had been known as Fidelity National Bank, and it had been a speck of a thing, with no more than $10 million in capital and seven employees. That's what everybody at the Associates and Gulf + Western wanted: a bank so tiny, so out-of-the-way, that nobody would notice what they were up to. Publicity, they knew, could only queer their deal. Even without publicity, it was a dicey proposition because, despite the comptroller's quick agreement that the loophole Kahr had found did indeed exist—and that the purchase of the bank by Gulf + Western was therefore legal—Volcker's Federal Reserve was also required to rule on the legality of the purchase. And the Fed had

remained ominously silent. If the Federal Reserve ruled against the acquisition, Gulf + Western would find itself in serious trouble with the government. But a year later, the Fed gave its reluctant approval, and that was that.

Now, truly, it seemed that anything was possible. Now it seemed as
though both the written and unwritten rules of American finance, which had
been so inviolable for so long, hadn't just gotten a little hazy; they had
disappeared entirely. "The genie was out of the bottle," wrote Tim Carrington of the *Wall Street Journal,* and the consequence was that companies
felt restrained only by the limits of their own imagination. The same month
Kahr and the Associates set up the first nonbank bank, an investment banker
named Sandy Lewis held the first in a series of meetings that would lead
American Express to buy the brokerage firm of Shearson Loeb Rhoades. In
April 1981, at about the same time that deal was completed, Prudential
Insurance bought Bache Securities, meaning that an insurance company
would be offering, in addition to insurance, stocks and bonds and mutual
funds. Dreyfus, the mutual fund company, bought a bank in New Jersey,
and quickly transformed it into a nonbank bank by selling off its commercial loan portfolio. Merrill Lynch soon followed suit. Fidelity Investments
bought a discount broker and set up a nonbank bank. Household Finance and
Beneficial both bought banks and quickly drew up plans to enter the credit
card business. Dillon, Read, perhaps the whitest of the white shoe investment banks, was bought by an investment company in California called
Sequoia Ventures, which was an arm of the Bechtel Group, the largest
construction company in the world. A construction company owned an
investment bank!

If anything, the nonfinancial companies like Bechtel were more enthusiastic about jumping into the fray than were the financial institutions. All of
a sudden, having a finance subsidiary of one sort or another was all the rage.
The Baldwin Piano & Organ Company had been content for a hundred years
to make pianos and organs. But in the early 1980s, it bought an insurance
company, changed its name to Baldwin United, and began selling annuities
through Merrill Lynch (with disastrous consequences, as it turned out).
Xerox Corporation, which had invented the copying machine, began offering an array of financial services. Kroger Company, the supermarket chain,
entered into an arrangement with an insurance company, allowing the latter
to set up counters in its stores. National Steel bought an S&L. RCA bought
a consumer finance company. American Can bought a string of insurance
companies, and then, in the mid-1980s, added the brokerage house of Smith
Barney. By the late 1980s, it had sold off its can divisions, and transformed
itself into a pure financial services company.[5]

And then there was Sears, the great retailer to the middle class, whose long, slow decline was beginning just as this financial services free-for-all was taking place. No company in America entered the money revolution so avidly, so hungrily, and so purposefully. It saw in financial services nothing less than its own salvation, and it felt confident that it had a huge built-in advantage over most of its potential competitors in the financial arena: the 24 million Americans who held a Sears charge card. In theory, those customers were all potential purchasers of Sears-offered mutual funds, or Sears-sponsored insurance. "Our goal," stated Sears chairman Edward Telling, "is to become the largest financial services entity." When Telling made this declaration, in the fall of 1981, Sears already owned the Allstate insurance group. In short order, the company announced that it was establishing a money market fund for Sears customers, that it was buying Coldwell Banker, the nation's largest real estate company, and that it was purchasing Dean Witter Reynolds, a large wirehouse. No wonder William Isaac had been so worried about Sears at those DIDC meetings: Sears really *was* trying to become a bank. Competitors, both on Wall Street and in the retail trade, snidely labeled the Sears scheme "Socks 'n' Stocks." But they were worried too.

At long last, the era A. P. Giannini had only been able to dream about, the era of the financial supermarket, had arrived. All the new entries into the financial services arena had a common theme: they all wanted to offer "one stop shopping" for financial products, or at least as close to one stop shopping as they could get. Never again would a customer need to juggle an array of relationships with a half-dozen different financial institutions. Now, the theory went, people would be able to deal with a single company to buy a house, to get life insurance, to invest for their children's college education, to get a credit card or a small loan, to put money away in a savings account and a dozen other things. For the companies involved, this hope was their great white whale.

Back in the 1920s and 1930s, Giannini had always assumed that banks would be the financial supermarkets. To him, that was the natural order of things: banks were the biggest and most important financial institutions in America, and banking was the central financial activity in American life. But it hadn't worked out that way. Instead, it seemed as though every kind of company *except* banks could transform themselves into financial supermarkets. Banks were still hindered by the laws that were supposed to be protecting them. For all the talk about the imminent demise of Glass–Steagall, the law was still standing—a bit the worse for wear perhaps but standing nonetheless. The McFadden Act, which prevented interstate banking, was also still on the books, as was the Bank Holding Company Act, which had granted banks some new powers to expand—but insisted that

such expansion be limited to areas that were "closely related" to commercial banking. So, for instance, when Citibank had tried to sell mutual
funds—hoping to do to the mutual fund companies what the fund companies
had been doing to it—the Investment Company Institute sued, claiming that
Citibank was in violation of the banking laws. The ICI won, and Citibank
was forced to withdraw its plan. For all the loopholes allowing the likes of
Baldwin United and Sears to break into the fortress of banking, there didn't
seem to be any loopholes that would allow banks to break out of that same
fortress.

Well, that's not quite true. There was one.

IN THE FALL OF 1980, not long after Andrew Kahr had set up the nation's
first nonbank bank, he and Mueller created a small company, which they
named First Deposit Corporation. Frustrated by their inability to land clients
who would agree to their terms, the two men concluded that starting their
own company might get them a little closer to their pot of gold. They would
still need to find a company willing to back Kahr's ideas, but the new plan
was to find just one such entity instead of dozens, linking First Deposit to
some larger, parent company.

Thanks to the mad rush by industrial companies into financial services,
their timing could not have been better. Mueller had friends at Parker Pen,
a company that was as eager to break into the financial services industry as
everyone else in corporate America. By the spring of 1981, Parker Pen had
purchased an 80 percent interest in First Deposit—with Kahr and Mueller
keeping the other 20 percent for themselves—and agreed to invest up to $15
million in its new division. During the course of the next year, Parker Pen
spent around $4 million buying a tiny bank in Tilton, New Hampshire, an
obscure S&L in Redding, California, and a life insurance company in Little
Rock, Arkansas. The first two institutions were transformed into nonbank
banks, and all three were folded into First Deposit. Kahr's involvement in
the Schwab One Account, which began around the same time Parker Pen
bought First Deposit, was likewise folded into his new company: his percentage of the proceeds from that deal became corporate rather than personal
assets.

A year later, Kahr was confident enough about First Deposit's prospects
to grant a rare interview to *Business Week* magazine.[6] Although Kahr spoke
in oblique terms, not wanting to tip his hand, he did mention home equity
loans as a possible new product, as well as a new kind of savings account
that would be "convenient, insured" and "offer tax advantages." He men-

tioned a Visa card. He talked about soliciting customers via telephone and direct mail, borrowing the marketing techniques of mutual fund companies rather than banks, whom he seemed to enjoy twitting. "Kahr believes that banks are hampered more by . . . their lack of imagination than by regulatory constraints," *Business Week* reported. "There is an unusual fluidity of customer relationships that makes it relatively cheap for a newcomer to go out and grab [bank] customers," Kahr said.

Unfortunately, Parker Pen's plans for First Deposit were quickly changing. The recession of the early 1980s had hurt the company badly, and by 1982, it was losing money. Having no other choice, it turned off First Deposit's money spigot. Its executives began talking about the need to "focus our resources . . . in the areas where we had expertise"—which were decidedly not financial services.

At this point, Kahr had some forty employees, divided among California, New Hampshire, and Arkansas. Parker Pen had not only stopped putting money into First Deposit, but was shopping its subsidiary around. And for all his talk, Kahr wasn't even close to developing a product. It would be an overstatement to say that First Deposit was in dire straits, but it was going to need some cash in the not-too-distant future to remain afloat, and it was hard to see where that cash might come from.

And then an odd thing happened. Rich Arnold, the chief financial officer at Schwab, whom Kahr had befriended when he had been working on the Schwab One Account, called him to say Schwab needed to buy Kahr out of their profit-sharing agreement. Could they negotiate something both sides could be happy with? Kahr's predicament being what it was, they certainly could. Putting aside his usual vehemence about the inviolability of his 20 percent share, he agreed to a deal that paid First Deposit $1.5 million in return for releasing Schwab from the profit-sharing agreement. That money gave Kahr a little breathing room. This was in November 1982.[7]

Why, though, was Schwab so insistent that its agreement with Andrew Kahr be rescinded? The answer was, Because it was a condition of Schwab's own soon-to-be completed sale. And who was purchasing Schwab? That was the oddest part of all. Charles Schwab & Co., which was by then America's largest and best-known discount broker, was in the process of being purchased by . . . BankAmerica.[8] If the deal went through, Chuck Schwab, who thought of himself as the quintessential entrepreneur, would be running just another subsidiary of the country's biggest bank. Well, maybe that's not *all* he'd be. Since the terms called for BankAmerica to pay for the discounter with stock, Chuck Schwab would also be the bank's largest stockholder.

Here was the loophole BankAmerica had found in the otherwise impregnable fortress of Glass–Steagall. Banks still couldn't buy insurance companies or sell mutual funds or take over Wall Street investment firms. But there was nothing in the law that said they couldn't buy discount brokerages. Of course, the main reason this loophole existed was because discounting had yet to be invented when the great Depression-era banking laws were written. But so what? The working assumption of loophole exploiters like Kahr had always been that if the law did not explicitly outlaw an activity, then that activity was, by definition, legal. To a large degree, both the courts and the regulators accepted this interpretation.[9] During the Reagan administration, certain deregulation-minded officials, particularly Comptroller of the Currency Todd Conover, openly encouraged the loophole-seekers, believing that the increased competition among financial firms would be good for consumers.

In the case at hand, Glass–Steagall forbade the underwriting of stocks and bonds by banks. But discounters didn't underwrite: all they did was make stock trades for customers. Of course, SRI had pointed out this loophole to the nation's bankers back in the mid-1970s, when it first began producing studies about the shape of the financial future. But it was only now, with the phrase ''financial supermarket'' a kind of mantra, hypnotizing corporate America, that a small handful of banks were willing to exploit this loophole. That BankAmerica should be one of them was somehow supremely fitting, given its history.

Given Schwab's, too.

ᑐ

HIS GRANDFATHER, A SAN FRANCISCO LAWYER, had once been retained by A. P. Giannini to conduct a delicate mission: he was hired to obtain the rights to the name ''Bank of America,'' which were then held by an East Coast bank. Schwab's grandfather succeeded in his task, and afterward he sent Giannini a bill for his services. Giannini thought the bill was too high, and initially, he refused to pay it. Finally, heated words were exchanged between the two men, which culminated in Giannini's angry vow that ''no Schwab will ever work for the Bank of America again!''

Later, when the top executives at Schwab & Co. heard this story, they speculated that their boss had agreed to be bought out by the giant bank because he wanted to gain some small measure of revenge for his grandfather's humiliation—he wanted to show Giannini, observing from the heavens, how wrong he had been about a Schwab ever working for Bank of America again. Although this was never one of those stories that was handed down to the rank and file, in the upper reaches of the firm, it became part of the lore of Schwab. Yet whatever grain of truth it contained, the story, like much of the Schwab lore, tended to obscure a grimmer reality.

The reality was this: Schwab sold his company not so much because he sought sweet vengeance, but because he was persuaded that he had no other choice. Year after year, Charles Schwab & Co. had grown so fast—quadrupling in size every two years—that it was often on the verge of being in violation of the SEC's capital requirements for brokerage firms. As a result, Schwab and his lieutenants were constantly foraging for money, just as they'd been doing since they first opened for business back in 1975.

Except it was different now. The stakes were higher. Schwab & Co. wasn't a small firm anymore; it was a company with a far-flung network of branch offices, staffed by some 800 employees. It had some 370,000 customers. It held a seat on the New York Stock Exchange, which had rather severe financial consequences, inasmuch as the NYSE capital requirements were twice the SEC's. Chuck Schwab had become a *player,* and his capital needs ran to the tens of millions of dollars. But it was debilitating, this endless search for money; worse, it was not always successful. His constant need for money was holding him back, preventing Schwab from becoming big the way he wanted to become big. Other discounters, such as Quick & Reilly, and even Fidelity, which had entered the discount business, were beginning to crowd Schwab as the 1980s began. With the BankAmerica deal, Schwab's capital worries would be over. He could expand to his heart's content. And one other thing: he would be extremely rich.


It's important to keep in mind that Charles Schwab & Co. was in no way immune to the forces that affected the fortunes of full-service wirehouses in the late 1970s and early 1980s. The stock market was as sluggish for Schwab as it was for Merrill Lynch. Inflation was influencing the financial decisions of Schwab customers, just as they were everyone else's. For Schwab, this was not entirely bad; the hard times could sometimes work to the company's advantage. In particular, as hard-core investors got tired of taking cold calls from desperate brokers, they started to switch their business to discounters, happy in the knowledge that no one from a discount firm would ever badger them with unsolicited stock tips. For most of its first decade of life, Schwab's business consisted primarily of catering to these hard-core investors, the kind of people who are compelled to invest no matter what the market is doing. Also, of course, discounters like Schwab are attractive during hard times because they charge lower commissions than do full-service wirehouses.

On the other hand, America is simply not a country full of hard-core investors. As SRI had shown in its early studies, the percentage of Americans who are willing to put money into a venture they consider risky is minimal. And when the market is going down, people tend to view stocks as an *extremely* risky venture. Schwab's 370,000 customers was impressive—for a discount broker. But in any larger context, it was still not much. Citibank had over 7 million credit card customers by the early 1980s. Fidelity had more customers than Schwab just in its money market funds. Discounting was still a minor theme, servicing a narrow niche. According to one estimate, all the discounters put together still did only 10 percent of the brokerage business in America.

Schwab's own growth was a bit illusory, too. True, it was still adding around twenty new branch offices a year, and was swallowing a number of smaller, regional discounters. But its pell-mell growth didn't seem to be leading anywhere; the company had come to resemble a hamster running inside a wheel. Corporate growth is supposed to be a means to an end; and the end is supposed to be larger profits. But where were Schwab's profits? The amount of money Schwab was making was not remotely commensurate with its size; as late as 1979, the company barely broke even. Quick & Reilly, Schwab's most direct competitor, was a much smaller company, and even gave bigger discounts on commissions, yet it made much more money than Schwab.

As ever, Schwab's problems were exacerbated by the company's own general ineptitude. "Ineptitude" is perhaps too harsh a word: the company was, after all, managing to transact the trades that customers requested (or most of them, anyway), to cope with the influx of new phone calls whenever a new branch office was opened (most of the time), to integrate (more or less) the newly acquired regional discounters into the Schwab operation. But there was never anything smooth about any of it; working for Schwab in those days usually meant leaving for home at the end of each working day feeling a little more behind than the day before. Schwab was a harried, frantic place. Mistakes piled up, long-range planning was nonexistent, and too many days were spent coping with the latest crisis.

Midlevel staffers would send out memos, anonymously, mocking the senior management. Others complained openly that Schwab's growth strategy was disastrous. "For a while," a former Schwab manager told *Business Week,* "they needed people so badly that they literally were pulling them in off Montgomery Street."[10] One former midmanager recalls that what rankled most in those days was that Schwab seemed to reward loyalty more than competence; even Rich Arnold, who was one of Schwab's top five executives, concedes that the management ranks were, as he puts it, "thin." The rank and file, he adds, were somewhat justified in their belief that their bosses were "hip shooters." The executives fought constantly: "It was a high conflict environment," recalls Arnold. And all the while, Schwab himself was the way he had always been: slightly aloof yet eager to keep everyone happy, intensely focused on marketing and slightly unfocused on other aspects of the business, keenly proud of his "outsider" status yet so anxious to be part of the establishment that he joined something called the Young Presidents Organization, made up of CEOs under the age of forty. And he was as unbending as ever in his unshakable belief that he could grow his way out of any problem. "He just always felt that because he knew marketing, he could always bring more people in the door," says a former executive.

In May 1980, as part of its ongoing efforts to raise money, Schwab announced plans for a public offering. The company hoped to raise about $5 million by selling 1.2 million shares of stock, at a price of $4 a share. If successful, the offering would not only temporarily solve the company's capital needs, it would also mark the first time a discount broker had gone public. But the offering never got off the ground. Two months later Schwab was forced to cancel it, a humiliating step that caused *Business Week* to question whether discounters could ever become "a credible part of the financial market mainstream."

Schwab and Arnold could list a half-dozen reasons why the offering had failed. The full-service firms didn't understand the discount business! None of the prestigious underwriters wanted to handle the deal! The underwriter who took the job undervalued the company! Wall Street still resented the West Coast upstarts! Well, maybe. And maybe the problem had less to do with some nefarious Wall Street conspiracy than with certain harsh facts about Schwab, facts that all the world could finally see, since they were laid out in the prospectus that accompanied the offering. All the crises, all the mistakes, all the accumulated problems—they were all there, and they didn't just take up a few paragraphs of boilerplate. They went on for pages. The most damning number was the company's error rate. A typical New York Stock Exchange firm makes a trading error 1.4 percent of the time. In 1978, Schwab's error rate was 3.4 percent; in 1979, it was 5.4 percent; and for the first half of 1980, according to the prospectus, it was a shameful 10.5 percent. Because brokers have to use their own capital to make up for such errors, that meant Schwab was spending a huge amount of its precious capital *just making up for its own mistakes*. This was a devastating admission. Schwab's explanation for this was that the new computer system was the source of the trouble. The state-of-the-art system they had installed in 1979 had had a lot of bugs in it, and the order takers hadn't gotten used to it yet, and it often broke down when trading got especially heavy, and . . . and . . . and . . .

. . . and it didn't matter. The prospectus scared investors away. When the underwriters began suggesting that $2.75 a share was a more realistic price than the $4 Schwab had counted on, Arnold persuaded Schwab to pull the deal off the table. Although they wound up raising $4 million by selling off 20 percent of the company in a private deal,[11] Schwab—both the man and the company—was embarrassed by the failure of the public offering. The embarrassment, in turn, resulted in some long overdue changes. In particular, Schwab finally hired a top executive who had actual management experience, with the expectation that after a short trial period he would become the company president and oversee its daily operations. The man's name was Lawrence Stupski, and if it's possible to describe a corporate bureaucrat as a breath of fresh air, that's what Stupski was. In the chaotic atmosphere that was Charles Schwab & Co., a corporate bureaucrat was what the company needed.

Still, what didn't change was the size of Schwab's appetite. He was still going to put growth before profits, because he still believed that was the quickest path to the kind of big-time success he craved. In the wake of the public offering debacle, however, Arnold took the trouble to put together a long-range forecast. It showed rather starkly that, even with the new infusion of money from the private placement, the company would exhaust its capital within two years if Schwab didn't slow down his expansion plans. Which meant that they would be right back where they had started.

And wouldn't you know it: that's when BankAmerica came calling.

Although Schwab didn't realize it at the time, it was actually he who made the first move, or more precisely, it was his impetuous, thirty-three-year-old strategic planner, Peter Moss, who did. In a way, Moss's initial approach to the bank was not unlike his decision, years earlier, to jump over the Schwab counter and reconcile his own account. It was an act of utter spontaneity that wound up having enormous consequences, not least of all for Moss himself.

While Schwab himself was shy and stiff and nonconfrontational in those early years, the people he tended to surround himself with were garrulous souls, unself-conscious talkers and arguers. Of no one was this truer than Moss, who was the most garrulous, the most argumentative, the most likely to say whatever he thought. He was also extremely tightly wound, and burdened with both an inflated sense of his own importance and a conviction of the correctness of his own ideas. Most people at Schwab found him both infuriating and endearing. One of his endearing qualities was that, of all of Schwab's lieutenants, Moss was the truest believer. Along with Chuck Schwab himself, Moss was the great Schwab dreamer, the most willing to see discounting as a righteous crusade.

Having picked up rumors that a number of banks were thinking about buying their way into the discount brokerage business, Moss took it upon himself to phone a contemporary at BankAmerica, a senior vice president named Stephen McLin, who was the bank's new head of strategic planning. This was in June of 1981. Moss had never met McLin in person, and had talked to him only once before on the phone. He had no authority whatsoever to make this contact. The two men talked in general terms about Schwab's capital needs and how BankAmerica might be able to help provide them. Neither man specifically mentioned the possibility of a merger, but they talked around it, hinting and feinting. They agreed to talk again.

BankAmerica was no longer the biggest bank in the world when Moss made his fateful phone call—a handful of Japanese and European banks had overtaken it—but it was still the biggest bank in America. It had around $120 billion in assets. It had recently reported profits of $600 million. It was still running neck and neck with Citicorp as the largest issuer of credit cards (though not for much longer). Fully a third of the citizens of California still did business with it. On the surface, it seemed like the place it had always been, the one that people used to call MotherBank.

But it wasn't. It wasn't close to being the same place that A. P. Giannini had founded; it wasn't even the same place it had been in the 1950s, when its executives had focused so shrewdly, and with such confidence, on middle-class consumers. Over the course of several decades, the bank had slowly atrophied, becoming nonchalant about its consumer base, sloppy in its lending practices, unoriginal in its marketing and advertising. It had become, in fact, a sprawling, bureaucratic, highly political place, so big that the left hand rarely knew what the right hand was doing, and so full of intrigue that the executive suites took on many of the characteristics of a medieval court.

One would not have known any of this from examining BankAmerica's profit-and-loss statements, which managed to remain curiously buoyant throughout the 1970s. And one wouldn't have known it from reading BankAmerica's press clippings, either; its problems would not burst into public view for another few years. But other bankers knew it; they could sense BankAmerica's vulnerability, and were quick to take advantage.

Crocker was the first bank in California to invest heavily in automatic teller machines, for example; ATMs were precisely the sort of consumer innovation that one would have expected from BankAmerica once upon a time. Security Pacific began to get the kind of reputation for product innovation that had once been BankAmerica's preserve. Wells Fargo began to do the kind of consumer marketing that had always been the larger bank's forte.

And on the other side of the country stood the greatest rival of them all: Citicorp. For a short time in the mid-1970s, Citicorp had actually grown larger than BankAmerica, only to see BankAmerica reclaim the title of "biggest bank in America" by around 1977. But even without being the largest, Citicorp had overtaken its West Coast adversary in every other way that mattered. The breathtaking risks it took, the fabulous national consumer franchise it had built, the secretive research and development facility it operated, the cutting-edge technology it invested in, and the sheer, haughty arrogance that characterized its every move—all of this and more were the envy of the nation's bankers. One hesitates, in hindsight, to give Citicorp too much credit, for by the early 1990s, Citi would be struggling to survive its own serious crisis, a good part of which was the result of directions taken a decade earlier. But at the time, there was no hesitation at all about giving Citicorp credit, not in the press, and not in banking circles, where the New York banking juggernaut was viewed with both fear and awe.

Throughout the 1970s, Citicorp had been a near obsession of BankAmerica's chairman, Tom Clausen.[12] This was not something he would ever admit, of course; the entire BankAmerica culture assumed a feigned indifference toward its East Coast rival. Still, you could see it in the things Clausen did: you could see it in the way he was constantly trying to do Walter Wriston one better. Wriston had made Citicorp a truly international bank, with large and profitable divisions in South America and Europe. So Clausen dived into South America and Europe too, making a series of bank takeovers in places like Argentina that turned out disastrously. Wriston had practically invented the business of lending money to Third World nations; so Clausen had to lend to Third World nations, too—to the bank's eventual regret. Citicorp gained a reputation for making giant interest rate bets; BankAmerica began playing the same game—and lost millions.

There was even talk that Clausen was goosing the numbers, using legal but unusually aggressive accounting moves so that BankAmerica could regain its status as the larger and more profitable of the two institutions. "The chief financial officer would call at the end of the last quarter," one former bank executive later told Moira Johnston, author of one of the two books written detailing the bank's travails, "and say, 'I need $2 billion in

five hours' ''—by which he meant $2 billion in loans, which could be added
to the bank's balance sheet. After the 1977 results were in, showing that
BankAmerica had earned $14 million more than Citicorp, Clausen boasted,
"We have regained our rightful position as the world's most profitable
bank." But he attributed this success to the bank's "conservatism," which
was ludicrous. By 1981, just as Clausen was retiring from his decade-long
reign as CEO, the previous fiscal year's balance sheet was so blatantly
massaged that it raised eyebrows in banking circles. It eventually became
clear that the accounting gimmicks were a kind of going-away present to
Clausen from his successor, so that the outgoing chairman would be able to
claim that profits had risen every year on his watch, something he badly
wanted to be able to do. However pleasing this may have been to Clausen,
it was hardly a sign of a bank with its eye on the ball.

Clausen's successor was a man named Samuel Armacost, and he was
surprisingly young for someone running so large and imposing an institution. When he took the helm at BankAmerica, he was forty-two years old,
two years younger than Schwab. He and Schwab shared similarities beyond
their relative youth: they were both Stanford grads, they both played a mean
game of golf, and they were both products of California's upper middle
class. Later, after the deal between their two companies had been struck,
these surface similarities would be much commented upon, for they helped
draw the two men to each other.

But in other ways, they were quite different. Armacost had a smooth
corporate sheen that Schwab lacked. His was the easy grace—"a jaunty
confidence and country club athleticism," as Johnston later put it—of someone who is comfortable with his status as an insider; Schwab was insecure
about his place in the world, and did a bad job of hiding it. Schwab tended
to see things in stark and simple terms; Armacost saw the world around him
as layered and complex. Schwab, despite his role as the company spokesman, was such a poor public speaker that he finally hired a coach to help him
improve; Armacost was almost preternaturally glib. Most of all, though,
Armacost had an arrogance that lay just under the veneer of that polished
surface. "He couldn't see his own weaknesses," recalls one man who
worked for Armacost in the mid-1980s, "and he didn't appreciate anyone
pointing them out." Schwab, who had known failure and wanted desperately to be liked, was anything but arrogant. In time, it was these differences
that would be stressed, for they helped drive the two men apart. But that
would come later.

*     *     *

In August 1981, McLin and Moss had a second conversation, this time talking more openly about a possible merger. A month after that, the two men had lunch, by which time McLin had talked to Armacost, who had told him to pursue a possible deal. It was after this lunch that McLin stated formally that BankAmerica was interested in pursuing a buyout of Schwab. Moss, alas, had not yet informed Schwab that he had opened this dialogue with his BankAmerica counterpart; when he finally did so, Schwab was not enthusiastic. "After all the struggling we've done," Moss recalls him saying, "why should we sell our birthright now?" But after some urging from Moss and Arnold, Schwab reluctantly allowed a lunch to be scheduled in which the participants would be Moss, McLin, Schwab, and Armacost. It took place two weeks later.

There is a moment in every deal when the thing begins to take on a life of its own—when it acquires a momentum that can seem almost independent of the participants. Even though nothing has been signed, or even agreed to, the parties stop thinking about it as simply an interesting possibility and start thinking of it as an inevitability. It seems fair to say that that moment arrived in the BankAmerica–Schwab deal when Schwab and Armacost had lunch together on that late September day in 1981.

They dined in Armacost's private dining room. It stood on the 52nd floor of the bank's gleaming skyscraper in the heart of the San Francisco financial district. Uniformed waiters served beautifully prepared food on exquisite china. The hushed, privileged atmosphere bespoke money and status—one of which Schwab needed and the other of which he craved. Armacost was charming, and the two men hit it off. They saw each other (mistakenly) as kindred spirits, and by the time the lunch had ended, they were also seeing each other's organizations as of a piece. Armacost and McLin put forward the argument that BankAmerica and Schwab "fit" together. The bank's history as an institution oriented toward consumers, one that had always embraced the mass market, meshed with Schwab's own history and orientation. Because of this similarity, the two organizations—and the two men leading them—would see things the same way. They could help each other grow. And so on. As the lunch was ending, Armacost gave Schwab a copy of an in-house history the bank had published, which emphasized A. P. Giannini's populist leanings. "Chuck," recalls Arnold, "was enamored of that."

Events moved quickly after that. Armacost and a team of BankAmerica executives trooped over to Schwab's offices for a tour. (McLin was particularly impressed with the Schwab computer system, which for all its problems was far more sophisticated than anything BankAmerica had.) Then another lunch, this time attended only by the two principals, followed by a series of meetings between the two men. McLin, sensing Schwab's weakness, wrote a private memo to Armacost suggesting that he should appeal to Schwab's ego. This Armacost did brilliantly. After agreeing not to change the Schwab name, to allow the discounter to remain as a free-standing unit, and to give Schwab the power to run his former company as he saw fit, Armacost threw in the clincher. Schwab, he said, would join BankAmerica's prestigious board of directors. After that, it was just a question of price.

And yet, however much Schwab had been seduced by Armacost, he still entered into the BankAmerica deal with a very clear sense of its purpose. Once his company became a part of BankAmerica, its capital needs would be solved. That was the most important thing. "He was tired of fighting for capital," recalls Moss. Everything else about the deal—the alleged "synergies" between the two companies, the chance to be a part of a "financial supermarket," even Schwab's treasured position on the board of directors—were incidental to that main purpose. Seduced he may have been, but Chuck Schwab understood quite concretely what he was getting out of Armacost.

The trickier question was what Armacost was getting out of Schwab. Schwab, with its 800 employees, was tiny compared to BankAmerica, with its 80,000 employees; its revenues were never going to make much difference to BankAmerica's bottom line. Moreover, while Schwab had many qualities that BankAmerica's executives found appealing—not only its advanced technology and its marketing panache, but its impressive demographics (the typical Schwab customer made around $20,000 a year more than the typical BankAmerica customer)—these were not traits that would easily translate from the smaller institution to the larger one. It was hard to see, even at the time, how each would be able to use the other to some mutual advantage.

But Armacost did not appear to be buying Schwab because the deal made such good business sense. Far more likely was the possibility that he was doing it because it would allow him to etch out his own identity as a bold leader, and because it would mean that for once, BankAmerica, rather than Citicorp, was doing something innovative. In the end, he appeared to be doing it because it seemed like the perfect way to proclaim the beginning of the Armacost era. Which is to say, his reasons had more to do with the internal culture of BankAmerica than with serving the needs of the bank's customers. Inside the bank, the purchase had its intended effect. "Everything stopped when we heard about it," one executive told Gary Hector, the author of the second book about the bank's problems. "[E]veryone was talking about the bank moving forward."

They heard about it officially on November 22, 1981, just two months after the principals first met in the BankAmerica dining room. The purchase price was $53 million, less (Hector reports) than the cost of installing six-months' worth of ATMs. Even so, Schwab had not come cheaply; since it had never earned as much as $2 million in any year, BankAmerica was paying thirty times earnings for the privilege of owning America's leading discount broker. To pay for the acquisition, BankAmerica would issue 2.2 million shares[13] of stock to shareholders in the privately held Schwab—Schwab and his executives, Uncle Bill's heirs, First Nationwide Savings, which had a 20 percent stake in Schwab, and a handful of others.

Still, a merger involving a bank can't be completed just because both sides have agreed to it. It needed the specific approval of Paul Volcker's Federal Reserve, which had to rule on the legality of a bank owning a discount broker. Volcker being Volcker, there was no way this was going to be done quickly. Legal papers were drawn up, pilgrimages made to the Federal Reserve building in Washington, briefings given to the Fed staff and its governors. And then everybody went back home to San Francisco and waited. And waited . . . and waited. . . .

And while they waited, spring arrived, and BankAmerica was forced to issue the first in a series of disappointing quarterly results. And while they waited, summer arrived, and BankAmerica's stock began to drop. And while they waited, fall arrived, and the bull market began.


The bull market! Isn't *that* the event that had the potential to eliminate Schwab's debilitating need for capital and to change the fortunes of the company radically? Isn't that what Chuck Schwab had been counting on all this time, as he'd struggled to build his company? Surprisingly, it wasn't. Strange as it may seem, the people at Schwab had never really thought much about what a bull market might mean to them. Perhaps that was because they had not collectively experienced one, or maybe it was because they all had enough to think about just getting through each day. But once the bull market began, it was rather obvious what effect it would have on Schwab. It was manna from heaven. The phones were clotted with customers who wanted to buy stocks; in the space of just a few months, Schwab added 100,000 people to its customer base. The branch offices were filled with people from the moment they opened for business and were nearly as full when it was time to close. The computers were humming. And most of all, the company that could never seem to scare up enough money to meet its needs was awash in commission revenues. Having never made as much as $2 million a year, Schwab was suddenly earning around $3 million a *month;* in the last five months of 1982, Schwab earned more money than it had made in the previous seven years. It suddenly appeared that Schwab no longer needed the backing of the biggest bank in the country.

More to the point, the terms of the deal, which had seemed so generous the previous November, didn't look so extravagant anymore. At the time the merger was announced, BankAmerica had appeared strong, and Schwab had appeared weak. Now, Schwab was the strong one and BankAmerica the weak one. In the fall of 1982, BankAmerica's stock dropped from 26½ to 19½; that meant that the 2.2 million shares Schwab stockholders were slated to receive had dropped in value from $53 million to less than $43 million. And even that original $53 million price raised a troubling question: if Schwab was a bigger, healthier company now, should it still be content to accept a price that was negotiated a year before, when its condition was far shakier?

Chuck Schwab's own answer to that question was unequivocal. It was "yes." He had agreed on a price, and if he were to reopen the negotiations, he would be going back on his word. No matter how much the circumstances had changed, this was not something he could do. "It became a point of honor with Chuck," says McLin. Peter Moss, however, was another story. The arrival of the bull market, combined with the steady stream of bad news about BankAmerica, had made him extremely agitated. Even though he himself had set the deal in motion, he now believed that it was a gigantic mistake, and in his state of high anxiety, he did what he had so often done in the past: he took matters into his own hands.

He wasn't going to get Schwab to back out of the merger; that was clear enough. When he tried to argue the point, Schwab told him it was too late to back out, and he was long past the point of entertaining contrary opinions. So then Moss went directly to Armacost, brashly telling the BankAmerica CEO that he thought there were problems with the deal. "What does Chuck think?" Armacost asked. "Chuck has some discomfort with it," Moss recalls replying, "but he's a gentleman and he thinks a deal is a deal." Armacost shrugged.

Even though both principals were determined to go through with it, Moss planted himself in the way. He asked Schwab to get a "fairness opinion" from one of the big investment houses.[14] Moss's hope was that the investment bankers would conclude that because of the bull market, the deal was no longer fair to the discounter. Schwab turned down his request. Moss then wrote a draft of a memo outlining his objections to the terms, intending to send it to the boards of both companies. Instead, someone snatched it from his secretary's desk and showed it to Schwab, who was furious. "I'm the biggest [Schwab] shareholder," Moss recalls Schwab telling him, "and I'm getting screwed the most. If I can deal with it, why can't everybody else?" Without telling Schwab, Moss visited McLin one weekend, pouring out his concerns. McLin was alarmed enough by this conversation to talk to Armacost, who in turn called Schwab, to see if there really were any problems. There weren't, insisted Schwab; he'd handle Moss. Now it was Schwab who was becoming agitated—at his strategic planner.

By now it was late November 1982. From Washington, BankAmerica began to hear rumblings that the Federal Reserve was close to issuing its ruling, and that it would be favorable. In San Francisco, both sides rushed to get the final documents ready so that they could be quickly signed once the ruling was made public. Nobody wanted to hear any more objections from Peter Moss. Yet it wasn't in Moss to let it go, or to chalk it up as one of life's disappointments. *He just couldn't stop.* His new tactic was to claim that the disclosure filings sent to the SEC were so incomplete as to border on fraud. In addition to the obvious material changes that had taken place within the two companies over the past few months—largely unmentioned in the filings—Moss had a list of facts, some more damaging than others, that had been left out of the documents.

This latest effort to undermine the merger led to a meeting with Stupski and a Schwab attorney. But when Moss laid out his charges, he was told (as he recalls it) that "I should keep my nose out of it." In early December, a new set of documents were issued, and though they included some additional disclosures, they did not touch upon Moss's main concerns. "I was pissed," Moss says now. "No question about it. I owned almost one and a half percent of the company. I was one of five corporate officers. I had initiated the deal. So I had no choice," he concludes with great sadness. "I hung myself out to dry."

On a Saturday in mid-December, Moss wrote one more draft of one more memo, the last memo he would ever write as an officer of Charles Schwab & Co. "It is my personal and moral duty," it began, "to inform you that I formally oppose the merger." And then he went on to list his objections in a lengthy, wrenching cri de coeur. After he finished, he was so distraught he couldn't sleep. The next day, Sunday, he went into the office to write the final version on his computer. But this memo didn't just go to Schwab or the top executives. This time, when he was done, he pressed a button on his computer that sent the memo electronically to every officer in the company, all the way down to the branch managers. On Monday morning, when they came to work and turned on their computers, the first thing they saw was Moss's memo. When Schwab himself saw it that morning, he became so angry that he did something he had rarely done in all the time he had been running the company. He called Peter Moss into his office and fired him.

Unbeknownst to Moss, at the same time he was composing his memo, Rich Arnold had reopened the issue of price with McLin and Armacost. The result of these new negotiations was reflected in a three-paragraph story tucked into the *Wall Street Journal* two days before Christmas. The story said simply that BankAmerica would be issuing 2.6 million shares for Schwab instead of 2.2 million. The added 400,000 shares brought the purchase price up to $52 million, close to the original price. It was still a steal for the bank, but it was better than it had been. Also, the day before that story, Schwab filed an amended set of documents at the SEC. Virtually every one of Moss's complaints was disclosed in the new documents.

But it was too late for Peter Moss. In January 1983, the Federal Reserve finally approved the BankAmerica–Schwab merger, and within two days Armacost and Schwab signed the necessary papers, making the buyout official. Schwab became the largest stockholder of BankAmerica and a member of its board. The significance of the deal was widely heralded by the financial press, which viewed it as the transaction that might finally ''break the back of Glass–Steagall,'' as Moira Johnston later put it. Peter Moss took pleasure in none of this. He was on the outside looking in, where he would remain, to his lasting regret. And although one could argue that he would have had to leave the company sooner or later anyway—as Schwab became more straitlaced and corporate, and less tolerant of people like Moss—he chose not to see it that way. Had he not written that memo, he would say later, he might still be there today. Moss spent the next decade in a series of different jobs, but always his heart remained with Schwab. Schwab's ''manifest destiny'' no longer included Peter Moss, and for Moss, nothing hurt more than that.

## CHAPTER 14

# The People's Nest Egg

## *April 1984*

THE EDITOR OF *Money* magazine, at the moment the bull market arrived, was a balding, pipe-smoking, leprechaunlike man with a voice so high-pitched he practically squeaked when he talked. He was fifty-three years old, and had held his current job—his first top editorial position—for a little more than two years. Already he had met with some success, at least according to the standard by which he was being judged: *Money* magazine turned its first-ever profit not long after he became its editor.[1]

Yet there was something about him, some combination of traits, that prevented some people at Time, Inc., which owned *Money* magazine, from taking him completely seriously. Operating in a profession that is incorrigibly pessimistic, he was a man of relentless optimism, with a sunny faith in America and its great institutions, among the greatest of which, in his opinion, was Time, Inc. (He used to tell people proudly that in all the years he had been working for the company—and accumulating Time stock in his profit-sharing plan—he had never sold a single share.) He percolated with uncontainable enthusiasm. He talked too much, lacking the social antennae that should have told him when other people were rolling their eyes. His workaholism seemed excessive. And his desire to ingratiate himself could cause him to say things that were simply silly. Once, when he saw a new editor stepping out of an elevator, he walked up to the man, offered his hellos, and then, having nothing else to say but feeling the need to say *something,* added, "That's a good elevator bank." Another time, after interviewing a high level government official at the White House, he asked to use the phone to call his wife. Later he told a colleague, "How many times in my life will I get someone to say to my wife, 'This is the White House'?" That was Marshall Loeb.

His ascension to the editorship of *Money* magazine was widely believed by his Time, Inc., colleagues to be a consolation prize.[2] He had joined the company in 1956 as a junior staff writer for *Time* magazine, and had spent the next twenty-four years rising through *Time*'s editorial ranks; his truest ambition, most of his colleagues believed, was one day to edit *Time*. And though he eventually became one of *Time*'s most senior editors, and even had his own column, it became clear at some point that that job was always going to remain outside his reach. Eventually, it became a question of what to do with Loeb—where to put this staunch company man. And since *Money* magazine was still struggling eight years after its birth . . . and since Loeb had spent most of his *Time* career writing and editing business stories . . . and since there was a feeling among the brass that Loeb deserved a shot at a top editing job somewhere in the company . . . and that's how Marshall Loeb became editor of *Money* magazine at the dawn of the 1980s.

Which is to say, that's how the money revolution got its most enthusiastic cheerleader. Just as personal finance was becoming complex instead of simple, and the middle class was starting to realize that it was going to have to sort through options, make choices, take control of its finances in a way it had never had to before, along came Marshall Loeb, promising (enthusiastically) to explain it all to his middle-class readers. Indeed, he relished the chance to do so, and not just because it was his job. He loved the idea that people had options they hadn't had before. "Just *think* of all the choices you had by then," he would joyously recall years later. "You had bond funds! You had tax-free bond funds! You had money market funds! You had *tax-free* money market funds!" He had real insight into the way America was changing; he could talk at great length, for instance, about how the middle class was finally gaining access to all the financial tools that had previously been available only to the rich. He understood the effect of inflation on middle-class behavior. He even liked the way the Age of Inflation had caused the subject of money to come out of the closet; he thought it was healthy for America to talk about its money. He was known to say that money was the new sex.

And when the bull market came along two and a half years into his tenure, Loeb could scarcely contain himself. Covering a roaring bull market is a little like covering a baseball team on a winning streak: the mood becomes so infectious that even the most objective reporter is bound to get a little jazzed about the goings-on. The bull market meshed perfectly with Loeb's own natural optimism. As the Dow made its historic climb, he began to use his magazine as a pulpit to plead with his readers to come into the market. "HOW TO START INVESTING . . . And Do It *Right*," promised one of his early bull market issues. "SECRETS OF SUCCESSFUL SMALL INVESTORS," screamed another: "How They've Outpaced the Pros—and How You Can Too."

Charlie Merrill, had he been alive, couldn't have said it better. Then again, with Marshall Loeb around, he didn't have to. Now it was Loeb who saw it as his solemn duty to champion the stock market to the middle class. And this time, it took.


*Money* magazine had been given life, it seems fair to say, before the need for it existed. The first issue went to press in September 1972,[3] the same month that Henry Brown and Bruce Bent were given permission by the SEC to unveil their newfangled money market fund. But who knew from money market funds? It was too early for people to start paying attention to such things; personal finance was still a simple affair.

Even the journalism of personal finance was simple back then, largely[4] monopolized by two people: Louis Rukeyser, whose show, "Wall Street Week," began its lengthy run in 1970, and Sylvia Porter, the syndicated columnist, who doled out her sensible, thrift-oriented advice three times a week. Most other people in the advice business were essentially stock touts, offering "tips" and other kinds of market advice in their (usually) over-priced newsletters. In the late 1970s and early 1980s, the best known of these was the flamboyant promoter Joe Granville,[5] who developed a huge following as a "market timer," until he made the unfortunate mistake of telling his followers to sell everything just as the bull market began in 1982.

If one wishes to be kind, one could claim that the Time, Inc., hierarchy was prescient in starting *Money* magazine. If one wishes to be less kind, one could claim that the Time, Inc., executives who conceived the idea for *Money* magazine were all well-to-do, and didn't fully realize that the options available to themselves as men of means were not available to most of the middle-class Americans they hoped would buy their new magazine.

Whatever the case, Time, Inc., plunged ahead. William Rukeyser, a senior editor at *Fortune* magazine, was plucked from that publication and brought in to edit the new magazine. And while he would seem to have personal finance in his genes—in addition to having Louis for a brother, his father was Merryle Rukeyser, a popular economist in his day—he viewed the subject as too narrow to carry the editorial burden of his new magazine. As a result, the most noteworthy aspect of *Money* magazine under Rukeyser was that it did not focus particularly on money. It evolved instead into a toned-down version of *Consumer Reports,* with annual ratings of automobiles, comparisons of vacation spots, grim warnings about defective prod-

ucts, and so on. Of the money-related features it did run, the most popular
was a column called "One Family's Finances," in which the members of a
family would lay out their finances, and then listen to three experts advise
them on how to tackle their problems. Rukeyser's *Money* was solid but
pedestrian; in its first few years, it went out to around 400,000 subscribers,
far below the number of readers a Time, Inc., magazine required to turn a
profit.

By 1975, more than two years after it had been started, *Money* was losing
several million dollars a year; among the top Time, Inc., executives, patience was wearing thin. "When the hell are we going to kill this thing?"
one executive was known to ask at the slightest provocation. By the spring
of that year, the rumors that the magazine would soon be shut down had
grown so insistent that the *Money* staff requested a chance to present their
case directly to the board of directors. This they apparently did convinc-
ingly. By the end of the meeting, they had extracted a commitment from the
company to invest another $1.7 million in the magazine, while promising
the board that if improvement were not visible by year's end, they themselves would recommend closing *Money* down. When 1975 had ended,
circulation was over 600,000, advertising pages were up, and *Money* had
begun to turn itself around.

There were two important ingredients to this turnaround. The first was
that Rukeyser, under pressure from his superiors, began putting a far greater
emphasis on money in *Money* magazine. The second was that this new
emphasis neatly coincided with the gradual realization among the middle
class that their financial underpinnings were being loosed from their moor-
ings. The OPEC oil embargo had taken place in 1974, and its effects were
still reverberating. In 1975, inflation was around 7 percent. Interest rates
were fluctuating—another new and unnerving phenomenon. And there were
new products: by the mid-1970s, one could find articles in *Money* about
tax-free municipal bond funds, about retirement accounts, about single-
premium annuities, and about money market funds. One could also find
stories about important new financial trends, such as the rise of the two-
income family and the effects of inflation. "I think," one Time, Inc.,
executive wrote to another, "it has found its niche and purpose."

And then, in March 1980, Rukeyser was moved back to *Fortune*, where
he was named editor, and was replaced by Marshall Loeb.

In a remarkably foresighted article he published in October 1982, on the
occasion of *Money*'s tenth anniversary—an article in which he correctly
predicted that American productivity would remain flat during the 1980s,

that real estate prices would begin dropping by the end of the decade, and that the dawning information revolution would completely change the nature of the American workplace—Marshall Loeb wrote this:

Despite [America's] problems, there will be plenty of opportunities to prosper through personal investments. The best investments may well be common stocks. Even after the market's recent leaps, shares remain extremely low. The Dow Jones industrials, adjusted for inflation, have crashed more than 60 percent in real terms since October 1972. Fairly soon, stocks should start benefiting from the recent reduction in America's income and capital-gains taxes, as well as the many steps taken by corporations during the recession to reduce bloated overhead and enhance efficiency. A sound course for the investor who does not constantly monitor his stocks would be to entrust his money to a mutual fund family. Such families allow you, easily and inexpensively, to switch your money around from stock funds to bond funds to money-market funds as changing conditions motivate you.

Here, in a nutshell, was Marshall Loeb's credo: buy stocks. And if you didn't want to buy stocks, buy mutual funds. Here is the distilled essence of what he believed, and what he preached. And for which, a decade later (by which time he had replaced Rukeyser at *Fortune*), he offered no apologies. "If I was optimistic about the stock market, I have been proven correct," he later insisted, noting that the market had quadrupled between August 1982 and May 1994. He added, "To the extent that *Money* recommended to its readers that carefully selected stocks and mutual funds might well be worthwhile investments for many people, then *Money* served its readers well."

Yet even with a bull market as magnificent as this one, there was a downside. A bull market did not mean that every stock went up every day—just as a bear market didn't mean that every stock went down every day. "If you had owned Bristol Myers over the last decade," Peter Lynch once said, "you would have made money whether the market was at 2,400 or 600. And if you had owned Avon Products, you would have lost money even if the market had gone to 10,000." Surely, he was right about that. Even in the best of times, the stock market was risky. One couldn't blindly dive in, no matter how rapidly the Dow Jones average was rising. This would seem to be a rather basic fact: people could lose as well as gain. Yet over time, a number of writers and editors came to believe that *Money* didn't dwell on the risks that came with investing. "We always felt, at least a number of us did, that we were probably too Pollyanish," recalls Robert Runde, who worked at *Money* from the mid-1970s to the mid-1980s. Once, at a staff retreat, Runde got up to complain about some of the articles the magazine had been running; his remarks were met with a stony silence.

To the surprise of almost everyone at Time, Inc., Loeb came to the job with a clear agenda. "I found *Money* to be a little too clinical and surgical and downscale, frankly," he says now. Loeb wanted a magazine that was more timely than the one his predecessor turned out, and maniacally focused on financial matters. He also wanted a magazine that spoke more directly to its middle-class readership. He had certain words he wanted on the cover of *Money* to convey the kind of magazine he was trying to edit. "Your" was a favored word, as were "now," "investments," and "best." If he could get a cover that said, "Your Best Investments Now," he was in heaven.

Much of this, it should be said, was praiseworthy. *Money* did need to start speaking more directly to the middle class. And its new single-minded emphasis on finances, at a time when inflation was raging out of control, was exactly right. Under Loeb, *Money* greatly expanded its coverage of mutual funds, and did a first-rate job of bringing to the attention of its readers such worthy new financial products as zero-coupon bonds. It often did offer cautious, one-step-at-a-time stock market advice aimed at new investors, as Loeb insists. Loeb also worked to make the magazine less New York–oriented, insisting that each editor make a trip once a year to some-place in middle America. He himself was constantly making such trips, always willing to address, say, a Rotary Club in Columbus, Ohio. He had a much clearer vision of his audience than Rukeyser had had—"a young professional anywhere in America" was his prototypical reader, says one former employee. And Loeb had a keen sense of the big picture: he was one of the very few people with a feel for the sweep and scope of the money revolution even as it was taking place. All of this was reflected in his magazine.

All of these things his staff would grant him, and other things, too: he was a nice boss; he made working at *Money* exciting instead of predictable; he raised the magazine's profile within the Time-Life building. Yet none of it could wash away the feeling that *Money* had begun to "pander to the reader," as a highly regarded senior editor named Robert Klein said years later. Loeb wanted a magazine as upbeat and as enthusiastic as he was, with an attitude toward the myriad financial choices facing Americans that approximated the kid-in-a-candy-store giddiness he felt himself. *Money* wasn't just reporting on those choices; it was also selling them, promising in the pages of the magazine far more than the money revolution could possibly deliver.

The money revolution did not promise, for example, that middle-class Americans would get rich. Yet *Money* magazine often implied that they would. "How to Turn $50,000 into $250,000 in Just Five Years," read a typical cover headline in March 1984. Inside, the magazine profiled seven people who had supposedly done just that, taking what the magazine described as "bold but intelligent risks." One of the seven, it turned out, was a silver speculator. A cover package entitled "The New Millionaires" included profiles of such "typical" young millionaires as Bruce McNall, the future owner of the Los Angeles Kings hockey team, who got rich dealing rare Greek and Roman coins, and Morris Seagal, the founder of Celestial Seasonings. Were readers really supposed to emulate them—or simply dream about it a little? The cover package that promised to show readers "How to Start Investing . . . And Do It *Right*" profiled a twenty-nine-year-old man who had allegedly "built $5,000 into $127,000 in three years." And on and on. An article that ran in July 1983 described a New Jersey doctor who had doubled his money by trading in index options. *Index options?* Yes, these issues also contained plenty of cautions, but what was bound to pop out at any reader was the opposite sensation—the notion that you, too, could get rich, just like these lucky souls who had made it into *Money* magazine. "While starting your own enterprise is still the best way to make a fortune, it's not impossible to get rich by working for someone else," *Money* advised, for instance, in its September 1981 cover package.

By the time the bull market began, the Loeb formula was pretty much set in stone—and would remain so well after he was gone. (In fact, it would become even more pronounced after he moved upstairs to assume the title of Editor of Magazine Development, something he did at the end of 1983. Even with his new job, he retained his title as editor of *Money*, and continued "to supervise all of *Money*'s editorial content and strategy," as his successor put it at the time.) The formula went like this: There would always be an upbeat headline on the cover, using whichever handful of Loeb's favorite cover words fit that month, and promoting some aspect of what one former *Money* reporter would later label "Happy Time Investing." It would often be accompanied by a photograph of a handsome financial expert or of some happy person or couple who had gotten rich beyond their wildest dreams by doing whatever it was the magazine was plugging that month. These cover models were real people, plucked from middle America, and attractive in a wholesome way. They were almost always white, though when the magazine would gather together subscribers for focus group sessions, the readers tended to remember not so much the color of their skin as the color of their teeth—their perfect, gleaming, white teeth. Then, inside the magazine, there would be more photographs of more happy, successful couples, enjoying the fruits of their winnings: driving their luxury automobile, standing in front of their gorgeous new home, dining in a gourmet restaurant, and so on. The clear implication was that if these people could do it, then so could you.

But could you? Could a country full of risk-conscious middle-income people really be expected to begin speculating in silver, as *Money* seemed to suggest? Was turning $5,000 into $127,000 in three years truly an appropriate goal? Or was something else going on here? Was the *Money* couple of the month the financial equivalent of the *Playboy* Playmate? Readers of *Money* would seem to have about as much chance of getting rich by following the strategies of the magazine's wholesome, attractive, wealthy exemplars as readers of *Playboy* did of sleeping with an anatomically perfect Playmate.

There were, in addition, more serious problems with *Money*'s approach. The first—and this is endemic in any periodical that offers financial advice—is that the strategies it put forward were terribly scattershot. One article featured options; the next heralded the financial possibilities in art collecting. One month it was offering a handful of small growth stocks its "experts" were high on; the next it was stressing the importance of having a portfolio full of big companies that could deliver slow but steady gains. A reader who came to *Money* because he was confused about the new choices he faced and was looking for help was likely to find that he had stepped instead into the magazine equivalent of a street bazaar—a place overflowing with goods, each more alluring than the next, while the merchants all shouted for attention. "To make a mockery of *Money*," recalled Robert Klein, "all you have to do is go through a year's worth and read all the contradictory advice." (He added, "*Money*'s real service was to keep people informed on what was good and bad among the many new investments.")

The magazine also contained "an unseemly hype," recalls Runde. "There was a lot of oversimplification," he adds. Other *Money* staffers agreed: "It bothered me that [it made investing] look easier than it was," says Flora Ling, the former head of research at *Money*, who nonetheless praised Loeb's vision. "With Rukeyser you could write negative stories," says Marlys Harris, a long-time *Money* writer. "But Marshall wouldn't let you write negative stuff." Another *Money* writer added: "Writers used to grumble a lot about the magazine's avoidance of certain negative aspects of personal finance." Robert Runde again: "The magazine pretended to offer something useful but really offered something glitzy." Robert Klein, the longtime senior editor: "I don't think *Money* explained the downside risks well enough." When *Money* staffers talked about the magazine's tendency to "pander" to readers, this is what they were referring to. ("Marshall *never* thought he was pandering," adds Ling, and Loeb himself insists that the magazine never did anything of the sort.)

And then there was the time Loeb put on the cover a former IRS employee who had just written a book about exploiting loopholes in the tax code. Loeb wanted to call the man a former IRS *agent*, to make his advice seem more authoritative, but the writer insisted that she couldn't do that because the man had never achieved an agent's status. So late on deadline night, after the writer had gone home, Loeb called in her editor and brought up the subject again. When the editor also demurred, Loeb pulled out a dictionary, looked up the word "agent," and then used the dictionary meaning—a rather different thing, of course, from the specific IRS meaning of the word—as his justification for making the change. (Loeb's recollection is that he asked the profile subject if the magazine could call him an IRS agent, and the man replied, "That's fine.") Whatever Loeb's justification, however, it does not change the fact that the man *had never been an agent of the IRS*.

This led to another in-house criticism of *Money* magazine. Just as the magazine was willing to stretch a little to be able to call a former IRS employee an "agent," so did a number of writers and editors feel that they were sometimes making the same kind of stretches in looking for stories as well. "Marshall established a stringer network to find the average people who fit into our special reports on such and such," says Klein. "Sometimes we had to stretch like crazy." He adds, "It's probably an occupational hazard of that approach." Runde concurs: "You were always being pressed to come up with the *most* vivid, the *most* photographable . . . everybody [*Money* profiled] had to be pretty. They had to be the perfect couple. Writers had to stretch a little to justify [their inclusion]." He adds, "It happened all the time."

Loeb has always denied in the strongest terms that *Money* stories were anything less than completely sound. "We did good journalism," he insists. (In specifically denying that any "stretching" occurred, he adds: "I never, never knowingly told an untruth or covered up relevant facts or twisted facts to create or slant a story.") And to those writers who objected to the new upbeat tone of *Money*, Loeb retorted that they just didn't understand America—they hadn't been beating the bushes the way he had; they didn't realize that there was a new mood sweeping the country. "He told me," recalls Marlys Harris, "that I was out of touch with the reawakening of America. I was too sixties." The upbeat magazine he was publishing was, in his own mind, simply a reflection of this new mood—a reflection of the way Americans were optimistic about their financial prospects, with an optimistic President in the White House and a bull market under way. His in-house critics, he believed, were acting the way journalists always acted; they were going out of their way to look for the dirt, to confirm their pessimistic worldview. And perhaps there was some truth to that. But as Robert Klein would later note, "It's a sacred trust to tell people what to do with their money. It represents the capital of their years of work."

What was undeniable, however, was that Loeb's formula worked. In the two and a half years between the time he took over the magazine and the time the bull market began, circulation rose to over 1 million; in the two and a half years after that, it grew by half as much again. In that time, it went from being a money loser to a consistently profitable magazine, earning around $5 million in 1982 and double that amount two years later. (It earns around $30 million today.) Plainly, people were buying whatever it was Loeb was selling; perhaps his magazine was reflecting a new mood in the country. By 1984, one top Time, Inc., executive could be heard describing Marshall Loeb—the same Marshall Loeb few on the editorial side had taken seriously for much of his career—as "the most valuable property we've got around here."

FOR ALL THE CHANGES Marshall Loeb made after he took over *Money*, there was one tradition that he knew well enough to leave alone. Some years before he arrived, the magazine's staff had gotten into the habit of devoting each February issue to a discussion of taxes.[6] The reason Rukeyser had begun the February tax issue tradition—and Loeb had stuck with it—was obvious to anyone who saw *Money*'s newsstand figures: that issue was always the biggest seller of the year. And the reason the issue was the biggest seller each year was equally obvious: Americans cared about taxes.

That may seem like the most self-evident of statements, but it's worth stating explicitly because taxes, like everything else having to do with personal finance, changed dramatically once inflation arrived. Since the 1940s, the nation's tax structure had combined high corporate and capital gains taxes with a progressive income tax that included rates that ranged from between 14 and 20 percent for lower income taxpayers to between 70 and 91 percent for the wealthiest taxpayers. The tax code, however, was replete with loopholes, exemptions, and shelters of every kind, which effectively drove down income tax bills, especially for the wealthy. Like so many other aspects of American society, the structure of the tax code went essentially unchallenged by most Americans: "Death and taxes," as the old saying goes.

In the mid-1970s this consensus—or at least this uncritical acceptance—began to crack, as the combination of inflation and flat productivity had a profound effect on the way Americans thought about their taxes. By then, wage increases did not so much reflect a new prosperity—as they had in the 1950s and 1960s—as they reflected the ratcheting effect of inflation. Wage hikes, although not necessarily creating more earning power, often pushed the recipient into a higher tax bracket. "Bracket creep" this phenomenon was called; it was one of the more fear-inducing phrases in the language of inflation.

In 1976, Jimmy Carter heightened the focus on the tax code by making it one of the major themes of his campaign. During his acceptance speech at the Democratic National Convention, he promised to eliminate the loopholes for the wealthy and to make the tax code fairer to the middle class. Two years later, some of his reforms (though not many; Congress wound up wresting control of Carter's tax bill from him) were embodied in the one major tax bill he signed during his presidency. In 1981, Ronald Reagan, who had also put taxes at the center of his presidential campaign—stressing, in his case, tax cuts instead of tax reform—pushed through legislation that reduced the overall tax rate by 25 percent over three years. That bill also indexed tax rates to inflation, thereby eliminating the scourge of bracket creep.

In many respects, the ferment over taxes fit neatly into the money revolution schema. The degree and frequency of changes in the tax code were such that the middle class had to begin paying attention to the details in a way they hadn't before. Just as with other areas of personal finance, people felt a need to take control of their own taxes—to plan ahead of time, to figure which exemptions might work for them—rather than simply hand over their forms to H&R Block every year and hope for the best.

Secondly, the "democratization" of the tax code was very much of a piece with the other changes one could see on the financial horizon. A good deal of this democratization came about because financial innovators created products that gave the middle class access to something that had once belonged solely to the wealthy—in this case, tax breaks. Fidelity's first municipal bond fund, introduced in 1976, was a classic example of such a product; Fidelity, in fact, openly promoted its new tax-free bond fund as a middle-class equalizer. "Municipal bonds," its brochures boasted, "they're not just for the wealthy anymore."

But the democratization also came about because Congress willed into existence a whole host of new middle-class tax breaks—energy tax credits, deductions for two-income families, tax-deferred annuities and retirement accounts, and more. Reagan's 1981 bill was so replete with middle-class tax cuts and exemptions that *Money* magazine calculated that a couple earning $50,000 could cut their taxes in half with a little advance planning, from $6,520 to $3,193. Is it any wonder people were paying attention?

There is one further thing that needs to be said about the connection between taxes and the money revolution. Odd as this may sound at first, a strong argument can be made that one middle-class tax break in particular played a surprisingly large role in luring the middle class into the stock market. That same 1981 tax bill contained a provision allowing any working person in America to lower his taxable income by $2,000 simply by putting that amount in a special tax-deferred retirement account, known as an Individual Retirement Account, or IRA for short.[7] At the time, no one really anticipated much interplay between IRAs and the stock market; it was generally assumed that IRA money would wind up in bank and thrift accounts. And at first, that's what happened. But over time, IRA money began gravitating away from banks and toward brokerage firms and mutual fund companies, drawn in part by the bull market and in part by a marketing blitz that dwarfed anything that had come before. With IRAs, Congress wound up creating yet another battle line in the continuing war between banks and thrifts on the one hand, and nonbank institutions on the other, for the savings of the middle class. With IRAs, the nature of America's postinflation behavior became that much clearer.

In 1982, the first year the new IRA rules went into effect, around 10 million American households had at least some savings in money market funds. These households, and the 15 million or so customers they represented, had become the most active customers of the mutual fund companies and brokerage houses that operated money funds, overshadowing old line equity investors who had remained in the market during the dog days of the 1970s.[8] Those people who lived in these 10 million households tended to be younger than their equity fund counterparts; although a quarter of them were over the age of sixty, their median age was still a relatively youthful forty, according to a survey conducted by the Investment Company Institute that year. They were also resolutely middle class. Although 63 percent of them had incomes over $30,000, only 8 percent had incomes over $70,000. These young, demographically attractive money fund users represented pretty much the only new customers the fund and brokerage industries had attracted in a decade. They also represented the future.

There was a rub, however. These new customers were still not *investors*—or rather, they didn't think of themselves as investors. They still thought of themselves as savers. Moving their money from a bank account to a money market fund had not changed that self-image at all. About half the nation's money fund customers held no other investments, for example, while over 53 percent of money fund customers flatly told the ICI surveyers that their "investment purpose" was "general savings." Money market funds had thus brought not only a new customer into the tent, but a new kind of customer: a bank customer. The trick now was to keep these new customers in the tent, while whetting their interest in the growing array of financial products fund companies had begun to offer. The trick, in other words, was to transform these savers into investors. Over the next five years, right up until that awful day in October 1987, when the stock market crashed, that is what the mutual fund industry went about doing, with no small amount of success.

To be sure, this process was propelled by broad, historical forces, such as the fact that baby boomers were reaching a stage in life where they had some disposable income they could put aside for investments. A related fact was that this same group was just beginning to inherit money from their parents. (Marshall Loeb was convinced that inheritance had an enormous, if little talked about, effect on the fortunes of the baby boom generation.) The bull market obviously had a great deal to do with luring savings from money market funds into stock and bond funds. The continuing desire to get double-digit yields played a role, especially once interest rates began to drop in the late summer of 1982.

But in this list of cause and effect, one ought not to overlook the surprising and subtle consequences of the new IRA rules. Consider: a person opening up an IRA was putting aside a sum of up to $2,000 annually that absolutely could not be withdrawn, without stiff penalties, until he had reached the age of fifty-nine and a half. This did not mean that that money was frozen, however; under the rules, it could be "rolled over" from one company to another once a year. So long as it remained in an IRA account, there was no penalty. In addition, IRA money could be moved *within* one of these companies, from one financial vehicle to another, as often as a customer liked.

It's not quite right to say that IRA funds became a form of play money for the middle class. Setting aside enough for retirement was—and remains—a serious affair, especially given the inadequacy of Social Security and the shrinking of pension benefits all over the country. It is right to say that because the pool of capital that made up an IRA could not be withdrawn for twenty or thirty years, many people viewed their IRAs as containing money they could experiment with. They could use an IRA to buy their first stock or their first mutual fund. They could put it in a money market fund first, and then, as they got bolder—and the bull market became more irresistible—shift some of it into something a little riskier. (This pattern was a frequent one.) IRAs gave people a way to try on the stock and bond markets for size, to see how they felt, and to become slowly comfortable with the idea of investing. The knowledge that the money couldn't easily be withdrawn acted as a psychological safety net, allowing investors to feel as though they could take a chance or two. If they made a mistake, they reasoned, there was still time to recoup—several decades perhaps. Over time, many people came to believe that it was imperative to maximize the returns they were getting on their IRA account, even at the risk of taking a loss. How else would they ever have enough to retire on? This, surely, is the classic definition of investment capital.

And in the scheme of things, the 10 million households with money market funds represented merely the first wave of prospective IRA customers. Every employed person in the middle class was a potential customer. At the time the new IRA rules went into effect, there were 36.5 million households with incomes of $20,000 or more. "This figure," wrote the ICI research department in an enthusiastic missive to its members, "translates to around 50 million individuals who are potential IRA purchasers. The IRA potential," the trade group exhorted its members, "is tremendous." Robert Metz, a financial writer for *The New York Times,* estimated that potential at around $50 billion. He wasn't even close; by 1992, IRA accounts held $724 billion.

Mimi Lieber, a consultant to the financial services industry, conducted a number of studies on IRAs and became convinced that IRAs were truly the financial device that brought home the realization that the American middle class was going to have to take control of its own financial future. "It was the first real incentive for a great number of Americans to put money away for the long term," she says now. "And these were generally people who up until then hadn't seen themselves as having any control over the long term." It was a device that made people feel both empowered and burdened, her studies showed. As much even as inflation, it caused people to begin learning what they could do with their money.

Edward Furash, the banking consultant, adds that in his view, the popularity of the IRA—and the consequent shift of the middle class from savers to investors—brought other, less sanguine repercussions. One of these repercussions was something he called Silas Marnerism. "Silas Marner," Furash explains, "used to like to sit and play with his money, to feel it go through his fingers. So a generation grew up believing that the pleasure of investing, a kind of sexual pleasure, came from counting your money. And it equated investing with astuteness: if you're a smart investor, you're a smart person. If you're good at managing your money, you're a good human being."

*     *     *

All of this, however, was a bit down the road, for the middle class did not catch on to the new, improved IRAs right away. It would still be another few years before Americans viewed IRAs as "the people's nest eggs," as *Times* columnist William Safire once labeled them.[9] During the first "tax season" after the new IRA rules went into effect—essentially the first three and a half months of 1982—some 2.5 million new IRA accounts were opened, containing around $5 billion. Given the high expectations, these figures were underwhelming. Even more underwhelming was the share of that money that had found its way to mutual funds: it was just 10 percent.

In 1983, however, as the tax deadline approached, there was a sudden dash to open IRAs—"an unbelievable rush," a spokesman for Merrill Lynch called it; "an explosion," added his counterpart at Fidelity. What was even more impressive, much of that money was going into equities. The Merrill Lynch spokesman told *Business Week* in 1983 that "the percentage of our IRA customers opening equity accounts is double" what it had been the previous year; indeed, during the second week in April, it was opening 9,000 IRA accounts a day. At T. Rowe Price, a large mutual fund company, 70 percent of its incoming IRA money was going to equity funds, compared to 28 percent in 1982. Fidelity was opening up 10,000 IRA accounts a week as the 1983 tax deadline grew close, half in equity funds. One market seer went so far as to claim that so much IRA money was being used to buy stocks or stock funds that it would be enough to "postpone any serious correction in the market." Yet that "unbelievable rush" that took place in March and April of 1983 genuinely surprised the fund companies and brokerage houses. "We scrambled to keep up with it," recalls Jane Jamieson, a Fidelity marketer[10] who worked on IRA accounts. "We were amazed at what came in." They were amazed because they still hadn't done much to promote IRAs; they hadn't even thought much about the possibilities inherent in IRAs. "No one," adds Jamieson, "stood up and took notice." Of course, it wasn't long before the mutual fund industry did begin to take notice, and, of course, nowhere was this more apparent than at Fidelity.

This one time, the person at Fidelity who first saw the true importance of a new financial device was not Ned Johnson. It was instead a newly hired executive named Charles L. Jarvie, the first high-level marketing person Johnson had ever hired who came from outside the fund industry. Jarvie's bona fides included a short, unhappy stint as a top executive of Dr Pepper, as well as an earlier, happier stretch with Procter & Gamble. "I'm a mass marketer," Chuck Jarvie would declare proudly; in his time at P&G, he had marketed Tide, the laundry detergent, and Pringles, the potato chip. Like most people who got their first taste of marketing at P&G, he took the lessons he learned there to heart. He was a huge proponent of "brand" management. He believed in having a wide variety of consumer products so that every possible taste could be satisfied by one company. And he believed in a marketing principle known as "the theory of discontinuity." He explains:

> That's a theory that says the way you really make money, and establish a business, is not by doing what already exists, but changing it in some way that is so fundamental that consumers have to react to it. Disposable diapers versus cloth diapers, detergents versus soap, television versus radio—these are all discontinuities. In the financial world at that time, there were two discontinuities, one created by the government, and the other created by inflation. The discontinuity created by inflation caused people to question the way they were saving. The discontinuity created by the government, the IRA, gave them a different way to save. And the company that could marry these two together could change the structure of the American savings system.

Is it any wonder that Jarvie was such a forceful proponent of IRAs? To him, they offered a once-in-a-career opportunity to reshape an entire industry. "Did they tell you I used to pound the table about IRAs?" he says now. "Did they tell you that I used to shout and scream that they'd never get another opportunity like this?"

Actually, they did mention the table pounding. The people who worked for Jarvie remember such scenes because they stood in such marked contrast to the less expressive behavior that was the norm at Fidelity. Jarvie, a native Texan, was not like other Fidelity executives. He was a physically imposing man, who was blunt and aggressive and impatient and competitive. Although he claimed to admire Johnson greatly, his methods were completely different from Johnson's, which perhaps explains why his stay at Fidelity lasted little more than a year. He was not, as they say in corporate America, "a good fit," at Fidelity, and by 1984, he was gone. But his blunt and aggressive and impatient emphasis on IRAs made him exactly what Fidelity—and the mutual fund industry—needed at that particular moment.

Jarvie arrived at Fidelity in the early part of 1983, and there were two things that immediately popped out at the former P&G man—the sorts of things that would pop out at any former P&G marketer. The first was that Fidelity was not stressing the Fidelity "brand." The Magellan Fund was being advertised as "Magellan," rather than "Fidelity Magellan." The same was true of the other funds. Each fund was set up as its own little company, with a budget and support staff and so on. There was surprisingly little effort put into "cross-selling" one product to customers who were in another product. Jarvie wanted both Fidelity and its customers to think of the company as a place where they were buying not just one fund but an entire "family" of funds. To this end, he pushed Fidelity to begin making it easy for people to switch from one fund to another.[11] "We had to create a relationship with the consumer rather than create investment vehicles for the consumer," he says now. This is commonplace today, but it wasn't then. The "family of funds" idea had been a vague undercurrent at Fidelity in the early 1980s; Jarvie was among those who helped bring it to the surface, where Johnson quickly embraced it.

The second thing Jarvie noticed was that despite the success of the money market fund to reach a new kind of middle-class customer, Fidelity was still largely geared to that smaller group of inveterate investors who had been its core customers prior to the Age of Inflation. Ned Johnson's idea of a great new product was the "select" funds Fidelity brought out in the early 1980s. Select funds, also known as sector funds, are mutual funds that invest only in a single industry. Because they are not diversified, however, such funds are inherently more volatile than other kinds of mutual funds, and are supposed to be aimed at only the most sophisticated investors, people who feel confident of their ability to gauge industry trends (and can afford to lose if they're wrong). Jarvie had a different perspective. "I'm part of the great unwashed," he would say later. "When I went to Fidelity, I didn't know anything about trading on margin, or calls and puts, or those other terms investors are familiar with. What I used to say—and I wasn't the only one there saying it—was that the majority of money out there is from people who want to save it safely at a higher rate of return. The mass market was not investors. The guy in Peoria who makes $30,000 a year doesn't think about the market the way Ned's father thought about the market." Jarvie's idea of a great new product was an IRA. The IRA, Jarvie believes, allowed Fidelity to say, "We're a company that provides a savings vehicle with investment opportunities rather than the other way around." It was a big difference.

By the summer of 1983, Jarvie had begun pounding his desk in earnest. Once at a meeting, Jamieson reports, he held up a newspaper clipping about IRAs, and said, *"This is the most significant fact of your business!"* He had Jamieson hold meetings with various Fidelity divisions "to instill religion in the rest of the company," as she puts it now. He held company rallies, in which people were asked to stand up and say publicly what they would do to support the coming IRA campaign. He created company slogans, and had IRA-related sweatshirts made up for everyone to wear. He did all the things a consumer goods company is likely to do when it prepares to unveil a major new product. Fidelity, however, had never seen anything like it.

Neither had the country. For the second part of Jarvie's campaign consisted of taking the IRA message into America itself. As the 1984 tax season drew near, a small group of Fidelity marketers began traveling across America, spreading the good word. (Schwab and Merrill Lynch were doing likewise, though on a less ambitious scale.) It didn't matter whether it was Chicago, Illinois, or Scottsbluff, Nebraska; if a town had a radio station and a newspaper, a Fidelity representative would travel there to be interviewed. As for the word itself, the Fidelity message was, first, that IRAs were a middle-class tax break everyone should take advantage of, and second, that mutual funds were the best IRA vehicles around. The fact that Fidelity offered a wide variety of funds did not go unmentioned, of course, but it wasn't at the top of the list. People needed to be comfortable with the idea of mutual funds before they would be comfortable handing $2,000 over to Fidelity. Jarvie understood that.

For those who were already comfortable with the idea of investing, the sell was much harder. Fidelity sent direct mail packages to *Money* magazine subscribers pitching its IRA efforts. It began a stock fund, called Freedom Fund, that only accepted IRA money. It began a strenuous effort to persuade its own money market customers—"people who already thought enough of Fidelity to send a check in the mail," says a former member of the IRA team—to open an IRA with Fidelity, preferably in a stock fund. And it rolled out its big gun: Magellan. Nineteen eighty-three had been another fabulous year for Lynch, who had turned in a 39 percent gain in a year when the S&P 500 was up 22 percent. Lynch's performance was the third best of any equity fund manager that year, and that was also the year that Magellan became the fund with the best ten-year record—a wonderfully promotable fact. In pushing Magellan as the perfect IRA vehicle, Fidelity quite naturally pointed to Lynch's consistently high returns, which stood in rather stark contrast to money fund and bank IRA returns, which had dropped into the single digits. There was nothing subtle about the company's approach. "We went after FDIT customers, and people who had money in tax-free bond funds, which were returning 7 percent," recalls a former Fidelity marketer. "We told them, through direct mail, that we had this thing returning 39 percent. We told them we had the number one fund in America."

One could argue that the potential risks that came with that 39 percent gain were not exactly stressed by Fidelity. One could make the case that the Fidelity hard sell was only slightly less disingenuous than the sort of thing one was likely to find in *Money* magazine. One could not, however, argue with the results. People wanted yield, and that's what Magellan offered; consequently the money streamed in. By 1985 the firm held $3.2 billion in IRA accounts, up from $400 million in 1982.

Fidelity's IRA marketing efforts soon came to resemble an all-out assault, with the entire company gearing up for D-Day, which, in this context, was April 15. IRA advertisements blanketed the country in the months leading up to the tax deadline. IRA promotions proliferated. A typical IRA press packet had become a thick and glossy thing, with packets containing story suggestions such as "Mutual Funds Are IRA Investment Choice for Many," and "The IRA Countdown Is On." Potential customers received something called a "Fidelity IRA Fund Selector," in which they were given, in easy-to-understand form, essential information on eleven funds Fidelity was promoting as IRA possibilities, from very aggressive (Magellan) to very conservative (Cash Reserves). The company put out pamphlets, got its spokesmen on television, eagerly talked to any reporter looking for information on IRAs. It's not too much to say that the entire company had begun banging the table about IRAs.

In 1986, when Congress repealed some of the tax benefits attached to IRAs,[12] more than $82 billion had come into mutual funds alone via IRAs or other retirement accounts. Fifteen million new IRA mutual fund accounts had been opened. At least as much money had arrived at brokerage firms the same way. Perhaps most important, IRA customers tended to be younger than those who didn't have IRAs, with a median household income of $51,000. Three quarters of them were married, a third held graduate degrees, and, best of all, they had "a greater tendency to accept a moderate amount of risk when investing," according to another of those ICI surveys. Although the mutual fund and brokerage industries complained loudly when IRAs lost some of their tax benefits, they had much to be thankful for by then. IRAs had done their job.[13]

THE IRA EXPERIENCE should suggest one other large cultural change that was taking place at Fidelity during this time: for the first time since the 1960s, the company was talking to the press. And not just talking to it, but actively courting it. For anyone who remembered the old days, the transformation was startling.

Johnson, of course, had always instinctively ducked the spotlight, just as his father always had; in his Brahman heart, he thought it a tawdry thing to want one's name in the paper. He'd also continued his father's long-standing ban on talking to the press. "If you got quoted in the paper," recalls Michael Kassen, a young Fidelity fund manager in the early 1980s, "you got into a lot of trouble."[14] All such calls were referred to the firm's public relations man, who would answer straightforward queries on an off-the-record basis. Anything beyond that—a feature story on a fund manager, say—just wasn't countenanced.

But you couldn't begin operating in the mass market and still adhere to that stricture—not when your competitors all had articulate spokesmen willing to tout the advantages of their products and funds, and not in an environment where hot fund managers became minicelebrities. Publications such as *Barron's* and *Money*—not to mention *USA Today* and *Glamour*—needed more than off-the-record information. They needed pithy quotes from fund managers. They needed interview time. They needed background information that would humanize financial stories. These needs were voracious and never-ending, and if Fidelity was not willing to supply them, then its competitors would.

As obvious as this would seem to be on the face of it, Johnson still resisted. "[Publicity] was a subject of extended discussion within the company," recalls Jarvie. "Finally, Ned said we could go ahead so long as he didn't have to talk to reporters himself." Jarvie continues: "So we sat down with *Money* and *Forbes* and *USA Today,* and we talked about how we wanted to participate in the mass market, and how we would be more than willing to work with them. And we came out of it with—I wouldn't say a 'partnership,' that's too strong a word—but with a very strong relationship with *Money* magazine." Thus, in April 1983, when *Money* was putting together a mutual fund package, Fidelity was finally ready to allow one of its own fund managers to appear on the cover.

They still remember that cover story at Fidelity. They remember it because it turned out to be an important moment in the life of the company: it marked the first time since Tsai's departure that a fund manager had been instructed to cooperate with a magazine—cooperation that included not just talking to a *Money* writer but posing outdoors for five hours, on a cold day in February, posing with a squash racket. They remember it because its aftermath offered unequivocal proof that such cooperation made good business sense. And they remember it because, to the general surprise of most Fidelity hands, Marshall Loeb did not pick Peter Lynch to be his cover boy. He picked Michael Kassen.

He picked, that is, a thirty-year-old mutual fund manager who had been managing money for little more than a year, and whose fund, Select Technology, was one of those "select" funds. But Kassen was younger than Lynch, he had grown up in Cleveland (middle America!), and he had the kind of cherubic good looks that Loeb favored in his cover subjects. And he was unquestionably the hot fund manager of the moment. No industry group had done better since the start of the bull market than the technology sector, and no fund manager had benefited from that more than Kassen. In eight months, his fund was up a remarkable 131 percent; *Money* was always a sucker for gaudy, short-term numbers like that. And having chosen Kassen, *Money* ran the following headline to accompany the photograph of Kassen: "How to Invest in Mutual Funds. They're the Safest Surest Way to Invest in a Surging Market."

To be sure, the big mutual fund article inside had its share of cautions about the risks involved in mutual fund investing. But none of those cautions could be found in the profile of Kassen, who was probably the worst person imaginable to represent the "safe" and "sure" aspects of mutual funds. His fund was both highly speculative and enormously risky—by their very nature, "sector" funds, which only invested in a single industry, were filled with risk, and were aimed only at the most sophisticated investors.

You can almost guess what happened next. In April, when the issue hit the newsstands, Select Technology held $200 million, which was already a sizable sum for a select fund. Two months later, the fund was closing in on $650 million. Millions of dollars were pouring in every day, so much money that Kassen was having trouble investing it all. "It was like watching time-lapse photography of a flower," he recalls. "Surreal." Although he himself was embarrassed by the story, Fidelity was ecstatic. After that, there was never any question about whether the company should respond to press inquiries.

And then—*poof!*—his joyride was over. In August 1983, technology stocks crashed, and so did Kassen's fund. He was working furiously now, trying to keep his head above water, and by any objective measure, he succeeded brilliantly. In the second half of 1983, technology stocks were down 20 percent, yet Select Technology dropped only 10 percent. "I was actually prouder of my performance when the fund was going down than when it was going up," Kassen said later, and however chagrined he was about the *Money* magazine experience, he came away from it feeling as though he had learned something important. He had been given a humbling reminder that a fund manager didn't walk on water simply because a magazine said he did, and that even a good fund manager could not defy the market. "You can't become a fund manager because you want to become famous," he says now. "You have to know your benchmarks and take your satisfactions from them. I think," he adds, "that what happened to me served as a pretty good example to the young fund managers who came up behind me."

As for all those people who put money in Kassen's mutual fund after reading about it in *Money,* they learned a few things, too. They learned that the search for yield could be dangerous. They learned that some mutual funds were a good deal "safer" and "surer" than others. They learned that just because a fund had returned 131 percent in eight months didn't mean it would continue doing so. They learned that there was a great deal of difference between being a saver and being an investor. Unfortunately, none of these lessons had been learned from reading about the Select Technology fund in *Money* magazine. They had been learned with cold, hard cash.

# CHAPTER 15

# The Pleasure Palace in the Sky

## *May 1984*

O<small>NE OF THE</small> defining characteristics of the 1980s, perhaps *the* defining characteristic, was the willingness of American society to take on debt. This, at least, is the conventional wisdom as it's been handed down; it is what "the eighties" have come to mean. Just as the fifties would conjure up Joe McCarthy and the suburbs, and the sixties would bring to mind Vietnam, so would the phrase "the eighties" act as a kind of shorthand for living beyond our means. Debt is what turned "the eighties" into a term of opprobrium.

It is unarguably true that debt drove the decade; as is often the case, the conventional wisdom about the 1980s is irrefutable on the face of it. Virtually every person we now characterize as "a creature of the eighties"— Donald Trump, Ivan Boesky, Michael Milken, Henry Kravis, Boone Pickens, Robert Campeau, Carl Icahn, and a hundred others—was fundamentally a creature of debt. It was their embrace of debt that brought them fame and fortune, and for some of them, it was that same embrace that brought them crashing back to earth. Debt gave rise to the hostile takeover movement. Debt drove the leveraged buyout craze. In a way, debt even made Ronald Reagan possible; had he not been willing to add $1 trillion to the national debt, his presidential joyride would not have been nearly as smooth. Surely you recall that the 1980s was when the United States went from being the world's largest creditor nation to its largest debtor nation.

And it wasn't just them—the government and the business moguls. It was us, too. According to Alfred L. Malabre, Jr., a *Wall Street Journal* economics columnist who wrote an anti debt book entitled *Beyond Our Means,* of the more than $7 trillion worth of debt accumulated by American society by the mid-1980s, fully a quarter was owed by individuals. Half a decade later, the financial journalist James Grant could write: "If, in the early decades of the century, it was impossible for a working man or woman to secure a loan from a legitimate lender, in the 1980s he or she could hardly refuse one. The descendants of the clientele of loan sharks became the valued credit-card 'members' of leading banks. In the 1980s the home-equity loan proliferated, and personal bankruptcy lost its stigma.''

The statistical evidence did, indeed, seem to suggest that we had become addicted to debt—perhaps not as addicted as Donald Trump, but hooked nonetheless. The total consumer debt[1] that had been so worrisome during the Age of Inflation? It more than doubled, rising from just under $300 billion to just over $600 billion between 1980 and 1987. The amount of that debt that could be attributed to credit cards? It nearly tripled in the same time period. Home equity loans? A negligible factor as the 1980s began, they had become an enormous source of new debt by the middle of the decade, accounting for nearly $80 billion in new debt in 1986 alone. The percentage of household income devoted to making interest payments, which had stood at 2.5 percent in 1953, had risen to 8 percent by 1985. And the ratio of household installment debt to household disposable income—a crucial sta-tistic in figuring out how indebted Americans were—jumped from around 14 percent in 1983 to 25 percent just three years later.

The anecdotal evidence was, if anything, even more riveting. There were ''credit card junkies'' out there, and they weren't very hard to find. A team of academics who wrote a book about bankruptcy found dozens of them, people such as the Voelkers[2] of South Texas, whose assets amounted to no more than $3,000, who had ''no obvious tale of woe,'' yet who managed to rack up $15,000 worth of debt, $12,000 of which had been put on their credit cards. This was their second go-round with bankruptcy. A front-page story in the *Wall Street Journal* told the sad tale of the Wards of Connect-icut, a two-income family whose Christmas was practically out of Dickens, primarily because they had lost control of their credit card debt, which got as high as $35,000. ''It never crossed my mind that I'd have to pay it back,'' a chagrined Peter Ward told the *Journal*. The *Journal* itself had a credit card junkie in its midst; its front-page editor was forced to resign less than a year after joining the paper after running up enormous credit card debts. A cover story in *New York* magazine about ''the new debtors'' began this way:

> One young stockbroker woke up [one day] with three mortgages on two apartments totaling $300,000, another $200,000 in outstanding loans . . . and an annual income that had dropped to $60,000. A mother on a credit card binge started lying to her husband, claiming the new clothes she'd bought her children were actually old and he just didn't remember them. A waiter at Maxwell's Plum tried his hand at Wall Street and ended up in bankruptcy court.

Tales like these are becoming a regular coda to the go-go eighties, an era when Americans piled up debt at a record pace. . . .

To anyone with a feel for the history of consumer credit in this country, however, the furor sparked by these anecdotes and statistics, as alarming as they were, had an awfully familiar ring. It was remarkably similar to the outcry that had taken place nearly twenty years before, when banks were busy drowning America in a sea of unsolicited credit cards. James Grant's condemnation of increased consumer credit was not so different, except in tone, from Wright Patman's far cruder denunciations in the 1960s. Many of the stories written in the mid-1980s could have taken their cues straight from Betty Furness, who had been so fearful of what middle-class Americans would do once they came into possession of credit cards. And if one went back a bit further, to the 1950s, when installment credit had been the great worry, one could see obvious parallels between Galbraith's *The Affluent Society* and Malabre's mid-1980s work, *Beyond Our Means*. Both books attempted to raise the specter of a debt-ridden America; both sought to wake Americans up before it was too late; and both books failed miserably in this task. A mere book was never going to get Americans to stop using credit.

History, thus, begged the question: was the personal[3] debt being accumulated in the 1980s really all that unprecedented? Or was there less going on here than met the eye? The banking industry, not surprisingly, felt quite strongly that it was the latter, and was, as ever, embittered by the bad press consumer credit garnered. "The popular press jumped in," complained one industry publication, referring to that moment in 1986 when consumer debt ratios reached their high-water mark, "predicting overextension and widespread bankruptcies, and making the usual sanctimonious comparisons between American borrowers and European savers." Despite the obvious ax they were grinding, the bankers had a point. First of all, that 1986 debt-to-income ratio of 25 percent—the figure, more than any other, that prompted the outpouring of worry—turned out to be an aberration. The following year, that ratio began to decline, and it continued to do so into the 1990s. Secondly, there were at least a few statistics that seemed to suggest that a more sanguine view was called for. For instance: while household debt had grown as a percentage of income, it had declined as a percentage of household *assets*. It wasn't only the nation's credit card bankers who took comfort from this fact; so did the Federal Reserve: "[M]ore than 80 percent of the families that have consumer installment debt also have financial assets or home equity sufficient to permit liquidating their debt in emergencies," wrote the authors of a Fed study published in the fall of 1987. "This finding appears to hold for more than half of the families with high payments relative to their income.''

Third, the rise in personal bankruptcies, which were approaching 600,000 a year by 1986 and were a prominent feature of most stories about debt, turned out to be a particularly unreliable barometer of the supposed new recklessness. In 1978, the bankruptcy code had been rewritten by Congress to make it easier for individuals to file for bankruptcy. What's more, as that team of academics discovered as they pored over the files of bankruptcy courts around the country, there was no glib "eighties" explanation for why people sought bankruptcy. Yes, there were people whose indebtedness was due to their own "cavalier foolishness." But the files they inspected also held tales of "heartache, revenge, optimism, disappointment [and] unavoidable disaster."[4]

Most tellingly, it was simply not possible to read any of the hundreds of stories published in the 1980s about bankrupt Americans and completely agree with Grant's conclusion that "personal bankruptcy lost its stigma." On the contrary: it was rare to find bankrupt Americans in these stories who were willing to speak on the record—they were too humiliated. Granted anonymity, they usually admitted as much. The mother profiled in *New York* magazine—the one who lied to her husband about her spending—would later recall that she broke down and cried when finally confronted with her behavior. "There's a stigma, I know," sighed "Barbara," a single mother interviewed by the *St. Petersburg Times*. Almost everyone who talked about their bankruptcy said something along those lines.

In some ways, that was the oddest thing about the accumulation of debt in the 1980s: people may have been using credit cards more freely than ever before, but they didn't *feel* all that differently about it than they had twenty years before, when credit cards were relatively new. For many Americans, the act of taking that little piece of encoded plastic out of their wallets and handing it to a merchant could still evoke a swirl of conflicting emotions: eagerness and nervousness, excitement and fear, a deep ambivalence. Americans, said Mimi Lieber, who did some landmark research into the attitudes of Americans toward credit cards, still had a "love-hate relationship" with their credit cards, even in the free-spending 1980s. Credit cards were a status symbol. Credit cards were temptation incarnate. Credit cards could get you access to things that were otherwise out of reach. Credit cards could ruin your life. Credit cards could bring great joy. Credit cards could bring enormous misery. Of all the symbols of the American consumer society, credit cards had a hold on the subconscious that was matched—in a completely different way—only by the automobile.

Without question, credit cards had become deeply interwoven into

middle-class life by the 1980s. By 1984, 71 percent of all Americans between seventeen and sixty-five carried a credit card, and by 1986, the
average outstanding balance carried by a "revolver" was $1,472—up from
$649 in 1970. A quarter of all installment loan payments by then were credit
card payments. The banking industry, in sum, had accomplished what it had
set out to do some twenty-five years before: it had made credit cards indispensable. You couldn't rent a car without one. If you stayed in a hotel, ate
in a fancy restaurant, ordered something from a mail order catalog, or flew
in an airplane, the odds were that you used a credit card to pay for it.
Borrowing money was something people now did as a matter of course.
"Nowadays," concluded Lieber in a study she published in 1985, " 'Can
we afford this yet?' generally means 'Can we afford *to borrow* for this
yet?' "

Yet in that same study, Lieber also found that many people were sub-
consciously unhappy about this turn of events—and some were quite consciously unhappy. Americans, she wrote, had "many conflicting values
about being in debt, and what people do is not always in sync with what they
believe. There is often resistance to borrowing even by those who seem to
be borrowing most freely." Sometimes, she found, people deceived themselves about their borrowing habits; they preferred to think of their credit
card as a convenient payment device rather than a loan device—even when
they didn't pay their balances in full. Many people tended to view things that
were clearly luxuries, such as vacation homes, as necessities when they had
to borrow money to attain them. Quite often, people expressed enormous
resentment when banks kept dangling new "preapproved" card solicitations
or quietly doubled their credit limits. Americans really did understand how
easy it was to get hold of ten or fifteen cards, and get into serious trouble.
The banks, people complained, seemed to *want* them to get into trouble;
why else would they keep sending solicitations?[5] Most startling of all,
Lieber discovered that even in the mid-1980s, 55 percent of the people she
polled believed that it was "not OK to borrow." Around 60 percent of these
people who believed that had credit cards. Half of them borrowed regularly.

So why was there such a proliferation of borrowing when it was surrounded by so much ambivalence? Lieber had two explanations. The first
was that many Americans in the 1980s truly did feel optimistic about the
future. Borrowing has always tended to rise rapidly at such times, because
people feel more comfortable about their ability to repay their debts; this was
the same psychology that drove much of the borrowing in the 1950s.

Lieber's second reason was that the psychological detritus left over from
the Age of Inflation was driving Americans to borrow. Although inflation
was well under control by the mid-1980s, the habits that had been formed

during that earlier era were still prevalent. "Although inflation is more in check in 1985," Lieber wrote, "consumers continue to act as if the rapid conversion of income to possessions is the order of the day. No more pressing message has caught their attention and made them change the assumptions that now lead so many into accepting debt as a prudent way of handling finances."

*The rapid conversion of income to possessions.* During the Age of Inflation, this is what America had learned. What had become obvious in the postinflation age is how deeply this lesson had embedded itself in the country's psyche—and how impossible it was to erase.

AH, BUT TO BE A CREDIT CARD BANKER in the early and mid-1980s! Unlike so many of their customers, the bankers who toiled in the credit card vineyard were not burdened with feelings of guilt or ambivalence. They were deliriously happy. This was their moment in the sun. In the 1980s, credit cards were the most profitable activity in all of banking. No longer was the credit card division the banking equivalent of Butte, Montana—the place where J. Edgar Hoover used to exile out-of-favor FBI agents. Now, the credit card division was where the bank put its comers, most of whom had dreams of becoming the next John Reed. As for John Reed himself, he became the chairman of Citicorp, when Wriston retired in August 1984. By then, of course, Citi had long since overtaken BankAmerica as the largest bank in the country. That's where credit cards could take a smart banker in the 1980s; it could take him right to the top.

Everything had finally fallen into place. The drop in the exorbitant interest rates of the early 1980s drastically lowered the cost of money for the bankers, while the end to the recession spurred credit card use. The annual fee was firmly in place, and that made a big difference.[6] For big issuers like First Chicago and Chase Manhattan, who followed Citibank's example and set up subsidiaries in credit-card-friendly states, usury laws had been effectively neutered, allowing them to charge whatever interest rate the market would bear. Happily for the credit card bankers (though not for their customers) the market continued to bear 18 percent and higher. And all this was happening as the lessons of inflation were kicking in, which provided Americans with the mental justification for accumulating debt as a financial strategy. One might also add that the material desires of the baby boom generation were kicking in, too, its members having reached the stage of life when they were most likely to rely on credit to meet their needs and wants.

The profits banks made from credit cards were gigantic—there's no other way to describe them. There were times in the middle of the decade when Citibank's credit card operation earned back the entire half a billion dollars it had lost in the late 1970s—*every year*. Other banks could report similarly eye-popping earnings. By 1985, close to 8 million Americans held either a Citibank Visa or a MasterCard, and were using them to ring up close to $8 billion in charges. These numbers continued to grow, until by the early 1990s Citi had more than 30 million cards in circulation; by then one out of every five American households contained at least one Citibank cardholder, and the subsidiary was earning almost $1 billion a year.

And yet it was a different business from the one it used to be. As the credit card business matured, it changed in ways that could never have been imagined by the credit card pioneers. It had become a highly automated business, of course, but that was the least of it. A product that had been initially created as a way to bond a bank to its customers now had almost nothing to do with either local merchants or local depositors. The merchant business was now in the hands of a handful of specialized companies that existed solely to service merchant accounts. And studies showed that local depositors usually had credit card accounts with some faraway institution, like Chase Manhattan or First Chicago. Quite often credit card customers didn't even know which bank issued their card. All they knew—and all they cared about—was that it was a MasterCard or Visa card. That little piece of encoded plastic was now nothing more than a commodity.

It had also become a fundamentally impersonal business. Credit-worthiness was determined by complicated credit "scoring" formulas spewed out by computers. Giant credit rating agencies sprang up to service the institutions issuing credit cards, compiling computerized credit histories on tens of millions of Americans.[7] The search for new customers became a sophisticated game of demographics and ZIP codes. Just like other modern financial institutions, banks began hiring anonymous telephone operators to "interact" with their credit card customers; these people became known as "customer service representatives," and their performance was measured statistically: how quickly did they answer each call? How quickly did they end the call? How many customers did they "interact with" in an hour?

Finally, the losses that resulted from this impersonal method of granting consumer credit became part of the new numbers game. Such losses were a statistical inevitability, of course; indeed, the number crunchers in the back office could usually gauge in advance how high they would go in a particular season. Nobody in banking believed anymore that losses were avoidable— not when you were mailing solicitations to people on the other side of the country, some of whom would turn out to be credit junkies, others of whom would lose their jobs or face some financial catastrophe that credit cards could delay but not prevent. But no one in banking cared anymore; one thing that often surprised people filing for bankruptcy was how their bank seemed to greet their insolvency with a big yawn. For the banks, the business had become one of controlling losses rather than preventing them, keeping them within a certain statistically acceptable range. Anything under 3 percent—which in the case of Citibank in the mid-1980s, amounted to around 250,000 people a year—was considered acceptable. That's where things stood by the 1980s: the once-terrifying thought that 250,000 customers would be unable to pay back their debts had become No Big Deal.

Lamentable though this all seems on the face of it—lamentable in many ways though it was—it is important to remember that there was nothing especially atypical about the way the credit card business had evolved; it was very much of a piece with the evolving nature of America itself. Large swatches of American life had become more impersonal over the years, as anonymity and privacy gradually displaced community as a reigning American value. This was never more obvious than when money was involved; given a choice (for example) between friendly local merchants who had to charge higher prices, and an antiseptic chain store that could offer discounts, Americans chose the latter every time. By the 1980s, people who might once have shopped in local stores now bought their goods by mail order. Impersonal Wal-Marts replaced communal downtowns. Even door-to-door salesmen gave way to telephone cold calls—many of which were programmed so that the listener didn't even hear a human being; he heard a recorded message. There were hundreds of similar examples; what they suggested, ultimately, was that Americans liked the gradual impersonalization of their lives a good deal more than they let on And if credit cards had helped accelerate this trend (as they surely had), they were also part of it, swept along by the potency of this powerful change. No matter how one felt about credit cards or the bankers who issued them, they did not operate outside the generally accepted parameters of American life. No successful business ever does.

Of all the credit card executives who had reason to be pleased with how successful a business it had become, none had more reason than Dee Hock. The organization he had devised in the dark days of 1970 had performed, to a remarkable degree, exactly the way he had said it would. It had been singularly responsible for making credit cards both a financial success and a commodity that most Americans felt compelled to carry. Along the way, Visa had overtaken MasterCard as the more widely used credit card; by the mid-1980s Visa had cards in the hands of 53 percent of the public compared to 46 percent for MasterCard. And Visa had penetrated not just the United States but most of the globe; its ability to act as a form of international currency was among Hock's proudest accomplishments: "No other business or political entity," he once boasted in a speech, "has approached [this feat], not even the United Nations." Bank cards had become the dominant form of credit card, and were poised to take on their last genuine nemesis, American Express, something they would do with increasing success through the 1980s and into the 1990s.

For these efforts, Hock had reaped his share of rewards. By the early 1980s, he was reportedly paid a salary package worth around $800,000 a year. And he was rewarded as well with the knowledge that he remained the single most compelling figure in his universe;[8] Spencer Nilson, the newsletter publisher, regularly placed Hock at or near the top in his occasional compilations of the most important figures in the credit card industry. Above all, even though banks could now issue the cards of both credit card organizations, and even though the two systems had become virtually indistinguishable in the eyes of the public, Visa still remained the superior organization to those in the know.

Except in one respect. The bankers who sat on the MasterCard board could say without hesitation that theirs was an organization that did the bidding of its member banks—who, after all, were the owners of the system. The bankers who sat on the Visa board never had the same feeling; they were too busy feuding with their employee, Dee Hock. Which is perhaps why, despite everything he had done, these were not the best of times for Hock. In many ways, they were the worst of times.

The crux of the matter was that the bankers considered Hock's work essentially finished, while Hock believed that he was just getting warmed up. They wanted him to run the "switch,"compile useful data, help stamp out credit card fraud, and handle marketing and advertising for Visa. These were all things Visa did more or less as a matter of course; it was the bread and butter of the place. Hock, on the other hand, wanted Visa to go head-to-head with American Express in the traveler's check business. He wanted to ensure that Visa would be the beating heart of electronic banking.[9] He wanted to create a Visa debit card program that was every bit as successful as the Visa credit card. Hock had a dozen ideas like that, all of which he firmly believed would be beneficial to banking, and which he strove relentlessly to turn into reality. His membership, however, became uneasy with Hock's big ambitions for Visa, and by the 1980s, they had come to believe, in the main, that Hock was trying to dominate banking, and even control it. He was acting more like a competitor than a facilitator, they believed. By 1983, a writer for *Fortune* magazine could quote Hock quoting Emerson—

"To be great is to be misunderstood"—and then quip, "The fifty-four-year-old Hock must be very great indeed, for he has been involved in an awful lot of misunderstandings."

There were two misunderstandings that stood out from all the others. The first occurred in 1979, when Hock managed to persuade J. C. Penney Company to accept Visa. Landing Penney was a tremendous coup, for it was the first nationwide retail chain to accept the Visa card, and once it did so, the resistance of most other national retailers quickly evaporated. (Sears remained the lone holdout, and didn't begin accepting bank cards until 1993.) Yet despite the obvious significance of this breakthrough, many Visa members were infuriated when the details of the deal became known. First, they complained, Hock had not informed anyone on the board about the negotiations,[10] but had instead sprung it on the board at the very end of a two-day board meeting. Although the board approved the deal after a protracted debate, it felt sucker-punched. More importantly, the Penney's deal had been shaped in such a way that the retailer would be interacting directly with Visa and not with a member bank. This, most emphatically, was not the way it was supposed to work. Lining up merchants—even huge national merchants—was what banks were supposed to do, and the merchant discount was what bankers were supposed to reap as their reward. As word of the Visa–Penney arrangement got out, there was an outcry from the member banks, who viewed it as an unwarranted incursion onto their turf. Board members, taken aback by the fury of the member banks, and chagrined at the way they had allowed Hock to corner them, quickly approved a new Visa bylaw specifically forbidding Visa from ever again negotiating directly with a prospective merchant.[11] (The Penney arrangement was allowed to stand, however.) The furor over J. C. Penney was the first time the growing divisions between Hock and the Visa membership had burst into the open, and the wounds created by that first big feud never fully healed.

The second major rift came a few years later. It centered on an issue that both Hock and his membership viewed as among the most important that bankers faced as the 1980s dawned—an issue with the potential to shape the future of banking, and to further the prospects of a viable, alternative "payment system." Naturally, that made it an issue about which Hock and most of the nation's bankers had firmly held, passionately felt, and diametrically opposed positions. The issue was debit cards.

Debit cards and credit cards are different members of the same species. They look nearly identical, of course, and they share an ability to trigger the back office electronics that make it possible to transact banking business without stepping into a bank. But there are important differences. Whereas a credit card gives a user access to an unsecured loan, a debit card gives a user access to his *deposits*—that is, to money he already has in the bank rather than money he is borrowing from the bank. One way to use a debit card is to insert it into an automatic teller machine, which electronically connects a cardholder to his checking and savings accounts. When he withdraws some of that money, even when the ATM he is using is located on the other side of the country, the funds are instantly deducted from his balance. A second way to use a debit card is as a payment device at a checkout counter.[12] Indeed, to the merchant, a debit card and a credit card work almost exactly the same way; the main difference is that most debit cards require a PIN (PIN stands for "personal identification number") to work, which in turn requires the installation of an additional piece of equipment so that the cardholder can punch in his number. To the user of the card, the key difference is that after he's bought something with a debit card, he never has to pay off the debt at the end of the month since no debt has been created. The card has burrowed its way electronically into the customer's bank account, and withdrawn the money needed to make the purchase.

It's not hard to understand the appeal of debit cards to Hock. A successful Visa debit card would bring him that much closer to his goal of having Visa develop into America's preeminent payment system. He believed, in particular, that those consumers who used credit cards primarily for reasons of convenience (as opposed to those who used it primarily as a borrowing device) would be drawn to a debit card. He also believed that a debit card, far more than a credit card, could be marketed as an alternative to checks at places like grocery stores. Because checks were used far more frequently by Americans than credit cards, they were, to Hock's way of thinking, every bit as much the enemy as American Express.

Finally, Hock saw debit cards as the first step toward his climactic idea, which *Business Week* once accurately labeled the "all-in-one card." If Hock had his way, Americans would one day carry a single card that acted as an "access device"[13]—a card that gave customers a means to get at not just their deposits, but all their financial assets. The choice of which asset to use—"a credit asset, a deposit asset, an investment asset, a mortgage equity asset, cash value of life insurance, or any other asset," as Hock once described it in a speech—would be "the customer's prerogative." Hock was convinced that this all-encompassing device would be so valuable that customers would willingly pay upward of $200 in annual fees for it—rather than the $15 or $20 they now so grumpily paid for credit cards. A card such as this one had the potential to place banking at the center of the financial lives of Americans again, the way it had been before all those other institutions began crashing through the walls of banking. It would forcefully bind a customer to his bank—though it was also true that that bank no longer had to be the one across the street; it could just as easily be one across the country.

The only problem with Dee Hock's big idea was that the rest of the world stubbornly refused to go along. Forget about the all-in-one card; Hock couldn't even sell the world on the simple debit card. Throughout the 1970s, customers were oblivious to the alleged advantages of debit cards, preferring to stick with those old standbys, checks and credit cards.[14] Merchants resisted the technology necessary to allow debit card transactions at the point of sale. But the fiercest resistance came from Visa's own member banks. Hock launched Visa's first debit card in the mid-1970s; some five years later, only 130 banks marketed them. It wasn't so much that bankers were against the idea of debit cards. But they were violently opposed to the idea of a *Visa* debit card. They wanted debit cards that they controlled, not Dee Hock. And they wanted Visa and Hock as far away from their customers' deposits as possible. "As long as he kept to credit cards, banks were willing to give him leeway," explains Ken Larkin:

> The moment you get into the debit card, you're talking about more than $1 trillion [residing in the nation's savings and checking accounts]. You're hitting bankers where they live. They weren't going to let anybody, *especially* Dee Hock, tell them how to manage their deposit stream.

Debit cards thus evolved in their own peculiar way, quite apart from Dee Hock's grand designs. Hock's dream of using debit cards in stores faded somewhat, despite periodic attempts to revive it. The interest just wasn't there, at least not then.[15] Instead, most debit card activity in America centered around ATM use, which grew rapidly in the late 1970s and early 1980s, and became as much a staple of American financial life as the credit card itself. In the beginning, most ATM systems were proprietary, meaning that customers could use their cards only in the very small handful of machines operated by their own bank. This, of course, put severe limits on their usefulness, and led in time to the emergence of a wide variety of ATM networks, which linked machines in different parts of the country to a centralized switch. Just as it had once taken years for a national credit card system to evolve—years of chaos and losses and wrong turns—so did it now take years for a clearcut nationwide ATM system to evolve—years that were, in their own way, chaotic and costly and full of wrong turns. The difference, however, was that in the 1980s, as the ATM systems were sorting themselves out, the networks and the technology that the nation's bankers were so frantically putting together was already in place. It existed at Visa. And *still* the nation's bankers refused to run their debit card business through Visa computers. That's how opposed they were to Dee Hock's vision.

The leader of the opposition was a man named D. Dale Browning, who was himself an important, if little-known, figure in the money revolution. A high-ranking official with the Denver-based Colorado National Bank, Browning had run the bank's credit card division since 1968.[16] He was one of the pioneers, having earned his stripes the same way so many of his colleagues had, by extricating his bank from its disastrous initial foray into credit cards and transforming it into a successful business. Like Hock, Browning had also been interested in debit cards very early on, and ultimately, that's where he made his mark. Colorado National was one of the few Visa banks that even tried to market Hock's first debit card. Later, it became the first bank in the state to install ATMs, and it was also among the first in the country to create a small ATM network, which started in Colorado and gradually extended into fifteen neighboring states. Browning's network was called the Plus System, and it was one of around 100 regional and local networks that had sprung up.

Obviously, Browning and Hock went way back. In the old days, they had been, if not friends exactly, certainly allies; Browning had been deeply involved in the movement by the BankAmericard licensees to break away from Bank of America. "Hock was exactly the right person in the right place," says Browning today. Hock once asked Browning to come work for him at Visa, an offer Browning turned down. "I knew it would be hard to work for Dee," he says.

Gradually, the relationship deteriorated, for there was no banker in the Visa system whose views diverged more sharply from Hock's.[17] By the early 1980s, credit cards had become tremendously important to Colorado National; although it only had $3.5 billion in assets, it had $1 billion in credit card loans outstanding. It ran a large processing center that handled card transactions for many smaller banks. Almost half of its employees worked in the credit card division. Given this importance, Browning was hardly likely to stand by and allow Dee Hock to dictate to the member banks, even if the two men had been in general agreement. But he and Hock rarely saw eye to eye on anything. "Dale always took the position that if Dee did it, it was wrong," sighs Frederick Hammer, a former Chase Manhattan executive and Visa board member. "Dee was just so arrogant and dogmatic," says Browning now. "That was his great flaw. He just didn't seem to know how to cope in an environment of consensus." One might also point out that Browning could be every bit as stubborn as Hock when he thought he was right. But he was, most certainly, able to "cope in an environment of consensus" without much difficulty. In their coming battles, this would be to Browning's great advantage: he was an easy man to deal with, and Hock was not.

Sometime in the fall of 1981, Hock discovered that Colorado National had instigated serious discussions with other banks about establishing America's first nationwide ATM network, which would be an extension of the regional Plus System that Browning had already set up. This was a move that had the potential to do for ATMs what the creation of NBI had done for credit cards—to make them not just useful but very nearly indispensable. And in a way, Hock should have been flattered. Browning's model for his new organization was transparently Visa, from its centralized switch mechanism to its joint ownership by the member banks to its lofty operating principles.[18] But of course Hock was not flattered. He was enraged. He considered Browning's talks an act of treachery, particularly since Visa had seen one debit card product after another languish—cards that were technological marvels, but which no one used because banks wouldn't market them and stores wouldn't adapt to them. Not long before he found out about Browning's plans, Hock had made yet another effort to get Visa into debit cards, announcing a hugely ambitious plan for a Visa ATM network that would span the globe. For Hock's plan to work, however, he needed to link Visa's computers to the thousands of ATMs owned by member banks. That was also something Visa had the technological wherewithal to pull off, but it could only happen if the nation's most important credit card banks got behind the effort, and the most influential credit card bankers actively supported it. Instead, as Hock saw it, one such banker had decided to stab the new effort in the back.

In November 1981, Hock and Visa's general counsel, Bennett Katz, flew out to Denver, where they confronted Browning and his boss, Bruce Rockwell, who was also Colorado National's representative on the Visa board. It was an angry, unpleasant session. Hock accused Browning (as Browning recalls it) of "trying to compromise the Visa ATM program, and creating divisiveness among the Visa members. I said, 'Dee, we're going to do this. You've left me no choice.' " And from Browning's perspective, that was the absolute truth. Visa's plans called for every ATM owned by a bank that was a Visa member to take any and all Visa debit cards—even if the issuing bank was across the street rather than across the country. For Hock, this was an unbreakable rule: no Visa member could exclude another Visa member's card. The entire system, he believed, stood on that principle of "universality."

To bankers like Browning, however, it was completely unacceptable that an ATM machine owned and operated by Colorado National Bank would have to accept ATM cards issued by its Denver competitors simply because they were Visa banks. Browning was happy to have a California bank connected to his network, but he was damned if he was going to let a local bank in. All over the country, bankers felt the same way: competitive advantage was more important that universality.[19] Since Browning's plan called for the member banks to be able to exclude local competitors from the Plus System, most bankers found Browning's proposed network far more appealing than Hock's.

Hock was still angry when he got back to California. He phoned several bankers who were going in with Browning, trying to persuade them to pull out. When that failed, he called in one of his executives and told the man he was being placed in charge of the Visa ATM program. "I want you to have 3,000 ATMs on line in ninety days," Hock commanded. The executive spent two days making a few discreet inquiries to banks where he had friends, and soon discovered the humiliating truth. Even though the Visa board had authorized the Visa ATM network, and even though a number of bankers had made commitments to accept the Visa card, none of them really had any serious plans about linking up with Visa. *Not one.* Dale Browning had won.

"I think the Plus System is a pimple on the ass of progress," one Visa executive says, echoing the sentiment of many of his colleagues. And maybe it is. Maybe if the bankers had followed Hock's vision, debit cards would have led to the next great leap in the money revolution, instead of performing the rather mundane function of allowing people to withdraw cash from a hole in a machine, which is still what they are primarily used for today, at least in America.[20] But the bankers were tired of vision. And they were tired of Hock.

Clearly, his time was drawing to a close. In 1980, Hock told a reporter that he hadn't expected to last three years as the head of Visa—he had always assumed that the battles would be so draining that his first three-year contract would never be renewed. As it turns out, his analysis was not wrong; only his timing was. By the early 1980s, when the battles finally did become draining, he had been the head of Visa for more than a decade. In that time, he had done some remarkable things, but the psychic toll it took to get them done—not just on him, but on everyone around him—got heavier with each passing year. In late 1979, in an attempt to relieve the toll,

Hock took a short leave of absence, time he spent puttering in his garden and rereading his favorite books. For most Visa bankers, it was as if a great hovering storm cloud had suddenly been lifted, and the sun was allowed to shine through. For the first time in years, it was easy to deal with Visa. And then Hock returned, and everything immediately reverted to the way it had been before.

Hock had changed since the early days; everyone could see it. By the early 1980s, one didn't hear much about how charismatic Dee Hock could be, or how inspiring. He was more like a coach who'd been delivering the same half-time speech for too many years. He grew secretive and mistrustful, especially toward the board members who disagreed with him. He seemed obsessed with preventing press leaks while also becoming hypersensitive about press criticism. The annual fight over Hock's salary had turned into a battle at least as contentious and bitter as the fights over ATM networks. Even at this late date, Hock still had close to two dozen people reporting to him, still ran meetings that lasted for hours, still went over the tiniest details—ever in search, it seemed to his staff, of mistakes he could pounce on.

In the minds of both Visa board members and his own staff, the thing that came to crystallize the kind of leader Hock had become was, of all things, office space. More precisely, it was a floor of a new skyscraper in downtown San Francisco, where Hock and his top dozen executives moved in 1983, establishing a new headquarters for Visa, even though the vast majority of the staff remained twenty miles down the road in San Mateo.[21] In retrospect, it was an odd item for the board to fixate on, since, as a genuine "issue," it paled in comparison to such controversies as ATM networks. Yet it loomed so large that years later, Visa board members who had long since forgotten the particulars of the big, important battles could recall with great precision every detail of the 44th floor of 101 California Street: Dee Hock's floor.

One-oh-one California was a sleek, postmodern skyscraper in the heart of the San Francisco financial district. Because Visa was among the first tenants to sign on, Hock was given much leeway to plan the space Visa would occupy. This he did with the same attention to detail that had always characterized him. He was involved in picking out the chairs used in the reception areas. He was involved in deciding where to put the wall plugs. He picked out every painting that hung from the walls. And since board meetings would have to have food brought in, he was even involved in picking out the place settings.

And when he was done, Hock had designed the single most exquisite office space anyone connected to Visa had ever seen. "The pleasure palace in the sky," one former Visa hand describes it. "A goddamn Taj Mahal," says another. It had the plushest rugs, the most elegant marble, the most tasteful wood paneling. It had a sauna and a steam room. The boardroom came equipped with state-of-the-art translation booths. And then there was Hock's own corner office, which was the pièce de résistance of the 44th floor. To get to it, one stepped down into a magnificently carpeted alcove, where one encountered walls lined with stunning, set-in bookshelves, on which sat beautifully bound copies of Hock's favorite books. Objets d'art were scattered about. "It was like stepping into a museum," recalls a Visa executive. Across from the bookshelves were windows that offered a sweeping panorama of San Francisco. Set off to the side was Hock's private dining room.

"I'll never forget our first meeting there," says Colorado National's Bruce Rockwell. "We all looked around in amazement." But it wasn't the kind of amazement that comes of having experienced something wonderful; it was the kind that comes of wondering if someone has just taken leave of his senses. As the shock wore off, there came the realization that Dee Hock, *who was their employee*, had planned and executed and paid for this move without ever informing the members of the Visa board. (*Just like the J. C. Penney deal.*) From that starting point, it was only a matter of time before the board began to see Hock's move to 101 California as the perfect metaphor for everything they had come to dislike about him. It was, as they saw it, the office of an empire builder. It was the office of an autocrat. It was the office of someone who ran roughshod over his membership. The small-town bankers who had always been Hock's staunchest allies were especially offended by the office, for it reminded them how much more money he made than anyone at their bank.[22] (*And all he did was run a switch.*) And when it turned out that at the same time Hock was moving into 101 California, he was also buying up some small companies working on debit card technology, while planning one last push to make debit transactions viable in stores (*at a cost of $170 million*), well, at that point, it was pretty much over.

With hindsight, one can spot an occasional clue that Hock sensed his time at Visa was coming to an end. Perhaps the strongest such clue was a speech he made to the American Bankers Association convention in September 1983, just three months after moving into 101 California—a speech so powerful and so passionate that Spencer Nilson devoted an entire issue of his newsletter to reprinting it. It's hard to read that speech now and not see it as a valedictory, but it's a peculiar valedictory, filled with barely disguised bitterness, the final public summation of a martyr about to walk to his death.

"Regarding speculation about the grandiose, mysterious Visa plan to monopolize payment systems," Hock said as his speech reached its crescendo,

> most of it arises from Visa's preoccupation with the management of change which requires a clear sense of direction without regard to a precise plan. It . . . has often caused us to launch products or put forth ideas ahead of their time. When events then validate our perception, many choose not to attribute it to such ordinary things as hard work, common sense or blind chance, but to more titillating things such as grand plans, ulterior motives, and ingenious schemes. It is so flattering to be attributed with great ingenuity and skill that I hesitate to disabuse you of it. It isn't all bad. Unfortunately, there are no trolls under the bridge, the sky is not falling, and no one is huffing and puffing to blow your house down. Visa is just a group of ordinary people extraordinarily committed to banking, who enjoy a unique vantage point from which to assess the future and attempt to persuade you to their version of it, and who, just like you, are struggling to understand and cope with radical change.

The following January, Hock announced his retirement. "I am under contract to write a book," he said in a prepared statement. "I have an interest in teaching and government. I have a ranch to run. I will resume painting. . . . Directors, for some time, have been aware of my desire to pursue other interests well before age 60. . . ." The clear implication was that the resignation was instigated by Hock, and that it was motivated by his desire to do something different with his life. But several directors remember the events precipitating Hock's announcement rather differently.

According to them, consensus on the Visa board had completely broken down, and Hock had lost his ability to control the board members, as his support continued to dwindle. During board meetings, Bruce Rockwell from Colorado National would display his contempt for Hock by reading the newspaper while the Visa president was speaking; when Hock had finished, Rockwell would pipe up, "Well now, let's get back to reality." Then, during a big Visa meeting held in Greece, an argument broke out between Hock and the board—an argument that grew so heated that Hock threatened to resign if the board refused to support him. In the past, whenever Hock had used this tactic, his backers on the board had always rallied around him, and urged him to stay. This time, the chairman of the Visa Board accepted Hock's resignation. "I understand," the board chairman said.

The next day Hock reversed his decision to resign. "At that point," recalls one former board member, "it was only a matter of time." A few months later, as a committee of Visa board members met to "redefine the Visa mission"—a euphemism for clipping Hock's wings—Hock walked in and said, "Let's face it, I don't have any support." And with those words, he quit. "Dee finally overran his supply line," says the same former board member.

In that same prepared statement, Hock claimed he would be staying on for another eighteen months before handing Visa over to an as-yet-unnamed successor. Not surprisingly, it didn't work out that way. So in May 1984, four months after Hock's first announcement, there came a second announcement from Visa: Charles Russell, Hock's longtime No. 2, would be taking over, effective immediately. Within days, Hock was gone. There were no grand going-away parties, no gold watches, no last-minute bonus payments in appreciation for all he had done. At the age of fifty-four, he walked away from Visa, turning his back on the business he had once dominated, and retired to the ranch he owned in a small California coastal town. Even those who had worked closest with him saw Hock only a handful of times over the intervening decade, and years later, when former Visa bankers and employees took time to remember the old days, they often asked the same question: "Whatever happened to Dee Hock?"

AT AROUND THE SAME TIME Dee Hock was exiting the credit card industry, Parker Pen was exiting the financial services business, none the worse for wear. Though it was ostensibly getting out in order to concentrate on its main pen business, it could not legitimately claim to have ever been very distracted by its investment in Andrew Kahr's First Deposit Corporation. The investment itself, around $4 million, was fairly insignificant for a company of Parker Pen's size, and though it had no profits to show for its involvement with Kahr, it had no serious losses, either, largely because Kahr had not rolled out a single new financial product in the time he had been affiliated with Parker Pen. For three years, he'd been fiddling with ideas—"flexible premium deferred annuities," "home equity access accounts," "a composite deposit product" (whatever *that* was),[23] and a dozen others. But for one reason or another, the products never got off the ground; either the tests Kahr conducted were not sufficiently encouraging,[24] or Kahr became disenchanted with his idea. For a man who made no secret of his desire for the big score, Kahr seemed strangely reluctant to take the first shot.

All of that was about to change, however. By early 1984, Parker Pen had found a potential buyer for its stake in First Deposit: an aggressive but obscure insurance company called Capital Holdings, based in Louisville, Kentucky. The company was very much a financial innovator: this was the firm, for instance, that had set up the joint venture with Kroger to establish "financial centers" at Kroger supermarkets. Not surprisingly, Capital Holdings was much taken with the idea of having the likes of Andrew Kahr in the fold—so taken that it was prepared to lay out $10 million for the 80 percent of First Deposit owned by Parker Pen. Before completing any deal, however, Capital Holdings wanted to be satisfied that Kahr was prepared to focus on one thing: it wanted him to devise a product that First Deposit could bring to market, and that would make them all a lot of money, *now*. Unfortunately, the one product Kahr absolutely knew he could bring to market quickly—and where his probability of success was extremely high—was the product he was most resistant to creating. It was a credit card.

After all, he had already trod the credit card path once, for the Associates, creating in the process something both smashingly successful and innovative. The idea of generating profits at First Deposit without doing something equally pathbreaking, was, well, *"embarrassing,"* as a former First Deposit employee would later recall. Whatever Kahr did next had to be at least as great, if not greater, than anything he had done before; it had to be the capstone of his career.

"He wants to create the perfect product," Thomas Simons, the late CEO[25] of Capital Holdings, once complained to Kahr's partner, Adolph Mueller, "and I've never seen a perfect product." Mueller, as it happens, could not have agreed more: for two years, he had been trying to persuade Kahr to stop fooling around, put out a credit card that would make them all rich, and be done with it. So frustrated had he become by Kahr's refusal that he planned to ask Capital Holdings to buy out his own 10 percent stake in First Deposit. He'd had enough.

Simons's fears about Kahr kept him from completing the purchase of First Deposit. The two men would have meetings in which Kahr would present Simons with a half-dozen ideas, spewing out his rapidfire explanations of how they would work, and why they would set the financial world on its ear. And Simons would respond with the only question that interested him: Which of these products could Kahr deliver first, and when could he deliver it?

Finally, after a frustrating, all-day session that took place just before the deal was supposed to be completed, Mueller took Simons aside. "I know you're worried about Andrew," Mueller remembers saying, "but you don't need to worry about him. He will do the job. He has got to make this work, and he knows it. His credibility is on the line. He also wants to make money—and he *will* make money." Simons called back the next day to say that the only way he would go through with the deal was if Mueller agreed to stay with First Deposit, so that he would have an ally on the premises as he stepped up his efforts to get Kahr to bring a product out quickly. When Mueller assented, the deal was struck. The transaction was completed in March 1984.

Not that Simons needed an ally. He was by all accounts a persuasive man—"not a brilliant guy, but a guy who has faith in people," says Mueller. He was also unrelenting: "He just wouldn't let up," adds Mueller. "He'd have drinks with you, and he'd be friendly, *but he just wouldn't let up.*" Not long after the buyout, Kahr and Mueller had dinner with Simons, during which Kahr presented the Capital Holdings CEO with a list of three potential products. One was a credit card. Simons bore in. "Why can't you come out with this?" he demanded to know. "You've already done it."

"Well," Mueller remembers Kahr replying, "it's been done."

"Dammit," said Simons, dropping his friendly demeanor, "tell me when this product is coming out!"

Kahr was trapped. He had put the credit card on his business plan, and he couldn't erase it now. "I'll tell you exactly when it's going to come out," he said angrily. "It'll come out 120 days after our first successful test."

Now it was Simons turn to be angry. "If I operated on that premise, I would never have been more than a dogcatcher," he said. "You will never come out with a product because you are scared to death of standing on your own."

Here, in his frustration, Simons had stumbled onto the means of persuading Andrew Kahr to do what he wanted. You couldn't cajole Kahr or even argue with him; you had to throw down a gauntlet. When Kahr got home after dinner, he spent the entire night devising a new business plan, which he presented to Simons at breakfast early the next morning. Kahr's manner was brazenly derogatory; he kept telling Simons that he was interfering with Kahr's business, and coercing him to do something he didn't want to do— and shouldn't have to do under the terms of his contract. "But if this is what you want, this is what you're going to get," he said. "Here's the credit card plan, and it'll be out in six months."

"Well, Andrew," said Simons, breaking into a smile, "I think you're overreacting a little, but I'll buy this."

"And that," concludes Mueller, "is how we got in the credit card business."


Like so many of his insights, the central idea behind Kahr's credit card product had come to him very early. One of his first consulting jobs after moving to San Francisco in the early 1970s was with Wells Fargo bank, where he spent some time in the credit card department. The department was in the usual state of early 1970s chaos, and when Kahr was first assigned to work there, he reacted with open contempt: "Credit cards," he sneered, "are just a new way banks have found to see if they can lose more money."

Yet he found that his time in the credit card department "illuminated the beacon for me." In fact, Kahr came away with several distinct illuminations. The first had to do with the running of a credit card back office. In Kahr's pitiless view, Wells Fargo's back office employees spent far too much of their time spinning their wheels—"wasting their time, getting lousy results, being arbitrary, giving a poor account of themselves" is Kahr's memorable (though probably overly strong) description of their activities. He quickly came to the view that he—and they—could get far better results if the work in the back office was rigorously systemized, so that virtually everything employees did in the course of a workday was executed according to a fixed set of strict criteria. Imposing such unflinching rigor on the structure of the back office, Kahr believed, would cause people "to work hard and produce more," yet would be "more satisfying" to the employees involved, even though they had far less freedom than they'd had previously. It would also give Wells Fargo a set of measurable standards, which was something that most credit card operations still lacked in the early 1970s. What criteria do you use to decide when to close an account that's delinquent? How far over their credit limit should you let people charge? How often did you telephone a customer in arrears, and what exactly should you say when you got him on the phone? Kahr, in fact, was particularly interested in systemizing the collections end of the business, which he felt was very haphazardly managed.[26] These questions, and a hundred just like them, could be answered, after close study and experimentation, in such a way as to maximize results. To some small degree, Kahr was able to impose a few of his ideas at Wells Fargo, and came away thinking that if he ever got the chance to do it on a larger scale, it might well give him the kind of competitive advantage he was always looking for.

His second revelation was that *everything* about credit cards, not just the structure of the back office, meshed remarkably well with Kahr's mathematical cast of mind. The credit card business is surprisingly compatible with the kind of complicated mathematical modeling that came so naturally to Kahr. It was a business, he would later note, where one could do demonstrably better "by using data, by testing, by gaining insights that could lead to successful levels of improvements." He adds, "When I saw that credit cards were amenable to very systematic, rigorous, reiterative thinking, I felt like I had come home."

Finally, he recalls, choosing his words carefully, "I saw that there were things that could be done to better build a profitable customer [base]." By this, he is referring to the most basic fact of all about the credit card business: profits are derived from customers who use the card to go into debt, rather from those who pay their balances in full. It was during his stint at Wells Fargo that Kahr first began to realize that if one could get hold of the right data, and analyze it properly, one could predict the kind of person most likely to become a "profitable customer." Or, rather, Andrew Kahr could predict it.

Building this kind of customer base was a key part of Kahr's work with the Associates, and his ability to predict behavior, on the basis of incomprehensible streams of numbers, was the reason close to 90 percent of the finance company's first credit card customers were "revolvers." Indeed, during his time with the Associates, Kahr became so annoyed at those who paid off their balances each month that he wanted to cut them off, by refusing to renew their cards when they expired. This was one Kahr idea that was met with an unequivocal rejection. You just couldn't do that, the executives told him. And they were right; it would have been a public relations disaster.

Yet from his Wells Fargo days onward, this was Kahr's ideal: to create a customer base where every single customer was "profitable." And that meant finding the person "who gets in debt, stays in debt, and always pays [the minimum balance] on time," says John Decker, a former First Deposit hand, choosing his words with a good deal less care than Kahr himself. Decker continues, "The way you make a credit card profitable is very simple. You get people to borrow a lot of money. That is the most important thing. Secondly, you identify people who are likely not to become delinquent. And thirdly, you make it easy for them to get into debt." At both the Associates and First Deposit, this concept was at the core of Andrew Kahr's credit products.

The truth of Decker's blunt comment, it has to be said, is indisputable. But it's an ugly truth, which is why it is virtually never spoken aloud among bankers, and why even Kahr shies away from phrasing it as straightforwardly as Decker. Credit card bankers don't want to see themselves as people whose essential goal is to entice customers to pile on debt—even though, as the years progressed and the business grew increasingly cutthroat, that's frequently what they became. This ugly truth is the reason the credit card industry has so often felt itself on the defensive, why it has been the object of continual criticism from consumer advocates and credit counselors and congressmen over the years, why even Americans who can afford to pay their credit card bills each month can resent the banks that make the cards available to them. It harkens back to our centuries-old Puritanical feelings about debt, our feeling, as a society, that those who dangle the lure of debt in front of us—notwithstanding our own eagerness to take on that debt—are doing something wrong. Not illegal, but wrong.

Even in modern, debt-embracing America, this cultural baggage serves a useful purpose: it acts as a brake on the credit card industry, a prick of conscience that at least slows down the search for new ways to get people to take on credit card debt. Andrew Kahr was—and is—a brilliant man, but his was a mathematical brilliance, cold and ruthlessly logical. He was neither a philosopher nor a moralist; to him, if something was not illegal, it was, therefore, possible. "I never went to work feeling that I was there to improve the world," he says. "I'm in business to make money, not only stay out of jail but off the front page and so on." He adds: "I [think] that if you're in business doing something consistently and you make money over a period of years, it implies fairly strongly that you're producing [something of] value. . . . I never tire of saying that it's the guy who goes broke who's socially destructive." Unencumbered by the societal baggage that held others back, Kahr was only too happy to take credit cards to their logical conclusion—which he did brilliantly. The same mind that brought us the CMA and the nonbank bank now brought us a credit card that dangled the lure of debt more nakedly than anyone ever had before.

There were a number of ways Kahr created his "profitable" customer base at First Deposit. He eliminated the annual fee on his "First Select" Visa card (as it was called), which gave it appeal among a segment of the population, while also rebating 1 percent of the price of every purchase, which furthered that appeal. He eliminated the grace period, while adding a number of penalty fees—for missing a payment deadline, for instance. He imposed a higher interest rate than just about anyone else in the country. The First Select card carried an interest rate that approached 22 percent when banks were charging 18 or 19 percent, for Kahr knew that "the most profitable customers are not very price sensitive." What they were sensitive to, Kahr also knew, was the minimum they had to pay each month, so while First Deposit was charging 22 percent interest, it was dropping the minimum payment to the lowest of any institution in the country. Requiring only the tiniest sliver of principal repayment, the First Select card more closely resembled the repayment structure of a home mortgage than a traditional credit card. Finally—and this was a classic Kahr twist, which he had first used at the Associates—in order to accept the card, one also had to accept a check from First Deposit that ranged from $1,000 to $3,000. This check served as a cash advance, and in its direct mail packages, First Deposit promoted the check as a way to pay off other credit card debt. The ostensible appeal to the consumer was that, although his total debt load would not go down (in fact, it would go up), the monthly minimum payment would be much lower than it had been—half as much in many cases. Of course the appeal for First Deposit was more clear-cut: the minute a cardholder cashed the check, he began paying interest. If the cardholder refused the check, he didn't get the credit card. That was one of the ways Kahr ensured that First Deposit's customers were "profitable."

Here was the other way: from his Wells Fargo experience, Kahr knew that there was a particular group of Americans who combined the two behavioral traits he was looking for: a willingness to use a credit card to build up debt, and a fierce unwillingness to default on that debt. Kahr himself will not divulge who these people are, but from the veiled comments of others, one can make a calculated guess. They are most likely middle class, though not upper middle class. They're strivers, perhaps the first generation in their family to break into the white collar work force. They live on the right side of the tracks, though perhaps a little closer to the tracks than they might like. They're young enough to harbor no fear of debt, though their station in life does cause them to fear for their credit rating, which is why they go to great lengths to avoid becoming delinquent. One source describes them as "the lower end of the yuppies, making good money, but spending ahead of their income, [yet] with a predictable ability to increase their income." For his part, Kahr will only concede that "we were never aiming at the affluent market." This same source adds that at most banks, the people who fit this description make up around 10 percent of the credit card portfolio. From a banker's perspective, however, they're the 10 percent who made money for the bank.

Yet even after Kahr knew, in a broad sense, who these people were, how did he track them down, sitting in his small office in San Francisco? This is also a *verboten* subject; Kahr's technique for targeting the profitable 10 percent was, and remains, First Deposit's trade secret. Suffice it to say that it brought to bear all his considerable skill at analyzing data in innovative ways—data about demographics, about spending preferences, about dozens of different traits and tendencies. He was using, he says now, "all the instruments of analysis, using the most fervent and intense application of the available techniques to deal with the complicated issue of behavior." He would get lists of names from credit agencies based on one set of data,[27] set those names into a complex matrix, match them against other lists based on other data, and the names that emerged from this lengthy sifting process would be the ones to get solicitations for the First Select card. Then he would track their credit card behavior, always refining his criteria, so that the next time he sifted through the American middle class, his success ratio would be higher. "We would generate thousands and thousands of pages of data that Andrew would analyze," recalls Mueller. It was all very mysterious, even to most First Deposit employees. Within the company, they used to call the process, with some amusement, Kahr's "black box." But it was no joke. By the time Kahr was done, four years later, his little black box had come up with 350,000 active customers, and First Deposit itself had about $1 billion in credit card receivables. Say what you will about First Deposit's credit card product, but you cannot deny its success. By the end of the 1980s, little First Deposit was the sixth most profitable credit card operation in America.

Most triumphant entrepreneurs look back on the start-up phase of their business with great fondness; Andrew Kahr looks back on First Deposit's start-up phase with something akin to horror. "I always hated the credit card business," Kahr once said, but the more likely truth is that he would have hated any business he was charged with running. Running things was never what he was cut out to do. He hated being responsible for everything and everybody. He hated having to write progress reports and job descriptions. He hated knowing that people were going to make mistakes in the middle of the night when he wasn't around—First Deposit had twenty-four-hour customer service lines almost from the start—which he would then have to fix the next day. He hated the feeling, he recalls, of being "constantly the victim of whoever rings on the phone or whoever walks up to your desk, and furthermore there [are] these forms to be filled out and work to be done that can never be completed." And he hated working as hard as he did at First Deposit. "I think," he says dryly, "that when all is said and done, being a consultant and not working too hard has a lot of advantages over facing all the odds."

The First Deposit "headquarters" was a small second floor office above a jewelry shop in the San Francisco financial district. Coming to work every day, where who-knows-what new disaster awaited him, he felt less like an owner than a glorified manager. Once there was a health scare, when some two thirds of his employees got sick because of some unknown condition in the building. Kahr had to decide whether to have the office evacuated (which he did), and though no one became seriously ill, the experience, which most managers would have long forgotten, has stuck with him. "It was all up to me," he says now, unhappily. "People in Louisville weren't going to make any decisions, and none of my subordinates were going to lift a finger. That certainly is one of the experiences in my life that I would have most wanted to avoid. Basically I felt that people's health might depend on a trade-off I might have to make." Kahr did not find such decisions challenging. He found them torturous.

But he never walked away, much as he might have wanted to. He stuck with First Deposit. And he did so, in all likelihood, because he had no choice, just as Mueller had suggested to Simons. His reputation *was* at stake. This *was* his best shot at making the kind of money he'd always wanted to make. And so he threw himself into it—spending hundreds of hours poring over data, refining the "black box," perfecting the direct mail pitch, while also doing all the unpleasant things that came with being the boss. He made it work, and the people who knew him—and knew how miserable he was—admired his willingness to stay with it.

For someone not connected to the company, though, no matter how much one admired Kahr's gifts, it would always be difficult to get past the fact that his success rested on his willingness to create this . . . *thing,* this credit card that seemed so blatantly manipulative, and so coldly immune to the societal forces that kept most banks from openly trying to drown people in debt. "A lot of people say Andrew has no compassion or ethics," Mueller once said, as he launched into a defense of his former partner. But that's not true. "A lot of people" said no such things about Kahr personally, because few people knew who he was. But they did say such things about his company. Although the details are murky, First Deposit seems to have been involved in several disputes with regulators, who didn't like one aspect or another of the First Select card. Other bankers frowned on First Deposit, believing Kahr had crossed a line that shouldn't have been crossed. A number of customers complained bitterly about the First Select card—once they realized how it really worked. At least one lawsuit was filed against the company, which was settled quietly, before it could create any adverse publicity.

The loudest critics, however, were the credit card consumer groups, which found First Deposit's direct mail packages appalling. The most prominent such group, the Bankcard Holders of America, held a press conference in November 1986, to draw attention to what it described as "misleading and deceptive advertising tactics [designed] to lure in credit card customers." It flagged five examples of such behavior (including one offer from Bank of America), but its lead example was the First Select Visa solicitation, which, it charged, "is one of the most misleading advertisements in circulation." First Deposit, the group continued, "disguised" its high interest rate in the fine print of its brochure, along with the fact that a potential customer had no choice but to accept a check in order to get the card. The First Deposit solicitation stressed that "you can save on monthly payments," but ignored the effect this had on the customer's pocketbook—namely, that he was ultimately going to pay more, not less. "If a cardholder paid off only the minimum required each month," Bankcard Holders of America reported, "a $1,000 outstanding balance would take a First Select cardholder *forty-four* years to pay off. . . .'' When the cardholder had finally erased the debt, the advocacy group added, he would have wound up paying a total of $4,950 in interest.

The sad thing is, it was all true. In all likelihood, Kahr had written that solicitation. Even if he hadn't, it surely would have been written according to his instructions, and with his approval. And though there was nothing illegal about the come-ons in the First Select offer, there soon would be. Reportedly, the First Select offer helped prod Congress into strengthening Proxmire's old Truth in Lending Act, in order to force First Deposit and others to be more straightforward about the terms of their credit card offerings. The new law passed in 1988.

But that was no longer a concern of Andrew Kahr's. He was on his way out the door by then. In March 1988, after four years of running First Deposit, with the business running smoothly and a hand-picked successor in place, Kahr retired as CEO. By early 1989, he had sold his stock in First Deposit to Capital Holdings, for a price he won't divulge but was probably around $25 million, based on what other credit card portfolios were being sold for. For the next several years, he turned away all offers of consulting work that came his way, preferring to spend his time in the south of France, where he bought a house and lived half the time. He enjoyed spending time with his family, and tutoring his daughters at home. At the age of forty-seven, this brilliant man, whose fingerprints were all over the money revolution, had finally reached the place he'd been trying to get to all his life. He was rich. He was free.

## CHAPTER 16

# The Bull's Last Stampede

## *January 1987*

W ELL, MAYBE THE one-stop financial supermarket wasn't such a hot idea after all. Maybe socks and stocks weren't quite as "synergistic" as its proponents had so blithely assumed. Maybe multinational corporations like General Electric, foreign banks like Credit Suisse, and powerful travel and entertainment companies like American Express weren't cut out to operate investment banks like Kidder Peabody, First Boston, and Shearson Lehman Brothers[1] (respectively), whose cultures and mores were so alien to their own. And maybe young, hungry, entrepreneurial discount brokerages like Charles Schwab & Co. didn't fit all that easily within the confines of giant banks like BankAmerica, even if the law did permit such couplings. Maybe, in fact, they didn't fit at all.

In the immediate aftermath of the Schwab–BankAmerica deal, there occurred what one might call the period of euphoric delusion, that marvelous time when the wonderful plans both sides have been dreaming up all these months finally seem within reach. It did not last long. Upon closer inspection, those wonderful plans too often turned out to make very little business sense, and the Schwab side, especially, found itself in the awkward position of having to shoot down numerous schemes proposed by the bank's executives. To those who had pushed for the buyout, it was like watching the air leak out of a tire.

Euphoria was thus followed by disillusionment. This period lasted much longer—about two years, all told—and was marked by continued public insistence from both Schwab and Armacost that the merger was going along swimmingly, when each man knew privately that it wasn't going well at all. The supposed synergies between the bank and the discounter turned out to be practically nonexistent; the only attempt at cross-selling that actually worked was a direct mail solicitation for a Bank of America Gold card that was mailed to Schwab's upscale customers.

In addition, the gulf between Schwab's culture and the bank's was too wide to be easily bridged. Schwab by then had grown to the point where it had about ninety branches and over 1,500 employees, but it was still dwarfed by BankAmerica. Schwab had a loose (to say the least) management structure; BankAmerica had layers of middle managers, and a chain of command so rigid it was practically calcified. Schwab officials had lucrative bonus arrangements based on the firm's future profits; the vast majority of Bank-America officials earned flat salaries. Schwab executives drove Porches and Jaguars; BankAmerica executives drove four-door sedans. Ultimately, Schwab ran an entrepreneurial company and Armacost a bureaucratic one, and practices one saw as standard operating procedure, the other saw as insanity.

Finally, Schwab's and Armacost's disillusionment extended not only to their new partnership, but to each other. Now that they were joined at the hip, the few things they had in common receded into insignificance. Now their differences came more powerfully into focus, causing them to view each other skeptically at first, then disdainfully, and, by the end, with something close to contempt. "Chuck would go to Sam," recalls someone who was there, "and ask, 'How much does it cost you to get a customer?' And Sam would say, 'Gosh, I don't know, Chuck. We've got a lot of different businesses; I can't quote you a single number.' " Schwab would come away from such discussions shaking his head in disbelief: "How can you run a business if you don't know how much it costs to get a new customer?" he would complain to his aides. Armacost would come away from the same discussions believing that Schwab did not have an inkling of what it took to run a highly complex organism like BankAmerica. "Sam saw Chuck as being brash, naive, almost juvenile," this same source recalls. "Chuck saw Sam as being arrogant, incapable of taking advice, and unwilling to do the things he needed to do to turn the bank around."

And then came the moment two and a half years after the buyout, when BankAmerica was finally forced to publicly admit that it was in serious trouble. In July 1985, the bank announced a second quarter loss of $338 million. It was not only the first quarterly loss in BankAmerica's history, it was the second largest quarterly loss in United States banking history. Worse, it came just a month and a half after Armacost had predicted that the bank would break even in the second quarter. That second quarter loss had many ramifications, but among the most significant was that the Schwab–BankAmerica relationship entered its final phase. With that disclosure, the period of guerrilla warfare began.

\*     \*     \*

It turns out that Schwab gained everything it was going to gain from the buyout on the day the papers were signed. It wasn't the bank's immense capital Schwab needed by then; it was credibility. There had been a tendency previously to associate discount brokers with penny stock operators and boiler-room scam artists, but when Schwab became a subsidiary of BankAmerica, that all changed. The bank's imprimatur instantly cloaked Schwab—and the entire discount industry—in a blanket of respectability.

It also turns out that even after the purchase of Schwab, the two companies continued to go in opposite directions. If anything, the divergence between their prospective fortunes accelerated. Schwab, as ever, was growing rapidly, but this time, it was able to tap into its own revenue stream to add new branches, hire new staff, move into a new and bigger headquarters, and so on. Better yet, this growth could not be attributed solely to the arrival of the bull market, for it was during this period—roughly, 1982 to 1985—that Chuck Schwab proved, beyond all doubt, that he was powerfully in touch with the needs and desires of the new middle-class investor. It was also during this period that he took the first steps to move the firm beyond its narrow discount niche, turning it into something that would appeal to a broader audience. Schwab's instincts told him that the firm's real future lay with these new investors, and of course he was right.

One could see this new emphasis in the firm's promotion of its money market fund—hardly the sort of financial vehicle aimed at hard-core stock traders. One could see it in Schwab's willingness to offer brokered certificates of deposit, or in its IRA advertisements, which were almost as heavy-handed as Fidelity's. Schwab's answer to the Merrill Lynch CMA, the Schwab One Account, was far more oriented to smaller investors; it required a minimum of $5,000 (compared to $20,000 for the CMA), and it charged no annual fee. Chuck Schwab himself was a big fan of no-load mutual funds; aside from his BankAmerica stock, his portfolio consisted primarily of no-load funds. This interest led him in 1984 to one of his best ideas: the establishment of a Schwab "mutual fund marketplace," where customers could invest in a variety of no-load funds simply by calling Schwab. In effect, Schwab created his own "family of funds," using other companies' funds. By the end of 1985, Schwab was approaching 1.2 million customers, compared to some 375,000 just prior to the buyout, and its revenues had more than tripled, going from around $67 million to more than $200 million. Most significant of all, 1985 was the first year Schwab could report profits that were remotely in line with its income. It made $20 million that year.

And what was BankAmerica doing during this same time? "It was consuming itself," to borrow Rich Arnold's nicely turned phrase. The Armacost era was a very odd time at the bank; in hindsight, it was almost otherworldly. Serious problems—with bad loans, quality control, antiquated computers, and a California public no longer enamored of the bank—had become apparent even before Armacost assumed the CEO's post. Yet Armacost seemed aggressively oblivious to all of it. *Problems?* Armacost seemed to dismiss them with a wave of his hand. *Quality control?* Armacost was so unconcerned that he wouldn't even name a chief operating officer to oversee the bank's day-to-day affairs. *Loans?* As free a lender as Clausen had been, Armacost made him look like Scrooge. There began during his tenure what the writer Gary Hector would later describe as "a reckless, uncontrolled surge of lending." That this was the same kind of mindless lending that would later damage such major East Coast banks as, well, as Citicorp doesn't make BankAmerica's mistakes any less forgivable. Its problems foreshadowed the crisis that overtook banking in the early 1990s, a crisis that the bankers very much brought on themselves. Armacost just beat them all to it.

When people told Armacost that he had a disaster in the making, he practically pressed his hands against his ears, so anxious was he to avoid hearing bad news. The subject caused him to grow cold and stony and hard, and he often ended the conversation abruptly. Schwab was one person who continued to press Armacost to face the bank's problems; it was one of the key reasons their relationship soured. But Armacost wouldn't even listen to the federal bank examiners, who by 1984, had begun to question seriously whether the bank was out of control. The examiners wrote several blistering reports in 1984 and 1985, which Armacost bitterly disputed, even trying to get them watered down. When that didn't work, he told his board of directors that the bank was being unfairly singled out by overzealous regulators, who were trying to make up for their failure to sniff out an earlier crisis at Chicago's Continental Illinois. BankAmerica's new leader was in denial. There's no other way to describe it.

It was in that summer of 1985, when the bank's problems burst out into the open, that the widening breach between Schwab and Armacost became a chasm. That May, Schwab went to see Armacost, and implored him to be upfront about the bank's problems, and to begin doing something about them. According to Gary Hector, Schwab came away from that meeting "aghast." It was there that Schwab learned that Armacost would be announcing a "probable" earnings drop in the second quarter. "Schwab fumed," Hector continues, "pushing Armacost to issue a clear statement of how bad things were going to be, to make it plain that the company was going to show no profit in the second quarter.'' Of course at that point, even Schwab had no idea how bad things were going to turn out to be.

A few days later, after Armacost issued an announcement that the second quarter would be break-even at best, Schwab took his first drastic action: he began dumping his BankAmerica stock. In thirteen days in June, he sold off about a third of his shares,[2] at an average price that was some three dollars below the price at the time of the buyout. Because of Schwab's position on the board, this sale was duly reported to the SEC, which meant the news wound up in the newspapers. The sale of that much stock sent an unmistakable signal: BankAmerica's largest shareholder had lost faith in the bank.

Then came July, and the news that the second quarter loss was $338 million; Schwab took his second drastic action. Wanting to know (as Hector would later put it) ''whether Armacost had covered up the company's loan problems,'' Schwab hired the accounting firm of Deloitte Haskins & Sells to conduct what amounted to an audit of the bank's publicly available numbers going back to the early 1980s. In its report to Schwab, Deloitte showed how BankAmerica officials had, in effect, manipulated its loan loss reserve in order to report higher profits than circumstances warranted. Indeed, the Deloitte report strongly implied that this had been going on since before BankAmerica had completed its purchase of Schwab & Co.

In August, when the BankAmerica board met for the first time since the announcement of the loss, Schwab took his third drastic action. After the meeting began, he passed around copies of the Deloitte study, arguing as he did that contrary to Armacost's assertions, the bank was understating its potential loan losses, and that a full-fledged audit was needed. He got nowhere; none of the other board members would even second the motion. He then urged the board to take a step that was, if anything, more radical: he wanted it to eliminate the dividend paid to stockholders. This was the holy of holies at BankAmerica, and Schwab knew it. But he felt that the bank needed to use the money it was paying out to shareholders (himself included; Schwab received $1 million a year in BankAmerica dividends) to turn itself around. This time his motion was voted on, and though the board decided to trim the dividend a bit, he essentially lost again. Finally, he said openly the things he had been telling Armacost privately. ''The bank must trim employment,'' Schwab argued,[3] ''trim expenses by such means as selling the corporate jet . . . cut executive pay, rescind the recent directors' fees increase [and] reassess the loan management system.'' For the third time, the board declined to take Schwab's advice. But there could be no doubt where Schwab stood. He had become a dissident board member. To Armacost, he had become the enemy.

And still Schwab wasn't done. Having been rebuffed by the full board, Schwab flew to Washington, where he met quietly with several of the outside board members,[4] again pressing his concerns. One more time, he was rebuffed. As winter approached, he took his next drastic action. He went to Armacost, and said that he wanted to buy back his company from the bank. Armacost's reply was brief. Charles Schwab & Co., he told Charles Schwab, was not for sale.

It was over for Schwab. He was done trying to reason with Armacost; that was hopeless. And any remaining thoughts he had about pitching in to help the bank right itself, those were also gone by the end of 1985. The buyout, Schwab now believed, had been a terrible mistake, no matter how wealthy it had made him, or how much credibility it had given his industry. And he wanted out. To that end, Schwab visited at least one investment bank, searching for ideas on how to extricate his company from the bank, an action that infuriated Armacost when he found out about it. Schwab continued to sell off his BankAmerica stock, even as it continued to drop in price. He dallied with at least one of the corporate sharks[5] who were circling the wounded bank, hoping to take it over. That such a takeover would mean the departure of Armacost did not appear to bother Schwab in the least. And while Schwab continued to attend BankAmerica board meetings, his heart wasn't in it anymore. His heart was back at Schwab, which was doing splendidly. Then again, that was the same reason Armacost was unwilling to let go of it. The Schwab purchase was about the only thing that had gone right for him since he had become CEO.

In July 1986, the bank announced a second quarter loss that was even more staggering than the previous year's: $640 million.[6] Yet at its August meeting, instead of tackling the growing crisis, the board of directors spent most of its time putting in place multimillion-dollar golden parachutes for the executives in the event of a takeover. A few days later, Schwab took the most drastic step of all: he resigned from the board. The stock dropped to $13 a share. Although he refused to comment on the move, the message could not have been clearer. Later, when Schwab finally felt he could speak candidly, he told the writer Moira Johnston that "it was a great, liberating thing to be free from the bank's problems." Adds Johnston, "He felt the exhilaration soldiers feel when a decisive campaign is about to begin."

The "campaign," of course, was to get his company back. Although this was something Armacost had vowed would never happen on his watch,

Armacost's watch was nearing its conclusion. Less than two months after Schwab left the board, the bank's directors finally gave up on Armacost and ousted him. In his place, they installed—implausibly, it seemed at the time—Tom Clausen. Clausen, who had done so much to create the bank's problems, was being brought back to fix them. Even more implausibly, Clausen succeeded in this task—though he did so largely by importing executives from rival banks such as Wells Fargo. One such man, Richard Rosenberg, eventually succeeded Clausen as CEO.

Among the first things Clausen did upon resuming his old post was to let the word out that the bank's discount brokerage unit was up for sale. But this was not quite the good news Schwab had hoped for. Clausen planned to *auction* it. If Schwab wanted to retake his firm, he would have to stand in line with everyone else. Schwab found out about the planned auction when he received a phone call from a junior investment banker at Salomon Brothers saying that he'd be arriving the next day to begin gathering the financial information needed to sell off the firm. Word quickly leaked out that the bank hoped to get between $300 million and $400 million from the sale.

Schwab had no intention of paying $300 million for the company; the figure he had in mind was more in the range of $190 million. He also had no intention of allowing Schwab to be put on the block. How could he be sure it would end up in friendly hands? Clausen received around fifty calls expressing interest in Schwab, one of which came from Leslie C. Quick, the founder of Quick & Reilly, the nation's second-largest discounter, who was Schwab's fiercest rival and most vocal critic.[7] The thought of Les Quick buying his company was more than Schwab could bear.

What is a bit surprising, in retrospect, is the realization that someone in Schwab's position—an ex-board member who had sold almost all of his stock, and was merely the head of a profitable, soon-to-be-sold subsidiary—thought he could have a say in its eventual disposition. The bigger surprise is that even without his stock and his board seat, Schwab still had some cards he could play. They were unpleasant cards to be sure; they could only make a nasty situation nastier. But Schwab didn't much care about niceties. If this was his hand, he'd play it.

His first card was his contract with BankAmerica. It would soon expire, and there was nothing in it to prevent him from walking across the street and starting a rival firm. In addition, if Schwab left, he had every right to take his name with him. Astonishingly, the bank had allowed Schwab to retain control of the name "Charles Schwab & Co." Thus, any potential buyer had to know that if it bought the firm, it faced the prospect of getting neither Schwab himself nor the use of his name on the front door. This was not the sort of information that was likely to spur a spirited auction.

These facts were relayed, via various back channels, to Clausen, along with the news of Schwab's trump card. If Clausen insisted on auctioning off the firm, Schwab let it be known that he would sue the bank to have the original buyout undone. His grounds would be that BankAmerica had misled him back in 1982, when it had hidden its growing problems behind a facade of nice-sounding, but overstated, profit statements. Besides killing any potential sale, such a move would create a legal nightmare for the bank, as angry shareholders followed Schwab with suits of their own. To act on such a threat would be to declare war on the bank. Arnold used to call it the "red button" strategy.

"Where I come from," one board member later told Gary Hector, "they call this blackmail. We shoot blackmailers." Another outraged director wanted to sue Schwab before he could sue the bank—and fire him while they were at it. But cooler heads prevailed. Clausen, using his own back channels, made it known to Schwab that the auction would be put on hold, and that Schwab would be given first crack at buying his firm—though not for $190 million, which the bank felt was a humiliatingly low number, especially since Schwab was closing in on $60 million in annual profits by the end of 1986.

The climactic meeting to negotiate the price was held in mid-December 1986. The bank never really had a chance. Schwab brought along a friend of his, George Roberts, a principal in the well-known leveraged-buyout firm of Kohlberg, Kravis & Roberts. During the meeting, Roberts played good cop to Schwab's bad cop. Schwab spent most of the meeting telling the bank officials that he would not budge from his original low-ball bid; Roberts, meanwhile, was walking these same officials through some sleight-of-hand financing he had devised that would allow the bank at least to save face.[8] When the papers were signed a few months later, and Schwab finally had his company back, the bank was able to announce a sale price of $280 million. But the executives at Schwab knew better. The true price had been $190 million—and of that amount, only $16.5 million in equity had been raised by the firm's new owners, who consisted primarily of the top executives. The rest was borrowed money. It was a classic leveraged buyout.

After the deal was signed, and the two companies were officially separated, they broke open some champagne in Schwab's office, and in the firm's San Francisco headquarters, people wore little buttons that read, "Schwab . . . Free At Last!" But mainly, the celebration was subdued. Most Schwab employees were too busy to spend much time celebrating; in the early part of 1987 the firm felt like an oversized version of its old self, when the entire staff had too much to do, and could never seem to catch up no matter how late they stayed or how many new people they hired. As for Schwab himself, he had his own reasons for cutting short the celebration. His mind was elsewhere. After a few sips of the champagne, he turned to Arnold and said quietly: "I want you to get started on a public offering."

Arnold was startled. "I said, 'Chuck, come on! We've just pulled off a phenomenal deal.' " Arnold went on to argue that if they could show several strong years while the company remained in private hands, they could then take Schwab public a few years down the road and make a killing. This is the normal course for a leveraged buyout.

"I know markets," Arnold recalls him replying nervously. "You never know when the top is coming."

This conversation took place on March 31, 1987. That day, the Dow Jones Industrial Average closed at 2,304.69. The top was coming soon.

AT THE END OF 1984, with the Dow Jones average at 1211.57—and poised, after a lull, to make its next great surge—there were 1,246 mutual funds in America. Their number had tripled in a decade, and would nearly triple again before the 1980s were over, by which time there would be more mutual funds than there were stocks on the New York Stock Exchange. There were growth funds that specialized in large stocks, and growth funds that concentrated on small stocks. There were income funds that allowed junk bonds in the portfolio, and income funds that didn't. There were funds that only accepted IRA money. There were short-term bond funds and long-term bond funds, and funds that combined stocks and bonds. There were balanced funds and overseas funds, sector funds and convertible securities funds, aggressive funds and conservative funds, funds that stressed undervalued stocks and funds that stressed contrarian ideas.

There was a fund for everybody, which didn't necessarily mean that everybody was happy. Part of the original appeal of mutual funds was that they seemed to offer a path into the stock market that was both simpler and safer than the old call-a-broker-and-buy-a-stock route. The proliferation of funds, however, had made the universe of mutual funds at least as bewildering as the universe of stocks had always been. Yet while the middle class had once been able to turn its back on stocks and bonds with no real adverse consequences, many people didn't feel that they had that luxury anymore. They felt that they had to have at least a portion of their money in the market, and a good many of them also felt that mutual funds were the investment vehicle that made the most sense. Twenty-eight million mutual fund accounts had been opened by 1984, and that number was rising every year.

But how could middle-class investors know which fund to choose? Which of those 1,246 mutual funds would speak to them directly, cutting through the growing cacophony of conflicting information and advice? For even as the funds themselves were proliferating, so was the information one could find about them. A dozen different magazines published ratings of mutual funds. Fund companies were doubling and tripling their advertising budgets. Article after article anointed this or that hot young fund manager as the new Peter Lynch. Halfway through the bull market, this was becoming the critical question for the nation's mutual fund companies. How could they ensure that their company's products would be the ones to rise above the growing din? How could they be *heard*? And as this need became more pronounced, it led to the next subtle evolution of the mutual fund industry. Within many fund companies, power began accruing to those who sold the funds—the marketers—at the expense of those who ran them—the portfolio managers. Not surprisingly, Fidelity was among the companies where this shift was most apparent—to the delight of the marketers and the dismay of the fund managers.

It was, in fact, one of those hot young fund managers anointed as the new Peter Lynch who would soon come to personify this shift—whose fate as a Fidelity fund manager would seem, afterward, to mark the moment when the marketers had triumphed. When he left Fidelity, after a short, bittersweet tenure, to strike out on his own—the first star portfolio manager to do so since Gerald Tsai twenty years before—he became (somewhat against his will) Exhibit A to those who believed that the company's soul now lay in marketing. There was irony in this, to be sure, for his status as a hot young thing was in no small part the result of the efforts of Fidelity's marketing staff. During the bull market the marketers had learned how to take a manager's good performance record and use it to transform him into a star. And however reluctant Ned Johnson may have once been to create stars—indeed, however ambivalent he remained still—he had learned to put that ambivalence aside.[9] Stars generated publicity, publicity brought in assets, and more assets meant a larger slice of the market. If you were in the mutual fund business, that's how you played the game.

The young man's name was Paul Stuka, and he was among the seemingly endless supply of young fund managers who were spawned in the Fidelity hothouse of the mid-1980s. Stuka's ''class'' of money managers contained a handful of other stars, including Michael Kassen, *Money* magazine's cover boy, George Noble, a twenty-nine-year-old whiz kid whose fund, Fidelity Overseas, was the top performing mutual fund in the country in 1985, and Thomas Sweeney, who was all of twenty-seven when he grabbed hold of a newly created fund, Capital Appreciation, and made it one of the hottest funds in the country in its first few years of life.[10] Stuka's fund was called Fidelity OTC Portfolio (OTC stands for Over-the-Counter, which encompasses the thousands of stocks not listed on either the New York or American stock exchanges), and he was also twenty-nine when he got his big chance, at the tail end of 1984. Half a year later, by which time he had turned thirty, OTC Portfolio was up 51 percent, the second best six-month return of any fund. Instantly, the press descended. *Business Week* photographed him leaning casually against a wall, eating a fruit cup. "The Rookie Running a Hot New Fund," read the headline. *Money* magazine described his "tousled hair and puckish grin." *USA Today* and *The New York Times* probed his feelings about the market. And not long after that, he was gone.

It was a different experience, being a Fidelity fund manager in the mid-1980s; it wasn't the way it had been for, say, Peter Lynch a decade before. There was a great deal more pressure, and a great deal more scrutiny. And Fidelity was such a bigger place now—not bureaucratic exactly, but filled with thousands of people who worked in buildings all across downtown Boston,[11] people you never saw and didn't know, but all of whom seemed to need something from you *right now*. Gone were the days when a portfolio manager could toil in obscurity for a few years, gradually developing a suitable stock-picking style, while laying a foundation that would lead to a decent performance record down the road. Now, the Fidelity marketing forces wanted a track record it could promote right away; it wasn't willing to wait years while a new fund manager worked out the kinks. Indeed, one key reason Fidelity created OTC Portfolio was that the firm's executives believed (correctly) that over-the-counter stocks were nearing the bottom, and would soon start rising. They wanted a new fund that would be positioned to rise right along with the OTC market. Which they could then sell to the public as a top performing mutual fund.

From the moment the fund was devised, Stuka was the obvious choice to run it. He had joined Fidelity four and a half years before, dropping out of Harvard's MBA program two months early because he was so anxious to begin work. Like all future Fidelity fund managers, he started as a stock analyst, covering the oil industry. But he quickly gained a reputation as someone with a nose for over-the-counter stocks, most of which are not covered on a regular basis by Wall Street analysts,[12] and are thus ignored by most portfolio managers. What began as a quirky little sideline soon became Stuka's main focus. Promotions, first to fund assistant and then to the manager of a select fund, quickly followed.

Stuka was also a Lynch protégé. This was another aspect of life in the equity shop that had grown in importance by the mid-1980s, for Lynch's stature had made him the de facto head of the growth fund managers. It was crucial for young analysts to impress Lynch because when the time came to name a new portfolio manager, Lynch's recommendation would be an important factor. In Stuka's case, it didn't hurt that his Holy Cross–Worcester, Massachusetts–Catholic background was somewhat similar to Lynch's own background. More importantly, Stuka's OTC bias meshed nicely with Lynch's own penchant for finding obscure, unwatched stocks that he could add to the ever-expanding list of stocks he held in the Magellan Fund. The best way for an analyst to catch Lynch's eye was to recommend a stock that Lynch knew little about—and then have it go up in value. Stuka did this regularly.

They started Stuka off with $100,000. It was "house money"—seed capital supplied by Fidelity. OTC Portfolio was not open to the public, not right away; the Fidelity modus operandi during the 1980s was to keep a new fund under wraps for a short time, and observe how the fund manager did with the pocket change he had been handed without the whole world watching. Each trade the new fund manager made was closely tracked, and every move he made examined. Of course, Lynch had been watched at the beginning, but it was different then: it was Ned Johnson popping in to ask about this or that. Now there were formal meetings, during which the new fund manager was grilled by a handful of veterans: Why did you buy this stock? Why did you sell only a portion of that position? "The first meeting," recalls Stuka, "I got beat up pretty badly."

But when the OTC market began rising, Stuka's new fund began rising even faster, and the decision was made to open the fund to the public. Here, of course, was a second reason new funds were begun away from the glare of publicity: if things worked out the way they were supposed to, the fund manager would have an advertisable track record very soon after he began taking money from the public. To attract money into this unknown mutual fund, Fidelity could waive the load; such decisions were a key component of mutual fund marketing. Then, once the fund was hot, the firm could slap on a 2 or 3 percent load, since most people didn't mind paying a small price to get into a hot fund. In time, this became the classic Fidelity marketing strategy.

Did it work? Every time. It worked with George Noble's Overseas Fund, which had $2 billion in assets within two years, and with Tom

Sweeney's Capital Appreciation Fund, which had $1.5 billion in its first two years. And it certainly worked with Stuka's OTC Portfolio. In the "old days," it took years for a new fund to gain substantial assets: Value Fund, started in 1980, didn't have $30 million until 1984. OTC Portfolio had that much money within four months. That was April 1985. By July it had $55 million; by October $81 million; by December $162 million. And then it really took off, quadrupling in size over the next six months, until it held close to $1 billion. "There was an appetite for products [like OTC Portfolio and Overseas]," says Fidelity's current head of marketing, Roger Servison. But that's a bit disingenuous. It was an appetite Fidelity did a great deal to whet.

Some of the portfolio managers had a term for those times when the marketing department decided to whet an appetite for a fund. "Gunning the fund," they called it. If you were a Fidelity portfolio manager who had had a hot quarter or six months, you could be pretty well assured that the marketers would gun your fund. Gunning the fund might include fiddling with the load, and it would always include increasing the fund's advertising budget, as ads touting the fund's wonderful recent performance would begin to appear regularly in *The New York Times,* the *Wall Street Journal,* and other newspapers and magazines.[13] It meant sending out direct mail packages to current customers and prospective ones, while prodding the nation's financial press to write stories about the latest hot fund manager to come out of Fidelity (invariably described by the public relations department as appealing and down-to-earth and brimming over with common sense, especially for someone so young). And the fund manager himself would be paraded before the press, the better to acquaint the public with his luminous talent. Fidelity spent around $100 million in advertising in 1986; when a top Fidelity executive once asked its top marketer at the time, a man named Rodger Lawson, why the company had to have seven different ads every Sunday in *The New York Times* business section, Lawson replied simply, "Because they all work." Indeed they did. Between 1984 and 1986 Fidelity's customer base rose from around 400,000 households to over 1 million, while the assets it managed grew from around $30 billion to close to $70 billion. Lawson gunned a lot of funds.

And what if a fund manager became uncomfortable with the way his fund was being promoted? What if he thought his fund was attracting more assets than he could profitably invest? What if he wanted the marketers to turn down the throttle, or shut the fund to new investors? In general, if a Fidelity fund manager had such complaints, he was out of luck. Other fund companies might close a fund to the public if it got too big; Vanguard, Fidelity's fiercest mutual fund competitor, did so with its most popular fund, Windsor, when it hit the $9 billion mark. But this was unthinkable at Fidelity during the bull market.

Stuka was among the portfolio managers who complained. He had been able to handle the inflow of money during 1985, but he became less and less comfortable as 1986 unfolded, and the fund began adding more assets in a month than it had gained its entire first year. He'd come into the office on a Monday morning, and discovered that the fund had gained another $10 million over the weekend—money he was supposed to put to work imme- diately. He couldn't do it. He couldn't find enough of his favorite small stocks to invest the assets that were pouring in. He began letting assets sit in money market funds; at one point 16 percent of the fund was in cash, which was practically a punishable offense at Fidelity. After all, cash hold- ings dragged down yield and hurt the marketing department's chances of peddling the fund. "They used to come down hard on fund managers who held too much of the fund's assets in cash," recalls a former Fidelity hand.
   Finally, Stuka asked Fidelity to stop advertising his fund. He knew what he was asking: "There's no overt statement at Fidelity that the funds have to keep growing and the ads have to keep running," he says. "You just pick it up from the feel of the place." Stuka adds, "If Peter Lynch could run $5 billion, you felt foolish complaining about having to run $500 million."
   Later, Lawson would claim that there were times when Fidelity did stop advertising a fund, at least temporarily, at the request of a fund manager. But this was not one of those times. It was Lawson's apparent opinion that the over-the-counter market was more than big enough to absorb $1 billion, and that the problem lay, essentially, with Stuka's fund managing style. Stuka needed to adapt, the way Peter Lynch had adapted when Magellan got big. He needed to find bigger OTC stocks, like Microsoft and Apple Com- puter, and end his fixation on those unknown little gems he preferred. Request denied.
   Later, too, the *Wall Street Journal* would recount how Stuka had "felt pushed into some bad choices, particularly in high-technology stocks." Stuka didn't name names, but he didn't have to; it was obvious who he felt had pushed him. It was an open secret in the equity department at Fidelity that the marketers occasionally pushed portfolio managers to invest in a particular category of bond or security, the better to pump up the fund's return. At the same time, Stuka's performance dropped substantially, which Stuka later attributed to his large cash position. "Looking back," he said, "you'd have been better off just throwing money at the market—and I wasn't willing to do that."
   So instead he left. He walked out in a flurry of publicity and hurt feel-

ings—Lynch was said to be especially hurt by Stuka's departure—rented an office a few blocks away from his old quarters, and set about raising capital for a new fund he planned to start. He raised around $20 million, a nice, manageable sum that would allow him to revert to the kind of investing he had always loved, ferreting out those unknown OTC stocks he favored. He could return to being the fund manager he'd been before the marketers took over his fund. Or so he implied to the many reporters who came calling, none of whom seemed to take note of the two advertisements that hung, framed, on his new office wall. They were mementos from his time at Fidelity. One screamed, "The Nation's Number Two Fund!" The other, equally insistent, read, "OTC UP 97.4%."

Not long after he had left Fidelity himself, in the summer of 1991, Rodger Lawson would recall the hot young things at Fidelity that he had done so much to create. "The little prima donnas," he called them dismissively. "George," he said a few minutes later, referring to George Noble, "we got a couple of good years out of George." The implication was clear: George Noble, like all the hot young things, was replaceable, and indeed, interchangeable—not unlike a football player who's been injured once too often. Only Peter Lynch was exempt from Lawson's dim view of the portfolio managers; Lynch, says Lawson, "was excellent to work with, always got back to me, was always responsible." That is to say: Lynch was acceptable because he didn't try to buck the marketing department.

But what was the point of that? What Lynch understood, and "the little prima donnas" did not, was that Lawson's ascension, and the rise of marketing in general, was not something that came about by accident. That's not the way Fidelity worked. The young fund managers, most of whom arrived as wet-behind-the-ears analysts prior to the start of the bull market, might long for the good old days when Fidelity still had the feel of a mutual fund boutique, a place that revolved around the equity department. It was easy for them to see Lawson as the enemy, since he personified everything they hated about how Fidelity had changed. But the old timers knew better. They understood that Lawson was the symbol, not the cause. Fidelity had changed during the bull market not because Lawson wanted it to change, but because Ned Johnson did.

Not that Johnson ever said as much; that's something that hadn't changed at Fidelity. No, the way one intuited Johnson's goals was by watching him hire executives and watching him spend money. When, in carly 1985, he brought in Lawson, a former marketing executive at Dreyfus, which was one of Fidelity's biggest rivals, it meant something. And when he began spending hundreds of millions of dollars on advertising and promotion, on new telephone centers in Salt Lake City and Dallas, on bigger and better technology, on 2,000 new employees a year, on twenty-four-hour telephone service, that meant something, too. It meant that Ned Johnson's ambitions had not abated. If anything, the bull market had only stoked them.

"He just left me alone," Lawson would later recall. That's the way Ned Johnson operated. He left Lawson alone to change the company irrevocably, just as he had left Jarvie alone when he was changing the company. Johnson's longtime associate and number two man, an executive named Samuel Bodman, was said to resist many of the changes, believing that funds were getting too big, and that they would ultimately suffer as a result. "He was the only one opposing the marketing juggernaut," recalls a former Fidelity fund manager. Bodman was beloved by the portfolio managers, who saw him as their great defender, but the ship was moving in a different direction, and eventually Bodman realized that there was nothing he could do to stop it. Lawson was the new power in the company, and in his leave-no-fingerprints way, Johnson was allowing Lawson's ascension to take place. So Bodman left. He left, it was also said, with a great deal of money, as he sold back his accumulated shares in the company. But his leaving was tinged with sadness because it was yet another signal that the old Fidelity no longer existed.

This sense of loss, however, was felt only inside the company. To most customers, Fidelity felt completely different. What they knew about Fidelity was that when they picked up the phone, at any hour of the night or day, somebody at Fidelity was ready to answer. They knew that when they turned to the business section of the paper each morning, there was a Fidelity ad staring out at them. They knew—how could they not know?—that OTC was up 97.4 percent, that Overseas was the nation's number one fund, and that Peter Lynch was, well, Peter Lynch was pretty much God. That's all that seemed to matter as the bull market entered its fifth year, careening toward the cliff.

⌒

IT's 1987 NOW. More precisely, it's eight days into 1987, and the Dow Jones average, which has already risen almost 100 points since the year began, closes for the first time ever over the 2000 point mark.[14] If we lived in a world where momentous events were still signaled by the ringing of bells in the town square, that's what we would have heard that January day: we would have heard bells tolling joyously. Instead, we live in a world where such events are signaled by the emphasis they are given on the network news shows and in the nation's newspapers. It is there that this milestone is celebrated, as reporters and news commentators agree that we have just witnessed a signature moment in a bull market that shows no signs of slowing down.[15]

*Slowing down?* That's a laugh. It took from August 1982 until December 1985 for the Dow Jones average to double. There were occasions during those three-plus years when it appeared as though the bull market might be over—when the market wavered, or gave back several hundred points, as it did in the first half of 1984. But toward the end of 1985, with the Dow around 1500, the market began to gather new momentum, rolling over anything in its path. In 1986 the Dow rose an impressive 400 points, ending just under 1900. Eight days into 1987, the 2000 point barrier was breached. And after that things really got crazy.

There were a number of ways to measure the craziness. One way was simply to observe the market, to watch it leapfrog month after month, in a series of awesome strides. Between January and April 1987, the Dow added another 400 points—equaling the entire gain of the previous year. Then, after dropping 150 points over the next month and a half, it began hurtling upward again, gaining close to 500 points in a scant ninety days, until by late August it had topped 2700. During that latter stretch, thirty- and forty-point days became almost commonplace. There were three fifty-point days in that span and one seventy-point day. It was a riveting thing to watch. There were days when people would walk into a Schwab or Fidelity branch office, watch the stock tape for a while, and walk out knowing they had seen the Dow Jones average rise twenty points during their lunch hour. Middle-class Americans did that in the middle of 1987: they walked to a brokerage office on their lunch hour just to watch the market go up. There were also days when the market went down, of course, sometimes by as much as forty or fifty points, but those days were the equivalent of hitting an airpocket—momentarily scary and instantly reversed.[16]

Yet watching the market rocket upward, mesmerizing though it was, was perhaps the least illuminating way to understand the effect it was having on America. For that, one had to look toward Main Street as well as Wall Street. By 1987, the bull market had spread well beyond the pages of *Barron's* and the *Wall Street Journal*, and had leached into the larger culture. Each evening, network anchormen announced the latest rise in the Dow Jones average—a piece of news they'd reported sporadically before, if at all. *USA Today*, a newspaper with a shrewd sense of middle-class concerns, heralded the bull market at every opportunity. Rupert Murdoch, the publisher of downscale tabloid newspapers, began running contests revolving around the stock market. Other cultural artifacts emerged: bull market

T-shirts, bull market games, bull market songs. Plainly, this was not the cognoscenti's bull market, the way it had been in the 1950s. By 1987, 55 million mutual fund accounts had been opened, holding more than $750 billion, while the number of people owning individual stocks was closing in on 40 million. The middle class was not only aware of this bull market, it was part of it.

Peter Lynch likes to recall that by the early part of 1987, whenever he went to a cocktail party, he would be surrounded by people wanting to talk about the market. But instead of asking his advice on stocks, they would offer theirs. That, says Lynch, is when he began to realize that things were veering a bit out of control. One could get the same feeling by looking at *Money* magazine, circa 1987; the covers of nine of the first eleven issues in 1987 promised sure-fire strategies for making money in the market. But the bull market had also found its way into other, less likely Time, Inc., publications, such as *People* magazine, which ran one article on a formerly obscure money manager named Martin Zweig,[17] and another, a few months later, about a summer camp devoted to teaching preteens about the stock market. In Rhode Island, a psychologist began advertising himself as the country's first "investor psychologist." The "Stock Doc," he called himself.

During this same time, a handful of new investment gurus emerged, heirs to Howard Ruff and Joe Granville. Their new prominence also seemed to suggest that things were getting out of hand. Probably the best known of the new gurus was Robert Prechter, a thirty-seven-year-old market technician who lived in Gainesville, Georgia, and was proclaiming loudly that the Dow would top 3600 before the bull market ended. This was an extremely appealing message to a great many people, to say the least, and reaped him an enormous amount of publicity. It also helped get him some 20,000 subscribers to his own highly priced newsletter. What was strange about Prechter's appeal was not so much his message, but what it was based on. Prechter believed in something called the Elliot Wave Theory, which, to put it bluntly, was virtually incomprehensible to anyone but him. It didn't seem to matter. Prechter was saying what people wanted to hear, at a time when they wanted to hear it. So he gained followers.

The first part of 1987 was a time of true euphoria, when investing seemed like fun and the prospect of losing money seemed dim. Just as middle-class Americans had once talked about real estate at dinner parties, now they talked about the stock market. The smell of money was in the air. This, after all, was the era that glorified the conspicuously wealthy and made heroes out of corporate-takeover artists. Some of the more adventurous of the new breed of middle-class investors even began speculating in rumored takeover stocks, though they played this game at a distinct disadvantage, since they usually got these rumors from the *Wall Street Journal*—which meant, essentially, that they were the last to know. Still, the rumors were often right; many of these Main Street speculators made money.


Does it need to be pointed out that Wall Street was every bit as euphoric as Main Street? Perhaps not. With trading volume on the New York Stock Exchange closing in on 180 million shares a day—nearly double what it had been at the beginning of the bull market—commission income stood at record levels. Money was pouring in. Employment in the securities industry went from 1.7 million to 2.3 million in four years. Fidelity quadrupled in size during the bull market; it had some 8,000 people on the payroll by August 1987. Merrill Lynch moved into yet another new headquarters building, this one in the World Financial Center, with plans eventually to take over a second World Financial Center skyscraper. There were no brakes on this expansion, no words of caution from company elders. It was as if Wall Street believed, right along with its customers, that the bull market would never end, that they'd all get rich and that everyone would live happily ever after.

Oddly enough, Merrill Lynch was one firm that wasn't necessarily getting rich during these grandest days of the bull market. It was still an enormous, powerful firm, with $7.1 billion in revenues and $2.7 billion in accumulated capital. But its profits had increased a scant 11 percent between 1980 and 1985; the far smaller Salomon Brothers made twice as much money, and Citicorp four times as much. Plainly, Merrill Lynch was suffering, at least in part,[18] from its unwillingness to completely embrace the logic of the money revolution—logic that it had first stumbled onto, years before, with its own CMA. That logic said that gathering assets would be the crucial skill once the regulatory barriers were dismantled. And that had indeed turned out to be the case. But at Merrill Lynch, despite having a large and well-run mutual fund division, the company still stressed commission revenue. So the brokers worked the phones the way they always had, making hundreds of cold calls, trying to persuade people to buy this stock or sell that one. Even the mutual fund division held to the commission system; a customer had to pay a load as high as 6 percent to get into a Merrill Lynch mutual fund, which was out of line with customer expectations—though very much in line with the expectations of the firm's brokers. In stressing commissions, and pushing brokers to make cold calls, Merrill Lynch was misreading the new middle-class investor. The new investor was reading *Money* magazine and watching Louis Rukeyser. The new investor had learned that he had to start

taking responsibility for his own financial life. If the new investor was going
to make a mistake in the market, it would be his own mistake, rather than
a mistake some broker put him into.

Yet in the face of these huge attitudinal changes, Merrill Lynch seemed
oblivious. It kept hiring new brokers,[19] and kept throwing them into the
branch offices, with the expectation that they would persuade people to buy
stocks, and make money for the firm. And when, late in the summer of
1987, a veteran broker went to his supervisor to suggest that the firm begin
holding seminars on how to protect clients in the bear market that was sure
to come, he got nowhere. It would be too damaging to the morale of all the
new brokers, the supervisor replied, who were working the bull market for
all it was worth. Besides, the manager added happily, "We're not going to
have a bear market. The market is going to 3600!"

But it wasn't going to 3600, at least not then. It's obvious now—and it
should have been obvious at the time—that the first eight months of 1987
marked the final, frenzied run-up that always comes before the awful fall.
There had been just such a run-up before the crash of 1929, too, and it had
been marked by the same kind of euphoria, the same forgetfulness that bull
markets always end and bear markets always follow, the same complacency,
the same willful suspension of disbelief.

That's what it all added up to, this gnawing sense one had that things were
getting out of hand. The bull market was almost over. Yet no one seemed
able to read the signs that practically stared them in the face—signs that
would seem painfully apparent afterward. "When it will end is anybody's
guess," a *New York Times* reporter could actually write in an August story
about the bull market—a story published barely three weeks before the bull
reached its peak. "Experts say the traditional signs of a dying bull market
have not yet appeared: excessive optimism, heavy issuance of new stock,
and sudden participation by small investors who normally do not buy
stocks." But that's *exactly* what had appeared. Excessive optimism was
everywhere. Issuance of new stock was rampant. And as for the "sudden
participation by small investors," all one had to do to see that was spend a
little time listening to the phone calls pouring into places like Fidelity and
Schwab, as people who barely knew the difference between a stock and a
bond began throwing their savings into the market. In that same article, the
*Times* reported that stock and bond funds—"the primary investment vehicle
of small investors," the paper called them—had seen their combined assets
grow from $53.7 billion to $430 billion since 1982. Where in the world did
the *Times* think this money came from? It came from the "sudden partici-

pation'' of the middle class. There was no other place it *could* have come from.

''The market climbs a wall of worry.'' So goes one of the great truisms of the stock market. What happened in the summer of 1987 was that everybody stopped worrying—sophisticated investors as well as rank novices, Wall Street as well as Main Street. If the history of the market tells us anything at all, it tells us that there is no surer sign that the end is near.

## CHAPTER 17

# "This Is a War over Here"

## *October 1987*

IT'S NOT QUITE right to say that *nobody* saw the crash coming. Somebody always sees it coming. In 1929, Charlie Merrill saw it coming, and his efforts to pull his clients, and his firm, out of the market before disaster struck helped cement his legend. The Go-Go Years had their own set of doomsayers, including the popular economists Eliot Janeway and John Kenneth Galbraith, both of whom drew urgent parallels between the overheated market of the 1960s and the conditions that existed in 1929. The former was so outspoken about the coming bear market that he earned the nickname "Calamity Janeway."

And it was no different in 1987. In January, and again in October, *The Atlantic Monthly* magazine ran articles (one by Galbraith, the other by government official turned investment banker Peter G. Peterson) that virtually predicted a market collapse. In *Harper's,* financial writer L. J. Davis weighed in with a similar assessment, as did Michael M. Thomas in *The Nation.* Elaine Garzarelli, a quantitative analyst for Shearson Lehman Brothers, turned bearish in early September; by mid-October, she was so sure that the end was near that when she appeared on CNN a week before the crash, she said flatly that the stock market was on the verge of collapse. James Grant, of *Grant's Interest Rate Observer,* was similarly convinced that a market "cataclysm" (as he put it) was around the corner. Alan Greene, a prominent Wall Street money manager, was a bear. Jim Rogers, the well-known investor and Columbia University finance professor, was a bear. And there were others. It was, in all, a surprisingly long list.

And they each had their own special reason for being bearish: they each had some little signal that told them the market was about to crash. Garzarelli's signals were her complex technical indicators, which, she would later crow, were 92 percent bearish by mid-October 1987. Greene, an old-fashioned value investor, believed that the standard market barometers were sending bearish signals; he pointed in particular to the way stock prices were running at twenty-three times earnings, far higher than what is considered healthy.[1] Michael Thomas thought he saw his signal in the rush by the middle class to invest in mutual funds, feeling that these investors would be the ones to trigger a market crash: "If, Heaven forfend, a pane of glass fell on Peter Lynch," Thomas wrote, "all hell could break loose, possibly setting off a ripple, then a wave, then a torrent of redemptions." And Rogers had the most idiosyncratic signal of all. Speaking at a luncheon early in 1987, he began pointing out the warning signs he saw: "Do you know," he said as ran down his list, "that there is a fellow at Fidelity running $1 billion who's only twenty-nine years old?" Everyone chuckled, but they understood Rogers's message: when Americans were entrusting that much money to twenty-nine-year-old fund managers, it surely meant that the market was out of control. As it happens, the twenty-nine-year-old in question was sitting in the audience that day; for years afterward, George Noble would regale people with that story.

The point is, the bears were prescient; they were forceful; and in some cases (Garzarelli's especially), they were practically begging people to get out of the market. Yet it was only later, after their prophecies had come true, that their forceful statements were underlined, their prescient articles clipped, their videotaped pleadings replayed over and over again. It was only when the crash had transformed them into the newest stars in the financial galaxy (this, again, was doubly true of the strikingly attractive Garzarelli) that we realized they were the ones who'd been right—as opposed to, say, Robert Prechter.

But then, how could we possibly know beforehand who was going to turn out to be right and who was going to be wrong? We never know ahead of time what the market is going to do: that's what makes it so interesting and so nerve-racking all at once. It's only in hindsight that the path it takes seems preordained, and the signals it sends seem obvious. When we're in the middle of it, nothing seems preordained or obvious. We are deluged with contradictory advice, as every market "expert" argues his position as loudly as he can. When a market gets as crazy as the one in 1987, those voices can start to drown each other out, until they have become merely noise.

Thus, in 1987, for every bear there were at least as many bulls who could make the bullish case sound every bit as convincing. For every Alan Greene saying that p/e ratios were out of whack, there was an investor like George Soros, far better known than Greene, claiming that in this market old-fashioned p/e ratios didn't matter anymore. For every Elaine Garzarelli on CNN, there was someone every bit the bull on the same show. Dan Dorfman, *USA Today*'s financial columnist, used to write two columns a week in 1987; it sometimes seemed as though the Tuesday column was devoted to the opinions of a well-known bear, while the Friday column gave equal time to a well-known bull. The new middle-class investor, turning to Dorfman for answers, was likely to find instead exactly the noise he was trying to flee. After the market peaked that August, and began dropping quickly in September, the mood shifted from euphoria to fear; among the investing public a single question rang out: *what were they supposed to do?*

Unlike the experts with their conflicting opinions, the middle-class investor didn't even have the courage of his convictions; when it came to the market, he didn't *have* any convictions. He was new at this. He didn't have the faintest idea about whether, or when, he should get out. And what was worse, even when he paid attention the way he was supposed to, his path became no clearer. Paying attention taught him that Alan Greene disagreed with George Soros—but it didn't teach him who was right. In September of 1987, as the market dropped forty-six points one day and gained seventy-five points another, as it ricocheted from 2700 to below 2500 and then back up to 2600 again, this was not a pleasant sensation. It was paralyzing.

The middle class was discovering something else about the money revolution: taking control of one's finances was not necessarily an enjoyable experience—not when the market seemed to be suddenly going against you and you felt as though you had no place to turn for help. And it was certainly not simple either—not when every day brought news of some new financial product that had to be investigated, and that was as likely to be offered by General Electric as by Fidelity. There were moments when all the changes wrought by the money revolution could seem terrifying, for their net result was to force people to make choices about where to put their money, *and every single choice entailed risk*. What if you moved your money into a nice, safe money fund and the market went up another 1,000 points? What if you stayed in the market and it crashed?

The bull market had lasted five years, almost to the day. During that time the Dow Jones average had more than tripled. In the first eight months of 1987, as the bull made its final surge, the Dow Jones average had gone from under 2000 to over 2700. It had been a wild, glorious ride. But as it wound down that September, this is what had become most clear: as Americans had gradually gone from being savers to investors, they had also gradually taken more risks with their money. And now, with the prospect of a crash just around the corner, there was no turning back, no matter how much they might want to. The world had changed too much for that.

It had been easy being a saver. It had been easy when the options were few, and interest rates were regulated, and handling one's money was a simple affair. It was hard being an investor. Nothing was simple anymore. People felt naked, alone, adrift in an ocean of choice. What the middle-class investor most longed for that September—for someone to take him by the hand and *tell him what to do*—that was the one thing the money revolution couldn't supply.

And what was Fidelity saying that August and September, as the market seesawed violently, and its customers became increasingly anxious about what lay ahead? Fidelity wasn't saying much of anything. It continued to do what it had done throughout the bull market: provide an ever-expanding menu of choices, as its mutual fund factory churned out new funds, and its marketing department sold them. This is how it had come to view its mission. "People want control," Rodger Lawson told one interviewer at the time, outlining Fidelity's worldview. "They want to make their own decisions." Well, maybe. On the other hand, Fidelity heavily influenced those decisions with its torrential marketing campaigns. And though it may not have been saying anything overtly to its customers, its own actions seemed to suggest that it, too, had become a bit nervous about what the end of the bull market might mean. In the early part of 1987, Ned Johnson made the decision that Fidelity would stop advertising Magellan—not that it did much good; the fund still swelled by an additional $4 billion that year. Soon afterward, the company began to downplay most of the other aggressive stock funds as well. If and when the downturn came, those funds would be the ones hit hardest. In their place, Fidelity began promoting some of the more conservative funds, such as Puritan Fund and Balanced Fund, which were bound to perform better in a down market.

There was, however, a more significant move Johnson could have made to protect his customers from the full force of the coming crash. He could have changed the company's firm but unspoken rule that Fidelity's stock funds had to be fully invested at all times. He could have let it be known, as the market began to tumble, that it would be all right for the fund managers to shelter some assets in cash. But Johnson did no such thing. He had always believed that people who handed over their money to Fidelity did so in the expectation that it would be invested in the market. That belief did not change once the market peaked in 1987.

Surely, though, Johnson was giving his customers too much credit. Most middle-class investors found mutual funds appealing precisely because they wanted someone more knowledgeable than they to make market decisions on their behalf. The decision about whether or not to be fully invested was exactly the kind of judgment a novice investor would want his fund manager to make. Yet after everything that had happened during the past decade— after all his prescient moves to draw middle-class money to his company— Johnson still seemed to perceive his customers as investing sophisticates, which they were not. If, late in the summer of 1987, he had allowed his fund managers to begin moving some assets out of stocks and into cash, he might have saved his customers some money. But this he was not yet ready to do; in his own way, he was also hanging on to an image of Fidelity that no longer reflected reality.


It's not as if Fidelity employees didn't sense what was coming either. As August turned to September, the 1,500 telephone operators the company employed could feel the winds shifting, as the customers they talked to became more nervous with each passing day. And while Peter Lynch might still proclaim his disinterest in the overall condition of the market, other Fidelity fund managers were not nearly so willing to attach the blinders that Lynch wore with such supposed ease.[2]

If one had been able to eavesdrop on Fidelity in late August, just as the market was peaking, one would surely have detected the growing trepidation; the air was thick with nervous talk, and the expectation that bad days lay ahead. Here, for instance, were a group of seventeen Fidelity portfolio managers gathered for their regular monthly meeting. These were the people who ran Fidelity's "equity income" group, which consisted of more conservative funds like Puritan and Balanced, rather than the aggressive growth funds, of which Magellan was the prototype. Francis Cabour, one of the grand old men of Fidelity and manager of the conservative Balanced Fund,[3] was at this meeting. Beth Terrana, thirty years old, the company's only female hot young thing, whose Growth and Income Fund had outperformed many of the pure growth funds in the eighteen months she had run it, was there, too. So was semiretired Leo Dworsky, who had managed Contrafund for sixteen consecutive years, a company record. Leading the meeting was Bruce Johnstone, who at the time headed both this group and his own large fund, Equity-Income, which had returned 600 percent over the past decade, and bulged with $4.5 billion worth of conservative middle-class money. After Lynch, he was probably Fidelity's best-known fund manager.

The Lynch credo notwithstanding, the meeting was nothing but a discussion of the state of the market; that was uppermost on everybody's mind. They talked about the continuing flurry of hostile takeovers and leveraged buyouts, which was propping up the bull market in this late stage. They talked about industries that still might offer decent buying opportunities. They talked about any market-related thoughts that popped into their heads.

"I think inflation is going to be a problem next year," one participant opined. "Salomon Brothers says it will hit 6½ percent in 1988." Although he was skeptical, Johnstone turned to a blackboard behind him and wrote, "Inflation." "I think we should be looking at food companies," said Beth Terrana. "They all have cash on their balance sheets and lots of free cash flow; most of them have solid franchises, and their stock is selling at a discount to the market on a p/e basis." Johnstone turned again to the board and wrote, "Food companies."

Eventually the discussion turned to the central issue: how much longer could the bull market last? "There is no way you can justify this market on the fundamentals," Cabour said vehemently. "I don't care what anybody says." Cabour was well known for his conservative view of the market, but on this morning, no one in the room disagreed with him.

"The Fed has been priming the pump only because the economy is in desperate, desperate shape," said Johnstone. "If they ever start tightening the money supply . . ."

"Consumer borrowing has declined to a level that, in the past, has meant a recession," said an analyst.

"The Nikkei is a rigged market," said Terrana. "It's not going to last forever." The Nikkei was the Japanese stock market, whose gains had far outpaced the Dow Jones average. It was another one of those things Americans had had to learn about: all the overseas mutual funds were heavily invested in Japan.

As they went around the table, the mood became increasingly black:

"Valuation is a dirty word all of a sudden."

"I got a call from a guy I haven't heard from in fifteen years asking me if I was still at Fidelity. He wanted me to tell him whether he should pull his money out of the market."

"I went to a funeral and the guy didn't want to talk about his dead wife. He wanted to talk about where to invest."

"I don't know about you guys but I think the big risk is that the Fed pulls the punchbowl from the market *and* consumer spending stops."

After listening to everyone speak his piece, Johnstone piped up. "Four or five months ago," he said, "we thought we were in the ninth inning. Now it looks like we're in extra innings." At that, everyone laughed, but it was an edgy laugh, the kind that means the joke has struck close to the bone.

"This meeting sure is bearish," Terrana said with a sigh.

As the meeting drew to a close, a young woman, new to Fidelity, suddenly asked for a straw poll on when the bull market would end. It was an embarrassing moment. Every fund manager in the room suddenly looked down at his shoes. The young woman persisted. Again the assembled portfolio managers demurred, more firmly this time. Here were seventeen market experts, the very people the middle class had come to rely on to guide them through the money revolution, each one of them working the bull market for every last dime. Yet they were no longer willing to look the thing square in the eye.

ON SEPTEMBER 22, 1987, CHARLES SCHWAB & CO. WENT PUBLIC. It was, in almost every respect, an astounding deal. Less than six months after it had broken away from BankAmerica, the company sold 8 million shares on the New York Stock Exchange, at a price of $16.50 a share, instantly raising $132 million in capital. Those 8 million shares, however, represented only a third of the total outstanding, meaning that the offering established a market value for the company of around $400 million. To put it another way, the market was saying that Schwab was worth more than twice what its executives had paid BankAmerica to buy it back the previous March. The $16.50 share price also meant that Schwab stock sold at a p/e ratio of 15, significantly higher than other brokerage stocks. Although the offering prospectus had been full of cautionary notes, investors—many of them Schwab's own customers—had been undeterred. On the contrary, demand for the stock had been so strong that Schwab had been able to offer more stock, and at a higher price, than originally planned. And, of course, the deal made Chuck Schwab and his immediate circle of executives instant multimillionaires. Schwab, who had put up $9 million during the buyout for a little less than a third of the company, was worth well over $100 million after the stock offering.

And the timing of the deal! In hindsight, that was the most spectacular part of all. On September 22, the Dow Jones average opened at 2492.82. That was more than 200 points below its late-August peak,[4] though no one yet knew for sure that the bull market had ended. Wall Street was describing the month-long skid as a "sell-off" or a "correction"—a temporary phenomenon in any case. On the very day Schwab chose to sell stock to the public, hope was suddenly renewed when the market did an abrupt about-face, and rose an unheard-of seventy-five points. Thus did Schwab sell its shares into the biggest one-day gain in the history of the Dow Jones average.[5]

But of course this was not the reason, finally, why the Schwab offering would turn out to be so memorable. It was remembered because it beat the crash of 1987 by a hair: a scant eighteen trading sessions stood between Schwab's offering and Black Monday. Clearly, Chuck Schwab's instinct had been right back in March when he had insisted on putting together a public offering while his firm was still celebrating its break from Bank-America. Had there been the slightest hitch along the way the deal would never have taken place. The crash would have wiped the offering off the table, and Schwab would have been back in his familiar position of having to scramble for capital.

And that's the best-case scenario. A far more plausible scenario is that, had the offering not taken place, the entire company would have been wiped off the table, or at least swallowed up by someone bigger and better capitalized. So, yes, Chuck Schwab had very good instincts. But the timing of the offering confirmed something else about him, as if it still needed confirmation. He was lucky. And he was luckiest when he most needed to be. Never did he need it more than in the aftermath of the crash of 1987.

One of Peter Lynch's favorite factoids, which he loved to trot out when visiting journalists came calling, was that between 1955 and 1985, the market dropped some 1,500 points—on Mondays. The Monday decline phenomenon fit all too nicely with one of Lynch's pet theories, which is why he trotted it out so often: Americans, he believed, did too much "negative" thinking, which affected their ability to be objective about buying and selling stocks. "The reason for the Monday decline," Lynch would assert, "is that on the weekend everyone becomes an amateur economist." They read the gloomy articles in the Sunday papers, and became gloomy themselves. Naturally, when the market opened on Monday, they wanted to sell. "It's no coincidence," Lynch would later add, "that in 1987, the market crashed on a Monday."

One hesitates to give much credence to a theory as off-the-cuff as this one, but at the very least, Lynch was right about Black Monday. The bull market took its last breath on Tuesday, October 13, when the Dow Jones average rose thirty-seven points. On Wednesday, the market dropped ninety-five points. On Thursday, it dropped another fifty-seven points. And on Friday, October 16, the market virtually gave out, losing 108 points—almost 5 percent of its value—as a record 338 million shares were traded. In a week's time, the Dow had lost 11 percent of its value, making it the single worst week in the stock market since World War II.

And then came the weekend. . . .

Did the American middle class think about the stock market that weekend? How could it not? The drop in the Dow Jones average wasn't just news for the business section, it was all over the front page. It led the television news shows. Newsletter writers all over the country sent out emergency advisories to their subscribers advising them to get out, or stay in, depending on whether the writer was a bear or a bull.[6] Brokers spent the weekend calling clients. Mutual fund companies placed soothing ads in the Sunday papers, many of which suggested that bond funds might be a good place for customers to put their money. Once upon a time, there might have been some chortling about the apparent end of the bull market, as Main Street sat back and waited for Wall Street to get its comeuppance. But the divide between Main Street and Wall Street was too narrow now for that kind of smugness: Main Street's money was now so commingled with Wall Street's that anything hurting the latter would also hurt the former. That was one of the logical consequences of bringing Wall Street to Main Street.

Did the American middle class think about the stock market that weekend? It thought about little else. Or at least it seemed that way to the phone operators at Schwab, at Fidelity, at Dreyfus, at Vanguard, at T. Rowe Price, at every financial institution that had captured middle-class savings during the money revolution and transformed it into middle-class investments. At all the mutual fund companies and brokerage houses, the phone lines were jammed; Fidelity alone received 80,000 calls from customers that weekend, the majority of whom were doing exactly what you'd expect novice investors to do in the face of a 108 point market drop. They were bailing out. But since the the stock exchanges were closed, Fidelity could not comply with its customers' wishes until Monday morning. And because Fidelity's funds had little in the way of cash cushions, when Monday came, the company would have to sell hundreds of millions of dollars worth of stock into a very fragile market to meet the demand for redemptions. This was a very troubling prospect. And that's why the people who ran the likes of Fidelity and Schwab and Vanguard knew—absolutely *knew*—what was going to happen next. It's not too much to say that everyone on Wall Street knew what was going to happen next.

John Phalen, Jr., the head of the New York Stock Exchange, would later tell reporters that he came to work that day expecting the market to fall at least 200 points. Robert Farrell, the highly regarded market analyst for Merrill Lynch, told his colleagues early Monday morning that it could be "a calamitous day." A Dallas money manager named Richard W. Fisher was dining that Sunday night with Margaret Thatcher and her son Mark, who lived in Dallas. During dinner one of the guests made a call to find out how the markets were doing in Asia, where Monday morning had already arrived. They were collapsing. That's when they all knew. At Fidelity, company executives held meetings all weekend, totting up the stocks they were going to have to sell on Monday, trying to come up with some strategy to lessen the effect on the overall market. When the figure reached $1 billion worth of stock, they knew that theirs was a hopeless exercise. You couldn't dump $1 billion worth of stocks in a single day and not have it affect the market. You just couldn't.

And then came Monday. . . .

The crash itself was a blur, a day that would be remembered by those who participated in it as being surreal. *Was it really happening?* Could it really be possible that stocks—big, important stocks, like IBM and Merck— couldn't open because there were no buyers, only sellers? Or was it some kind of weird nightmare that would go away if they could just rouse themselves from it? There were times that day when stock traders felt as though they were standing outside their own bodies, watching themselves with a bizarre detachment as they frantically attempted to unload stocks. These feelings were especially pronounced late in the afternoon, when the market, after seeming to stabilize—having already dropped by more than 300 points—suddenly took one last stomach-wrenching swoon, and fell about 200 points in the last hour of trading. The last hour was the apocalypse. Having opened that day at 2246, the Dow Jones average closed at 1738—a 508 point free fall. That amounted to a staggering 22 percent loss, the largest one-day drop ever.[7] On the exchange floor, in the trading rooms of the brokerage firms, in the offices of everyone on Wall Street, people just sat there, numb, speechless, completely overwhelmed by what they were seeing.

"Monday was the longest day of my life," wrote one such Wall Street personage, the author and investment adviser John Spooner, writing in the *Boston Globe*. "Shock and shutdown set in around noon. . . . The entire day was like walking through a dream. I had no center; I was watching a Fellini movie but I was in it at the same time." That evening, after the market had closed and Wall Street employees began bumping into each other at restaurants or bars, they found it difficult to talk about the day. Instead, an eerie silence took hold, as people seemed to realize that words were inadequate to describe what they had just been through. Sometimes, people would start laughing, for no reason. By the next morning, the first crash jokes were being passed around. "What do you say to a thirty-year-old investment banker?" went one. "Waiter!"

Those feelings of numbness, of awe, of fear, of standing in the middle of a horrific nightmare—they existed on Main Street, too. In Miami, an investor named Arthur Kane, wiped out by the crash, it was reported,[8] because most of his $11 million portfolio had been bought on margin, walked into the office of his Merrill Lynch broker, pulled out a .357 Magnum, and opened fire. By the time his shooting spree had ended, Kane had seriously wounded his broker and killed the Merrill Lynch office manager. Then he turned the gun on himself and fired one last time.

In 1929, of course, the sight of distraught investors jumping to their death became one of the resonant images of that crash. In 1987, the sight of distraught investors walking into their brokerage offices and opening fire did not, thank goodness, become one of the resonant images of Black Monday: it only happened that one time in Miami.[9] Rather, the images one saw that day, and in the chaotic days that followed, were pictures of people simply staring, disbelieving, their jaws agape, as they watched every tick of the Dow Jones average. In San Francisco, one could walk into the Schwab office and see dozens of middle-class investors, milling around, peering helplessly at the digital Dow as it flashed across a large screen. In New York, one could see the same thing at Fidelity's large investment center at Park Avenue and 52nd Street, where so many people gathered that when reporters went in search of "average investors" to interview about the crash, they headed for Park and 52nd rather than a Wall Street location.

In Boston, on the day after the crash—a day that was as scary as Black Monday, as the Dow lurched insanely from 200 points up to 150 points down, and then back up again[10]—people stood outside a Fidelity center in the financial district, staring into a storefront window, where a flashy digital sign transmitted the latest numbers. By lunchtime, the crowd had grown so large, and so transfixed, that the police asked the company to turn off the sign so that traffic could get through. Fidelity complied. No one moved. Truck drivers honked their horns angrily. Still no one moved. They were in a market-induced trance. Inside, late in the afternoon, one could find more than twenty people huddled in a corner around two Quotron machines. They had been there all day, and they looked tired and dazed—the way people look when they're in the middle of an all-night poker game, when they're sick of playing, and the game seems stale, and all they want to do is quit and go home. But they couldn't go home, not until the market closed. They were in too deep. Thus did the middle-class react to the crash of 1987.

The biggest problem most people had was getting through to their brokers or fund companies on the telephone. Having taught Americans that they could transact all their financial business over the telephone, financial institutions now reaped what they had sown. Phone lines were constantly busy, and customers became infuriated when they couldn't get through, not even at 3:00 A.M. At Schwab, the computer system was completely overwhelmed by 8:00 A.M. Monday morning: it simply did not have the capacity to handle the volume of trades—approaching 60,000 a day, when 15,000 was the norm—or phone calls. The toll-free phone system collapsed, and for several days, customers got only a busy signal. By Wednesday the entire computer system had shut down, and Schwab was reduced to running apologies in California newspapers. Other discounters simply stopped answering the phones. Because of Ned Johnson's lust for computer technology, Fidelity did better than most; that week, it handled an average of 300,000 calls a day—a half-million poured in on Tuesday alone—and while most customers got through, they had to spend up to an hour on hold.[11] Quite a few of the calls were fielded by mid-level executives, pulled away from their other work to help answer the flood of telephone calls.

Fidelity came out of the crash pretty well. Although the company received some blame for supposedly helping to trigger the events of Black Monday—it had dumped $500 million worth of stock in the first hour of trading, and by the time the day had ended, it had accounted for 4.5 percent of the sell-off—its systems stood up pretty well. And to a large degree, so did its assets. Toward the end of the week, the *Boston Globe* was reporting that the assets Fidelity had under management had shrunk from $88 billion to $75 billion. But that was more the result of market losses than customers fleeing the company. Not surprisingly, the firm's money funds swelled considerably that week.

As for Peter Lynch, he was playing golf in Ireland when the crash came, his first day of a much-delayed vacation. Because of the time difference, he finished his round of golf two hours before the opening of the stock exchange, and then checked into a hotel where he spent the next five and a half hours on the phone to Boston. On Tuesday, he worked the phone from the airport, pleading with the Irish operators to keep the line open: "We're talking about hundreds of millions of dollars here," he implored. By Wednesday he was back in his office. Later, his travails became one of the mini-sagas to come out of the crash, but in truth, it wouldn't have mattered much if he had been around. On Black Monday, Magellan lost 17 percent of its value, compared to the 22 percent drop in the Dow, while shrinking in size from $11 billion to $7.7 billion. Given its nature as an aggressive growth fund, and its mandate to be fully invested at all times, that is about the best one could have expected. Balanced Fund, which Cabour managed, was down only 6 percent. By the middle of the week, Fidelity's fund managers had begun to buy stocks again. For them, the worst was over.

⤲

THE WORST WAS NOT OVER FOR SCHWAB.

Early in the morning of October 29, ten days after Black Monday, Charles Schwab was forced to admit that his newly public company—whose stock he had so proudly sold to his own customers—had lost $22 million in the crash. Needing to get the word out before the markets opened in the east, Schwab made the announcement at 6:00 A.M., in a hotel conference room in downtown San Francisco, before a gauntlet of cameras and reporters. The loss was large enough, Schwab conceded, that it would wipe out virtually all the profits the firm had made during the last half of 1987. When trading opened that day, Schwab's stock, which had already tumbled from $16.50 to around $8 a share in the previous weeks, tumbled some more, to $6.50. "I am profoundly unhappy," Schwab said that morning. He wasn't the only one.

It was, all in all, a startling admission Schwab made that morning, revealing the degree to which Schwab had temporarily lost control of his company, as he tended to do whenever the company went on one of its big growth spurts. "It's always easy to look good when the market is going up," says one former employee—when new customers are walking in at the rate of 34,000 a month, and a new branch office is being opened every month, and new employees are being hired as fast as they can apply for jobs. When the crash came, Schwab's lack of control could no longer be hidden. Schwab was a mess the week of the crash; as late as Wednesday the computer systems still weren't working, and people still couldn't get through on the phones. And when customers did get through, it didn't necessarily mean that their trades were executed promptly. Thousands of orders got backed up in the chaos of the crash, and that was among the reasons for the $22 million loss. Whenever the company was late executing a trade, and the price continued to fall in the meantime, Schwab had to make up the difference to the customer.

Far more than the late orders, however, Schwab had been hurt for another reason: it had allowed a small number of customers to trade so-called naked options, which are an extremely dangerous form of stock speculation. This too was part of losing control. No command decision had even been made about option trading; it was just one of those things that seemed to have happened at Schwab when no one was paying much attention.*

In fact, a single customer, based in Hong Kong and conducting his business through Schwab's small Hong Kong branch, was responsible for $13 million of the $22 million loss. The customer's account had grown so large that on Black Monday he had margin calls of $124 million. Although the customer's name was not divulged, the magnitude of Schwab's error was clear to everyone at the press conference. "That someone was not aware of the potential for this kind of swing was just unforgivable," a brokerage source later told the *Wall Street Journal,* and Schwab himself pretty much conceded the point. Looking glumly into the cameras, he vowed that the firm would never again allow an account to grow that large, and that the firm would put much stricter controls on its options selling. "We don't like it," he told the press, reading from a script, "it will never happen again, but that's the way it is." He also insisted that despite the loss, the firm was not in financial trouble. Thanks to its miraculously timed public offering, this was quite true.

The unnamed Hong Kong investor with the $124 million in margin calls was the big story the next day. As embarrassing as it was, the Schwab staff had to feel relieved. For what never got reported was how much worse it might have been—indeed, how much worse it very nearly was. The reporters attending the press conference that Thursday morning never knew that the public relations staff had written two different scripts for the affair. In one, the loss was $22 million, after tax, and the company, though chagrined, was largely out of harm's way. In the other, the loss was $100 million, pretax, and the company, its capital suddenly wiped out and finding itself in violation of its loan covenants, was in serious jeopardy. Partly because *Business Week* was feverishly chasing the story of the Hong Kong investor, partly because rumors were circulating on Wall Street that Schwab was in trouble—and partly because, as a publicly traded company, Schwab had a duty to disclose bad news promptly—the company's executives had decided to hold a press conference even before they knew the outcome of their dealings in Hong Kong. As late as Wednesday evening, when Chuck

---

* Options work much like commodities, acting essentially to bind a customer to a promise to buy or sell an underlying stock, or basket of stocks, at a later date. To put it another way, an option is a bet on the future price of a stock, or on the direction of the market itself. What makes it so dangerous is that options traders put up very little of the purchase price at the time they buy their option; in the case of a "naked" option, they put up no money at all. Should the market suddenly turn against them, the margin calls can be enormous. And should the customer be unable to meet the margin call, then the responsibility for paying up falls on the brokerage firm that sold him the option in the first place.

Schwab left the office to go home, he still didn't know which script he would
be using the next day. It wasn't until 5:00 A.M. Thursday, an hour before the
press conference, that the word came through that they would be able to use
the script with the lesser amount. That's how close to the edge Schwab came
during the crash of 1987.

The investor's name, the *Wall Street Journal* later learned,[12] was Teh Huei
"Ted" Wang. He was fifty-two years old. Together with his wife Nina, he
ran a company called the Chinachem Group, which was, as the *Journal*
described it, "a closely held property and construction concern in Hong
Kong." In the Hong Kong brokerage community, however, the multimil-
lionaire real estate developer was best known for his weakness for stock
speculation. His appetite for betting on the market appeared to be insatiable,
and he also appeared to have the means to back it up. There were those at
Schwab who were convinced, afterward, that he was worth in the range of
$1.5 billion, his money scattered in accounts across the globe. There were
those in Hong Kong who were apparently convinced of the same thing. In
1983, Wang had been abducted from his car and held for eight days, while
his kidnappers negotiated with his wife on an appropriate ransom. She
reportedly paid $11 million to get her husband back.

   Schwab had had an office in Hong Kong since 1981; it was the company's
one overseas branch. The decision to establish an outpost there had been
typical: someone with potential investment capital wanted to open a branch
in Hong Kong, so the deed was done. For much of its existence, the office
lost money, though not enough to cause anyone at Schwab to agitate for
closing it down. More recently, it had made a great deal of money for the
company, so much so that Schwab had begun drawing up plans to expand
his presence in the Far East.

   The profits, it turns out, had been due largely to the trading habits of
Wang, as well as a handful of other, smaller options players in Hong Kong,
all of whom generated enormous commissions. Wang himself had been a
customer in good standing for some three years, and afterward, Schwab
officials would point to this long-standing relationship as evidence that
things were not as out of control as they had seemed—that Wang and
Schwab had enough history together to allay any fears about his ability to
meet margin calls. In making this claim, however, the Schwab forces con-
veniently left out a crucial fact. True, for most of the time that Wang did
business with Schwab, he'd been a big customer, but he only did about a
third of his trades with Schwab. Wang took many of his biggest trades
elsewhere, primarily to Drexel Burnham Lambert.

The more painful fact is that Wang decided to move *all* his business to Schwab a mere three months before the crash, after he reportedly had a falling out with his Drexel broker. Only then did the Schwab Hong Kong office realize what an amazing amount of trading Wang did. It is not uncommon for a serious options player to be juggling hundreds of separate contracts at any one time; Wang was juggling thousands of contracts—nay, tens of thousands. When the crash came, he had upward of 42,000 contracts outstanding; it took five Schwab accountants several days just to untangle his positions. In addition, instead of buying an options contract outright, Wang preferred to short-sell options, an action that greatly increased both his potential gains and his potential risks. By October 1987, his main strategy was to short "put" options. Since a put option is a bet that the market is going down, Wang, in effect, was betting against the speculators who were betting against the market. What he was doing, of course, was gambling, in the highest stakes game he could find.

Obviously, if you spent most of the bull market shorting put options, you made a lot of money. Wang did indeed make a lot of money—possibly as much as $100 million. It's equally obvious, though, that if you continued shorting put options through August and September 1987, when the market was making its jagged trip downward—and Wang had consolidated all his trading with Schwab—your losing days would far outnumber your winning days. This was also true of Wang. Yet right up until the crash, he always met his margin calls—met them promptly and without complaint. The week before Black Monday, he had wired $10 million to Schwab in response to a margin call. One suspects that if Schwab officials had taken the time to focus on the sheer size of the account, they would have realized that Wang was a disaster waiting to happen. But they never got around to focusing on the account, in part because the firm lacked the kind of controls that would have alerted the executives to the danger lurking in Hong Kong. But they also missed it because disaster *hadn't* happened. The warning bells that a missed margin call would have triggered never went off.

On Sunday, October 18, the day before the crash, most of the top executives of the company attended a wedding; their head of marketing was getting married. After the 100 point drop on Friday, the groom already knew his honeymoon was going to be postponed, and his Schwab colleagues were distracted that Sunday afternoon, worried about what Monday would bring. Nervously, they broached the subject of Hong Kong among themselves. A bit too late, they had finally become aware of the existence of Mr. Wang and his account. As a result of the Friday drop, he had a $27 million margin call due Monday morning.

Which, amazingly, he made, well before the market opened. By then, however, warning bells were going off everywhere. Most Schwab managers were in the office by 5:00 A.M. on Black Monday; by 6:30 A.M., when the market opened on the East Coast, it was obvious to everyone that the day was going to be catastrophic. Schwab's main office wouldn't open its doors for hours, yet the place was already in a state of complete chaos: computers not working, phone lines overloaded, people racing about frantically trying to patch things up. And hovering over all this frantic activity was the fearful specter of a customer no one in San Francisco knew a thing about whose account had the potential to ruin them. Desperately, Schwab executives tried to track Wang's account on their computer screens. They couldn't do it: his losses, which were mounting by the minute, were already so large that they disabled the computer, which was not programmed to absorb an account that size. One top executive was later described by a colleague as "strung out." Another former executive recalls that there were people who were "kind of delirious."

By midmorning, Schwab's bankers at Security Pacific were sniffing around, trying to find out if the firm's problems were causing it to be in violation of its loan covenants. They weren't—not yet anyway—though the calls were a reminder of how serious the situation was, and how much hinged on what was happening half a world away. Half a world away, however, things were not good. Wang's margin calls were now over $100 million—money for which Schwab would be liable if Wang did not come through. Early on Black Monday, he had come up with another $13 million, on top of the $27 million he had paid earlier. But as the market continued to disintegrate, he stopped making margin calls. By day's end, Wang owed Schwab $84 million—and the firm could no longer reach him.

Surely, this should not have come as a shock to the Schwab troops: how much of a surprise can it be to learn that a man who is unexpectedly saddled with $84 million worth of debt is not taking phone calls? But Schwab officials, especially those in the Hong Kong branch, did seem surprised. Worse, they seemed at a loss as to what to do next. As was so often the case at Schwab, what happened next was less the result of some boldly conceived, decisively executed plan of action than it was the result of one man's impulsive decision to do something fast. By midmorning Monday, even before the market had made its final 200 point dive, a Schwab executive named Robert Rosseau had put himself on a plane to Hong Kong. When he arrived—to do what, exactly, he wasn't yet sure—it was 8:00 P.M., Hong Kong time.

*     *     *

Robert Rosseau was to Schwab what Chuck Jarvie had been to Fidelity: a man who was fundamentally miscast at the company yet who turned out to be exactly the right person for one small, critical moment. Like Jarvie at Fidelity, Rosseau joined the company at a fairly high level—he was the head of retail services—but never really fit with the other executives, and lasted little more than a year. "There was a clique at Schwab," he says now, and he was never going to be part of it. Arguing among the executives had long been a part of the company culture, but Rosseau didn't just argue, he confronted. He was too combative, too brusque, and most of all too quick to criticize the company's management practices and its other executives. His criticisms, though often right, were brutal: "My branch managers had an impossible job," he would later say. "The branches were too small. They didn't have scheduled lunches or breaks. The phones were sporadic." He believed that the company was run in slipshod fashion, and no one seemed especially interested in doing anything about it. It is perhaps not a surprise that Schwab executives don't have much good to say about Rosseau, even though he was directly responsible for salvaging the desperate situation unfolding in Hong Kong. A powerfully built Vietnam veteran, he did so with relish. "I had ten days of very little sleep, and just sheer, intense pressure all the time," he says with a smile. "It was by far the most interesting thing I've ever done in my life."

So what do you do when you're trying to rope in a customer who owes you $84 million? You do everything you can think of. You hire detectives to trace both the man and his money.[13] You get interpreters to help you wend your way through the maze of regulators and bureaucrats and other people you need to deal with. You get the best local lawyers you can find, and attempt to tie your customer up in the courts. You also hire another, competing lawyer, and have him come in when everyone else has gone home to second-guess the strategy.

And if you're Bob Rosseau, with a flair for the dramatic, you tell your lawyer things like, "We're talking about the life of the company. You *will* prevail!" And when the lawyer replies in a huff, "I don't do business that way," you shout back at him, "You push until they threaten to put you in *jail*! Is that *clear*?" When you set up your operation in a Hong Kong office building, you paper the windows over so no one can see in, and bring in your own private phone lines to keep the phones from being tapped, and tape all your phone calls, since you may need to listen to them again. You give the whole thing the flavor of a covert operation—which to some extent it is. "I had to use all my skills as a street fighter," he would later say with relish.

Tuesday, his first day in Hong Kong, was a bad day for Rosseau. First, the lawyer Schwab had retained in Hong Kong went to court to get a judge to freeze Wang's assets. But the lawyer had made several errors, and the case was thrown out of court—though the door was left open for Schwab to return with the same request at a later date. Rosseau, of course, immediately fired the lawyer (''I said, 'You messed up.' I said, 'You're goddamn lucky the judge gave us a sliver.' '') and hired a better-connected firm. He made them work all night rewriting the request.

Then, in the afternoon, the Schwab executives began calling in. ''They were trying to run the thing from San Francisco,'' Rosseau recalls with annoyance. (''I said, 'Look guys, I don't have *time* to entertain you people.' I said, 'You get fifteen minutes for a conference call.' I said, 'This is a *war* over here.' '')

Wednesday was a little better, as Rosseau and his hastily put-together team began untangling Wang's byzantine finances—he apparently had some 200 different shell corporations through which he would move money. And Thursday was pretty good. That's when the new lawyer went to court and got the order they wanted, the one that tied up Wang's assets. By Friday, Rosseau had identified enough of Wang's assets—and had locked them up firmly enough—that the investor had no choice but to start dealing with Schwab.

Or, rather, the investor's wife had no choice, for with Ted Wang refusing to deal face-to-face with Rosseau, it was Nina Wang who wound up doing most of the negotiating. She turned out to be a big player in the market herself, though she stayed away from the kind of speculative options trading her husband favored. She was not one to flaunt her wealth, or even, it would appear, spend very much of it. She was also a smart, tough negotiator who absolutely understood the leverage she held. First, the shell corporations through which Wang did most of his trading offered him some limited liability, meaning that he was never going to have to pay 100 percent on the dollar. And second, Rosseau was in a tremendous hurry to come to an agreement because Schwab needed to disclose the extent of its loss as quickly as possible. Hence, the longer Mrs. Wang dragged out the negotiations, the more favorable they were likely to be.

They played what amounted to a week-long high-stakes chess match. They both implicitly understood that the Wangs would not have to pay the full amount of the margin call—Schwab's mistake in allowing the account to get so out of hand would have to result in some pain for the company—and so they dickered over the size of the settlement, over how much would be paid at once and how much over time, over which assets would be liquidated to make the payments. These meetings, which lasted for hours, and were conducted both face-to-face and through lawyers, were tense but cordial. As the days passed and the settlement grew closer, an odd respect grew between the two adversaries.

The agreement they came up with called for the Wangs to pay off $67 million of their obligation, with Schwab absorbing the rest. In addition, Mrs. Wang and Rosseau agreed that she would pay only a portion of the money up front, with the rest to be paid off in a series of installments, the last of which would be due at the end of December. This is the deal that Rosseau phoned into Schwab's San Francisco headquarters early that Thursday morning, causing the top executives, he would later say, "to do cartwheels in the office." That is the deal that was reported in the press.

Rosseau did not return to San Francisco right away. He stayed in Hong Kong until the last payment was made, which Mrs. Wang handed to him over dinner one night. The two former adversaries talked about the ordeal they had both just been through, like soldiers recalling a memorable battle. She asked him which of her moves had been wrong, and what she should have done differently. And then she asked him if he wanted to go to work for the Wangs. Rosseau said no; it was time to go home.

In early November, when the *Journal* came across Wang's name in some court filings in Chicago, a reporter called her for a comment. "It's too dangerous to talk to the press," she said. "Talk to my lawyer." In this, she appears to have been right. Years later, the story wafted back that Mr. Wang had reportedly been kidnapped a second time. This time the ransom was set at $60 million. Nina Wang was said to have paid $30 million to free her husband, but it wasn't enough. When police broke into the apartment of the suspected kidnappers, they found the money but not her husband. Ted Wang, it was said, has never been seen since.

## CHAPTER 18

# Peter Lynch's Long Good-bye

## *March 1990*

SEVEN MONTHS AFTER the market crash, on a cool, foggy May morning in 1988, ten people walked into a large, unadorned conference room somewhere in Maryland, and took seats around a long table. They included eight men and two women, their ages ranging from early thirties to late seventies. One of the men was a minister; another was a retired engineer; three were small business owners. Of the two women, the younger was a tour operator who listed her hobbies as gardening and traveling, while the older woman, a homemaker, said that she enjoyed cooking and investing. This latter interest, in fact, was the reason these ten, randomly selected people had been brought together. This was a focus group session, being conducted by one of America's large financial institutions.[1] It wanted to hear the middle-class talk about its money.

Was it really only a decade ago that middle-class Americans were horrified at the thought of talking openly about their money? These middle-class Americans were quite comfortable talking about their money, eager to do so, in fact. They'd had a lot on their minds since the crash. The Dow Jones average, on this May day, had opened at 1951.09. In seven months, it had regained over 200 of the 500 points it had lost on Black Monday; fears that the crash of 1987 would lead to the next great Depression had pretty much vanished. The more sanguine view—that the crash had simply been a long overdue correction that unfortunately occurred in a single day—had taken hold. Just the same, no one in the room took much solace from the Dow's climb. The market's ride had been a bumpy one, with thirty- and forty-point one-day swings far too common for comfort. The Dow could get above 2100 one day (as it did April 12), only to drop below 2000 a week later. People were scared: "The big jumps make me very insecure," one man said. "I can't work eight hours a day at my job and then know what's going on in the stock market. If it's going down, I'm stuck."

They were confused:

- "I feel like an ostrich with my head in the sand. I don't know what to do. It's just too much."
- "I have a heckuva problem knowing where to put my money with the market conditions that exist today. I feel as though I don't have any good choices. I keep hoping someone will tell me what to do."
- "One day you hear interest rates are going up. The next day you hear they are going down. What's going on?"

They felt tremendous resentment toward the big institutional investors, who, they were convinced, held all the advantages:

- "Last year, there was a mob psychology. Everybody was doing the same thing. And then the smart people who run the pension funds started to get out, while all the dumb people, like myself, stayed in."
- "I feel as though the institutional people said, 'We've made enough, let's get out.' The minor investors didn't have a chance by comparison."

They felt foolish:

- "I raced into the market a month before the crash, trying to make a short-term profit. It's the only time I've *ever* tried to make a short-term profit. I wanted to use the money to build a house. I lost my shirt."
- "Every time I start to make money, I listen to someone or read something and make a mistake."

And, overwhelmingly, they felt that the October crash had sobered them up:

- "I'm much more cautious now."
- "I've moved into bond funds since the crash."
- "I'm still willing to take the risk, but I'm more sober about it now."

*I'm still willing to take the risk.* Here, surely, was the key to everything: here was what separated the 1987 market crash from all the bear markets that had come before it. Always before, the ugly aftermath of a long bull market had been accompanied by the sound of scurrying feet, as panicked small investors turned tail and ran as far from the market as they could. But after the crash of 1987, small investors did not turn and run, at least not in huge numbers.[2] The New York Stock Exchange, in one of its regular shareholder surveys, found almost no drop-off in the number of stockholders in the year after the crash. The fund companies all noticed the same thing: new sales were slow, and business was sluggish, but customers simply did not flee the way they had feared. They *moved* their money, in ways that reflected a new caution,[3] shifting assets from an aggressive fund to a less aggressive one, from an equity fund to a bond fund, from a bond fund to a money market fund. But they kept their assets in the company.

A year after the crash, both *The New York Times* and the *Wall Street Journal* ran long articles about the state of the market; both concluded that investors were skittish, and that the market, as the *Journal* put it, was "battling a pervasive malaise." "October is in the back of everyone's mind, day in and day out," one market expert told the paper. But skittish investors were better than no investors at all. For anyone who had worked at a mutual fund company in the early 1970s, and had watched in dismay as customers pulled assets out, it was an astonishing change. It was, indeed, a revolutionary change. Even the largest one-day drop in history could not push the middle-class out of the stock market. "The 1980s taught investors that risk lay not in playing the investment game unsuccessfully, but in not playing at all," concluded John Rekenthaler, an editor of *Morningstar Mutual Funds,* an authoritative mutual fund periodical.[4]

That Americans would stay in the market, despite their fears and feelings of inadequacy, was easy enough to understand. The stock market was now seen as one of the financial tools at the disposal of the middle-class. Despite the crash, it still offered the possibility of gains that could not be matched anywhere else. *Offered,* not guaranteed: people understood that now. If they put money in the bank now, it was not out of panic; it was because bank long-term CDs were offering high rates that they wanted to lock in. The days when banks were the big winners after a market downturn—those days were emphatically over.

That mutual funds would remain America's favorite way to invest after the crash was a somewhat more complicated issue. Consultant Edward Furash views the aftermath of the 1987 crash as the ultimate triumph of the fund companies: "From 1972 to 1987," he notes, "the fund companies created the first financial industry that truly understood how to merchandise." Furash continues:

> The multi-fund company, the ease of picking funds and switching from one to another, the idea that you laid out a buffet and that consumers picked out flavors from the buffet—that was all part of that merchandising effort. They catered to the ego needs of the emerging investor who said, "I'm not giving

my money to some schmuck broker!''. . . People who gave their money to brokers tended to blame their brokers when they lost money in the crash, but people who put their money in mutual funds tended to blame themselves. And the reason is that the fund industry had convinced the American consumer, during this 15 year period, that *he* was responsible for where he put his money, and for what happened to it.

This focus on merchandising also meshed perfectly with the habits developed by the baby boom generation, who were the predominant purchasers of mutual funds. So theorized Don Phillips, the publisher of *Morningstar Mutual Funds:* ''One of the great hidden advantages of the fund industry,'' he wrote, ''is that by packaging investments in consumer wrapping, mutual funds tap into the consumption skills baby boomers have spent their lifetimes refining. . . . [F]unds make investing very much like shopping.''

Both these views have much to commend them. But there were other reasons why mutual funds caught on in the 1980s. They were easy to understand and to use. They offered performance measures that people could grab onto. They were the focus of a huge amount of press coverage. And the ''stars'' of the mutual fund industry—the money managers who captured the public's fancy, such as Peter Lynch, or John Templeton, who ran his own successful fund company, or John Neff, who managed the legendary Windsor Fund at Vanguard—were a far cry from the gunslingers of old. They were diligent stock pickers who didn't cut corners or sacrifice long-term performance in order to chalk up gaudy short-term numbers, as the gunslingers of the 1960s had so often done. Rarely has any American industry had a better group of headliners to serve as role models and spokesmen. The sports equivalent would have been if Michael Jordan had never gambled; Charles Barkley had never spit at a fan; Magic Johnson had never become infected with HIV as a result of his own reckless sexual behavior.

Not least, mutual funds became the investment vehicle of the middle-class because they still struck people as making a great deal of sense. If anything, mutual funds made more sense than ever after the crash. For one thing, even the most aggressive mutual funds outperformed the market on Black Monday, and in so doing provided at least a little comfort to small investors. More importantly, as the financial life of the middle-class became ever more complicated, connected irrevocably to such arcana as the state of the Japanese market and the shape of the yield curve, Americans took increasing solace in the central notion behind mutual funds—that by putting money in a fund, they were hiring a professional to make market decisions they felt increasingly incapable of making themselves. It wasn't the perfect solution—financial consumers still had to sort through thousands of funds to find those that appealed to them. And an investment in a mutual fund certainly did not eliminate all worries, not by a long shot. But for millions of people, mutual funds were the most reassuring of financial products.

There was nothing more apparent from that postcrash focus group session than this. "I don't have time to track my particular investments," said one man, as the others nodded their agreement. "So I'm willing to give a portion of my profits to a professional who tracks every twitch in the market. It's a security blanket."

Another man chimed in: "The big difference for me, before and after the crash, is that I've moved to mutual funds."

And a third: "With a mutual fund, you can look at their historic track record. I don't think the managers themselves know why they beat the market. But you can *see* if they've done it consistently."

A few moments later, the moderator asked the participants about how they viewed the differences between mutual fund companies and banks. Once again, their answers showed how powerful the mutual fund idea had become. Most of the people in the room actually preferred dealing with a mutual fund company over dealing with a bank. Virtually all of them believed the fund companies offered better service. None had the slightest qualms about sending checks for $5,000 or $10,000, via the post office, to a fund company on the other side of the country. Several even felt that their money was safer in a mutual fund than in a federally regulated bank or S&L. It was hard to imagine a more profound change in America's financial attitudes.

Except maybe this: As the focus group session was drawing to a close, the moderator suddenly asked her charges, "Is investing enjoyable or a chore?"

There was a pause, as the participants contemplated her question. Then one man replied: "It's neither. It's a necessity. It's a fact of life."

NONE OF THIS IS TO SAY that America's financial institutions didn't suffer after Black Monday. Even though investors didn't flee—and, indeed, even though it only took fifteen months for the market to regain every penny lost in the crash—there were rough times ahead for just about any company even tangentially connected to Wall Street. The big brokerage houses suffered because, although customers weren't shedding their portfolios en masse, they weren't adding to them either. In general, they were standing pat, which meant they weren't generating any commissions. The smaller, more prestigious underwriting firms suffered because the market for public offerings dried up after the crash. Firms that had bet their future on the continued growth of the mergers and acquisition business suffered because the drop in stock prices pretty much killed off corporate takeovers. Mutual fund companies suffered because a great deal of the assets they held moved to money market funds, where profits were razor thin. The *Wall Street Journal* suffered because the brokerage ads that had made the paper so fat during the bull market dropped off dramatically.

Even *Money* magazine suffered, as its own ad pages, heavily weighted toward financial firms, took a temporary dip. It also suffered a credibility problem, after its November 1987 issue was published with the classically upbeat headline, "Mutual Funds: New Ways to Pick Winners." Because the November issue had been printed before October 19, nobody wound up with more egg on their faces than the editors of *Money*. The December cover, however, saw an abrupt about-face. "SAFEST Places to Put Your Money NOW," it read, and for the next few years, the magazine suddenly seemed to have the word "safety" branded on the cover of every new issue. *Money* was suddenly full of the same caution as its readers—and for the same reason. The crash had sobered it up.

Yet *Money* magazine wound up rebounding much more quickly than the *Wall Street Journal*. By the end of 1988, *Money* had regained whatever ad pages and readers it had lost after the crash, and did so well over the next few years that it became one of the most profitable monthly magazines in America. The *Journal*, meanwhile, continued to lose both readers and ad pages, despite its unrivaled excellence. In one important way, this made a certain sense. In spite of the *Journal*'s reputation for producing superb journalism, the paper had never been completely in tune with the money revolution prior to Black Monday. *Money* magazine, on the other hand, had consciously linked its fortunes to the money revolution from the day Marshall Loeb walked in the door, and that explicit linkage continued long after he had walked out four years later. It is revealing of the magazine's mind-set that in late 1987 it conducted a joint focus group session with at least one large fund company—a company it both covered and accepted advertising from. It justified its action by saying that the two of them, the fund company and the magazine, were in the same basic business.

In a broad sense, one could see the same phenomenon at most of the financial institutions affected by the crash. The general rule of thumb seemed to be: the more a company's business reflected the enormous changes that had taken place during the money revolution, the more quickly it recovered.

Merrill Lynch offered a rather striking example of this. Yes, the firm had seen the money revolution coming back when Donald Regan ran the firm, and had even tried to get in front of the coming changes. But it had never been willing to abandon its old ways completely, and after Regan left, a good deal of backsliding took place. It still saw itself as a place where profits were made less by gathering assets than by having thousands of glib, hard-charging, won't-take-no-for-an-answer brokers persuade people to buy or sell stocks and bonds. Its culture still emphasized the needs and wants of its brokers rather than the needs and wants of its customers. And the "wire-house" side of the business, which was still huge, lived and died on commission revenue, just as it always had. Is it any wonder Merrill Lynch suffered after the crash?

In early January 1988, Merrill Lynch announced its first layoffs in more than a decade; 200 people were let go immediately, and 3,000 followed them out the door at the end of the month. That same month, Merrill Lynch announced that it was raising the commissions it charged retail customers by 27 percent. In late June, *Fortune* magazine weighed in with a brutal assessment of the firm's short-term prospects. Under the stinging headline, "Merrill Lynch: The Stumbling Herd," the lengthy article pointed out, among other things, that the firm had "screwed up the bull market" (as one Wall Street source put it); it had lost market share and turned in mediocre profits for most of the 1980s. An anonymous competitor speculated that if Merrill Lynch didn't turn around quickly, one of the giant Japanese firms might take it over. Donald Regan, also quoted in the article, seemed to go out of his way to encourage a merger of some sort, on the grounds that Merrill Lynch management was ill-equipped to cope with the demands of the changing financial universe. "Merrill," he said bluntly, "is not smart enough to start lending money de novo." This was the article that caused the executives of the firm to turn against their old boss.

The next year, 1989, was even worse. That was the year Merrill Lynch made plans to move out of one of its two World Financial Center headquarters buildings, laid off another 2,200 employees, eliminated a half-dozen different businesses, announced junk bond losses of $158 million, took a "restructuring" charge of $470 million, and wound up with a year-end loss of $213.4 million. And on it went. In 1990, even though the firm was back in the black, its stock continued to fall, while its employment rolls dropped from around 50,000 before the crash to under 40,000. It wasn't until 1991 that Merrill Lynch could truly be said to have put the crash of 1987 behind it. Of the changes it had put in place by then, one stands out. It had finally reformulated its fee and commission structure in such a way as to make the business of gathering assets into its mutual funds and cash management accounts a significantly profitable activity. As a result, it became less reliant on the commissions generated by its brokers. Well, better late than never.

Contrast this with the postcrash experience of the mutual fund companies. In spite of Black Monday, the assets held by mutual fund companies actually grew slightly in 1987. Although plenty of people moved out of funds in the second half of the year, the total held in equity, bond, and income funds went from $424 billion in 1986 to $454 billion in 1987, while the money held in money market and short-term municipal bond funds rose from $292 billion to $316 billion. The statistics clearly illustrated the way people had moved their money around right after the crash. In October 1987, the assets held in the various stock fund categories dropped by $15 billion. That same month, the assets in money market funds rose by $15 billion.

In 1988, a year generally described as "sluggish" for the fund companies, and the first year since 1979 that more people took money out of equity funds than put money in, the mutual fund industry still managed to see its total assets rise by about $35 billion, and ended the year at well over $800 billion. By 1989, the same year Merrill Lynch was losing $213 million, the mutual fund industry was recording its second best year in history. According to the ICI's figures, more than 20 percent of all new money that landed in any kind of savings or investment vehicle that year found its way into a mutual fund.[5]

At the individual fund companies, the story was pretty much the same. They breathed a sigh of relief in 1987, saw slow growth in 1988, and then watched in amazement as their business took off again in 1989. Were there problems? Of course there were. With customers so concerned with safety, several fund companies promoted a new idea called asset allocation funds, which were supposed to be more diversified (and hence safer) than traditional equity mutual funds. But asset allocation funds did poorly, and customers abandoned them. Many companies saw their first layoffs in more than a decade in 1988; Fidelity laid off 2,000 people that year, which amounted to about a quarter of its workforce. But they only had to do it once, and by 1989 most companies were expanding again, albeit cautiously. Fidelity came out with a new line of no-frills money market and short-term bond funds called Spartan funds, where costs were cut to the bone in order to boost yield. They were an instant sensation. Dreyfus, which had a similar product line, found similar success.

There are exceptions to every rule, and to the rule that those companies aligned with the money revolution did better after the crash than those that weren't, the exception was Schwab. To be sure, Schwab's postcrash life wasn't as grim as the struggle endured by many of the full-service wirehouses, but it was far more trying than the relatively pain-free experience of the mutual fund companies. What Schwab's ordeal probably proved was that in the face of hard times, vision and foresight—which Schwab demonstrably had—needs to be accompanied by competent management—which Schwab demonstrably lacked. Schwab suffered not because it hadn't grabbed onto the money revolution with sufficient fervor, but because it had performed miserably in the crash. When telephones aren't answered for days at a time, when the orders that are taken aren't executed promptly, when the entire firm seems to be having a nervous breakdown at the very moment customers are most dependent on it—that's not the sort of thing people tend to forget. In the past, customers had always been forgiving of Schwab's lapses. This time, they weren't.

"Discount Broker Sees Big Board Trades Off 10%," exclaimed a late 1987 headline in the *Wall Street Journal,* in a story reporting Schwab's forecast for the following year. Although this prediction turned out to be pretty close to the mark, it did not necessarily follow that Schwab's own business would only be off 10 percent. In fact, all through 1988 and into the early part of 1989, Schwab's trading volume ran at between 40 and 50 percent below its 1987 level—well below the level the company needed to sustain just to cover its overhead. Schwab struggled to get its costs down, firing 5 percent of its staff in February, mandating pay cuts for all its executives,[6] and canceling its ambitious expansion plans. Except for the much-publicized fourth quarter of 1987, Schwab managed to stay in the black, but just barely. In the second quarter of 1988, the company announced an 84 percent drop in earnings; by the time the year had ended, Schwab reported profits of only $7.4 million—a figure that had more in common with the Schwab of the early 1980s than the Schwab of the late bull market. During that same period of time, the stock price never got above $6 a share. It was, in all, a difficult time. People who were there remember in particular one top executive who seemed openly panic-stricken in the latter part of 1987 because the crash had brought him to the brink of bankruptcy. Just prior to Black Monday, he had borrowed a large sum of money against his Schwab stock. Now he had to meet margin calls, just like any other customer.

What most of these people will also say, though, is that the crash was the best thing that ever happened to Schwab. Schwab's brush with disaster in Hong Kong, and the hard times that followed, caused the company to focus on its long-term problems in a way it had never done before. For one thing Schwab himself stopped pretending that he had management skills and kicked himself even further upstairs. While holding on to the title "chairman and chief executive officer" (he also remained the firm's largest stockholder), he finally ceded most real control of the day-to-day operations to Stupski, who in turn promoted another executive, David Pottruck, to oversee the core discount brokerage business. Pottruck was a brute of a man, a hard-charging executive who got a kick out of telling interviewers that he was a wrestler—an example, he seemed to think, of his "toughness." Pottruck was a divisive figure within the firm, precisely because he was so un-Schwab-like in his dealings with people. But the harsh truth was, Schwab needed someone un-Schwab-like to do the hard things that had to be done. These were tasks Pottruck was more than happy to take on.

Secondly, the firm began to take steps to further broaden its image, and to get away from being perceived strictly—or even primarily—as a discount broker. Although Schwab had been moving slowly in this direction for some time, the crash accelerated that move. One smart thing the company did was to realize that the needs of old-line independent investors were different from those of the baby boomers who had come to stocks and bonds for the first time during the bull market. Schwab began creating different services to cater to those different needs. It put greater emphasis on its mutual fund marketplace, while exploring for the first time the idea of putting out its own mutual fund—an index fund that would mirror the performance of the larger market.[7] The fund, called the Schwab 1000, was surprisingly successful when it came to market in 1990, even though its introduction was accompanied by very little fanfare. The company also put new stress on another customer segment with high potential: the tens of thousands of small financial planners, scattered across the country, who had very specific needs from a brokerage house. This too became a burgeoning business.

Finally, the company began the arduous process of straightening itself out. The executives went on retreats, where they underwent exercises intended to stress teamwork and leadership. Certain of them were replaced, and new faces brought in. The firm spent millions of dollars making the computer system fail-safe, so that it could withstand the next big market move; it modernized the phone system; and it put those who answered the phones through rigorous training—so that they actually knew what they were doing when they started work. Schwab had always talked about the need for customer service, and though he had always been sincere, his words had never meant anything concrete within the company's culture. Now they did.

By early 1990, you could see the effect of the changes: Schwab reported 1989 earnings that were double what they had been in 1988 while its total assets under management grew by 43 percent. Transactions were up to 13,000 a day—still around 5,000 a day under the 1987 peak, but more than enough to be profitable again. Its customer service was dramatically better; customers quickly noticed the difference.

In truth, though, the changes that had taken place at Schwab were evident even before 1990. In the fall of 1989, just a few days after the Dow Jones average hit an all-time high of 2791,[8] the market made another of its terrible swoons when it fell 190 points on October 12. This time, however, Schwab was ready. With its souped-up computers, its beefed-up telephone answering staff, its new customer service ethos well in place, it handled the so-called minicrash with ease. That was the moment when it was clear that Schwab was for real.

Then again, middle-class investors also seemed to handle the minicrash with surprising ease. This time, there wasn't even a hint of panic among small investors, nor were there any big moves to sell stocks or transfer out of equity funds. On the contrary: "[M]any individuals stood ready to bargain-hunt," marveled *Morningstar Mutual Funds*. Investment companies that conducted focus group research after the crash discovered, to their amazement, that most of their customers were taking the same sanguine view of the minicrash: it was a short-term event, they said, and they were in the market for the long haul. Therefore, although the market drop made them nervous, they were determined not to let it affect their judgment. The crash of 1987 had had its own lessons to teach, and the middle-class had absorbed them.

EVER SO SLOWLY, interest rates began climbing in the late 1980s. Except to a bond trader, it was barely noticeable at first, as the yield on the short-term Treasury bill rose from 5.18 percent in October of 1986 to 5.70 a year and a half later. But in April 1988, T-bill rates lurched forward a quarter of a percent, and the month after that, it went up another third of a percent, and it kept jumping like that, taking dramatic, visible leaps, until it approached 9 percent in March of 1989. As T-bill rates rose, so did the yields on all the financial instruments that were tied to those rates in one way or another: certificates of deposit, deregulated bank passbook accounts, money market deposit accounts, and, not least, money market funds. If assets had gravitated to money market funds after the October crash because Americans were looking for a safe harbor, assets gravitated to them at the end of the decade for an entirely different reason. For the first time in years, money funds quenched the thirst for yield.

We had come, by then, to take them utterly for granted. We mailed off large checks to be "deposited" into our money market funds without a moment's hesitation, and with the absolute expectation that the funds would do what they had always done. They would offer check writing, liquidity, and ease of use. And even though money funds lacked Federal Deposit Insurance, they would offer safety, too. In the years since Bruce Bent and Henry Brown had first created them, we had come to think of money market funds as a form of savings account, and that perception was the secret of their success.

But of course we had one other expectation when we put our savings in money market funds: we expected them to outperform savings accounts. For the first decade of their existence, when money funds could offer market interest while banks could not, that had been their principal selling point. But even after interest rate deregulation money funds still offered higher rates than competing bank vehicles, sometimes as much as 2 percent more than the typical savings account rate. Given the way people now thought about yield, that was significant.

Which is why, as the 1980s progressed, money gradually trickled back into money funds. By 1986, money funds had regained all the assets lost in the immediate aftermath of deregulation. Two years later, as T-bill rates rose, the trickle became a flood. By the end of 1988, money fund assets were approaching $300 billion, which they passed in the first few days of May 1989; fifteen months later, they smashed the $400 billion barrier.

It would be nice to be able to say that money market funds outperformed bank accounts purely because their costs were lower, or because they were more flexible, or because the short-term nature of their holdings made it possible for money fund managers to adjust quickly to changing circumstances. And while these were all important factors, they weren't the only ways money funds boosted yield, and hadn't been for some time. Just as investors had learned to search for yield, so had fund companies learned to "stretch for yield"—even with their money market funds. Once money funds had held primarily Jumbo CDs and government securities; now they were all heavily invested in short-term commercial paper, which paid higher interest than Treasury bills.[9] Indeed, while the SEC forbade money market funds to invest in truly dangerous bonds, such as junk bonds, the agency did allow them to invest in several grades of corporate debt, including A2-rated paper, which was considered slightly riskier than prime-grade A1-rated paper. Even this small increase in risk commanded an increased interest coupon, which is why money fund managers liked A2 paper. A money fund manager could also make what amounted to an interest rate bet by stretching out the duration of the fund's paper at times when rates were high. One small fund in Toledo, Ohio, made just such a bet in 1989, pushing the average maturity of its debt to a hair-raising 116 days. (The bet paid off; by year's end, the fund was the sixth-highest-yielding fund in the country.) And finally, many money funds participated in so-called repurchase agreements, in which T-bills were used as collateral against short-term loans made by money funds to the firms that owned the T-bills. This, too, was considered a relatively safe transaction, though not as safe as buying the T-bill outright. The predictable result was that "repos" also pushed up yield a bit.

The crucial point is that all these approaches implied a degree of risk that would have surprised the millions of people who had been taught to equate their money fund with a savings account. It wasn't a huge amount of risk, but it was *some* risk, and it was precisely that small risk that made it possible for money funds to outperform T-bills—not to mention short-term certificates of deposit, money market deposit accounts, and so on. This, of course, is one of the immutable laws of investing: you have to take risks to generate rewards, and the larger the risks, the greater the potential rewards.

Was it inevitable that some money fund manager was going to stretch too far in pushing for a little extra yield? Probably. That, too, would seem to be one of the immutable laws of investing—though it's more likely one of the immutable laws of human nature. Someone always takes a good idea too far, and ends up losing instead of gaining. And so it was that on two separate occasions, once in the spring of 1989 and again in the spring of 1990, A2-rated corporate paper held by a handful of money market funds defaulted. As a result of these defaults, the money funds in question were in danger of "breaking the dollar"—that is, dropping to 99 cents a share, and costing investors some principal for the first time ever. If that were to happen, the money fund industry would be faced with the prospect of seeing its worst nightmare come true. Fund companies had always harbored the unspoken fear that if one money fund ever broke the dollar, it could create an unprecedented panic, and that people would rush to move their savings back into the bank, where it really was completely safe, since it was insured.[10] To put it another way: their nightmare was that one mistake would destroy the entire business.

Later, various spokesmen for the mutual fund industry, which ran most of the nation's money market funds, would claim that they had always told people that putting money in a money fund was a form of investing. They had always made it plain that money funds lacked Federal Deposit Insurance, they insisted. This was true only in the most literal sense. Such claims could be found in the fine print of money fund advertisements and in the boilerplate of prospectuses—that is, in those places where the law required them to be found. The larger truth was something else: practically from the start the fund industry had been quite content to have people view money market funds as the equivalent of savings accounts. It understood completely that the blurring of the distinction between a bank deposit and a money fund investment worked to their advantage.

This also explains why, when it came down to it, the companies whose money funds held the defaulted paper were unwilling to take their chances and let events play themselves out. Every single fund company involved chose not to let its money market fund absorb the loss. Instead, the parent companies purchased the defaulted paper from their money funds at face value, so that the parent, not the money market fund, would be the one tagged with the loss. Value Line, whose money market fund was caught with $22.6 million worth of defaulted paper in the 1989 incident, wound up taking a "$7.5 million after-tax charge to its earnings," after purchasing the paper from its fund, according to *Barron's*. And in 1990, when a company called Mortgage Realty and Trust abruptly filed for bankruptcy, triggering the second incident, T. Rowe Price was left holding $64 million worth of Mortgage Realty and Trust paper in its money market fund. Once again, the parent company unhesitatingly bought the paper from its money fund.

*Barron's*, which was the only publication to report on the problem with any skepticism, darkly invoked the word "cover-up" to describe the way the fund industry acted after the defaults. And there was something vaguely cover-up-like about the whole affair. With the exception of T. Rowe Price, the fund companies involved said nothing about the defaults—to this day, it's not known who all of them are. The normally voluble ICI was uncharacteristically circumspect. William Donoghue, the money funds' great defender, studiously downplayed the defaults. Without any real proof, *Barron's* alluded to "a secret industry bailout agreement to protect investors for any principal losses."[11] Certainly, the behavior of the companies involved would seem to suggest the existence of such an agreement. On the other hand, the firms involved didn't need a secret agreement to know what they had to do. They all knew how much was at stake.

Even T. Rowe Price, the one company that did come clean, couched its explanation in terms that were, if not misleading, at least self-serving. "It was a relatively small amount—less than 1 percent of a $4.8 billion fund," company spokesman Steven Norwitz said later. "I'm not even sure we would have broken the dollar. But," he added, "we had to purchase the notes to remove the uncertainty in the minds of investors. The most important thing was to retain the confidence of the investors." Left unsaid was the reason it was so critical to "retain the confidence of the investors": only if investors continued to believe that money funds were safe—and not just safe *but as safe as bank accounts*—would they continue to feel comfortable pouring their savings into them. In a weird way, money funds did turn out to be insured after all. It was the discipline of the marketplace that insured the funds, the palpable fear that allowing a money fund investor to lose principal could bring the entire industry tumbling down. In some ways, this fear served customers better than deposit insurance.

What had to offer the greatest relief to the fund industry, though, was how little attention was paid to the two incidents. Mutual fund companies received few calls from customers about the defaults. And the press, aside from *Barron's*, yawned at the story. As a direct result of the two defaults, the SEC tightened its money market regulations to make funds safer;[12] even that action didn't get much publicity. The defaults amounted to the single greatest crisis faced by the money fund industry since interest rate deregulation, yet most people were unaware that anything unusual had taken place. Less than four months after the second incident, money funds blithely broke the $400 billion barrier, as if nothing had happened. From the point of view of investors, nothing had.

⌒

THE DEGREE TO WHICH PETER LYNCH WAS AN ANOMALY—the great, magnificent exception to the rule—was never more apparent than at the end of the 1980s. "Hot" fund managers, who could turn in a great quarter or a great year, or even several good years in a row, were plentiful by then. The publicists for all the fund companies knew how to dangle the bait of performance, and the press knew exactly what to do after taking the bait. The number of "stars" who streaked across the mutual fund sky, cometlike, proliferated throughout the decade. When a new fund like Fidelity's Capital Appreciation burst upon the scene with an impressive 20 percent-plus gain in 1987, in spite of the market crash, it garnered kudos and attention, and its young manager, Tom Sweeney, was soon labeled the "next Peter Lynch." And then two years later, Capital Appreciation's performance sagged, and reporters stopped referring to Sweeney as the next Peter Lynch. This sort of thing happened all the time. What Lynch did in the late 1980s proved just how difficult an act his would be to follow.

Throughout the decade, Lynch's consistently superior performance record, and that of a small handful of other highly touted fund managers, obscured something important about mutual funds in the 1980s. The members of this elite group were *all* the exceptions to the rule. Because they got the lion's share of attention, it was easy for middle-class investors to forget sometimes that not every fund manager was a Peter Lynch or a John Neff, and not every fund delivered returns that regularly exceeded the S&P 500 index or the Dow Jones average. On the contrary: it was hard to beat the S&P 500 on a regular basis, especially in a decade like the 1980s, when the index itself rose so spectacularly, gaining more than 340 percent from the start of the bull market to the end of the 1980s. It was not something just anybody could do. And thus, the startling, much overlooked truth: the vast majority of the nation's fund managers *underperformed* the S&P 500 during the 1980s. When the numbers were totted up, the S&P 500 had risen at an annual rate of 17.55 percent during the 1980s, while average annual equity mutual fund had risen at an annual rate of 15.43 percent.[13] That, it turns out, was the rule.

There are several reasons why this awkward fact was so readily overlooked. The first is that even without beating the S&P 500, equity mutual funds did extremely well in the 1980s. Even though beating the market benchmarks is supposed to be the goal of an equity fund manager, the goal for most investors is somewhat different. For them, the objective is to earn a nice double-digit return. Thus, if they can get an annual return of 15.43 on their money, they are generally quite content, even if that figure doesn't match the market index. In fact, in a year such as 1985, when the S&P 500 rose by 32 percent, many investors were extremely happy when their mutual fund "only" returned, say, 25 percent. Under the circumstances, happiness was an appropriate response.

But there's another reason why this underperformance did not get the attention it might have: it implied a logic most people were unwilling to pursue. If most fund managers couldn't beat the S&P 500, then maybe the central notion behind mutual funds—that it made sense to have a professional fund manager make investment decisions on one's behalf—wasn't quite as reassuring as people assumed. Maybe, in fact, it made more sense to rely on vehicles such as index funds, where it didn't matter a whit who managed the fund, since all the fund did was mirror the performance of the S&P 500. Such funds would never beat the market, but they wouldn't lag it either. Maybe the entire foundation upon which Wall Street was built—the notion that it was possible, by dint of hard work and good, sound fundamental analysis, to pick winning stocks on a regular basis—was flawed. There were many economists in academia and even on Wall Street who believed exactly that, and who could make the case that stock picking could be done just as well by throwing darts at a stock market table as by studying companies, reading balance sheets, examining the fundamentals, and so on.[14] The experience of the nation's mutual fund managers in the 1980s would certainly lend support to this alternative theory, however much the mutual fund industry might reject it—and however much the public might shrink from it.

That's another reason why its "stars" were ultimately so important to the success of mutual funds. Great fund managers Neff and Lynch and Templeton were the beacons of hope, the bearers of the good news that there *were* people who could beat the market regularly, and that it therefore made sense to entrust these people (and others like them) with one's money. Ever since Gerry Tsai, the public relations departments at most fund companies had made it their business to promote star funds and star fund managers, while the financial sections of the nation's newspapers and magazines made it their business to cover those stars. There was nothing especially calculated about this; it was what they were geared to do anyway. This was how public relations departments and the press promoted and covered most aspects of American life, sports or politics or the movies. With mutual funds, as with these other spheres, the light of publicity was like a laser, homing in on a specific, often heroic, image at the expense of a larger, more illuminating, landscape.

Even when the laser of publicity did bore in on someone who was underperforming, it was usually aimed at a star who was falling fast. In the late 1980s, the most prominent such example was Elaine Garzarelli, the woman who had "called the crash." Just two months before Black Monday, in a move intended to take advantage of the celebrity aura that had begun to surround her even before her famous "call," her employer, Shearson Lehman Brothers, set up a mutual fund for Garzarelli to run. Thanks largely to the postcrash publicity that came her way, she quickly found herself handling more than $700 million worth of middle-class assets. Yet despite her long experience as a topflight market technician, she had never managed an equity fund before. So perhaps it's not surprising that in 1988, with the world watching her every move, she fell flat on her face. That year, while the S&P 500 rose 22 percent, her fund was down 12 percent; of the nation's 160 capital appreciation funds, hers was ranked last. "I got whipsawed," she conceded gamely. Through it all, she continued to grant interviews and pose for photographs, but she seemed jumpy now whenever she came face to face with the laser of publicity—still eager, it seemed, to bask in its glow, but fearful of it, knowing that its glare was liable to be as harsh as it had once been radiant and warm.


The laser was also aimed at Peter Lynch in the late 1980s. Having so visibly slipped in 1987—caught on vacation when Black Monday arrived, and then failing to beat the S&P 500 for only the second time in his career—Lynch felt the glare in all its cruel intensity. Or so it seemed to him. He looked around him after the crash, and all he saw were "critics," who were pointing at him, mocking him, waiting for him to fail so that they could shout at once: "We told you so." He became nearly obsessed by the criticism, stung by its lash. "My wife would get these zingers at the supermarket," he complained years later. "They were the kind of zingers you had to translate. People would say, 'I really feel badly that Peter's having a bad year.' What they meant was, 'Boy, am I glad they finally caught up with him.' " To a *Wall Street Journal* reporter, he added, "A lot of people were saying that Magellan was . . . hopeless [because of its size]. Some said Fidelity was being a pig for keeping the fund open." To a *USA Today* reporter he said, "My mother used to tell me, 'Don't get mad, get even.' "

A more disinterested observer, however, might be moved to ask: *what* critics? Where was this deluge of criticism that made Lynch want to "get even"? It was certainly not to be found in the *Wall Street Journal* or *The New York Times,* nor in *Money* magazine or *USA Today,* nor on Rukeyser's "Wall Street Week" or PBS's "Nightly Business Report." Reporters and commentators treated Robert Prechter savagely for being wrong about the crash;[15] Lynch received nothing even remotely comparable. Oh, he caught a few half-hearted jabs here and there; when the *Boston Globe* ran a story early in 1988 about the possibility of layoffs at Fidelity, it incorrectly linked the action to "Magellan's sluggish performance," which infuriated Lynch. And from time to time, someone would suggest that Magellan was getting too big to beat the market.[16] But far more typical was the story in *Time* magazine that first reported that Lynch had been in Ireland playing golf on Black Monday. The writer recounted the tale of Lynch's difficulties with deference and sympathy, ending his article by strongly hinting that Lynch and Magellan would quickly rebound. The article seemed intended not to bury Lynch but to praise him. If Magellan and its steward were, in fact, being assaulted by criticism, it was an awfully strange assault. Only one person on earth could hear it.

And yet here was Lynch, throwing himself into his work like never before, determined to prove "his critics" wrong. Since 1982, Lynch had done a full day's work each Saturday; after the crash, he began to put in four hours each Sunday as well. He'd always been a sports junkie; after the crash, he stopped going to games. He didn't have time anymore. He began bringing work home, something he hated doing. He was missing family events that he'd always managed to attend before: a recital, a game, a weekend away with his wife and children. Because of his preference for smaller companies, Magellan's roster of stocks actually expanded after the crash. Which meant that Lynch had to visit even more companies and make even more phone calls and read even more balance sheets and analysts' reports.

But *why?* He had grown tired of managing a multibillion-dollar fund by then. He was tired of the grind. No matter how much he did, there was always more to do; no matter where he was, at least part of his mind was on

Magellan. He had begun to think about quitting at least three years before the crash, and those feelings only increased after Black Monday. So why was he piling on even more work, staying in the office even longer hours, and seeing his family even less frequently than before?

His own explanation—that it was those damnable critics who egged him on—simply doesn't make sense. A far more likely possibility is that during this last phase of his fabled career, Lynch was being pushed by his own ego. To say this, admittedly, is to contradict in some small measure the public image Lynch has cultivated over the years—that of a self-effacing money manager whose only gift was for hard work, and whose only reward came in knowing that those who had entrusted their money to him—one out of every hundred American families by the late 1980s—were getting a decent return. This self-image contained its share of truth, to be sure. But the people around him also knew that he did not lack for ego; they'd seen it plenty of times. They knew that he took a nearly overweening pride in his accomplishments, and that it meant a great deal to him to be known as America's best mutual fund manager. He had developed, over the years, a mixture of personality traits that one more commonly associates with great athletes. A burning desire to succeed was combined with an extremely thin skin; a genuine yearning to give the fans (or shareholders) their money's worth was combined with a need for adulation; sincerity was mixed with self-absorption; humility mingled with hubris. After Lynch's stumble on Black Monday, these traits provided him with all the fuel he needed: they gave him a powerful desire to prove to the world that he could still run the biggest equity mutual fund America had ever seen better than anyone who had ever lived. Quite possibly, he had to prove it to himself as well.

And so that's what he did. His performance the year after the crash was a genuinely wondrous thing, quite possibly the greatest single year of his career, and anyone who knew anything about money management could only stand back and marvel. "Lynch's 1988 performance was marked by a quiet dignity and a level of professionalism that in some ways outshone his more-heralded early work," swooned *Morningstar,* which named Lynch its 1988 Portfolio Manager of the Year.[17] It was also marked by many of the traits that had long characterized his stock picking: for instance, a willingness to take huge bets on particular industries that others were shunning. In 1988, one of the bets Lynch made was on his own out-of-favor industry: when most analysts were predicting disastrous times ahead for mutual funds, Lynch was shrewdly scooping up shares of Dreyfus and T. Rowe Price. He had, as ever, the ability to block out the white noise of the market, and to focus instead on those mundane midsized companies he understood so well—the companies that earned their money by making the goods and providing the services the middle-class wanted. The crash, in other words, did not cause Peter Lynch to change the way he bought and sold stocks, nor did it put even the slightest dent in the confidence he had in his instincts and judgments. The market as a whole rebounded smartly in 1988—the S&P 500 wound up with a gain of 16.6 percent—but Magellan did much better than that. At year's end, it was up almost 23 percent. What made this gain even more remarkable was that Lynch was maneuvering some $9 billion through the shoals of the market by then—"His multibillion handicap," *Morningstar* labeled it. In 1989, the handicap became larger, for as the market continued to move upward, Magellan swelled to over $12.5 billion. That year, the S&P 500 finished up an almost unbeatable 31.7 percent. And yet Magellan still beat it, by a solid 3 percent. By then, nobody was suggesting that the fund was too big to beat the market. Not so long as Peter Lynch was running it.

And it was then—when Lynch could truly say that he had nothing left to prove—that he quit.

Twenty-five years before, when the nation's first big-name portfolio manager had quit Fidelity, it had been an event of no small moment. But it was nothing compared to the commotion created by Lynch's announcement, in March of 1990, that he would be retiring in two months. When Gerry Tsai left Fidelity in 1965, there were 170 mutual funds in existence, holding a total of $35 billion in assets. Although mutual funds were considered the "hot" investment vehicle of the moment, the total number of accounts had not even cracked 7 million. When Peter Lynch made it known that he would be stepping down as manager of the Magellan Fund, the total number of mutual funds stood at 3,108. The number of mutual fund accounts stood at well over 60 million. Almost unbelievably, the assets in those 60 million-plus accounts now exceeded $1 trillion. The ICI calculated that more than one out of every four American households had some money in a mutual fund by 1990. Given this context, Peter Lynch's resignation wasn't just a news item. It was *news*. It affected millions who had money in Magellan, and it was of very real interest to the tens of millions more who followed Lynch's career the way they might follow the career of Mick Jagger or Robert Redford. During his thirteen years at the helm of Magellan, Lynch had been many things: a stock picker extraordinaire, an exemplar for his industry, a powerful magnet for Fidelity, even a best-selling author, a status he attained after his first book, *One Up on Wall Street*, was published in 1989. The buzz surrounding his resignation proved that he was something else as well: a household name.

To the dozens of reporters angling to get the "real story" of his retirement, Lynch said the same things: he was quitting, first of all, so that he could spend more time with his family. He was quitting because he had recently turned forty-six, which was the same age his father had been when he had died; the birthday had made him feel "a little more mortal," he told *People* magazine. He was quitting because he had made plenty of money, and he didn't feel any compelling need to make more. He was quitting because he was tired of the grind. He was quitting because he wanted to start going to ball games again. He was quitting because he wanted to recapture his life.

At the moment of his retirement, it was Lynch's best side that shone through—the guileless, plainspoken, boy scout side that the public had always found so appealing. Reporters looking for a hidden agenda came up empty. The reigning theory of the skeptics held that Lynch would leave Fidelity and set up his own fund; he flatly denied it and, of course, did no such thing. Ross Perot was among those unconvinced of Lynch's sincerity; he came to Boston one day and spent seven hours trying to persuade him to set up a joint venture with the Dallas billionaire—to no avail. No, the motives Lynch gave for quitting were the real ones. And unlike Ross Perot, the middle-class investors who had handed him their assets trusted his explanation, just as they had once trusted him with their money. After his announcement, people stopped Lynch in the street just to thank him for making it possible for them to send a child to college, or put an addition on their home. Hundreds of others wrote him letters bearing the same message. He was clearly moved by such sentiments. As for those who claimed that he would soon become restless, he wasn't worried. He would still be a presence at Fidelity—loyalty being another Lynch virtue now on display. He ran a foundation, which he could now devote more time to. He sat on a number of boards, including that of his beloved Boston College. He would still be managing money, but it would be his own and his foundation's, rather than the savings of 1.1 million American families. And if, after all that, he was still bored he could always write another best-selling book.


The great fear at Fidelity, Rodger Lawson once said, was that Peter Lynch would walk out of work one day and be hit by a bus. That is always the danger when you hop aboard the shoulders of a star and let him carry you as far as he can. Lynch had carried Fidelity a very long way indeed: not long before his retirement, the company's assets had surpassed $100 billion, making Fidelity the first mutual fund company to reach that landmark. Of that amount, 11 percent resided in Magellan, which had become such a cash cow that it generated more than $150 million annually for Fidelity.[18] And while one can never know precisely how much more was drawn into the company's other funds because of the glow that surrounded Lynch, it is safe to say that it was a lot. Peter Lynch was the franchise. His mere presence brought in assets. And now he *had* been hit by a bus, at least in a marketing sense.

It was easy to envision Magellan shareholders, upon hearing the news about Lynch, pulling assets out of the fund in a wild stampede. But that didn't happen. Instead, Magellan shareholders took the news with remarkable calm. When Fidelity's marketers did focus group research after the Lynch announcement, they discovered, to their immense relief, that the vast majority of Magellan shareholders were inclined to be patient; they would give Lynch's replacement time to prove himself before deciding whether to stay in or get out. This would also give Fidelity time to prove itself, to show that its pool of talent went deeper than Lynch, and that the company was far more than one supremely gifted fund manager. Of course it wouldn't hurt if the person Ned Johnson picked to be the new Magellan manager turned out, somehow, to be the *real* "new Peter Lynch." But who could know for sure?

The new man's name was Morris Smith, and if the truth be told, becoming known as the "new Peter Lynch" was not high on his list of life's goals. He was thirty-two years old, the father of three young children. He had been with Fidelity since 1982, first as an analyst and then as the manager of Fidelity's OTC Portfolio, which he had inherited when Paul Stuka left, and where he gained a reputation (as *Morningstar* would later characterize it) "for both his dependability and his lack of color, consistently beating the competition by a moderate amount." What he shared with Lynch was an MBA from Wharton, a capacity for hard work, a belief that fund managers succeeded by concentrating on companies instead of "the market," and a deep religious faith. Smith was an Orthodox Jew, which meant that he had to be home every Friday by sundown, no matter how much work he had to leave behind. What he did not share with his predecessor was a willingness to assume the public roles that had always come so naturally to Lynch. Instead, Smith harbored a deep distrust of the publicity machinery; if he had his way, he would never talk to a reporter. But how could you manage Magellan and not talk to reporters? It was like trying to run for election without holding a news conference.

Not that Smith didn't try. After an initial flurry of bland interviews, Smith hunkered down. Requests from reporters to talk to him were denied, while he changed the fund's stock holdings to conform to his own preferences.

Although he talked a great deal in the beginning about the similarities between his investing style and Lynch's, such talk was a smokescreen, intended to calm nervous Magellan shareholders. In fact, Smith's methods were quite different from Lynch's, and within six months of his taking charge, Magellan was a completely different beast. It held about 800 stocks instead of 1,700, and it was concentrated on large companies rather than the midsized companies Lynch had always favored. It held 10 million shares of Phillip Morris, for instance, a $750 million position. *Morningstar* again: "Smith's decision with Magellan to concentrate on proven growth stocks (mostly health care and other consumer staples) meshed perfectly with his usual pattern of caution."

Later, Smith would claim, speaking in the clichés he had come to master, that he had been happy to have been asked to follow Lynch at Magellan. "It was the supreme challenge," he said. "It was nice that they asked me." The evidence, however, suggested otherwise. Smith hated being a public person, yet that's what he became the moment he inherited Magellan, even before he had bought or sold a single share of stock. The amount of work involved was staggering, and his task was made more difficult by the demands of his religion. The pressure on him to do well was intense; he felt, according to one friend, as if the fate of the entire company rested on him alone. This friend compared him to a football halfback who is handed the ball thirty-five times a game—"Sooner or later, Morris is going to break down," he said. And unlike Lynch, Smith really was the subject of a great deal of early criticism, some of it quite unfair. The lowest point came when the *Boston Globe* began running a little box called "The Morris Smith Watch" every Sunday. Under a picture of Smith and an early quote of his ("All I can promise is that I'll give it my best shot"), the newspaper printed a graph comparing Magellan's performance during the preceding week with that of the S&P 500. The feature ran for about a year.

The Morris Smith Watch finally ended when it became clear that Morris Smith was going to do just fine as the Magellan manager. After a rocky start, Smith began to exceed the market averages consistently. In the two years between May 1990 and May 1992, the S&P index rose 20.6 percent, the Dow Jones average went up 22.8 percent—and Smith's Magellan was up 28.2 percent. Given the size of the fund, this was about as well as anyone could have done. Smith was still dull as dishwater, but who cared? Investors certainly didn't. As the market continued to make gains during his tenure— the Dow Jones average exceeded 2900 for the first time ever in June of 1990, cracked the 3000 barrier the following April, and topped 3100 by the end of 1991—Americans once again flocked to Magellan, just as they had during the Lynch era. By the spring of 1992, the fund held $20 billion in assets, $7 billion of which had come into the fund in the two years since Lynch had left. No other equity fund came close. That any number of smaller, more nimble growth funds beat Magellan handily didn't seem to matter; millions of people seemed quite content to beat the market by 4 percent a year, if they could do it in Magellan. That Magellan finally lost its position as the top-ranking mutual fund for the previous ten years didn't seem to matter either. Even without Lynch, Magellan remained the most extraordinary mutual fund in the history of the business, and Americans still gravitated to it, despite having thousands of alternatives to choose from. In the post-Lynch era, that was Fidelity's triumph. That was Morris Smith's accomplishment.

And it was at that moment—knowing that he had nothing left to prove—that Smith did the most Lynch-like thing of his entire tenure. Two years after taking over Magellan, burned out by the unending grind, the pressure, the publicity, and the lack of time for his family, Morris Smith quit.

# CHAPTER 19

# The Triumph of Main Street

## *August 1993*

T HE BOMBING RAIDS began on the 17th of January, 1991. It was a Thursday night, 3:00 A.M. in Iraq but prime time in the United States, and all over the country, Americans flipping on their television sets suddenly found themselves watching the outbreak of war, live and in color. Reporters, standing on the roof of the Al Rashid Hotel in downtown Baghdad, breathlessly described what viewers could see quite plainly for themselves: the sudden bursts of light, like a fireworks display, as American bombs lit up the sky; the stutter of antiaircraft fire from Iraqi defenders; the brilliant midair explosions as American Patriots appeared to intercept Iraqi Scud missiles. The next day, the Dow Jones average rose 114.60—the second-largest one-day gain in history. The link between this bullish occurrence and the bullish events of the night before was plain: Americans were euphoric about the war's initial success, and so was the market.

Markets have always been affected by the great events of the day. The Cuban missile crisis, the Kennedy assassination, and Richard Nixon's resignation[1] are only a few of the more historic events that have jarred the stock market, even though they were not ostensibly market-related. With those previous cataclysms, though, the movement of the stock market had been considered an insignificant by-product of the moment—of concern to Wall Street, perhaps, but not worthy of serious attention from most Americans. At such momentous times as those, how the market reacted didn't matter very much.

In this new era, however, the movement of the market mattered a great deal, not just to Wall Street but to tens of millions of Americans. That concern was on vivid display in the weeks and months leading up to the Gulf War. To a degree that would once have been thought unseemly, people were viewing the prospect of war through the prism of their own personal finances. Andrew Tobias, the well-known financial writer, wrote an advice column in *Time* magazine under the cover title: "The Crisis: What to Do with Your Money." Shearson Lehman Hutton sent out a mailgram that began: "Mid East Crisis: how it will affect your investments." In hundreds of newspapers and magazines and newsletters, one could find financial advice based on the likelihood that war would soon break out. One could also see people acting on that advice. The near-universal opinion of the experts was that the market would drop dramatically once hostilities began: "Within hours of the gunfire, look for stock prices to fall 150 points or more on the Dow," *Money* magazine predicted. Was it any surprise, then, that in early January 1991, a few weeks before the hostilities began, "wary investors [seeking] a haven amid war fears" (as the *Wall Street Journal* put it) moved more than $24 billion into the haven of money market funds? That was a one-month record. Of course it then turned out that the near-universal opinion was as wrong as a thing could be, and that the millions of Americans who acted on this advice wound up leaving billions of dollars in potential gains on the table. One was tempted to say: serves them right.[2]

But that's too harsh a judgment. It was only natural that people would be paying attention to the market as the Gulf War approached, and it was asking too much to expect them to shut out the stock market at the very moment when the world around them seemed most uncertain. Regarding the movement of the stock market, Americans had become ever vigilant. How could it be otherwise? The market had become an integral facet of their lives. It held money for their children's college tuition, money to get them through an emergency, money for that great vacation they were saving for, money for retirement.

There was, at Fidelity, a distinct moment when everyone in the company suddenly understood the extent to which the stock market had become a part of everyday life in America. The moment was January 28, 1986—the day the space shuttle *Challenger* exploded. In the first few hours after the explosion, the telephones were utterly, eerily, silent. But then, as the initial shock wore off, the phone lines were suddenly jammed, as customers clamored to find an answer to one slightly perverse question: *What's it going to mean for the market?* As we entered the last decade of the twentieth century, that question was never far from the surface. Whenever anything important happened anywhere in the world, we instinctively asked: What was it going to mean for the market? What was it going to mean for us? By the early 1990s, the money revolution had so captured the day that it was nearly impossible to imagine a scenario that would cause us to stop asking that question.

THE 1990S WERE MARKED by many of the other tendencies and habits that had been first formed during the Age of Inflation and carved in stone during the 1980s. Some of these practices were more obvious than others. One of the less obvious ones—perhaps because it had become so unremarkable that no one bothered to write about it anymore—was the willingness of Americans to use credit cards in order to borrow ever-larger sums of money to buy ever-more expensive things. Every year, without fail, the dollar figures connected to credit card use continued their upward climb, just as they had for the last thirty years.[3] By 1993, Americans were using their bank credit cards to charge more than $400 billion worth of goods. Credit card debt amounted to 35 percent of installment debt—up from 25 percent in 1989. In a nation where 70 million households had bank cards, there were 300 million cards in circulation, and 220 million active accounts—that is, there were more than three active accounts per household.

Another habit was the continual search for yield, a quest that had acquired, over time, a restless, overwrought quality quite out of proportion to any real need for so pressing a search. Indeed, what both these examples perhaps best illustrated was the way the behavioral patterns formed during the money revolution had become almost knee-jerk. In a sense, the first half of the 1990s resembled nothing so much as the first half of the 1950s, when an entire generation of Americans, acting on habits formed during the Depression, missed out on the greatest bull market of this century. Now it was the habits formed during the Age of Inflation that were proving impossible to dislodge—even though the 1990s were offering a rather different set of economic circumstances.

With the exception of one year, 1990,[4] inflation was no longer the dominant economic motif—disinflation was. This was partly due to the recession that took hold in 1992; facing hard times, people weren't willing to pay ever-higher prices, and undertook to find less expensive alternatives. But it was also due to trends that were in evidence even after the recession had ended. The new global economy, the enormous economic power of discounters such as Wal-Mart, the move away from "name" brands and toward generic products—these were all factors that exerted a downward pressure on prices. Fast food restaurants, having saturated the country, were forced to compete with each other by lowering prices. Cheap generic cigarettes began cutting deeply into the market share of the big, established brands, forcing companies like RJR Nabisco and Phillip Morris to lower prices on well-known brands such as Winston and Marlboro. A vicious price war broke out among computer manufacturers. The price of gasoline at the pump in 1993 approached prices not seen since the late 1970s. There were dozens of similar examples. Even the price of a house was not immune from this trend. After almost twenty years of spiraling upward, housing prices finally stopped rising in many sections of the country. In some sections, they actually went down.

By all rights, Americans should have been rejoicing at this turn of events. But many weren't. Homeowners, in particular, were dismayed when they realized that their chief economic asset had stopped rising in value; many had come to view the built-in capital gain provided by a 10 or 15 percent annual rise in the price of their home as practically a God-given right. But there was no such right. Houses were commodities. They reacted to the laws of supply and demand. And, as with every other aspect of personal finance in America, buying a house meant taking some risk. To their chagrin, millions of Americans were now relearning this most basic of truths.

Even the more generalized phenomenon of disinflation was not necessarily greeted with cheers. Just as one generation of Americans continued to conjure up images of the Depression well into the late 1950s and early 1960s, so did the next generation of Americans continue to conjure up inflation fears. People seemed to be looking over their shoulders, half expecting inflation to break out again—or more likely, believing it had never left. In the summer of 1992, at a time when inflation was lower than it had been since the 1950s, *Business Week* cited a survey in which consumers said they expected inflation to grow by almost 5 percent during the next year. By the end of 1992, the Consumer Price Index had risen 1.7 percent—a negligible amount. Yet a decade after inflation had been tamed, people remained haunted by it.

Alongside disinflation, another new phenomenon arose. Throughout the 1980s, interest rates had risen and fallen constantly, but in the early 1990s, all they seemed to do was fall. In March of 1989, three-month T-bills were yielding 8.82 percent, while the "long bond"—the benchmark thirty-year Treasury bond—was yielding 9.17 percent. Over the next three and a half years, yields floated steadily downward, until by the fall of 1993, the yield on the long bond had dropped to 5.86 percent, while short-term T-bill yields had absolutely fallen through the floor, and stood at 2.5 percent. Short-term rates hadn't been so low in thirty years.

It was an astonishing thing, to have interest rates fall this far; it was also, without question, a good thing. Low interest rates allowed businesses to borrow money more cheaply. They made it possible for homeowners to refinance their mortgages, substantially reducing their payments. For those who did not own homes, low rates provided hope that an important part of the American Dream was within reach. The drop in bond yields also triggered a fabulous bond rally,[5] allowing millions of Americans—who by the end of 1991 had put some $440 billion into bond funds—to reap a windfall.

Yet because this was a country that had learned to adapt to higher interest rates, there was surprisingly little cheering over this occurrence, either. Thirty years ago, Americans would likely have focused on the effect of low interest rates on lending and borrowing; now they tended to focus on the effect such rates had on savings. From that vantage point, what they saw was decidedly unpleasant. As Treasury yields dropped, so did the interest paid out on the various savings vehicles at their disposal. In 1989, for example, a typical one-year certificate of deposit had an interest rate of just under 10 percent. By 1993, that same one-year CD yielded less than 3 percent interest. The yield on money market funds, which in a handful of cases had topped 10 percent in early 1989, dropped to 2.63 percent by July 1993. This marked an all-time low.

So instead of leading to rejoicing, the drop in T-bill rates was accompanied by a chorus of complaints that lower rates were cutting into people's incomes. ''People have got their backs against the wall,'' one expert told the *Wall Street Journal* when most interest rates dropped under 3 percent. And feeling that way, millions of Americans began looking desperately for alternative places to put their money—looking for those higher yields that they simply couldn't live without anymore. Not even in the early 1980s did the search for yield have the urgency it had in the first part of the 1990s.

You could see it every April and October, when most six-month CDs came due: the nation's personal finance writers rushed into print with suggestions about where readers could capture higher returns. You could see it in the way middle-class money began flowing out of banks, with a speed that hadn't been seen since the bad old days of Regulation Q. Between the summer of 1991 and the summer of 1992, bank CDs lost 17 cents of every dollar they had held—a $200 billion outflow. Money fund assets also diminished. As ever, the mutual fund companies hastened to the breach with new financial products designed to meet their customers' desire for higher yields. In just the first six months of 1993, the industry brought out an astounding 207 new bond funds. These funds, with names like Benham Adjustable Rate Government Securities, Fidelity Short Term World Income Fund, T. Rowe Price Adjustable Rate U.S. Government, and Vanguard Fixed-Income I/T U.S. Treasury, were all designed to do one thing: generate yields that were higher than those investors could get in traditional savings vehicles—a category that included, by now, their own money market funds.

Were these new funds riskier than old-fashioned CDs and money market funds? *Of course they were*. These were true bond funds. They lacked dollar pricing, meaning investors could track the daily fluctuations of principal as well as yield. More importantly, even if these new funds relied on various hedging techniques to give them an extra dollop of safety—as many of them did—they were still ultimately at the mercy of the bond market. If interest rates were to take a sharp, unexpected upswing, investors would lose principal. If the swing was sharp enough, they could lose quite a bit: a 1 percentage point rise in the yield of the thirty-year Treasury bond could cost an investor as much as 12.5 percent of his principal.

Did people understand the risks they were taking? It was easy enough to find "experts" who feared that they didn't; the *Wall Street Journal* unearthed a Baruch College finance professor who said, "A lot of people who are making their investments now have never seen what could happen with their funds in a bear market." But it seems more likely that they did understand. "Even though we know the bond market is not the best thing to put our money in now," said one middle-class investor at the time, "it seems the least of all evils." They understood, but they were willing to take the risk because a higher yield was a narcotic they had to have. The result of America's yield addiction was striking: by the end of 1993, bond funds held more than $760 billion in assets—60 percent of which had arrived since the beginning of the decade. For mutual fund companies, it must have seemed as though the only thing better than high interest, so crucial to the growth of the industry a decade ago, was low interest rates, which were so crucial now.

There is no question that the anxiety people felt as rates went down was real. What is questionable is whether that anxiety was justified. During the late 1970s and early 1980s, high yields and high inflation had gone hand in hand—a tendency that had disguised the true nature of interest rates. For instance, if your money market fund had yielded 11 percent in 1979, that did not mean that your money's earning power had grown by 11 percent. It hadn't—because the inflation rate had risen by 9 percent that year. Thus, in 1979, the earning power of the assets in your money fund had actually grown by 2 percent—the spread between the fund's yield and the inflation rate. Two percent was the real interest rate in 1979.

Was it worth chasing yield to lasso a 2 percent return? Back then, it was; during times of high inflation, as the value of money is constantly eroded, anyone who doesn't at least try to keep pace with inflation can be hurt badly. But a decade later, the situation was completely reversed: now it was low interest rates and low inflation rates that were going hand in hand. Now, while your money market fund was yielding 3 percent, the inflation rate was still below the fund's return. As a result, real interest rates in the 1990s were somewhere in the range of 1.5 percent. To put it another way: *real interest rates in the 1990s were almost exactly what they had been during the Age of Inflation.* This is what people missed as they hunted so frantically for higher yields in the 1990s. And that's why, when the bond market did finally turn in early 1994, people got hurt. Many of them lost money they had viewed as "savings." By the end of the first quarter, the typical municipal bond fund had dropped almost 6 percent—a "debacle," *The New York Times* called it. That's where chasing yield could lead sometimes: it could lead to losses. This was something people had understood implicitly but were now having to deal with rather explicitly. Not surprisingly, assets began to flow back into money market funds.

⟡

FOR THE NATION'S CREDIT CARD BANKERS, the new decade began with a severe, unpleasant jolt. The 1990s weren't even three months old when AT&T began soliciting customers for a new credit card it had begun distributing under its name.[6] The phone company had been in the credit card business for years, of course, with a card that allowed customers to charge long-distance calls. No banker was likely to perceive such a card as a threat. But the new AT&T Universal Card was very much a threat, for it was a true bank card, connected to MasterCard just like any other bank card,[7] and providing customers the same access to stores and services.

And quite a bank card it was, too. Like many of the large card issuers, AT&T offered rental car insurance, emergency medical assistance, and twenty-four-hour customer service to its cardholders—these were all standard "add-ons" that had been created as the competition for new customers had intensified. Like a number of the more ambitious card issuers, the phone company also offered no-fee traveler's checks, a complete year-end statement, and a twenty-four-hour travel agency. Customers who used the AT&T card to make long-distance calls received a 10 percent discount—an add-on that no other card issuer could match, obviously. But perhaps most ominous of all for the nation's banks, AT&T was the first credit card issuer in recent times to break the hegemony of the annual fee. At a time when annual fees had become an institutionalized part of the business, AT&T was publicly proclaiming that any cardholder who got in on the ground floor would never have to pay one.[8] The company's shrewd refusal to say how long this offer would last had the effect of creating a small riot, as people rushed to order the card before it was too late. The very first day the card was made available, AT&T received over 260,000 phone calls from Americans requesting the card. Within four months AT&T had generated 2.5 million credit card accounts. Within a year, it had 8 million cards in circulation, issued to 4.5 million households. It was the fifth-largest bank card issuer in the country, trailing only the biggest of the big boys: Citibank, Chase Manhattan, First Chicago, and BankAmerica.

Here, come to life, was every banker's worst nightmare; here was the reason they had objected to Dee Hock's vision all those years. This fearsome new competitor wasn't a Citibank or even a Household Finance, which, though not a bank was at least a traditional lender. *It was the phone company!* Who gave the phone company the right to issue a bank credit card? the bankers asked themselves. It infuriated them that this was happening, a sentiment that was given perhaps its rawest display in the spring of 1991, when a top Citibank credit card executive[9] made an impassioned speech at a bankers' conference. "Banks have invested, by my estimate, $50 billion in the MasterCard and Visa systems," the man railed, his voice rising in anger with every sentence:

> The bank credit card has changed the role of currency. It has given consumers a wider range of choices. Because it is the most egalitarian of bank products, it is popular everywhere. It is a necessity in modern life. It is one of the business success stories of the century. Should this business be franchised away for free? Should we be giving our competition a subsidy to steal away our customers? What we're doing borders on economic hara-kari!

Yet there was nothing the banks could do to stop AT&T's incursion. Too many barriers had fallen, and too much history had preceded it. When Dee Hock sweet-talked the Visa board into first accepting the Merrill Lynch CMA card, and then the Associates card and others like it, he paved the way for the entry of an AT&T.

Ultimately, AT&T's entry into credit cards has turned out to be an enormously important event. Never mind that by 1992, AT&T was the second-largest issuer of bank credit cards, behind only Citibank. Or that its initial, successful foray into credit cards has been followed by similar moves by other large, well-known industrial companies, most notably Ford and General Motors. Or that nonbanks now control a remarkable 43 percent of the gross volume of Visa and MasterCard charges—up from 7 percent in 1987. Of far more moment, the AT&T entry has completely changed the dynamics of the credit card business—to the detriment of the nation's banks, but to the great benefit of the nation's consumers. Once AT&T stripped away the annual fee, banks had to do likewise. They tried to hold the line at first, but as they saw customers slipping away they quietly began trying to hold on to them by offering to waive the annual fee. By the spring of 1991, James Grant reported in *Grant's Interest Rate Observer,* it was not uncommon for a customer to call his credit card bank, planning to cancel his card because he had acquired a no-annual-fee card, only to be told, "In the interest of customer service, we'll waive the fee for this year." Soon thereafter, a number of banks began publicly trumpeting their new no-annual-fee policy. Thus did the banks try to turn lemons into lemonade.

Did elimination of annual fees cut into bank profits? You bet it did. One authoritative study conducted in late 1990 concluded that "annual fees represent the difference between profit and loss on a per-account basis"— that's how important they had become to the business. "No-annual-fee" offers not only stripped banks of a key source of revenue, but they also attracted precisely those customers most banks didn't want: the ones who paid off their balances each month. In late 1991, Spencer Nilson reported that convenience users would "cost" the banking industry $1.21 billion that year. For banks, the introduction of the AT&T Universal Card brought consequences that were painful indeed—and made more so when competitive pressures caused banks to begin lowering the interest rates they charged on credit cards, a trend that also started in the early 1990s.

But so what? Banks had gotten greedy in the 1980s. Even after credit cards had become the most lucrative part of the entire banking business, banks had uniformly resisted lowering interest rates or annual fees. "When profits are high, new entrants come in, just like it says in the economic textbooks," shrugs Charlene Sullivan, a Purdue University economics professor and credit card expert. And if some banks—most notably Citibank, with some 30 million credit cards in circulation, generating, at times, 60 percent of the profits for the entire company—felt they had no choice but to grab every cent from their credit card customers to make up for the huge problems they were facing elsewhere,[10] well, that wasn't AT&T's fault. It wasn't our fault either. And if AT&T's entry into credit cards caused the nation's banks to begin giving middle-class consumers a break—"in the interest of customer service"—so much the better. All in all, it was about time.

ON JULY 1, 1992, MORRIS SMITH HANDED OFF THE MAGELLAN FUND to his successor, Jeffrey Vinik, and headed to Israel with his family, where they planned to spend the next year. It almost goes without saying that Vinik was young (thirty-three years old), that he had a reputation as a prodigious worker, that he claimed to look at the market, as he liked to put it, "from the bottom up," company by company, and that he was a rising star at

Fidelity. Far more than Smith, Vinik had etched out a public reputation as a stellar stock picker in the years before he assumed the helm of Fidelity's flagship fund. His first major stint as a fund manager had come in early 1989, when he had been put in charge of Contrafund, one of Fidelity's oldest and most distinguished mutual funds. Over the next twenty-one months, Contrafund gained 34.5 percent, while the S&P 500 was going up 17 percent. Then the company gave him the more conservatively oriented Growth & Income Fund, with almost $4 billion in assets; again, Vinik turned in terrific numbers: over the next nineteen months, Growth & Income gained 55 percent compared to the S&P 500's 39 percent rise.

Although in interviews Vinik stressed (of course!) his admiration for his predecessor's record, and his partiality toward Smith's methods, he was a far more apt manager of Magellan than Smith, at least from marketing's point of view. His style was flashier. The press didn't appear to bother him. In some indefinable way, he embraced the job in a way Morris Smith never had—he looked like he was enjoying himself as he managed the most closely watched mutual fund in the country. He certainly didn't give the impression that he was being ground down; for one thing, he made it a point to leave the office every day at 5:30. And as a stock picker, while he spent most of his time doing the kind of one-company-at-a-time research that was Fidelity's trademark, he was also something of a market timer, who made big industry bets when he sensed the market was headed in their direction. In this, he resembled no one so much as Gerry Tsai.

The *Boston Globe,* having learned its lesson, did not run a Jeff Vinik Watch. It's a good thing it didn't. For although "past performance is no guarantee of future results"—to quote the SEC-mandated boilerplate that can be found in the fine print of all mutual fund advertising—Vinik's past performance did, indeed, cause people to expect him to produce results. And this he did. At first, Magellan lagged the S&P 500, as Vinik repositioned the fund to suit his own style—which was geared more to the small and midsized companies Lynch had always preferred—which of course brought out the critics. *Business Week* went so far as to suggest that his strategy was "just so-so." But by July 1993, just four months after the *Business Week* article—and a year into Vinik's tenure—Magellan was obliterating the S&P 500. It was up over 20 percent in that time, while the market benchmark had risen 12 percent. "My bets," Vinik crowed to the *Wall Street Journal,* "have paid off."

By the end of 1993, Magellan had turned in an amazing 21 percent gain for the year, again thrashing the S&P 500, which rose less than 10 percent. And all the while, the fund just kept growing and growing and growing; at year's end, it was well over $30 billion and counting. It was nearly twice as large as the next biggest fund. In contemplating the fund, one was finally reduced to tipping one's cap in admiration. By all rights, Magellan's monstrous size should have made Vinik's performance impossible. Indeed, by all rights, people should have stopped putting their money in Magellan, now that there were over 4,500 mutual funds that competed with it for assets, any number of which had sterling track records and the backing of powerful marketing campaigns. Yet Magellan remained unstoppable. Truly, there was nothing like it in the financial universe. In all likelihood, there never would be again.

Fidelity itself seemed pretty unstoppable in the 1990s. Its "family of funds" ran to more than 200 offerings by 1994, and the company was constantly coming up with new ones to take advantage of market trends, or cater to perceived investor tastes. In 1993, when global investing suddenly became the rage, the marketing department wasted no time bringing out a Latin America fund (up 42.9 percent in five months!), a Southeast Asia fund (up 36.5 percent!), a Global Balanced fund (up 31.2 percent!), a New Markets Income fund (up 30.4 percent!). In just five months, Southeast Asia had $750 million in assets—even with Rodger Lawson gone, no one could gun a fund like Fidelity. After Lawson left, though, Fidelity became more willing to close an occasional fund when the situation warranted. It did so, for instance, with a hot new fund called Low Priced Stock, after the fund manager was so deluged with new money that he was unable to find enough attractive low-priced stocks to absorb the cash. Meanwhile, Fidelity's equity shop continued to turn out promotable new mutual fund stars, not just Vinik but others such as Beth Terrana, Brad Lewis, Will Danoff,[11] and Robert Beckwitt. The latter's stewardship of Fidelity's Asset Manager fund almost single-handedly revived the entire "asset allocation" category.

Fidelity had its critics, of course; its size and its swagger made it an inviting target. From inside the company, the case against it was that it had lost the flavor of the old days, and had become bureaucratic and political. Employees complained that Johnson "threw away" tens of millions of dollars on idiosyncratic projects—money that, by all rights, should have found its way to the bottom line. This mattered because executives at Fidelity had generous profit-sharing arrangements—which would have been even more generous if Johnson could have been persuaded to stop spending the "profits" so freely. But of course he couldn't be persuaded. Fidelity was a private company, and one reason Ned Johnson insisted on keeping it private was so that he could run it the way he wanted, without having to answer to anybody.

From outside the company, the case against Fidelity was that it had become a voracious money machine—sucking in assets with carefully calibrated ads, and then charging fees and loads that "robbed" investors of gains that were "rightfully" theirs. Yet one of the most vocal critics of excessive mutual fund fees, the *Morningstar* organization, published an article that came to the defense of Fidelity against such charges. After conducting a study of the overall performance of Fidelity's equity funds, *Morningstar* concluded the average Fidelity equity fund not only beat the market averages the great majority of the time—it beat them by a lot. This was true *even after excluding Magellan,* and it caused *Morningstar* to proclaim that Fidelity was "the winningest equity-fund manager in existence." Its secondary point, though, was that those who criticized Johnson for being greedy were missing something important. He had plunged much of the money the company had made from its loads right back into Fidelity—to pay for its research department and its computer technology and a dozen other things that gave the company its edge. And even with all the fees and loads, Fidelity had still done awfully well by its shareholders. Perhaps this helps explain why, by the end of 1993, Fidelity held $268 billion in assets, making it twice as large as its nearest competitor, Vanguard. It also held, by then, almost $100 billion more in assets than Citibank.

Ned Johnson was sixty-three years old in 1993. Nobody thought of him as a flake anymore; instead, his "genius" was so widely heralded as to inflict some mild embarrassment on his Brahman sensibilities. He was, as ever, involved in a million different things, buying companies and jumping into new ventures as they caught his fancy. Fidelity owned a voice-mail system in London and a chain of small newspapers in Massachusetts, a life insurance company and a string of art stores. It even published a personal finance magazine, called *Worth,* which was one of two new magazines that had arisen to compete with *Money* magazine for the attention of the new middle-class investor.[12] Early on, *Worth* was rumored to be losing millions of dollars but however much it was, it did not amount to much more than pocket change for Johnson. His majority ownership of Fidelity Investments made him worth "at least" $1.7 billion, according to *Forbes* magazine's estimate. This was the twenty-sixth-largest fortune in the United States. His instinct for the money revolution had made him wealthier than David Rockefeller.

Although he gave no outward inkling that he was considering retirement, Fidelity watchers could not help but notice that another Johnson had joined him at the company. Her name was Abigail Johnson, and she was Ned Johnson's thirty-one-year-old daughter, "a slender, self-possessed woman," according to the *Wall Street Journal,* who, after a typically lengthy stint as an analyst, had become a hot fund manager in her own right. Given a fund to run in 1993, the newly created Dividend Growth Fund, she steered it to a 17 percent gain in eight months, beating the S&P 500 by a solid 8 percent.[13] This performance attracted attention, of course, and reporters came calling. And when they did, they wanted to know whether she was being groomed to succeed her father. "I can't see into the future," she replied crisply, adding that such speculation was "completely premature." But then, what would you expect a Johnson to say? What would Ned Johnson have said twenty-five years before, if he had been asked about following in his own father's footsteps? Johnsons didn't display ambition; they didn't reveal their innermost thoughts; they didn't talk to the press about their deepest hopes and fondest dreams. They learned their trade and did their job and waited their turn. And when the day came, as it surely would, they gracefully assumed the mantle they had always known would be theirs.

JANUARY 18, 1991, THAT DAY WHEN THE DOW JONES AVERAGE ROSE 114 points after the first bombing raid over Baghdad, turned out to be more than simply a momentous response to a momentous event. In market terms, it turned out to be a harbinger, the same way that Friday the 13th of August 1982 had been a harbinger. That earlier date, you'll recall, would later be memorialized as the Day the Bull Market Began. And January 18, 1991, we now know, was also the day a bull market began—the bull market of the early 1990s, the fifth of this century.

It was a strange one, especially at first. Whereas America had become aware of the 1980s bull market within months of its start, this new bull began quietly, despite its explosive first day. For a long time, the rise in stock prices received very little attention, even though the Dow kept setting new records. People didn't seem to trust what was happening, nor did they seem willing to speak about it out loud, as if such idle talk might cause the balloon to burst.

It wasn't until the summer of 1993 that the financial press awakened from its long sleep, and realized they had been living through a powerful bull market the past two and a half years. In mid-August, when the Dow passed an important watershed—the 3600 barrier—the *Wall Street Journal* heralded the moment with a lengthy front-page story. A few weeks later, *The New York Times* wrote essentially the same story for its front page. At that point, the quiet bull was a secret no more.

There were two aspects of this bull market that seemed to take the press by surprise. The first was that stock prices in the 1990s were moving not to Wall Street's tune but to Main Street's—where, as the *Times* put it, "a whole generation of savers, seeking alternatives to the 2 and 3 percent returns available at banks, [were] now being transformed into investors." Well, yes, though one had to wonder how anyone who had been paying even the slightest attention during the last twenty years could have found this surprising. Still, it was true enough. If the 1980s bull market was the first in which the middle class participated on an equal footing with Wall Street, this one marked something even more significant: this was the first bull market that owed its very existence to the steady infusion of middle-class money. "The baby boomers are doing to the stock market what they did to the housing market," one wag told a *Times* columnist—meaning that just as the demand for housing in the 1970s had driven up housing prices, now the demand for investment returns was driving up stock prices. One could decry this state of affairs—one could worry that the "unsophisticated" small investor would panic at the first sign of trouble and bring the whole thing tumbling down. Or one could applaud it, seeing it as a democratic trend in a democratic society: "Never before in American history have so many middle-class people enjoyed something at least faintly resembling the 'private banking' available to the rich," noted Ron Chernow, the author of several fine business biographies. "The culture of investing has become an abiding part of the American scene."

Whichever view one took, however, one could not deny the reality. The so-called smart money did not lord it over the financial markets anymore. "The modest sums of the thrifty," as Charlie Merrill had once described our money, now had as much to do with deciding whether markets would go up or down as any Wall Street trader. Surely, this had to rank as one of the momentous changes in modern American life. In some crucial way, it completed the revolution.

The press's second finding was even less surprising than the first. It was that the primary means by which the middle class had taken control of the financial markets was through mutual funds. "Since the start of the current bull market," the *Times* noted in that same front-page story, "more than $450 billion has poured into mutual funds—which include stock, bond and money market funds. . . ." By the end of 1993, nearly a third of American households had a mutual fund investment of one sort or another. Indeed, rare was the baby boomer household that *didn't* rely on mutual funds, or more likely, on a variety of mutual funds. One well-known household that was heavily invested in mutual funds was the one at 1600 Pennsylvania Avenue, where Bill and Hillary Clinton resided. According to their financial disclosure statements, the President kept his cash in a money market fund with Charles Schwab and divided his IRA money between the Janus Fund and the Strong Opportunity Fund. Hillary Rodham Clinton had as much as

$180,000 invested in seven different mutual funds, including GT Pacific Growth, Federated Prime Cash Series, and Thomson funds. Like many people of their generation, the Clintons appeared to keep only minimal amounts in the bank.

Indeed, by the early 1990s, mutual funds had come to dominate the financial universe. They drove the stock market and the government bond market, of course. But they also drove the short-term commercial paper market, the junk bond market, many foreign stock markets, and even the risky derivative market. There were days when Fidelity alone accounted for up to 10 percent of the volume on the New York Stock Exchange. The Vanguard Group had well over $100 billion in assets. Merrill Lynch, which was revived by the 1990s bull market—its total assets exceeding $500 billion, which amounted to a staggering 2.4 percent of all the financial assets in the United States—had a mutual fund division that held around $123 billion. Charles Schwab & Co., which had become a truly solid company in the 1990s, began a program in 1993 to solidify its mutual fund presence. Called OneSource, it allowed investors to switch among 200 different funds—including some well-known names like Janus and Twentieth Century—without having to pay transaction fees. The program gathered over $20 billion in assets in practically the blink of an eye, but more than that, it signaled that Schwab was not competing with Quick & Reilly anymore. It was competing with Fidelity and Vanguard. Discounting was only one part of what it did. By early 1994, it could claim 2.7 million active customers, and more than $1 billion in annual revenues; it, too, had more than $100 billion under management.

Even banks began peddling mutual funds. By the fall of 1993, over 100 banks were offering mutual funds, and they held about 10 percent of all mutual fund assets. On Capitol Hill, one heard talk from time to time that the entry of banks into the mutual fund business was a dangerous thing, putting people's savings at risk. It violated the spirit, if not the letter, of Glass–Steagall, it was said. But such talk usually evaporated quickly. It was hard to get too worked up about Glass–Steagall, not when AT&T could issue credit cards, and Citicorp could underwrite insurance, and John Hancock, the insurance company, could offer brokered deposits. And not when Merrill Lynch managed more money in IRA accounts than the 100 largest banks combined, and Fidelity Investments held $100 billion more in customer assets than the biggest bank in the United States. The only thing banks still had left was deposit insurance, but as a magnet for money, deposit insurance had long ago lost its pull. In December 1993, Mellon Bank announced that it was purchasing the Dreyfus Corporation, one of the oldest names in the mutual fund business, which held around $80 billion in assets.

The news was greeted with a general yawn. Around the same time, the ICI announced that the mutual fund industry, which had crossed the $1 trillion barrier just three years before, was poised to pass the $2 trillion mark. There could be no clearer sign of how the world had changed.

⌒

AND YET, AND YET . . .

And yet one was still left wondering about the new investors themselves. It wasn't that they were "unsophisticated"; their market behavior since the crash should have put that one to rest. Nor was it that they failed to appreciate the potential benefits the new world had created for them. They understood those benefits completely. They also appreciated the fact, as Ron Chernow put it, that they had to "either actively manage their own financial futures or suffer in the future." Thus did they salt away funds for retirement, and move money around to get a higher return. Thus did they jump into risky and exotic foreign funds with some of their money—and put other funds into conservative bond and asset allocation funds. Thus did they subscribe to newsletters and pore over the stock tables each day. Thus did they take control, as they knew they had to.

They did all these things, but they did not do them with any particular joy. The joy had gone out of it after the crash. They accepted the new world, but they did not embrace it. It still made them nervous. "Every year," remarked Mimi Lieber, "people were different both in terms of their sophistication and their anxiety. The more they knew, the more it scared them." And though they had become investors, they did not yet believe in their own investing abilities, or trust their market instincts. They feared the possibility of loss more than they relished the potential for gain. In 1992 and 1993, America experienced one of the most glorious market moments ever—twin bull markets in stocks and bonds—and people wondered: When will the next crash come? After everything that had happened, they remained unsure of themselves—and slightly envious of those lucky few who had the investing skills they felt they would never acquire.

One of the lucky few, of course, was Peter Lynch. Through the years, he had remained steadfast in his belief that the rest of us could do as well in the market as he had done: "I've said before that an amateur who devotes a small amount of study to companies in an industry he or she knows something about can outperform 95 percent of the paid experts. . . ." he wrote. He wrote those words, as it happens, in his second best-selling book, entitled *Beating the Street*, which he worked on after retiring from Magellan, and which, by March of 1993, he was busily promoting. He traveled to

Dallas and Washington and Los Angeles and Chicago, and everywhere he went, people pointed him out, or stopped him on the street to ask for an autograph or a stock tip, or shook his hand. *He* may have believed that we could outperform the pros, but *we* didn't believe it, not for a second. Indeed, it was precisely because we didn't believe it that we were buying his book. We were convinced that Peter Lynch could pick stocks better than anyone, and in appreciation of that gift, we had bestowed upon him the kind of celebrity status that caused people to point him out in the street and ask for his autograph.

One day that March, during lunch hour, Lynch went to a popular bookstore in the Chicago financial district to sign copies of his new book. Even before he got to the store, a long line had formed; within fifteen minutes of his arrival, the line snaked most of the way around the store. Young women, describing themselves as "your biggest fans here," giggled. People asked him nervously about one stock or another—"What do you think about Starbucks?" "Can IBM come back?"—hoping to gain the courage to buy or sell. Someone asked him to inscribe the book with the words, "Buy low, sell high." "I'll write it," he said, "but I don't believe it. I believe you should buy low and you should buy high. If you didn't buy Home Depot because you thought it was too high, you made a big mistake." The man looked at Lynch sheepishly. Someone else talked to Lynch about a stock of his that, he claimed, had doubled. "Why did you buy it?" Lynch asked. "Because I thought it was going to go up," the man boasted. "That's a lousy reason," Lynch replied. "If it has doubled, you should sell it today and be thankful." This man too walked away sheepishly.

Even the store manager couldn't resist the urge to talk about her portfolio. "We got into stocks late," she told Lynch after the customers had left, and he was signing extra books. "Our broker put us into this company that makes Velcro." Lynch immediately perked up, as he always does when he thinks he's about to learn something. "Oh, yeah," he said, "isn't that a little company up in New Hampshire?" The woman didn't know. "What does your broker say about it?" She didn't know that either. Her broker had told her to buy the stock, and she had bought it, and that was about it. Thus did the middle class cope with the 1990s, with the stock market, with the money revolution.

Peter Lynch, meanwhile, went back to signing books.

# Acknowledgments

IT'S IMPOSSIBLE, I've discovered, to write a book like this one, which attempts to meld history with journalism, without relying on the work of the many journalists who took one step or another on this path before me. Because the money revolution encompasses so many different aspects of American finance over such a span of time, there were hundreds of such reporters, working at newspapers as varied as *The New York Times* and the *Salt Lake Tribune*, toiling anonymously (as was the case for many years) at the newsweeklies and *Business Week*, reporting for large-circulation magazines such as *Forbes* and *Fortune* and small-circulation trade publications such as *The Nilson Report* and *Financial Services Week*. In the notes that follow, I've tried to acknowledge my more obvious debts to particular writers and publications, but I would be remiss if I did not take a moment here to express my gratitude to all those reporters who covered the many and varied aspects of the money revolution. Their work was the foundation upon which I was able to construct this book, and it was invariably solid.

I am also indebted to the many people who generously spent time with me over the past six years answering my questions about the evolution of personal finance in America. There were more than 250 of them before I was done; and a number of them must have wondered if they'd ever be rid of me, for I kept coming back for another interview or another question. Nonetheless they always took the time to answer my questions, usually with good cheer. A good portion of those I interviewed are listed in the chapter notes; however, a number of sources agreed to be interviewed only if I did not identify them. Though I can't name them personally, I appreciate the help they gave me.

The life of a business writer can be made immeasurably easier—or more difficult—by the help (or lack of it) that he receives from public relations departments. Three public relations departments made my life easier: Charles Schwab & Co., under the irrepressible Hugo Quackenbush and his assistant, Nancy Mitchell; the Investment Company Institute, where I received help from a small army of people, including L. Eric Kanter and Laurie Strollo; and Fidelity Investments, where Joy Smith was always ready to respond to a query or set up an interview. I also received a great deal of valuable assistance from the former head of Fidelity's public relations department, the late Rab Bertelsen, who really understood what I was trying to do and did everything he could to help me accomplish it. Among the public relations people I encountered along the way, I would also like to thank Jane Ginsburg at Benham Capital Management Group, Jean Peters at Capital Holdings Corp., Kelly Williams at AT&T, Barbara Orlando at *Money* magazine, Richard Woods at MasterCard, Barbara Gertz at *Morningstar Mutual Funds,* Tracey Gordon and Darla Hastings at Fidelity, William Clark and Fred Yager at Merrill Lynch, Susan Sherwood at Bank of America, Steven E. Norwitz at T. Rowe Price, and Daniel Brigham at Visa.

I was aided by a number of librarians and archivists, including Martin Elzy and his staff at the Jimmy Carter Library in Atlanta, William F. Sherman at the National Archives in Washington, D.C., Marilyn B. Ghausi, the corporate archivist at BankAmerica, Mary L. Callinan, the Chief Librarian at *The American Banker,* Sarah Pritchard and the staff of the Neilson Library at Smith College, and Elise Feeley at the Forbes Library in Northampton, Massachusetts, who tracked down numerous stray facts. I would also like to thank Stephen Szekely of Payment Systems, Inc., as well as Spencer Nilson and his associate David Robertson of *The Nilson Report.* The former allowed me to look through PSI's extensive library of credit card–related material, while the latter gave me access to back issues of *The Nilson Report*—a rare gift indeed, as anyone familiar with Nilson will immediately recognize. Kenneth Larkin also supplied me with a number of documents that aided my task. Several other people who provided documents asked that they not be named.

I first began thinking about the incredible changes surrounding personal finance in the early part of 1987, when Lee Eisenberg, then the editor of *Esquire,* asked me to write a story about Fidelity Investments and the 1980s bull market. I knew very quickly that there was a book in the material I was gathering and that I wanted to write it. I am grateful to Lee for giving me the chance to explore in that early story the germ of the idea that eventually became this book. I'd also like to thank David Hirshey and Laura Marmor, who helped shepherd that original *Esquire* story into print. I am even more indebted to another editor, Art Cooper at *GQ,* who gave me a magazine home when I was badly in need of one, and whose generosity, friendship, and unflagging support made it possible for me to complete this book at a time when I had begun to doubt that I'd ever reach that goal. Martin Beiser, who edits my column in *GQ*, became one of the people I most relied on for advice. My relationship with *GQ* is one of the most satisfying of my writing life, and I'm grateful for it.

During the past few years, I've had a terrific crew of researchers and fact checkers. Ron Cesar pulled together much useful material in the early stages of my reporting; Erin Gray, Melissa Jones, Jen Vander Weyden, Portia Keating, and Ben Horowitz all ably assisted me in the latter stages. Lisa Levchuk, Robin Shank, Wes Brown, and, especially, Colleen Sackheim transcribed my taped interviews.

I am lucky to have a group of friends who were willing to take the time to read a very long manuscript in its various stages and help keep me on track throughout. Nicholas Lemann read the book in two different stages and offered his usual sound counsel. Robert Nylen, Norman Sims, and Daniel Akst all read early portions of the book and made many helpful suggestions. James Fallows critiqued an early draft of Chapter Nine. Barry Werth, Elinor Lipman, Michael Zonis, and Martin Beiser read a draft of the completed manuscript and offered their guidance. I am especially appreciative of the efforts of Randall Stross, Norman Pearlstine, and Daniel Okrent, whose close reading of the manuscript and detailed suggestions made this a much better book than it would otherwise have been.

There are other kinds of help one needs to get through a project of this duration, and I got plenty of it. My parents, Rosalie D. Nocera and the late Amato Nocera, and my in-laws Barbara B. Rose and the late Stuart Rose offered large doses of moral support. I'd also like to thank Andrew and Janet Rose, Mary and Luca Cafiero, Phillip Weiss and Cynthia Kling, Julie Michaels, Fred Rose and Anne Gregor, Barry Wadsworth, Paul Nocera, Larry Gondelman and Pauline Sobel, John Koten, Will Dana, Elizabeth Pochoda, Tina Jordan, David Shipley, Sally Dinkel, Bob Thompson, Charlie Peters, Maynard Parker, Mark Whitaker, Katy Roberts, Michael Hirshorn, Jane Bryant Quinn, Kurt Brouwer, Fred Woodward, Timothy Noah and Marjorie Williams, Andrew Zimbalist, Andrew Kuether, Susan Feldman, Sue Zesiger, Ellen Ryder, Kit Nylen, Bob Gray, Joan Hughes, Suzanne Russin, Malcolm B. Smith, Lisa Newman, Marty Wohl, Eric Kobren, and Christina Platt for various kindnesses along the way. Thomas Henriksen of the Hoover Institution gave me a place to hang my hat during two reporting stints in northern California. On both occasions, Wendy Minkin was indispensable, as she is for most everyone who passes through the Hoover. Robert Samuelson of *Newsweek* made an off-handed comment one day that got me thinking about credit and credit cards, something that had not been part of my original plan.

I feel blessed to have had Alice Mayhew as my editor and Esther Newberg as my agent. In some ways, Alice grasped the full dimensions of what I was trying to do before I grasped them myself. Her consistently shrewd advice, unending supply of patience, and uncanny ability to cut to the heart of things were all qualities I came to depend on. Esther Newberg's steadfastness, straightforwardness, and insistent belief in this book were every bit as important. They were both true partners in this endeavor. I'd also like to thank, at ICM, Amanda Beesley, Sloan Harris, and Kathy Pohl, and, at Simon & Schuster, Eric Steel, Eric Rayman, Sarah Baker, Larry Ratzkin, Lydia Buechler, and Ann Finlayson for their help.

I've discovered something else about writing a book: as it becomes part of the writer's life, it becomes part of his family's as well. My family always embraced this part of our life together, seeing it not as a burden—which it surely was at times for them—but as a part of our collective adventure as a family. My children, Katherine, Amato, and Nicholas, were an endless source of joy and sustenance. My wife, Julie Rose, has been my companion in this project, as she has been in everything we've done together during our married life. There is nothing I am more thankful for than that and no debt I more look forward to repaying.

# Notes

## INTRODUCTION:
### The Money Revolution

1. To be sure, it was once an even more important selling season than it is today. As will be discussed in greater detail in Chapter 14, between 1982 and 1986, every working American could get a $2,000 tax deduction by putting that amount in an IRA. This deduction, of course, gave IRAs much of their initial allure. However, in the Tax Reform Act of 1986, Congress stripped the deduction from Americans who had pension plans at work and earned more than $35,000 (or $50,000 for married couples), though IRAs did retain some of their other tax advantages. This change has caused the spring "tax season" to be less dramatic than it used to be—though still dramatic enough that many mutual fund companies still do close to 50 percent of their business during "IRA season."

## CHAPTER 1
### The Drop, September 1958

The story of the creation of BankAmericard comes primarily from interviews with former Bank of America executives, including Kenneth V. Larkin, Joseph Williams, Samuel Stewart, and John A. Dillon. Phillip S. Hayman, a former marketer with Bank of America (and later Visa), wrote, in 1962, the in-house history of BankAmericard that I refer to in the text; we also had several telephone conversations. Books that were helpful with the early history of the bank include *Breaking the Bank: The Decline of BankAmerica*, by Gary Hector, and *Roller Coaster: The Bank of America and the Future of American Banking*, by Moira Johnston. *The Big Store: Inside the Crisis and Revolution at Sears*, by Donald R. Katz, contains an illuminating history of credit in America, while Lewis Mandell's *The Credit Card Industry: A History* and Terry Galanoy's *Charge It: Inside the Credit Card Conspiracy* both offer concise histories of the origins of BankAmericard. John Kenneth Galbraith's *The Affluent Society* makes the case against installment loans and the consumer society about as powerfully as it can be made. *The Good Life: The Meaning of Success for the American Middle Class*, by Loren Baritz, also tackles the effects of the consumer society, though from a more modern (and sanguine) perspective. Other sources I relied on include the following: "A History of Bank Credit Cards," a study by Gavin Spofford and Robert H. Grant for the Federal Home Loan Bank Board, dated June 2, 1975; "History of Charge and Credit Cards," by Visa U.S.A.; *Bank Cards* and *Banking and the Plastic Card*, two books put out by the American Bankers Association; various issues of *The Nilson Report*, the most authoritative credit card industry newsletter; and newspaper articles from the *Fresno Bee*. The Bank of America corporate archivist supplied me with numerous documents relating to the founding of BankAmericard. At the time I interviewed Alex "Pete" Hart, he was the head of MasterCard; he has since left that position to return to the banking industry.

1. In 1959, of course, California would drop to the third-largest state when Alaska was admitted to the union.
2. The bank's reach was so immense that it held more than 30 percent of all the deposits in the state of California, and had a banking relationship, in one form or another, with 60 percent of the state's population. No bank in the country, before or since, has ever approached that kind of dominance.
3. Sears began granting credit as early as 1910; by the 1950s, more than 25 million Americans had a Sears charge plate. "Sears gave the masses credit because banks would not," notes Katz in *The Big Store*. "Much of the rise in the standard of living of the American masses was thought within the company to have been promoted by Sears and its credit policies—and many historians of economic development have tended to agree."
4. Katz again: "It was actually the Great Depression that opened up consumer credit beyond the realms of Sears and one or two other companies, because it was then that poorer Americans demonstrated that they pay their bills—even when times are tough."
5. American Express, in fact, got into the charge card business two weeks after Bank of America.
6. This legend, which McNamara honed to a fare-thee-well, may well be apocryphal. Oddly enough, McNamara sold the business in 1953 because, as one writer explained, "he realized that many Americans were suspicious of credit, and he thought they were likely to remain so."
7. It would be a good two decades before banks began imposing annual fees on credit cards. Indeed, the fact that it cost nothing to obtain a credit card was a key selling point in the early years.
8. The circumstances of Williams's departure are unclear. Several old BofA hands say he was forced out, which Williams adamantly denies. In any case, after leaving Bank of America, he started a credit card in New York, called Unicard, which was both successful and profitable. When he eventually sold his company to American Express, he received enough American Express stock to become a wealthy man, much to the amazement of his former Bank of America colleagues.
9. This, according to Hayman's in-house history.

## CHAPTER 2
### The Man with the Golden Touch, February 1966

Charlie Merrill's life has never been recounted in a full-length published biography, but there are some unpublished accounts in existence, which were written shortly after he died, apparently at the behest of his daughter. "Chain of Fortune," by Stanley Frank, is the more useful—and less hagiographic—of the two. Two of James Merrill's books, written more than thirty years apart, *The Seraglio* and *A Different Person: A Memoir*, contain sharp and insightful portraits of his father. *The Seraglio*, which Merrill wrote when he was a young man, is a work of fiction, but a very thinly disguised one; it captures Charlie Merrill during the latter part of his life, after he had been stricken with heart disease. In the mid-1980s, Merrill Lynch commissioned a history of the firm, entitled *A Legacy of Leadership*, a good portion of which is devoted to the founder's life and times. Donald Regan, Roger Birks, John Fitzgerald, and William Clark were among the present and former Merrill Lynch executives I interviewed who had known Merrill. A lengthy story in the May 1972 issue of *Fortune* magazine, "The Merrill Lynch Bull Is Loose on Wall Street," includes a profile of Merrill. *Share Ownership in America: 1959* was the survey conducted by the New York Stock

Exchange that is mentioned in the text. *The Go-Go Years* by John Brooks, *The Money Game* by "Adam Smith"—a.k.a. George J. W. Goodman—and *The Reckoning* by David Halberstam all tell the story of Gerry Tsai. The big Tsai story in *Newsweek,* entitled "Tsai and the 'Go-Go' Funds," was published in the May 13, 1968, issue. In addition, *Business Week* wrote several lengthy stories about Tsai, including "Fresh face in money management" (February 20, 1965) and "Tsai touch no longer seems so golden" (March 4, 1972). Years later, Tsai spoke to *Institutional Investor* magazine about the Go-Go Years; that interview can be found in the June 1987 issue. Past and present Fidelity employees who spoke to me about Edward Johnson 2d include Peter Lynch, the late Rab Bertelsen, Daniel Prigmore, Leo Dworsky, Joseph Midwood, Caleb Loring, Richard M. Reilly, Alan Holliday, and Warren Casey.

1. Magowan stepped down as CEO of Safeway in 1993, when he became the managing partner of the San Francisco Giants. He remained, however, chairman of the Safeway board of directors.
2. Though it should be said that his memoirs are tempered by much genuine fondness and love: "I find my father at the Excelsior Hotel," he writes in *A Different Person.* "He kisses me affectionately. It is always a pleasure to set eyes upon him: silver haired, his round face lightly tanned, a small, compact figure in smart clothes. I am his youngest child; he has a daughter and son by his first wife. I've come to think of him as less paternal than grandfatherly. He was after all over forty at my birth, and two or three heart attacks have added a decade to his age. Conversation is happily just now out of the question, what with the two American factotums who met his ship, the come-and-go of waiters with sandwiches and tea, and the excited claims of his traveling companions."
3. Cassatt & Co. was a small Philadelphia firm that was merged into the other two. As Merrill bought other firms over the years, the name would evolve; the final change took place in 1958, the year after Merrill's death, when Winthrop Smith took over the firm, and his last name replaced Beane.
4. Or the wives of these middle managers: according to the NYSE's statistics, one out of three shareholders was a housewife.
5. Peter Lynch, the great former manager of Fidelity Magellan, has an intriguing theory about why so many Americans missed the bull market of the 1950s and early 1960s. The country, in his view, had become so obsessed with the Cold War and the threat of nuclear war that it largely forgot about its own growing prosperity. "People were building fall-out shelters instead of buying stocks," he once told me.
6. In Merrill's defense, it should be noted that in his day, mutual funds were not the "investor friendly" financial tool they have since become. For instance, many mutual fund operators charged exhorbitant fees, often as much as half the initial investment, making it extremely difficult for the investor to make a profit in any reasonable length of time. Another problem was the distribution system: although many funds were sold by brokers, many others were peddled mainly by college students going door-to-door. Indeed, one theory as to why Merrill so loathed them was that he considered mutual fund operators charlatans, barely a step above penny stock promoters. If this was his view, he was hardly alone.
7. In that same interview, Tsai also said, somewhat more sagely, "If I were starting my life all over again, after twenty-five years or so of managing portfolios, I wouldn't give a hoot about the relative performance of other funds. . . . You can't manage a portfolio as if you're running a race every five minutes. That's stupid; it really is."

## CHAPTER 3
### Delusions and the Madness of Bankers, November 1966

So far as I can tell, Lewis Mandell's book, *The Credit Card Industry: A History,* is the only published history of the credit card business; it contains a thumbnail account of the credit card drops of the late 1960s. The Spofford and Grant study, "A History of Bank Credit Cards," offers a chronology of the expansion of credit cards and the formation of the BankAmericard and Interbank systems. *The Bank Book,* by "Morgan Irving" (aka Charles Sopkin), gives a powerful sense of what it was like to work in a bank as the credit card losses began piling up. Three speeches—by former Proxmire aide Kenneth A. McLean ("Public Policy Implications of Credit Card Growth," June 1970); former BankAmericard executive Conrad Johnson ("Those Were the Days, My Friends . . . ," date unknown); and Kenneth Larkin ("Opening Remarks to the National Installment Credit Conference," March 1967)—contain much useful history.

Other published sources I drew on include the following: *The American Banker,* which ran a series on credit cards during the week of May 17, 1971; the proceedings of the National Installment Credit Conference, 1967; "Fundamentals of Bank Credit Cards," a study conducted for the Eastern States Bankcard Association by Don D. Jutilla; "The Story of Interbank," by Edward E. Bontems (*Banker's Monthly,* July 15, 1968); "Credit Card America," by Nancy Shepherdson (*American Heritage,* November 1991); "The Chicago Bank Credit Card Fiasco," by Harold S. Taylor (*The Banker's Magazine,* Winter 1968); and "Chicago's credit card crisis" (*Business Week,* July 15, 1967). A congressional hearing into "Unsolicited Bank Credit Cards" was held in June 1967, by the House Committee on Banking and Currency. A Senate inquiry into "Bank Credit-Card and Check-Credit Plans" was conducted on October 9, 1968, by the subcommittee on Financial Institutions. The *Life* magazine article quoted in the chapter, "A Little Gift from Your Friendly Banker" (March 27, 1970), was written by Paul O'Neill. A scathing appraisal of credit cards can be found in the 1970 book *Credit Cardsmanship,* by Martin J. Meyer. Important interviews include Kenneth Larkin, John Dillon, Darold Hoops, Leighton Johnson, Jr., Kenneth McLean, George Fesus, and Charles Holstein.

Numerous people spoke to me about Dee Hock. In addition to those listed above, they include Charles Russell, Bennett Katz, Thomas Honey, Dan Brigham, Richard Rossi, Don D. Jutilla, Guy W. Botts, Stephen Szekely, and Linda Fenner Zimmer. Spencer Nilson and his associate, David Robertson, allowed me to look through back issues of *The Nilson Report* for items relating to Hock, which were plentiful. The most comprehensive account of Hock's life was compiled by a writer named Susan Chace, who profiled Hock for *The New Yorker* around 1980. Her piece, however, never ran. A 1981 Harvard Business School case study, "Visa International: The Management of Change," was prepared by J. Stewart Dougherty under the supervision of Robert G. Eccles, Jr.

1. One of Larkin's favorite facts is that in July 1967, when Master Charge was finally introduced, BankAmericard had its best month ever. He happily surmises that the competition's saturation advertising rebounded to Bank of America's advantage.
2. A number of other important pieces of credit card legislation bear Proxmire's stamp. It was he who pushed through the Truth in Lending law, forcing credit cards to publish their annual percentage rate (instead of the monthly rate as the banks preferred), and other consumer-oriented disclosures that are now a required part of the monthly statement. Also, he wrote the law limiting to $50 the amount for which a consumer would be held liable if his cards were stolen. Although the banks bitterly opposed this law, Proxmire did them a huge service, for in one fell swoop he eliminated the source of much anxiety, and thus helped make credit cards that much more acceptable in American life.

3. This description comes from an odd but entertaining work, entitled *The Bank Book*, authored by one "Morgan Irving." In fact, Irving was the pen name for a New York banker named Charles Sopkin; the book itself is a vivid, if overly wry, sketch of life inside his bank, which he calls First Mutual Trust.

4. Since renamed First Chicago, that bank is today one of the top five issuers of credit cards—and one of the savviest marketers.

5. In fact, thanks to a law passed during the Depression, finance companies had the right to charge as much as 33 percent, even in states with usury ceilings.

6. It was just as bad, if not worse, among the banks issuing Master Charge cards. Perhaps the most absurdly memorable moment came when a bank in Pittsburgh placed tiny pins in the imprinters it rented to its merchants. The pins were intended to destroy competing cards—which they did, even when the cards had been issued by other Master Charge banks.

## CHAPTER 4
## The Great Wall of Q, February 1970

Publicity-shy though he is, Ned Johnson has been the subject of numerous articles over the years. I wrote one of them, for *Esquire* magazine in February 1988, under the headline "The Ga-Ga Years." Some of the better magazine profiles include the following: "The Son Also Rises," by Michael VerMuelen (*Institutional Investor*, February 1986); "Why Fidelity Is the Master of Mutual Funds," by Alex Taylor (*Fortune*, September 1, 1986); "Ned Johnson of FMR: Watch your flank, Merrill Lynch," by Richard Phalon (*Forbes*, October 26, 1981); and "Semper Fidelity," by Margaret Pantridge (*Boston Magazine*, March 1992). Pantridge's article is by far the best at capturing the essence of Johnson, and at tracking down his life's story; she is the reporter, for instance, who elicited the quotes from Arthur DuBow, his college roommate. Eric Kobren, the editor of the newsletter *Fidelity Insight*, also publishes an annual *Independent Guide to Fidelity Funds;* it includes a smart, concise history of the company. Peter Lynch, Joseph Midwood, Alan Holliday, Bo Burlingham, Leo Dworsky, John O'Brien, Caleb Loring, Warren Casey, Roger Servison, Richard M. Reilly, Daniel Prigmore, and Johnson himself were among those who granted me interviews. Rab Bertelsen spent the two years before he died gathering information for his own book—intended to be a history of the Johnson family and Fidelity—much of which overlapped with my own research needs. Yet he was never less than generous in sharing what he had learned with me. Much of what Rab told me eventually found its way into this chapter.

The story of the invention of the money market mutual fund comes primarily from the inventors themselves, Henry Brown, Bruce Bent, and James Benham. Brown gave me an unpublished chapter of a book he was working on that contains his account of the creation of the Reserve Fund. Donald E. Farrar and William Donoghue talked to me about the early days of money market funds. Edward Furash and Kurt Brouwer helped supply the Big Picture. *The New York Times* article Bent and Brown credit with saving their money market fund— "Overnight Mutual Funds for Surplus Cash," by Robert D. Hershey, Jr.—ran on January 7, 1973. Other published sources include the following: *The Dow Jones–Irwin Guide to Buying and Selling Treasury Securities*, by Harold M. Berlin; *Capital Ideas: The Improbable Origins of Modern Wall Street*, by Peter M. Bernstein; *How to Prosper During the Coming Bad Years*, by Howard Ruff; the original prospectuses for the Reserve Fund, the Capital Preservation Fund, and Fidelity Daily Income Trust; and two "Change Agents" columns that ran in *Changing Times* magazine, one on Bent (March 1989) and the other on Benham (November 1989). The anonymous labor leader who predicted "riots in supermarkets" was quoted in the March 4, 1974, issue of *Newsweek*.

1. The name was derived from the fact that the market's seeming upsurge was actually being driven almost exclusively by fifty or so overheated "glamor" stocks.
2. The lawsuit was known as *Moses* v. *Bergen,* and the attorney who brought it, who was perhaps the most reviled man on Wall Street in his heyday because of his propensity for filing—and winning—lawsuits against investment firms, was named Abe Pomerantz.
3. Essentially the court ruled that Fidelity should have been trying to find ways to ensure that commission "give-ups," as they were called, wound up in the hands of the fund's shareholders, instead of the brokerage houses that sold its funds or offered investment research. Although a lower court had agreed with Fidelity's contention that this was not possible under current NYSE rules, the appeals court said that Fidelity had breached its fiduciary duty to the shareholders of its various funds.
4. During the last years of his life, Mr. Johnson suffered from Alzheimer's. He died in 1984, at the age of eighty-six.
5. They were rare because the elder Johnson was not so sure his portfolio managers should fraternize with each other; he feared it might dull their competitive instincts.
6. Loring was also Mr. Johnson's longtime personal lawyer.
7. Government debt securities are classified as either Treasury bills, Treasury notes, or Treasury bonds, depending on their duration. T-bills are those that come due in a year or less; T-notes have fixed maturities of between one and ten years; and Treasury bonds are those that have a fixed maturity of longer than ten years. The shortest-term T-bill is a thirteen-week security; the longest-term bond is the Treasury's benchmark thirty-year bond—the so-called long bond. For the purposes of a money market fund manager, it is the short-term T-bills that make sense because they allow the fund manager to adapt quickly to any changes in market interest rates—which, of course, is the point of the exercise.
8. The yield of a money market fund is more properly thought of as a kind of dividend, since mutual funds, by definition, cannot produce "interest."
9. This is called the expense ratio: of late, the Reserve Fund's expense ratio has been around 0.99 percent of assets, which is a bit under the average for a money market fund.
10. And promptly sued Merrill Lynch. In October 1973, a court ruled that, as a *New York Times* account put it, "Benham had a moral and legal duty to tell clients what he actually thought about the stock market, and that Merrill Lynch had no right to force him to do otherwise."
11. It should be pointed out that there are at least three countervailing arguments on behalf of Regulation Q. The first is that, in return for accepting low interest rates, depositors received something of value from the government: deposit insurance. Secondly, because most banks (and all S&Ls) had made many long-term loans at 5 and 6 percent interest, forcing them to pay rates that were higher than that to depositors would seriously jeopardize the health of many institutions. And third, if Reg Q was lifted, banks and S&Ls would lapse back into the behavior that had gotten them into trouble during the Depression: paying excessively high interest rates to attract deposits. Indeed, when passbook rates were finally deregulated in the early 1980s, that is precisely what the S&L industry did and this reckless behavior played a role in the S&L crisis of the late 1980s. The debate over the purpose and value of Regulation Q will be examined in closer detail in Chapter 11.
12. Since most loads in the early 1970s were around 8 percent, a load on a money market fund would have made them completely impractical. The lack of a load, however, was yet another reason why brokers were uninterested in selling them.

## CHAPTER 5
## "Here Come the Revolutionaries," July 1970

A good deal of the information that found its way into this chapter was contained in a cache of old NBI documents that had been saved by Don Jutilla of Puget Sound Tele-Services. In the late 1960s and early 1970s, Jutilla had been among the BankAmericard licensees who aided Hock in breaking away from the BofA; he graciously made those documents available to me. They include a speech Hock made in Hawaii before the Licensee Executive Committee in September 1969; I've quoted it in the chapter, and drawn from it liberally in piecing together the chronology of events. I also drew on other works: Mandell's *The Credit Card Industry: A History;* the Spofford and Grant study; Susan Chace's unpublished article; *The American Banker* series; NBI annual reports; a study conducted by Payment Systems, Inc., for American Express, entitled "Visa: A Competitive Assessment" (1977); an article from *Business Week,* "Bank Cards Take over the Country" (August 4, 1975); and back issues of *The Nilson Report.* Interviews with former Hock associates include Charles Russell, Aram Tootelian, David A. Huemer, Dan Brigham, Frederick Hammer, Guy W. Botts, Don Jutilla, Robert Miller, Bennett Katz, Irwin Derman, Kenneth Larkin, Leighton Johnson, John Dillon, Richard Rossi, and D. Dale Browning. Interviews with Donald Baker, Adolph Mueller, Stephen M. Pollan, Stephen Szekely, and Lewis Mandell were also helpful. As I mention in the chapter, the information concerning American attitudes toward credit cards comes from Mandell's 1972 book, *Credit Card Use in the United States.* Mimi Lieber also helped guide my thinking about America's ambiguous attitudes toward credit cards.

1. The emphasis is mine. It's startling to note that even with close to 4,000 banks in the old BankAmericard system, bankers were still stuffing sales drafts into envelopes and mailing them to all the other banks in the system for reimbursement.
2. In a September 1969 memo to the membership, Hock described the principles he and the other three arrived at thusly: "That the organization be given sufficient powers to make, implement, and enforce decisions involving the needs of the system; that these powers should rest in a board small enough to work effectively, yet large enough to represent all interests and areas adequately; that the board should be constructed so as to prevent any single bank, or group of banks, from exercising control; that duplicate levels of management should not be created but that for greater efficiency and economy, the new organization should combine all existing structures [the need was to simplify, not complicate]; that every bank heavily and directly involved in BankAmericard should be entitled to voting membership; that assessments should not exceed the present royalties; that voting and funding should be based on a common formula, which should be directly related to each member's proportionate share of the system; that no bank should be financially damaged, or otherwise left in a lesser position, as a result of the reorganization; that the plan must offer enough advantages to gain voluntary acceptance from a majority of the licensees; that all existing contractual obligations must be honored for any bank which might decide not to accept the plan; . . . and finally that the unique position of the Bank of America in the system must be recognized, properly compensated, and that their ability to provide sustaining assistance during any transitional period should be utilized."
3. Later reduced to eighteen members.
4. Indeed, the big banks chafed at this voting system, feeling that Hock had rigged the game in favor of the small banks. "Hock was the world's greatest bank populist," complains Larkin, a description with which Hock himself would probably agree.
5. Larkin was also among the five Bank of America representatives on the board. As the number of BofA seats dwindled, Larkin would retain his seat until finally he was the lone

Bank of America man left on the board. He resigned the seat when he retired from the bank, in 1984.

6. He is now a professor of finance and associate dean at the University of Connecticut School of Business.

7. The banking industry has long known this to be the case. Until quite recently, surveys consistently found that people cared less about the rate than about the minimum monthly charge. So long as they could make the minimum payment, they were willing to overlook the onerous interest rate they were paying.

8. The statistic that is always used here is the credit card default rate, which in the best of times hovers between 2 and 3 percent, and in the worst of times can get up to 5 and 6 percent. That statistic allows the banking industry to argue, somewhat misleadingly, that between 94 and 98 percent of cardholders are "responsible" users of credit. What the statistic fails to take into account, of course, is that those 2 to 6 percent in default are a constantly rotating group of people.

9. The smaller, so-called Class B banks, which issued cards but had no merchant accounts, came on the system later.

10. Proxmire wants it known that he only obtained a credit card for "identification purposes," and has never used it to run up debt. Even this protestation speaks to the power of Hock's system, however, for it is precisely the willingness of a merchant to accept that a Visa (or MasterCard) can instantly identify a potential buyer of goods—simply by virtue of having the card—that gives that card a potency well beyond its role as an instigator of debt.

## CHAPTER 6
### The Luckiest Entrepreneur, May 1975

The key published source for this chapter, it almost goes without saying, is *The Last Days of the Club,* Chris Welles's stellar, sturdy, and comprehensive history of the tumultuous events leading up to Mayday. Welles also recounted Donald Regan's tenure as chairman of Merrill Lynch for *Institutional Investor* magazine, in an article entitled "The Making of a Treasury Secretary" (March 1981). In addition, I found Charles Schwab's 1984 book, *How to Be Your Own Stockbroker,* to be quite helpful, particularly its one autobiographical chapter. The *Wall Street Journal* article mentioned in the beginning of the chapter was headlined "Merrill Lynch Boosts Fees Average 3% on Most Transactions Under $5,000," and published on April 30, 1975. The New York Stock Exchange survey mentioned near the end of the chapter was called *Public Attitudes Toward Investing.* It came out in July 1978. Of the dozens of articles that recount either Schwab's rise or, more broadly, the rise of discount brokers, I found four especially useful: "The Schwab Story," by Jordan Cohn (*Continental Magazine,* August 1986); "One Tiny Discount Brokerage Leaps to Top, Propelled by End of Fixed Fees," by Barbara Bry (*Los Angeles Times,* November 25, 1979); "Charles Schwab: Stock Market Maverick," by George Leeson (*San Francisco Sunday Examiner and Chronicle,* December 16, 1979); and "Brokers No Longer Ignore Discounters," by Christopher Elias (*The New York Times,* March 4, 1979). "Diary of a Decade," by Pamela Savage Forbat (*Registered Representative,* September 1986), offers a good overview of the era. Among those interviewed for this chapter were Charles Schwab, Richard Arnold, Peter Moss, Hugo Quackenbush, Barbara Wolff, James Fuller, Donald Baker, Donald E. Farrar, John McQuown, Donald Regan, Thomas Chrystie, Ross Kenzie, and John Fitzgerald. A number of longtime Schwab employees recorded their recollections of the early days for a company video, entitled "Charles Schwab: A Living Portrait."

1. Among the earliest discount brokers was Carl Icahn, who went on to become one of America's best-known—and most feared—financiers, but only after he had given up on discounting.
2. There is, of course, one group of businessmen who are specifically (and inexplicably) granted an exemption from the nation's antitrust laws: the owners of major league baseball teams.
3. One of the ways the stock exchange got Americans to invest in stocks in the 1950s was with crude appeals to patriotism, making the claim that buying a stock was a way of fighting Communism. That was the kind of appeal that would have been scoffed at twenty years later.
4. Not all the firms that failed were small, either. The most notable failure was F. I. DuPont, Glore Forgan & Company, which Ross Perot famously tried to save, only to liquidate it after absorbing a staggering $100 million in losses.
5. Haack was so sure that his speech would be considered an act of heresy that he took the unusual step of refusing to show it to anyone associated with the stock exchange ahead of time. He feared—no doubt correctly—that if the exchange got wind of what he planned to say, it would force him to cancel the appearance.
6. This was a complete bluff. Privately, Needham was a realist, who saw deregulated commissions as inevitable, and who argued that member firms should accept reality. His fondest hope was that in return for agreeing to competitive pricing, the stock exchange would be allowed to freeze out the emerging third markets, like NASDAQ. The SEC, however, never let it happen, and in the end, it was the exchange that was forced to adapt to technology and competitors like NASDAQ.
7. Merrill Lynch's long-running television campaign, "Merrill Lynch Is Bullish on America," was first unveiled in the fall of 1971, during that year's World Series.
8. In later interviews, Regan would claim that he had graciously "stepped aside" so that Haack could be first to call for reform. But this seems implausible, given the degree of secrecy surrounding Haack's speech; it's much more likely that Regan found out about it the way the rest of Wall Street did: by either hearing the speech at the Waldorf or reading about it in the next day's newspaper.
9. Regan's instincts about the importance of deregulated commissions were completely right. That commission prices for institutional investors dropped by some 50 percent on Mayday, and now stand at around a few pennies a share, is the least of it. Just about everything that happened on Wall Street in the 1980s—from the rise of Drexel Burnham Lambert, to the creation of the powerful mergers and acquisition departments, to the replacement of the largely genteel WASP culture that had long characterized Wall Street to one that was populated with Jews and ethnics—was attributable in some way to Mayday. It is the seminal event in the history of modern Wall Street.
10. Regan's most withering scorn was reserved for the specialist firms whose monopoly was most blatant: "They stood there at their post, allowed to trade for their own account, and made a *fortune*! The *bastards*!''
11. Actually, Merrill Lynch first announced that it planned to *raise* the commission prices it charged institutional investors. This was something other Wall Street firms were also trying to do. The price hike, however, did not stick, and within two weeks Merrill Lynch was forced to rescind it.
12. This anecdote may be apocryphal. Kenzie denies that he ever taped trainees' hands to the phone, even though it is part of the lore of Merrill Lynch.
13. Schwab paid himself only $24,000 in those early years.

## CHAPTER 7
### The World's Most Hated Bank, August 1977

Information about Andrew Kahr and SRI comes primarily from interviews with former associates of Kahr's, among them Carl Spetzler, Barbara Casey, James Fuller, Mary Falvey Fuller, John McQuown, Howard Raiffa, Rex Brown, Robert Schlaiffer, and Adolph Mueller. Kahr granted me several lengthy interviews. I was given access to a sizable number of old SRI documents, including the landmark "Consumer Financial Decisions" study. Other published sources include the following: *The Big Store*, by Donald Katz; "The NOW Account Decision . . . Profitability, Pricing, Strategies," a study by Neil B. Murphy and Lewis Mandell for the Bank Administration Institute; the *Flow of Funds Account*, which is put out quarterly by the Federal Reserve Board of Governors; and *Financial Reform in the 1980s*, by Thomas F. Cargill and Gillian G. Garcia.

The list of stories that have been written over the years about Wriston, Reed, and Citicorp is long indeed. These I found most helpful: "The Money Machine," by John Brooks (*The New Yorker*, January 5, 1981); "John Reed's Charge to the Top," written by John Taylor and reported by Michele Whitney and Walecia Konrad (*Manhattan, Inc.*, September 1984); "Champion of the City," by Peter Field and Nigel Adam (*Euromoney*, October 1983); "Walt's triumphant farewell," by Cary Reich (*Institutional Investor*, July 1983); "Citicorp After Wriston," by Edward Boyer (*Fortune*, July 9, 1984); "How Citicorp restructured for the 'eighties," by Alena Wels (*Euromoney*, April 1980); "Citicorp's Atypical Leader," by Fred R. Bleakley (*The New York Times*, June 21, 1984); "John Reed builds his dream house," by Suzanna Andrews (*Institutional Investor*, March 1987); and "The Real John Reed Stands Up," by Robert A. Bennett (*The New York Times Magazine*, April 2, 1989). Books include *Risk and Other Four Letter Words*, by Walter Wriston, and *Global Dreams: Imperial Corporations and the New World Order*, by Richard J. Barnet and John Cavanagh. The famous speech of Wriston's quoted in the chapter was delivered in the spring of 1980 before the Reserve City Bankers Association and reprinted in *The American Banker* (April 11, 1980). Three studies were helpful: "Competition Gameplan: Citicorp and Financial Services in the 1980s," by Cheryl Hollis (RND Ventures Division, September 1984); "First National City Bank Operating Group (A and B)," a Harvard Business School case study written by John A. Seeger, under the supervision of Jay W. Lorsch and Cyrus F. Gibson; and "The Visa Value Exchange Philosophy—Its Radical Impact on Competition" (*The Duffy Report*, October 1980). Spencer Nilson described Citibank as "the world's most hated bank" in *The Nilson Report*, no. 133 (February 1976). The Citibank public relations department sent me some historical documents that were mildly useful. Richard Kane, James Bailey, David Phillips, Hans H. Angermueller, Michael Levine, Stephen Szekely, and Stuart Reale were among those interviewed for this chapter.

1. Not until 1981 were financial institutions outside New England allowed to establish NOW accounts.

2. The university and its nonprofit think tank went their separate ways during the Vietnam War, when SRI's classified work for the Defense Department made it a lightning rod for student protests. Still, while SRI lost Stanford's name and backing, the university continued to collect 1 percent of SRI's income.

3. In the mid-1970s, when Spetzler was beginning his work, one could count more than 13,000 banks, 5,000 S&Ls, 22,000 credit unions, and 4,000 securities firms.

4. The Federal Reserve would eventually do a similar study, far more detailed than SRI's, but not until 1983.

5. Katz's book is about the efforts of Sears' management, in the mid-1980s, to turn the company around. Among the things Sears did, of course, was make a heavy investment

in financial services, buying companies like Dean Witter Reynolds and Allstate Insurance, and issuing an all-purpose credit card, the Discover card. Kahr is mentioned in the book because he was among those at Sears consulted with as it was forming its financial services' strategy.

6. McQuown has had his fingers in any number of financial innovations, but he is primarily known as one of the creators of the "index fund"—a form of mutual fund that does not try to beat the market but simply tries to match it, by mirroring the ups and downs of such market benchmarks as the S&P 500. As the founder of Wells Fargo's nascent Management Sciences division in the mid-1960s, McQuown led the effort to create the nation's first successful index fund for the bank's trust department. More than twenty-five years later, he and several colleagues came up with another successful index fund, this time for Schwab, which Schwab has marketed under the name "The Schwab 1000 Fund."

7. Citibank became a wholly owned subsidiary of the new holding company.

8. The writer is John Taylor, now of *Esquire*, writing in the September 1984 inaugural issue of the now-defunct *Manhattan, Inc.* Taylor's byline, however, was not attached to the article, which was headlined "John Reed's Charge to the Top." It was described instead as having been "reported by" Michele Whitney and Walecia Konrad.

9. Reed was not the head of the Operating Group; he reported to another executive higher up the ladder than he. However, he was the one given the mandate to clean up the back office—and the free hand to carry it out however he saw fit.

10. Hock's regrets notwithstanding, BankAmericard (later Visa) was the big winner after duality because it had far fewer banks than did Interbank. Before duality, Interbank had a third more cards in circulation than BankAmericard. Within two years of duality, Visa overtook its archrival, a position it would never cede.

11. The big banks especially, however, were very glad to be rid of the name "BankAmericard" on the front of their cards. It had always been a sore spot that the card was emblazoned with the logo of a competitor.

12. Hock's rationale, as usual, was not unpersuasive. He believed that if a credit card was going to be accepted all across the nation, it had to *look* the same all across the nation. He was acting on his strong belief that customers and merchants valued universality above all else. When bankers argued that they should be able to put their own logos on the front of the card, Hock responded by saying that that would be fine *after* the Visa logo had become so recognizable that it no longer needed to be the dominant feature of the card. Of course, Hock's view of when the Visa logo was recognizable and the bankers' view of the same were utterly at odds, and the struggle over the size and position of the various logos became one of the most bitter and long-standing disagreements between Hock and his membership.

## CHAPTER 8
## The Discreet Charms of the CMA, September 1977

My portrait of Donald Regan owes a fair amount to Regan himself, including his autobiography, *For the Record*, and a lengthy interview he consented to. I also drew on Peggy Noonan's *What I Saw at the Revolution: A Political Life in the Reagan Era*, Chris Welles's March 1981 profile in *Institutional Investor*, and interviews with a handful of former Regan associates, including Roger Birks, Thomas Chrystic, Robert Rittereiser, John Fitzgerald, Sandy Lewis, Ross Kenzie, John Orb, William Clark, and John Kelly. Other interviews include Scott Black, Eric Kobren, Kurt Brouwer, and John L. Steffens. Carol J. Loomis's May 1972 *Fortune* article, "The Merrill Lynch Bull Is Loose on Wall Street," provided a good deal of broader information on the firm, as did Chris Welles's profile of Birks, "Merrill Lynch's new jockey" (*Institutional Investor*, September 1981). Other published sources include *The Big Store*, by Donald Katz, "Why Merrill Lynch Wants to Sell You a House," by Charles G. Burck (*Fortune*, January 29, 1979), and "A Legacy of Leadership," the in-house history compiled by the Merrill Lynch public relations department. The *Fortune* magazine article that created the rift between Regan and his old associates was headlined "Merrill Lynch: The Stumbling Herd" (June 20, 1988); the *Forbes* article that effectively announced that Regan was running the firm was called "The Quiet Revolution" (October 1, 1969).

Tim Carrington's book, *The Year They Sold Wall Street*, although primarily about the merger between American Express and Shearson Loeb Rhoades, contains a smart and straightforward account of the creation of the cash management account. *Investor's Daily* published a three-part series on the CMA, which ran on August 27, 28, and 31, 1987. Eric K. Clemons and Michael C. Row wrote a 1988 case study of the CMA for the Wharton School. *Fortune* ran two lengthy CMA stories, "Merrill Lynch Quacks like a Bank," by Martin Mayer (October 20, 1980), and "Merrill Lynch's Latest Bombshell for Bankers," by Lee Smith (April 19, 1982). *Forbes* ran "A buyer's guide to the financial supermarket," by William G. Flanagan with Janet Bamford on August 1, 1983. In addition to those listed above, Paul Stein and Dennis Hess of Merrill Lynch spoke to me about the creation of the CMA, as did Andrew Kahr, James Fuller, Carl Spetzler, and John McQuown. The article by Nicholas Lemann quoted at the end of the chapter was entitled "How the Seventies Changed America" (*American Heritage*, July/August 1991).

1. Essentially, Regan believed Merrill Lynch was perfectly situated to "cross-sell" insurance and real estate to the firm's stock and bond customers. "All that type of stuff was a natural with our securities business, where you were investing your extra money or even your business funds in money market funds," he once said exuberantly. "And here we have a real estate division, where we can either build you a shopping center or rent you a store or find you a home. Name what you want!"

2. He remained Treasury Secretary through Ronald Reagan's reelection, and then switched jobs with James Baker, who had been Reagan's chief of staff during the President's first term. He was forced to resign in 1987 after the Iran–Contra scandal broke. Though not involved in the scandal itself, Regan was generally deemed to have done a poor job of protecting the President—and had gotten on the wrong side of Nancy Reagan, two factors that spelled his demise.

3. In an interview he granted shortly after taking over from Regan, Birks firmly denied that he saw his role as a mere "caretaker." But his subsequent actions spoke louder than his words; four years later, when Birks himself left Merrill Lynch, the Regan strategy was very much intact.

4. Rittereiser would become much better known some years later, when he was named the chairman of E. F. Hutton, which was then struggling to survive a series of devastating scandals. The job turned out to be a thankless one, however, for the firm was beyond saving. After arranging for the firm to be bought out by Shearson Lehman Brothers, Rittereiser left.

5. The talks broke off supposedly because neither Regan nor Robinson was willing to be the Number 2 man in the merged entity.

6. This fixation stemmed from his long-held view that the financial consumer, assaulted from all sides by financial salesmen, was in a state of utter confusion. Spetzler believed that the consumer would be far better off if he only had to listen to one person—his "personal" financial planner. The planner would assume the task of guiding the consumer toward the choices best suited for him. As splendid as Spetzler could make this

system sound, it never happened. No one has ever been able to devise a way to make financial planning for the middle class both free of bias and profitable.

7. To his lasting regret, Chrystie agreed. Merrill Lynch would lose somewhere around $16 million on its financial planning project before finally pulling the plug.

8. From *The Year They Sold Wall Street*, by Tim Carrington.

9. The bank Chrystie found was City National Bank & Trust in Columbus, Ohio. Now known as Bank One, it has a much-deserved reputation as one of the most innovative consumer banks in the country.

10. Not that Hock dared admit this out loud. "This is just a small little pilot," he soft-pedaled the CMA when it came up for a vote before the NBI board. "It's just going to be for a couple of rich people."

11. Actually, the free credit balances weren't *completely* lost: the CMA still gave the firm an overnight float, before the customers' money was swept away into the CMA money fund.

12. It was not the only such means, I should point out. Merrill Lynch's mutual fund division, which I have slighted in this account, would become an asset-gathering behemoth in its own right. As of early 1994, it ranked third, behind Fidelity and Vanguard, with $123 billion in assets.

13. That resistance reached its peak at the end of 1978, when, at the end of one of the more ribald partners' meetings, the CMA was given the "golden turd" award, as the worst product of the year.

## CHAPTER 9
## The Great Inflation, July 1979

Every modern administration leaves behind a voluminous record of memos and documents, and the Carter administration is no exception. Most White House documents from the Carter era reside in the archives of the Jimmy Carter Library in Atlanta, Georgia, but at the time I looked through them (summer 1991), many were still being vetted by the library staff, and had not yet been made available to the public. These included the files of Charles Schultze, Barry Bosworth, Alfred Kahn, and G. William Miller—four of Carter's top economic aides. Of the files I was able to see, Stuart Eizenstat's were the most helpful. In addition, Alfred Kahn, Anne Wexler, Alvin From, and Hendrick Hertzberg allowed me to cull from their personal files of old White House documents.

The public record of any administration is, of course, equally voluminous. More than most chapters, I was able to piece together a chronology of the Carter administration's anti-inflation efforts simply by tracking the coverage in *The New York Times*, the *Washington Post*, the *Wall Street Journal*, and *Congressional Quarterly*. A *Times* four-part series, "Living with Inflation: Who Wins, Who Loses," ran the week of April 22, 1979; the first article, by Peter T. Kilborn, includes the anecdote about "Nancy T." Steven Rattner and Meryl Gordon gave me a sense of what it was like to cover "the inflation beat" as a reporter in the late 1970s and early 1980s. James Fallows's monumental two-part series in *The Atlantic*, "The Passionless Presidency" (May and June 1979), illuminates Carter's character, while "Economic Advice in the Carter Administration," a paper written by W. Carl Bivens of the Georgia Institute of Technology, offers an overview of economic policy in the Carter White House. Robert Samuelson's columns and articles in *National Journal* contain the best contemporary analysis of the Carter administration's efforts to deal with inflation. Elizabeth Drew's analysis of Carter's malaise speech, quoted in the chapter, ran in the August 29, 1979, issue of *The New Yorker*. The James Reston column concerning Alfred Kahn was headlined "The New Aga Kahn" (*The New York Times*, April 13, 1979). Books I used include the following: *America in Search of Itself: The Making of the President 1956–1980*, by Theodore H. White; *Secrets of the Temple*, by William Greider; *Memos to the President: A Guide Through Macroeconomics for the Busy Policymaker*, by Charles L. Schultze; *Changing Fortunes: The World's Money and the Threat to American Leadership*, by Paul A. Volcker and Toyoo Gyohten; *A Time of Passion*, by Charles Morris; *Keeping Faith: Memoirs of a President*, by Jimmy Carter; and *The Roaring '80s*, by "Adam Smith." Charles Schultze, Barry Bosworth, Alfred Kahn, Alvin From, Alice Rogoff, David Rubenstein, Susan Irving, Lyle Gramley, Stuart Eizenstat, Anne Wexler, Paul Jensen, Orin Kramer, Robert Carswell, John Dunlop, Curt Hessler, and Roger Altman were among those interviewed for this chapter.

1. The Consumer Price Index rose 12.3 percent that year.
2. Keynesians, of course, are the followers of the great British liberal economist, John Maynard Keynes, whose theories about the effect of government policy on a nation's economy were akin to tablets handed down from the heavens for at least the first three decades after World War II. Indeed, the intractable nature of inflation played no small role in causing the Keynesian consensus to break down. With the Keynesians having lost their way, other competing theories, such as the theory of monetarism proposed by Milton Friedman and the conservative Chicago school were able to get a hearing in establishment Washington that they would not have otherwise received.
3. The person who most strenuously argued for the recession option was Michael Blumenthal, who was Carter's first Treasury Secretary.
4. There was one other option Carter had: he could impose wage and price controls, as Nixon had in the early 1970s. Here, however, Carter's objection was not philosophical but practical. Every one of his economic advisers believed that Nixon's program had been a fiasco, creating distortions in the economy, building resentments over the inevitable exceptions and loopholes, and in the end, not so much stopping inflation as temporarily bottling it up. Once mandatory controls were lifted, prices simply exploded, rising at a disastrous annual rate of 35 percent over the next six months.
5. Not that they needed much prodding. George Meany, the grand old man of labor, who still headed the AFL-CIO at the age of eighty-two, openly loathed Carter. And the feeling—at least among White House aides—was mutual. In the files of the Carter White House one can find dozens of memos and documents that attest to the animosity that existed between labor and the White House, including one note telling Carter of Meany's desire to have a meeting with the President. Scrawled in the margin, an anonymous aide had written: "Right now, Meany looks like shit, and we look good and he knows it."
6. Carter's rationale for pushing for a quick, though inflationary, settlement was that a prolonged coal strike could cripple the country's energy supplies. However, this was a case where Carter clearly panicked; most of his advisers knew full well that enough coal had been stockpiled to last for months—and they told him so.
7. After the success of the United Mine Workers, Teamster president Frank E. Fitzsimmons told reporters: "The miners got 37 percent. You think I'm going to the table for anything less?"
8. "Don't ask me to psychoanalyze myself," Kahn says now. "Maybe I felt that the truth was so obvious it was pointless to try to conceal it. Or maybe I thought no one would respect me if I didn't say what I believe."
9. "[The chairwoman] was absolutely right," Kahn says now. "The policy was inexcusable. Someone in the administration told me that it would 'only' add 1/10th of a percent to the CPI. I would sweat blood for 1/10th of a percent!"
10. By the time Bosworth made these remarks, in the early fall of 1979, he had quit the

administration in frustration and returned to the Brookings Institution, from whence he had come.

11. From also played a critical role in winning back the middle class in the 1990s. After Walter Mondale's devastating defeat at the hands of Ronald Reagan in 1984, he co-founded the Democratic Leadership Council, a group whose specific aim was to reconnect the Democratic Party to the middle class. Another cofounder was Bill Clinton. From was among those who urged Clinton to enter the 1992 presidential race; and during the campaign he was an important behind-the-scenes adviser. He was also a deputy director of Clinton's transition team, though he was never offered a high job in the administration himself, and wound up back at the DLC once the new President took office.

12. This was a $15 billion deficit in a $615 billion budget, which is to say, it was *minuscule* compared to the deficits that would come later.

13. "I had little or nothing to contribute," Volcker later wrote, "but the exercise provided an interesting insight for me. . . . Day after day, what I seemed to be seeing before my eyes was a president with basically conservative instincts finding his . . . decisions challenged by advisers sensitive both to particular interests and to the more liberal traditions of his party."

14. There were more than a few people inside the White House who agreed. Al From, for one, conveyed his sense of disgust by putting quotation marks around the word "new" when he wrote memos about Carter's "new" program.

15. An economist named Al Sommers, who had helped convince Kahn of the worth of credit controls, later told the inflation czar, "Volcker did for the reputation of credit controls what the Boston Strangler did for the reputation of door-to-door salesmen."

## CHAPTER 10
## "Please Don't Take It Away!" March 1981

Mimi Lieber, Marshall Loeb, Edward Furash, and Cynthia Glassman are four people who have thought hard about the effect of inflation on middle-class financial behavior; my interviews with them helped shape this chapter. "How the Seventies Changed America," by Nicholas Lemann (*American Heritage*, July/August 1991), was also full of Big Picture nuggets and useful data. "Better Now Mentality" (*Time*, February 18, 1980), "The Consumer Credit Spiral," by Karen Arenson (*The New York Times*, July 29, 1979), and "Consumer Resigned to Inflation: Learning New Ways to Hedge," by Peter T. Kilborn (*The New York Times*, April 22, 1979), were particularly helpful contemporaneous articles; the latter contains the lament at the passing of thirty-year fixed mortgages. *The New York Times* article by Christopher Rupkey quoted in the text was headlined "The Have It All Now Generation" (May 13, 1979); the speech by Kenneth Larkin was before the Colorado Bankers Association (February 18, 1980). The authors of the USC study mentioned by Larkin in that speech—"Social Changes Affecting the Consumer Finance Industry, Period 1980–2000"—are Dana Bramlett and Anthony Wiener. Although I was able to track down Wiener, I was never able to obtain the complete study.

Much of the general credit data in this chapter comes from the Federal Reserve; most of the data relating specifically to credit cards comes from *The Nilson Report*. *The Nilson Report* was also a useful guidepost in chronicling the credit card-related events described in this chapter, such as the imposition of annual fees, as was Lewis Mandell's book, *The Credit Card Industry: A History*, and two speeches by Dee Hock, "Industry Questions and Their Answers" (September 13, 1979) and "Credit Controls and Payment Cards" (April 3, 1980). *The American Banker* closely covered the effect of Jimmy Carter's credit controls on the credit card industry. The annual fee study mentioned in the chapter was done for Bank of

America in 1974. Interviews include Richard Kane, David Phillips, Hans Angermueller, David Huemer, Stephen Szekely, Kenneth Larkin, Frederick Hammer, Bennett Katz, Daniel Brigham, and George Fesus.

The story of the Utah money market fund battle comes primarily from the participants, including James Lee, Desmond Barker, Robert Reeder, Robert Sykes, Peter Billings, Kay Conable, Sherman Harmer, Jr., Mirvin Borthick, David Silver, Matthew Fink, Donald Farrar, and Paul Stein. The Utah legislature keeps dictabelt recordings of past sessions; I was able to listen to the debate and the subsequent vote in both the Senate and the House. Robert H. Woody, the business editor for the *Salt Lake Tribune,* wrote virtually every article the paper ran on the battle. The Investment Company Institute's annual Mutual Fund Fact Books contain most of the money market fund asset figures found in the chapter. Other published sources include "Money Market Funds: A Round-table Discussion" (*The Wall Street Transcript,* October 12, 1980), Hearings before the Subcommittee on Financial Institutions on "Oversight of the Supervision and Regulation of Money Market Mutual Funds and the Effects of the Funds on Financial Markets" (January 24 and 30, 1980), "How Dreyfus Plans to Beat the Banks," by Gary Hector (*Fortune,* March 21, 1983), and *William E. Donoghue's Complete Money Market Guide,* by William E. Donoghue with Thomas Tilling. I also interviewed William Donoghue.

1. In 1980, for instance, real income for a typical American family—that is, income after the effects of inflation were taken into account—dropped 5.5 percent.

2. The man making the estimate was the indefatigable newsletter publisher Spencer Nilson, writing in the April 1979 issue of *The Nilson Report.* His data is generally accepted as the most authoritative that is publicly available, and is regularly used as such in numerous media. However, it's worth noting that because Nilson traffics in information that the giant card organizations consider proprietary, neither Visa nor MasterCard has ever confirmed—or denied—the accuracy of Nilson's figures.

3. If one includes other credit cards, such as department store or oil company cards, the number jumps to 7.1 cards per person, again according to Nilson.

4. American Express's success in those days was due almost entirely to its snob appeal; it shrewdly positioned itself as the charge card for the elite, while casting Visa and MasterCard as the cards for the masses. When Visa and MasterCard developed their own "prestige" gold cards in the mid-1980s, they began to steal away the "status" business that had always gravitated to American Express as a matter of course. By the early 1990s, those inroads had become so serious that American Express's charge card division, which was at the heart of the entire enterprise, was reporting serious quarterly losses.

5. These figures exclude home mortgage debt.

6. For his part, Dee Hock was publicly estimating that banks would lose, in the aggregate, more than $1 billion on their card operations in 1980 if conditions didn't improve.

7. There was a third problem, it should be mentioned, but one that took much longer to get under control: credit card fraud. Unlike the other two problems, however, there was no simple solution, just a long, hard slog to reduce it.

8. Such charges were usually considered a violation of the usury laws, an interpretation the courts generally upheld. When Citibank, for instance, added a 50 cent–per–month charge in the mid-1970s to any account that was paid in full, New York banking authorities responded swiftly. Citing its usury laws, the regulators forced Citibank to rescind the monthly charge, and to refund more than $1.5 million in such charges to its customers.

9. In the House of Representatives, the key congressmen were much more sympathetic to the banks and S&Ls, with such powerful figures as banking committee chairman Henry Reuss calling for regulations that would limit the interest money market funds could pay out.

10. In fact, Garn did believe that money market funds had an unfair advantage over the nation's banks. But during the Utah battle, he was conspicuous mainly by his absence, speaking publicly—and equivocally—on the subject only once during the entire fight.

## CHAPTER 11
## Mr. Regan Goes to Washington, September 1981

The National Archives in Washington, D.C., hold most of the old records of the now-defunct DIDC; they were the principal source for the material in this chapter. I also interviewed a number of the participants in the events surrounding the DIDC, including Donald Regan, Todd Conover, Richard Pratt, Sen. Jake Garn, M. Danny Wall, Kenneth McLean, Beryl Sprinkle, Peter Wallison, Roger Mehle, Neal Soss, Norman Ture, Steven Entin, and William Donoghue. Donoghue's newsletter, *Donoghue's Money Fund Report,* covered the DIDC meetings closer than virtually any other publication. *Secrets of the Temple,* by William Grieder, and *Volcker: Portrait of the Money Man,* by William R. Neikirk, both profile the former Federal Reserve chairman at great length, and discuss the recession that resulted from his monetary policy. Volcker himself tackles the same subject in his book *Changing Fortunes: The World's Money and the Threat to American Leadership,* which he wrote with Toyoo Gyohten, a former high-ranking bureaucrat at the Japanese Ministry of Finance. Other books include *For the Record,* by Donald Regan, *What I Saw at the Revolution,* by Peggy Noonan, *Financial Reform in the 1980s,* by Thomas F. Cargill and Gillian G. Garcia, and *Behind the Scenes,* by Michael Deaver. Other published sources: "The Making of a Treasury Secretary," by Chris Welles (*Institutional Investor,* March 1981); "A Brand New Game for Savers," by Susan Dentzler (*Newsweek,* December 27, 1982); "A Big Brawl in Banking," by Charles P. Alexander (*Time,* January 17, 1983); "A Bonanza for the Banks," by David Pauly (*Newsweek,* January 3, 1983); and "Psychic Dividends: In Spite of Low Yields, Savings Accounts Still Satisfy Many People," by John Helyar (the *Wall Street Journal,* April 15, 1981). Kenneth McLean provided me with a copy of a paper he wrote, "Legislative Background of the DIDMCA." Information on money fund yields are drawn either from the monthly listing in *Money* magazine or the weekly listing in the *Wall Street Journal;* figures on money fund assets come from the Investment Company Institute's annual Mutual Fund Fact Books.

1. It would take years before the real consequence of this provision became clear, but ultimately, raising the amount covered by deposit insurance played a huge role in the S&L crisis of the late 1980s. It allowed unscrupulous S&L operators to rope in deposits by offering higher-than-average interest rates; much of the money that flowed into those S&Ls came from brokerage firms like Merrill Lynch, which would raise money from customers and then place it, in insured increments of $100,000, at these S&Ls. In lending out that money, the S&Ls did not fear the consequences of making excessively risky loans, since the deposits were insured by the government. And indeed, when S&Ls began to fail all over the country, it was the government that wound up picking up the tab.

2. A "time deposit" is a savings vehicle in which money is held for a specified time; by contrast, a vehicle such as a passbook account, from which money can be withdrawn at any time without penalty, is called a "demand deposit."

3. The only certificates of deposit that offered market rates of interest were jumbo CDs, which required a minimum deposit of $100,000. All other CDs were regulated in varying degrees, so that while most of them could offer higher interest than passbook accounts, they still did not approach the yields being generated by money market funds.

4. The government's rationale for regulating premiums was that the gifts constituted a kind

of interest; hence, expensive premiums were seen as a means of evading Regulation Q.

5. S&Ls were granted the differential because Congress believed that their role as the chief mortgage lender in America was so crucial—and their alternate means of attracting deposits so circumscribed—that they deserved this small advantage over commercial banks.

6. Banks, of course, were faced with the same essential dilemma; they also needed to attract deposits. The reason their problems were not as serious as those facing the thrift industry was that they were not nearly so dependent on passbook accounts for deposits, or on mortgages for loans.

7. There is no doubt, however, that the outflow of funds from banks and S&Ls to money funds was at least slowed down by the introduction of money market certificates. Three years after their creation, these certificates held over $450 billion, more than twice the assets held by money funds. Most of that money, however, came from deposits already in the bank.

8. In retrospect, the government's decision to keep the S&L industry alive in the early 1980s was a disastrous one. Though the industry had long been the primary mortgage lender in America, that wasn't the case by the 1980s, when thousands of other financial institutions were issuing mortgages. The circumstances that had made the S&L industry unique and important in America had evaporated. Had Congress and the bank regulators been willing to admit that S&Ls had outlived their usefulness, and had been willing to shut down the industry in the early 1980s, it would have been far less costly to the country, and far less painful than what would come later.

9. Bernard Ramsey, a former chairman of Merrill Lynch's executive committee, would later tell Chris Welles that "[the Treasury] job is something Don has wanted for a long time. . . . He had a long-term plan to get it."

10. He was not the first choice, however. William Simon, the financier perhaps best known as Gerald Ford's "energy czar" was the person the new administration wanted. But Simon wanted an enormous amount of autonomy, and when it became clear he wasn't going to get it, he withdrew his name from consideration. That cleared the path for Regan.

11. This phrase belongs to Chris Welles.

12. "I think he found it easy to believe that taxes were too high," dryly notes this same former aide. It's worth noting, however, that at his confirmation hearings, Regan lapsed into what Chris Welles would later describe as "deviationist thinking," arguing that cutting government spending was more important than cutting taxes. For this he was sharply rebuked by the White House, and by the time he next testified before Congress, he had learned his lesson. His recitation of supply-side theory was so enthusiastic that both Jack Kemp and the *Wall Street Journal* editorial page were moved to praise him.

13. The change in chairmen came about because Republicans, riding Ronald Reagan's coattails, captured the Senate in the 1980 election; thus, men such as Garn, who had spent years as ranking minority members of one committee or another, suddenly became committee chairmen.

14. Because the meetings were open to the public, such thinking out loud was highly unusual. Most of the time, Regan's proposals were scripted well in advance of the meeting, his arguments typed up for him by aides.

15. In his defense, Volcker would later write, "In the end, there is only one excuse for pursuing such strongly restrictive monetary policies. That is the simple conviction that over time the economy will work better, more efficiently, and more fairly, with better prospects and more saving, in an environment of reasonable price stability."

16. It was common wisdom at Fidelity, for instance, that more money fund checks were written out to pay off American Express bills than for any other purpose.

17. Not surprisingly, the lawsuit had been brought by the National Savings and Loan League, whose entire argument revolved around the fact that the schedule had not been put out for public comment prior to its passage, and hence was invalid. That the maneuver succeeded does not mean that it wasn't an act of desperation. It was.

18. Donoghue would later describe the efforts of the DIDC to invent new financial products as akin to "watching a bunch of academics design a sports car with square wheels."

19. This is, indeed, one of the great mysteries—with real world interest rates so high, why was *any* money in passbook accounts, much less $350 billion? The answer, as Andrew Kahr had surmised back when he was analyzing data for SRI, was that inertia was a powerful force when it came to one's finances. "For a lot of people, it would take a stick of dynamite lit under them to force a change," one bank executive told John Helyar of the *Wall Street Journal,* who explored the subject in the spring of 1981. "Why so much in savings accounts?" another bank official told Helyar. "Ignorance . . . fear . . . laziness."

20. Lord, the acting comptroller of the currency, was a nonvoting member of the committee.

21. In theory, the new account was thought to be a way to get around the political impossibility of tackling Reg Q head-on while still making market interest rates available to the middle class. For the most part, this was true, though savers who had less than $2,500—the minimum amount needed to open one of these new accounts—were still locked out of market rates at the bank, at least for another few years. When Regulation Q was finally abolished in 1986, the world had changed so much—and the idea of market rates had become so widely accepted even among bankers—that the event was scarcely noticed.

22. Volcker loathed interest-bearing checking accounts because, for complicated technical reasons, they made it much more difficult to keep track of the money supply.

## CHAPTER 12
### The Maestro of Magellan, August 1982

Peter Lynch has written (with the help of John Rothchild) two books: *One Up on Wall Street* and *Beating the Street*. Both contain a great deal of information about Lynch's beliefs about investing, and are dotted with anecdotes about some of his more famous stock picks, such as his decision to put Hanes in Magellan's portfolio after seeing his wife buy L'Eggs pantyhose at the supermarket. *One Up on Wall Street* also contains a short autobiographical section, which was useful. Back when Lynch was running Magellan, I was able to spend a day with him; after he had resigned as fund manager, he granted me two lengthy interviews. And, of course, every publication that is even faintly aware of the mutual fund boom—from Morningstar, the mutual fund monitoring organization, to *People* magazine—has weighed in with articles about Lynch over the years. Many of the ones that recount his history as Magellan's fund manager were written in the wake of his retirement, including these: "Lynch quits while he's at the top," by Jim Henderson (*USA Today,* March 29, 1990); "Confessions of an Investaholic" (*Financial World,* March 20, 1990); and "Mutual Loss: Both Fidelity Investors and Firm Are at Sea as Magellan Boss Goes," by Christopher Chipello, Michael Siconolfi, and Jonathan Clements (the *Wall Street Journal,* March 29, 1990). Lynch gave several long interviews to *Barron's* that were helpful: "Lynch Lore" (July 22, 1985) and "Neff and Lynch: Contrasting Styles, Comparable Success" (August 10, 1987). Eric Kobren's newsletter, *Fidelity Insight,* was a consistent source of information about Fidelity, as were *Morningstar Mutual Funds* newsletter and Fidelity's annual reports. In addition to the articles mentioned as sources for Chapter 4, I found useful information in the following: "The Master of Magellan," by Julie Rohrer (*Institutional Investor,* September 1987); "Clash of the Titans," by Ellen Spragins (*SmartMoney*, October 1993); "Streaking Ahead with the Mutual Funds," by Jerry Edgerton (*Money*, April 1983); "Go-Go Again," by Jack Egan (*New York*, January 17, 1983); "Braving the Boom in Mutual Funds," by Richard Lynch (*Money*, January 1986); "Magellan's Peter Lynch hedges his bets," by Richard Eisenberg (*Money*, January 1986); "Fidelity's Secret: Faithful Service," by Jaclyn Fierman (*Fortune*, May 7, 1990); and "Can Fidelity Maintain Its Frenzied Growth," by Thomas J. Lueck (*The New York Times*, March 16, 1986). Most of the statistical information about Magellan was supplied by the Fidelity public relations department; most of the information concerning the beginnings of the bull market comes from either Dow Jones or the *Wall Street Journal*. Interviews for this chapter include Ned Johnson, Leo Dworsky, Roger Servison, Michael Kassen, Morris Smith, Bo Burlingham, John O'Brien, Rab Bertelsen, Eric Kobren, Kurt Brouwer, Joseph Midwood, Edward Furash, Roger Harris, and Richard Reilly. The New York Stock Exchange survey mentioned in the text is the same one quoted in Chapter 6.

1. Over 455 million shares were traded that week, an amount that today would constitute a slow week.
2. He acquired this nickname in the late 1970s because of his incessantly dour interest rate predictions.
3. How powerful was this bull market? When the 1950s began, the Dow Jones average stood at 198.89.
4. There were several instances in which Merrill Lynch brokers were reprimanded by their superiors for refusing to accept business from people who just wanted to open money fund accounts, not trade stocks.
5. It also helped create a huge new market for municipal bonds; as of 1993, there was $1.2 trillion worth of municipal bond debt outstanding, and municipal bond funds were the most voracious buyers of that debt.
6. What is true of the municipal bond market is doubly true of the junk bond market. Michael Milken, who created the junk bond market, was able to place his bond issues among a network of bond buyers, some of which were junk bond portfolio managers. But after his fall from grace, junk bond funds became the saviors of the junk bond market. Their voracious appetite made it possible for others to step into and issue junk bonds, and they also brought some stability to the market that hadn't existed before.

    I should also point out here that one person who was part of Milken's buyer network was a woman named Patricia Ostrander, who managed Fidelity's junk bond fund during Milken's heyday. She is one of the sadder peripheral figures in the Milken scandal, for long after Milken went to jail, she was accused of accepting gratuities—in the form of special deals that went into her own account—in return for steering Fidelity business to Milken. She was convicted after a trial in which Milken testified for the defense, sentenced to two months in jail, fined $100,000, and barred from the securities industry.
7. On the other hand, most people weren't able to put $1,000 into Magellan when Lynch took it over in 1977 because it was closed to new investors. Only *existing* shareholders (of which there were relatively few) ever had the chance to reap the full 2,700 percent return. In fact, since Magellan wasn't open to new investors until the middle of 1981, they missed out on Lynch's two most impressive years: 1979, when Magellan gained 52 percent versus 18 percent for the S&P 500, and 1980, when it was Magellan's 70 percent against the S&P 500's 32 percent gain. Indeed, Magellan's average return during Lynch's tenure was over 28 percent a year; when you subtract those early years, before it was opened to the public, the average annual return drops to around 20 percent a year. This is nothing to sneeze at, of course, but it's considerably less than the figures usually

attached to Lynch's name. One could argue that middle-class investors were drawn into Magellan on the basis of a total return figure that was never within their reach.

8. Fidelity is, and always has been, a private company, owned primarily by the Johnson family. Johnson did, however, parcel out small ownership stakes to key employees such as Lynch, as well as "phantom" stock to a wider group of executives, as a kind of profit-sharing plan. However, the rule was that anyone leaving Fidelity had to sell his shares back to the company. Lynch still retains his shares because he is still associated with Fidelity, even though he no longer manages Magellan.

9. The most prominent no-load company is the Vanguard Group, run by Jack Bogle, who is the most outspoken executive in the entire mutual fund industry. His outspokenness is largely on behalf of what he believes are the superior moral values of no-load fund companies over the low-load companies like Fidelity. It's worth pointing out that although Bogle took a very different route from Johnson, it has also turned out to be extremely successful. Vanguard today is the nation's second-largest mutual fund group, with assets well over $100 billion.

## CHAPTER 13
## Socks 'n' Stocks, November 1982

Andrew Kahr's business history has not been documented by any journalist before, so I relied primarily on interviews to fill in this part of the story. In addition to Kahr himself, those who spoke to me include John McQuown, George Evans, David Woody, Adolph Mueller, James Fuller, and Rich Arnold. The *Business Week* interview with Kahr ran on April 5, 1982, under the headline "Parker Pen slips into financial services." The *Wall Street Journal* ran an article about Kahr's abrupt resignation as a trustee of the CMA Money Trust on September 4, 1980 ("Trustee of a Merrill Lynch Fund Is Ousted After Calling a Managing Fee Excessive"). *The Big Store,* by Donald Katz, discusses Kahr's involvement with Sears as it was preparing to dive into the financial services area. Tim Carrington's *The Year They Sold Wall Street* was an important source of information about the frenzy surrounding the "financial supermarket" idea. *The American Banker* covered the creation of the nonbank bank. "The Perils of Financial Services" (*Business Week,* August 20, 1984) discusses in detail the push by nonfinancial companies to get into the financial services arena.

The story of BankAmerica, on the other hand, has been well told, both in newspaper and magazine accounts of the time, and in two books, *Roller Coaster,* by Moira Johnston, and *Breaking the Bank,* by Gary Hector. I relied heavily on the books for my own retelling of BankAmerica's mid-1980s decline, and less heavily for my retelling of the purchase of Charles Schwab & Co. by the bank. Other published sources include the following: the *Wall Street Letter,* May 19, 1980; "Discount Brokers Square Off in Feud Over Who's Bigger" (the *Wall Street Journal,* September 29, 1981); "Charles Schwab vs. Les Quick: Discount Brokering's Main Event," by Anthony Bianco (*Business Week,* May 12, 1986); "A Big Setback for Discount Brokers" (*Business Week,* August 18, 1980); "BankAmerica-Schwab Would Not Violate Glass–Steagall," and opinion by the Department of Justice filed with the Federal Reserve and reprinted in the *American Banker* (July 20, 1982); "BankAmerica's elusive headstart in brokerage" (*Business Week,* August 2, 1982); and "Fed Clears Bid by BankAmerica to Buy Schwab" (the *Wall Street Journal,* January 10, 1983). Peter Moss, Rich Arnold, Hugo Quackenbush, Steven McLin, David S. Pottruck, Barbara Wolff, and Charles Schwab were among those interviewed.

1. Money market funds, like all other mutual funds, have boards of trustees, ostensibly to look out for the interests of the funds' shareholders.

2. At the time, Gulf + Western was run by a man named Charles Bluhdorn, one of the

legendary conglomerateurs of the age. When Bluhdorn died, he was succeeded by Martin Davis, who began selling off many of the companies Bluhdorn had assembled under the G + W umbrella. One of the last companies he sold was the Associates, which had become by the early 1990s an enormously profitable subsidiary; Ford Motor Company, which bought the Associates, paid $4 billion for it. Davis's goal was to transform the corporation into a pure media and entertainment company, and after he had shed the Associates, that's what he had. He renamed it Paramount Communications. (In 1994 Paramount was bought by Viacom.) I should point out that Simon & Schuster, the publisher of this book, is a division of Paramount.

3. The credit card project Kahr set up for the Associates was virtually the same project he had previously proposed to both Household Finance and Beneficial Finance, both of which were larger than the Associates and were also being squeezed by the rise of bank credit cards in America.

4. The details of Kahr's credit card design, and their implications, are discussed in greater detail in Chapter 15.

5. The architect of this corporate transformation was none other than Tsai, who had joined American Can as a high-ranking adviser to the CEO. By the time American Can bought Smith Barney, Tsai had become the CEO himself. He changed the name of the company to Primerica, and after the crash of 1987—an event that badly wounded Smith Barney—he sold Primerica to the legendary Wall Street figure Sanford Weill, who would go on to turn it into a truly diversified, and truly powerful, financial entity.

6. The magazine described him as a "brilliant thinker" but "something of an enfant terrible." It also quoted John Fischer, senior vice president of Bank One in Columbus, Ohio, which was processing the CMA credit card, as saying, "Andy Kahr is a super-intelligent guy, but I know very few people who get along with him."

7. This is Arnold's version of the story. Mueller's version of the same story is quite a bit different, and a good deal more entertaining. According to him, the contract between First Deposit and Schwab stipulated that the discounter would "undertake to develop and market nonbrokerage financial services" only through First Deposit. Mueller continues:

> When it was announced that BofA was in negotiations to buy Schwab, we remained deathly silent. Finally when the deal was signed, we delicately broached the subject. We said, by the way, we have this clause in our contract. . . . Some lawyer must have been fired over that one. So they gave us $1.5 million worth of BofA stock, and we canceled the whole thing.

8. Like most big banks, Bank of America formed a holding company during the 1970s. It was named BankAmerica, and the bank itself (which was still called Bank of America) became a wholly owned subsidiary of the larger corporate entity. Because it is the corporation, rather than the bank, that purchased Charles Schwab & Co., I've begun using the name of the holding company at this point in the text. For much the same reason, I've begun using "Citicorp" rather than "Citibank" in these latter chapters when it seems appropriate.

9. Though not necessarily Congress. Indeed, because of congressional anger over the nonbank bank loophole, a law was passed in the mid-1980s specifically closing the loophole. The law did, however, grandfather in the sixty or so nonbank banks already in existence.

10. Montgomery Street is the San Francisco equivalent of Wall Street.

11. The buyer was First Nationwide Savings, the seventh-largest S&L in the country, which was run by Anthony M. Frank, who knew Schwab through the Young Presidents Or-

ganization. Frank later became the nation's Postmaster General during the Bush Administration.

12. His full name was Alden Winship Clausen, but he was universally known as Tom.

13. According to Hector, Schwab was given the choice of locking in the $53 million purchase price, or accepting the 2.2 million shares, which of course might fall in price by the time the deal was completed. He took the stock, which shows, if nothing else, how very little he understood about BankAmerica's true condition when he agreed to the buyout.

14. Earlier, BankAmerica had gotten its own fairness opinion from Salomon Brothers, which has signed off on the fairness of the terms.

## CHAPTER 14
## The People's Nest Egg, April 1984

My views about *Money* magazine were initially formed by reading the magazine; the *Money* public relations office sent me a copy of every back issue since the magazine was started in 1972. I was also able to obtain a number of documents relating to the founding of *Money* from the Time, Inc., archives. Two books about the company, *Right Places, Right Times*, by Hedley Donovan, and *The World of Time Inc.*, by Curtis Prendergast with Geoffrey Colvin, contain brief accounts of *Money*'s launch and eventual success. Dean Rotbart, the publisher of the newsletter *TJFR* (*The Journalist & Financial Reporting*) devoted an entire issue to *Money* magazine in October 1987. Primarily, though, I relied on interviews with present and former *Money* staffers and Time, Inc., executives. Among those interviewed were Marshall Loeb, William Rukeyser, Henry Grunwald, Ray Cave, Marlys Harris, Patricia Dreyfus, the late Hedley Donovan, Nancy Pechar, Keith Johnson, Walter Isaacson, Brad Darrich, John Crandell, Malcolm Carter, Christopher Byron, the late Robert Klein, Andrew Heiskell, Michael Klingensmith, Otto Fuerenberger, Robert Runde, and Flora Ling.

Coverage of "IRA season"—roughly mid-February through mid-April—was extensive in the early and mid-1980s. The bulk of the coverage that I wound up drawing from was published by *The New York Times*, which ran numerous articles along the lines of: "I.R.A.'s Get Off to Slow Start" (March 22, 1982); "I.R.A.'s a Hit with Taxpayer," by Robert A. Bennett (April 15, 1983); and "I.R.A. Investments Up $35 Billion in '84," by Leonard Sloane (January 21, 1985). The *Business Week* article quoted in the chapter was entitled "A Rush of IRA Money Is Buoying Equities" (April 25, 1983); the William Safire column, "The People's Nest Eggs," ran on April 4, 1985. The Investment Company Institute study, "Investors' Interest in Mutual Fund IRAs," was issued in March 1983. I also drew on a 1982 "Survey of Mutual Fund Shareholders," which was put out by the ICI, and a 1987 study by the Federal Reserve, "Responses to Deregulation." Changes in the tax code are discussed in *Showdown at Gucci Gulch,* by Jeffrey H. Birnbaum and Alan S. Murray. "The American Way," an article by William E. Brownlee in *The Wilson Quarterly* (spring 1989), also deals with the tax code. Edward Furash, Mimi Lieber, David Silver, Roger Servison, Rab Bertelsen, Michael Hines, Charles L. Jarvie, Jane Jamieson, and Roger Harris were among those I interviewed about IRAs.

1. At Time, Inc., the editors of the company's various magazines are called "managing editors." In the interest of clarity, I've called them simply "editors" in this account, since that better reflects their roles as the top editorial executives of the individual magazines.

2. I should note that Henry Grunwald, then the editor-in-chief of all the Time, Inc.,

publications, denies that Loeb's promotion was a consolation prize. And Loeb himself has never claimed to feel that way about it.

3. I mean that literally: the inaugural issue of *Money* was actually the October 1972 issue, which means it went to the printer during the month of September.

4. Largely, but not entirely. In addition to Rukeyser, Porter's trailblazing colleagues in personal finance journalism included Jane Bryant Quinn and Knight Kiplinger. The former, like Porter, was a columnist, while the latter started a magazine called *Changing Times* (since renamed *Kiplinger's Personal Finance*), which was *Money*'s quiet, and quietly successful, predecessor.

5. *Barron's* would later describe Granville's road shows as "Barnum-like spectacles replete with costumes, balloons and bikini-clad women." The paper continues: "In May [1980], he was hauled on stage in Atlantic City in a coffin filled with ticker tape. . . . He had 'quaffed a number of vodka tonics,' he later conceded and, at one point, had to be helped from the stage. . . . More warmly received was his debut at Carnegie Hall on June 25, where, between other acts, he clowned around on a Steinway concert grand, and, as he recalled it later, was brought back 'for three curtain calls and a wild standing ovation.' "

6. Although Loeb stuck with the February tax issue, he couldn't resist adding that special Loeb touch. In February 1981, his first such issue, he put an ostentatiously wealthy man on the cover, with the subhead: "How this man earns $1,000,000 but pays no income tax."

7. A family in which one spouse worked and one didn't could put aside a slightly higher amount: $2,250 instead of $2,000.

8. Prior to the start of the bull market, there were around 5 million people who had money in equity mutual funds, for instance.

9. Then again, it took Safire some time to come to that view, too. He wrote his column in praise of IRAs in April 1985.

10. Jamieson has since become Fidelity's senior vice president for corporate communications.

11. Perhaps the most critical element in making it easy for people to switch funds was a decision Fidelity made to impose only one load on assets that were already in a Fidelity fund. Thus, if you had paid a 3 percent load to get into Magellan, and then switched to the more conservative Equity-Income, which also had a 3 percent load, you would not be charged another 3 percent on the original sum you invested. This same feature also did a great deal to help Fidelity hold on to its customers; having paid one load, people were loath to pull their money out and put it into another fund company that would also charge a load.

12. In the Tax Reform Act of 1986, Congress took away the immediate $2,000 tax write-off that had given IRAs so much of their initial appeal. However, the capital gains on the money already in an IRA account—and, indeed, on money added to IRAs even after the law was changed—remained tax-deferred until it was withdrawn. For this reason, IRA accounts have continued to grow, though not as impressively as they did during the mid-1980s.

13. Indeed, they had. As of 1992, almost 30 percent of the $724 billion held in IRA accounts could be found in mutual funds, with another 28 percent in self-directed brokerage accounts. Only 18 percent of IRA accounts are with banks, and only 12 percent with thrifts.

14. Even Peter Lynch was not supposed to speak to the press, though he was allowed, in the one great exception to the rule, to make occasional guest appearances on "Wall Street Week."

## CHAPTER 15
## The Pleasure Palace in the Sky, May 1984

The growing tension between Hock and the Visa bankers began to leach into the press in the early 1980s. One can find mention of their various disputes in such articles as "Visa Stirs up the Big Banks—Again," by Arthur Louis (*Fortune*, October 3, 1983), "Visa's bid to keep the banks on board" (*Business Week*, April 26, 1982), "The iconoclast who made Visa No. 1" (*Business Week*, December 22, 1980), and "Visa's Vietnam?" by Eamonn Fingleton (*Forbes*, October 26, 1981). Still, the depth of feeling toward Hock was best illuminated in a clip I found in Spencer Nilson's files. A banker had ripped out the 1982 *Business Week* article and sent it to Nilson with a note that said, "Hock is fond of dictionary usage; he . . . ought to take a good look under 'truth.' " The J. C. Penney dispute was well-covered in both *The Nilson Report* and the *American Banker*. Hock's "all-in-one card" idea was described by *Business Week* ("Visa's vision of an all-in-one card," October 1982). Hock's resignation and departure were also covered in the *American Banker*. I relied on four Hock speeches: "Consumer Payment Systems of the 80s" (September 17, 1980); "Financial Markets of the Future" (April 30, 1984); "Alice and the Bank Bird Dog II" (February 27, 1984); and "Retail Banking in the Future: 1968 Revisited, Orwell's *1984* or Common Sense?" (September 23, 1983). The latter is the speech quoted at length in the chapter. Kenneth Larkin, Frederick Hammer, Paul Kahn, Guy W. Botts, Thomas Honey, Bennett Katz, Charles Russell, Daniel Brigham, Irwin Derman, Robert Miller, Bruce Rockwell, and D. Dale Browning were among those interviewed.

I interviewed Andrew Kahr, Adolph Mueller, and John Decker about the creation of the First Select credit card. Elgie Holstein and Gerri Detweiler, then of the Bankcard Holders of America, talked to me about First Select, and also showed me their file of First Select material; it included the press release detailing BHA's complaints about the old First Select mailings. A small handful of other people spoke to me—conversations that were usually brief and oblique—about First Deposit; invariably they asked that their names not be used. Payment Systems, Inc., and *The Nilson Report* both published data detailing First Deposit's success. *Financial Services Week* (March 19, 1984) detailed the sale of First Deposit to Capital Holding Corporation. *New Hampshire Business Review* ran a rare lengthy article about First Deposit ("N.H.'s Fastest-Growing Bank—It's in Tilton," by Michael Kitch, September 25, 1987). "Bank Accused of High Visa Charges," by Laura Paull-Borga (*San Francisco Examiner*, March 28, 1986), details the filing of a $10 million class action lawsuit against First Deposit accusing it "of exploiting its Visa credit-card users through excessive and hidden charges." According to court documents, the suit was settled in January 1988, with First Deposit paying $80,000, half of which went to the plaintiffs' attorneys, with the other half going to charity.

The statistics on credit and credit cards that begin this chapter are drawn from a variety of published sources, including the following: "Changes in Consumer Debt: Evidence from the 1983 and 1986 Surveys of Consumer Finance," a Federal Reserve study published in the *Federal Reserve Bulletin*, October 1987; "The Growth of Consumer Debt," a Federal Reserve study published in the June 1985 *Federal Reserve Bulletin;* "Increasing Indebtedness and Financial Stability in the United States," a paper by Benjamin M. Friedman delivered at a symposium on Debt, Financial Stability and Public Policy sponsored by the Federal Reserve Bank of Kansas City (August 1986); "Caught in the Eighties," by Michael Stone (*New York*, April 24, 1989); "Hooked on Plastic: Middle Class Family Takes a Harsh Cure for Credit Card Abuse," by Dana Milbank (the *Wall Street Journal*, January 8, 1991); "Mounting Doubts About Debt," by Barbara Rudolph (*Time*, March 31, 1986); "Why Consumers Are Paying Down Debt," by Liam Carmody (*Credit Card Management*, July/

August 1988); "Despite heavy debt, credit card holders charge on," by David Ballingrud (*St. Petersburg Times,* January 27, 1991). I also relied on various issues of *Grant's Interest Rate Observer* and *Credit Card Management* magazine. Books include *Beyond Our Means,* by Alfred L. Malabre, Jr., *As We Forgive Our Debtors: Bankruptcy and Consumer Credit in America,* by Teresa A. Sullivan, Elizabeth Warren, and Jay Lawrence Westbrook, *Money of the Mind,* by James Grant, and *The Credit Card Industry: A History,* by Lewis Mandell. The study by Mimi Lieber mentioned in the chapter was entitled "The Money Study 1985: Analysis of Credit Markets."

1. As usual, the statistics that follow exclude mortgage figures.
2. These are fictitious names; the authors of *As We Forgive Our Debtors,* from which this example is taken, made a point of changing names and some identifying data.
3. I want to stress here that I'm talking about the debt accumulated by individuals, rather than corporate or government debt. The growth of corporate debt, in particular, was unquestionably a new phenomenon, driven by a radically new way of thinking about debt as a tool, rather than a hindrance for business.
4. These findings also contradicted the belief of most bankers that—to quote again from *As We Forgive Our Debtors*—"bankruptcy has become a haven for middle class sharpies who bathe in the cleansing waters of bankruptcy rather than pay debts they are quite able to pay."
5. The simple answer to the question is, first, that banks had no way of knowing what other credit cards a potential customer had, and secondly, that banks always hoped that the people who took their credit card would stop using other cards. That it didn't always work out that way was, in their view, the price they paid for being in the credit card business.
6. According to one authoritative estimate, Citicorp earned more of its credit card profits from fees than from interest.
7. These histories were often erroneous, doing grievous harm to people who needed credit, and yet because they were on computer, they were extremely difficult to have erased from one's record. That, along with the privacy issues raised by such credit agencies, made the rating agencies quite controversial, and by the early 1990s, Congress had enacted legislation to rein them in, just as it had once enacted legislation to control certain aspects of credit cards.
8. Arguably his only real competitor in this regard was John Reed, who had no compunction about using Citicorp's heft to move the credit card industry in one direction or another he wanted it to go—sometimes successfully and sometimes not.
9. In this account, I've had to give short shrift to the electronic banking debates that embroiled much of the industry—and the government—in the 1970s and early 1980s, and in which Dee Hock was one of the more vocal debaters. Here, however, is an excerpt from a publicity brochure put out by Visa in 1990, which owes much to Hock's original view of electronic banking, and will give the reader a small glimpse into his vision:

> Today, American families practically need a business manager to handle the administrative overhead of daily life—innumerable bills to be sorted, paid and recorded; funds to be shuttled between accounts; statements to be checked; account balances to be verified. And then there are all the payment devices that must be carried—ATM cards to get cash; cash for small purchases; checks for groceries; credit cards for larger purchases.
>
> Wouldn't it be more efficient if we could transact all this business through one system? A system that would automatically transfer monthly bills—the phone, the utilities, even the mortgage—on the correct days. A system that could make

a direct debit to our accounts for small purchases and groceries so that we wouldn't always need to have cash and checks with us. A system that would keep track of all these transactions and provide us with a single, simple statement each month.

Wouldn't that kind of system make the business of daily life much simpler? Visa thinks so.

10. Hock's explanation was that the secrecy was at Penney's insistence, and he had no choice but to go along.

11. As it happens, Hock himself introduced this bylaw. But this was a preemptive move. Had he not introduced the bylaw, the board members would have—and would have passed it.

12. Of course, it would also be easy enough to have one debit card perform both ATM and payment functions; in fact, to some small degree it is already happening, especially at gasoline stations, a good number of which allow customers to buy their gas with an ATM card.

13. I'm borrowing this astute phrase from the credit card consultant Helene Duffy, who used it in the lengthy report she wrote about Hock's various "payment device" strategies.

14. It was generally thought that convenience users resisted debit cards because they valued the float that credit cards provided. Among the experts who believed this, incidentally, was Donald Baker, the Justice Department antitrust lawyer who had done so much to break up the New York Stock Exchange's monopoly. Baker was keenly interested in credit cards and electronic banking, which were filled with thorny antitrust issues, and he understood the business as well as or better than most bankers. "I saw an ad for a Visa debit card at one bank back in 1980," he would later recall. "The ads said, 'Looks like a credit card, works like a check.' I thought, 'Why would anyone want *that*?' "

15. "Before debit cards become widely acceptable . . . three things will have to happen," according to a study by the A. J. Wood Research Corporation, conducted in 1980. "First, alternative payment methods (primarily credit cards and checks) will have to become less attractive. . . . Second, the debit cards themselves will have to offer some explicit inducements. . . . The third prerequisite for widespread use of debit cards is consumers getting accustomed to the absence of canceled checks as receipts for transactions." The authors of the study predicted that these conditions would be met by the mid-1980s, but it's only now that debit cards are becoming accepted as a form of payment.

16. In time, Browning rose all the way to the top at Colorado National, becoming president and CEO, a position from which he stepped down in December 1992. He is currently the president and CEO of Plus System, Inc., the ATM network he founded.

17. I should point out here that despite Browning's prominence among the Visa bankers, he was not a member of the board during Hock's tenure. That was reserved for Browning's boss Bruce Rockwell, who was then the president of Colorado National. I should also point out that it didn't matter much: Rockwell took the Colorado National position at board meetings, which of course was the Browning position. When the battle between Browning and Hock over the future of debit cards accelerated in the early 1980s, however, Rockwell usually refrained from voting, citing the obvious conflict of interest.

18. Indeed, the similarity even extends to the emergence of a single competing network. Not long after Browning laid the groundwork for Plus, a banker in California named Alex "Pete" Hart drew up plans for a competing network, which he called Cirrus. To complete the symmetry, Plus today is owned by Visa, whereas Cirrus is owned by MasterCard. And Pete Hart, of course, later became the head of MasterCard.

19. Although it didn't do him much good, Hock's view turned out to be the correct one. As bankers came to realize the overriding importance of universality to their customers, they

began linking their own machines with their competitors'. Today, in fact, many machines accept both Plus and Cirrus cards—and the two ATM systems have become, for most people, as interchangeable as Visa and MasterCard.

20. In Europe, debit cards are used much the way Hock envisioned—in stores, in parking lots, at roadway tolls, and so on. To some degree, a debit card in Europe has the same "almost-a-necessity" status as the credit card does here. Many parking lots, for instance, don't even have attendants anymore; if you can't pay by debit card, you can't get in.

21. Although this was not an issue with the board, the executives who were quartered in 101 California disliked it because it was simply too far away from their own staffs back in San Mateo. They found that they were constantly shuttling back and forth between the two places—a difficult and annoying thing to have to do during rush hour, say. So many of the executives were spending so much time in San Mateo that Hock actually ordered them to spend at least two days a week in the San Francisco office.

22. Big city bankers, such as Chase Manhattan's Hammer, were more accustomed to salaries like Hock's, and were not bothered by how much he made. Indeed, Hammer believes that Hock was underpaid, because unlike many of the bankers who complained about his salary, he received no equity stake in the enterprise, and had no "golden parachute."

23. These three product descriptions are Kahr's own, in typically cryptic remarks he made to the newsletter *Financial Services Week*.

24. One reason these early product ideas never got past the planning stages is that they were bewilderingly complex. Kahr's annuity product, for instance, would have allowed consumers to put money in an account where it would be tax-deferred until accessed by check or debit card. He attempted to market it through the auspices of Jerry Falwell's Moral Majority, but it was simply too complicated to be explained in a punchy direct mail package.

25. Simons died in August 1988.

26. "I had a feeling," Kahr once said, "I could have made a lot more money faster if I had just concentrated on collections, and bought uncollectible accounts [from banks]."

27. One reason this was so complicated—and why there has been so few attempts to replicate Kahr's efforts, despite First Deposit's tremendous success—was that it is against the law to simply ask a credit rating agency for a list of names of people who carry debt but aren't delinquent. Thus the questions had to be broad, and Kahr had to be able to infer from other kinds of data which people were likely to be hard-core revolvers.

## CHAPTER 16
## The Bulls' Last Stampede, January 1987

As with Chapter 13, I relied a great deal on the books by Gary Hector and Moira Johnston in recounting Schwab's break with BankAmerica. This was supplemented by data gleaned from the prospectus for the August 1987 Schwab public offering, as well as contemporaneous newspaper and magazine accounts, primarily from the *Wall Street Journal*. Other useful articles include "Charles Schwab Is Feeling Fettered," by Gary Hector (*Fortune*, January 20, 1986); "Mavericks in Brokerage and Insurance," by Rod Willis (*Management Review*, September 1986); and "Charles Schwab Is Bullish on Charles Schwab & Company," by Mark Dowie (*San Francisco* magazine, February 1987). Interviews with Stephen McLin and Rich Arnold were quite helpful. Less helpful were current Schwab officials, who were reluctant to rehash the negotiations. It turns out that I was conducting these interviews just months prior to the publication of Johnston's book. Schwab executives had the galleys, and, worried about the blunt tone Chuck Schwab had taken with her, they were trying to persuade her to tone down his remarks. They do not appear to have succeeded.

Paul Stuka's departure from Fidelity was widely publicized at the time. The *Wall Street Journal* article quoted in the chapter, "Paul Stuka Is Leaving to Form 'Hedge Fund' That Invests in Securities," by Jan Wong, ran on June 16, 1986; the *Business Week* article mentioned in the text, "The Rookie Running a Hot New Fund," by Lois Therrien, was published August 12, 1985. Another useful article was "Paul S. Stuka: Ex–Fidelity fund manager now plays the market for the well-heeled," by Jane Fitz Simon (the *Boston Globe*, February 3, 1987). I interviewed Stuka not long after he had left Fidelity. I also interviewed Rodger Lawson. Several former Fidelity fund managers spoke to me about Fidelity's marketing emphasis but asked that their names not be used.

The volume and dollar figures connected to the market run-up in 1987 come either from Dow Jones or the *Wall Street Journal*. Other published sources include "Stock Doctor Eases Investors' Anxieties," by Bob Powell (*Providence Business News*, July 27, 1987); "Mutual Funds Are Popular Again, Fueled by Strong Marketing Effort," by Randall Smith (the *Wall Street Journal*, July 13, 1984); "A Frenzy to Market Mutual Funds," by Robert A. Bennett (*The New York Times*, April 26, 1987); "How High the Bull," by John J. Curran (*Fortune*, February 6, 1984); "How I Spent My Summer: At Camp with My New Friends N.Y.S.E. and Dow, Buying Phillips Oil on Margin," by Gail Cameron Wescott (*People*, August 18, 1986); and "Scoring Big on Wall Street, Says a Stock Market Pro, Means Knowing That the Trend Is Your Friend," by Maggie Mahar (*People*, May 12, 1986). Robert Prechter's prophecies were covered most fervently by *Barron's*. The *New York Times* article quoted at the end of the chapter, "5-Year Stock Rally: The Far Reaching Impact," by Leslie Wayne, ran on August 3, 1987.

1. Trying to keep track of Shearson's corporate name changes during the 1980s is a little like trying to hit a moving target. The investment firm American Express bought in 1981 was Shearson Loeb Rhoades. In 1985, the parent company bought Lehman Brothers, Kuhn Loeb and merged it into Shearson; the resulting firm was called Shearson Lehman Brothers. And a few years later, the failing wirehouse, E. F. Hutton, was folded into Shearson. At that point, the name was changed to Shearson Lehman Hutton. In the early 1990s, by the way, American Express sold the wirehouse side of Shearson to Sanford Weill's Primerica, which merged it with Smith Barney. It was then renamed Smith Barney Shearson.

2. Schwab was the subject of a stockholder suit, alleging he had dumped his stock knowing in advance of the upcoming loss. But he didn't. Because Armacost was in the habit of telling his board as little as possible, Schwab was as surprised as anyone when the size of the loss was announced a few weeks after he had sold his stock.

3. This, according to Moira Johnston, author of *Roller Coaster*.

4. The meeting was held in Washington because the other key dissident on the board, former defense secretary Robert McNamara, lived there. The meeting was held in McNamara's living room.

5. The best known of these sharks and the one Schwab appeared to support was Sanford Weill, who by then had left Shearson and was looking for a way to get back into business. His "takeover bid" amounted to a promise to raise $1 billion in new capital for BankAmerica if the board would push Armacost aside and name him (Weill) CEO. Not surprisingly, the proposal was rejected.

6. Hector recounts Armacost's reaction upon learning for the first time how big that loss would be. "It was fun while it lasted," he is supposed to have remarked, knowing that those numbers would seal his fate.

7. Schwab told a reporter from *Business Week* that the idea of Quick & Reilly buying his company was "a joke" because the two firms were so "fundamentally different." Quick retorted, "He's right. We know how to make money and they don't."

8. Roberts, though a friend of Schwab's, did not do this work out of the goodness of his heart. In return for his aid, Roberts got a small but significant slice in Schwab, which he later distributed among his partners.

9. The ambivalence stemmed from the obvious: besides being the antithesis of the "team-work" ethic Johnson wanted in the equity department, "star" fund managers had the company over a barrel. They could demand more money, and if they didn't get it, they could quit and strike out on their own, using their newly acquired fame as a magnet to attract assets. This happened infrequently during the early 1980s—and more frequently in the late 1980s.

10. Capital Appreciation was intended to be an aggressive, anything-goes growth fund, like Magellan, but aimed at investors who felt that Magellan had gotten too large to outperform the market. Sweeney's best year with the fund was his first, 1987, when he steered Capital Appreciation to an impressive 20 percent gain—despite the market crash that October.

11. Rather than build a giant headquarters building, Johnson preferred to buy existing real estate in the financial district and put Fidelity divisions in those buildings. By the end of the 1980s, the company had offices in a dozen different downtown locations—and Fidelity's real estate holdings had appreciated dramatically.

12. This is not entirely true: as the electronically based NASDAQ exchange has grown in size and scope, becoming a legitimate competitor to the New York Stock Exchange, quite a few large companies have stuck with NASDAQ and eschewed the NYSE. The most prominent of these companies are in the computer industry, including such giants as Microsoft, Apple Computer, and Intel.

13. But not, oddly enough, television. Johnson was skeptical of the power of television advertising, and consequently Fidelity was among the last major financial institutions in America to run television commercials, far behind the likes of Merrill Lynch, Schwab, and Citibank. Even today, its television presence is minimal, while its print advertising is omnipresent.

14. The closing price of the Dow Jones average that day was 2002.25.

15. On the other hand, most market professionals—as opposed to reporters and small in-vestors—appeared to be blasé about the milestone. "Two thousand is one point higher than 1,999," yawned one Wall Street analyst. Indeed, the majority opinion on Wall Street was that the Dow would quickly drop back below the 2,000-point mark because it was overvalued.

16. The most nerve-racking days were certain Fridays that came to be known as "triple witching hours." They occurred four times a year, when three important index contracts expired, and investors had to either buy or sell the underlying stocks.

17. Later, of course, Zweig would become fairly well known as a regular panelist on "Wall Street Week."

18. The other important reason Merrill Lynch was hurting was that it had simply gotten sloppy. Among other things, it entered a handful of businesses, such as mortgage-backed securities, that it knew nothing about. In the case of mortgage-backed securities, for instance, it wound up losing an astonishing $225 million when a young trader made a huge wrong bet—and there was no one at the firm who knew enough even to question his trading. This was said to be the single largest loss from one trade in the history of Wall Street.

19. These new brokers had a rather different mind-set from that of the brokers who came to the firm in the postwar years, to say the least. One of them would later recall that his training session was dominated by "parties and drinking and drugs and sex. There was an exaggerated, euphoric state of mind," he adds.

## CHAPTER 17
## "This Is a War over Here," October 1987

I spent a good deal of 1987 working on an article about Fidelity and the bull market for *Esquire* magazine ("The Ga-Ga Years," February 1988); I was allowed to sit in on the meeting described in this chapter for that story. A number of other scenes—such as the scene outside the Fidelity investment center the day after the crash—were things I saw while reporting the *Esquire* story. Of course, every media outlet in the country covered the crash of 1987; my files bulge with stories from the *Wall Street Journal* and *The New York Times*. Among the more important, for my purposes, were the following: "Investor-Slayer Led Double Life," by Jon Nordheimer (*The New York Times*, October 20, 1987); "Terrible Tuesday: How the Stock Market Almost Disintegrated a Day After the Crash," by James B. Stewart and Daniel Hertzberg (the *Wall Street Journal*, November 20, 1987); "Trade Tangle: Brokers' Back Offices Stagger Under Load, Exasperating Clients," by Steve Swartz (the *Wall Street Journal*, October 23, 1987); "The Events That Changed the World," by James Sterngold (*The New York Times*, October 26, 1987); "Fidelity Investments Keeps It in the Family During Crash," by Christopher J. Chipello and Gary Putka (the *Wall Street Journal*, October 23, 1987); and "It Was Like Being in a Fellini Film," by John D. Spooner (the *Boston Globe*, November 3, 1987). Frederick Ungehauer first recounted Peter Lynch's crash travails in *Time* magazine ("Up, Up, then Doooown," January 4, 1988). The Report of The Presidential Task Force on Market Mechanisms analyzed the events that led to Black Monday. "Are Stocks Too High?" by John Curran (*Fortune*, September 28, 1987) is the article in which George Soros and Alan Greene are quoted, offering their divergent opinion about the state of the market. "Why This Is 1929 All Over Again," by Michael M. Thomas (*The Nation*, May 16, 1987), "The Next Panic," by L. J. Davis (*Harper's*, May 1987), and "The Morning After," by Peter G. Peterson (*The Atlantic*, October 1987), offer their respective doomsday predictions. "Calling the Crash: Pessimistic Predictions by Analyst at Shearson Make Her a Star," by James B. Stewart (the *Wall Street Journal*), recounts Elaine Garzarelli's famous "call." Virtually every person I interviewed in the financial services industry had some little nugget about the October crash to offer.

I interviewed Robert Rosseau, Barry Snowbarger, Woodson Hobbes, Hugo Quackenbush, Tom D. Seip, John Coghlan, Lawrence Stupski, David Pottruck, Rich Arnold, and Guy Bryant about events surrounding Charles Schwab & Co. during the crash. Richard B. Schmitt of the *Wall Street Journal* is the reporter who revealed Wang's name, as well as a number of details about his life, including the 1983 kidnapping ("Investor Linked to Schwab Loss Named in Papers," November 2, 1987).

1. Greene made his concerns known in an article that ran in *Fortune* magazine less than a month before the crash—an article that, in general, downplayed the comments of naysayers such as him. On the cover of that issue sat legendary investor George Soros, smiling confidently into the camera; the headline read: "George Soros, who may well be Wall Street's most successful investor, thinks the volatile market could climb a lot more." Incidentally, Marshall Loeb was editing *Fortune* by then.
2. Later, even Lynch would concede he had become concerned about the overall state of the market in the early part of 1987. "We went over 2100 on January 19," he told an interviewer from *Time* magazine, "then 2200 a month later. Then 2300 in March, 2400 in April, 2500 in July. Then you get 2600 in August and 2700 a week later. Bang! Bang! These were scary numbers."
3. Cabour began managing Balanced Fund in early 1987, after recovering from a heart attack. For the seven years prior to his illness, he had managed the large and popular

Puritan Fund, where he cemented his reputation for being a fund manager with conservative instincts who could still reap consistent market gains.

4. For the record, the bull market reached its top on August 25, when it closed at 2722.42.

5. This record would soon be eclipsed: on the day after the October 19 crash, the stock market rose 102 points.

6. Robert Prechter is among those who issued an All Points Bulletin to his subscribers, telling them to flee the market just before the crash. His warning, however, came just days before the crash, and could not prevent him from becoming the new Joe Granville in its aftermath—the well-known forecaster with a large following whose predictions turned out to be dead wrong.

7. The volume that day also set a record it has never again approached. Over 600 million shares were traded on Black Monday.

8. This initial story was true only insofar as it went. Arthur Kane was indeed a distraught investor wiped out by the crash, as well as a midlevel (and reputedly mild-mannered) federal bureaucrat. However, reporters soon learned that Kane had another identity. His real name was Arthur Katz, who a decade before had been a Kansas City lawyer embroiled in what *The New York Times* called "a bogus auto accident scheme." He received his new identity from the government after testifying against the other lawyers involved in the scam, and joined the federal witness protection program.

9. One important reason the crash of 1987 was not as devastating to investors as the crash of 1929 was because most Americans did not buy stocks on margin in the 1980s. In 1929, taking on margin debt to buy stocks was a widely used technique designed to "leverage" an investor's purchasing power. When the crash came, however, and people could not make their margin calls, that same debt became their undoing.

10. The Dow finally closed that day with a gain of 102 points, but that did not reflect the true state of the overall stock market. All the broader averages were down substantially, and the *Wall Street Journal* would later claim that the market had been on the verge of total meltdown that day. Peter Lynch called it "the worst day of my career."

11. Fidelity also instituted a temporary policy of waiting seven days before redeeming its customers' mutual fund shares. While this did not make customers happy, it allowed Fidelity a week's time to sell the necessary stock, thus lessening the effect of the selling into the market.

12. The unmasking of Wang was largely an accident, it would appear; a court order was mistakenly left unsealed. To this day Schwab officials refuse to divulge his name, even though it has been published.

13. Hong Kong has a bank secrecy law, so tracing money can be difficult.

## CHAPTER 18
### Peter Lynch's Long Good-bye, March 1990

Stock market postmortems were a dominant strain of article in business publications during the year after the October crash. Among those I drew from were "Dreary Street: In Wake of the Crash, Stock Market Turns Cautious—and Dull," by Douglas R. Sease (the *Wall Street Journal,* April 11, 1988); "Six Months Later: The Crash," by Sarah Bartlett (*Business Week,* April 18, 1988); and "The Uncertain Legacy of the Crash," by Louis Uchitelle (*The New York Times,* April 3, 1988). The *Times* ran a five-part series entitled "Market Meltdown: The Lessons of October" the week of December 13, 1987. The ongoing analysis in *Morningstar Mutual Funds* was obviously helpful, as was the analysis provided by Edward Furash. Most of the mutual fund statistics in the chapter are culled from the ICI's annual

Mutual Fund Fact Books. The New York Stock Exchange study mentioned in the chapter was entitled "Shareownership 1990" (undated). The ICI study mentioned was entitled "After the October 1987 Market Break" (October 1988). The struggles of Schwab and Merrill Lynch in the late 1980s were most closely covered in the *Wall Street Journal*. Also helpful were "Merrill Lynch Visits the Fat Farm," by Saul Hansell (*Institutional Investor,* November 1990); "Merrill Lynch: The Stumbling Herd," by Brett Duval Fromson (*Fortune,* June 20, 1988); "For Discount Brokers, the Crash Still Isn't Over," (*Business Week,* December 1988); "Suddenly, the Envy of the Street Is . . . Schwab?" (*Business Week,* March 19, 1990); "Repositioning a Leading Stockbroker," by Kent Dorwin (*Long Range Planning,* vol. 21, no. 6, 1988); "Charles Schwab," a research report by Ram Capoor of Morgan Stanley; and "Trends: An Analysis of Emerging Trends in the Securities Industry," a study produced by the Securities Industry Association (December 29, 1989).

The best story about the money market fund crisis was written by Jonathan R. Laing of *Barron's* ("Never Say Never," March 26, 1990). "Fund Run by Garzarelli Fares Poorly Since Crash," by Randall Smith (the *Wall Street Journal,* October 6, 1988) and "Where Have All the Gurus Gone?" by Stan Hinton (*The Washington Post,* April 23, 1989) document Garzarelli's postcrash troubles. The departure of Lynch and arrival (and subsequent departure) of Morris Smith as manager of Fidelity Magellan was written about in numerous publications. To the Lynch stories mentioned in the notes for Chapter 12, I would add "Changing of the Guard," a *Morningstar* commentary (April 20, 1990). Morris Smith stories include "Morris Smith, We Hardly Knew Ye," by Geoffrey Smith (*Business Week,* May 11, 1992); "Morris, We Hardly Knew You," by Kimberly Blanton (the *Boston Globe,* April 30, 1992); and "Magellan Myths" (*Morningstar Mutual Funds,* April 30, 1993). The postcrash article that so infuriated Lynch was "Fidelity Runs into a Wall," by Hank Gilman (the *Boston Globe,* February 28, 1988). Lynch, Garzarelli, and Smith were among those interviewed for this chapter.

1. One of the promises made to focus group participants is that their anonymity will be preserved. For this reason, the institution that showed me the tape of this session did so on the condition that I not disclose the firm's identity.

2. Some who tried to cut and run, but were unable to because of the phone overload in the days after Black Monday, would later profess gratitude that the phones had been tied up, and they had been prevented, in effect, from panicking.

3. Acccording to a survey done by the Investment Company Institute, in the year before the crash, 23 percent of fund owners labeled "safety of investment" as their most important objective; a year later, 77 percent of fund owners felt that way.

4. Begun in 1986, and intended to offer unbiased, but tough-minded, ratings of mutual funds, *Morningstar Mutual Funds* has since become the premier source of information about mutual funds, overtaking such longtime fund raters as Lipper Analytical Services, which for many years had the "fund rating" market cornered.

5. This figure had been exceeded only twice before: in 1986, when the bull market was in full fury, and in 1981 when, prior to banking deregulation, money flocked into unregulated money market funds.

6. On the other hand, top Schwab executives could certainly afford a pay cut. In 1987, Chuck Schwab was paid $6.1 million, while company president Lawrence Stupski took in almost $4.2 million. The two men were ranked first and second in the *San Francisco Chronicle*'s list of the Bay Area's "top 100 earners."

7. One reason Schwab was attracted to an index fund, as opposed to a more traditional mutual fund, is that such a passive fund seemed to fit with the essentially passive nature

of discounting. It also would not be seen as competition to the several hundred mutual funds Schwab carried as part of its mutual fund marketplace. By the way, one of the people who created the Schwab 1000 was Andrew Kahr's old friend John McQuown.

8. That figure gives an indication of how quickly the market bounced back: in just two years, the Dow Jones average had regained not only the money lost in the crash, but the additional 500 points that the market had dropped in August and September of 1987. The 2791 achieved by the Dow in October 1989 was sixty-nine points higher than the bull market peak in August of 1987.

9. In fact, as of early 1990, money market funds owned more than $175 billion worth of commercial paper—more than a third of the total commercial paper issued.

10. "I'd be lying if I said that we'd never thought about the possibility of a general run on money funds, but please don't quote me on it," one anonymous executive told *Barron's* in the spring of 1990. "Anything might trigger it. A cluster of commercial-paper defaults, a loss of confidence in the brokerage industry, some principal losses that fund sponsors decided not to cover, a spate of feature stories on the evening news or in *USA Today*—anything."

11. It attributed this allusion to "hints" from "Donoghue, among others."

12. Although its first impulse was to resist the regulations, in time, most mutual fund companies came to support the tighter rules, seeing it as a necessary safety net for the entire industry. It's also worth noting that the SEC drew up these tighter regulations precisely because the agency understood the implicit promise the money fund industry had made to its customers—namely that the assets residing in money funds would always be safe.

13. In their defense, not all equity fund managers were *trying* to beat the S&P 500. The goal of an income-oriented fund, for instance, was quite different from the goal of an aggressive growth fund, and the manager of such a fund would certainly be happy with a 10 percent gain in a year the S&P 500 went up, say, 12 or 13 percent. Still, the main point remains: during the 1980s, most equity fund managers underperformed the most widely accepted market benchmark.

14. This competing theory is called the Random Walk theory. Its best-known popularizer is Burton G. Malkiel, an economics professor at Princeton University and the author of *A Random Walk Down Wall Street* (W. W. Norton & Company), a book that has come to be regarded, in the twenty years since it was first published, as a classic. Among his other roles, Malkiel serves as a director of the Vanguard Group. This is only fitting, since Vanguard, despite being the home to John Neff and the Windsor Fund, is the company that has most eagerly embraced the implications of Random Walk. It has done so by offering an impressive line of index funds, which it markets fiercely and quite successfully.

15. The fusillade of criticism heaped on Prechter so wounded him that he withdrew almost completely from the public arena—canceling previously scheduled appearances, turning down almost all interview requests, and in general, getting as far away from the laser of publicity as he could.

16. The primary critic of not just Magellan but all of Fidelity, was Jack Bogle, the head of Vanguard. A cantankerous, outspoken man, Bogle created the impression of being the world's biggest Fidelity hater, which was not far from wrong.

But he also ran his company in a completely different fashion from Ned Johnson: all Vanguard funds were no-load, and it was a point of pride with Bogle that he kept costs to a bare minimum in order to pass the savings on to his shareholders. Thus, from Bogle's point of view, Johnson's system of attaching fees and loads to Fidelity mutual funds, especially once they became popular, was unconscionable.

Bogle also loathed Fidelity's marketing emphasis. "There's too much hype," he once told *SmartMoney* magazine. "To treat investments as packaged products, like toothpaste or Budweiser—I find that disgusting." Johnson's mild reply: "There is more than one way to run a mutual fund company."

17. Actually, *Morningstar Mutual Funds* didn't begin regularly picking a Portfolio Manager of the Year until 1991. The Lynch award for 1988 was an after-the-fact designation, as the newsletter's editors attempted to show readers what they would have done if they had chosen a manager of the year in 1988.

18. It was on this point that Jack Bogle, and other Fidelity critics, were most critical of Ned Johnson. If Magellan generated that much cash, they argued, Fidelity should lower the fees on the fund, and, in effect, give some of that money back to the shareholders. The counterarguments made by Johnson and Lynch were, first, that the fees were not out of line with other low-load funds; second, that people wouldn't pay the fees if they didn't believe they were getting their money's worth; and, third, that even with the fees, Magellan still managed to return a higher yield over the long term than virtually every other mutual fund in existence.

## CHAPTER 19
## The Triumph of Main Street, August 1993

The last scene in the book—Peter Lynch's book signing in Chicago—is one I witnessed; I spent that day with him. I also spent several days in Jacksonville, Florida, at the headquarters of AT&T's credit card venture. Among the AT&T executives I interviewed were Paul Kahn, Victor Pelson, Robert Ranelli, Frederick Winckler, Cynthia Hazouri, Peter Gallagher, and Mary Kay Emmerich. As ever, Stephen Szekely of Payment Systems, Inc., and *The Nilson Report* were sources of credit card data and insight. The article in *Grant's Interest Rate Observer* quoted in the chapter was headlined "Credit-Card Fees: Just Ask" (March 15, 1991).

As the full shape of the money revolution has become clearer—and the degree to which mutual funds have become a dominant form of investment in America—there has been an explosion of articles and information. *The New York Times* is now running a regular investment section each Saturday; many papers and magazines offer quarterly roundups of mutual fund results; and two new magazines, *Worth* and *SmartMoney*, have sprung up to report on various aspects of the money revolution. "Mutual Funds: The Battle for Your Dollar," by Jon Friedman (*Business Week*, June 11, 1990) offers a good overview of the shape of things. "New, Calmer Investor Predicted for 1990s," by Michael Hines (*COMPASS Readings*, April 1990), offers the view of a high-ranking Fidelity marketer on the evolution of investor psychology at the turn of the decade. "The Mutual Fund Time Bomb," by Jonathan Burton (*Worth*, July/August 1993), gives a less sanguine outlook on the same subject. "The New Global Investor," by Jeffrey M. Laderman (*Business Week*, October 11, 1993), discusses the rise of overseas investing. "The End of Banking as We Know It," a series of articles that ran in the *Wall Street Journal* beginning on July 7, 1993, tackles that aspect of the money revolution.

Articles about Fidelity were equally voluminous. Among the many that were useful: "Clash of the Titans," by Ellyn E. Spragins (*SmartMoney*, October 1993); "And It Just Keeps Rolling In," by Kimberly Blanton (the *Boston Globe*, September 5, 1993); "Fidelity Jumps Feet First into the Fray," by Geoffrey Smith (*Business Week*, May 25, 1992); "Jeff Vinik: Insider Interview," by Fred W. Frailey (*Kiplinger's Personal Finance Magazine*, October 1992); and "Jeffrey Vinik's Nest Egg," by Thomas Watterson (the *Boston Globe*, January 17, 1993). Various issues of *Fidelity Insight* and *Morningstar Mutual Funds* were invariably helpful. Among those interviewed were Ned Johnson, Rab Bertelsen, Peter Lynch, Rodger Lawson, J. D. Martine, and Michael Hines. Most Fidelity-related statistics were supplied by the Fidelity public relations department; a number of mutual fund statistics were supplied by the ICI public relations department. Articles quoted or mentioned in the chapter include "Lifestyles Suffer from Low Interest," by Harriet Johnson Brackey and Denise Kalette (*USA Today,* November 13, 1991); "Betting on the Baby Boom Bull Market," by Floyd Norris (*The New York Times,* October 31, 1993); and "The Bull Markets to Come," by Ron Chernow (the *Wall Street Journal,* August 30, 1993). The two articles that effectively "announced" the 1990s bull market were "Investment Soars in Mutual Funds, Causing Concern," by Leslie Wayne (*The New York Times,* September 7, 1993), and "Higher Still: Bulls Push Industrials to over 3,600 Points, but Bears Stay Bearish," by Anita Raghavan, Sara Calian, and Steven E. Levingston (the *Wall Street Journal,* August 19, 1993).

1. Actually, Nixon's resignation, which took place in the middle of a terrible bear market, caused the Dow Jones average to rally temporarily.
2. Or rather, serves *us* right. I confess that I was among those who moved money from a growth fund to a money market fund, in anticipation of the war's effect on the markets.
3. This was so even in 1991, when for the first time since 1958, total installment credit in the United States fell. Despite a drop of 1 percent in consumer credit, credit card charge volume still managed a 5.9 percent gain.
4. The Consumer Price Index rose 6.1 percent in 1990.
5. As the new class of investors had learned by then, the value of a bond increases when interest rates drop.
6. The original head of AT&T's new credit card division was a man named Paul Kahn, who was always described in the papers as a former credit card executive with First Chicago, which was the third-largest issuer in the country at the time of AT&T's entry into the business. Kahn, however, had made a number of stops during his career, one of which was First Deposit, where he was initially hired by Andrew Kahr to run the day-to-day operation once the First Select card was up and running. Kahn, however, feuded with Kahr over the latter's plans, and his stay at First Deposit was a short one.
7. How times had changed, though! Visa, which had once been the organization actively encouraging the participation of nonbanks like the Associates and Merrill Lynch in the bank card business, refused to admit AT&T into its system. MasterCard, on the other hand, took the exact position that Visa had once taken—that new entrants helped spur competition, and that refusing to allow nonbanks into the system could lead to antitrust problems with the Justice Department. Consumers, of course, could not have cared less whether their AT&T card was a MasterCard or a Visa, since they viewed the two organizations as interchangeable.
8. The only caveat was that a cardholder had to use his AT&T Universal Card at least once every year; if he failed to do that, then AT&T would regain the right to impose an annual fee.
9. His name was Richard Srednicki, and he was Citibank's General Manager for Master-Card and Visa programs. He spoke at a National Credit Card Forum, which was held in San Diego in late March 1991. Of course, the irony of having a Citibank man complaining about the incursions of a powerful competitor into "its" territory is almost too rich to bear.
10. Citicorp's problems in the late 1980s and early 1990s have been well documented. Suffice it to say here that the root cause of its problems was the same kind of reckless lending that had earlier done so much harm to BankAmerica. To prop itself up, and pump badly needed capital into the bank, Citicorp even had to sell a 10 percent stake to a Saudi prince, an action that had to be humiliating to John Reed. As for Reed himself,

he was the subject of numerous rumors throughout the early 1990s that his days as CEO were numbered because of the bank's poor performance and mounting losses. But miraculously, he survived, and by the beginning of 1994, Citicorp's health seemed restored. I should note that even in its darkest days, Citi's credit card operation continued to churn out hundreds of millions of dollars in profits. It may be an exaggeration to say that its credit cards saved the bank, but it's probably not much of one.

11. Lewis ran a fund called Disciplined Equity, which combined quantitative criteria and fundamental stock picking; it was up 22 percent in 1993. Danoff managed Contrafund, which he turned into one of the hottest funds in the shop—up 27 percent in 1993, it also had swelled to nearly $6 billion in assets. Terrana, who earned her stripes running first Growth & Income and then Equity-Income, moved to Fidelity Fund in 1993.

12. The other new magazine, which was titled *SmartMoney,* is published jointly by Hearst, publisher of such magazines as *Esquire, Cosmopolitan,* and *Town and Country,* and Dow Jones, publisher of the *Wall Street Journal.*

13. In April 1994, she moved from the $80 million Dividend Growth Fund to the $1.3 billion OTC Fund.

# Selected Bibliography

Baritz, Loren. *The Good Life: The Meaning of Success for the American Middle Class*. New York: Alfred A. Knopf, 1989.

Barnet, Richard J., and John Cavanagh. *Global Dreams: Imperial Corporations and the New World Order*. New York: Simon & Schuster, 1994.

Baxter, William F., Paul H. Cootner, and Kenneth E. Scott. *Retail Banking in the Electronic Age: The Law and Economics of Electronic Funds Transfer*. Montclair: Allanheld, Osmun and Company, 1977.

Berlin, Howard M. *The Dow Jones–Irwin Guide to Buying and Selling Treasury Securities*. Homewood, Ill.: Dow Jones–Irwin, 1984.

Bernstein, Peter L. *Capital Ideas: The Improbable Origins of Modern Wall Street*. New York: Free Press, 1992.

Birnbaum, Jeffrey H., and Alan S. Murray. *Showdown at Gucci Gulch: Lawmakers, Lobbyists, and the Unlikely Triumph of Tax Reform*. New York: Vintage Books, 1988.

Brooks, John. *The Go-Go Years*. New York: E. P. Dutton, 1973.

Cargill, Thomas F., and Gillian G. Garcia. *Financial Reform in the 1980s*. Stanford, Cal.: Hoover Institution Press, 1985.

Carrington, Tim. *The Year They Sold Wall Street*. New York: Penguin Books, 1985.

Carter, Jimmy. *Keeping Faith: Memoirs of a President*. New York: Bantam Books, 1982.

Deaver, Michael K., with Mickey Herskowitz. *Behind the Scenes: In Which the Author Talks About Ronald and Nancy Reagan . . . and Himself*. New York: Morrow, 1987.

Donoghue, William E., with Thomas Tilling. *William E. Donoghue's Complete Money Market Guide: The Simple Low-Risk Way You Can Profit from Inflation and Fluctuating Interest Rates*. New York: Harper and Row, 1981.

————. *William E. Donoghue's No-Load Mutual Fund Guide: How to Take Advantage of the Investment Opportunities of the Eighties*. Toronto: Bantam Books, 1983.

Donovan, Hedley. *Right Places, Right Times: Forty Years in Journalism Not Counting My Paper Route*. New York: Henry Holt and Company, 1989.

Eichler, Ned. *The Thrift Debacle*. Los Angeles: University of California Press, 1989.

Galanoy, Terry. *Charge It: Inside the Credit Card Conspiracy*. New York: G. P. Putnam's Sons, 1981.

Galbraith, John Kenneth. *The Affluent Society*. Boston: Houghton Mifflin, 1958.

————. *The Great Crash: 1929*. Boston: Houghton Mifflin, 1955.

Gart, Alan. *The Insider's Guide to the Financial Services Revolution*. New York: McGraw-Hill Book Company, 1984.

Grant, James. *Money of the Mind: Borrowing and Lending in America from the Civil War to Michael Milken.* New York: Farrar, Straus, Giroux, 1992.

Greider, William. *Secrets of the Temple: How the Federal Reserve Runs the Country*. New York: Simon & Schuster, 1987.

Halberstam, David. *The Reckoning*. New York: Morrow, 1986.

Hayes, Samuel L., III, ed. *Wall Street and Regulation*. Boston: Harvard Business School Press, 1987.

Hector, Gary. *Breaking the Bank: The Decline of BankAmerica*. Boston: Little, Brown and Company, 1988.

"Irving, Morgan." *The Bank Book*. Boston: Little, Brown and Company, 1973.

Johnston, Moira. *Roller Coaster: The Bank of America and the Future of American Banking*. New York: Ticknor and Fields, 1990.

Katz, Donald R. *The Big Store: Inside the Crisis and Revolution at Sears*. New York: Viking, 1987.

Klein, Robert J. *The "Money" Book of Money: Your Personal Financial Planner*. Boston: Little, Brown and Company, 1987.

Lowy, Martin. *High Rollers: Inside the Savings and Loan Debacle*. New York: Praeger, 1991.

Lynch, Peter, with John Rothchild. *Beating the Street: The Best-Selling Author of "One Up on Wall Street" Shows You How to Pick Winning Stocks and Develop a Strategy for Mutual Funds*. New York: Simon & Schuster, 1993.

———. *One Up on Wall Street: How to Use What You Already Know to Make Money in the Market*. New York: Simon & Schuster, 1989.

Malabre, Alfred L. *Beyond Our Means: How America's Long Years of Debt, Deficits and Reckless Borrowing Now Threaten to Overwhelm Us*. New York: Random House, 1987.

Malkiel, Burton G. *A Random Walk Down Wall Street*, 4th ed. New York: W. W. Norton and Company, 1985.

Mandell, Lewis. *The Credit Card Industry: A History*. Boston: Twayne Publishers, 1990.

———. *Credit Card Use in the United States*. Ann Arbor: Braun and Brumfield, 1972.

Mayer, Martin. *The Bankers*. New York: Weybright and Talley.

———. *The Greatest-Ever Bank Robbery: The Collapse of the Savings and Loan Industry*. New York: C. Scribner's Sons, 1990.

———. *The Money Bazaars: Understanding the Banking Revolution Around Us*. New York: E. P. Dutton, 1984.

Meyer, Martin J. *Credit-Cardsmanship: How to Survive the Credit Card Nightmare and Turn Plastic into Gold*. Lynbrook, N.Y.: Farnsworth Publishing Company, 1971.

Merrill, James Ingram. *A Different Person: A Memoir*. New York: Alfred A. Knopf, 1993.

———. *The Seraglio*. New York: Alfred A. Knopf, 1957.

Morris, Charles R. *A Time of Passion: America, 1960–1980*. New York: Harper and Row, 1984.

Neikirk, William R. *Volcker: Portrait of the Money Man*. New York: Congdon and Weed, 1987.

Noonan, Peggy. *What I Saw at the Revolution: A Political Life in the Reagan Era*. New York: Random House, 1989.

Pendergast, Curtis, with Geoffrey Colvin. *The World of Time, Inc.: The Intimate History of a Changing Enterprise*. Vol. 3, *1960–1980*. Ed. Robert Lubar. New York: Atheneum, 1986.

Perez, Robert C. *Marketing Financial Services*. New York: Praeger, 1983.

Prechter, Robert Rougelot, and Alfred John Frost. *Elliot Wave Principle: Key to Stock Market Profits*. Gainesville, Ga.: New Classics Library, 1978.

Quinn, Jane Bryant. *Making the Most of Your Money: Smart Ways to Create Wealth and Plan Your Finances in the 90s*. New York: Simon & Schuster, 1991.

Regan, Donald T. *A View from the Street*. New York: New American Library, 1972.

———. *For the Record: From Wall Street to Washington*. San Diego: Harcourt Brace Jovanovich, 1988.

Rothchild, John. *A Fool and His Money: The Odyssey of an Average Investor.* New York: Viking, 1988.

Ruff, Howard J. *From A to Z: A Timeless Money Making Odyssey through the First Four Years of America's Leading Financial Advisory Service.* San Ramon, Cal.: Target Publishers, 1980.

————. *How to Prosper During the Coming Bad Years.* New York: Times Books, 1979.

Schultze, Charles L. *Memos to the President: A Guide through Macroeconomics for the Busy Policymaker.* Washington: Brookings Institution, 1992.

Schwab, Charles. *How to Be Your Own Stockbroker.* New York: Macmillan Publishing Company, 1984.

Seidman, L. William. *Full Faith and Credit: The Great S&L Debacle and Other Washington Sagas.* New York: Times Books, 1993.

"Smith, Adam." *The Money Game.* New York: Vintage Books, 1976.

————. *The Roaring 80s.* New York: Summit Books, 1988.

Sullivan, Teresa A., Elizabeth Warren, and Jay Lawrence Westbrook. *As We Forgive Our Debtors: Bankruptcy and Consumer Credit in America.* Oxford: Oxford University Press, 1989.

Sykes, Jay G. *Proxmire.* Washington: Robert B. Luce, 1972.

Tobias, Andrew. *The Only Investment Guide You'll Ever Need.* New York: Harcourt Brace Jovanovich, 1978.

————. *The Only Other Investment Guide You'll Ever Need.* New York: Bantam, 1989.

Volcker, Paul A., and Toyoo Gyohten. *Changing Fortunes: The World's Money and the Threat to American Leadership.* New York: Times Books, 1992.

Welles, Chris. *The Last Days of the Club.* New York: E. P. Dutton and Company, 1975.

White, Theodore H. *America in Search of Itself: The Making of the President, 1956–1980.* New York: Harper and Row, 1982.

Williams, Bordon. *Financial Survival in the Age of New Money.* New York: Simon & Schuster, 1981.

Wriston, Walter B. *Risk and Other Four-Letter Words.* New York: Harper and Row, 1987.

# Index

adjustable rate mortgages (ARMs), 188
*Affluent Society, The* (Galbraith), 21, 299
airline industry, deregulation of, 175
air traffic controllers strike, 228
Allstate Insurance, 258
*America in Search of Itself* (White), 177–78
American Bankers Association, 199
American Can, 257
American Express, 61, 154, 252–53
  bank credit cards vs., 104, 190–91
  brokerage firm acquired by, 257
  charge cards issued by, 24, 60
  computerized authorization and, 101–2
  Visa competition for, 305, 307
Anderson, Charles, 128
anti-Semitism, 201
Apple Computer, 106
Armacost, Samuel, 268–70, 272, 273, 274, 325, 326, 327–31
Arnold, Rich, 121, 260, 263–64, 265, 269, 274, 327, 332, 333
Associates, The, 253–56, 316, 319, 320, 397
AT&T, 396–98
automatic teller machines (ATMs), 137, 143, 267, 271, 307, 308–11

baby boom generation, 287, 369, 403
Bache Securities, 257
Bacon, Sir Francis, 64
Baker, Donald I., 113
balanced budget, 169, 184, 186
Baldwin United, 257
BankAmerica, *see* Bank of America
BankAmericard:
  competition for, 53
  computer systems for, 25–26, 56, 100–105
  delinquent accounts of, 28, 30
  fraudulent use of, 30, 32
  initial development of, 23, 24–33
  interchange system for, 67–68, 92, 103–4
  international operations of, 104, 144–145
  mass mailings of, 15–16, 26–32
  merchants signed by, 26, 27, 28–30, 32
  out-of-state banks licensed for, 55–56, 62, 66, 89–90, 91, 92
  profitability of, 31, 32–33, 55
  promotional efforts for, 26, 28–29, 32, 104
  sales authorization for, 68–69, 90, 101–3
  sales volume for, 33, 104
  separate organization created for, 89–93, 309; *see also* National Bank-Americard, Inc.
  as Visa, 16, 62, 144–45, 146; *see also* Visa
BankAmericard Service Exchange, 101–03
Bankcard Holders of America, 323–24
Bank Holding Company Act (1960), 256, 258–59
banking, banks:
  branch systems for, 18–20, 145
  corporate clients vs. middle-class customers of, 17
  credit card competition among, 53–62, 147
  credit card duality and, 144
  credit card profits of, 302–3, 398
  fund companies vs., 370, 404
  interest rates regulated for, 77, 197–98, 207–12, 215–18, 221–26
  interstate, 145
  legislative definition of, 256
  marketing efforts of, 16–17, 208–9
  money market deposit account devised for, 226–28
  money market funds fought by, 199–206
  mutual funds offered by, 404–5
  passbook account assets levels for, 197, 211

regulatory policies on, 18–19, 54, 77, 140–41, 145, 197–98, 207–26, 256–259, 260–61, 328
stock market downturns and, 368
*see also specific banks*
Bank of America (BankAmerica):
BankAmericard separated from, 90–93, 104, 309
Citicorp vs., 16, 18, 140, 267–68, 270, 302, 328
credit card business of, 323, 325, 397; *see also* BankAmericard; Visa
credit cards introduced by, 15–16, 23–30
development of, 17–18, 19–20, 266
managerial style at, 266, 326
middle-class customers as focus for, 17–18, 22, 23, 267, 269
money market accounts at, 227
personal loan procedures at, 22–23
profitability of, 267–68, 326, 327–29, 330
Schwab merger with, 260–74, 325–33, 352
share prices for, 272
size of, 16, 18, 19–20, 140, 266, 267–268, 302
Bank of Italy, 17–18
bankruptcy, personal, 298, 300, 304
Baritz, Loren, 21
Barker, Desmond, 204
BASE I, 101–3
BASE II, 103–4
Baumol, William, 113
*Beating the Street* (Lynch), 405–6
Bechtel Group, 134, 257
Beckwitt, Robert, 400
Beise, Clark, 31, 32–33
Beneficial Finance Co., 252, 257
Benham, James, 76, 78, 79–81, 82–83, 87
Benham Adjustable Rate Government Securities, 394
Benham Capital Management, 81
Bent, Bruce R., 76–84, 87, 277
Bernstein, Peter L., 70
*Beyond Our Means* (Malabre), 297, 299
Billings, Peter, 199–200
Birks, Roger, 151, 161
Black Monday, market crash on:
aftermath of, 358–65, 366–76, 382–85
mutual fund performance on, 357–58, 369
onset of, 346–55
Wall Street brokerages on, 355–57, 362
Bodman, Samuel, 340
Boesky, Ivan, 297
Bogle, Jack, 236
bond funds, 237, 285, 394–95, 396
Borthick, Mirvin R., 200, 202, 206
Boston Coach, 235
Bosworth, Barry, 179, 187
Braun, Ted, 155
brokerage business(es):
capital requirements for, 262
computer technology in, 88, 121, 158, 159, 235, 236, 264–65, 269, 357, 358, 374, 404
customers' free credit balances used by, 81, 157
discount, 106–7, 111–12, 118–20, 261, 262, 263, 327
know-your-customer rule of, 119–20
mass marketing techniques for, 41–44
nationwide distribution networks in, 41, 43
small investors brought into, 41–52
*see also specific brokerage firms*
Brooks, John, 46, 47, 50, 51, 140
Brown, Henry B. R., 76–84, 87, 277, 377
Browning, D. Dale, 309–11
Buchanan, Ann, 153
Bush, George, 168, 214
*Business Week*, 259–60

Cabour, Francis, 350, 351, 358
Campeau, Robert, 297
Capital Appreciation Fund, 335, 350, 358
Capital Fund, 46, 47–48, 49, 234
Capital Holdings, 315–17, 324
Capital Preservation Fund, 76, 80–81, 82–83
Carrington, Tim, 257
Carte Blanche, 53, 56, 190
Carter, Jimmy, 167–86
credit control program of, 184–86, 196
deregulation backed by, 207, 212
inflation problems and, 167–86, 207, 228
tax reforms of, 285
Casey, Barbara, 134–35, 148
cash management account(s) (CMAs), 155–63
checking privileges for, 156, 199
credit cards for, 156, 158, 159, 255, 397

cash management account(s)
(CMAs) (*cont.*)
   development of, 139, 150–59, 250
   introduction of, 159–63, 254
   Schwab One Account vs., 253, 327
   state legislative efforts against, 199–
      206
certificates of deposit (CDs), 78, 140,
   238, 394
chain stores, 37–38, 41, 306
*Challenger* shuttle explosion, 391
Chase Manhattan Bank, 24, 62, 139, 302,
   397
chasing yield, 220, 394–96
checking accounts:
   bank interest payments and, 207
   in money market funds, 84–88, 100,
      127, 156
   at S&Ls, 127
checks, two-party vs. three-party, 202
Chemical Bank, 143
Chernow, Ron, 403, 405
Chinachem Group, 360
Chrysler Corporation, 174, 241
Chrystie, Thomas, 154, 156–60, 215–16
Citibank (Citicorp), 135, 139–48
   Bank of America vs., 16, 18, 267–68,
      270, 302, 328
   competitiveness of, 139–41, 267–68
   consumer business developed at, 18,
      143–44, 145
   in credit card business, 53, 139, 144,
      145–48, 194, 263, 266, 302–3, 304,
      397, 398
   deregulation of interest rates pressed by,
      217, 218
   growth rate of, 139, 140, 143
   holding company for, 140
   as international bank, 267
   management of, 302
   Merrill Lynch profits vs., 343
   mutual fund sales prohibited for, 259
   Operating Group revamped at, 142–43
   profitability of, 398
   ruthless corporate culture at, 140,
      142
   size of, 16, 18, 139, 140, 302, 401
Civil Aeronautics Board, 175
Clausen, Tom, 267–68, 331, 332
Clinton, Bill, 403, 404
Clinton, Hillary Rodham, 403–4
CMAs, *see* cash management accounts
Coldwell Banker, 258

Colorado Bank Board, 162
Colorado National Bank, 309–11
commissions, deregulation of, 106, 112,
   115–16, 117–18
computer industry, employee compensation
   in, 122
computer technology:
   on Black Monday, 357, 358, 362
   in brokerage businesses, 88, 121, 158,
      159, 235, 236, 264–65, 269, 357,
      358, 374, 404
   for cash management account, 159
   for credit card business, 25–26, 54, 56,
      63, 100–105, 190, 303
   financial complexity masked by, 100–
      101
   on stock exchange, 114
Congress, U.S.:
   banking regulations and, 19, 198, 207,
      210, 218, 222–26
   credit card issues in, 60–61
   tax bills passed by, 285–86, 293
Connell, Lawrence, Jr., 197
Conover, Todd, 211, 217, 261
Consumer Bankers Association, 143
consumer debt:
   cultural ambivalence toward, 300–301,
      319–20
   generationally-based views on, 192–93
   growth of, 20–22, 23–24, 297–302
   inflationary economy and, 184–86, 191–
      193, 301–2
Consumer Financial Decisions, 130, 134–
   139, 148, 263
Continental Illinois Bank, 59, 328
Coolidge, Calvin, 38–39
corporate takeovers, 297, 342–43, 350–51,
   370–71
Council on Wage and Price Stability
   (COWPS), 172, 179, 186
credit card(s):
   annual fees for, 195–96, 320, 396–98
   cardholders' financial control increased
      by, 26, 33, 93–96
   cash advance check offered with, 320–
      321, 323
   check writing vs., 95
   on CMAs, 156, 158, 159, 255
   computerization and, 25–26, 54, 56, 63,
      100–105, 190, 303
   creditworthiness and, 25, 29–31, 303–4
   customer service interactions for, 303
   debit cards vs., 306–11

direct mail solicitations for, 146
fraud linked with, 30, 32, 58
impersonalization furthered by, 303–4
imprudent use of, 298–99
indispensability of, 301
interest charges on, 25, 59, 60, 95,
    193–95, 320
introduction of, 15–16, 23–33
loans floated on, 195
minimum payments for, 320–21, 323
one-month grace period on, 25
public acceptance for, 31, 32, 33, 190,
    300–302, 319–20, 392
sales authorization for, 68–69, 101–3
spending facilitated by, 93–94, 95–
    96
statistics on usage of, 33, 62, 94–95,
    104, 190, 191, 298, 301, 392
stolen, 31, 58, 90
see also BankAmericard; Visa
credit card business(es):
    back office operations of, 318
    bank domination of, 190–91
    bank interchange system for, 67–68
    competition for, 53–62
    consumer groups on, 323–24
    critics of, 31, 58–61, 299
    duality issue for, 144
    finance companies in, 253–57
    industry newsletter on, 61
    merchant discounts in, 25, 32, 60
    misleading solicitations for, 323–24
    nationwide systems of, 55–56, 62
    nonbank issuers in, 396–97
    profitability of, 25, 31, 32–33, 55, 61,
        193–94, 302–3
    promotional efforts of, 26, 28–29, 32,
        59, 104
    select customer base for, 318–24
    unsolicited mailings of, 15–16, 26–32,
        56–61, 62, 145
Credit Card Use in the United States
    (Mandell), 94
credit controls, inflationary spiral and,
    184–85
credit rating agencies, 145, 303
credit unions, 197
Crocker Bank, 267
cross-selling, 138, 291

Danoff, Will, 400
Davis, L. J., 346
Dean Witter Reynolds, 258

debit cards, 156, 306–11, 313
debt-to-income ratios, 298, 299–300
decision analysis, 128–29, 133
Decker, John, 319
Deloitte Haskins & Sells, 329
Democratic Party, 167–68
Depository Institutions Deregulation and
    Monetary Control Act (1980), 207–
    208
Depository Institutions Deregulation Com-
    mittee (DIDC):
    money market deposit account for banks
        devised by, 226–28
    on passbook interest rates, 208–9, 212–
        213, 216–18, 219–25
Depression, 19, 21, 24, 77, 131, 167
Dillon, Read, 257
Diners Club, 24, 26
direct mail marketing, 110
discontinuity, theory of, 290
discount brokerages, 106–7, 111–12, 118–
    120, 261, 262, 263, 327
    see also Fidelity Investments; Charles
        Schwab & Company
disinflation, 392–93
dollar pricing, 84
Donaldson, Lufkin & Jenrette, 114,
    116
Donoghue, William, 76, 197, 209, 227–
    228, 379
Dorfman, Dan, 348
Doriot, Georges, 132, 251
Dow Jones Industrial Average, 45, 70,
    231–33, 279, 333, 340–42, 348,
    351–358, 366, 375–76, 388, 390,
    402
Drew, Elizabeth, 176–77
Drexel Burnham Lambert, 360, 361
Dreyfus Corporation, 86, 257, 339, 373,
    384, 404–5
DuBow, Arthur, 72–73
Duffy, Helene, 148
Dworsky, Leo, 70, 234, 350

Edie, Lionel D., 154
Eisenhower, Dwight, 22
Eizenstat, Stuart, 173, 179
elections, presidential, 167–68, 169,
    186
Electronic Data Systems, 106
Emerson, Ralph Waldo, 305
Essex Fund, 238, 245
Evans, George, 254

Everything Card, 54, 56
Execu-Charge card, 255

Falvey, Mary, 135
Farrell, Robert, 354
FDIT (Fidelity Daily Income Trust), 84–
    88, 237
Federal Deposit Insurance Corporation
    (FDIC), 207, 208, 217, 378
Federal Home Loan Bank Board
    (FHLBB), 80, 81, 208, 217
Federal Reserve Board:
    bank acquisitions approved by, 256–57,
        271, 273, 274
    chairmanship of, 176
    consumer debt studied by, 299–300
    inflation problems and, 180–82
    political independence of, 181
Fidelity Fund, 49
Fidelity Investments, 233–49
    on Black Monday, 354, 355, 356,
        357–58
    bull market's end anticipated at, 349–52
    *Challenger* explosion and, 391
    commission policies at, 235–36, 248,
        336–37
    company atmosphere at, 244, 247, 290–
        291, 335, 336, 339–40, 350, 400
    computerization at, 88, 235, 236, 357
    direct customer access to, 87–88
    equity department at, 85, 234, 238,
        350–52, 400
    global investments of, 400
    IRA accounts at, 289–93, 327
    management of, 48–49, 50, 52, 70, 71–
        74, 85–86, 234–36, 400–402
    marketing department at, 334–40
    money market funds at, 84–88, 234,
        235, 237–38, 239, 263
    mutual funds volume at, 48, 70, 404
    nonbank bank run by, 257
    parent company of, 70
    portfolio managers at, 49–50, 240–49,
        334–39, 347, 380–89, 398–400
    postcrash layoffs at, 373, 383
    promotional efforts of, 238, 247, 285,
        290–95, 327, 337, 349
    as retail company, 86–88, 234–37, 262
    Spartan funds offered by, 373
    tax-free bonds at, 237, 285
    total assets of, 386, 401, 404
    variety of funds offered by, 237, 238,
        349, 373, 400

Fidelity Management and Research, 46, 70
Fidelity mutual funds:
    Asset Manager, 400
    Balanced Fund, 349, 350, 358
    Capital Appreciation, 335, 337, 380
    Capital Fund, 46, 47–48, 49, 234
    Cash Reserves, 237, 293
    Contrafund, 238, 399
    Daily Income Trust (FDIT), 84–88, 237
    Dividend Growth Fund, 402
    Equity-Income Fund, 350
    Freedom Fund, 292
    Growth and Income Fund, 350, 399
    Low Priced Stock, 400
    Magellan Fund, *see* Magellan Fund
    Mercury Fund, 238
    OTC Portfolio, 335–39, 340, 387
    Overseas, 335, 336, 337, 340
    Puritan, 238, 349, 350
    Salem Fund, 238
    Select Technology, 294–96
    Short Term World Income, 394
    Trend Fund, 50, 70, 72, 74, 234
Fidelity National Bank, 256
finance companies, 17, 20, 22, 65, 253–57
financial services industry:
    blurring of institutional differences in,
        126–27, 129–30
    components of, 9
    consumer inertia and, 137–38
    cross-selling in, 138, 291
    deregulation of, 207–13, 215–26
    employment levels in, 343
    regulatory apparatus for, 129
    SRI comprehensive study of, 130,
        134–39
First Chicago, 302, 397
First Commander Corporation, 111
First DeKalb Bank, 227
First Deposit Corporation, 259–60
    select credit system developed for,
        315–24
First National Bank (Chicago), 59, 62
First National City Bank of New York, 53,
    56
    *see also* Citibank
First Nationwide Savings, 251, 271
First Select Visa card, 320–22, 323–24
Fisher, Richard W., 354–55
Florsheim Shoes, 28
Flying Tiger Airlines, 240
Ford, Gerald, 169, 171, 181
Ford Motor Co., 242, 397

Forsgren, Afton, 204
Franklin, Benjamin, 20
Fraser, Douglas, 174, 175
Friedman, Milton, 182
From, Alvin, 174, 179, 180
Fuller, James, 130, 135, 158, 252, 253
Furash, Edward, 83, 100, 192, 227, 236, 288, 368–69
Furness, Betty, 60–61, 299

Galbraith, John Kenneth, 21, 22, 299, 346
Gallup Organization, 135
Garbo, Greta, 47
Garn, Jake, 201, 213, 216, 223–24, 225–26
Garzarelli, Elaine, 346, 347, 348, 382
General Electric Credit Corporation, 252
General Foods, 140
General Motors, 397
Giannini, A. P., 17–19, 20, 23, 35, 140, 258, 261, 269
Glass-Steagall Act (1933), 19, 130, 141, 150, 216, 258, 261, 274, 404
Go-Go Years, 47–48, 50–52, 243, 346
gold funds, 237, 247
Gorbachev, Mikhail, 85
Gotbaum, Josh, 179
Grant, James, 297–98, 299, 300, 346, 398
Granville, Joe, 277, 342
Greene, Alan, 346–47, 348
Greider, William, 181, 185
Gulf + Western, 253, 254, 256–57

Haack, Robert, 115, 116
Hammer, Frederick, 309
Hanes Corp., 246
Harmer, Sherman, Jr., 204, 205–6
Harris, Marlys, 281, 283
Hart, Alex ''Pete,'' 33
Harvard Business School, 64, 128, 133, 135
Haselton, Ronald, 127
Hector, Gary, 270, 271, 328–29, 332
Hock, Dee Ward, 146
    background of, 63, 64–66
    CMA debit/credit card approved by, 159, 397
    computerization instituted by, 101–5
    corporate rituals disliked by, 65–66
    on credit cards as basic exchange medium, 62–63, 96, 99, 159, 304–5, 397

debit card system urged by, 306–11, 313
duality opposed by, 144
management style of, 96–100, 306–15
new BankAmericard organization created by, 89–93
office space designed by, 312–13
retirement of, 313–15
salary of, 93, 99, 104, 305, 312
Visa name change and, 144–45
Visa run by, 62–64, 190, 255, 304–15
Holliday, Alan, 87
home equity loans, 137, 156, 298
Honey, Thomas, 99–100
hostile takeovers, 297, 350–51
House Banking and Commerce Committee, 58, 60
Household Finance, 252, 257
housing market, 178, 188–89, 393, 403
How to Prosper During the Coming Bad Years (Ruff), 82
E. F. Hutton, 118, 239

Iacocca, Lee, 241
IBM, 45, 102, 355
Icahn, Carl, 297
ICI (Investment Company Institute), 199, 202, 259, 286, 293, 373, 385
inflation, 167–86
    Carter presidency damaged by, 168–86
    cause of, 169
    chasing yield instigated by, 220
    consumer debt and, 184–86, 191–93, 301–2
    disinflation vs., 392–93
    federal policies on, 76, 167–86, 219, 228
    interest rates and, 76–77, 180, 181–83, 184
    middle class fears of, 176–78, 180
    money market funds and, 76, 82, 83, 197–98
    partisan politics and, 167–68
    real estate investments during, 189, 233
    S&L investment during, 210–11
    societal adaptations to, 187–90
    special interest politics fueled by, 167
    spiral effect of, 169–70, 228
    unemployment problems vs., 169, 180
    usury laws and, 193–95
inheritance, 287
installment loans, 22
Interbank, 54, 56, 57, 102, 103, 104

interest rates:
federal regulation of, 77–78, 80, 141,
163, 190, 197–98, 207–13, 215–18,
221–27
1990s drop in, 393–96
Investment Company Act (1940), 75, 78
Investment Indicators, 110–11
IRA (Individual Retirement Account),
286–93, 327, 404
Isaac, William, 217, 218, 222, 224, 258

Jamieson, Jane, 289–91
Janeway, Eliot, 346
Janus Fund, 403, 404
Jarvie, Charles L., 289–92, 294, 340,
363
Jobs, Steve, 106
John Hancock Insurance Co., 404
Johnson, Abigail, 401–2
Johnson, Edward Crosby, 2nd, 48–50, 52,
70, 71, 73, 74
Johnson, Edward Crosby (Ned), 3rd:
computer systems developed by, 74,
235, 236, 357
Fidelity management by, 50, 52, 70,
72–74, 85–86, 108, 234–39, 241,
243, 248, 289, 291, 293–94, 339–40,
400–402
funds managed by, 50, 72, 74, 234,
245, 246
market crash onset and, 349–50
money market fund with check writing
devised by, 84–88, 127
personnel policies of, 243, 244, 245,
246–47, 248, 334, 336, 339, 340,
387
retail marketing concepts instituted by,
86–88, 235–36, 237
variety of funds backed by, 237, 291
wealth of, 401
Johnson, Lyndon, 60, 76, 169
Johnston, Moira, 267, 268, 274, 330
Johnstone, Bruce, 350, 351
Jordan, Hamilton, 179, 180
junk bonds, 237

Kahn, Alfred, 172–75, 179, 180–81, 183,
184–85, 186
Kahr, Andrew, 130–39, 141
background of, 132–34
cash management account devised
by, 139, 155, 156, 157, 158, 250,
253

credit card products developed by, 253–
257, 315–24
entrepreneurial efforts of, 251–52, 259–
260, 315–17, 322–23
regulatory loopholes exploited by, 131,
250, 254–57, 261
on SRI survey, 134–39
wealth desired by, 133–34, 250, 251,
252, 316, 324
Kane, Arthur, 356
Kane, Richard, 145, 147, 194
Kassen, Michael, 293–96, 334–35
Katz, Bennett, 310
Katz, Donald, 131
Kaufman, Henry, 232
Kennedy, Edward, 181, 183
Kennedy, John F., 45, 170, 390
Kenzie, Ross, 119
Kerr-McGee, 186
Keynesian economic theory, 169, 182,
183
Klein, Robert, 280, 282, 283, 284
Kohlberg, Kravis & Roberts, 332
Kravis, Henry, 297
Kroger Company, 257, 316

labor, inflationary wage settlements and,
170, 171, 174, 228
Larkin, Kenneth:
BankAmericard/Bank of America separation and, 69, 90–91, 93
on BankAmericard development, 27, 29,
31, 32
career of, 22, 192
on consumer use of credit, 94, 192
on Hock, 90, 104–5, 308
on introduction of annual fees, 196
national BankAmericard system suggested by, 55–56
on Reed's consumer efforts, 143–44
on small personal loans, 22
Lawson, Roger, 337, 338, 339–40, 349,
386, 400
Lee, James B., 200, 201, 202, 204,
206
Lemann, Nicholas, 163
Lewis, Brad, 400
Lewis, Sandy, 257
Liberty Bonds, 38
Lieber, Mimi, 288, 300, 301–2, 405
*Life*, 59
Ling, Flora, 282
loads, 50

Loeb, Marshall, 275–85, 294
  on baby boomers' inheritances, 287
  career of, 275–76, 281, 371
  on money as conversation topic, 189
  views of, 276–77, 279–84
Lord, Charles, 218, 222
Loring, Caleb, 73, 74
Lynch, Eddie, 36, 38, 39
Lynch, Peter, 239–49
  background of, 239–40, 243–44,
    336
  books written by, 385, 405–6
  investment choices of, 241–42, 246,
    336
  Magellan Fund managed by, 240–49,
    292, 335, 336, 338, 357–58, 382–85,
    399
  Magellan management after, 388–89
  on Monday market declines, 353
  on overall market conditions, 246, 279,
    342, 350
  protegé of, 336, 339
  as public figure, 240, 249, 294, 334,
    340, 380, 381–86
  resignation of, 384, 385–87

McCrory Corp., 37
McFadden Act (1927), 19, 141, 145, 216,
  258
McKinsey & Company, 135
McLin, Stephen, 266, 269–70, 272, 273,
  274
McNall, Bruce, 281
McNamara, Frank X., 24
McQuown, John, 132, 135, 252–53
Mafia, 58, 90
Magellan Fund, 238, 350
  advertising for, 290, 349
  Black Monday losses of, 357–58, 383
  gains made by, 74, 242, 249, 292–93
  investment choices for, 241–42, 246,
    336
  loads on, 248
  portfolio management for, 74, 239, 240–
    249, 338, 383–89, 398–400
  public access to, 245, 247, 248
  total assets of, 242, 248, 349, 388–89,
    399–400
Magowan, Peter, 38
Magowan, Robert, 153
Malabre, Alfred L., Jr., 297, 299
Mandell, Lewis, 20, 21, 94–96
Manhattan Fund, 50–51

MasterCard (Master Charge):
  computerization for, 67, 101, 102, 103
  formation of, 53, 56
  nonbank issuers and, 255, 396
  several banks joined in, 53, 57, 62
  Visa use vs., 144, 304–5
Mayday, 106, 112, 117–18
Mellon Bank, 404
Merrill, Charles Edward, 34–46, 116
  background of, 36–37, 155
  brokers salaried by, 42, 118, 161
  chain stores financed by, 37–38
  death of, 34, 35
  ill health of, 34–35, 43, 44
  market crash foreseen by, 38–39, 346
  middle-class investors served by, 35, 37,
    41–46, 107–8, 231, 238, 277, 403
  mutual funds disliked by, 46
  personal life of, 39–40, 152
  Regan vs., 150, 151, 152, 153
Merrill, Hellen, 39
Merrill, James, 39–40
Charles E. Merrill & Co., 35
Merrill Lynch:
  banking services at, 141, 149–50, 156
  bank purchased by, 257
  broker compensation at, 41, 42, 118,
    151, 161, 343–44
  cash management accounts developed
    for, see cash management accounts
  commissions raised by, 107–8, 112,
    117–18, 372
  debit/credit card from, 156, 158, 159
  discount brokerage underestimated by,
    118–19
  diversification goals of, 149–50, 154–
    155, 156
  early development of, 35, 37–39, 40–
    44
  headquarters of, 118, 343, 372
  holding company for, 156
  institutional business of, 117, 118, 151,
    154
  investor education campaign at, 43
  IRA accounts at, 289, 292, 404
  management styles at, 116, 150–55,
    160, 214–15
  mass marketing efforts of, 41–44, 45–
    46, 116, 161–62
  Money Trust, 250–51
  mutual funds at, 46, 154, 343, 404
  nationwide distribution network for, 41,
    43, 123, 145

Merrill Lynch (*cont.*)
  postcrash decline of, 371–72
  profitability of, 43, 118, 150–51, 343,
    372, 373
  as public company, 116–17, 151
  Ready Asset Trust, 200, 215, 233
  real estate business at, 149, 151–52
  shooting of employees at, 356
  slogan of, 151
  trading volume at, 43, 155
  Utah money fund restrictions opposed
    by, 199–206
Merrill Lynch, E. A. Pierce, and Cassatt &
  Co., 41
Merrill Lynch, Pierce, Fenner & Beane, 35
Metz, Robert, 288
Michigan, University of, 94
Microsoft, 241–42, 338
Midwest Bank Cards, 54, 57
Milken, Michael, 297
Miller, G. William, 176, 185
Miller, Robert, 99
Minarek, Joseph, 192
Mobil Oil, 23–24
Mondale, Walter, 176
monetarists, 182
*Money,* 275–86, 292
  bullish slant of, 276–77, 279–84, 292,
    342
  covers for, 280, 281–82, 294–96, 342
  on Gulf War, 391
  for middle class investors, 280–81, 401
  money fund yields listed by, 220
  postcrash editorial shift of, 371
  soundness of news coverage in, 295–96
money market certificates, 198–99, 210–
  211
money market funds, 75–88
  bank equivalent to, 226–28
  bank-led efforts against, 199–206
  for cash management accounts, 155–56
  with check-writing privileges, 84–88,
    100, 127, 156
  consumer demographics for, 286–87
  dollar pricing used for, 83–84
  growth of, 197, 211, 219–20, 224–25,
    377, 380
  inflation and, 76, 82, 83, 197–98
  initial approval for, 75–81
  investment management for, 377–78
  management fees for, 250–51
  protection against: risk in, 378–80
  in repurchase agreements, 377–78

as saving vehicle vs. investment vehicle,
  75, 126, 287, 377, 378
selling of, 81–84, 87–88
state legislative efforts on, 199–206
tax-free, 237
total assets of, 197, 211, 219–20, 224–
  225, 227, 377, 380
in yield comparisons, 220, 227, 237–38,
  376, 377
see also specific brokerage firms; specific
  money market funds
money revolution:
  inflation-based behavior and, 168
  principal elements of, 126–27
Morgan, J. P., 37
*Morningstar,* 401
Morris, Charles, 169–70
Mortgage Realty and Trust, 379
Moss, Peter, 109, 121, 265–66, 269, 270,
  272–74
Mueller, Adolph, 132, 252–53, 254, 259,
  316–17, 321, 323
municipal bond funds, 237, 285, 396
Murdoch, Rupert, 341
mutual funds:
  banks prohibited from sales of, 259
  bond funds, 237, 285, 394–95, 396
  defined, 46
  direct retail sales of, 88, 235–36, 248
  fees for, 50, 83, 248, 336–37
  in Go-Go Years, 47–48, 50–52
  gold funds, 237
  largest, 200
  lobbying organization for, 199
  low-load, 248
  merchandising effort for, 368–69
  money market, *see* money market funds
  net redemption in, 70–71
  no-load, 110, 248, 327
  performance funds, 48
  popularity of, 46, 48, 333–34, 342,
    368–70, 385, 403–4
  portfolio managers' power shifted to
    marketers of, 334–40
  postcrash performance of, 372–73
  press coverage on, 369, 382–83
  proliferation of, 333–34, 385, 400
  SEC regulation of, 75, 80–81
  sector funds, 291, 295–96
  splitting commissions on, 71
  star portfolio managers for, 47, 49–50,
    240–41, 334–39, 369, 380–89, 398–
    400

state registration of, 111
total assets in, 342, 344, 373, 385, 405
*see also specific brokerage firms; specific mutual funds*

Nader, Ralph, 93, 175
naked options, 358–59
NASDAQ, 114
National BankAmericard Inc. (NBI):
  computerization of, 101–4, 190
  duality opposed by, 144
  establishment of, 91–93, 190
  management style at, 96–100
  organizational structure of, 91–92
National Bank of Commerce, 66
National Credit Union Administration, 197, 208
Needham, James, 116
Neff, John, 369, 380, 381–82
Negotiable Order of Withdrawal (NOW) account, 126–27
net redemptions, 70
*New York,* 298–99, 300
*New Yorker,* 176–77
New York Stock Exchange (NYSE):
  brokerage commissions and, 71, 106, 112, 114–16
  capital requirements for members of, 262
  as clubby monopoly, 112–14
  mutual funds vs. stocks on, 333
  presidents of, 115, 116
  shareholder surveys by, 120, 368
  trading volume on, 343
*New York Times,* 177, 188, 193
Nikkei Index, 351
Nilson, Spencer, 139–40, 190–91, 193, 305, 313, 398
*Nilson Report,* 61
Nixon, Richard, 76, 79, 80, 114, 169, 390
Noble, George, 335, 336, 339, 347
Noonan, Peggy, 150
Norwitz, Steven, 379
NOW (Negotiable Order of Withdrawal) accounts, 126–27

"Of Usury" (Bacon), 64
oil prices, 170, 175, 176, 186
Olin, John, 162
OneSource, 404
*One Up on Wall Street* (Lynch), 385
OPEC, 170, 175, 176, 278

option trading, 358–59, 360–62
Overcash, Reece, 254
Overseas Fund, 335, 336, 337, 340

Pacific Stock Exchange, 121
Parker Pen, 259, 260, 315–16
Patman, Wright, 57–58, 60, 67, 93, 299
J.C. Penney Company, 306, 313
performance funds, 48
Perot, H. Ross, 106, 386
Persian Gulf War (1991), 390–91
Peterson, Peter G., 346
Phalen, John, Jr., 354
Phillip Morris, 388, 392
Phillips, David, 145, 146
Phillips, Don, 369
Pierce, Edward, 40
E. A. Pierce & Co., 40–41
Plus System, 309, 310, 311, 313, 314
politics, inflation and, 167–68
Pollan, Stephen M., 94
Porter, Sylvia, 277
portfolio managers:
  as industry stars, 47, 49–50, 240–41, 334–39, 369, 380–89, 398–400
  marketing department power vs., 334–40
Pottruck, David, 374–75
Powell, Jody, 179, 180, 186
Pratt, Richard, 217, 218, 222, 226
Prechter, Robert, 342, 347
Presley, Elvis, 121–22
prime rate, 140, 180, 182–83, 184
Procter & Gamble, 289–90
Proxmire, William, 174, 184, 198, 216
  bank deregulation and, 207, 212, 225
  credit cards and, 60, 61, 104, 324
Prudential Insurance, 224, 257

Quackenbush, Hugo, 107, 111, 124–25
Quick, Leslie C., 331
Quick & Reilly, 262, 263, 331, 404

Rafshoon, Gerald, 172
Raiffa, Howard, 132–33
Ready Asset Trust, 200, 215, 233
Reagan, Ronald, 150, 211, 213
  air traffic controllers fired by, 228
  economic policies of, 167–68, 186, 214, 219, 225, 261, 285–86
real estate, inflationary-period investments in, 189, 233
recessions, 183, 185–86, 219, 392
Reed, John S., 141–48, 194, 302

Regan, Donald, 149–55, 161
    background of, 151, 152–53
    on brokerage commissions, 107–8, 116,
        117, 119, 140
    CMA development and, 155, 157–58,
        159–60
    management style of, 150–55, 160,
        214–15, 216
    Merrill Lynch run by, 46, 116–17, 118,
        141, 149–52, 153–55, 233, 371–72
    as Treasury Secretary, 151, 154, 213–
        218, 221–26
Regulation Q, 77–78, 80, 141, 163, 190,
        197, 207–12, 215–18, 221–22, 225
Rekenthaler, John, 368
Republican Party, 168, 213
repurchase agreements, 377–78
Reserve Fund, 75, 81, 83–84, 86
Reserve Management Corporation, 76
Reston, James, 173
Rittereiser, Robert, 151–52
RJR Nabisco, 392
Roberts, George, 232
Robinson, James, 154
Rockefeller, David, 401
Rockwell, Bruce, 310, 313, 314
Rogers, Jim, 346, 347
Rogers, William, 214
Rogoff, Alice, 179
Ronczy, Edward, 177
Ronczy, Josephine, 177
Roosevelt, Franklin, 19, 131, 167
Rosenberg, Richard, 331
Rosseau, Robert, 362–65
Rubenstein, David, 179–80
Ruff, Howard, 82, 342
Rukeyser, Louis, 232, 241, 249, 277,
        343
Rukeyser, Merryle, 277
Rukeyser, William, 277–78, 282, 284
Runde, Robert, 279, 282, 283
Rupkey, Christopher, 192–93
Russell, Charles, 315

Safeway Stores, 37, 38
Safire, William, 289
St. Germain, Fernand, 209, 223, 224–26
Salomon Brothers, 232, 331, 343, 351
Samuelson, Paul, 113
Samuelson, Robert, 179
savings and loans (S&Ls):
    checking accounts at, 127
    congressional support for, 222–23
    federal regulation of, 80, 127, 207–13,
        215–18
    inflationary impact on, 210–11
    interest paid by, 136, 210–13, 217–18,
        221–26
    lending restrictions eased for, 225
    money market assets levels vs., 197,
        211
savings habits, 136, 138
Schlaiffer, Robert, 133
Schultze, Charles, 172, 182, 185
Schwab, Charles:
    in advertisements, 124–25
    background of, 106, 109–12, 261–62
    BankAmerica merger and, 260–62, 264–
        266, 268–74, 325–33
    on Black Monday losses, 358, 359–60
    business style of, 108–9, 110, 253, 264,
        265, 374, 375
    discount brokerage begun by, 104, 111–
        112, 127
    Schwab public offerings and, 264–65,
        333, 352–53
Schwab, William, 110, 111, 122–23, 124,
        271
Charles Schwab & Company:
    advertisements for, 124–25, 327
    BankAmerica merger with, 260–74,
        325–33, 352
    Black Monday and, 356, 357, 358–65,
        373–74
    branch offices of, 122–24, 262, 360
    business volume at, 120–21, 123, 271–
        272, 327, 358, 374, 404
    computer system at, 121, 264–65, 269,
        357, 358, 362, 375
    as discount brokerage, 106–7, 112, 118–
        119, 122, 263, 327, 375
    employees at, 120, 121, 125, 236, 262,
        374
    IRAs promoted by, 292
    management style at, 108–9, 120–22,
        263–64, 265, 274, 326, 332–33, 358–
        359, 363, 374–75
    mutual funds at, 327, 375, 404
    no-advice policy of, 119–20
    postcrash improvements at, 373–76
    problems of rapid growth for, 262,
        263–65
    profitability of, 263, 327, 332, 374,
        375
    public offerings of, 264–65, 333,
        352–53